MW01537246

THE AMISH REMEDIES

1000+ TRANSFORMATIVE REMEDIES AND RITUALS TO HEAL NATURALLY AND FIND INNER PEACE. HARNESS NATURE'S WISDOM TO HEAL YOUR FAMILY AND SOOTHE YOUR SOUL.

EMILY GREEN

Copyright 2025 by (Emily Green) - All rights reserved.

This document is geared towards providing exact and reliable information regarding the topic and issue covered. The publication is sold with the idea that the publisher is not required to render accounting, officially permitted, or otherwise, qualified services. If advice is necessary, legal, or professional, a practiced individual in the profession should be ordered.

- From a Declaration of Principles which was accepted and approved equally by a Committee of the American Bar Association and a Committee of Publishers and Associations.

In no way is it legal to reproduce, duplicate, or transmit any part of this document in either electronic means or in printed format. Recording of this publication is strictly prohibited and any storage of this document is not allowed unless with written permission from the publisher. All rights reserved.

The information provided herein is stated to be truthful and consistent, in that any liability, in terms of inattention or otherwise, by any usage or abuse of any policies, processes, or directions contained within is the solitary and utter responsibility of the recipient reader. Under no circumstances will any legal responsibility or blame be held against the publisher for any reparation, damages, or monetary loss due to the information herein, either directly or indirectly.

Respective authors own all copyrights not held by the publisher.

The information herein is offered for informational purposes solely and is universal as so. The presentation of the information is without contract or any type of guaranteed assurance.

The trademarks that are used are without any consent, and the publication of the trademark is without permission or backing by the trademark owner. All trademarks and brands within this book are for clarifying purposes only and are owned by the owners themselves, not affiliated with this document.

TABLE OF CONTENTS

Book 36
Crafting Herbal Drinks Beyond Tea

Book 37
Zero-Waste Herbalism

Book 38
Herbal Support for Chronic Conditions

Book 39
Herbal Support for Athletes

Book 40
Preserving and Sharing Herbal Knowledge

INTRODUCTION

For centuries, herbs have been at the heart of traditional medicine, weaving their way into the lives of countless cultures across the globe. Long before the advent of modern pharmaceuticals, our ancestors relied on nature's bounty to heal wounds, treat illnesses, and sustain overall well-being. From the calming chamomile tea used to soothe frayed nerves to the invigorating power of ginseng, herbs have been humanity's trusted allies in health and healing.

Today, as the world grows increasingly complex and reliant on synthetic solutions, many people are rediscovering the profound benefits of herbal healing. This resurgence reflects not only a desire to return to natural methods but also a recognition of the environmental and personal toll that over-reliance on pharmaceuticals and chemicals can have. Embracing herbs as a part of your lifestyle allows you to connect with nature's wisdom, restore balance in your body, and build a healthier, more sustainable future.

This book is your invitation to step into the ancient yet ever-evolving world of herbal medicine. Whether you're entirely new to the practice or have dabbled in creating herbal teas and remedies, this guide will provide you with the tools, knowledge, and inspiration to transform your approach to health and wellness.

Why a Home Apothecary is Essential

A home apothecary is much more than a cupboard filled with jars of dried herbs. It is a personal sanctuary of health, wellness, and tradition—a space where healing meets sustainability. In a fast-paced world filled with synthetic products and processed solutions, having a home apothecary allows you to regain control over your family's health while fostering a deeper connection to the natural world.

1. Empowerment and Independence: When you build a home apothecary, you empower yourself to address minor health concerns independently. From soothing a child's fever with a gentle herbal syrup to calming your own anxiety with a nervine tea, your apothecary equips you with safe, effective alternatives to over-the-counter medications.

2. Sustainability and Eco-Consciousness: By cultivating and preserving your own herbs or sourcing them from ethical suppliers, you contribute to a greener planet. A home apothecary encourages zero-waste practices, reduces packaging waste, and allows you to align your wellness journey with your environmental values.

3. Cost-Effectiveness: While the initial investment in creating your apothecary may seem significant, the long-term savings are undeniable. Herbs, when properly stored, can last for months or even years, providing you with countless remedies at a fraction of the cost of pharmaceuticals or commercial wellness products.

4. Connection to Tradition: A home apothecary is a living testament to the healing traditions passed down through generations. When you blend a tea or craft a tincture, you're participating in a timeless ritual, connecting with the wisdom of countless healers who came before you.

5. Customized Care: Every individual is unique, and so are their health needs. A home apothecary allows you to tailor remedies to your specific concerns. Whether you're addressing seasonal allergies, digestive discomfort, or emotional stress, your apothecary can be curated to suit your personal wellness journey.

How to Safely Use Herbs for Wellness

While herbs offer incredible benefits, it's essential to approach their use with care and respect. Unlike pharmaceuticals, which are standardized and mass-produced, herbs are living entities with unique properties that vary depending on their species, growth conditions, and preparation methods. To harness their healing potential safely, consider the following principles:

1. Understand Herbal Actions and Dosages: Herbs work in various ways—some stimulate the immune system, while others calm the nervous system or promote digestion. Familiarize yourself with the specific actions of the herbs in your apothecary and use recommended dosages to avoid overuse or adverse reactions.

2. Start Small: If you're new to herbalism, begin with gentle, well-known herbs such as chamomile, peppermint, or calendula. These are safe for most people and easy to incorporate into daily routines.

3. Research Potential Interactions: Herbs can interact with medications or other herbs. For example, St. John's Wort may reduce the effectiveness of certain antidepressants or birth control pills. Always consult reliable resources or a qualified herbalist if you're unsure about a combination.

4. Know Your Allergies: Just like foods, herbs can cause allergic reactions in some individuals. Introduce new herbs slowly and monitor for any signs of irritation or sensitivity.

5. Use High-Quality Ingredients: The effectiveness of an herbal remedy depends largely on the quality of the herbs used. Source your herbs from reputable suppliers or grow them yourself to ensure they're free from pesticides, contaminants, or adulteration.

6. Learn Proper Preparation Techniques: Different herbs require different preparation methods to unlock their benefits. For example, roots and barks are best extracted through decoctions, while delicate flowers and leaves are better suited for infusions. This book will guide you through these techniques step by step.

7. Store Herbs Properly: To preserve potency, store dried herbs in airtight containers, away from direct sunlight and moisture. Proper storage ensures your remedies remain effective for as long as possible.

8. Consult Professionals When Needed: While herbalism can address many common health concerns, it's not a substitute for professional medical care. For chronic or severe conditions, always seek advice from a qualified healthcare provider.

By practicing herbalism safely and responsibly, you can build a lasting relationship with nature's remedies and create a foundation of trust in your apothecary.

Understanding the Structure of This Book

This book is designed to be your comprehensive guide to herbal healing, offering both foundational knowledge and practical applications. Its structure is intentional, ensuring that you can easily navigate the content whether you're a complete beginner or someone looking to deepen your expertise.

1. Introduction and Foundations: The opening chapters introduce you to the philosophy and principles of herbalism. You'll learn about herbal actions, safety guidelines, and how to start your home apothecary with confidence.

2. Growing and Harvesting: For those who wish to cultivate their own herbs, this book provides guidance on planting, harvesting, and wildcrafting responsibly. You'll discover how to grow a sustainable herb garden, identify wild plants, and preserve your harvest.

3. Preparation Techniques: Understanding how to prepare herbs is essential. This section covers methods such as infusions, decoctions, tinctures, salves, and syrups, ensuring you can unlock the full potential of your herbs.

4. Remedies for Specific Needs: The heart of this book lies in its remedy-focused chapters, organized by health concerns. From respiratory health to skincare, digestive support, and stress relief, you'll find step-by-step recipes and instructions tailored to common ailments.

5. Seasonal and Specialty Practices: Herbalism is deeply connected to the rhythms of nature. This book explores seasonal practices, beauty rituals, and advanced techniques like creating herbal wines or zero-waste solutions.

6. Community and Legacy: Herbalism is not just a practice—it's a way of life. The final chapters encourage you to document your journey, share your knowledge with others, and create a legacy with your apothecary.

7. Appendices and Resources: For quick reference, the appendices include dosage charts, safety guidelines, and a glossary of terms. These resources ensure that you can access essential information whenever you need it.

Each chapter is filled with actionable insights, easy-to-follow recipes, and vibrant illustrations to make your learning journey enjoyable and accessible. Whether you prefer to read this book cover to cover or jump to specific sections, its structure allows you to tailor your experience to your needs.

Embarking on the path of herbal healing is both an empowering and rewarding endeavor. With the guidance of this book, you'll gain the knowledge, confidence, and skills to care for yourself and your loved ones naturally. As you build your home apothecary, remember that herbalism is not just about remedies—it's about embracing a holistic lifestyle that nurtures the body, mind, and spirit.

Now, let's begin this transformative journey and rediscover the wisdom of nature's healing power.

BOOK 1

THE FOUNDATIONS OF HERBALISM

Herbalism is an ancient practice that has stood the test of time, offering people a natural and holistic way to nurture health and well-being. To begin your journey into herbal healing, it's essential to start with a solid foundation. This book is designed to provide you with the core knowledge necessary to understand, appreciate, and practice herbalism effectively and safely.

We'll begin by exploring the roots of herbalism, including its rich history and its relevance in modern times. You'll discover how herbalism differs from conventional medicine and why it continues to be a trusted approach to wellness for millions around the world. The first chapter is an accessible guide for beginners, introducing the principles, methods, and scope of herbalism.

Next, we'll dive into herbal actions—the unique ways herbs work in the body—and the benefits they provide. From adaptogens to nervines, you'll gain clarity on the terms and concepts essential for crafting effective remedies. The book also explores the philosophy behind holistic healing, emphasizing the importance of treating the whole person, not just symptoms.

Finally, we'll address the ethical considerations of herbal practice, including sustainability, respect for cultural traditions, and safety. By the end of this book, you'll be well-prepared to confidently step into the world of herbalism with a strong, informed foundation.

What is Herbalism? A Beginner's Guide

Herbalism, the art and science of using plants for medicinal purposes, is one of humanity's oldest healing traditions. Long before the development of modern pharmaceuticals, people turned to nature to address their physical, emotional, and spiritual needs. From the roots and barks of ancient trees to the leaves and flowers of delicate herbs, plants have been a source of healing and nourishment for thousands of years.

At its core, herbalism seeks to harness the natural compounds found in plants to promote health and restore balance in the body. It views the body as a dynamic system, where physical, emotional, and environmental factors are interconnected. This holistic approach to health is what sets herbalism apart from many conventional medical practices, which often focus solely on treating symptoms rather than addressing the root causes of illness.

For beginners, herbalism may seem like an overwhelming field with its vast array of plants, preparation methods, and terminologies. However, starting with a basic understanding of its principles, benefits, and practices can demystify the process and open the door to a lifetime of healing knowledge.

The Origins and Evolution of Herbalism

Herbalism's roots stretch back to the dawn of human civilization. Archeological evidence suggests that even ancient hunter-gatherers used plants for medicinal purposes, guided by observation and experimentation. Over time, herbal practices evolved into sophisticated systems of medicine, each shaped by the unique cultures and environments in which they developed.

- Ancient Egypt and Mesopotamia: Ancient Egyptian medical texts, such as the Ebers Papyrus, document the use of plants like garlic, aloe, and myrrh for healing wounds, improving digestion, and embalming the dead. In Mesopotamia, clay tablets record recipes for herbal remedies used in rituals and treatments.
- Traditional Chinese Medicine (TCM): TCM has relied on herbalism for over 3,000 years, combining plant-based remedies with acupuncture, qi balancing, and dietary therapy. Iconic herbs such as ginseng, licorice root, and astragalus are still widely used today.
- Ayurveda: Originating in India, Ayurveda emphasizes balance between the body's energies, or doshas, and incorporates herbs like turmeric, ashwagandha, and neem to address various imbalances.
- Western Herbal Traditions: Rooted in the

teachings of ancient Greece and Rome, Western herbalism was greatly influenced by figures such as Hippocrates, Dioscorides, and Galen. During the Middle Ages, European monasteries preserved and advanced herbal knowledge.

Herbalism has continued to evolve, blending ancient wisdom with modern scientific research. Today, herbalists combine traditional practices with evidence-based approaches, making it more accessible and relevant than ever.

Key Principles of Herbalism

Understanding the principles of herbalism provides a solid foundation for beginners. These guiding concepts emphasize the holistic nature of herbal healing and its integration with the rhythms of nature.

1. The Body's Innate Healing Ability

Herbalism respects the body's natural ability to heal itself. Herbs are used to support and enhance this process, rather than suppress symptoms. For example, elderberry is often used to boost the immune system during a cold, helping the body fight off the infection more effectively.

2. Holistic Approach

Herbalism views health as a balance of physical, emotional, and environmental factors. A herbalist might recommend a combination of remedies to address not only a digestive issue but also related stress or dietary habits.

3. Synergy of Herbs

In herbalism, the whole plant is often used, rather than isolating a single compound. This practice takes advantage of the plant's synergy—how its components work together to create a more potent effect.

4. Individualized Care

Every person is unique, and herbalism acknowledges this by tailoring remedies to the individual's specific needs. Two people with the same symptoms might receive different recommendations based on their constitution, lifestyle, and preferences.

5. Sustainability and Respect for Nature

Herbalism emphasizes responsible foraging, ethical sourcing, and sustainable cultivation practices to protect the environment and ensure the long-term availability of medicinal plants.

Benefits of Herbalism

Herbalism offers numerous benefits, making it an appealing choice for those seeking natural and holistic approaches to health. Here are some of the key advantages:

1. Accessibility Many medicinal herbs are readily available and can be grown at home, making herbalism a cost-effective alternative to conventional treatments. Even beginners can start with common herbs like chamomile, peppermint, and rosemary.

2. Fewer Side Effects

When used responsibly, herbs are generally gentler on the body than synthetic drugs. For example, ginger can alleviate nausea without the drowsiness often associated with pharmaceutical options.

3. Comprehensive Wellness

Herbs often address multiple aspects of health simultaneously. For instance, adaptogens like ashwagandha not only reduce stress but also improve energy levels and support immune function.

4. Connection to Nature

Herbalism encourages a deeper relationship with the natural world. Whether you're harvesting fresh herbs from your garden or foraging in the wild, the practice fosters mindfulness and respect for the environment.

Types of Herbal Practices

Herbalism encompasses a wide range of practices, each with its unique methods and philosophies. Beginners may choose to explore one or more of these approaches:

1. Culinary Herbalism

Incorporating herbs into food and beverages is one of the simplest ways to experience their benefits. Common examples include using garlic for its antimicrobial properties or turmeric for its anti-inflammatory effects.

2. Medicinal Preparations

Herbal remedies can be prepared in various forms, such as teas, tinctures, salves, and capsules. Each method extracts different active compounds, making it important to choose the right preparation for the intended purpose.

3. Aromatherapy This practice uses essential oils derived from herbs to promote physical and emotional well-being. Lavender oil, for instance, is widely used for relaxation and stress relief.

4. Wildcrafting and Foraging

Gathering wild herbs connects practitioners to their local ecosystems and encourages sustainable practices. However, proper plant identification and ethical harvesting are crucial to avoid harm to both the environment and oneself.

Getting Started with Herbalism

For beginners, stepping into the world of herbalism can feel daunting. Here are practical steps to help you get started:

1. Start with a Few Herbs

Choose 3–5 easy-to-use herbs that address common needs in your household. Chamomile for relaxation, peppermint for digestion, and calendula for skin health are excellent starting points.

2. Learn Through Observation

Pay attention to how your body responds to different herbs. Keep a journal to record your experiences, noting any changes in symptoms, energy levels, or mood.

3. Invest in Reliable Resources

Equip yourself with trustworthy books, courses, or workshops to build your knowledge. Always cross-reference information to ensure accuracy.

4. Experiment with Simple Preparations

Begin with teas and infusions, which are straightforward and require minimal equipment. As your confidence grows, explore tinctures, salves, and other preparations.

5. Connect with Nature

Spend time outdoors to observe plants in their natural habitats. This practice enhances your understanding of herbs and their role in the ecosystem.

Common Myths About Herbalism

As you embark on your herbal journey, it's important to separate fact from fiction. Here are a few common myths and the truths behind them:

1. "Herbs Are Completely Safe"

While herbs are natural, they are not inherently risk-free. Proper dosages, contraindications, and individual sensitivities must be considered.

2. "Herbalism Is Not Scientific"

Modern research increasingly validates the efficacy of many traditional herbal remedies. For example, studies support the use of echinacea for immune support and turmeric for reducing inflammation.

3. "Herbs Work Instantly"

Unlike pharmaceuticals, herbs often work gradually, addressing the root causes of imbalances rather than providing quick fixes.

The Future of Herbalism

Herbalism is experiencing a revival in today's world, as people seek natural and sustainable alternatives to modern healthcare. With advancements in research and technology, herbal medicine is bridging the gap between tradition and science, offering evidence-based solutions for a wide range of health concerns.

By embracing herbalism, you're not only honoring an ancient tradition but also contributing to a movement that values health, sustainability, and a deep connection to the natural world.

Herbalism is a journey of exploration, empowerment, and healing. As a beginner, you don't need to know everything all at once. By starting with a basic understanding of its principles and practices, you'll gain the confidence to incorporate herbs into your daily life. Remember, every great herbalist began with a single step—learning about one herb, making one remedy, and embracing the wisdom of nature.

Let this chapter be the foundation of your herbal journey, guiding you toward greater health, self-reliance, and a deeper connection with the world around you. With curiosity and commitment, you're well on your way to discovering the transformative power of herbal healing.

Understanding Herbal Actions and Benefits

Herbal medicine is a powerful, versatile approach to health, rooted in the natural properties of plants. At the heart of this practice lies an essential understanding: herbs interact with the body in specific ways, guided by their "actions." These actions—such as calming the nervous system, reducing inflammation, or stimulating digestion—are the foundation of how herbs support wellness. By learning about herbal actions and their associated benefits, you'll be able to select the right herbs for specific health goals with confidence.

This chapter explores the most common herbal actions, explains their role in health and healing, and provides examples of herbs associated with each action. Whether you're addressing a particular ailment or simply looking to maintain balance and vitality, understanding these principles is key to harnessing the full potential of herbal remedies.

What Are Herbal Actions?

Herbal actions describe the effects herbs have on the body. They provide a systematic way to categorize herbs based on their primary uses, making it easier to match an herb to a specific need. For example, chamomile is a calmative because it soothes the nervous system, while ginger is a carminative because it relieves digestive discomfort.

These actions are not isolated; many herbs possess multiple actions that work synergistically to support overall health. For instance, lavender is both a nervine (calming the nerves) and a carminative (soothing the digestive system). This versatility is one of the reasons herbal medicine is so effective and widely practiced.

Categories of Herbal Actions and Their Benefits

Below are some of the most common herbal actions, along with examples of herbs that embody these properties.

1. Adaptogens

Definition: Adaptogens are herbs that help the body adapt to stress and maintain balance. They support the adrenal system, enhance energy levels, and improve resilience against physical and emotional challenges.

Benefits:

- Reduce fatigue and improve stamina.
- Enhance mental clarity and focus.
- Support the body during periods of stress or recovery.

Examples:

- Ashwagandha: Promotes relaxation and reduces cortisol levels.
- Rhodiola: Improves energy and reduces mental fatigue.
- Holy Basil (Tulsi): Supports emotional balance and reduces inflammation.

2. Nervines

Definition: Nervines are herbs that support the nervous system, either by calming or stimulating it. They are often used to manage stress, anxiety, and insomnia.

Benefits:

- Soothe frazzled nerves and reduce anxiety.
- Promote restful sleep.
- Enhance focus and concentration.

Examples:

- Chamomile: Gentle and calming, ideal for relaxation.
- Passionflower: Supports sleep and reduces tension.
- Lemon Balm: Uplifting and calming, often used for stress relief.

3. Carminatives

Definition: Carminatives are herbs that ease digestive discomfort by reducing gas, bloating, and cramping. They often have aromatic properties that stimulate digestion.

Benefits:

- Relieve indigestion, bloating, and flatulence.
- Support healthy digestion and nutrient absorption.
- Reduce spasms in the digestive tract.

Examples:

- Peppermint: Eases gas and soothes an upset stomach.
- Fennel: Relieves bloating and cramping.
- Ginger: Stimulates digestion and reduces nausea.

4. Anti-Inflammatories

Definition: Anti-inflammatory herbs reduce inflammation in the body, addressing both acute and chronic conditions.

Benefits:

- Relieve joint pain and swelling.
- Support recovery from injuries.
- Manage chronic inflammatory conditions like arthritis.

Examples:

- Turmeric: Contains curcumin, a potent anti-inflammatory compound.
- Boswellia (Frankincense): Reduces inflammation in joints and connective tissue.
- Willow Bark: A natural pain reliever with anti-inflammatory properties.

5. Antispasmodics

Definition: Antispasmodics relax muscle spasms, making them useful for conditions involving cramping or tension.

Benefits:

- Relieve menstrual cramps and muscle spasms.
- Soothe digestive cramping.
- Ease tension headaches.

Examples:

- Cramp Bark: Effective for menstrual cramps and uterine spasms.
- Valerian: Relaxes muscles and promotes restful sleep.
- Peppermint: Calms spasms in the digestive tract.

6. Immunomodulators

Definition: Immunomodulators are herbs that regulate and support the immune system, making them valuable for both boosting immunity and calming overactive immune responses.

Benefits:

- Strengthen the immune system during illness.
- Help manage autoimmune conditions.
- Reduce susceptibility to infections.

Examples:

- Echinacea: Boosts immune function and reduces the severity of colds.

- Astragalus: Enhances overall immune resilience.
- Reishi Mushroom: Balances the immune system and supports long-term health.

7. Expectorants

Definition: Expectorants help clear mucus from the respiratory system, making them useful for colds, coughs, and congestion.

Benefits:

- Loosen and expel mucus from the lungs.
- Soothe irritation in the respiratory tract.
- Support recovery from respiratory infections.

Examples:

- Licorice Root: Soothes inflamed airways and loosens mucus.
- Mullein: Clears mucus and supports lung health.
- Thyme: Antimicrobial and expectorant, ideal for coughs.

8. Astringents

Definition: Astringents tighten and tone tissues, making them useful for wounds, bleeding, and diarrhea.

Benefits:

- Heal minor cuts and abrasions.
- Reduce excessive bleeding or discharge.
- Support digestive health by firming tissues.

Examples:

- Witch Hazel: Commonly used for skin care and wound healing.
- Yarrow: Stops bleeding and supports wound healing.
- Raspberry Leaf: Tones the uterus and supports digestive health.

9. Diuretics

Definition: Diuretics promote the elimination of excess water and toxins through the kidneys.

Benefits:

- Reduce water retention and swelling.
- Support kidney and bladder health.
- Help eliminate toxins from the body.

Examples:

- Dandelion Leaf: A gentle diuretic that also provides potassium.
- Nettle: Supports kidney health and reduces inflammation.
- Parsley: Promotes urination and detoxification.

10. Hepatics

Definition: Hepatics are herbs that support liver health by improving detoxification and bile production.

Benefits:

- Enhance liver detoxification processes.
- Support digestion of fats.
- Improve overall energy and metabolism.

Examples:

- Milk Thistle: Protects liver cells and supports detoxification.
- Artichoke Leaf: Stimulates bile production and aids digestion.
- Dandelion Root: Detoxifies the liver and promotes digestion.

How to Apply Herbal Actions in Daily Life

Understanding herbal actions is not just about theory—it's about application. Here are a few practical ways to incorporate herbal actions into your daily routine:

1. Address Specific Needs: If you experience occasional anxiety, reach for nervines like chamomile or lemon balm. For sore muscles, consider an anti-inflammatory herb like turmeric.
2. Create Custom Blends: Many herbal remedies combine multiple actions to address complex needs. For example, a tea blend for relaxation might include nervines (like passionflower), carminatives (like peppermint), and adaptogens (like ashwagandha).
3. Seasonal Wellness: Use herbs that align with seasonal changes. In winter, immune-boosting herbs like echinacea and elderberry are ideal. In summer, cooling herbs like peppermint and hibiscus are refreshing.
4. Experiment and Observe: Every individual responds differently to herbs. Keep a journal to track how specific herbs affect your body and adjust your remedies accordingly.

Herbal actions form the foundation of understanding how herbs interact with the body. By familiarizing yourself with these categories, you gain the ability to select the right herbs for specific health goals and create remedies that address multiple needs. Whether you're calming frazzled nerves, boosting your immune system, or relieving digestive discomfort, herbal actions provide a clear roadmap to natural healing.

As you explore the vast world of herbal medicine, remember that the key lies in balance and experimentation. Herbs are not quick fixes but partners in your wellness journey, offering gentle, effective support that aligns with the body's natural rhythms. By mastering herbal actions, you take the first step toward crafting remedies that empower and heal.

The Philosophy of Holistic Healing

Holistic healing is not merely a practice but a philosophy that views health as a dynamic interplay of physical, mental, emotional, and spiritual well-being. Unlike conventional medicine, which often isolates symptoms and treats them independently, holistic healing seeks to address the root causes of imbalance while nurturing the whole person. It emphasizes the interconnectedness of all aspects of health, recognizing that a person's environment, lifestyle, and emotional state significantly influence their physical health.

Herbalism, as a cornerstone of holistic healing, embodies this philosophy. It embraces the belief that true health is achieved when the body, mind, and spirit function in harmony. This chapter delves into the core principles of holistic healing, exploring its relationship with herbalism and offering insights into how this approach can transform not just health, but also one's outlook on life.

The Core Principles of Holistic Healing

1. The Body as a Whole System: in holistic healing, the body is seen as an integrated system rather than a collection of separate parts. Every organ, tissue, and cell works in concert to maintain balance. When one system falters, others are affected. For example, chronic stress (a mental and emotional factor) can lead to digestive issues (a physical symptom). Holistic healing seeks to identify these connections and address them at their source.

Herbalism applies this principle by using remedies that support multiple systems. For instance, adaptogens like ashwagandha not only help the body cope with stress but also improve immune function and energy levels, addressing a cascade of interconnected issues.

2. Focus on Root Causes, Not Just Symptoms: conventional treatments often focus on suppressing symptoms, offering quick relief but rarely addressing the underlying issue. Holistic healing goes deeper, seeking the root cause of illness or imbalance. For example, instead of merely taking painkillers for recurring headaches, a holistic practitioner might explore potential causes such as dehydration, stress, or dietary deficiencies. Herbal remedies are tailored to this approach. For instance, a tea made from ginger and peppermint might alleviate the headache (a symptom) while improving digestion (a potential root cause) and reducing inflammation (a contributing factor).

3. Prevention Over Cure: prevention is a cornerstone of holistic healing. The philosophy emphasizes proactive care—strengthening the body's resilience before illness arises. This involves maintaining a balanced lifestyle, eating nourishing foods, managing stress, and integrating natural remedies into daily routines. Herbal tonics like elderberry syrup or nettle tea embody this preventive approach. They support immune health and provide essential nutrients, reducing the likelihood of illness during challenging times, such as flu season.

4. Balance and Harmony: holistic healing recognizes that health is about balance—balancing the body's internal systems, as well as its relationship with external factors like environment, relationships, and work-life dynamics. Traditional systems like Ayurveda and Traditional Chinese Medicine (TCM) have long emphasized balance, whether it's maintaining equilibrium between the doshas (Ayurveda) or yin and yang (TCM). Herbalism incorporates balance by combining herbs with complementary actions. A calming tea might include nervines like chamomile to soothe the mind and carminatives like fennel to ease digestion, creating a harmonious blend.

5. The Healing Power of Nature: holistic healing draws heavily from nature, embracing the idea that the earth provides everything we need to thrive. Herbs, essential oils, and natural foods are seen as gifts that support the body's natural healing processes. This principle fosters a deep connection to the natural world, encouraging sustainable and respectful practices. For example, wildcrafting herbs (responsibly gathering wild plants) not only provides potent remedies but also deepens one's relationship with the environment. The act of preparing a tea, tincture, or salve becomes a ritual of gratitude and mindfulness.

6. Patient Empowerment Holistic healing empowers individuals to take an active role in their health. Rather than being passive recipients of care, people are encouraged to make informed decisions, listen to their bodies, and embrace practices that nurture wellness. Herbalism naturally supports this empowerment. By learning to identify, grow, and prepare herbs, individuals gain the tools to address minor ailments at home, reducing dependence on conventional medications.

The Role of Herbalism in Holistic Healing

Herbalism is a natural extension of holistic healing, as it works with the body's innate healing mechanisms rather than against them. Herbs are not quick fixes but allies in promoting long-term balance and health. Here's how herbalism aligns with holistic principles:

1. Gentle, Gradual Healing: Unlike pharmaceuticals that often act aggressively on specific symptoms, herbs work gently, supporting the body's natural processes. For instance, rather than suppressing a cough, expectorant herbs like mullein help clear mucus, allowing the body to heal more effectively.

2. Multi-System Support: Many herbs have a broad range of actions, addressing multiple aspects of health simultaneously. For example, calendula not only promotes wound healing but also supports the lymphatic system and soothes inflamed tissues, making it a versatile ally in holistic care.

3. Individualized Care: Herbalism thrives on customization. A skilled herbalist considers the individual's unique constitution, lifestyle,

and emotional state when creating remedies. This personalized approach ensures that the chosen herbs address the person as a whole, rather than just their symptoms.

4. Ritual and Mindfulness: Preparing and using herbal remedies fosters mindfulness, turning the act of healing into a ritual. Whether it's brewing a cup of tea or massaging a salve into sore muscles, these moments of care enhance the connection between body and mind.

The Emotional and Spiritual Dimensions of Healing

Holistic healing recognizes that emotions and spirituality play a vital role in overall well-being. Negative emotions like stress, fear, and anger can manifest physically, leading to illness or prolonged recovery times. Conversely, cultivating positive emotions like gratitude and hope can accelerate healing and promote resilience.

1. Emotional Support through Herbs

Certain herbs are particularly effective for emotional healing. For instance:

- » Lemon Balm: Uplifting and calming, ideal for easing anxiety.
- » Rose: Soothes grief and nurtures the heart.
- » Holy Basil (Tulsi): Supports emotional resilience and clears mental fog.

2. Herbal Rituals for the Spirit

Herbs have long been used in spiritual practices. Smudging with sage, crafting herbal sachets, or sipping ceremonial teas are all ways to connect with the spiritual dimensions of herbalism. These rituals remind us that healing extends beyond the physical, touching the realms of purpose, connection, and meaning.

Practical Applications of Holistic Healing

To integrate holistic healing into daily life, consider the following practices:

1. Daily Herbal Rituals

Start your day with a grounding tea made from adaptogens like ashwagandha or rhodiola. In the evening, unwind with a nervine tea of chamomile and lavender to promote restful sleep.

2. Journaling for Awareness

Keep a health journal to track your physical, emotional, and mental states. Noticing patterns—like how stress impacts digestion—can guide you toward holistic solutions.

3. Seasonal Practices

Adjust your herbal routines to align with the seasons. In spring, detox with liver-supporting herbs like dandelion. In winter, boost immunity with elderberry and echinacea.

4. Mindful Eating

Incorporate culinary herbs like garlic, turmeric, and ginger into your meals for both flavor and health benefits. These small, intentional choices contribute to holistic well-being.

Challenges and Misconceptions in Holistic Healing

1. Patience and Commitment

Holistic healing is not a quick fix. It requires patience, as the focus is on long-term balance rather than immediate symptom relief. This slower pace can be challenging for those accustomed to instant results.

2. Misunderstanding the Role of Holistic Healing

Holistic healing is not an alternative to conventional medicine but a complement to it. Serious conditions often require the expertise of medical professionals, and holistic approaches should support—not replace—necessary interventions.

The philosophy of holistic healing offers a profound shift in how we view health and wellness. By addressing the whole person—body, mind, and spirit—it goes beyond symptom management to foster deep and lasting balance. Herbalism, as a key component of this approach, empowers individuals to take charge of their health while reconnecting with the natural world.

As you continue your journey into holistic healing, remember that every choice you make—whether it's sipping a calming tea, taking a mindful walk in nature, or addressing emotional stress—is a step toward greater harmony and well-being. Holistic healing is not just about curing illness; it's about cultivating a life that feels whole, vibrant, and aligned with the rhythms of nature.

Essential Ethics in Herbal Practice

Introduction to Ethical Herbalism

Herbalism is a practice deeply rooted in tradition, sustainability, and respect for nature. As stewards of this ancient art, herbalists have a responsibility to approach their work with ethical care and mindfulness. The ethics of herbalism encompass more than just proper plant usage; they also involve responsible harvesting, cultural sensitivity, environmental preservation, and ensuring the safety of those who use herbal remedies.

This chapter explores the essential ethical considerations in herbal practice. Whether you're foraging in the wild, purchasing herbs, or preparing remedies for others, adhering to these principles ensures that your work aligns with the values of respect, responsibility, and integrity that are fundamental to the herbalist's path.

1. Respecting the Environment

The foundation of ethical herbalism lies in respecting the environment from which we source our herbs. Plants are living beings, and their ecosystems are complex and interconnected. Overharvesting or careless foraging can disrupt these ecosystems, threatening plant populations and the wildlife that depend on them.

1. Sustainable Harvesting Practices
   » Take Only What You Need: Harvest only a small portion of any plant population, typically no more than 10–20%. This allows the plant community to regenerate and thrive.
   » Focus on Abundant Plants: Prioritize harvesting plants that are plentiful in your area, avoiding those that are rare or at risk.
   » Harvest at the Right Time: Learn the optimal time to harvest each plant to ensure its potency and ability to reproduce. For example, roots are often best harvested in the fall when the plant's energy is stored underground.

2. Avoiding Harmful Practices
   » Don't Disturb Habitats: Be mindful of your impact on the surrounding environment, avoiding practices that could harm wildlife or other plants.

   » Avoid Overharvesting Wild Plants: Certain herbs, like ginseng and goldenseal, have been overharvested to the point of endangerment. Refrain from gathering these plants in the wild unless you're part of a regulated conservation effort.

3. Planting and Giving Back
   » Ethical foraging involves giving back to the environment. This could mean scattering seeds, planting native species, or supporting rewilding efforts. By replenishing what you take, you contribute to the sustainability of herbal resources for future generations.

2. Cultural Sensitivity and Respect

Herbalism has deep roots in indigenous and traditional cultures around the world. Many of the herbs and techniques we use today come from practices that have been developed, refined, and preserved by these communities for centuries. It is vital to honor and respect the origins of these practices.

1. Acknowledging Cultural Contributions
   » Learn the History: Educate yourself about the cultural significance of the herbs and practices you use. For example, white sage, widely used for smudging, holds spiritual significance for many Indigenous American tribes.
   » Give Credit: When sharing herbal knowledge, acknowledge its cultural origins to avoid appropriating traditions without recognition.

2. Avoiding Cultural Appropriation
   » Be cautious not to exploit or commercialize cultural practices in a way that disrespects their sacredness. For example, mass-market smudging kits often strip away the spiritual context of the practice.

3. Supporting Indigenous Communities
   » Purchase herbs and products directly from Indigenous growers and producers whenever possible. This supports the communities that have preserved these traditions and ensures that your practices contribute to their well-being.

3. Ensuring Safety and Informed Use

As an herbalist, your first responsibility is to ensure the safety and well-being of yourself and others. Ethical practice means providing accurate information, being transparent about the limitations of herbal remedies, and avoiding harm.

1. Knowledge and Education
   » Know Your Herbs: Familiarize yourself with the actions, uses, and potential contraindications of each herb you work with. For example, St. John's Wort can interact with certain medications, reducing their effectiveness.
   » Keep Learning: Herbalism is a dynamic field with ongoing research. Stay informed about new findings, safety concerns, and best practices.

2. Honesty About Limitations
   » Be clear that herbal remedies are not a substitute for professional medical care. Encourage people to seek medical advice for serious or chronic conditions and use herbs as a complementary approach when appropriate.

3. Safe Dosages and Preparations
   » Always use correct dosages and preparation methods to avoid adverse effects. For example, while yarrow is excellent for wound healing, it should not be ingested in large amounts as it may cause digestive upset.

4. Labeling and Instructions
   » If you're providing remedies to others, ensure that they're labeled clearly with the name of the herb, preparation method, dosage instructions, and potential warnings.

4. Transparency and Integrity

Ethical herbalism involves being transparent and honest in all aspects of your practice, from sourcing herbs to working with clients or sharing knowledge.

1. Ethical Sourcing
   » Purchase herbs from reputable suppliers who prioritize organic, sustainable, and fair-trade practices. This ensures that the herbs you use are free from pesticides and grown with respect for the environment and workers.

2. Avoiding Exploitation
   » If you're selling herbal products or services, ensure that your pricing is fair and accessible. Avoid overstating the benefits of herbs or making unrealistic claims.

3. Full Disclosure
   » Be honest about the origin of your herbs and remedies. If a product contains synthetic additives or non-organic ingredients, disclose this information.

5. Personal Responsibility and Self-Care

As a practitioner, your own well-being is a critical part of ethical herbalism. The energy and intention you bring to your practice affect the quality of your work and the trust you build with others.

1. Commit to Self-Care
   » Herbalism can be physically and emotionally demanding, especially if you're foraging, preparing remedies, or working with others. Incorporate self-care practices into your routine to maintain balance.

2. Respect Your Limits
   » Know when to refer someone to a more experienced herbalist or a healthcare professional. Ethical practice means recognizing your boundaries and prioritizing the best care for others.

6. Environmental and Community Advocacy

Ethical herbalists are often advocates for environmental and community health. Your work has the potential to influence not just individuals, but entire ecosystems and social structures.

1. Educate Others
   » Share your knowledge of sustainable practices, ethical harvesting, and the importance of biodiversity. Encourage others to adopt environmentally friendly habits in their herbal practices.

2. Support Conservation Efforts
   » Get involved in initiatives to protect endangered plants, conserve wild spaces, and promote the reintroduction of native species.

3. Build Community
    »   Herbalism has always been a community-centered practice. Host workshops, collaborate with local growers, and create spaces for sharing knowledge and resources.

7. Embracing the Spirit of Herbalism

Beyond the practical aspects, ethical herbalism is a deeply spiritual practice. It calls for mindfulness, gratitude, and a profound connection to the natural world.

1. Mindful Harvesting
    »   Approach your work with reverence. When harvesting, take a moment to express gratitude to the plants and the earth for their gifts.

2. Ritual and Intention
    »   Infuse your herbal practices with intention, whether it's through meditation, prayer, or quiet reflection. These rituals not only enhance the potency of your remedies but also deepen your connection to the plants.

3. Fostering Gratitude
    »   Recognize that herbalism is a gift passed down through generations. Honor the traditions, the plants, and the communities that make this practice possible.

Ethical herbalism is about more than using plants to heal—it's about cultivating a practice rooted in respect, responsibility, and mindfulness. By honoring the environment, respecting cultural traditions, ensuring safety, and practicing transparency, you can align your herbal work with the highest ethical standards.

As you continue your journey, remember that every decision you make—whether it's how you harvest a plant or how you share a remedy—has a ripple effect. Ethical herbalism is not just a practice but a way of life, one that nurtures both people and the planet. By embodying these principles, you contribute to a tradition of healing that is as sustainable and compassionate as it is powerful.

BOOK 2

THE ANATOMY OF AN HERB

Herbs are nature's intricate masterpieces, with each part serving a unique purpose in promoting health and vitality. Understanding the anatomy of an herb—its roots, stems, leaves, flowers, and seeds—provides valuable insight into how these plants work and how to use them effectively. Every component has its own healing properties, and learning how to identify and utilize them is a cornerstone of herbal practice.

In this book, we'll explore the fascinating roles of different plant parts, from roots that ground and stabilize to flowers that radiate gentle, healing energy. You'll learn how various components contribute to an herb's medicinal qualities and why certain parts are harvested for specific remedies.

We'll also cover seasonal harvesting techniques to ensure maximum potency and efficacy, as well as practical tips for identifying herbs in the wild or your garden. By the end of this book, you'll have a deeper appreciation for the complexity of herbs and the knowledge to harvest and use them with confidence. This foundational understanding is key to unlocking the full potential of herbal healing in your apothecary.

The Role of Roots, Stems, Leaves, and Flowers

Herbs are nature's powerhouse healers, and understanding their anatomy unlocks their full potential in herbal medicine. Each part of an herb—roots, stems, leaves, and flowers—plays a unique role in the plant's life and in its medicinal properties. By studying these components, you'll gain a deeper appreciation of how herbs work and how to use them effectively in your remedies.

This chapter explores the unique roles of each plant part, their associated medicinal properties, and how to harvest and prepare them for maximum efficacy. Whether you're crafting a tea, tincture, or salve, knowing which part of the herb to use is key to creating potent and effective remedies.

The Role of Roots

Roots anchor plants to the earth, providing stability and absorbing water and nutrients from the soil. This grounding function mirrors their medicinal properties, as roots are often associated with nourishment, strengthening, and grounding in herbal medicine.

1. Medicinal Properties of Roots
   - » Nourishment and Strength: Many roots, such as dandelion and burdock, are rich in vitamins, minerals, and other nutrients, making them excellent for overall health and vitality.
   - » Detoxification: Roots like milk thistle and chicory support liver health, aiding the body in detoxifying harmful substances.
   - » Adaptogenic Support: Adaptogenic roots like ashwagandha and licorice help the body adapt to stress and restore balance.

2. Common Roots and Their Uses
   - » Dandelion Root: Supports liver detoxification and promotes digestion.
   - » Ginger Root: Relieves nausea, improves circulation, and reduces inflammation.
   - » Valerian Root: Acts as a sedative, promoting relaxation and restful sleep.

3. Harvesting Roots
   - » Roots are best harvested in the fall when the plant's energy has returned to the root system. This ensures the highest concentration of nutrients and medicinal compounds.
   - » Use a digging fork or spade to carefully loosen the soil and avoid damaging the root.

The Role of Stems

Stems serve as the plant's framework, providing support and acting as conduits for transporting water, nutrients, and sugars between the roots and leaves. In herbal medicine, stems are often overlooked but can have valuable therapeutic properties.

1. Medicinal Properties of Stems
   - » Structural Support: Stems often contain compounds that mirror their structural role in the plant, such as silica, which supports connective tissue and bone health.
   - » Circulatory Benefits: Certain stems, like celery, have diuretic properties that promote healthy circulation and reduce water retention.
   - » Astringency: Many stems have astringent properties, making them useful in tonics for tightening and toning tissues.

2. Common Stems and Their Uses
   - » Cinnamon Bark (a modified stem): Known for its warming, circulatory-boosting properties and antimicrobial benefits.
   - » Horsetail Stem: Rich in silica, it supports bone health and strengthens hair and nails.
   - » Raspberry Cane: Used in traditional remedies for its mild astringent properties.

3. Harvesting Stems
   - » Stems are typically harvested during the plant's active growth phase, often in spring or summer. For woody stems, pruning tools may be needed to cut them cleanly.

The Role of Leaves

Leaves are the workhorses of the plant, responsible for photosynthesis—the process of converting sunlight into energy. This vital function reflects their importance in herbal medicine, as leaves often contain a high concentration of active compounds.

1. Medicinal Properties of Leaves
   - » Cooling and Soothing: Leaves like peppermint and chamomile are known for their calming effects on the digestive system and nervous system.
   - » Nutrient-Rich: Many leaves, such as nettle and moringa, are packed with vitamins and minerals, making them ideal for nourishing teas and powders.
   - » Antimicrobial and Immune-Boosting: Leaves like oregano and thyme have powerful antimicrobial properties, supporting the immune system.

2. Common Leaves and Their Uses
   - » Nettle Leaves: Rich in iron and other nutrients, they support energy and combat fatigue.
   - » Mint Leaves: Soothe digestion and provide a refreshing flavor in teas and tinctures.
   - » Sage Leaves: Known for their antimicrobial properties and use in respiratory health.

3. Harvesting Leaves
   - » Leaves should be harvested when they are fresh and vibrant, typically in the morning after the dew has dried. Avoid harvesting damaged or yellowing leaves, as they may have reduced potency.

The Role of Flowers

Flowers are the reproductive centers of plants, often brightly colored and fragrant to attract pollinators. In herbal medicine, flowers are prized for their delicate yet potent properties, offering a range of therapeutic benefits.

1. Medicinal Properties of Flowers
   - » Calming and Uplifting: Many flowers, like lavender and chamomile, are used for their soothing effects on the mind and body.
   - » Anti-Inflammatory and Antioxidant: Flowers like calendula and hibiscus contain compounds that reduce inflammation and combat oxidative stress.
   - » Skin Healing: Flowers such as calendula are often used in salves and creams for their ability to soothe and heal skin irritations.

2. Common Flowers and Their Uses
   - » Chamomile: Calms the nervous system, aids digestion, and promotes restful sleep.
   - » Calendula: Soothes skin irritations and supports wound healing.
   - » Lavender: Eases anxiety, promotes relaxation, and can be used in skin care remedies.

3. Harvesting Flowers
   - » Flowers are best harvested in the morning, just as they open and before the heat

of the day diminishes their essential oils. Use scissors or pruning shears to cut flowers carefully without damaging the plant.

Working with Different Plant Parts

Each plant part requires specific preparation techniques to extract its medicinal properties effectively. Here are some common methods:

1. Roots: Often prepared as decoctions (simmered in water) to extract their dense, water-soluble compounds.
2. Stems: Used in teas or tinctures, depending on their texture and properties.
3. Leaves: Ideal for infusions, where they are steeped in hot water to release their active compounds.
4. Flowers: Typically used in infusions or as ingredients in salves and oils due to their delicate nature.

The Synergy of Plant Parts

In many cases, different parts of the same plant can be used together to create a more holistic remedy. For example:

- Dandelion: The root supports liver detoxification, while the leaves act as a diuretic to flush out toxins.
- Elder: The flowers help reduce fever and promote sweating, while the berries boost immune function.

This synergy reflects the interconnectedness of plants and their ability to address multiple aspects of health simultaneously.

Understanding the roles of roots, stems, leaves, and flowers is fundamental to becoming a skilled herbalist. Each part of a plant offers unique properties and benefits, contributing to its overall medicinal value. By learning how to identify, harvest, and prepare these components, you'll gain the knowledge to craft remedies that harness the full power of herbs. This foundational understanding not only enhances your herbal practice but also deepens your connection to the plants and their remarkable capabilities.

How Different Parts Serve Different Purposes

Every part of an herb has its unique role, not only in the life of the plant but also in its medicinal applications. From the deep-reaching roots to the delicate flowers, each part contains distinct compounds that contribute to its overall healing potential. Understanding how different parts of a plant serve specific purposes is essential for crafting effective herbal remedies. This chapter dives into the functions of roots, stems, leaves, flowers, and other plant parts, exploring how they can be used individually or synergistically to address various health needs.

Roots: Foundations of Strength and Stability

Roots are the anchors of a plant, providing stability, drawing nutrients and water from the soil, and storing energy. In herbal medicine, roots often mirror these functions, offering grounding and nourishing properties that support overall vitality.

1. Primary Uses of Roots
   » Nourishment and Fortification: Roots like dandelion and burdock are rich in vitamins, minerals, and prebiotic fibers, making them excellent for supporting digestion and overall health.
   » Adaptogenic Support: Roots such as ashwagandha and Siberian ginseng help the body adapt to stress, balance hormones, and boost resilience.
   » Detoxification: Many roots, including yellow dock and chicory, are used to support liver detoxification and promote the elimination of toxins.

2. Key Compounds Found in Roots
   » Inulin: A prebiotic fiber that supports gut health (e.g., dandelion root).
   » Saponins: Compounds that enhance immune function and support hormonal balance (e.g., licorice root).
   » Alkaloids: Bioactive compounds with therapeutic properties, often found in medicinal roots like goldenseal.

3. Application of Roots
   » Roots are typically prepared as decoctions, tinctures, or powders, allowing their

dense and robust compounds to be effectively extracted.

Stems: Channels of Energy and Support

Stems act as conduits, transporting water, nutrients, and energy throughout the plant. While often overlooked in herbal medicine, stems play an important role in supporting structural integrity and contributing unique compounds to remedies.

1. Primary Uses of Stems
   » Strength and Flexibility: Stems like horsetail contain silica, which strengthens connective tissues, bones, and hair.
   » Circulatory Support: Certain stems, such as cinnamon bark (technically a modified stem), improve circulation and provide warming properties.
   » Astringency and Toning: Woody stems, like raspberry cane, are mildly astringent and can tone tissues when used in teas or washes.

2. Key Compounds Found in Stems
   » Silica: Promotes bone and joint health (e.g., horsetail stems).
   » Cinnamaldehyde: Found in cinnamon, offering anti-inflammatory and antimicrobial benefits.
   » Tannins: Present in woody stems, helping tighten and tone tissues.

3. Application of Stems
   » Stems are often dried and used in teas, tinctures, or decoctions. Woody stems may require longer steeping times to release their beneficial compounds.

Leaves: The Powerhouses of Healing

Leaves are the primary sites of photosynthesis, converting sunlight into energy to sustain the plant. This vital role is reflected in their medicinal properties, as leaves often contain a high concentration of bioactive compounds that promote healing and balance.

1. Primary Uses of Leaves
   » Soothing and Cooling: Leaves like peppermint and lemon balm are known for their calming and refreshing effects.
   » Nutritional Support: Leaves such as nettle

and moringa are nutrient-dense and are often used to combat deficiencies.
   » Immune and Respiratory Support: Herbs like thyme and oregano have antimicrobial properties that boost immune function and clear the respiratory tract.

2. Key Compounds Found in Leaves
   » Volatile Oils: Found in aromatic leaves like mint and basil, offering antimicrobial and digestive benefits.
   » Chlorophyll: Present in green leaves, supporting detoxification and oxygenation.
   » Flavonoids: Potent antioxidants that protect cells from damage (e.g., in green tea leaves).

3. Application of Leaves
   » Leaves are often used in infusions, tinctures, and powders. Their delicate nature makes them ideal for quick steeping methods that preserve their aromatic compounds.

Flowers: Delicate Yet Powerful

Flowers are the reproductive centers of plants, often containing concentrated essential oils and delicate compounds. Their beauty and fragrance are matched by their therapeutic properties, which range from calming the mind to soothing the skin.

1. Primary Uses of Flowers
   » Calming the Nervous System: Flowers like chamomile and lavender are used to reduce anxiety, promote relaxation, and improve sleep quality.
   » Skin Healing: Flowers such as calendula are often used in salves and creams to soothe irritated or inflamed skin.
   » Digestive Support: Some flowers, like fennel and hibiscus, aid in digestion and support the elimination of toxins.

2. Key Compounds Found in Flowers
   » Essential Oils: Provide soothing, antimicrobial, and uplifting properties (e.g., lavender and rose).
   » Mucilage: Found in marshmallow flowers, helping to soothe irritated tissues.
   » Anthocyanins: Potent antioxidants in

brightly colored flowers like hibiscus, promoting cardiovascular health.

3. Application of Flowers
   » Flowers are often prepared as infusions, salves, or oils. Their delicate nature makes them ideal for topical and aromatic uses as well.

Fruits and Seeds: Concentrated Energy

Fruits and seeds represent the culmination of a plant's life cycle, containing concentrated energy and nutrients. In herbal medicine, they are often used for their tonic and restorative properties.

1. Primary Uses of Fruits and Seeds
   » Digestive Health: Seeds like fennel and anise ease bloating and support healthy digestion.
   » Nutritional Boost: Fruits such as rose hips are rich in vitamins and antioxidants, supporting immune health.
   » Hormonal Support: Seeds like milk thistle and fenugreek are used to balance hormones and support liver function.

2. Key Compounds Found in Fruits and Seeds
   » Essential Fatty Acids: Found in seeds like flax and chia, supporting brain and heart health.
   » Vitamin C: Present in fruits like rose hips, boosting immunity and collagen production.
   » Lignans: Found in seeds like flax, offering hormone-regulating benefits.

3. Application of Fruits and Seeds
   » Fruits and seeds can be used in teas, tinctures, or oils. For example, rose hip tea provides a nourishing boost of vitamin C, while fennel seed tea aids digestion.

Synergy Between Plant Parts

While each plant part serves a specific purpose, their real power emerges when used together. The combination of different parts can create a more comprehensive remedy that addresses multiple aspects of health.

1. Elder Plant Synergy:
   » Flowers promote sweating to reduce fever, while the berries strengthen the immune system.

2. Dandelion Plant Synergy:
   » Roots support liver detoxification, and leaves act as a diuretic to flush toxins from the body.

This holistic approach mirrors the interconnectedness of the plant itself and the body systems it supports.

Understanding the Plant's Lifecycle

The medicinal properties of a plant's parts can vary depending on its stage of growth. For example:

- Young Leaves: Tend to be more tender and nutrient-rich, ideal for infusions.
- Mature Roots: Store more energy and medicinal compounds, best harvested in fall.

Recognizing these changes ensures that you harvest and use the plant at its peak potency.

Understanding how different parts of an herb serve distinct purposes is a vital skill for any herbalist. Roots ground and detoxify, stems support and channel energy, leaves nourish and protect, flowers calm and uplift, and seeds provide concentrated nutrition. By learning the unique properties and applications of each part, you'll be better equipped to craft remedies that harness the full potential of the plant. This knowledge not only enriches your herbal practice but also deepens your connection to the plants and their remarkable abilities to heal and sustain.

Seasonal Harvesting for Maximum Potency

In herbal medicine, timing is everything. The potency and efficacy of herbs depend heavily on when and how they are harvested. Plants are living organisms with cycles of growth, flowering, fruiting, and dormancy, and their medicinal compounds fluctuate throughout these stages. By understanding the seasons and the life cycles of plants, herbalists can harvest herbs at their peak potency, ensuring the highest quality remedies.

This chapter explores the art and science of seasonal harvesting. It provides guidance on identifying the best times to collect roots, stems, leaves, flowers, and seeds, as well as practical tips for harvesting sustainably. Whether you're foraging in the wild or tending your own herb garden, this knowledge is key to maximizing the effectiveness of your herbal preparations.

The Importance of Seasonal Harvesting

1. Optimal Potency Plants produce different compounds at different times in their life cycle. For example:
   » Roots store energy and nutrients during the plant's dormant phase.
   » Flowers are at their most potent just as they bloom.
   » Leaves contain the highest levels of chlorophyll and nutrients during active growth.
2. Respecting the Plant's Lifecycle Harvesting at the wrong time can damage or even kill the plant. For example, overharvesting roots before the plant has a chance to seed can deplete the population.
3. Sustainability and Regeneration Seasonal harvesting allows plants to regenerate naturally, ensuring their availability for future generations. Ethical timing and methods protect ecosystems and biodiversity.

Seasonal Guide to Harvesting Herbs

Spring Harvest: The Season of Renewal

Spring is a time of new growth, making it ideal for harvesting fresh, tender parts of plants. During this season, energy is concentrated in the above-ground parts as plants awaken from dormancy.

1. What to Harvest in Spring
   » Young Leaves: Nettles, dandelion greens, and chickweed are nutrient-dense in spring and perfect for teas or tinctures.
   » Early Flowers: Spring-blooming flowers like violet, lilac, and hawthorn are potent and aromatic during this season.
   » Fresh Stems: New growth on plants like raspberry or blackberry canes can be harvested for their astringent properties.
2. Tips for Spring Harvesting
   » Harvest leaves and flowers in the morning after the dew has dried but before the sun diminishes their essential oils.

» Use scissors or pruning shears to cut delicate parts cleanly without damaging the plant.

Summer Harvest: The Season of Abundance

Summer is the peak growing season for many herbs, with plants concentrating their energy in flowers, leaves, and fruits. This is the ideal time to harvest most aerial parts of plants.

1. What to Harvest in Summer
   » Flowers: Chamomile, lavender, and calendula flowers are at their most potent during early bloom.
   » Mature Leaves: Herbs like basil, mint, and lemon balm thrive in summer and are perfect for culinary and medicinal uses.
   » Aromatic Herbs: Plants like rosemary, thyme, and oregano have the highest concentration of essential oils during this time.
2. Tips for Summer Harvesting
   » Harvest flowers just as they open, as this is when their essential oils are most concentrated.
   » Pinch or prune leaves regularly to encourage new growth, particularly in herbs like basil and mint.
   » For culinary herbs, harvest just before the plant flowers for the best flavor.

Fall Harvest: The Season of Roots and Fruits

As plants prepare for dormancy, energy moves downward into their roots. Fall is the ideal time to harvest roots, fruits, and seeds, as they contain the plant's stored nutrients and energy.

1. What to Harvest in Fall
   » Roots: Burdock, dandelion, and echinacea roots are at their peak potency in the fall.
   » Berries and Fruits: Elderberries, rose hips, and hawthorn berries are ripe and ready for harvest.
   » Seeds: Collect seeds from herbs like fennel, dill, and milk thistle for culinary or medicinal use.
2. Tips for Fall Harvesting
   » Use a digging fork to carefully loosen the soil around roots, avoiding damage.
   » Collect fruits and berries at peak ripeness

to ensure the highest concentration of nutrients.

» Dry seeds thoroughly before storing them to prevent mold.

Winter Harvest: The Season of Dormancy

Winter is a quiet time in the plant world, but some herbs remain active underground or in evergreen foliage. Winter harvesting is limited but can yield valuable remedies.

1. What to Harvest in Winter

   » Evergreen Leaves: Rosemary, pine needles, and sage retain their potency through the colder months.
   » Roots: In mild climates, roots like valerian and horseradish can still be dug up during winter.

2. Tips for Winter Harvesting

   » Focus on harvesting only what you need, as plant growth is slow and regeneration takes time.
   » Protect your hands and tools from the cold, as winter harvesting can be physically demanding.

Practical Tips for Harvesting Herbs

1. Timing of Harvest

   » Morning Harvesting: Most herbs are best harvested in the morning, after dew has evaporated but before the heat of the day diminishes their potency.
   » Avoid Wet Weather: Harvesting during wet conditions can lead to mold and spoilage.

2. Tools and Equipment

   » Use sharp scissors, pruning shears, or knives for clean cuts to minimize damage to the plant.
   » Carry a basket or cloth bag to allow for airflow and prevent crushing delicate parts.

3. Signs of Readiness

   » Flowers: Look for buds that are just beginning to open.
   » Leaves: Harvest when leaves are vibrant and free from yellowing or damage.
   » Roots: Harvest when the plant's aboveground growth begins to die back in the fall.

4. Handling and Storage

   » Gently clean roots and leaves to remove dirt or insects, but avoid washing flowers unless absolutely necessary.
   » Dry herbs in a well-ventilated, dark space to preserve their color, aroma, and potency.

Ethical and Sustainable Harvesting Practices

1. Harvest with Intent

   » Take only what you need and leave enough for the plant to regenerate and for wildlife that depends on it.
   » Avoid overharvesting rare or endangered plants; consider growing these species in your garden instead.

2. Know Your Plants

   » Learn to identify herbs accurately to avoid accidental harvesting of toxic or look-alike plants.
   » Study the habitat and growth patterns of the plants you intend to harvest to ensure sustainable practices.

3. Support Biodiversity

   » Rotate your harvesting areas to prevent overuse of a single location.
   » Consider planting native herbs in your garden to reduce the pressure on wild populations.

The Science of Seasonal Potency

Scientific research has confirmed that plants' chemical compositions vary with the seasons. For example:

• Echinacea: The root contains higher concentrations of alkylamides in the fall, enhancing its immune-supportive properties.
• Rosemary: Its essential oil content peaks in the summer when the plant receives the most sunlight.

Understanding these variations allows herbalists to harness the full power of each plant part at the right time.

Seasonal harvesting is both an art and a science, requiring careful observation, knowledge, and respect for nature. By aligning your harvesting practices with the natural rhythms of plants, you can ensure maximum potency in your remedies while supporting the health and sustainability of the environment. This seasonal awareness not only enhances the quality of your herbal preparations but also deepens your connection to the plants and the ecosystems they inhabit. As you practice seasonal harvesting, you'll gain a greater appreciation for the cycles of nature and the profound wisdom they offer.

Tips for Proper Herb Identification

Proper herb identification is a cornerstone of herbalism. Misidentifying plants can lead to ineffective remedies, wasted effort, or even harmful outcomes. With countless species of plants—many of which look remarkably similar—it's essential to develop a systematic approach to identifying herbs confidently and accurately.

This chapter explores the tools, techniques, and best practices for proper herb identification. Whether you're foraging in the wild, cultivating a garden, or purchasing dried herbs, learning to identify plants correctly ensures the safety, potency, and effectiveness of your herbal remedies.

Why Proper Herb Identification is Essential

1. Safety First Some plants are toxic or can cause allergic reactions if misused. For example, the leaves of edible elderberry (Sambucus nigra) can be confused with those of poisonous water hemlock (Cicuta spp.). Correct identification ensures you avoid dangerous plants.
2. Maximizing Potency Different species of plants, and even different parts of the same plant, contain varying levels of active compounds. Harvesting the wrong species or using the incorrect part can reduce the effectiveness of your remedies.
3. Respect for Nature Accurate identification helps prevent overharvesting rare or endangered plants, allowing you to focus on sustainable and abundant species.

Essential Tools for Herb Identification

Investing in the right tools can make herb identification easier and more accurate. Here are the essentials:

1. Field Guidebooks
   » Choose region-specific guidebooks with clear photographs and detailed descriptions.
   » Look for guides that include information on plant habitats, growth patterns, and potential look-alikes.
2. Plant Identification Apps
   » Use apps like PlantSnap or iNaturalist to supplement your knowledge. While these apps are helpful, always cross-reference with a reliable guidebook or expert.
3. Magnifying Glass or Hand Lens
   » A 10x magnifying glass allows you to examine small details, such as leaf veins, flower structures, and trichomes (plant hairs).
4. Notebook and Camera
   » Document your observations with photos and detailed notes about the plant's size, location, and surrounding environment. This helps with later identification and learning.
5. Herbarium Samples
   » Collect and press samples of plants you've confidently identified. Creating your own herbarium (a collection of preserved plant specimens) provides a personal reference library.

Key Features for Identifying Herbs

When identifying herbs, focus on specific features that distinguish one plant from another. By learning to observe these characteristics, you can confidently differentiate between similar-looking plants.

1. Leaves

Leaves are often the most distinctive part of a plant. Consider these aspects:

- Shape: Leaves can be round, lance-shaped, heart-shaped, or deeply lobed.
- Edges: Look for smooth, serrated, or wavy margins.
- Veins: Observe whether the veins are parallel (as in grasses) or branching (as in most herbs).
- Arrangement: Note how leaves are posi-

tioned on the stem—alternately, opposite, or in whorls.

Example: Stinging nettle (Urtica dioica) has serrated, heart-shaped leaves arranged oppositely, which helps distinguish it from similar plants like dead nettle (Lamium purpureum).

2. Flowers

Flowers are key to identifying plants, as they often have unique colors, shapes, and structures.

- Number of Petals: Count the petals or look for patterns (e.g., five-petaled flowers are common in the rose family).
- Color: Observe the flower's hue and whether it changes over time.
- Shape: Look for distinctive forms like tubular (mint family), bell-shaped (bluebell), or composite (dandelion).

Example: Yarrow (Achillea millefolium) has clusters of tiny, white flowers with a flat-topped appearance, helping to differentiate it from similar-looking plants like Queen Anne's lace (Daucus carota).

3. Stems

The stem's texture, shape, and growth pattern can provide critical clues:

- Square vs. Round: Plants in the mint family (Lamiaceae) often have square stems.
- Hairy vs. Smooth: Examine whether the stem is covered in hairs, as in mullein, or smooth, as in dandelion.
- Hollow vs. Solid: Some plants, like fennel, have hollow stems, which can help distinguish them from look-alikes.

4. Roots

Roots are typically examined after harvest, but they can offer important identification features:

- Shape: Taproots (e.g., dandelion) differ from fibrous roots (e.g., grasses).
- Color and Texture: Note whether the root is woody, fleshy, or brittle.

Example: Burdock (Arctium lappa) has a long, deep taproot, distinguishing it from other plants with similar above-ground features.

5. Habitat and Growth Pattern

The environment where a plant grows often provides important clues:

- Soil Type: Some plants, like plantain, prefer compacted soil, while others, like horsetail, thrive in wet, sandy areas.
- Light and Shade: Observe whether the plant grows in full sun, partial shade, or deep forested areas.
- Growth Pattern: Consider whether the plant grows as a single specimen, in clusters, or spreads aggressively.

Common Pitfalls and How to Avoid Them

Even experienced herbalists can make mistakes. Here's how to avoid common pitfalls:

1. Confusing Look-Alikes
   » Some plants have toxic look-alikes. For instance, hemlock (poisonous) resembles Queen Anne's lace (edible). Always double-check key features like flowers and stems.
2. Relying on a Single Feature
   » Avoid identifying a plant based on one characteristic alone. Use a combination of features—leaves, flowers, stems, and habitat—for accurate identification.
3. Assuming Garden Plants Are Always Safe
   » Many garden plants, such as foxglove and monkshood, are toxic despite their beauty. Be cautious with plants you didn't intentionally cultivate.
4. Harvesting Without Certainty
   » If you're unsure about a plant's identity, don't harvest it. Take photos, make notes, and consult guidebooks or experts before proceeding.

Building Confidence in Identification

1. Start Small
   » Begin by learning a few easy-to-identify herbs, such as dandelion, chamomile, and mint. Master these before expanding your knowledge.
2. Learn Through Repetition
   » Spend time observing the same plant

throughout its lifecycle. This helps you understand how its features change with the seasons.

3. Join a Community
   » Connect with local herbalists, foraging groups, or botany clubs. Group outings provide hands-on learning and mentorship opportunities.

4. Practice Drawing
   » Sketching plants encourages close observation and helps you remember details better than photos alone.

Ethical and Sustainable Identification Practices

Proper herb identification goes hand-in-hand with ethical harvesting. Always follow these principles:

- Harvest Responsibly: Take only what you need and leave enough for the plant to thrive and reproduce.
- Avoid Endangered Species: Learn which plants in your area are protected or at risk, and avoid harvesting them.
- Share Knowledge: Educate others about responsible foraging and proper identification techniques.

When to Consult an Expert

Sometimes, identifying a plant requires more expertise than a beginner may have. Consult an experienced herbalist, botanist, or local extension office if:

- You encounter a plant with no clear match in your guidebooks.
- You suspect the plant may have toxic look-alikes.
- You want to confirm the identity of a plant before using it medicinally.

Mastering herb identification is an ongoing process that requires patience, observation, and practice. By focusing on key plant features, using reliable tools, and consulting trusted resources, you'll build confidence in identifying herbs accurately. This knowledge not only ensures the safety and efficacy of your remedies but also deepens your connection to the natural world. With each plant you identify, you become a more skilled and ethical herbalist, equipped to create powerful remedies that honor both people and the environment.

BOOK 3

STARTING YOUR MEDICINE

A home apothecary is the heart of any herbalist's practice—a dedicated space where your herbs, tools, and knowledge come together to create healing remedies. Whether you're just starting out or looking to refine your existing setup, this book will guide you step-by-step in building an organized, functional, and affordable apothecary tailored to your needs.

We'll begin by exploring the essential tools and equipment every herbalist needs, from mortar and pestle to tincture bottles. Next, you'll learn how to choose the right storage solutions to keep your herbs fresh and potent, ensuring they're ready whenever you need them. Organization is key to an efficient apothecary, and this book will show you how to arrange your herbs and supplies for quick and easy access.

Finally, for those on a budget, we'll share creative tips for building an apothecary without overspending. From repurposing household items to sourcing affordable supplies, you'll discover that starting your apothecary can be both economical and rewarding. By the end of this book, you'll have all the tools and knowledge you need to create a space that supports your herbal journey with ease and inspiration.

Tools and Equipment You'll Need

Starting your home apothecary begins with gathering the right tools and equipment. Just as a chef relies on knives and pots, an herbalist depends on a variety of specialized tools to prepare, process, and store herbs effectively. The good news is that building your toolkit doesn't have to be expensive or overwhelming. Many of the items you'll need are likely already in your kitchen or can be sourced affordably.

This chapter will guide you through the essential tools and equipment every herbalist should have, explaining their uses and offering tips for selecting high-quality, long-lasting items. Whether you're crafting teas, tinctures, salves, or syrups,

these tools will help you create remedies with precision and care.

Essential Tools for Herbal Preparation

1. Mortar and Pestle
   » Purpose: A mortar and pestle is used to grind, crush, or powder herbs. It's especially useful for breaking down dried roots, seeds, and spices.
   » Tips for Choosing: Look for a sturdy, non-porous material such as granite or ceramic. A heavy base provides stability during use.

2. Scissors and Pruners
   » Purpose: These are essential for harvesting herbs, trimming leaves, and cutting stems.
   » Tips for Choosing: Invest in sharp, rust-resistant tools. Pruners are ideal for woody stems, while scissors work well for softer parts like flowers and leaves.

3. Fine-Mesh Strainer or Cheesecloth
   » Purpose: Used to strain teas, tinctures, or infused oils, removing plant material and ensuring a smooth final product.
   » Tips for Choosing: Stainless steel strainers are durable and easy to clean, while cheesecloth is perfect for finer filtration.

4. Measuring Cups and Spoons
   » Purpose: Accurate measurement is crucial for herbal preparations, especially when working with tinctures or teas.
   » Tips for Choosing: Opt for stainless steel or glass measuring tools, as they're durable and won't absorb strong herbal aromas.

5. Glass Jars and Bottles
   » Purpose: Glass containers are ideal for storing dried herbs, tinctures, syrups, and infused oils. They preserve freshness and don't react with herbal compounds.
   » Tips for Choosing: Amber or cobalt glass

bottles protect against light exposure, prolonging shelf life. Wide-mouth jars are best for dried herbs.

6. Funnels
   » Purpose: Essential for transferring liquids into jars or bottles without spilling.
   » Tips for Choosing: A set of funnels in various sizes (preferably stainless steel or BPA-free plastic) ensures versatility for different container types.

7. Digital Scale
   » Purpose: Precise weighing of herbs is important, especially when crafting tinctures, capsules, or teas with specific dosages.
   » Tips for Choosing: Select a scale with a capacity to weigh both small (grams) and larger (ounces) quantities.

8. Mixing Bowls
   » Purpose: These are used for blending dried herbs or mixing ingredients for salves and lotions.
   » Tips for Choosing: Glass or stainless steel bowls are non-reactive and easy to clean.

Specialized Tools for Advanced Preparations

1. Double Boiler
   » Purpose: A double boiler is used to gently heat oils or waxes without burning them, making it ideal for salves, balms, and lip gloss.
   » Tips for Choosing: You can buy a dedicated double boiler or improvise with a heat-safe bowl placed over a pot of simmering water.

2. Coffee Grinder or Herb Grinder
   » Purpose: A grinder is perfect for pulverizing dried herbs into fine powders, especially for capsules or herbal blends.
   » Tips for Choosing: Dedicate one grinder to herbal use, as herbs can impart strong flavors or aromas.

3. Tincture Press
   » Purpose: This tool is used to press out every last drop of liquid from plant material after tincturing or oil infusion.
   » Tips for Choosing: While a tincture press

is an investment, it can save time and increase efficiency when working with large batches.

4. Pipettes or Droppers
   » Purpose: Used for measuring and dispensing small amounts of tinctures or oils.
   » Tips for Choosing: Look for glass pipettes, as they are reusable and durable.

5. Dehydrator
   » Purpose: A dehydrator is perfect for drying fresh herbs quickly and evenly, preserving their color, aroma, and potency.
   » Tips for Choosing: Choose a model with adjustable temperature settings to prevent overheating delicate herbs.

6. Capsule Filler
   » Purpose: This tool makes filling capsules with powdered herbs quick and efficient.
   » Tips for Choosing: Capsule fillers come in various sizes (e.g., size "0" or "00" capsules). Select one that matches the size of your capsules.

Safety and Sanitation Tools

Maintaining cleanliness and safety is vital in herbal preparation. Proper sanitation ensures your remedies are free of contaminants and safe for use.

1. Sanitizing Supplies
   » Purpose: Disinfecting jars, bottles, and tools prevents microbial growth.
   » Tips for Choosing: Use food-grade sanitizers or boil tools in water before use.

2. Gloves and Apron
   » Purpose: Gloves protect your hands when handling strong or irritating herbs, while an apron keeps your workspace clean.
   » Tips for Choosing: Choose latex-free gloves if you have sensitivities and a washable apron for easy cleanup.

3. Labels and Markers
   » Purpose: Labeling ensures you can identify stored herbs, tinctures, or oils. Include details like the herb name, preparation date, and any special instructions.
   » Tips for Choosing: Use waterproof la-

bels and permanent markers to prevent smudging or fading.

DIY and Budget-Friendly Alternatives

Building an apothecary doesn't have to break the bank. Many tools can be repurposed or sourced affordably:

1. Repurposed Kitchen Tools
    »   A standard kitchen pot can serve as a double boiler.
    »   Clean spice jars make excellent storage containers for small batches of herbs.
2. Thrift Store Finds
    »   Look for glass jars, mixing bowls, and strainers at secondhand shops. Just be sure to clean them thoroughly before use.
3. Household Substitutions
    »   Muslin or clean cotton cloth can replace cheesecloth for straining.
    »   A small cutting board and sharp knife can substitute for expensive herb cutters.

Organizing Your Tools

Once you've gathered your tools, organize them in a way that's accessible and efficient:

*   Store small items like droppers, funnels, and pipettes in labeled bins or drawers.
*   Use shelves or wall hooks for larger tools like grinders or double boilers.
*   Keep sanitizing supplies and labels within easy reach for quick and safe preparation.

Having the right tools and equipment is an essential first step in building your home apothecary. These tools empower you to prepare herbal remedies with precision, safety, and efficiency. Whether you're crafting a simple tea or experimenting with tinctures and salves, a well-equipped workspace ensures you're ready for any herbal project. Remember, many tools can be repurposed or sourced affordably, making it easy to start your apothecary on any budget. As you grow in your herbal practice, your toolkit will evolve, becoming a reflection of your skills and creativity.

Choosing the Right Storage Solutions

Proper storage is essential to maintaining the potency, quality, and safety of your herbs and herbal preparations. Whether you're working with dried herbs, tinctures, infused oils, or salves, choosing the right storage solutions will help preserve their efficacy and extend their shelf life. Each type of herbal preparation has unique storage requirements, and understanding these will ensure your apothecary remains organized and functional.

1. Glass Containers for Dried Herbs

Dried herbs are the cornerstone of most home apothecaries, and their storage directly impacts their potency. Glass containers are ideal for preserving dried herbs as they are non-reactive, airtight, and provide a clear view of their contents.

*   Airtight Lids: Always choose containers with airtight lids to prevent exposure to moisture, which can lead to mold growth.
*   Amber or Cobalt Glass: Colored glass protects herbs from UV light, which can degrade their active compounds over time. If using clear glass, store jars in a dark, cool space.
*   Wide-Mouth Jars: These make it easier to access herbs without damaging delicate leaves or flowers.

Label jars with the herb name, harvest date, and any specific notes about the batch. Avoid storing dried herbs in plastic, as it can trap moisture and leach chemicals over time.

3. Metal Tins for Teas and Powders

Teas and finely powdered herbs require storage solutions that prevent clumping and preserve freshness. Metal tins are a popular choice because they are lightweight, durable, and provide excellent protection from light and air.

*   Food-Grade Tins: Ensure that the tins are food-safe and free from any coatings that could react with herbal compounds.
*   Sealed Lids: Look for tins with snug-fitting or twist-off lids to keep contents fresh.
*   Moisture Control: Include silica gel packets or moisture-absorbing pads to prevent caking in powdered herbs.

Metal tins are also aesthetically pleasing and can be labeled or decorated for a personal touch.

4. Glass Bottles for Tinctures and Extracts

Tinctures and liquid extracts are highly concentrated preparations that require careful storage to maintain their potency. Glass bottles, particularly amber or cobalt varieties, are the gold standard for storing these remedies.

- Dropper Bottles: Ideal for tinctures, as they allow precise dosing and minimize contamination.
- Spray Bottles: Useful for aromatic or topical applications like room sprays or herbal mists.
- Secure Caps: Ensure that bottles have tight-fitting caps to prevent leaks and exposure to air.

Store tinctures in a cool, dark place to prevent the degradation of alcohol or glycerin bases. Label each bottle with the herb, solvent used, and the preparation date.

5. Oil-Proof Containers for Infused Oils

Infused oils are prone to spoilage due to their fat content, so proper storage is critical. Use glass bottles or jars that are specifically designed to handle oils.

- Dark Glass Bottles: Amber or green glass helps protect oils from light exposure, which can lead to rancidity.
- Small Containers: Divide oils into smaller bottles to minimize exposure to air each time you use them.
- Leak-Proof Seals: Choose bottles with secure seals to prevent leaks and spills.

Refrigerate infused oils when possible to extend their shelf life, especially if water content from fresh herbs was introduced during the infusion process.

6. Containers for Salves, Balms, and Creams

Topical preparations like salves and creams require durable, easy-to-access containers that protect against contamination.

- Metal Tins or Glass Jars: Metal tins are lightweight and portable, while glass jars are elegant and reusable. Both are excellent for storing thicker formulations.
- Plastic-Free Options: Avoid plastic containers, as they can leach chemicals into your products over time.
- Wide-Mouth Jars: These make it easy to scoop out thick preparations like balms without wasting product.

Store salves and balms in a cool, dark space to prevent melting or separation of ingredients.

7. Freezer Storage for Bulk Herbs

If you harvest or purchase herbs in large quantities, freezing can be a useful method for long-term storage. Freezing helps retain freshness and prevents the degradation of sensitive compounds.

- Vacuum-Sealed Bags: Remove as much air as possible to prevent freezer burn and preserve potency.
- Glass Freezer Containers: Use glass containers with airtight lids that can withstand low temperatures.
- Labeling for Rotation: Clearly label and date each batch so you can use the oldest herbs first.

Frozen herbs are best used within one year to ensure their quality and medicinal properties remain intact.

7. Organizing and Labeling Your Storage

A well-organized apothecary saves time, reduces waste, and ensures that you always know what you have on hand.

- Categorize by Use: Group herbs by their function, such as respiratory support, digestive health, or skincare, so you can find what you need quickly.
- Alphabetical Arrangement: Arrange jars and bottles alphabetically for easy reference.
- Use Clear Labels: Every container should have a label with the following information:
  » Herb name (common and Latin)
  » Date of harvest or preparation
  » Expiration or best-by date
  » Additional notes (e.g., wild-harvested, organic)

8. Ideal Storage Environment

The environment where you store your herbs plays a significant role in their longevity. Temperature, light, moisture, and air exposure are critical factors to control.

- Temperature: Keep your apothecary cool, ideally between 60–70°F (15–21°C), to prevent degradation of delicate compounds.
- Light: Store containers away from direct sunlight. Even with colored glass, excessive light exposure can reduce potency.
- Humidity: Dried herbs should be stored in a

low-humidity environment to prevent mold growth.

- Air Exposure: Always seal containers tightly after use to minimize oxidation and moisture absorption.

9. Rotating Stock

To ensure that you're using herbs and remedies at their peak, implement a first-in, first-out (FIFO) system. Use older batches before newer ones to avoid waste. Regularly inspect your stock for signs of spoilage, such as discoloration, off smells, or mold.

10. Creative and Budget-Friendly Storage Ideas

Building your apothecary doesn't have to be expensive. Consider these cost-effective storage solutions:

- Repurpose Jars: Reuse cleaned glass jars from food items like pasta sauce or pickles for storing dried herbs.
- Thrift Store Finds: Search for vintage tins, glass containers, or wooden storage boxes at secondhand shops.
- DIY Labels: Create custom labels using printable templates or washi tape for a personal touch.

11. Special Considerations for Traveling with Herbs

If you need to take your herbal remedies on the go, use portable and durable storage options:

- Travel Tins: Small tins are perfect for salves and balms.
- Roller Bottles: These are convenient for carrying essential oils or liquid blends.
- Pill Organizers: Use them to store capsules or small quantities of dried herbs for daily use.

Proper storage solutions are the foundation of an effective and organized apothecary. By choosing the right containers and maintaining an optimal environment, you'll preserve the quality and potency of your herbs and remedies, ensuring they're ready whenever you need them.

Organizing Herbs for Quick Access

An organized apothecary is essential for efficiency and ease of use. Whether you're preparing a tincture, blending a tea, or crafting a salve, quick access to your herbs and tools can save time and energy. Proper organization also ensures that your herbs remain fresh, potent, and easy to identify, preventing waste and confusion.

This chapter provides practical strategies and creative solutions for organizing your herbs and supplies, tailored to fit your space, preferences, and needs. From labeling systems to storage layouts, these tips will help you create a functional and aesthetically pleasing apothecary that inspires your herbal practice.

1. Start with an Inventory

Before organizing your herbs, it's important to take stock of what you already have. This step will help you avoid duplications, identify any gaps in your collection, and determine the storage solutions you need.

- Create a List: Write down every herb in your apothecary, noting its name, form (dried, tincture, powder), and quantity.
- Assess Freshness: Check each herb for signs of spoilage, such as discoloration, off smells, or mold. Discard anything that is expired or degraded.
- Group by Type: Categorize herbs by their form (e.g., dried herbs, tinctures, salves) or use (e.g., digestive support, immune boosters).

2. Categorize Herbs for Easy Retrieval

Organizing herbs into categories makes it easy to locate what you need quickly. Here are some common ways to categorize herbs:

By Function or Use

- Group herbs based on their therapeutic properties, such as:
  » Respiratory Health: Eucalyptus, thyme, mullein.
  » Digestive Support: Peppermint, fennel, ginger.
  » Stress Relief: Chamomile, lemon balm, ashwagandha.
- This method is especially helpful when preparing remedies for specific conditions.

By Form

- Dried Herbs: Store all dried herbs together in jars or tins.
- Tinctures and Extracts: Keep liquid prepara-

tions in one section, arranged by herb name or purpose.

- Powders: Group powdered herbs separately to avoid mixing them with whole herbs.
- Pre-Made Products: Salves, oils, and capsules can have their own designated area.

Alphabetically

- Organize your herbs alphabetically for quick reference, particularly if you have a large collection. This method is straightforward and works well for dried herbs and tinctures.

3. Use Proper Containers for Storage

The containers you use play a significant role in maintaining your herbs' quality and making them easy to access.

- Dried Herbs: Use clear or colored glass jars with airtight lids to preserve freshness. Wide-mouth jars are ideal for easy scooping.
- Tinctures and Oils: Store in amber or cobalt glass bottles with dropper caps for precision.
- Teas and Powders: Metal tins or glass jars with tight seals prevent clumping and contamination.
- Small Quantities: Use spice jars or mini containers for frequently used herbs, keeping larger bulk supplies in storage.

Label each container clearly with the herb's name (common and Latin), preparation date, and expiration date.

4. Optimize Your Storage Space

Whether you have a dedicated room or a small shelf, optimizing your storage space is key to an efficient apothecary. Consider these layout ideas:

Vertical Storage

- Use wall-mounted shelves or tiered racks to store jars and bottles vertically, maximizing space while keeping everything visible.
- Install hooks or pegboards for hanging lightweight tools like strainers and funnels.

Drawers and Cabinets

- Dedicate drawers or cabinet shelves to specific categories of herbs and tools.
- Use dividers or bins within drawers to separate smaller items like labels, pipettes, or scoops.

Portable Storage

- For those with limited space, consider a rolling cart or portable storage box. These can be moved as needed and hold all your essential herbs and tools.

Display Options

- Arrange herbs in an attractive, visible manner to inspire your practice. Glass jars on open shelves not only look appealing but also make it easy to see what you have.

5. Labeling for Clarity

A clear labeling system is crucial for quick and accurate access to your herbs. Follow these tips to create effective labels:

- Include Essential Information:
  » Herb name (common and Latin).
  » Date of harvest or preparation.
  » Expiration date or best-by date.
  » Special notes (e.g., "wild-harvested," "organic").
- Use Durable Labels:
  » Choose waterproof labels or write with permanent markers to prevent smudging.
- Color-Coding:
  » Use different colors for categories (e.g., green for dried herbs, blue for tinctures) to identify items at a glance.

6. Implement a System for Rotation

To prevent herbs from losing potency or going to waste, adopt a first-in, first-out (FIFO) system:

- Date Everything: Clearly label each container with its preparation date.
- Prioritize Older Stock: Use older herbs before opening new batches.
- Set Alerts: Create reminders to review your inventory every few months to check for expiring items.

7. Accessibility and Workflow

Arrange your apothecary to support your workflow. Frequently used items should be easy to reach, while bulk or specialty items can be stored in less accessible areas.

Create a "Work Zone"

- Dedicate a surface or counter for preparing remedies.
- Keep tools like funnels, scales, and mixing bowls nearby.

Ready-to-Use Kits

- Assemble kits for specific purposes (e.g., "cold and flu," "stress relief") with all the necessary herbs and tools. This saves time during preparation.

8. Digital and Physical Recordkeeping

Keeping track of your apothecary's contents ensures that you always know what you have and what needs replenishing.

Digital Inventory

- Use a spreadsheet or herbal app to log your herbs, their quantities, and their preparation details. This allows for easy updates and tracking.
- Include sections for:
  » Herb name.
  » Storage location.
  » Preparation date and type.
  » Notes on usage.

Physical Records

- Maintain a binder or notebook with the same information. Include printouts of labels, recipes, and notes for quick reference.

9. Tips for Preventing Clutter

Over time, apothecaries can become cluttered with unused herbs, expired remedies, or redundant tools. Regular maintenance is key to keeping your space functional.

- Quarterly Reviews:
  » Go through your inventory every three months to remove expired items and reorganize shelves.
- Consolidate Supplies:
  » Combine partial jars of the same herb to save space.
- Declutter Tools:
  » Donate or repurpose tools that you no longer use.

10. Personalizing Your Apothecary

Your apothecary is more than a storage space—it's a reflection of your herbal journey. Add personal touches to make it inspiring and enjoyable to use.

- Decorative Elements:
  » Use wooden shelves, woven baskets, or vintage jars to add charm.
- Inspiration Board:
  » Hang recipes, quotes, or photographs that inspire your practice.
- Aroma and Atmosphere:
  » Place small sachets of dried lavender or rose petals in your apothecary to create a pleasant, calming scent.

Organizing your herbs for quick access not only saves time but also enhances the joy and efficiency of your herbal practice. By categorizing, labeling, and optimizing your storage space, you'll create an apothecary that's as functional as it is inspiring.

Building Your Apothecary on a Budget

Creating a home apothecary can feel like an intimidating investment, especially when you're just starting out. However, with thoughtful planning and resourcefulness, you can build a well-equipped apothecary without breaking the bank. A budget-friendly apothecary focuses on prioritizing essentials, repurposing items, sourcing herbs wisely, and gradually expanding as your knowledge and needs grow.

This chapter will guide you through cost-saving strategies to build a functional and efficient apothecary, proving that herbal medicine is accessible to everyone, regardless of budget.

1. Prioritize the Essentials

When starting your apothecary, it's tempting to gather a wide range of tools and herbs. However, focusing on the essentials allows you to create a practical setup without unnecessary expenses.

Essential Tools

- Mortar and Pestle: A small, affordable mortar and pestle is perfect for grinding herbs.

Alternatively, use a heavy bowl and the back of a spoon.

- Strainers or Cheesecloth: A fine-mesh kitchen strainer or an inexpensive piece of cheesecloth works well for filtering teas and tinctures.
- Glass Jars and Bottles: Start with jars and bottles you already have at home, such as cleaned food jars or small spice containers.
- Measuring Tools: Basic measuring spoons and cups are sufficient for most herbal preparations.

Basic Herbs

Start with a small selection of versatile and commonly used herbs that address a range of health concerns:

- Chamomile: Calming and great for teas.
- Peppermint: Soothes digestion and relieves headaches.
- Lavender: Useful for relaxation and skin care.
- Dandelion Root: Supports liver health and digestion.
- Ginger: A versatile herb for nausea, inflammation, and immune support.

By focusing on multi-purpose herbs, you can create remedies for various needs without buying an extensive inventory.

2. Repurpose Household Items

Many everyday household items can be repurposed for your apothecary, reducing the need to buy new tools and containers.

Storage Solutions

- Glass Jars: Reuse jars from sauces, jams, or pickles. Clean them thoroughly and remove labels with warm, soapy water and vinegar.
- Metal Tins: Repurpose small tins from candies or mints to store teas, salves, or powdered herbs.
- Cardboard Boxes: Use sturdy boxes to create compartments for organizing jars and tools.

Preparation Tools

- Mixing Bowls: Any kitchen bowl can be used for blending herbs or preparing salves.
- Funnels: Make a DIY funnel by cutting the top off a plastic bottle.
- Scoops and Spoons: Old teaspoons or measuring scoops can double as tools for portioning herbs.

Repurposing not only saves money but also aligns with the sustainable values of herbalism.

3. Source Herbs Affordably

Herbs are the foundation of any apothecary, and sourcing them affordably ensures you can build your collection without overspending.

Grow Your Own Herbs

Growing your own herbs is one of the most cost-effective ways to stock your apothecary. Start with easy-to-grow plants like basil, mint, calendula, and parsley. Even a small windowsill garden can produce enough herbs for basic remedies.

Wildcrafting

Foraging for wild herbs is another budget-friendly option, but it requires knowledge and care:

- Learn Plant Identification: Use field guides or attend local foraging workshops to confidently identify plants.
- Harvest Responsibly: Take only what you need, leaving enough for the plant to regenerate and for wildlife to thrive.
- Focus on Abundant Herbs: Look for common, non-threatened plants like dandelion, plantain, and nettle.

Buy in Bulk

Purchasing herbs in bulk from reputable suppliers is often cheaper than buying pre-packaged amounts. Look for organic or sustainably sourced options from trusted vendors. Consider splitting bulk purchases with friends or local herbalists to reduce costs.

Local Farmers and Markets

Visit farmers' markets to find fresh, affordable herbs. Many small-scale farmers grow organic herbs and may offer discounts for bulk purchases.

4. Make Your Own Preparations

Pre-made herbal products can be expensive, but making your own remedies at home is both economical and empowering.

Infusions and Teas

Herbal teas are one of the simplest and most affordable remedies to prepare. Use dried or fresh herbs and steep them in boiling water to create infusions for relaxation, digestion, or immune support.

Tinctures

Tinctures are easy to make at home using herbs and an alcohol base like vodka or brandy. While the initial cost of alcohol may seem high, a single bottle can produce multiple batches of tinctures.

Infused Oils

Infused oils can be created by steeping herbs in carrier oils like olive or coconut oil. These oils can be used on their own or as a base for salves and balms.

Salves and Balms

Making salves requires just a few ingredients: infused oil, beeswax, and optional essential oils. By investing in these staples, you can produce multiple jars of salves for a fraction of the cost of store-bought products.

5. Create a Budget-Friendly Storage System

Organizing your apothecary doesn't require fancy shelves or expensive organizers. Focus on functionality and creativity.

DIY Shelving

* Use recycled wooden crates or old bookshelves to create storage for jars and tools.
* Install simple wall-mounted shelves to maximize vertical space.

Labeling

Handwritten labels on paper or masking tape are inexpensive and effective. Include the herb name, preparation date, and any important notes.

Bins and Baskets

Sort herbs and tools into bins or baskets grouped by category, such as "Teas," "Tinctures," or "Salves."

6. Join a Herbal Community

Connecting with other herbalists can help you save money and expand your knowledge.

Herbal Swaps

Participate in herbal swaps where members exchange herbs, seeds, or remedies. This is a great way to diversify your collection without spending money.

Workshops and Events

Many herbal workshops offer free or low-cost opportunities to learn skills and access resources. Check local libraries, community centers, or online forums for events.

Shared Tools

Consider sharing tools like dehydrators or tincture presses with a community group to reduce individual costs.

7. Take Advantage of Free Resources

The internet is a treasure trove of free herbal knowledge. Explore websites, blogs, and forums dedicated to herbalism.

DIY Recipes

Search for free recipes for teas, tinctures, and salves. Many experienced herbalists share detailed instructions online.

Plant Identification Apps

Use free or low-cost apps like iNaturalist to help identify herbs in your area.

E-Books and Online Courses

Many organizations offer free e-books or introductory courses on herbalism. These resources provide valuable knowledge without requiring a financial investment.

8. Gradually Expand Your Apothecary

Building your apothecary doesn't have to happen all at once. Take a gradual approach, adding new tools, herbs, and preparations over time as your needs and skills grow.

Start Small

Focus on one or two remedies, such as a calming tea blend or a basic salve, before expanding into more complex preparations.

Seasonal Additions

Use each season to add specific herbs to your apothecary. For example:

- Spring: Fresh greens like dandelion and nettle.
- Summer: Flowers like chamomile and calendula.
- Fall: Roots like burdock and echinacea.

Upgrade Over Time

As your budget allows, invest in higher-quality tools or bulk herb orders. Gradual upgrades prevent overwhelming upfront costs.

With creativity, resourcefulness, and a focus on the essentials, you can build an effective and inspiring apothecary on any budget. This process is not only economical but also deeply rewarding, as it connects you with the traditions of herbalism while nurturing your health naturally.

BOOK 4

HERBAL PREPARATIONS 101

Herbal preparations are the heart of transforming raw herbs into potent remedies that support health and well-being. From soothing teas to powerful tinctures, understanding how to properly prepare herbs allows you to harness their full therapeutic potential. Whether you're a beginner or looking to refine your skills, this book provides a comprehensive guide to creating a variety of herbal remedies with confidence and precision.

We'll begin by exploring the foundational techniques of infusions, decoctions, and tinctures, giving you the tools to craft remedies tailored to your needs. Next, you'll learn to make herbal powders and capsules, a convenient way to incorporate herbs into your daily routine. For topical applications, we'll guide you through the art of creating salves, balms, and ointments to nourish and heal the skin. Finally, we'll delve into glycerites and non-alcoholic extracts, ideal for those seeking alcohol-free alternatives for themselves or their families.

This book emphasizes practical, step-by-step instructions, empowering you to master each method. By the end, you'll have the knowledge and skills to turn simple herbs into versatile, effective preparations, building a solid foundation for your herbal practice. Let's begin this exciting journey into the art and science of herbal medicine!

Decoding Infusions, Decoctions, and Tinctures

Herbal preparations like infusions, decoctions, and tinctures are foundational methods for extracting the healing properties of herbs. Each technique is unique, depending on the part of the herb being used and the desired outcome. Understanding how to prepare and use these methods is key to maximizing the potency and benefits of your herbal remedies.

Infusions

Infusions are the simplest form of herbal preparation, often used for delicate plant parts like leaves and flowers. This method involves steeping herbs in hot water to extract their nutrients and active compounds. Infusions are ideal for teas or water-based herbal remedies.

How to Prepare an Infusion:

1. Heat water to a boil.
2. Place 1–2 teaspoons of dried herbs (or 1 tablespoon of fresh herbs) per cup of water into a heatproof container.
3. Pour the hot water over the herbs.
4. Cover the container and let steep for 5–15 minutes.
5. Strain and enjoy warm or cold.

Decoctions

Decoctions are used for tougher plant materials, such as roots, barks, and seeds, which require longer and more intense boiling to release their medicinal compounds.

How to Prepare a Decoction:

1. Add 1–2 tablespoons of the herb to a saucepan with 1 cup of water.
2. Bring to a boil, then reduce heat to a simmer for 15–30 minutes.
3. Strain the liquid into a mug or container.
4. Drink immediately or store for later use.

Tinctures

Tinctures are concentrated herbal extracts made using alcohol or other solvents to draw out and preserve the plant's active constituents. They are potent, long-lasting, and versatile, often used in small doses.

How to Prepare a Tincture:

1. Chop fresh herbs or use dried herbs and place them in a clean glass jar.
2. Pour alcohol (vodka or brandy) over the herbs to completely cover them.

3. Seal the jar and store in a cool, dark place, shaking it daily for 4–6 weeks.
4. Strain the liquid into a dropper bottle for storage.

Practical Remedies for Infusions, Decoctions, and Non-Alcoholic Tinctures

This section showcases practical remedies for crafting effective infusions, decoctions, and non-alcoholic tinctures at home. These remedies are designed to support common health needs such as relaxation, immune support, and digestion. The methods are simple, cost-effective, and tailored to make your herbal practice more accessible and functional.

1. Relaxing Lavender and Lemon Balm Infusion

Ingredients:

- 1 teaspoon dried lavender flowers
- 1 teaspoon dried lemon balm leaves
- 1 cup boiling water

Instructions:

1. Add lavender and lemon balm to a heatproof mug.
2. Pour boiling water over the herbs and cover to trap steam.
3. Let steep for 10–12 minutes.
4. Strain the herbs and drink warm.

Uses/Benefits: Calms the nervous system, reduces stress, and promotes restful sleep.

Dosage/How to Use:

- Drink 1 cup in the evening or before bedtime.

Storage Tips:

- Prepare fresh for each use.

Safety Notes:

- Avoid if allergic to plants in the mint family.

2. Immune-Boosting Elderberry and Ginger Decoction

Ingredients:

- 1/2 cup dried elderberries
- 1 tablespoon fresh ginger slices
- 4 cups water

Instructions:

1. Combine elderberries, ginger, and water in a saucepan.
2. Bring to a boil, then simmer for 30 minutes.
3. Strain into a clean jar and let cool.
4. Sweeten with honey if desired (optional).

Uses/Benefits: Strengthens the immune system and reduces the severity of colds and flu.

Dosage/How to Use:

- Take 1 tablespoon every 2–3 hours during illness or 1–2 tablespoons daily for prevention.

Storage Tips:

- Store in the refrigerator for up to 1 week.

Safety Notes:

- Avoid raw elderberries as they can be toxic.

3. Digestive Soothing Peppermint and Fennel Infusion

Ingredients:

- 1 teaspoon dried peppermint leaves
- 1/2 teaspoon fennel seeds
- 1 cup boiling water

Instructions:

1. Add peppermint and fennel seeds to a mug or teapot.
2. Pour boiling water over the herbs.
3. Cover and steep for 10 minutes.
4. Strain and sip slowly.

Uses/Benefits: Eases bloating, relieves indigestion, and calms nausea.

Dosage/How to Use:

- Drink 1 cup after meals as needed.

Storage Tips:

- Use fresh herbs for each preparation.

Safety Notes:

- Not suitable for individuals with acid reflux.

4. Energy-Boosting Ginseng and Licorice Decoction

Ingredients:

- 1 tablespoon dried ginseng root
- 1 teaspoon dried licorice root
- 3 cups water

Instructions:

1. Place ginseng and licorice root in a saucepan with water.
2. Bring to a boil, then simmer for 20–25 minutes.
3. Strain into a clean container and drink warm.

Uses/Benefits: Supports energy, reduces fatigue, and enhances focus.

Dosage/How to Use:

- Take 1 cup in the morning or early afternoon.

Storage Tips:

- Refrigerate unused decoction for up to 48 hours.

Safety Notes:

- Avoid prolonged use of licorice root if you have high blood pressure.

5. Chamomile and Honey Glycerite

Ingredients:

- 1/2 cup dried chamomile flowers
- 1/2 cup vegetable glycerin
- 1/4 cup distilled water

Instructions:

1. Combine chamomile, glycerin, and water in a glass jar.
2. Seal the jar and shake well to mix.
3. Store in a cool, dark place for 4–6 weeks, shaking daily.
4. Strain into a dropper bottle for use.

Uses/Benefits: Promotes relaxation, eases anxiety, and supports restful sleep.

Dosage/How to Use:

- Take 1–2 drops in water or tea before bed.

Storage Tips:

- Store in a dark, cool place for up to 1 year.

Safety Notes:

- Safe for children over 1 year old.

6. Pain-Relieving Willow Bark Decoction

Ingredients:

- 1 tablespoon dried willow bark
- 2 cups water

Instructions:

1. Combine willow bark and water in a saucepan.

2. Bring to a boil, then simmer for 20–30 minutes.
3. Strain into a clean container and drink warm.

Uses/Benefits: Provides mild pain relief and reduces inflammation.

Dosage/How to Use:

- Take 1/2 cup every 4–6 hours as needed.

Storage Tips:

- Keep refrigerated for up to 48 hours.

Safety Notes:

- Avoid if allergic to aspirin or similar compounds.

7. Cold Remedy Ginger and Cinnamon Decoction

Ingredients:

- 1 tablespoon fresh ginger slices
- 1 cinnamon stick
- 3 cups water

Instructions:

1. Place ginger and cinnamon in a saucepan with water.
2. Simmer for 20 minutes.
3. Strain into a mug and drink warm.

Uses/Benefits: Soothes sore throats, warms the body, and supports immunity.

Dosage/How to Use:

- Take 1 cup 2–3 times daily during illness.

Storage Tips:

- Store in the refrigerator for up to 2 days.

Safety Notes:

- Use caution with cinnamon if pregnant.

8. Rosemary and Lemon Focus Infusion

Ingredients:

- 1 teaspoon dried rosemary leaves
- 1 lemon slice
- 1 cup boiling water

Instructions:

1. Add rosemary and lemon slice to a mug.
2. Pour boiling water over the herbs.
3. Cover and steep for 10 minutes.
4. Strain and drink warm.

Uses/Benefits: Improves focus, enhances memory, and sharpens mental clarity.

Dosage/How to Use:

- Drink 1 cup in the morning or early afternoon.

Storage Tips:

- Prepare fresh for each use.

Safety Notes:

- Avoid rosemary in large amounts during pregnancy.

9. Echinacea and Mint Immune Glycerite

Ingredients:

- 1/2 cup dried echinacea root
- 1/4 cup fresh mint leaves
- 1/2 cup vegetable glycerin
- 1/4 cup distilled water

Instructions:

1. Combine echinacea, mint, glycerin, and water in a glass jar.
2. Seal the jar and shake well to mix.
3. Store in a cool, dark place for 4–6 weeks, shaking daily.
4. Strain into a dropper bottle for use.

Uses/Benefits: Strengthens immunity and supports faster recovery during illness.

Dosage/How to Use:

- Take 1–2 drops daily in water or tea during cold season.

Storage Tips:

- Keep in a dark, cool place for up to 1 year.

Safety Notes:

- Safe for alcohol-free users and children over 1 year.

10. Lemon Balm and Ginger Stress Relief Infusion

Ingredients:

- 1 teaspoon dried lemon balm leaves
- 1 teaspoon fresh ginger slices
- 1 cup boiling water

Instructions:

1. Add lemon balm and ginger to a mug.
2. Pour boiling water over the herbs.
3. Cover and steep for 10 minutes.

4. Strain and enjoy warm.

Uses/Benefits: Reduces stress, lifts mood, and soothes digestion.

Dosage/How to Use:

- Drink 1 cup 1–2 times daily as needed.

Storage Tips:

- Prepare fresh for each use.

Safety Notes:

- Avoid lemon balm if you have a thyroid condition.

Making Herbal Powders and Capsules

Herbal powders and capsules are among the most versatile and convenient ways to incorporate herbs into daily life. By grinding herbs into a fine powder, you can access their healing properties in a form that is easy to measure, blend, and use. Capsules, on the other hand, are an excellent way to take powdered herbs without dealing with their taste, making them ideal for those who prefer a quick and tasteless option.

This chapter explores the process of creating herbal powders and capsules, explaining how to prepare, store, and use them effectively. It also discusses the advantages of these methods and how they fit into a modern herbalist's toolkit. Whether you want to make powders for teas and tonics or fill capsules for precise dosing, this chapter provides the foundational knowledge you need to succeed.

Why Choose Powders and Capsules?

Herbal powders and capsules are highly practical forms of herbal medicine, offering several benefits:

1. Convenience: Powders can be stored for extended periods and easily incorporated into smoothies, teas, or recipes. Capsules provide a portable option for taking herbs on the go.
2. Taste Masking: Some herbs have a bitter or unpleasant taste. Encapsulating them makes them easy to consume without the need to mask their flavor.
3. Precision Dosing: Capsules allow for accurate dosing, ensuring consistent intake of herbal medicine.
4. Versatility: Powders can be used in multiple

ways, including making pastes, teas, or topical remedies.

How to Prepare Herbal Powders

Creating herbal powders involves drying, grinding, and storing herbs in a way that preserves their potency. Here's how to do it:

1. Drying the Herbs:

Begin with thoroughly dried herbs, as any residual moisture can cause spoilage. Air drying in a well-ventilated area is the most cost-effective method, but dehydrators can speed up the process.

2. Grinding the Herbs:

Use a coffee grinder, spice grinder, or mortar and pestle to grind the dried herbs into a fine powder. Ensure your equipment is clean and free from cross-contamination. For larger batches, consider investing in a high-powered grinder.

3. Sifting the Powder:

After grinding, sift the powder through a fine-mesh strainer to remove any large particles. This ensures a consistent texture, which is especially important for capsules.

4. Storing the Powder:

Store the finished powder in an airtight glass jar in a cool, dark place. Label the jar with the herb name, preparation date, and expiration date (usually 6–12 months from preparation).

How to Make Capsules

Capsules offer a convenient way to take herbal powders. Making your own capsules at home is cost-effective and allows you to control the quality and dosage of the herbs.

1. Choosing Capsules:

Opt for vegetable-based capsules, which are suitable for most dietary needs. They come in various sizes, with "00" being the most commonly used.

2. Filling the Capsules:

Capsule-filling machines make the process quick and efficient. Simply place the capsule halves in the machine, fill with the powdered herb, and close the capsules.

3. Blending Herbs:

Some herbs work better in combinations. For example, mixing turmeric powder with black pepper enhances its bioavailability. Experiment with blends that address specific health needs.

4. Storing Capsules:

Store filled capsules in an airtight container away from light and moisture. Properly stored capsules can last up to a year.

When to Use Powders vs. Capsules

The choice between powders and capsules depends on your preference and the intended use of the herb:

- Choose Powders: When making teas, tonics, or recipes where the herb's flavor and texture can be incorporated.
- Choose Capsules: For precise dosing or when the herb's flavor is unpleasant.

Safety Considerations

While herbal powders and capsules are generally safe, keep the following points in mind:

1. Quality Control: Ensure that your herbs are sourced from reputable suppliers to avoid contaminants or adulterants.
2. Dosage: Follow recommended dosages for each herb. Overuse of certain herbs can cause side effects.
3. Allergies and Sensitivities: Be aware of potential allergies or interactions with medications.

Practical Remedies Using Herbal Powders and Capsules

Below are 10 practical remedies using herbal powders and capsules to address various health needs. Each remedy provides detailed instructions and tips for preparation, storage, and safe usage.

11. Digestive Aid Ginger and Fennel Powder

Ingredients:

- 1 tablespoon dried ginger powder
- 1 tablespoon fennel seed powder

Instructions:

1. Mix ginger powder and fennel powder in a clean, dry container.
2. Store in an airtight jar.

Uses/Benefits: Relieves bloating, improves digestion, and eases nausea.

Dosage/How to Use:

- Take 1/2 teaspoon mixed in warm water or tea after meals.

Storage Tips:

- Keep in an airtight container for up to 6 months.

Safety Notes:

- Avoid ginger if you have a sensitive stomach or are prone to heartburn.

12. Immune Boosting Turmeric Capsule

Ingredients:

- 2 tablespoons turmeric powder
- 1 tablespoon black pepper powder
- Empty "00" vegetable capsules

Instructions:

1. Mix turmeric and black pepper powder thoroughly in a bowl.
2. Use a capsule-filling machine to fill capsules with the mixture.
3. Store capsules in a dry, airtight container.

Uses/Benefits: Boosts immunity, reduces inflammation, and supports overall health.

Dosage/How to Use:

- Take 1–2 capsules daily with food.

Storage Tips:

- Store capsules in a cool, dry place for up to 1 year.

Safety Notes:

- Consult with a healthcare provider if you're on blood thinners.

13. Energy-Enhancing Maca Root Powder

Ingredients:

- 1 teaspoon maca root powder
- 1 cup plant-based milk (e.g., almond or oat milk)

Instructions:

1. Stir maca powder into warm plant-based milk until fully dissolved.
2. Sweeten with honey or a natural sweetener if desired.

Uses/Benefits: Improves energy, enhances stamina, and supports hormone balance.

Dosage/How to Use:

- Drink once daily in the morning.

Storage Tips:

- Store maca powder in a sealed container away from light.

Safety Notes:

- Avoid if pregnant or breastfeeding unless advised by a healthcare provider.

14. Anti-Inflammatory Ashwagandha Capsules

Ingredients:

- 2 tablespoons ashwagandha powder
- Empty "00" vegetable capsules

Instructions:

1. Fill capsules with ashwagandha powder using a capsule-filling machine.
2. Store in a clean, dry container.

Uses/Benefits: Reduces inflammation, promotes stress resilience, and supports energy levels.

Dosage/How to Use:

- Take 1–2 capsules daily with water.

Storage Tips:

- Keep capsules in a cool, dry place for up to 1 year.

Safety Notes:

- Consult a doctor if taking medications for thyroid disorders.

15. Digestive Support Licorice Root and Slippery Elm Powder

Ingredients:

- 1 tablespoon licorice root powder
- 1 tablespoon slippery elm bark powder

Instructions:

1. Mix powders together in a dry container.
2. Store in an airtight jar.

Uses/Benefits: Soothes the digestive tract, relieves acid reflux, and supports gut health.

Dosage/How to Use:

- Mix 1/2 teaspoon in warm water and drink as needed.

Storage Tips:

- Keep in an airtight container for up to 6 months.

Safety Notes:

- Avoid prolonged use of licorice root if you have high blood pressure.

16. Mood-Lifting Cacao and Adaptogen Powder

Ingredients:

- 2 tablespoons raw cacao powder
- 1 tablespoon ashwagandha powder
- 1 tablespoon maca root powder

Instructions:

1. Mix all powders in a bowl until well combined.
2. Store in a sealed jar.

Uses/Benefits: Boosts mood, reduces stress, and enhances mental clarity.

Dosage/How to Use:

- Mix 1 teaspoon into warm milk or water and enjoy as a daily tonic.

Storage Tips:

- Store in a cool, dry place for up to 6 months.

Safety Notes:

- Avoid taking at night if you're sensitive to stimulants.

17. Joint Support Boswellia and Turmeric Capsules

Ingredients:

- 1 tablespoon boswellia powder
- 1 tablespoon turmeric powder
- Empty "00" vegetable capsules

Instructions:

1. Mix boswellia and turmeric powder thoroughly.
2. Use a capsule machine to fill capsules.
3. Store capsules in a sealed container.

Uses/Benefits: Reduces joint pain, supports mobility, and alleviates inflammation.

Dosage/How to Use:

- Take 1–2 capsules daily with meals.

Storage Tips:

- Store capsules in a cool, dry place for up to 1 year.

Safety Notes:

- Consult a healthcare provider if taking anti-inflammatory medications.

18. Nutritional Greens Powder Mix

Ingredients:

- 2 tablespoons spirulina powder
- 1 tablespoon wheatgrass powder
- 1 tablespoon moringa powder

Instructions:

1. Mix all powders in a clean bowl.
2. Store in an airtight jar.

Uses/Benefits: Provides a nutrient-dense boost for energy, detoxification, and overall health.

Dosage/How to Use:

- Mix 1 teaspoon into smoothies, juices, or water daily.

Storage Tips:

- Keep sealed and away from light for up to 6 months.

Safety Notes:

- Consult your doctor if you have thyroid conditions due to iodine content in spirulina.

19. Immune-Strengthening Astragalus Powder

Ingredients:

- 2 tablespoons astragalus root powder
- Empty "00" vegetable capsules

Instructions:

1. Fill capsules with astragalus powder using a capsule machine.
2. Store capsules in an airtight container.

Uses/Benefits: Boosts immunity, supports energy, and enhances resilience to illness.

Dosage/How to Use:

- Take 1–2 capsules daily with food.

Storage Tips:

- Store in a cool, dry place for up to 1 year.

Safety Notes:

- Avoid during active fever or illness.

20. Sleep Support Nutmeg and Chamomile Powder

Ingredients:

- 1/2 teaspoon nutmeg powder
- 1 teaspoon dried chamomile powder

Instructions:

1. Mix nutmeg and chamomile powders in a small container.
2. Store in a sealed jar.

Uses/Benefits: Promotes restful sleep, reduces anxiety, and calms the nervous system.

Dosage/How to Use:

- Mix 1/2 teaspoon into warm milk or tea 30 minutes before bed.

Storage Tips:

- Keep in an airtight container for up to 3 months.

Safety Notes:

- Use nutmeg in moderation; excessive amounts can have adverse effects.

Crafting Salves, Balms, and Ointments

Salves, balms, and ointments are indispensable in any herbalist's toolkit. These topical preparations are used to address a wide variety of skin concerns, such as soothing dryness, easing pain, or promoting wound healing. Made by infusing herbs into carrier oils and combining them with waxes and butters, they are simple to make and highly effective.

This chapter will guide you through the art of crafting salves, balms, and ointments. It covers the essential ingredients, tools, and step-by-step methods required to create these remedies at home. By understanding the foundational techniques, you can customize recipes to suit your specific needs and preferences.

Understanding Salves, Balms, and Ointments

These preparations differ slightly in texture and purpose, but their basic components and methods are similar:

1. Salves: Soft and spreadable, salves are made by blending infused oils with beeswax. They are ideal for soothing dry or irritated skin.
2. Balms: Firmer than salves, balms typically include butters (like shea or cocoa butter) for added nourishment and structure. Commonly used for lips, joints, and areas needing extra protection.
3. Ointments: Similar to salves but with a heavier consistency, ointments are often used for medicinal purposes like wound care or pain relief. They contain higher concentrations of oils and waxes.

Essential Ingredients

1. Herbs: Choose herbs suited to the purpose of the remedy, such as calendula for soothing or arnica for pain relief.
2. Carrier Oils: Olive, coconut, or almond oil are commonly used to extract the medicinal properties of herbs.
3. Waxes: Beeswax or plant-based waxes (like candelilla) provide structure and stability to the preparation.
4. Butters: Shea or cocoa butter adds nourishment and firmness, especially in balms.
5. Essential Oils (Optional): Add fragrance and enhance therapeutic benefits.

Basic Method for Crafting Salves

1. Infuse the Oil:
   - » Combine dried herbs and carrier oil in a jar.
   - » Heat gently in a double boiler for 2–3 hours or place in a sunny window for 4–6 weeks.
2. Strain the Oil:
   - » Use cheesecloth or a fine mesh strainer to remove herb particles.
3. Melt Wax:
   - » Heat beeswax or a plant-based wax in a double boiler until melted.
4. Combine:
   - » Mix the strained herbal oil with the melted wax and stir well.
5. Pour and Cool:
   - » Pour into clean containers and allow to cool before sealing.

Storage and Shelf Life

Store salves, balms, and ointments in airtight containers in a cool, dark place. Properly prepared remedies can last 6–12 months, depending on the stability of the oils used.

Practical Remedies for Salves, Balms, and Ointments

Below are 10 practical recipes to help you craft your own topical remedies at home.

21. Soothing Calendula Salve

Ingredients:

- 1 cup calendula-infused olive oil
- 1 ounce beeswax
- Optional: 10 drops lavender essential oil

Instructions:

1. Melt beeswax in a double boiler.
2. Add calendula-infused oil and stir until well combined.
3. Remove from heat and mix in lavender essential oil (if using).
4. Pour into small tins or jars and let cool.

Uses/Benefits: Calms irritated skin, reduces inflammation, and speeds up wound healing.

Storage Tips:

- Store in a cool, dry place for up to 1 year.

Safety Notes:

- Do a patch test before use if you have sensitive skin.

22. Pain-Relieving Arnica Balm

Ingredients:

- 1/2 cup arnica-infused oil
- 1 tablespoon shea butter
- 1 ounce beeswax

Instructions:

1. Melt beeswax and shea butter in a double boiler.
2. Add arnica-infused oil and stir thoroughly.
3. Pour into containers and let cool before sealing.

Uses/Benefits: Relieves muscle pain, reduces swelling, and soothes bruises.

Storage Tips:

- Keep in a dark, cool place for up to 9 months.

Safety Notes:

- Avoid using on broken skin.

23. Nourishing Cocoa Butter Lip Balm

Ingredients:

- 1 tablespoon cocoa butter
- 1 tablespoon coconut oil
- 1 teaspoon beeswax
- Optional: 3 drops peppermint essential oil

Instructions:

1. Melt cocoa butter, coconut oil, and beeswax in a double boiler.
2. Stir in peppermint essential oil (if using).
3. Pour into lip balm tubes or small pots and let cool.

Uses/Benefits: Hydrates and protects lips, leaving them soft and smooth.

Storage Tips:

- Store in a pocket or purse for up to 6 months.

Safety Notes:

- Avoid if allergic to cocoa butter.

24. Healing Comfrey Ointment

Ingredients:

- 1/2 cup comfrey-infused oil
- 1 ounce beeswax

Instructions:

1. Melt beeswax in a double boiler.
2. Add comfrey-infused oil and stir until combined.
3. Pour into jars and let cool.

Uses/Benefits: Promotes healing of cuts, scrapes, and minor wounds.

Storage Tips:

- Store in a sealed jar for up to 9 months.

Safety Notes:

- Not recommended for deep wounds or prolonged use.

25. Lavender Sleep Balm

Ingredients:

- 1/2 cup coconut oil
- 1 tablespoon beeswax

- 10 drops lavender essential oil

Instructions:

1. Melt coconut oil and beeswax in a double boiler.
2. Remove from heat and stir in lavender essential oil.
3. Pour into small tins and allow to cool.

Uses/Benefits: Promotes relaxation and supports restful sleep when applied to temples or wrists.

Storage Tips:

- Keep in a cool place for up to 1 year.

Safety Notes:

- Test on a small area before widespread use.

26. Anti-Inflammatory Turmeric Salve

Ingredients:

- 1/2 cup turmeric-infused oil
- 1 ounce beeswax

Instructions:

1. Melt beeswax in a double boiler.
2. Add turmeric-infused oil and stir well.
3. Pour into jars and let set.

Uses/Benefits: Eases joint pain and reduces inflammation.

Storage Tips:

- Store in a cool, dark place for up to 1 year.

Safety Notes:

- Avoid on light clothing as turmeric may stain.

27. Anti-Chap Hand Balm

Ingredients:

- 2 tablespoons shea butter
- 2 tablespoons olive oil
- 1 tablespoon beeswax

Instructions:

1. Melt all ingredients in a double boiler.
2. Pour into tins and let cool.

Uses/Benefits: Repairs dry, cracked hands and provides a protective barrier.

Storage Tips:

- Store in a dry place for up to 6 months.

28. Winter Chest Rub

Ingredients:

- 1/2 cup coconut oil
- 1 tablespoon beeswax
- 10 drops eucalyptus essential oil
- 10 drops peppermint essential oil

Instructions:

1. Melt coconut oil and beeswax in a double boiler.
2. Add essential oils and mix well.
3. Pour into jars and let cool.

Uses/Benefits: Soothes congestion and promotes easier breathing during colds.

Storage Tips:

- Keep in a cool place for up to 9 months.

29. Baby-Safe Diaper Balm

Ingredients:

- 1/2 cup calendula-infused oil
- 1 tablespoon shea butter
- 1 tablespoon beeswax

Instructions:

1. Melt beeswax and shea butter in a double boiler.
2. Stir in calendula-infused oil.
3. Pour into jars and let cool.

Uses/Benefits: Soothes diaper rash and protects sensitive skin.

Storage Tips:

- Store in a cool, dark place for up to 6 months.

30. Cooling Aloe Vera Balm

Ingredients:

- 1/4 cup aloe vera gel
- 1/4 cup coconut oil
- 1 tablespoon beeswax

Instructions:

1. Melt coconut oil and beeswax in a double boiler.
2. Remove from heat and gently fold in aloe vera gel.
3. Pour into jars and cool.

Uses/Benefits: Relieves sunburn and soothes irritated skin.

Storage Tips:

- Store in the refrigerator for up to 3 months.

Exploring Glycerites and Non-Alcoholic Extracts

Glycerites and non-alcoholic extracts are wonderful alternatives to traditional tinctures for those who want to avoid alcohol-based preparations. These gentle yet effective remedies are particularly suitable for children, pregnant individuals, and anyone with sensitivities or preferences against alcohol.

Glycerites use vegetable glycerin—a sweet, syrupy liquid derived from plant oils—as the primary solvent. Non-alcoholic extracts can also be made with apple cider vinegar, water, or other natural bases. This chapter delves into the preparation, benefits, and practical applications of glycerites and non-alcoholic extracts, providing you with techniques to create versatile remedies tailored to your needs.

Why Glycerites and Non-Alcoholic Extracts?

1. Alcohol-Free: Suitable for all ages and situations where alcohol is not ideal.
2. Palatable: The natural sweetness of glycerin masks the bitterness of herbs, making remedies more enjoyable.
3. Versatile: Can be used in teas, smoothies, or taken directly by dropper.
4. Customizable: Allows for a wide range of herbal combinations to address specific health concerns.

How to Make Glycerites

1. Ingredients:
   - » Fresh or dried herbs
   - » Vegetable glycerin
   - » Distilled or filtered water
2. Preparation:
   - » Chop herbs finely to increase surface area for extraction.
   - » Mix glycerin and water in a 3:1 ratio.
   - » Place herbs in a jar, covering them completely with the liquid mixture.
   - » Seal the jar and shake well.
3. Steeping:
   - » Let the mixture steep for 4–6 weeks in a cool, dark place, shaking daily to enhance extraction.
4. Straining:
   - » Use cheesecloth or a fine-mesh strainer to separate the liquid from the plant material.
5. Storage:
   - » Pour into dark glass dropper bottles, label with the herb name and preparation date, and store in a cool, dark place.

How to Make Non-Alcoholic Vinegar Extracts

1. Ingredients:
   - » Herbs of choice
   - » Apple cider vinegar
2. Preparation:
   - » Fill a jar halfway with chopped herbs.
   - » Cover with apple cider vinegar, leaving some space at the top.
   - » Seal with a non-metal lid or place wax paper between the lid and jar to prevent corrosion.
3. Steeping:
   - » Let the mixture steep for 2–4 weeks, shaking occasionally.
4. Straining:
   - » Strain and pour the liquid into a clean glass bottle.
5. Storage:
   - » Store in a dark, cool place for up to 6 months.

Practical Remedies Using Glycerites and Non-Alcoholic Extracts

31. Calming Chamomile Glycerite

Ingredients:

- 1/2 cup fresh or dried chamomile flowers
- 1/2 cup vegetable glycerin
- 1/4 cup distilled water

Instructions:

1. Combine chamomile, glycerin, and water in a glass jar.
2. Seal the jar and shake well.

3. Let steep for 4–6 weeks, shaking daily.
4. Strain into a dropper bottle.

Uses/Benefits: Promotes relaxation, reduces stress, and supports restful sleep.

Dosage/How to Use:

- Take 1–2 drops under the tongue or in tea before bed.

Storage Tips:

- Store in a cool, dark place for up to 1 year.

32. Immune-Boosting Elderberry Glycerite

Ingredients:

- 1 cup fresh or dried elderberries
- 3/4 cup vegetable glycerin
- 1/4 cup distilled water

Instructions:

1. Add elderberries, glycerin, and water to a jar.
2. Shake well and let steep for 4 weeks.
3. Strain and store in a dark glass bottle.

Uses/Benefits: Strengthens immunity and shortens the duration of colds.

Dosage/How to Use:

- Take 1 dropper daily as a preventive or every 2 hours during illness.

Storage Tips:

- Keep in a dark, cool place for up to 1 year.

33. Digestive Soothing Peppermint Glycerite

Ingredients:

- 1/2 cup fresh peppermint leaves
- 1/2 cup vegetable glycerin
- 1/4 cup distilled water

Instructions:

1. Combine peppermint, glycerin, and water in a jar.
2. Seal, shake, and let steep for 4–6 weeks.
3. Strain and transfer to a dropper bottle.

Uses/Benefits: Eases bloating, nausea, and indigestion.

Dosage/How to Use:

- Take 1 dropper in water or tea after meals.

Storage Tips:

- Store in a cool, dark place for up to 1 year.

34. Apple Cider Vinegar Energy Tonic

Ingredients:

- 1 cup fresh ginger slices
- 2 cups apple cider vinegar

Instructions:

1. Place ginger in a jar and cover with apple cider vinegar.
2. Seal and let steep for 2 weeks.
3. Strain and store in a clean glass bottle.

Uses/Benefits: Boosts energy, supports digestion, and enhances circulation.

Dosage/How to Use:

- Mix 1 tablespoon in warm water and drink as needed.

Storage Tips:

- Keep in a cool, dark place for up to 6 months.

35. Stress Relief Lemon Balm Glycerite

Ingredients:

- 1/2 cup fresh lemon balm leaves
- 3/4 cup vegetable glycerin
- 1/4 cup distilled water

Instructions:

1. Add lemon balm, glycerin, and water to a jar.
2. Seal and shake well.
3. Let steep for 4 weeks, shaking daily.
4. Strain and store in dropper bottles.

Uses/Benefits: Calms the nervous system and reduces anxiety.

Dosage/How to Use:

- Take 1–2 drops as needed.

Storage Tips:

- Store in a dark place for up to 1 year.

36. Skin-Soothing Calendula Vinegar Extract

Ingredients:

- 1 cup calendula flowers
- 2 cups apple cider vinegar

Instructions:

1. Fill a jar halfway with calendula flowers.
2. Cover with apple cider vinegar.
3. Let steep for 3 weeks, then strain and bottle.

Uses/Benefits: Soothes irritated skin and can be used as a diluted rinse or compress.

Dosage/How to Use:

- Dilute 1 tablespoon in 1 cup of water for topical use.

Storage Tips:

- Store in a cool, dark place for up to 6 months.

37. Antioxidant Rose Glycerite

Ingredients:

- 1/2 cup fresh or dried rose petals
- 1/2 cup vegetable glycerin
- 1/4 cup distilled water

Instructions:

1. Combine rose petals, glycerin, and water in a jar.
2. Shake and steep for 4 weeks.
3. Strain and store in a dropper bottle.

Uses/Benefits: Supports skin health and reduces oxidative stress.

Dosage/How to Use:

- Take 1 dropper daily in water or tea.

Storage Tips:

- Store in a cool, dark place for up to 1 year.

38. Echinacea Immune Vinegar

Ingredients:

- 1 cup echinacea root
- 2 cups apple cider vinegar

Instructions:

1. Fill a jar halfway with echinacea root.
2. Cover with apple cider vinegar.
3. Steep for 3–4 weeks, then strain and store.

Uses/Benefits: Boosts immunity and reduces the severity of colds.

Dosage/How to Use:

- Take 1 tablespoon diluted in water daily.

Storage Tips:

- Keep in a cool, dark place for up to 6 months.

39. Anti-Inflammatory Turmeric Glycerite

Ingredients:

- 1/2 cup turmeric powder
- 1/2 cup vegetable glycerin
- 1/4 cup distilled water

Instructions:

1. Mix turmeric, glycerin, and water in a jar.
2. Shake and steep for 4 weeks.
3. Strain and store in a dropper bottle.

Uses/Benefits: Reduces inflammation and supports joint health.

Dosage/How to Use:

- Take 1 dropper daily with water or tea.

Storage Tips:

- Store in a cool, dark place for up to 1 year.

40. Warming Cinnamon Vinegar Extract

Ingredients:

- 1 cup cinnamon sticks
- 2 cups apple cider vinegar

Instructions:

1. Place cinnamon sticks in a jar and cover with vinegar.
2. Seal and steep for 3 weeks, shaking occasionally.
3. Strain and store in a glass bottle.

Uses/Benefits: Improves circulation and provides a warming effect.

Dosage/How to Use:

- Take 1 teaspoon in warm water or tea.

Storage Tips:

- Store in a dark, cool place for up to 6 months.

BOOK 5

GROWING YOUR OWN HERB GARDEN

Growing your own herb garden is one of the most rewarding ways to connect with nature while ensuring a sustainable supply of fresh, organic herbs for your remedies and culinary needs. Whether you're planting a few pots on a windowsill or cultivating a sprawling garden in your backyard, this book will guide you through the essential steps to create a thriving herb garden tailored to your space and climate.

In this book, you'll learn how to choose the best herbs for your region, implement organic gardening practices, and enhance your plants' growth with companion planting and proper soil care. You'll also discover how to avoid common gardening mistakes, ensuring your efforts yield healthy, vibrant herbs year-round.

Herb gardening is about more than growing plants—it's a journey of learning, patience, and connection with the earth. By cultivating your own herbs, you'll have fresh ingredients for remedies, teas, and meals while fostering a sense of empowerment and sustainability. Let's dive into the basics of growing a successful herb garden and nurturing your plants with care and purpose.

Selecting the Best Herbs for Your Climate

Choosing the right herbs for your climate is a foundational step in establishing a thriving herb garden. Herbs are resilient plants, but their growth and productivity depend significantly on their compatibility with the environment. Factors such as temperature, humidity, rainfall, and sunlight play crucial roles in determining which herbs will flourish in your garden. This chapter will guide you through understanding your climate, identifying suitable herbs, and making informed decisions to create a garden tailored to your location.

Understanding Your Climate

Your climate determines the types of herbs you can grow successfully. The first step in selecting the best herbs for your garden is to assess the local growing conditions. Broadly, climates fall into categories such as tropical, subtropical, temperate, and arid. Each type presents unique challenges and advantages for herb cultivation.

1. Tropical Climates

Tropical regions are characterized by high temperatures, high humidity, and abundant rainfall. These conditions are ideal for herbs that thrive in moisture-rich environments. Examples include basil, lemongrass, cilantro, and ginger.

2. Subtropical Climates

Subtropical areas experience milder winters and hot summers. Herbs like rosemary, thyme, oregano, and parsley adapt well to these conditions, as they can withstand moderate variations in temperature.

3. Temperate Climates

Temperate climates have distinct seasons, with cold winters and warm summers. Perennial herbs such as sage, mint, and chives thrive in these regions, as they can go dormant during winter and regrow in spring.

4. Arid Climates

Dry, hot climates are challenging but not impossible for herb gardening. Herbs like lavender, rosemary, and thyme are drought-tolerant and can survive with minimal water, provided they are given well-drained soil.

5. Microclimates

Even within a single region, microclimates can exist due to variations in elevation, proximity to water bodies, or urban heat islands. These localized conditions can influence which herbs perform best in specific parts of your garden.

Factors to Consider When Selecting Herbs

1. Temperature Tolerance

Herbs vary in their ability to tolerate temperature extremes. For instance, basil prefers warm weather and struggles in cold conditions, while thyme and sage can endure frost.

2. Sunlight Requirements

Most herbs require full sun (6–8 hours of direct sunlight daily) to grow well. However, some, such as parsley and mint, can tolerate partial shade, making them suitable for areas with less sun exposure.

3. Water Needs

Herbs like lavender and rosemary thrive in well-drained soil and require minimal watering, while basil and cilantro prefer consistently moist soil. Understanding the water needs of each herb ensures that you can provide optimal growing conditions.

4. Soil Type

Different herbs have varying soil preferences. Mediterranean herbs such as oregano and thyme prefer sandy, well-drained soil, while nutrient-rich loamy soil supports herbs like dill and parsley.

5. Seasonality

Some herbs are annuals, completing their life cycle in a single season (e.g., basil and cilantro), while others are perennials, growing back year after year (e.g., chives, rosemary). Knowing the lifecycle of each herb helps you plan your garden effectively.

Popular Herbs for Different Climates

Here are some commonly grown herbs categorized by their suitability to different climates:

1. Warm Climates (Tropical/Subtropical)

- » Basil: A heat-loving herb that grows rapidly in warm weather.
- » Lemongrass: Prefers high humidity and thrives in hot climates.
- » Cilantro: Grows well in tropical areas but may bolt quickly in extreme heat.

2. Cool Climates (Temperate)

- » Mint: Hardy and resilient, mint can tolerate cooler temperatures and regrows each spring.
- » Chives: A perennial herb that thrives in temperate regions, providing flavor and beauty to your garden.
- » Parsley: Prefers moderate temperatures and does well in partial shade.

3. Arid Climates (Dry)

- » Lavender: A drought-tolerant herb that thrives in arid conditions with plenty of sunlight.
- » Rosemary: Requires little water and grows well in sandy, well-drained soil.
- » Sage: An adaptable herb that tolerates heat and dry soil.

4. Adaptable Herbs

Some herbs, such as thyme, oregano, and dill, are highly adaptable and can grow in a variety of climates with proper care.

Companion Planting for Climate Optimization

Selecting the right herbs is only part of the equation. Companion planting can help maximize your garden's potential by creating beneficial relationships between plants. For example:

- Basil and Tomatoes: Planting basil near tomatoes can deter pests and enhance tomato flavor.
- Mint and Cabbage: Mint repels cabbage moths and other pests that harm cruciferous vegetables.
- Chives and Carrots: Chives improve carrot flavor and repel carrot flies.

Companion planting also allows you to create microclimates within your garden. Tall herbs like dill can provide shade for delicate plants, while dense foliage from thyme can act as a living mulch to retain soil moisture.

Starting with Easy-to-Grow Herbs

If you're new to gardening, consider starting with herbs that are easy to grow and forgiving of minor mistakes. Some beginner-friendly options include:

- Basil: A fast-growing herb that rewards you with abundant leaves for pesto and salads.
- Mint: Vigorous and hardy, mint grows well in containers or gardens but can spread aggressively if not contained.
- Parsley: A versatile herb that thrives in partial shade and requires minimal maintenance.

Herb Gardening in Containers

For those with limited space or challenging climates, container gardening offers an excellent alternative. Containers allow you to control soil quality, water levels, and sun exposure. Additionally, they can be moved to protect plants from extreme weather conditions.

1. Choose the Right Containers: Use pots with drainage holes to prevent waterlogging. Terracotta pots are excellent for herbs like rosemary and thyme, as they allow the soil to dry out between waterings.
2. Use Quality Potting Mix: A well-draining potting mix enriched with compost provides the nutrients herbs need to thrive.
3. Monitor Watering: Containers dry out more quickly than garden beds, so check soil moisture regularly.

Practical Tips for Selecting Herbs

1. Start Small: Begin with a few herbs suited to your climate and expand your garden as you gain confidence.
2. Research Native Plants: Native herbs are often well-adapted to your local environment and require less maintenance.
3. Experiment: Test a variety of herbs to see which ones perform best in your specific garden conditions.
4. Keep Records: Document your successes and challenges each season to refine your herb selection over time.

Selecting the best herbs for your climate is an essential first step in herb gardening. By understanding your region's conditions, evaluating the needs of different herbs, and experimenting with a variety of plants, you can create a flourishing herb garden that complements your environment. Whether you're growing drought-tolerant lavender in an arid landscape or nurturing parsley in a shaded temperate garden, the key is to start small, observe, and adapt. The herbs you choose today will lay the foundation for a productive and rewarding gardening journey.

Organic Gardening Practices for Beginners

Organic gardening is a sustainable and eco-friendly approach to cultivating plants without the use of synthetic chemicals or fertilizers. For beginners, adopting organic practices not only promotes healthier plants and soil but also supports the broader ecosystem, ensuring your garden is a haven for beneficial insects, wildlife, and biodiversity.

This chapter will guide you through the essential principles and techniques of organic gardening, laying the foundation for a thriving herb garden.

Understanding Organic Gardening

Organic gardening centers on working with nature rather than against it. It emphasizes soil health, natural pest management, and biodiversity. By using compost, crop rotation, and organic mulches, gardeners can maintain a healthy growing environment while reducing their environmental impact.

The main principles of organic gardening include:

1. Building Healthy Soil: Using organic matter like compost and mulch to enrich the soil.
2. Avoiding Chemicals: Eliminating synthetic pesticides, herbicides, and fertilizers in favor of natural alternatives.
3. Promoting Biodiversity: Encouraging a diverse ecosystem of plants, insects, and microorganisms.
4. Sustainability: Using resources efficiently to reduce waste and preserve the environment.

1. Preparing Your Garden

Before planting, it's important to prepare your garden space with organic principles in mind.

Choosing a Location

- Select a site that receives adequate sunlight for your chosen herbs, typically 6–8 hours daily.
- Ensure the area has good drainage to prevent waterlogged soil, which can lead to root rot.

Testing Your Soil

Healthy soil is the foundation of organic gardening. Start by testing your soil's pH and nutrient levels with a simple soil test kit.

- Adjusting Soil pH: Most herbs prefer slightly acidic to neutral soil with a pH of 6.0–7.0. Use lime to raise pH or sulfur to lower it if needed.
- Improving Soil Structure: Add organic matter like compost, aged manure, or peat moss to improve soil texture and fertility.

2. Composting: Nature's Recycling System

Compost is an essential component of organic gardening, providing nutrients to plants and improving soil health. Creating your own compost is an easy and cost-effective way to recycle kitchen and garden waste.

How to Start a Compost Pile

1. Select a Location: Choose a well-drained spot in your garden for your compost bin or pile.
2. Layer Materials: Alternate layers of "green" (nitrogen-rich) and "brown" (carbon-rich) materials:
   » Green: Fruit scraps, vegetable peels, coffee grounds, grass clippings.
   » Brown: Dry leaves, shredded newspaper, cardboard.
3. Maintain Balance: Aim for a ratio of 2 parts brown to 1 part green materials.
4. Turn Regularly: Aerate the pile weekly to speed up decomposition and prevent odors.

When is Compost Ready?

Compost is ready when it is dark, crumbly, and has an earthy smell. Use it as a soil amendment or top dressing for your herb garden.

3. Natural Fertilizers

In organic gardening, plants are fed through natural sources of nutrients rather than synthetic fertilizers. Natural fertilizers promote long-term soil health and reduce the risk of nutrient runoff.

Common Organic Fertilizers

- Compost: Provides a balanced mix of nutrients and improves soil structure.
- Aged Manure: A rich source of nitrogen but should be well-composted to prevent burning plants.
- Bone Meal: Supplies phosphorus to promote strong roots and flowering.
- Seaweed or Kelp: Adds trace minerals and stimulates plant growth.

How to Apply Fertilizers

- Mix compost or aged manure into the soil before planting.
- Use liquid seaweed or fish emulsion as a foliar spray for a quick nutrient boost.

4. Managing Pests and Diseases Organically

One of the challenges in gardening is dealing with pests and diseases. Organic gardening relies on prevention, natural remedies, and beneficial insects to manage these issues.

Preventing Pests and Diseases

- Diversity: Plant a variety of herbs and flowers to attract beneficial insects and confuse pests.

- Healthy Plants: Well-nourished plants are more resistant to pests and diseases.
- Crop Rotation: Avoid planting the same herbs in the same spot year after year to reduce pest build-up.

Natural Pest Control Methods

1. Handpicking: Remove larger pests like caterpillars or beetles by hand.
2. Neem Oil: A natural pesticide that deters insects without harming beneficial ones.
3. Diatomaceous Earth: A powder that dehydrates soft-bodied insects like slugs.
4. Companion Planting: Plant pest-repellent herbs like basil or marigold near vulnerable crops.

Encouraging Beneficial Insects

Ladybugs, lacewings, and parasitic wasps are natural predators of garden pests. To attract them, plant flowers like dill, fennel, and calendula.

5. Mulching for Weed Control and Moisture Retention

Mulch is a gardener's best friend in organic gardening. It suppresses weeds, conserves moisture, and regulates soil temperature.

Types of Organic Mulch

- Straw: Effective for suppressing weeds and breaking down into the soil.
- Wood Chips: Long-lasting and excellent for pathways or perennial beds.
- Grass Clippings: Add nitrogen as they decompose but should be applied thinly to avoid matting.

How to Apply Mulch

- Spread a 2–3 inch layer of mulch around your herbs, keeping it a few inches away from the stems to prevent rot.

6. Watering Wisely

Watering is a critical part of organic gardening. Overwatering can lead to root rot, while underwatering stresses plants.

Best Practices for Watering

1. Water Early: Water in the morning to reduce evaporation and allow plants to dry before evening.
2. Deep, Infrequent Watering: Encourage deep

root growth by watering thoroughly but less frequently.

3. Use Drip Irrigation: Directs water to the roots, minimizing waste and reducing disease risk.

7. Encouraging Pollinators

Pollinators like bees, butterflies, and hummingbirds are vital for the success of your herb garden. Attract them by planting flowers and herbs that provide nectar and pollen.

Herbs That Attract Pollinators

- Lavender
- Thyme
- Basil
- Mint

Creating a Pollinator-Friendly Garden

- Avoid pesticides that harm bees and other beneficial insects.
- Provide water sources like shallow dishes with stones for insects to rest on.

8. Seasonal Care and Maintenance

Organic gardening is an ongoing process that requires attention throughout the year. Seasonal tasks ensure your garden remains productive and healthy.

Spring

- Prepare the soil with compost and organic fertilizers.
- Plant cool-season herbs like parsley and cilantro.

Summer

- Mulch to retain moisture and protect plants from heat stress.
- Harvest herbs regularly to encourage new growth.

Fall

- Plant perennials like sage and thyme.
- Collect leaves for compost or mulch.

Winter

- Protect tender herbs with frost covers or move pots indoors.
- Plan next year's garden and order seeds early.

9. Organic Gardening and Sustainability

Organic gardening goes beyond growing plants; it's about fostering a sustainable relationship with nature. By avoiding chemicals, conserving resources, and supporting local biodiversity, you're contributing to a healthier planet.

Reducing Waste

- Compost kitchen scraps and garden clippings.
- Reuse containers and repurpose materials for garden projects.

Saving Seeds

Saving seeds from your herbs is a sustainable way to ensure a steady supply of plants while preserving heirloom varieties.

Organic gardening is more than a technique—it's a philosophy that prioritizes harmony with nature. By adopting these beginner-friendly practices, you'll create a thriving herb garden that supports healthy plants, vibrant soil, and a balanced ecosystem. As you gain confidence, you'll discover that organic gardening is not only better for the environment but also deeply rewarding, connecting you to the rhythms of the natural world.

Companion Planting and Soil Care

Companion planting and soil care are two of the most critical aspects of a thriving herb garden. Together, they create a harmonious environment where plants grow stronger, pests are minimized, and soil fertility is maintained. Companion planting involves strategically pairing plants that benefit each other, while proper soil care ensures that your herbs receive the nutrients they need for optimal growth.

This chapter explores the principles of companion planting and soil care, offering practical techniques to create a sustainable, productive garden.

Companion Planting: The Basics

Companion planting is a gardening practice that involves grouping plants together to maximize their growth and health. Some plants enhance each other's growth, deter pests, or improve soil conditions, while others may compete for resources or attract harmful insects. Knowing which plants work well together can transform your garden into a self-sustaining ecosystem.

Benefits of Companion Planting

1. Pest Control

Certain plants emit natural chemicals or scents that repel pests. For example, basil deters aphids and whiteflies, making it an excellent companion for tomatoes and peppers.

2. Pollinator Attraction

Herbs like thyme, dill, and lavender attract bees, butterflies, and other pollinators, which are essential for the reproduction of many plants.

3. Enhanced Growth

Some plants improve the flavor, yield, or growth of their companions. For instance, planting chives near carrots enhances their flavor and deters carrot flies.

4. Efficient Use of Space

Companion planting allows you to grow more in less space by combining plants with complementary growth habits. For example, low-growing herbs like oregano can be planted under taller herbs like dill.

5. Weed Suppression

Dense plantings of compatible herbs can act as a living mulch, suppressing weed growth and retaining soil moisture.

Companion Planting Examples for Herbs

1. Basil and Tomatoes

Basil enhances the flavor of tomatoes and repels pests like aphids and mosquitoes.

2. Rosemary and Cabbage

Rosemary deters cabbage moths and other pests that attack cruciferous vegetables.

3. Dill and Lettuce

Dill attracts beneficial insects like ladybugs, which feed on aphids that can harm lettuce.

4. Thyme and Strawberries

Thyme deters worms and beetles that attack strawberries.

5. Chives and Carrots

Chives repel carrot flies and improve carrot flavor.

6. Lavender and Roses

Lavender repels pests like aphids and enhances the beauty and fragrance of roses.

Plants to Avoid Pairing

Not all plants make good companions. Some compete for nutrients or attract pests that harm their neighbors. For example:

- Fennel inhibits the growth of most herbs and vegetables.
- Mint spreads aggressively and can overtake neighboring plants unless contained.

Designing a Companion Planting Layout

1. Group by Compatibility: Place herbs with similar water, sunlight, and soil needs together.
2. Layering: Use taller plants to provide shade for sun-sensitive herbs, like cilantro, in hot climates.
3. Border Planting: Plant pest-repelling herbs, such as marigolds or nasturtiums, around the edges of your garden to create a natural barrier.
4. Intercropping: Combine fast-growing herbs like radishes or parsley with slower-growing plants like basil to maximize space.

Soil Care: The Foundation of Healthy Plants

Soil is the lifeblood of your garden, providing nutrients, water, and support to your plants. Healthy soil is teeming with microorganisms, organic matter, and a balance of essential nutrients. Without proper soil care, even the best companion planting techniques will fall short.

Understanding Soil Composition

Soil is composed of three main particles: sand, silt, and clay. The ideal soil type for most herbs is loamy soil, which balances drainage and nutrient retention. Loamy soil consists of:

- 40% sand: For drainage and aeration.
- 40% silt: To hold nutrients and moisture.
- 20% clay: To bind the soil and provide structure.

Improving Soil Quality

1. Add Organic Matter

Organic matter, such as compost, aged manure, and leaf mold, enriches the soil, improves its texture, and supports microbial life.

2. Maintain Soil pH

Most herbs thrive in slightly acidic to neutral soil

with a pH of 6.0–7.0. Adjust soil pH using lime (to raise pH) or sulfur (to lower pH) if necessary.

3. Aerate the Soil

Regularly loosening the soil with a garden fork or tiller improves drainage and allows roots to access oxygen.

4. Use Cover Crops

Planting cover crops like clover or rye during the off-season prevents soil erosion, suppresses weeds, and adds nutrients back to the soil.

Fertilizing Your Herb Garden

Herbs generally require less fertilization than other plants, as excessive nutrients can lead to weak, leggy growth. Use organic fertilizers sparingly to avoid overfeeding.

Types of Organic Fertilizers

- Compost: Provides a balanced mix of nutrients.
- Bone Meal: Adds phosphorus to promote strong roots and flowering.
- Wood Ash: Supplies potassium, but should be used in moderation.
- Seaweed or Kelp: Provides trace minerals and boosts plant immunity.

When to Fertilize

- Light feeders like thyme and oregano may only need an application of compost once a year.
- Heavy feeders like basil benefit from monthly doses of diluted compost tea or seaweed extract.

Maintaining Soil Health

1. Mulching Mulch helps retain moisture, suppress weeds, and regulate soil temperature. Use organic mulches like straw, wood chips, or grass clippings.
2. Rotate Crops

Rotate plant families each season to prevent nutrient depletion and reduce pest and disease build-up.

3. Avoid Soil Compaction

Compacted soil restricts root growth and water penetration. Avoid walking on planting beds and use stepping stones if needed.

4. Encourage Microbial Life

Healthy soil is alive with microorganisms that break down organic matter and release nutrients. Avoid synthetic chemicals that kill beneficial microbes.

Watering and Soil Moisture Management

1. Water Deeply: Encourage deep root growth by watering thoroughly but less frequently.
2. Drip Irrigation: Use a drip irrigation system to deliver water directly to the roots, minimizing waste.
3. Check Moisture Levels: Insert your finger into the soil; if it feels dry 1–2 inches below the surface, it's time to water.

Integrated Companion Planting and Soil Care

Companion planting and soil care are interdependent practices. Together, they create a self-sustaining cycle of growth and renewal in your garden.

1. Use Cover Crops as Companions: Clover and vetch fix nitrogen in the soil, benefiting nutrient-hungry herbs like basil and parsley.
2. Plant Nitrogen-Fixing Herbs: Herbs like fenugreek and clover enrich the soil by fixing nitrogen, reducing the need for fertilizers.
3. Alternate Deep and Shallow Rooters: Pair deep-rooted herbs like comfrey with shallow-rooted ones like cilantro to maximize soil nutrient uptake.

Common Mistakes in Companion Planting and Soil Care

1. Overcrowding: Planting too closely can lead to competition for nutrients and increased risk of disease.
2. Ignoring Soil pH: Failing to test and adjust soil pH can stunt herb growth.
3. Over-Mulching: Applying too much mulch can suffocate roots and promote mold growth.
4. Poor Companion Pairing: Pairing incompatible plants, like fennel and most herbs, can inhibit growth.

Practical Example: A Companion Planting and Soil Care Plan

Garden Setup Example:

- Front Row: Basil and parsley (full sun, moderate feeders).
- Middle Row: Chives and carrots (companion pairing for pest control).
- Back Row: Lavender and thyme (drought-tolerant, nutrient-light).

Soil Preparation Steps:

1. Add 2 inches of compost to the topsoil and till gently.
2. Test soil pH and adjust with lime or sulfur as needed.
3. Mulch the planting rows with straw to retain moisture.

Maintenance Plan:

- Fertilize basil monthly with diluted compost tea.
- Hand-weed weekly to prevent competition.
- Rotate parsley and carrots to new rows next season.

Companion planting and soil care are the cornerstones of a healthy, sustainable herb garden. By strategically pairing plants and maintaining soil fertility, you can create a thriving environment that minimizes pests, maximizes growth, and reduces the need for chemical inputs. With careful planning and consistent effort, your garden will not only produce abundant, flavorful herbs but also support a balanced ecosystem that nurtures plants, insects, and soil life alike.

Common Gardening Mistakes and How to Avoid Them

Gardening is a rewarding experience, but like any skill, it comes with a learning curve. Even seasoned gardeners make mistakes, and beginners often face challenges that can lead to frustration or underwhelming results. The good news is that most common gardening mistakes can be avoided with a bit of knowledge and planning. This chapter explores the pitfalls that gardeners often encounter and provides practical advice to overcome them, ensuring your herb garden thrives.

Mistake 1: Choosing the Wrong Location

The location of your garden plays a critical role in its success. Many herbs require specific conditions to thrive, and planting in an unsuitable spot can lead to poor growth or plant failure.

How It Happens:

- Planting in areas with insufficient sunlight for sun-loving herbs like basil and thyme.
- Placing herbs in low-lying areas prone to waterlogging.
- Ignoring microclimates that may expose plants to excessive wind or shade.

How to Avoid It:

1. Assess Sunlight: Most herbs need at least 6–8 hours of direct sunlight daily. Observe your garden throughout the day to identify the sunniest spots.
2. Consider Drainage: Avoid areas where water tends to pool after rain. If drainage is an issue, consider raised beds or container gardening.
3. Account for Wind: Protect delicate herbs like cilantro from strong winds by planting near barriers such as hedges or fences.

Mistake 2: Overwatering or Underwatering

Watering issues are among the most common mistakes gardeners make. Both overwatering and underwatering can stress plants and hinder their growth.

How It Happens:

- Assuming all herbs have the same water requirements.
- Watering too frequently, leading to root rot.
- Neglecting plants during hot or dry weather.

How to Avoid It:

1. Understand Water Needs: Group herbs with similar water requirements together. For example:
   » Drought-tolerant herbs like rosemary, sage, and thyme prefer dry soil.
   » Moisture-loving herbs like basil and parsley need consistent watering.
2. Water at the Right Time: Water in the early morning to minimize evaporation and fungal diseases.
3. Check Soil Moisture: Insert your finger into the soil; if it's dry 1–2 inches below the surface, it's time to water.

Mistake 3: Neglecting Soil Health

Soil is the foundation of any garden, yet many gardeners overlook its importance. Poor soil quality can result in nutrient deficiencies, stunted growth, and weak plants.

How It Happens:

- Planting without testing or amending the soil.
- Using soil that is too compacted or lacks organic matter.
- Relying solely on chemical fertilizers, which can deplete soil health over time.

How to Avoid It:

1. Test Your Soil: Use a soil test kit to check pH and nutrient levels. Most herbs prefer slightly acidic to neutral soil (pH 6.0–7.0).
2. Amend with Organic Matter: Add compost, aged manure, or leaf mold to enrich the soil and improve texture.
3. Avoid Over-Tilling: Excessive tilling can disturb beneficial microbes and lead to erosion. Focus on maintaining soil structure.

Mistake 4: Planting Too Closely

Planting herbs too close together can lead to overcrowding, which restricts airflow, increases competition for nutrients, and encourages the spread of diseases.

How It Happens:

- Underestimating the mature size of plants.
- Overplanting in small spaces.
- Ignoring spacing recommendations on seed packets or plant labels.

How to Avoid It:

1. Plan Ahead: Research the mature size of each herb and follow spacing guidelines.
2. Thin Seedlings: When growing from seed, thin out seedlings to the recommended spacing once they sprout.
3. Use Containers for Overflow: If you run out of space in your garden, grow additional herbs in pots.

Mistake 5: Ignoring Pests and Diseases

Pests and diseases are inevitable in any garden, but ignoring early signs can result in widespread damage.

How It Happens:

- Failing to monitor plants regularly.
- Using harmful pesticides that kill beneficial insects.

- Planting the same herbs in the same location year after year, encouraging pests and diseases to build up.

How to Avoid It:

1. Inspect Plants Regularly: Check for signs of pests (e.g., holes in leaves, sticky residue) and diseases (e.g., discoloration, mold).
2. Encourage Beneficial Insects: Attract ladybugs, lacewings, and other natural predators by planting flowers like dill, fennel, and calendula.
3. Rotate Crops: Avoid planting the same herbs in the same spot each year to break pest and disease cycles.

Mistake 6: Using Poor-Quality Seeds or Plants

Starting with low-quality seeds or weak plants can set your garden up for failure from the beginning.

How It Happens:

- Buying seeds from unreliable sources.
- Choosing plants that look unhealthy or stressed at the nursery.
- Using old seeds without checking viability.

How to Avoid It:

1. Source Quality Seeds: Purchase seeds from reputable suppliers and check expiration dates.
2. Inspect Nursery Plants: Look for healthy leaves, strong stems, and no signs of pests or disease.
3. Conduct a Germination Test: Place seeds on a damp paper towel to see if they sprout before planting them in the soil.

Mistake 7: Neglecting Weeds

Weeds compete with herbs for sunlight, water, and nutrients. Allowing them to proliferate can choke out your desired plants and make your garden harder to manage.

How It Happens:

- Waiting too long to weed, allowing weeds to go to seed.
- Using herbicides that can harm nearby herbs.
- Failing to mulch, which leaves soil exposed for weeds to grow.

How to Avoid It:

1. Weed Early and Often: Remove weeds as soon as they appear to prevent them from spreading.
2. Use Mulch: Apply a 2–3 inch layer of organic mulch around your herbs to suppress weeds and retain moisture.
3. Hand-Pull Around Delicate Herbs: Use a gentle hand to pull weeds near shallow-rooted herbs to avoid disturbing their roots.

Mistake 8: Over-Fertilizing

While herbs benefit from nutrient-rich soil, over-fertilizing can lead to excessive foliage growth at the expense of flavor and potency.

How It Happens:

- Applying too much fertilizer or using high-nitrogen formulas.
- Fertilizing too frequently, especially during the growing season.
- Ignoring the nutrient needs of specific herbs.

How to Avoid It:

1. Fertilize Sparingly: Most herbs require minimal fertilization. Use compost or diluted organic fertilizers once every 4–6 weeks.
2. Focus on the Right Nutrients: Phosphorus promotes root development, while potassium enhances overall plant health.
3. Observe Plant Responses: Adjust fertilization based on how your plants are growing. Excessive growth may indicate over-fertilization.

Mistake 9: Failing to Harvest Properly

Harvesting herbs incorrectly or neglecting to harvest them at all can reduce their productivity and flavor.

How It Happens:

- Harvesting too much at once, weakening the plant.
- Waiting too long to harvest, resulting in over-mature or bitter-tasting leaves.
- Failing to prune regularly, which discourages new growth.

How to Avoid It:

1. Harvest Gradually: Remove no more than one-third of the plant at a time to allow for recovery.
2. Pick at the Right Time: Harvest herbs like basil and mint before they flower for the best flavor.
3. Prune Regularly: Pinch back leaves and stems to encourage bushier growth and prevent plants from becoming leggy.

Mistake 10: Giving Up Too Soon

Gardening takes time, patience, and practice. Many beginners become discouraged by early setbacks and abandon their gardens prematurely.

How It Happens:

- Expecting instant results without considering the learning curve.
- Failing to adapt to changing conditions or problems.
- Lacking a plan for ongoing maintenance.

How to Avoid It:

1. Start Small: Focus on a few easy-to-grow herbs like basil, mint, or chives.
2. Learn from Mistakes: Treat setbacks as opportunities to improve your skills and knowledge.
3. Celebrate Small Wins: Even a single successful harvest is a step forward!

Gardening is a journey filled with both challenges and rewards. By understanding and avoiding these common mistakes, you can create a healthier, more productive herb garden. Remember, every gardener makes mistakes—it's part of the process. With time, effort, and the strategies outlined in this chapter, you'll gain confidence and experience, transforming your garden into a flourishing haven of fresh, flavorful herbs.

BOOK 6

SUSTAINABLE WILDCRAFTING

Wildcrafting, or the practice of foraging for plants in their natural habitats, is a deeply rewarding way to connect with nature and source herbs for your remedies. However, it's essential to approach this practice with sustainability and respect for the environment in mind. Sustainable wildcrafting ensures that the plants we harvest continue to thrive, ecosystems remain balanced, and future generations can enjoy the abundance of wild herbs.

In this book, you'll learn the principles of responsible foraging, from understanding local ecosystems to recognizing ethical harvesting practices that protect plant populations. You'll also discover the tools and techniques needed for safe and efficient wildcrafting, along with methods to preserve and store your harvest for long-term use.

Sustainable wildcrafting is about more than gathering plants; it's a practice of stewardship, mindfulness, and reciprocity with the natural world. By understanding and following ethical guidelines, you'll not only enrich your herbal practice but also contribute to the health and vitality of the ecosystems you explore. Whether you're a beginner or an experienced forager, this book provides the knowledge and tools to wildcraft responsibly and sustainably. Let's dive into the art and ethics of sustainable wildcrafting.

Foraging Responsibly in Nature

Foraging, the act of gathering plants and herbs from the wild, is a timeless tradition that connects us to the natural world. It offers an opportunity to source fresh, potent herbs while deepening our understanding of local ecosystems. However, with this practice comes the responsibility to forage in a way that preserves the environment and ensures the sustainability of plant populations. This chapter will guide you through the principles and practices of responsible foraging, helping you develop a mindful and ethical approach to gathering herbs in nature.

Understanding the Importance of Responsible Foraging

Responsible foraging is about more than simply collecting plants; it's about maintaining a balance between human use and the natural ecosystems that support plant life. Overharvesting, habitat destruction, and lack of knowledge about local plants can have detrimental effects on ecosystems. By following responsible foraging practices, you can:

- Protect plant populations and ensure their continued availability.
- Support biodiversity by leaving habitats undisturbed.
- Build a deeper connection with the land and its natural rhythms.

Know the Rules and Regulations

Before setting out to forage, familiarize yourself with local laws and regulations regarding foraging in your area. Rules can vary depending on the location and type of land, such as:

- Public Lands: Many parks and nature reserves allow limited foraging, but some may prohibit it entirely to protect ecosystems.
- Private Property: Always obtain permission from landowners before foraging on private land.
- Endangered Species Protections: Learn about plants that are protected by law and avoid harvesting them to ensure their survival.

Understanding and respecting these rules is a crucial first step in responsible foraging.

Identify Plants Accurately

One of the most critical aspects of responsible foraging is accurate plant identification. Mistaking one plant for another can lead to overharvesting of the wrong species or, worse, ingestion of toxic plants.

1. Study Field Guides: Invest in region-specific

field guides with detailed photos and descriptions of plants.
2. Join Foraging Groups: Participate in guided foraging walks with experienced foragers who can help you identify plants in your area.
3. Learn Look-Alikes: Some edible plants have toxic look-alikes. For example, wild carrot (Queen Anne's lace) resembles poison hemlock. Understanding these differences is vital.
4. Use Multiple Resources: Cross-reference plants using books, apps, and online resources to ensure accurate identification.

Harvesting with Care

Once you've identified a plant, it's essential to harvest it in a way that minimizes harm to the environment and supports the plant's regeneration.

1. Take Only What You Need
   » Harvest sparingly, leaving at least 70–80% of the plant population intact. This ensures the plant can reproduce and support wildlife that depends on it.
2. Avoid Overharvesting in One Area
   » Spread your harvesting across multiple locations to avoid depleting a single area.
3. Respect Growth Cycles
   » Harvest herbs at the appropriate stage of their growth cycle for optimal potency. For example:
   ▪ Collect leaves before the plant flowers.
   ▪ Harvest seeds when they are fully mature.
   ▪ Gather roots during the plant's dormant season.
4. Use the Right Tools
   » Use sharp, clean tools like scissors or knives to make clean cuts and avoid damaging the plant.
5. Replant and Replenish
   » In cases where you harvest roots or whole plants, consider replanting seeds or cuttings to support regrowth.

Leave No Trace

Foraging should have minimal impact on the environment. By practicing "Leave No Trace"

principles, you can ensure that your presence in nature doesn't disrupt ecosystems.

1. Stay on Trails
   » Avoid trampling vegetation or disturbing wildlife by staying on established paths when possible.
2. Avoid Damaging Habitats
   » Refrain from uprooting plants unnecessarily or disrupting the soil, as this can lead to erosion and habitat degradation.
3. Pack Out Waste
   » Take all trash with you, including any packaging or food scraps, to keep the environment clean.

Respect Wildlife and Ecosystems

Plants are a vital part of the ecosystems they inhabit. Many animals rely on the same plants you may wish to harvest, and disrupting their food sources can have cascading effects.

1. Observe Wildlife
   » Avoid foraging in areas where animals are actively feeding or nesting.
2. Know Keystone Species
   » Some plants play a critical role in their ecosystems. For example, milkweed is essential for monarch butterflies. Harvesting such plants should be done sparingly or avoided altogether.
3. Support Biodiversity
   » Avoid removing all of one type of plant from an area to maintain ecological balance.

Building Knowledge Through Observation

Foraging is as much about learning as it is about gathering. Spend time observing plants in their natural habitats to understand their role in the ecosystem.

1. Notice Plant Communities
   » Plants often grow in association with other species. Observing these relationships can help you identify plants and understand their growing conditions.
2. Track Seasonal Changes

» Plants look different at various times of the year. Learning to recognize them in all stages of growth ensures successful foraging.

3. Journal Your Experiences

» Keep a foraging journal to document what you find, where you find it, and how you use it. Over time, this record will become an invaluable resource.

Foraging Ethics: Beyond Sustainability

Responsible foraging goes beyond ensuring sustainability—it also involves respecting the cultural and spiritual significance of plants.

1. Cultural Awareness

» Many plants have cultural or spiritual significance to Indigenous peoples and local communities. Learn about the history and uses of these plants and approach them with respect.

2. Mindful Harvesting

» Take a moment to appreciate the plant and its contribution to your well-being. Some foragers even practice a moment of gratitude before harvesting.

3. Sharing Knowledge

» Share your knowledge about responsible foraging with others to foster a community of ethical wildcrafters.

Planning Your Foraging Trips

Preparation is key to a successful and responsible foraging experience.

1. Research Locations

» Study maps and local resources to identify areas where foraging is allowed and plants are abundant.

2. Check Weather Conditions

» Avoid foraging in extreme weather to ensure your safety and minimize disturbance to the environment.

3. Pack Essentials

» Bring tools like a field guide, sharp scissors, paper bags (to avoid moisture buildup), gloves, and water.

What to Avoid While Foraging

1. Contaminated Areas

» Avoid foraging near roadsides, industrial sites, or areas treated with pesticides or herbicides.

2. Protected or Endangered Plants

» Learn to recognize plants that are rare or endangered and avoid harvesting them.

3. Large-Scale Harvesting

» Foraging is a personal practice and should never be done on a commercial scale without proper permits.

A Practical Example: Foraging Responsibly for Wild Mint

Wild mint is a common herb that grows near streams and wetlands. Here's how to forage responsibly:

1. Identify the plant using its distinct square stem and fragrant leaves.

2. Harvest sparingly, taking only the top third of each plant to encourage regrowth.

3. Avoid areas with stagnant water or signs of pollution.

4. Leave some plants untouched to support local wildlife and ensure the population thrives.

Foraging responsibly in nature is about more than gathering herbs—it's about building a relationship with the land, respecting its ecosystems, and ensuring its resources remain abundant for future generations. By following the principles outlined in this chapter, you can enjoy the rewards of wildcrafting while minimizing your impact on the environment. Responsible foraging is a practice of mindfulness, gratitude, and stewardship, allowing you to connect deeply with nature while supporting its health and vitality.

Ethical Harvesting of Wild Plants

Ethical harvesting of wild plants is the cornerstone of sustainable wildcrafting. It ensures that the ecosystems where plants thrive remain balanced and undisturbed while allowing humans to benefit from nature's bounty. As wildcrafting gains popularity, the need to harvest responsibly has become more critical than ever to prevent overharvesting and habitat destruction.

This chapter explores the principles and practices of ethical harvesting, focusing on how to gather wild plants in a way that supports regeneration, protects biodiversity, and nurtures your connection to the natural world.

Understanding Ethical Harvesting

Ethical harvesting is guided by the principle of reciprocity with nature. It's not just about taking plants for personal use; it's about giving back and ensuring that the environment remains healthy and abundant for future generations. Ethical harvesting means:

1. Respecting the plant's lifecycle and reproductive needs.
2. Ensuring the sustainability of plant populations.
3. Protecting habitats and ecosystems.

By approaching wildcrafting with mindfulness and care, you can become a steward of the land rather than a threat to it.

1. Know Your Plants

The first step in ethical harvesting is to know exactly what you're harvesting. Misidentification can lead to overharvesting of the wrong plants, harming ecosystems, or even poisoning yourself with toxic species.

Tips for Plant Identification:

- Use Reliable Resources: Invest in a regional field guide or download a foraging app with clear photographs and descriptions.
- Learn Plant Families: Understanding families like the mint family (square stems, aromatic leaves) or the carrot family (umbrella-shaped flowers) helps in identification.
- Observe Growth Stages: Learn how plants look in different seasons to avoid harvesting at inappropriate times.
- Seek Guidance: Join foraging groups or workshops to learn from experienced foragers.

2. Harvest Sparingly

One of the most important rules of ethical harvesting is to take only what you need. Overharvesting can deplete plant populations and disrupt ecosystems.

General Guidelines:

- Leave the Majority: Take no more than 10–30% of a plant population in any given area.
- Spread Out Harvesting: Avoid concentrating your harvest in one location. Instead, gather from multiple sites to minimize impact.
- Skip Sparse Populations: If a plant population is small or struggling, avoid harvesting entirely to allow it to recover and reproduce.

By harvesting sparingly, you ensure that the plant population remains robust and that animals relying on these plants have access to their food sources.

3. Understand Plant Life Cycles

Plants have specific life cycles, and harvesting at the wrong time can harm their ability to grow and reproduce.

Guidelines for Harvesting at the Right Time:

- Leaves: Collect leaves early in the growing season when they are tender and before the plant flowers.
- Flowers: Harvest flowers during full bloom, but leave some to ensure the plant can produce seeds.
- Roots: Harvest roots in the fall or early spring when the plant is dormant, and its energy is concentrated in the root system.
- Seeds: Wait until seeds are fully mature before collecting, and leave enough behind to allow for natural propagation.

4. Minimize Damage to Plants and Habitats

How you harvest matters as much as what you harvest. Ethical harvesting involves using techniques that minimize damage to plants and their surrounding environment.

Techniques for Minimal Impact:

- Use Proper Tools: Use sharp scissors, pruners, or knives to make clean cuts and avoid tearing plants.
- Avoid Uprooting: Harvest leaves, flowers, or seeds without pulling up the entire plant unless necessary.
- Restore the Area: Refill holes, scatter seeds, or cover disturbed soil to minimize the visual and ecological impact.

5. Respect Protected and Endangered Species

Some plants are rare, endangered, or play a critical role in their ecosystem. Harvesting these species can have far-reaching consequences and may even be illegal.

What You Can Do:

- Research Local Species: Learn which plants in your region are protected or at risk.
- Avoid Harvesting Endangered Plants: If you encounter a rare plant, admire it but leave it untouched.
- Report Illegal Activity: Notify local authorities if you witness illegal harvesting of protected plants.

6. Protect the Ecosystem

Plants are part of a larger ecosystem, supporting wildlife, insects, and soil health. Ethical harvesting means considering the broader impact of your actions.

Guidelines for Ecosystem Preservation:

- Leave Habitat Intact: Avoid disturbing animal habitats, such as nests or burrows, while foraging.
- Maintain Plant Diversity: Harvest a variety of plants rather than focusing on a single species to maintain ecological balance.
- Know Keystone Species: Some plants, like milkweed for monarch butterflies, are critical for specific wildlife and should be left untouched or harvested minimally.

7. Practice Reciprocity

Reciprocity is about giving back to nature in exchange for what you take. By practicing reciprocity, you honor the land and ensure its health and abundance.

Ways to Give Back:

- Replant Seeds: Scatter seeds from harvested plants to encourage regrowth.
- Remove Invasive Species: While harvesting, take the opportunity to remove invasive plants that threaten native species.
- Volunteer for Conservation Efforts: Join local groups that work to restore habitats and protect native plants.

8. Harvest with Gratitude

Ethical harvesting is a practice of mindfulness and gratitude. Taking a moment to appreciate the plants and their role in your life fosters a deeper connection with nature.

Simple Acts of Gratitude:

- Pause and Reflect: Before harvesting, take a moment to observe the plant and its surroundings.
- Offer Thanks: Many foragers say a small prayer or expression of gratitude to honor the plant.
- Be Mindful: Treat plants with care, recognizing their role in the ecosystem and your life.

9. Leave No Trace

The principle of "Leave No Trace" ensures that your foraging activities have minimal impact on the environment.

Steps to Leave No Trace:

- Pack Out Waste: Take all trash, including food wrappers or broken tools, with you.
- Stay on Trails: Avoid trampling vegetation or creating new paths.
- Restore the Landscape: Cover disturbed soil and ensure the area looks as natural as when you arrived.

10. Teaching and Sharing Knowledge

One of the most powerful ways to ensure ethical harvesting practices are upheld is by sharing your knowledge with others. Educating fellow foragers creates a community of responsible wildcrafters who care for the land.

Ways to Share Knowledge:

- Host Workshops: Teach others about plant identification and ethical harvesting techniques.
- Write or Blog: Share your experiences and tips online or in local publications.
- Join Foraging Groups: Engage with others in your area to promote responsible practices.

Practical Example: Ethical Harvesting of Dandelions

Dandelions are a common plant that many foragers seek for their roots, leaves, and flowers. Here's how to harvest them ethically:

1. Observe the Population: Ensure there are plenty of dandelions in the area before harvesting.
2. Take Only What You Need: Harvest leaves from multiple plants rather than stripping one plant bare.
3. Leave Enough for Wildlife: Dandelions are an early food source for bees and other pollinators. Leave flowers for them to feed on.
4. Replant Seeds: If you harvest roots, scatter seeds in the area to encourage regrowth.

Ethical harvesting is a practice of respect, mindfulness, and care for the natural world. By understanding plant life cycles, protecting ecosystems, and practicing reciprocity, you can ensure that your foraging activities benefit both you and the environment. Ethical wildcrafting is not just about gathering plants—it's about fostering a sustainable relationship with nature, where every action contributes to the health and balance of the land.

Tools for Safe and Sustainable Foraging

Foraging for wild plants is an enriching and practical activity that connects us to nature, but it requires preparation and the right tools to ensure safety and sustainability. Having the appropriate tools not only makes foraging more efficient but also minimizes damage to plants and their surrounding ecosystems. This chapter explores the essential tools and how to use them effectively to support safe and sustainable wildcrafting practices.

Why Tools Matter in Foraging

Foraging tools are designed to make the process of gathering plants easier, safer, and more respectful of the environment. The right tools can:

1. Prevent Damage to Plants: Proper tools help you harvest only the parts of the plant you need without harming the rest.
2. Ensure Personal Safety: Sharp tools and protective gear reduce the risk of accidents, especially when foraging in dense or rugged environments.
3. Enhance Efficiency: Tools allow you to gather, clean, and store plants quickly and effectively.
4. Support Sustainability: Tools like pruners and scissors enable precise harvesting, which

helps plants regenerate and protects their populations.

Essential Foraging Tools

When assembling your foraging kit, focus on tools that are versatile, lightweight, and durable. Here are some essential items to include:

1. Sharp Pruners or Scissors

Pruners or scissors are indispensable for cutting herbs, flowers, and stems cleanly. Clean cuts minimize damage to the plant and encourage regrowth.

How to Use Them:

- Use pruners for woody stems and thicker plants, such as rosemary or lavender.
- Use scissors for softer herbs, like mint or parsley.

Maintenance Tips:

- Clean and sanitize blades after each foraging trip to prevent the spread of plant diseases.
- Sharpen blades regularly to maintain efficiency.

2. Digging Tools

Small digging tools, such as trowels or hori-hori knives, are essential for harvesting roots or loosening compacted soil.

How to Use Them:

- Gently dig around the plant to expose the roots without damaging them.
- Avoid pulling plants out of the ground by hand, as this can harm the surrounding soil structure.

Maintenance Tips:

- Rinse tools after use to remove soil and debris.
- Apply a light coat of oil to metal parts to prevent rust.

3. Basket or Foraging Bag

A sturdy basket or foraging bag is necessary for carrying your harvest without crushing delicate plants. Choose breathable materials to prevent moisture buildup, which can lead to mold.

Features to Look For:

- Adjustable straps for hands-free carrying.

- Multiple compartments to separate different plants.

Sustainability Tip:

- Opt for reusable bags made from natural fibers, such as canvas or wicker.

4. Gloves

Protective gloves are essential when handling prickly plants, such as nettles, or when foraging in areas with thorny underbrush.

How to Choose Gloves:

- Lightweight gloves for general foraging.
- Heavy-duty gloves for handling tough or thorny plants.

Safety Note:

- Always inspect gloves for tears or wear before use.

5. Field Guide or Plant Identification App

Accurate plant identification is crucial for safe and ethical foraging. A reliable field guide or plant identification app can help you distinguish edible plants from toxic look-alikes.

Features to Look For:

- Region-specific guides with clear photos and descriptions.
- Apps that use image recognition to identify plants.

Tip:

- Carry a physical guide as a backup in case you lose internet access while foraging.

6. Notebook and Pen

A notebook allows you to record your observations, track plant locations, and document seasonal changes.

How to Use It:

- Note the location, date, and condition of plants you harvest.
- Sketch plants or describe their characteristics to aid future identification.

Bonus Tip:

- Over time, your notebook will become a valuable resource for understanding local plant cycles and ecosystems.

7. Pocket Knife

A pocket knife is a versatile tool for cutting stems, slicing roots, or trimming leaves. Compact and easy to carry, it's a must-have for any forager.

How to Use It Safely:

- Always cut away from your body to avoid injury.
- Keep the blade sharp for clean cuts and efficient use.

Maintenance:

- Clean and oil the blade after use to prevent rust.

8. Water Bottle

Foraging often involves walking long distances or exploring remote areas. Staying hydrated is essential for your safety and comfort.

Sustainability Tip:

- Use a reusable water bottle made from stainless steel or BPA-free plastic.

Bonus Tip:

- Bring extra water to rinse plants in the field before storing them.

9. First Aid Kit

Safety is a priority when foraging, especially in unfamiliar terrain. A small first aid kit can address minor injuries, such as cuts, scrapes, or insect bites.

What to Include:

- Bandages, antiseptic wipes, and tweezers.
- Insect repellent and sunscreen.

Pro Tip:

- Learn basic first aid skills to handle emergencies confidently.

10. Compass or GPS Device

Getting lost in the wild is a risk, even for experienced foragers. A compass or GPS device ensures you can navigate your way back safely.

How to Use It:

- Mark your starting point before venturing out.
- Use GPS to log the coordinates of productive foraging spots.

Backup Plan:

- Carry a paper map as a backup in case your GPS device runs out of battery.

Tools for Sustainable Practices

To ensure your foraging activities are sustainable, consider incorporating these tools into your kit:

1. Seed Packets or Envelopes

Bringing seed packets allows you to scatter seeds in areas where you've harvested plants, supporting their regeneration.

How to Use:

- Collect seeds from mature plants during foraging trips.
- Scatter them in suitable areas to encourage new growth.

2. Eco-Friendly Cleaning Supplies

Use biodegradable soap and a soft brush to clean tools after foraging. Keeping tools clean prevents the spread of plant diseases and reduces environmental impact.

3. Camera or Smartphone

Documenting plants with a camera helps you identify them later and share your findings with others.

Tips for Effective Photos:

- Capture close-ups of leaves, flowers, and stems for detailed identification.
- Take wider shots to show the plant's habitat and surroundings.

Caring for Your Tools

Proper maintenance of your tools ensures their longevity and effectiveness. Follow these tips to care for your foraging gear:

1. Clean After Each Use: Remove dirt, plant sap, and debris from tools and bags.
2. Sharpen Blades: Dull blades can damage plants and increase the risk of injury.
3. Store Properly: Keep tools in a dry, cool place to prevent rust and deterioration.

Organizing Your Foraging Kit

A well-organized foraging kit saves time and ensures you're prepared for every trip. Use a durable backpack or tool roll to store your gear, keeping essential items easily accessible.

Checklist for Your Kit:

- Pruners or scissors.
- Digging tool or hori-hori knife.
- Foraging bag or basket.
- Gloves.
- Field guide or plant identification app.
- Notebook and pen.
- Pocket knife.
- Water bottle.
- First aid kit.
- Compass or GPS device.

Having the right tools for foraging is essential for both your safety and the sustainability of the plants you harvest. Each tool plays a specific role, from accurately identifying plants to minimizing environmental impact. By assembling and maintaining a well-rounded foraging kit, you'll not only enhance your wildcrafting experience but also contribute to the health and vitality of the natural world. Equipped with these tools, you're ready to embark on safe, sustainable, and rewarding foraging adventures.

Preserving and Storing Wild Herbs

Preserving and storing wild herbs is an essential part of sustainable wildcrafting. Proper preservation techniques ensure that the herbs you harvest retain their potency, flavor, and medicinal properties for long-term use. From drying and freezing to crafting herbal preparations, understanding the best methods for storing your harvest can help you make the most of the herbs you collect.

This chapter explores practical and effective ways to preserve wild herbs, focusing on maintaining quality while respecting the time and effort invested in ethical harvesting.

Why Proper Preservation Matters

Wild herbs are at their peak potency and flavor immediately after harvesting. However, without proper preservation, herbs can quickly lose their medicinal properties and freshness. Preserving wild herbs correctly:

1. Retains Potency: Prevents the loss of essential oils, vitamins, and minerals.

2. Extends Shelf Life: Keeps herbs usable for months or even years.
3. Enhances Accessibility: Allows you to store herbs in convenient forms for remedies, teas, and cooking.
4. Reduces Waste: Ensures your hard-earned harvest doesn't spoil.

Preparing Herbs for Preservation

Before preserving wild herbs, proper preparation is essential to ensure they are clean, healthy, and ready for storage.

1. Cleaning Your Harvest

- Shake Off Dirt and Debris: Gently shake herbs to remove soil, insects, or loose debris.
- Rinse When Necessary: For herbs collected in dusty areas, rinse them briefly with cool water. Shake off excess moisture or pat dry with a clean towel.

Tip: Only rinse herbs if necessary, as excess moisture can slow drying and encourage mold growth.

2. Inspecting for Quality

- Choose Healthy Plants: Discard herbs with yellowed, wilted, or damaged leaves.
- Remove Pests: Inspect the plants for insects or eggs and remove them carefully.

Methods of Preserving Wild Herbs

There are several methods to preserve wild herbs, depending on how you plan to use them. Each method has its advantages and best practices.

1. Air Drying

Air drying is one of the simplest and most traditional ways to preserve herbs. It's ideal for hardy herbs like rosemary, thyme, and oregano.

Steps for Air Drying:

1. Bundle the Herbs: Gather small bunches of herbs and tie the stems together with twine or string.
2. Hang Upside Down: Hang the bundles in a warm, dry, and well-ventilated area out of direct sunlight.
3. Check for Dryness: Herbs are fully dried when the leaves crumble easily between your fingers, typically after 1–2 weeks.

Storage Tip: Store dried herbs in airtight glass jars, away from light and moisture.

2. Dehydrating

Using a dehydrator is a faster and more controlled method of drying herbs, particularly for those with high moisture content, like basil or mint.

Steps for Dehydrating:

1. Prepare the Herbs: Spread clean herbs in a single layer on the dehydrator trays.
2. Set the Temperature: Use the lowest heat setting (95–115°F or 35–46°C) to prevent loss of essential oils.
3. Monitor Progress: Check herbs every few hours; most herbs dry within 4–12 hours, depending on their moisture content.

Storage Tip: Store in glass containers with tight-fitting lids and label them with the herb name and drying date.

3. Freezing

Freezing is an excellent method for preserving delicate herbs like cilantro, dill, or chives. It helps retain their flavor, color, and nutrients.

Steps for Freezing:

1. Chop the Herbs: Wash and finely chop the herbs.
2. Portion in Ice Cubes: Place the chopped herbs into ice cube trays and cover with water or olive oil.
3. Freeze: Once frozen, transfer the cubes to freezer-safe bags or containers.

Usage Tip: Drop herb cubes directly into soups, stews, or sauces for added flavor.

4. Making Herbal Oils and Vinegars

Infusing herbs in oil or vinegar is a flavorful way to preserve their properties for culinary or medicinal use.

Steps for Herbal Oils:

1. Choose a Carrier Oil: Use olive oil, coconut oil, or almond oil as a base.
2. Add the Herbs: Fill a clean, dry jar with fresh or dried herbs and cover completely with oil.
3. Infuse: Let the mixture sit in a warm, sunny spot for 2–4 weeks, shaking daily.
4. Strain and Store: Strain the oil and store it in a dark glass bottle.

Steps for Herbal Vinegars:

1. Use Apple Cider Vinegar: Fill a jar with herbs and cover with apple cider vinegar.
2. Steep: Let sit for 2–3 weeks, shaking occasionally.
3. Strain and Store: Store the vinegar in a sterilized bottle.

Storage Tip: Keep infused oils and vinegars in a cool, dark place for 6–12 months.

5. Creating Herbal Powders

Grinding dried herbs into powders makes them easy to use in recipes or remedies.

Steps for Herbal Powders:

1. Dry the Herbs Thoroughly: Ensure herbs are completely dry before grinding.
2. Grind into Powder: Use a coffee grinder, spice grinder, or mortar and pestle to grind the herbs into a fine powder.
3. Store in Airtight Jars: Label jars with the herb name and grinding date.

Usage Tip: Use herbal powders in capsules, teas, or as seasonings.

Storing Preserved Herbs

Proper storage is key to maintaining the quality of preserved herbs. Follow these best practices:

1. Choose the Right Containers:
   » Use glass jars with tight-fitting lids to keep herbs fresh and prevent moisture entry.
   » Avoid plastic containers, which can retain odors and degrade over time.
2. Label Your Herbs:
   » Clearly label each container with the herb name and preservation date to keep track of freshness.
3. Store in a Cool, Dark Place:
   » Keep preserved herbs in a pantry, cabinet, or drawer away from heat and direct sunlight.
4. Check Regularly:
   » Periodically check for signs of spoilage, such as mold or discoloration, and discard affected herbs immediately.

Shelf Life of Preserved Herbs

The shelf life of preserved herbs depends on the method used:

- Dried Herbs: 6 months to 1 year.
- Frozen Herbs: Up to 1 year.
- Herbal Oils: 6–12 months (refrigeration extends shelf life).
- Herbal Vinegars: 6–12 months.
- Herbal Powders: 6 months (store in airtight containers).

Tip: Over time, herbs may lose potency. Crush a small amount between your fingers to test for aroma and flavor before use.

Combining Preservation Techniques

For maximum flexibility, consider combining preservation methods. For example:

- Freeze Fresh Herbs: Use a portion for soups and stews.
- Dry the Rest: Store dried herbs for teas or remedies.
- Create Oils or Vinegars: Infuse some herbs for culinary or medicinal applications.

Practical Example: Preserving and Storing Mint

Mint is a versatile herb used in teas, remedies, and cooking. Here's how to preserve it:

1. Air Drying: Tie mint into small bundles and hang upside down in a dry, shaded area. Once dry, crumble leaves into a jar for tea.
2. Freezing: Chop fresh mint, place in ice cube trays, and fill with water. Use cubes in drinks or sauces.
3. Infusing Vinegar: Add fresh mint leaves to apple cider vinegar, steep for 2 weeks, and use in salad dressings.

Preserving and storing wild herbs is as much an art as it is a science. By choosing the right methods and following best practices, you can ensure that your harvested herbs retain their potency, flavor, and medicinal properties. Whether you're drying, freezing, or creating infused oils, proper preservation allows you to enjoy the benefits of wild herbs long after the foraging season ends. With thoughtful preparation and care, your herb collection will become a valuable resource for remedies, teas, and culinary creations.

BOOK 7

HERBAL TEAS FOR EVERY OCCASION

Herbal teas are a timeless and comforting way to experience the healing power of plants. From energizing blends that keep you focused during busy days to soothing infusions that help you unwind after a long day, herbal teas offer a versatile and enjoyable path to wellness. Whether you're looking to boost your immune system, support digestion, or simply relax with a warm cup, there's a tea for every occasion.

This book guides you through the art of crafting herbal teas tailored to meet your specific needs. You'll discover the unique properties of individual herbs, learn how to blend them for maximum effectiveness, and explore recipes designed to support your energy, immunity, relaxation, and digestive health.

Herbal teas go beyond nourishment—they offer a sensory experience that connects us to the earth. Each cup is an invitation to slow down, savor, and nurture both body and mind. Whether you're a tea enthusiast or new to herbal brewing, this book equips you with the knowledge and recipes to create your own blends, transforming simple herbs into powerful allies for everyday health and balance. Let's dive into the world of herbal teas and unlock their potential for every occasion!

Energizing Blends for Busy Days

In today's fast-paced world, maintaining energy levels can feel like an ongoing challenge. Herbal teas offer a natural, caffeine-free way to invigorate the mind and body without the jitters associated with coffee or synthetic stimulants. By combining carefully selected herbs, you can create energizing blends that enhance focus, boost stamina, and combat fatigue.

Energizing herbal teas often contain adaptogens, which help the body adapt to stress and support sustained energy, as well as herbs that improve circulation and sharpen mental clarity. These blends are perfect for busy mornings, mid-afternoon slumps, or whenever you need a pick-me-up.

This chapter introduces 15 herbal tea recipes to help you power through your day. Each blend is easy to prepare, delicious, and packed with natural vitality. Whether you're facing a packed schedule or need a boost for an active lifestyle, these teas will keep you refreshed and energized.

41. Morning Energy Boost Tea

Ingredients:

- 1 tsp yerba mate
- 1 tsp peppermint leaves
- 1/2 tsp dried lemon peel

Instructions:

1. Steep ingredients in 1 cup of boiling water for 5–7 minutes.
2. Strain and enjoy.

Benefits: Provides gentle stimulation and mental clarity.

Storage Tips: Store dried ingredients in airtight jars for up to 6 months.

42. Adaptogen Energy Tea

Ingredients:

- 1 tsp ashwagandha root
- 1 tsp tulsi (holy basil)
- 1/2 tsp cinnamon

Instructions:

1. Simmer ashwagandha in 1 cup of water for 10 minutes.
2. Add tulsi and cinnamon, steep for 5 minutes, then strain.

Benefits: Reduces fatigue and increases stress resilience.

43. Peppermint and Ginseng Wake-Up Tea

Ingredients:

- 1 tsp peppermint leaves

- 1/2 tsp dried ginseng root
- 1 tsp green tea (optional for mild caffeine)

Instructions:

1. Steep all ingredients in hot water for 5–7 minutes.
2. Strain and drink.

Benefits: Boosts focus and revitalizes energy.

44. Citrus Sunrise Tea

Ingredients:

- 1 tsp dried orange peel
- 1 tsp lemongrass
- 1/2 tsp ginger root

Instructions:

1. Steep ingredients in boiling water for 5 minutes.
2. Strain and enjoy with a touch of honey.

Benefits: Refreshing and uplifting with a citrusy aroma.

45. Stamina Builder Tea

Ingredients:

- 1 tsp eleuthero root (Siberian ginseng)
- 1 tsp nettle leaves
- 1/2 tsp licorice root

Instructions:

1. Simmer eleuthero root in water for 10 minutes.
2. Add nettle and licorice root, steep for 5 minutes, then strain.

Benefits: Supports endurance and combats fatigue.

46. Minty Matcha Power Tea

Ingredients:

- 1 tsp matcha powder
- 1/2 tsp peppermint leaves
- 1 cup hot (not boiling) water

Instructions:

1. Whisk matcha powder into water.
2. Add peppermint and steep for 3–5 minutes. Strain if needed.

Benefits: Enhances alertness with a minty kick.

47. Cinnamon and Ginger Zest Tea

Ingredients:

- 1/2 tsp cinnamon bark
- 1/2 tsp ginger root
- 1/2 tsp cardamom pods

Instructions:

1. Simmer ingredients in water for 10 minutes.
2. Strain and enjoy warm.

Benefits: Warming and energizing, perfect for cold mornings.

48. Lemon Mint Green Tea

Ingredients:

- 1 tsp green tea
- 1/2 tsp dried lemon balm
- 1 tsp fresh lemon juice

Instructions:

1. Steep green tea and lemon balm in hot water for 5 minutes.
2. Add lemon juice before drinking.

Benefits: Combines antioxidants with a refreshing twist.

49. Herbal Energy Chai

Ingredients:

- 1 tsp chai spice blend (cinnamon, cardamom, clove)
- 1/2 tsp ashwagandha root
- 1 tsp rooibos tea

Instructions:

1. Simmer chai blend and ashwagandha in water for 10 minutes.
2. Add rooibos, steep for 5 minutes, and strain.

Benefits: A rich, caffeine-free energy booster.

50. Energizing Rosemary Tea

Ingredients:

- 1 tsp dried rosemary
- 1/2 tsp dried sage
- 1 tsp honey (optional)

Instructions:

1. Steep rosemary and sage in boiling water for 7 minutes.
2. Strain and sweeten with honey if desired.

Benefits: Improves memory and focus.

51. Zesty Hibiscus Tea

Ingredients:

- 1 tsp dried hibiscus flowers
- 1/2 tsp ginger root
- 1 tsp orange peel

Instructions:

1. Steep ingredients in hot water for 5–7 minutes.
2. Strain and enjoy.

Benefits: Refreshing and energizing with a tangy flavor.

52. Morning Matcha Lemonade

Ingredients:

- 1 tsp matcha powder
- 1 tsp fresh lemon juice
- 1 cup cold water

Instructions:

1. Whisk matcha powder in cold water.
2. Add lemon juice and serve over ice.

Benefits: Cool, refreshing energy for hot days.

53. Tulsi and Mint Revitalizer

Ingredients:

- 1 tsp tulsi (holy basil)
- 1 tsp peppermint leaves
- 1/2 tsp dried lemon peel

Instructions:

1. Steep ingredients in boiling water for 5 minutes.
2. Strain and enjoy.

Benefits: Balances energy and soothes the mind.

54. Spicy Energy Tea

Ingredients:

- 1/2 tsp cayenne pepper
- 1 tsp ginger root
- 1 tsp lemon juice

Instructions:

1. Simmer cayenne and ginger in water for 5 minutes.
2. Add lemon juice before drinking.

Benefits: Increases circulation and boosts energy.

55. Revive and Thrive Blend

Ingredients:

- 1 tsp nettle leaves
- 1/2 tsp ginseng root
- 1 tsp fresh orange juice

Instructions:

1. Steep nettle and ginseng in hot water for 7 minutes.
2. Add orange juice before serving.

Benefits: Restores vitality and supports focus.

These energizing tea blends are easy to prepare and packed with natural benefits to fuel your busy days. Let the power of herbs energize you!

Soothing Infusions for Relaxation

In a fast-paced world filled with stressors, soothing herbal infusions offer a gentle and natural way to relax and unwind. The right blend of herbs can calm the mind, ease tension, and promote a sense of tranquility, making them perfect for evenings or moments when you need a break from the chaos of life.

Relaxing herbal teas are often made with nervines—herbs that support the nervous system—and aromatic botanicals known for their calming effects. These blends work synergistically to promote relaxation without sedation, making them suitable for any time of day.

This chapter provides 15 soothing tea recipes designed to help you find peace and balance. Whether you're preparing for a restful night or seeking calm during a busy day, these infusions will guide you toward relaxation with every sip.

56. Lavender and Chamomile Calm Tea

Ingredients:

- 1 tsp dried lavender flowers
- 1 tsp dried chamomile flowers
- 1/2 tsp lemon balm

Instructions:

1. Steep all ingredients in boiling water for 5–7 minutes.
2. Strain and enjoy warm.

Benefits: Relieves stress and promotes gentle relaxation.

Storage Tips: Store dried herbs in airtight jars for up to 6 months.

57. Lemon Balm Serenity Tea

Ingredients:

- 1 tsp dried lemon balm
- 1/2 tsp dried peppermint leaves
- 1 tsp honey (optional)

Instructions:

1. Steep lemon balm and peppermint in hot water for 5 minutes.
2. Strain and sweeten with honey if desired.

Benefits: Eases tension and soothes the mind.

58. Valerian and Mint Sleep Aid Tea

Ingredients:

- 1/2 tsp valerian root
- 1 tsp dried peppermint
- 1/2 tsp dried passionflower

Instructions:

1. Simmer valerian root in water for 10 minutes.
2. Add peppermint and passionflower, steep for 5 minutes, and strain.

Benefits: Promotes restful sleep and calms the nervous system.

59. Hibiscus and Rose Petal Relaxation Tea

Ingredients:

- 1 tsp dried hibiscus flowers
- 1 tsp dried rose petals
- 1/2 tsp orange peel

Instructions:

1. Steep all ingredients in boiling water for 7 minutes.
2. Strain and serve warm or chilled.

Benefits: Uplifting yet calming, perfect for quiet moments.

60. Cinnamon and Vanilla Comfort Tea

Ingredients:

- 1/2 tsp cinnamon bark
- 1/2 tsp vanilla bean or extract
- 1 tsp dried chamomile

Instructions:

1. Simmer cinnamon and vanilla in water for 10 minutes.
2. Add chamomile, steep for 5 minutes, and strain.

Benefits: Soothes the senses and warms the spirit.

61. Holy Basil Stress Relief Tea

Ingredients:

- 1 tsp tulsi (holy basil)
- 1/2 tsp dried lemongrass
- 1 tsp fresh lemon juice

Instructions:

1. Steep tulsi and lemongrass in hot water for 5 minutes.
2. Add lemon juice before drinking.

Benefits: Reduces stress and restores balance.

62. Vanilla Rooibos Evening Tea

Ingredients:

- 1 tsp rooibos tea
- 1/2 tsp dried lavender
- 1/4 tsp vanilla extract

Instructions:

1. Steep rooibos and lavender in hot water for 5–7 minutes.
2. Add vanilla extract before serving.

Benefits: Naturally caffeine-free, perfect for evening relaxation.

63. Mint and Ginger Comfort Blend

Ingredients:

- 1 tsp fresh ginger slices
- 1 tsp dried peppermint leaves
- 1 tsp honey (optional)

Instructions:

1. Simmer ginger in water for 10 minutes.
2. Add peppermint, steep for 5 minutes, and strain.

Benefits: Soothes the stomach and calms the mind.

64. Relaxing Chamomile and Fennel Tea

Ingredients:

- 1 tsp dried chamomile flowers

- 1/2 tsp fennel seeds
- 1 tsp honey (optional)

Instructions:

1. Steep chamomile and fennel in hot water for 5 minutes.
2. Sweeten with honey if desired.

Benefits: Reduces bloating and encourages relaxation.

65. Rosemary and Lemon Tea

Ingredients:

- 1 tsp dried rosemary
- 1 tsp fresh lemon juice
- 1 tsp honey (optional)

Instructions:

1. Steep rosemary in boiling water for 7 minutes.
2. Add lemon juice and honey before serving.

Benefits: Sharpens the mind while gently relaxing the body.

66. Sage and Orange Zest Tea

Ingredients:

- 1 tsp dried sage leaves
- 1/2 tsp dried orange peel
- 1 tsp fresh orange juice

Instructions:

1. Steep sage and orange peel in hot water for 5 minutes.
2. Add orange juice before drinking.

Benefits: Grounds the mind and soothes nerves.

67. Cardamom and Rose Tranquility Tea

Ingredients:

- 1/2 tsp cardamom pods
- 1 tsp dried rose petals
- 1/2 tsp honey (optional)

Instructions:

1. Simmer cardamom in water for 10 minutes.
2. Add rose petals, steep for 5 minutes, and strain.

Benefits: Aromatic and calming, perfect for winding down.

68. Blueberry and Mint Relaxation Tea

Ingredients:

- 1 tsp dried blueberry leaves
- 1/2 tsp dried mint
- 1 tsp honey (optional)

Instructions:

1. Steep blueberry leaves and mint in hot water for 7 minutes.
2. Sweeten with honey if desired.

Benefits: Refreshing and calming, with a hint of sweetness.

69. Chamomile and Lavender Night Tea

Ingredients:

- 1 tsp dried chamomile flowers
- 1 tsp dried lavender flowers
- 1 tsp honey (optional)

Instructions:

1. Steep chamomile and lavender in boiling water for 7 minutes.
2. Strain and sweeten with honey if desired.

Benefits: Encourages restful sleep and calms the senses.

70. Lemon Verbena Relaxation Tea

Ingredients:

- 1 tsp dried lemon verbena
- 1/2 tsp dried lemon balm
- 1 tsp fresh lemon juice

Instructions:

1. Steep lemon verbena and lemon balm in hot water for 5–7 minutes.
2. Add lemon juice before drinking.

Benefits: Light, fragrant, and deeply calming.

These soothing tea blends are crafted to help you find moments of calm and relaxation throughout your day. With natural ingredients and simple recipes, they provide an easy path to tranquility, one cup at a time.

Immune-Boosting Teas for Cold Seasons

As the colder months approach, our immune systems often need extra support to fend off colds, flu, and seasonal ailments. Herbal teas offer a natural and delicious way to strengthen immunity, soothe symptoms, and promote overall health. Packed with antioxidants, vitamins, and immune-enhancing compounds, these teas can be your first line of defense against seasonal illnesses.

This chapter provides 15 immune-boosting tea recipes featuring herbs like echinacea, ginger, elderberry, and cinnamon, known for their ability to fortify the immune system. Whether you're looking to prevent sickness or speed up recovery, these teas offer warmth, comfort, and healing with every cup.

71. Echinacea and Lemon Immune Tea

Ingredients:

- 1 tsp dried echinacea leaves
- 1 tsp dried lemon balm
- 1 tsp fresh lemon juice

Instructions:

1. Steep echinacea and lemon balm in boiling water for 7 minutes.
2. Add lemon juice before serving.

Benefits: Strengthens the immune system and fights off early signs of illness.

Storage Tips: Store dried herbs in airtight jars for up to 6 months.

72. Ginger and Honey Immunity Tea

Ingredients:

- 1 tsp fresh ginger slices
- 1 tsp honey
- 1/2 tsp turmeric powder

Instructions:

1. Simmer ginger and turmeric in water for 10 minutes.
2. Strain and stir in honey before drinking.

Benefits: Anti-inflammatory and antibacterial properties support recovery and boost immunity.

73. Elderberry and Clove Winter Tea

Ingredients:

- 1 tsp dried elderberries
- 1/2 tsp cloves
- 1/2 tsp cinnamon

Instructions:

1. Simmer elderberries, cloves, and cinnamon in water for 10 minutes.

2. Strain and enjoy warm.

Benefits: Packed with antioxidants to fight colds and flu.

74. Lemon Ginger Turmeric Tea

Ingredients:

- 1 tsp fresh ginger slices
- 1/2 tsp turmeric powder
- 1 tsp fresh lemon juice

Instructions:

1. Simmer ginger and turmeric in water for 10 minutes.
2. Add lemon juice before serving.

Benefits: Boosts immunity and reduces inflammation.

75. Peppermint and Echinacea Tea

Ingredients:

- 1 tsp dried peppermint leaves
- 1 tsp dried echinacea flowers
- 1 tsp honey (optional)

Instructions:

1. Steep peppermint and echinacea in boiling water for 5–7 minutes.
2. Sweeten with honey if desired.

Benefits: Relieves congestion and strengthens immunity.

76. Cinnamon and Orange Peel Tea

Ingredients:

- 1 tsp cinnamon bark
- 1 tsp dried orange peel
- 1 tsp honey

Instructions:

1. Simmer cinnamon and orange peel in water for 10 minutes.
2. Strain and sweeten with honey.

Benefits: Rich in vitamin C and warming for cold days.

77. Spiced Apple Immune Tea

Ingredients:

- 1 cup fresh apple slices
- 1 tsp cinnamon bark
- 1/2 tsp ginger root

Instructions:

1. Simmer apple slices, cinnamon, and ginger in water for 10 minutes.
2. Strain and serve warm.

Benefits: Combines warmth and immune-boosting nutrients in a comforting tea.

78. Holy Basil (Tulsi) Immunity Tea

Ingredients:

- 1 tsp tulsi leaves
- 1/2 tsp dried ginger powder
- 1 tsp fresh lemon juice

Instructions:

1. Steep tulsi and ginger in hot water for 7 minutes.
2. Add lemon juice before drinking.

Benefits: Fights infections and promotes overall health.

79. Rosehip and Hibiscus Tea

Ingredients:

- 1 tsp dried rosehips
- 1 tsp dried hibiscus flowers
- 1/2 tsp honey

Instructions:

1. Steep rosehips and hibiscus in hot water for 5–7 minutes.
2. Sweeten with honey if desired.

Benefits: High in vitamin C, supports immunity and skin health.

80. Licorice Root and Ginger Tea

Ingredients:

- 1 tsp dried licorice root
- 1 tsp fresh ginger slices
- 1 tsp honey

Instructions:

1. Simmer licorice root and ginger in water for 10 minutes.
2. Strain and sweeten with honey before drinking.

Benefits: Soothes sore throats and boosts immune function.

81. Elderflower and Chamomile Tea

Ingredients:

- 1 tsp dried elderflowers
- 1 tsp dried chamomile flowers
- 1 tsp honey (optional)

Instructions:

1. Steep elderflowers and chamomile in boiling water for 7 minutes.
2. Sweeten with honey if desired.

Benefits: Combines calming and immune-strengthening effects.

82. Thyme and Honey Cold Tea

Ingredients:

- 1 tsp dried thyme leaves
- 1 tsp honey
- 1 tsp fresh lemon juice

Instructions:

1. Steep thyme in boiling water for 5–7 minutes.
2. Add honey and lemon juice before serving.

Benefits: Antimicrobial properties help fight colds and sore throats.

83. Turmeric and Cardamom Immune Tea

Ingredients:

- 1/2 tsp turmeric powder
- 1/2 tsp crushed cardamom pods
- 1 tsp honey

Instructions:

1. Simmer turmeric and cardamom in water for 10 minutes.
2. Strain and sweeten with honey.

Benefits: Anti-inflammatory and immunity-boosting properties.

84. Nettle and Mint Vitality Tea

Ingredients:

- 1 tsp dried nettle leaves
- 1 tsp dried peppermint leaves
- 1 tsp honey (optional)

Instructions:

1. Steep nettle and peppermint in boiling water for 7 minutes.
2. Sweeten with honey if desired.

Benefits: Supports vitality and strengthens the immune system.

85. Ginger, Clove, and Honey Cold Tea

Ingredients:

- 1 tsp fresh ginger slices
- 1/2 tsp cloves
- 1 tsp honey

Instructions:

1. Simmer ginger and cloves in water for 10 minutes.
2. Strain and stir in honey before drinking.

Benefits: Warming, soothing, and packed with antibacterial properties.

These immune-boosting teas are simple to prepare and provide natural support for your health during cold seasons. With each sip, you'll fortify your body and enjoy the warmth and comfort of herbal wellness.

Digestive Support Blends for Daily Wellness

Digestive health is essential for overall wellness, as a healthy gut helps your body absorb nutrients, supports immunity, and contributes to mental clarity. Herbal teas can play a significant role in maintaining digestive balance, soothing discomfort, and addressing common issues like bloating, indigestion, or nausea. The right combination of herbs offers gentle yet effective support for your digestive system.

This chapter features 15 carefully curated digestive support tea blends that promote daily gut health. From calming teas for post-meal relaxation to potent blends that tackle occasional discomfort, these recipes are easy to prepare and incorporate into your routine.

86. Peppermint Digestive Ease Tea

Ingredients:

- 1 tsp dried peppermint leaves
- 1/2 tsp fennel seeds
- 1 tsp honey (optional)

Instructions:

1. Steep peppermint and fennel in boiling water for 5–7 minutes.

2. Strain and sweeten with honey if desired.

Benefits: Relieves bloating and soothes indigestion.

Storage Tips: Store dried herbs in airtight containers for up to 6 months.

87. Ginger and Lemon Gut Support Tea

Ingredients:

- 1 tsp fresh ginger slices
- 1 tsp fresh lemon juice
- 1 tsp honey

Instructions:

1. Simmer ginger in water for 10 minutes.
2. Add lemon juice and honey before serving.

Benefits: Eases nausea and supports digestion.

88. Chamomile and Fennel Relaxation Tea

Ingredients:

- 1 tsp dried chamomile flowers
- 1/2 tsp fennel seeds
- 1 tsp honey (optional)

Instructions:

1. Steep chamomile and fennel in boiling water for 5 minutes.
2. Strain and sweeten with honey.

Benefits: Reduces stomach cramps and promotes relaxation.

89. Digestive Calm Cardamom Tea

Ingredients:

- 1/2 tsp crushed cardamom pods
- 1/2 tsp cinnamon bark
- 1 tsp fresh orange zest

Instructions:

1. Simmer cardamom and cinnamon in water for 10 minutes.
2. Add orange zest before straining and serving.

Benefits: Soothes the stomach and enhances digestion.

90. Lemon Balm and Peppermint Soothing Tea

Ingredients:

- 1 tsp dried lemon balm leaves

- 1 tsp dried peppermint leaves

Instructions:

1. Steep both ingredients in boiling water for 7 minutes.
2. Strain and enjoy warm.

Benefits: Calms the digestive tract and relieves gas.

91. Turmeric and Ginger Digestive Tonic

Ingredients:

- 1/2 tsp turmeric powder
- 1 tsp fresh ginger slices
- 1 tsp honey

Instructions:

1. Simmer turmeric and ginger in water for 10 minutes.
2. Strain and sweeten with honey.

Benefits: Reduces inflammation and improves gut health.

92. Licorice Root and Mint Comfort Tea

Ingredients:

- 1 tsp dried licorice root
- 1 tsp dried peppermint leaves

Instructions:

1. Simmer licorice root in water for 10 minutes.
2. Add peppermint, steep for 5 minutes, and strain.

Benefits: Eases acid reflux and soothes the stomach.

93. Rosemary and Fennel Tea

Ingredients:

- 1 tsp dried rosemary
- 1/2 tsp fennel seeds

Instructions:

1. Steep rosemary and fennel in boiling water for 5–7 minutes.
2. Strain and enjoy.

Benefits: Improves digestion and reduces bloating.

94. Cinnamon and Ginger Warming Tea

Ingredients:

- 1/2 tsp cinnamon bark
- 1 tsp fresh ginger slices

Instructions:

1. Simmer cinnamon and ginger in water for 10 minutes.
2. Strain and serve warm.

Benefits: Stimulates digestion and improves circulation.

95. Cumin and Coriander Digestive Tea

Ingredients:

- 1/2 tsp cumin seeds
- 1/2 tsp coriander seeds

Instructions:

1. Toast seeds lightly in a pan to release their aroma.
2. Simmer in water for 10 minutes, then strain.

Benefits: Supports digestion and relieves gas.

96. Holy Basil Gut Health Tea

Ingredients:

- 1 tsp tulsi (holy basil) leaves
- 1 tsp fresh lemon juice

Instructions:

1. Steep tulsi in hot water for 7 minutes.
2. Add lemon juice before drinking.

Benefits: Reduces stress and supports gut health.

97. Apple Cider Vinegar Digestive Boost Tea

Ingredients:

- 1 tsp apple cider vinegar
- 1 tsp honey
- 1 cup warm water

Instructions:

1. Mix all ingredients together and serve warm.

Benefits: Balances gut pH and promotes healthy digestion.

98. Nettle and Mint Detox Tea

Ingredients:

- 1 tsp dried nettle leaves
- 1 tsp dried peppermint leaves

Instructions:

1. Steep both ingredients in boiling water for 7 minutes.
2. Strain and enjoy.

Benefits: Cleanses the gut and promotes detoxification.

99. Chamomile and Ginger Digestive Harmony Tea

Ingredients:

- 1 tsp dried chamomile flowers
- 1 tsp fresh ginger slices

Instructions:

1. Steep chamomile and ginger in boiling water for 5 minutes.
2. Strain and enjoy.

Benefits: Soothes the stomach and calms nausea.

100. Digestive Reset Lemongrass Tea

Ingredients:

- 1 tsp dried lemongrass
- 1 tsp fresh lime juice

Instructions:

1. Steep lemongrass in boiling water for 5–7 minutes.
2. Add lime juice before serving.

Benefits: Refreshing and supportive for the digestive system.

These digestive-supporting tea blends are designed to help you maintain gut health and tackle common discomforts naturally. With these recipes, you can enjoy better digestion and daily wellness in every cup!

BOOK 8

CRAFTING HERBAL OILS AND INFUSIONS

Herbal oils and infusions are versatile creations that bring the healing properties of plants into your daily life. Whether used for skincare, massage, or relaxation, these oils offer a natural way to nourish the body, soothe aches, and promote overall wellness. By infusing herbs into carrier oils, you can unlock their therapeutic potential and create personalized products tailored to your needs.

This book introduces you to the art of crafting herbal oils and infusions, combining traditional knowledge with practical techniques. You'll learn how to choose the right herbs and carrier oils, prepare infusions safely, and create remedies for skincare, pain relief, and relaxation. Whether you're a beginner or an experienced herbalist, these recipes and methods will guide you in making high-quality, effective products at home.

From calming massage oils to soothing blends for sore muscles, the possibilities are endless when working with herbal infusions. Crafting these oils is more than just a skill—it's a creative and rewarding way to connect with the healing power of plants. Let's explore the world of herbal oils and discover how they can enrich your health and wellness routines.

Making Infused Oils for Skin and Massage

Herbal infused oils are one of the most versatile and accessible products you can create. They harness the healing properties of herbs while providing a nourishing, hydrating base for skincare and massage. Infused oils are excellent for soothing dry skin, calming inflammation, relieving muscle tension, and even promoting relaxation through aromatherapy.

Crafting infused oils allows you to tailor them to specific needs. Whether you're looking to support healthy skin or create a massage oil that eases soreness, the process is simple and rewarding. By combining dried herbs with carrier oils, you can extract beneficial compounds and preserve them for long-term use.

The following recipes guide you through creating infused oils for various skin and massage needs. These blends are made with accessible ingredients, practical techniques, and a focus on safety. Each remedy includes instructions, benefits, and storage tips to help you make the most of your creations.

101. Lavender-Calendula Infused Oil

Ingredients:

- 1 cup sweet almond oil
- 2 tbsp dried lavender flowers
- 2 tbsp dried calendula petals

Instructions:

1. Combine the herbs and oil in a clean jar.
2. Use the solar method (4–6 weeks) or heat method (2 hours).
3. Strain and store in a dark glass bottle.

Uses: Soothes irritated skin and promotes relaxation.

Storage Tips: Store in a cool, dry place for up to 12 months. Add a few drops of vitamin E oil to extend shelf life.

102. Arnica Muscle Recovery Oil

Ingredients:

- 1 cup grapeseed oil
- 1/4 cup dried arnica flowers

Instructions:

1. Heat arnica and oil on low for 2 hours.
2. Strain and store in a sterilized container.

Uses: Relieves muscle soreness and inflammation.

Storage Tips: Keep in a dark bottle and store in a cool location for 6–8 months.

103. Rose Petal Hydration Oil

Ingredients:

- 1 cup olive oil
- 1/4 cup dried rose petals

Instructions:

1. Infuse rose petals in olive oil using the solar method.
2. Strain and transfer to a glass container.

Uses: Softens and hydrates the skin.

Storage Tips: Store in a dark, airtight container away from sunlight. Use within 12 months.

104. Chamomile Baby Oil

Ingredients:

- 1 cup coconut oil
- 2 tbsp dried chamomile flowers

Instructions:

1. Combine chamomile and coconut oil in a jar.
2. Heat gently for 2 hours or infuse for 4 weeks.
3. Strain and store.

Uses: Gentle on baby's skin, perfect for bedtime massages.

Storage Tips: Refrigerate for up to 12 months to keep the coconut oil solid and fresh.

105. Peppermint Cooling Oil

Ingredients:

- 1 cup grapeseed oil
- 1/4 cup dried peppermint leaves

Instructions:

1. Heat peppermint and oil for 2 hours over low heat.
2. Strain and store in a sterilized bottle.

Uses: Cools and soothes the skin, great for summer massages.

Storage Tips: Keep in a cool, dark location and use within 6–9 months.

106. Calendula Healing Oil

Ingredients:

- 1 cup olive oil
- 1/4 cup dried calendula petals

Instructions:

1. Infuse calendula in olive oil using the solar method for 4 weeks.
2. Strain and store in a cool place.

Uses: Ideal for minor cuts, scrapes, and dry skin.

Storage Tips: Store in a dark glass container for up to 12 months.

107. Rosemary Invigorating Oil

Ingredients:

- 1 cup jojoba oil
- 2 tbsp dried rosemary leaves

Instructions:

1. Heat rosemary and jojoba oil on low for 2 hours.
2. Strain and transfer to a clean bottle.

Uses: Stimulates circulation and revitalizes tired muscles.

Storage Tips: Store in a cool, dark area and use within 9–12 months.

108. Lemon Balm Calming Oil

Ingredients:

- 1 cup sweet almond oil
- 1/4 cup dried lemon balm leaves

Instructions:

1. Infuse lemon balm in almond oil using the solar method.
2. Strain and store in a dark glass container.

Uses: Calms the skin and promotes relaxation.

Storage Tips: Keep in a cool, dry place and use within 6–9 months.

109. Eucalyptus Decongesting Oil

Ingredients:

- 1 cup grapeseed oil
- 1/4 cup dried eucalyptus leaves

Instructions:

1. Heat eucalyptus and oil for 2 hours.
2. Strain and store.

Uses: Relieves congestion when massaged on the chest.

Storage Tips: Store in a sealed container away from light and heat for up to 6 months.

110. Turmeric Anti-Inflammatory Oil

Ingredients:

- 1 cup coconut oil
- 2 tbsp dried turmeric root

Instructions:

1. Simmer turmeric in coconut oil for 2 hours.
2. Strain and store in a jar.

Uses: Reduces inflammation and soothes aching joints.

Storage Tips: Keep in a cool, dry place for up to 9 months.

111. Lavender and Rose Relaxation Oil

Ingredients:

- 1 cup olive oil
- 1 tbsp dried lavender flowers
- 1 tbsp dried rose petals

Instructions:

1. Combine the herbs and oil in a jar.
2. Infuse for 4 weeks or use the heat method.
3. Strain and store.

Uses: Perfect for a calming massage or bedtime routine.

Storage Tips: Store in an airtight container in a dark, cool place for up to 12 months.

112. Ginger Warming Massage Oil

Ingredients:

- 1 cup sesame oil
- 2 tbsp dried ginger root

Instructions:

1. Heat ginger and sesame oil gently for 2 hours.
2. Strain and store.

Uses: Eases muscle tension and promotes circulation.

Storage Tips: Keep in a dark, dry spot for up to 6 months.

113. Sage and Thyme Joint Relief Oil

Ingredients:

- 1 cup olive oil

- 1 tbsp dried sage leaves
- 1 tbsp dried thyme leaves

Instructions:

1. Combine sage, thyme, and olive oil in a clean jar.
2. Use the heat infusion method for 2 hours or the solar method for 4–6 weeks.
3. Strain and store in a sterilized bottle.

Uses: Eases joint pain and inflammation, perfect for massage.

Storage Tips: Store in a cool, dark place for up to 9 months.

114. Calendula and Lavender After-Sun Oil

Ingredients:

- 1 cup sweet almond oil
- 2 tbsp dried calendula petals
- 1 tbsp dried lavender flowers

Instructions:

1. Combine all ingredients in a jar.
2. Infuse using the solar method for 4 weeks.
3. Strain and transfer to a dark glass bottle.

Uses: Soothes sunburned or irritated skin and promotes healing.

Storage Tips: Keep in a cool, dark location and use within 12 months.

115. Basil and Mint Energizing Oil

Ingredients:

- 1 cup grapeseed oil
- 2 tbsp dried basil leaves
- 2 tbsp dried mint leaves

Instructions:

1. Heat the basil and mint in grapeseed oil on low heat for 2 hours.
2. Strain and store in a clean, dark container.

Uses: Refreshes the skin and invigorates tired muscles, great for morning massages.

Storage Tips: Store in a dark glass bottle in a cool, dry place for up to 6 months.

Creating Essential Oils at Home

Essential oils are concentrated extracts that capture the aromatic and therapeutic properties of plants. Unlike infused oils, which are made by steeping herbs in carrier oils, essential oils are extracted through processes such as steam distillation. These oils are incredibly potent, making them valuable for aromatherapy, skincare, and holistic wellness practices.

While creating essential oils at home may seem complex, it's entirely possible with the right tools and techniques. This chapter provides an introduction to crafting essential oils using simple methods and equipment. You'll also find recipes tailored to various needs, whether you're looking to relax, energize, or heal. Each recipe emphasizes safety and offers tips to maximize yield and quality.

By distilling your own essential oils, you not only gain a deeper connection to the plants but also the satisfaction of crafting products that are pure, personalized, and chemical-free. Let's explore the art of making essential oils at home.

Tools and Equipment for Essential Oil Extraction

To create essential oils, you'll need:

1. Distillation Equipment: A still or home distillation kit is essential for steam distillation, the most common method.
2. Fresh Herbs or Flowers: Freshly harvested plants yield the most oil.
3. Water: Used to create steam for the distillation process.
4. Glass Storage Bottles: Dark glass bottles are best for storing oils to protect them from light.

Method: Steam Distillation

Steam distillation is the preferred method for extracting essential oils at home. Here's a simplified process:

1. Prepare the Plant Material: Chop fresh herbs or flowers to increase surface area.
2. Set Up the Still: Fill the still with water and place the plant material in the designated chamber.
3. Heat the Water: Boil the water to produce steam, which passes through the plant material and captures the oil.
4. Condense the Steam: The steam travels through a condenser, where it cools and turns back into liquid.

5. Separate the Oil: The essential oil floats on top of the water and can be carefully separated.

Safety Notes

- Always use clean, sterilized equipment to prevent contamination.
- Test essential oils for skin sensitivity before applying.
- Keep essential oils out of reach of children and pets due to their potency.

116. Lavender Essential Oil

Ingredients:

- 2 cups fresh lavender flowers
- Water (as required for the still)

Instructions:

1. Add lavender to the distillation chamber and follow the steam distillation process.
2. Separate the oil and store in a dark glass bottle.

Uses: Calms the mind, reduces stress, and soothes irritated skin.

Storage Tips: Store in a cool, dark place for up to 12 months. Ensure the bottle is tightly sealed to preserve the aroma and potency.

117. Peppermint Essential Oil

Ingredients:

- 2 cups fresh peppermint leaves
- Water

Instructions:

1. Use steam distillation to extract oil from peppermint leaves.
2. Store in a sterilized, dark glass bottle.

Uses: Energizes, relieves headaches, and soothes digestive discomfort.

Storage Tips: Keep in a dry, cool area for up to 12 months. Avoid direct sunlight to prevent deterioration.

118. Rosemary Essential Oil

Ingredients:

- 2 cups fresh rosemary sprigs
- Water

Instructions:

1. Chop rosemary and place it in the still.

2. Extract the oil and store in a sterilized glass bottle.

Uses: Improves focus, boosts circulation, and strengthens hair.

Storage Tips: Store in a tightly sealed dark container away from heat and moisture for up to 1 year.

119. Lemon Essential Oil

Ingredients:

- Zest of 6 fresh lemons
- Water

Instructions:

1. Peel lemons, avoiding the pith, and place the zest in the still.
2. Extract oil and store.

Uses: Uplifts mood, cleanses, and purifies the air.

Storage Tips: Refrigerate for maximum freshness, or keep in a dark, cool cabinet for up to 9 months.

120. Eucalyptus Essential Oil

Ingredients:

- 2 cups fresh eucalyptus leaves
- Water

Instructions:

1. Use steam distillation to extract oil from eucalyptus leaves.
2. Store in a dark glass bottle.

Uses: Relieves congestion and supports respiratory health.

Storage Tips: Keep in a cool, dry place for up to 12 months. Ensure the lid is secure to maintain potency.

121. Orange Essential Oil

Ingredients:

- Zest of 6 fresh oranges
- Water

Instructions:

1. Place orange zest in the still and follow the distillation process.
2. Store oil in a sterilized bottle.

Uses: Uplifts mood and refreshes the mind.

Storage Tips: Store in the refrigerator or a dark, cool cabinet for up to 6–9 months.

122. Basil Essential Oil

Ingredients:

- 2 cups fresh basil leaves
- Water

Instructions:

1. Chop basil and place it in the still.
2. Extract oil and store properly.

Uses: Relieves fatigue and enhances focus.

Storage Tips: Keep in a dark glass container away from heat for up to 12 months.

123. Geranium Essential Oil

Ingredients:

- 2 cups fresh geranium flowers
- Water

Instructions:

1. Distill geranium flowers to extract oil.
2. Store in a dark bottle.

Uses: Balances hormones and nourishes the skin.

Storage Tips: Store in a cool, dry place for up to 12 months.

124. Clove Essential Oil

Ingredients:

- 2 cups fresh or dried cloves
- Water

Instructions:

1. Place cloves in the distillation chamber and extract oil.
2. Store in a sterilized container.

Uses: Relieves pain and acts as an antiseptic.

Storage Tips: Keep in a cool, dark location for up to 12 months.

125. Lemongrass Essential Oil

Ingredients:

- 2 cups fresh lemongrass stalks
- Water

Instructions:

1. Chop lemongrass and extract oil using steam distillation.
2. Store properly.

Uses: Repels insects and improves mood.

Storage Tips: Store in an airtight, dark glass bottle for up to 9 months.

126. Chamomile Essential Oil

Ingredients:

- 2 cups fresh chamomile flowers
- Water

Instructions:

1. Place chamomile flowers in the still and follow the steam distillation process.
2. Collect the essential oil and store in a dark glass bottle.

Uses: Promotes relaxation, reduces inflammation, and soothes sensitive skin.

Storage Tips: Keep in a cool, dark place for up to 12 months. Ensure the bottle is tightly sealed to maintain freshness.

127. Sage Essential Oil

Ingredients:

- 2 cups fresh sage leaves
- Water

Instructions:

1. Chop sage leaves and place them in the distillation chamber.
2. Extract the oil and store it in a sterilized container.

Uses: Helps improve focus, reduces stress, and supports respiratory health.

Storage Tips: Store in a dark, airtight container in a cool, dry place for up to 9–12 months.

128. Ginger Essential Oil

Ingredients:

- 1 cup fresh ginger root (sliced)
- Water

Instructions:

1. Slice the ginger root and place it in the still.
2. Use steam distillation to extract the oil.
3. Store the oil in a clean glass bottle.

Uses: Relieves nausea, soothes aching muscles, and stimulates circulation.

Storage Tips: Store in a tightly sealed container in a dark cabinet for up to 12 months.

129. Thyme Essential Oil

Ingredients:

- 2 cups fresh thyme sprigs
- Water

Instructions:

1. Place the thyme sprigs in the still and extract oil using steam distillation.
2. Separate the oil and store in a sterilized glass bottle.

Uses: Supports immunity, purifies the air, and helps alleviate respiratory issues.

Storage Tips: Store in a cool, dry area in a dark glass bottle for up to 12 months.

130. Ylang Ylang Essential Oil

Ingredients:

- 2 cups fresh ylang ylang flowers
- Water

Instructions:

1. Add ylang ylang flowers to the distillation chamber and perform steam distillation.
2. Collect the oil and store it in a dark glass bottle.

Uses: Uplifts mood, promotes relaxation, and enhances skin health.

Storage Tips: Keep in a cool, dark location for up to 9–12 months. Avoid exposure to heat and sunlight.

Using Carrier Oils to Enhance Benefits

Carrier oils are the unsung heroes of herbal and aromatherapy applications. Unlike essential oils, which are concentrated and volatile, carrier oils are fatty oils derived from seeds, nuts, or kernels. They are used to dilute essential oils, ensuring safe application while delivering their own nourishing benefits. Each carrier oil brings unique properties, such as hydration, anti-inflammatory effects, or antioxidant support, making them essential for crafting personalized remedies.

This chapter explores the various carrier oils available, their benefits, and how to pair them with essential oils to create effective blends. From lightweight oils like grapeseed to rich, hydrating options like coconut oil, you'll learn how to select the right carrier oil for your skin type or therapeutic goals.

The following 15 remedies combine carrier oils with essential oils to target specific needs, from soothing dry skin to relieving muscle tension. Each recipe is designed to maximize the benefits of both the carrier and essential oils while offering practical storage tips for maintaining freshness.

131. Sweet Almond Oil for Dry Skin

Ingredients:

- 2 tbsp sweet almond oil
- 2 drops lavender essential oil

Instructions:

1. Mix almond oil and lavender essential oil in a small bottle.
2. Massage into dry areas of the skin.

Uses: Hydrates and soothes flaky, dry skin.

Storage Tips: Store in a cool, dark place for up to 12 months.

132. Coconut Oil for Cracked Heels

Ingredients:

- 2 tbsp coconut oil (solid or melted)
- 2 drops tea tree essential oil

Instructions:

1. Combine coconut oil and tea tree oil.
2. Massage into cracked heels before bedtime.

Uses: Deeply moisturizes and protects against infections.

Storage Tips: Keep in a cool, dry area for up to 18 months.

133. Jojoba Oil for Oily Skin

Ingredients:

- 1 tbsp jojoba oil
- 2 drops geranium essential oil

Instructions:

1. Blend jojoba oil and geranium essential oil in a dropper bottle.
2. Apply sparingly to oily areas of the face.

Uses: Balances oil production and improves skin texture.

Storage Tips: Store in a dark glass bottle for up to 12 months.

134. Grapeseed Oil for Hair Growth

Ingredients:

- 2 tbsp grapeseed oil
- 3 drops rosemary essential oil

Instructions:

1. Combine grapeseed oil and rosemary oil.
2. Massage into the scalp and leave for 30 minutes before washing.

Uses: Strengthens hair follicles and promotes growth.

Storage Tips: Keep in a cool, dry place for up to 6 months.

135. Olive Oil for Cuticle Care

Ingredients:

- 1 tbsp olive oil
- 1 drop lemon essential oil

Instructions:

1. Mix olive oil and lemon essential oil.
2. Massage into cuticles daily.

Uses: Softens cuticles and promotes nail health.

Storage Tips: Store in a dark container for up to 12 months.

136. Argan Oil for Anti-Aging

Ingredients:

- 1 tbsp argan oil
- 2 drops frankincense essential oil

Instructions:

1. Combine argan oil and frankincense oil.
2. Apply to the face and neck before bedtime.

Uses: Reduces fine lines and promotes skin elasticity.

Storage Tips: Keep in a cool, dark place for up to 12 months.

137. Avocado Oil for Dry Scalp

Ingredients:

- 2 tbsp avocado oil
- 2 drops peppermint essential oil

Instructions:

1. Blend avocado oil and peppermint oil.
2. Massage into the scalp and rinse after 20 minutes.

Uses: Moisturizes and soothes a dry, itchy scalp.

Storage Tips: Store in a dark glass bottle for up to 8 months.

138. Sesame Oil for Joint Pain Relief

Ingredients:

- 2 tbsp sesame oil
- 2 drops ginger essential oil

Instructions:

1. Combine sesame oil and ginger oil.
2. Massage into joints and sore areas.

Uses: Reduces inflammation and relieves joint pain.

Storage Tips: Keep in a dark, cool place for up to 12 months.

139. Hemp Seed Oil for Sensitive Skin

Ingredients:

- 1 tbsp hemp seed oil
- 2 drops chamomile essential oil

Instructions:

1. Mix hemp seed oil and chamomile essential oil.
2. Gently apply to sensitive or irritated skin.

Uses: Calms redness and hydrates sensitive skin.

Storage Tips: Refrigerate after opening and use within 6 months.

140. Castor Oil for Eyebrow Growth

Ingredients:

- 1 tbsp castor oil
- 1 drop rosemary essential oil

Instructions:

1. Combine castor oil and rosemary oil.
2. Apply to eyebrows nightly using a clean brush or cotton swab.

Uses: Strengthens hair and encourages thicker growth.

Storage Tips: Store in a dark container for up to 12 months.

141. Rosehip Oil for Acne Scars

Ingredients:

- 1 tbsp rosehip oil
- 2 drops tea tree essential oil

Instructions:

1. Mix rosehip oil and tea tree essential oil.
2. Apply to acne scars or blemished areas.

Uses: Promotes skin healing and reduces scar appearance.

Storage Tips: Store in a cool, dark place for up to 6 months.

142. Apricot Kernel Oil for Massage

Ingredients:

- 2 tbsp apricot kernel oil
- 3 drops lavender essential oil

Instructions:

1. Combine apricot kernel oil and lavender oil.
2. Use as a relaxing massage oil.

Uses: Softens skin and promotes relaxation.

Storage Tips: Keep in a dark bottle for up to 12 months.

143. Walnut Oil for Muscle Soreness

Ingredients:

- 2 tbsp walnut oil
- 2 drops eucalyptus essential oil

Instructions:

1. Blend walnut oil and eucalyptus oil.
2. Massage into sore muscles.

Uses: Relieves muscle tension and promotes circulation.

Storage Tips: Store in a cool, dark place for up to 9 months.

144. Evening Primrose Oil for Eczema

Ingredients:

- 1 tbsp evening primrose oil
- 2 drops chamomile essential oil

Instructions:

1. Combine evening primrose oil and chamomile oil.
2. Apply to eczema-affected areas twice daily.

Uses: Reduces inflammation and soothes itchy skin.

Storage Tips: Refrigerate after opening and use within 6 months.

145. Sunflower Oil for Daily Moisturizing

Ingredients:

- 2 tbsp sunflower oil
- 1 drop rose essential oil

Instructions:

1. Mix sunflower oil and rose essential oil.
2. Apply as a light, daily moisturizer.

Uses: Hydrates skin without clogging pores.

Storage Tips: Store in a cool, dry place for up to 12 months.

Recipes for Pain Relief and Relaxation

Herbal oils, when combined with essential oils, can offer powerful remedies for pain relief and relaxation. Whether you're dealing with sore muscles, tension headaches, or simply looking to unwind after a long day, these blends provide natural solutions to soothe discomfort and promote calmness. By harnessing the therapeutic properties of carrier and essential oils, you can create personalized recipes that are effective and safe.

This chapter provides 15 recipes tailored to alleviate pain and enhance relaxation. Each remedy combines carefully chosen ingredients to target specific issues, such as joint pain, muscle soreness, or stress. With easy-to-follow instructions and practical storage tips, these recipes will help you create oils that bring comfort and peace to your daily routine.

146. Lavender and Peppermint Tension Relief Oil

Ingredients:

- 2 tbsp sweet almond oil
- 2 drops lavender essential oil
- 1 drop peppermint essential oil

Instructions:

1. Mix all ingredients in a small bottle.
2. Massage onto temples or neck to ease tension headaches.

Uses: Relieves tension and promotes relaxation.

Storage Tips: Store in a cool, dark place for up to 12 months.

147. Arnica and Rosemary Muscle Soothing Oil

Ingredients:

- 2 tbsp arnica-infused oil
- 3 drops rosemary essential oil

Instructions:

1. Blend arnica oil and rosemary essential oil.
2. Massage into sore muscles after exercise.

Uses: Reduces muscle soreness and improves circulation.

Storage Tips: Keep in a dark glass bottle for up to 9 months.

148. Ginger and Eucalyptus Joint Relief Oil

Ingredients:

- 2 tbsp sesame oil
- 2 drops ginger essential oil
- 2 drops eucalyptus essential oil

Instructions:

1. Combine ingredients in a bottle.
2. Apply to joints and massage gently.

Uses: Eases joint pain and inflammation.

Storage Tips: Store in a cool, dry place for up to 12 months.

149. Chamomile and Calendula Relaxation Oil

Ingredients:

- 2 tbsp coconut oil
- 2 drops chamomile essential oil
- 1 drop calendula-infused oil

Instructions:

1. Mix ingredients thoroughly.
2. Apply to the skin before bedtime for relaxation.

Uses: Calms the mind and soothes irritated skin.

Storage Tips: Keep in a cool, dark cabinet for up to 12 months.

150. Clove and Lavender Pain Relief Oil

Ingredients:

- 2 tbsp olive oil
- 1 drop clove essential oil
- 2 drops lavender essential oil

Instructions:

1. Blend ingredients in a sterilized bottle.
2. Massage into areas of localized pain.

Uses: Reduces pain and inflammation naturally.

Storage Tips: Store in an airtight container for up to 9 months.

151. Frankincense and Rosehip Stress Relief Oil

Ingredients:

- 2 tbsp rosehip oil
- 3 drops frankincense essential oil

Instructions:

1. Combine ingredients in a dropper bottle.
2. Apply to wrists or temples for stress relief.

Uses: Promotes calmness and emotional balance.

Storage Tips: Keep in a dark glass bottle for up to 12 months.

152. Peppermint and Lemongrass Cooling Oil

Ingredients:

- 2 tbsp grapeseed oil
- 2 drops peppermint essential oil
- 2 drops lemongrass essential oil

Instructions:

1. Blend all ingredients and store in a sterilized container.
2. Apply to sore, inflamed areas.

Uses: Provides a cooling sensation and soothes tired muscles.

Storage Tips: Store in a cool, dark place for up to 6 months.

153. Basil and Lavender Neck Massage Oil

Ingredients:

- 2 tbsp jojoba oil
- 2 drops basil essential oil
- 2 drops lavender essential oil

Instructions:

1. Combine the oils in a bottle.
2. Massage into the neck and shoulders.

Uses: Relieves neck tension and promotes relaxation.

Storage Tips: Keep in a dark bottle for up to 12 months.

154. Rosemary and Thyme Energizing Oil

Ingredients:

- 2 tbsp olive oil
- 2 drops rosemary essential oil
- 2 drops thyme essential oil

Instructions:

1. Mix ingredients in a bottle.
2. Massage onto the back or legs to energize sore muscles.

Uses: Improves circulation and relieves fatigue.

Storage Tips: Store in a cool, dry area for up to 12 months.

155. Ylang Ylang and Almond Relaxation Oil

Ingredients:

- 2 tbsp sweet almond oil
- 2 drops ylang ylang essential oil

Instructions:

1. Blend the oils together.
2. Apply to the chest or wrists for relaxation.

Uses: Promotes relaxation and reduces stress.

Storage Tips: Keep in a sealed container for up to 12 months.

156. Lemongrass and Ginger Warming Oil

Ingredients:

- 2 tbsp sesame oil
- 2 drops lemongrass essential oil
- 2 drops ginger essential oil

Instructions:

1. Mix the oils in a sterilized bottle.
2. Massage into sore areas for a warming effect.

Uses: Relieves stiffness and promotes relaxation.

Storage Tips: Store in a cool, dark place for up to 9 months.

157. Tea Tree and Eucalyptus Relief Oil

Ingredients:

- 2 tbsp grapeseed oil
- 2 drops tea tree essential oil
- 2 drops eucalyptus essential oil

Instructions:

1. Combine the oils in a bottle.
2. Apply to inflamed or painful areas.

Uses: Reduces swelling and relieves minor aches.

Storage Tips: Store in a dark glass bottle for up to 6 months.

158. Lavender and Chamomile Sleep Aid Oil

Ingredients:

- 2 tbsp coconut oil
- 2 drops lavender essential oil
- 2 drops chamomile essential oil

Instructions:

1. Mix ingredients in a clean bottle.
2. Apply to temples or wrists before bedtime.

Uses: Encourages restful sleep and relaxation.

Storage Tips: Store in a cool, dark area for up to 12 months.

159. Clary Sage and Rosehip Tension Relief Oil

Ingredients:

- 2 tbsp rosehip oil
- 2 drops clary sage essential oil

Instructions:

1. Combine ingredients and store in a sterilized bottle.
2. Massage onto the back of the neck to reduce tension.

Uses: Eases stress and promotes calmness.

Storage Tips: Keep in a dark container for up to 9 months.

160. Cinnamon and Orange Comfort Oil

Ingredients:

- 2 tbsp sweet almond oil
- 1 drop cinnamon essential oil
- 2 drops orange essential oil

Instructions:

1. Mix the oils in a clean bottle.
2. Massage into the lower back or feet.

Uses: Provides warmth and relaxation.

Storage Tips: Store in a cool, dry place for up to 12 months.

BOOK 9

HERBAL REMEDIES FOR RESPIRATORY HEALTH

Breathing is the foundation of life, and maintaining respiratory health is essential for overall well-being. From seasonal allergies and colds to chronic respiratory concerns, our lungs and airways often face challenges that impact our ability to breathe freely. Fortunately, nature offers a wealth of herbs and remedies to support the respiratory system, clear congestion, and promote healthy lung function.

This book explores the power of herbal remedies in addressing common respiratory issues. By using simple yet effective preparations such as steams, teas, syrups, and throat soothers, you can alleviate discomfort and breathe easier. Each chapter focuses on a specific aspect of respiratory health, from clearing congestion naturally to creating soothing remedies for coughs and sore throats.

With practical guidance and easy-to-follow recipes, you'll learn how to harness the therapeutic properties of herbs like eucalyptus, thyme, mullein, and licorice root. Whether you're looking to support your immune system during flu season or maintain long-term respiratory wellness, this book provides the tools and knowledge you need to care for yourself and your loved ones. Let's embark on a journey to breathe deeply and embrace the healing power of herbs for respiratory health.

Clearing Congestion Naturally

Respiratory congestion is a common issue caused by colds, flu, allergies, or environmental factors. It occurs when mucus builds up in the airways, making it difficult to breathe comfortably. Herbal remedies offer natural, effective solutions to help clear congestion without relying on over-the-counter medications. Many herbs contain properties that loosen mucus, reduce inflammation, and support overall respiratory health.

This chapter focuses on herbal remedies designed to clear congestion and restore easy breathing. These remedies include teas, steams, and topical applications, harnessing the power of decongestant and anti-inflammatory herbs. Whether you're dealing with sinus pressure, a stuffy nose, or chest congestion, these natural solutions provide relief while supporting your body's healing process.

Here are 15 herbal remedies to help you breathe easier and find relief from congestion. Each recipe is simple to prepare and uses accessible ingredients.

161. Eucalyptus Steam Inhalation

Ingredients:

- 5 drops eucalyptus essential oil
- 1 liter boiling water

Instructions:

1. Pour boiling water into a large bowl.
2. Add eucalyptus oil and cover your head with a towel.
3. Inhale the steam deeply for 5–10 minutes.

Uses: Clears nasal passages and soothes congestion.

Storage Tips: Use immediately; do not store.

162. Peppermint and Thyme Tea

Ingredients:

- 1 tsp dried peppermint leaves
- 1 tsp dried thyme leaves
- 1 cup boiling water

Instructions:

1. Steep herbs in boiling water for 5–7 minutes.
2. Strain and drink warm.

Uses: Loosens mucus and supports respiratory health.

Storage Tips: Consume immediately.

163. Garlic and Honey Syrup

Ingredients:

- 5 cloves fresh garlic (crushed)
- 1/4 cup raw honey

Instructions:

1. Mix crushed garlic with honey in a jar.
2. Let it sit for 12 hours, then strain.

Uses: Reduces chest congestion and boosts immunity.

Storage Tips: Store in the refrigerator for up to 2 weeks.

164. Ginger and Lemon Decongestant Tea

Ingredients:

- 1 tsp fresh ginger slices
- 1 tsp fresh lemon juice
- 1 cup boiling water

Instructions:

1. Steep ginger in boiling water for 10 minutes.
2. Add lemon juice and drink warm.

Uses: Eases nasal congestion and soothes the throat.

Storage Tips: Consume fresh.

165. Turmeric Milk

Ingredients:

- 1 cup warm milk (dairy or plant-based)
- 1/2 tsp turmeric powder
- 1 tsp honey

Instructions:

1. Mix turmeric and honey into warm milk.
2. Stir well and drink before bedtime.

Uses: Reduces inflammation and clears respiratory passages.

Storage Tips: Consume immediately.

166. Onion Vapor for Stuffy Nose

Ingredients:

- 1 medium onion (sliced)
- 1 liter boiling water

Instructions:

1. Place onion slices in a bowl.
2. Pour boiling water over them and inhale the steam.

Uses: Breaks down mucus and clears nasal passages.

Storage Tips: Use immediately.

167. Mullein and Honey Cough Tea

Ingredients:

- 1 tsp dried mullein leaves
- 1 cup boiling water
- 1 tsp honey

Instructions:

1. Steep mullein in boiling water for 10 minutes.
2. Strain, add honey, and drink warm.

Uses: Clears chest congestion and soothes coughs.

Storage Tips: Drink fresh.

168. Basil and Black Pepper Brew

Ingredients:

- 5 fresh basil leaves
- 1/2 tsp black pepper
- 1 cup boiling water

Instructions:

1. Steep basil and pepper in boiling water for 7 minutes.
2. Strain and drink warm.

Uses: Opens airways and reduces sinus pressure.

Storage Tips: Consume immediately.

169. Mustard Chest Rub

Ingredients:

- 1 tbsp mustard powder
- 2 tbsp coconut oil

Instructions:

1. Mix mustard powder with coconut oil to form a paste.
2. Rub onto the chest and cover with a warm cloth.

Uses: Relieves chest congestion and improves circulation.

Storage Tips: Store in a sealed jar for up to 1 week.

170. Thyme Steam Therapy

Ingredients:

- 2 tbsp dried thyme leaves
- 1 liter boiling water

Instructions:

1. Add thyme leaves to boiling water in a bowl.
2. Cover your head with a towel and inhale deeply for 10 minutes.

Uses: Reduces nasal congestion and clears airways.

Storage Tips: Use immediately.

171. Honey and Cinnamon Paste

Ingredients:

- 1 tbsp raw honey
- 1/2 tsp cinnamon powder

Instructions:

1. Mix honey and cinnamon into a paste.
2. Take 1 teaspoon twice daily.

Uses: Relieves congestion and supports immune function.

Storage Tips: Store in a sealed jar for up to 1 week.

172. Fenugreek Seed Tea

Ingredients:

- 1 tsp fenugreek seeds
- 1 cup boiling water

Instructions:

1. Simmer fenugreek seeds in water for 5 minutes.
2. Strain and drink warm.

Uses: Loosens mucus and eases chest congestion.

Storage Tips: Consume immediately.

173. Mint and Eucalyptus Chest Rub

Ingredients:

- 1 tbsp coconut oil
- 2 drops eucalyptus essential oil
- 1 drop peppermint essential oil

Instructions:

1. Mix coconut oil with essential oils.
2. Massage onto the chest before bedtime.

Uses: Opens airways and reduces congestion.

Storage Tips: Store in a sealed jar for up to 2 weeks.

174. Licorice Root Tea

Ingredients:

- 1 tsp dried licorice root
- 1 cup boiling water

Instructions:

1. Steep licorice root in boiling water for 10 minutes.
2. Strain and drink warm.

Uses: Soothes the throat and reduces respiratory inflammation.

Storage Tips: Drink fresh.

175. Saltwater Nasal Spray

Ingredients:

- 1/2 tsp salt
- 1 cup warm distilled water

Instructions:

1. Dissolve salt in warm distilled water.
2. Use a nasal spray bottle to apply.

Uses: Clears nasal passages and reduces sinus irritation.

Storage Tips: Store in the refrigerator for up to 1 week.

Remedies for Seasonal Allergies

Seasonal allergies, often known as hay fever, can bring discomfort through symptoms like sneezing, itchy eyes, nasal congestion, and sinus pressure. These reactions are typically caused by allergens such as pollen, dust, or mold. While over-the-counter medications provide relief, herbal remedies offer a natural, effective way to manage symptoms without unwanted side effects.

This chapter introduces 15 herbal remedies to help alleviate the discomfort of seasonal allergies. These recipes include teas, syrups, steams, and nasal rinses designed to soothe inflammation, boost immunity, and clear allergens from your system. By incorporating these remedies into your routine, you can manage seasonal allergies and enjoy the changing seasons more comfortably.

176. Nettle and Peppermint Allergy Tea

Ingredients:

- 1 tsp dried nettle leaves
- 1 tsp dried peppermint leaves
- 1 cup boiling water

Instructions:

1. Steep nettle and peppermint in boiling water for 5–7 minutes.
2. Strain and drink warm.

Uses: Reduces inflammation and alleviates nasal congestion.

Storage Tips: Consume immediately.

177. Chamomile and Lemon Balm Infusion

Ingredients:

- 1 tsp dried chamomile flowers
- 1 tsp dried lemon balm leaves
- 1 cup boiling water

Instructions:

1. Steep chamomile and lemon balm in boiling water for 5 minutes.
2. Strain and drink warm.

Uses: Calms irritated sinuses and reduces allergic reactions.

Storage Tips: Drink fresh.

178. Turmeric and Ginger Immunity Shot

Ingredients:

- 1/2 tsp turmeric powder
- 1 tsp fresh ginger juice
- 1 tsp honey
- 1/4 cup warm water

Instructions:

1. Mix all ingredients in a small cup.
2. Drink the shot in the morning.

Uses: Boosts immunity and reduces inflammation.

Storage Tips: Prepare fresh daily.

179. Eucalyptus Steam for Sinus Relief

Ingredients:

- 5 drops eucalyptus essential oil
- 1 liter boiling water

Instructions:

1. Add eucalyptus oil to boiling water in a bowl.
2. Cover your head with a towel and inhale deeply for 5–10 minutes.

Uses: Clears sinuses and reduces nasal irritation.

Storage Tips: Use immediately.

180. Quercetin-Rich Herbal Tea

Ingredients:

- 1 tsp dried elderflower
- 1 tsp dried hibiscus flowers
- 1 cup boiling water

Instructions:

1. Steep elderflower and hibiscus in boiling water for 7 minutes.
2. Strain and drink warm.

Uses: Provides natural antihistamine effects.

Storage Tips: Consume immediately.

181. Apple Cider Vinegar and Honey Drink

Ingredients:

- 1 tbsp apple cider vinegar
- 1 tsp honey
- 1 cup warm water

Instructions:

1. Mix apple cider vinegar and honey into warm water.
2. Drink before meals.

Uses: Reduces mucus production and supports the immune system.

Storage Tips: Prepare fresh for each use.

182. Lavender and Lemon Soothing Tea

Ingredients:

- 1 tsp dried lavender flowers
- 1 tsp fresh lemon juice
- 1 cup boiling water

Instructions:

1. Steep lavender in boiling water for 5 minutes.
2. Add lemon juice and drink warm.

Uses: Reduces allergy-induced stress and calms the respiratory system.

Storage Tips: Drink fresh.

183. Holy Basil (Tulsi) Tea

Ingredients:

- 1 tsp dried holy basil leaves
- 1 cup boiling water

Instructions:

1. Steep tulsi in boiling water for 7 minutes.
2. Strain and drink warm.

Uses: Supports respiratory health and reduces inflammation.

Storage Tips: Consume immediately.

184. DIY Nasal Rinse

Ingredients:

- 1/2 tsp salt
- 1/4 tsp baking soda
- 1 cup warm distilled water

Instructions:

1. Dissolve salt and baking soda in warm water.
2. Use a nasal spray bottle or neti pot to rinse nasal passages.

Uses: Removes allergens and clears nasal congestion.

Storage Tips: Store in a sterilized bottle for up to 1 week.

185. Licorice Root Allergy Tea

Ingredients:

- 1 tsp dried licorice root
- 1 cup boiling water

Instructions:

1. Steep licorice root in boiling water for 10 minutes.
2. Strain and drink warm.

Uses: Soothes inflammation and eases breathing.

Storage Tips: Consume fresh.

186. Mint and Basil Sinus Relief Tea

Ingredients:

- 1 tsp dried mint leaves
- 1 tsp fresh basil leaves
- 1 cup boiling water

Instructions:

1. Steep mint and basil in boiling water for 7 minutes.
2. Strain and drink warm.

Uses: Reduces sinus pressure and clears congestion.

Storage Tips: Drink fresh.

187. Black Seed Oil Nasal Rub

Ingredients:

- 1 tsp black seed oil
- 2 drops eucalyptus essential oil

Instructions:

1. Mix black seed oil with eucalyptus oil.
2. Apply gently to the sides of the nose and chest.

Uses: Reduces inflammation and supports easy breathing.

Storage Tips: Store in a cool, dark place for up to 6 months.

188. Fennel and Ginger Soothing Tea

Ingredients:

- 1 tsp fennel seeds
- 1 tsp fresh ginger slices
- 1 cup boiling water

Instructions:

1. Steep fennel seeds and ginger in boiling water for 10 minutes.
2. Strain and drink warm.

Uses: Eases sinus irritation and calms inflammation.

Storage Tips: Consume immediately.

189. Cinnamon and Honey Immunity Booster

Ingredients:

- 1/2 tsp cinnamon powder
- 1 tsp honey
- 1/4 cup warm water

Instructions:

1. Mix cinnamon and honey in warm water.
2. Drink daily in the morning.

Uses: Reduces allergic reactions and boosts immunity.

Storage Tips: Prepare fresh daily.

190. Mullein Leaf Steam Therapy

Ingredients:

- 1 tbsp dried mullein leaves
- 1 liter boiling water

Instructions:

1. Add mullein leaves to boiling water in a bowl.
2. Cover your head with a towel and inhale deeply for 5–10 minutes.

Uses: Clears nasal passages and soothes inflamed airways.

Storage Tips: Use immediately.

Supporting Lung Health with Herbal Steams

Herbal steams are one of the simplest and most effective ways to support lung health. The warmth and moisture from the steam loosen mucus, clear the airways, and deliver the therapeutic properties of herbs directly to your respiratory system. This method is especially helpful for addressing congestion, improving breathing, and soothing irritated airways caused by colds, allergies, or environmental irritants.

In this chapter, we explore 15 herbal steam recipes designed to support lung health and enhance respiratory wellness. By using easily accessible herbs such as eucalyptus, thyme, peppermint, and chamomile, you can create personalized steam blends tailored to your specific needs. Each remedy is designed to cleanse and nourish your lungs while promoting relaxation and overall well-being.

191. Eucalyptus and Mint Steam

Ingredients:

- 3 drops eucalyptus essential oil
- 2 drops peppermint essential oil
- 1 liter boiling water

Instructions:

1. Add the essential oils to a bowl of boiling water.
2. Cover your head with a towel and inhale deeply for 5–10 minutes.

Uses: Clears nasal passages and supports lung function.

Storage Tips: Prepare fresh for each use.

192. Thyme and Rosemary Steam

Ingredients:

- 2 tbsp dried thyme leaves
- 1 tbsp dried rosemary leaves
- 1 liter boiling water

Instructions:

1. Add thyme and rosemary to the boiling water.

2. Inhale the steam deeply for 10 minutes.

Uses: Reduces congestion and fights respiratory infections.

Storage Tips: Use immediately.

193. Chamomile and Lavender Steam

Ingredients:

- 1 tbsp dried chamomile flowers
- 1 tbsp dried lavender flowers
- 1 liter boiling water

Instructions:

1. Steep chamomile and lavender in boiling water for 5 minutes.
2. Inhale the aromatic steam deeply.

Uses: Soothes irritated airways and promotes relaxation.

Storage Tips: Consume immediately; do not store.

194. Peppermint and Basil Steam

Ingredients:

- 1 tsp dried peppermint leaves
- 1 tsp fresh basil leaves
- 1 liter boiling water

Instructions:

1. Add the herbs to boiling water.
2. Cover your head with a towel and breathe in the steam.

Uses: Opens airways and alleviates sinus congestion.

Storage Tips: Prepare fresh for each session.

195. Ginger and Lemon Steam

Ingredients:

- 1 tbsp fresh ginger slices
- 1 tbsp lemon zest
- 1 liter boiling water

Instructions:

1. Add ginger and lemon zest to the boiling water.
2. Inhale the steam deeply for 10 minutes.

Uses: Loosens mucus and soothes inflamed airways.

Storage Tips: Discard after use.

196. Sage and Clove Steam

Ingredients:

- 1 tbsp dried sage leaves
- 5 cloves
- 1 liter boiling water

Instructions:

1. Add sage and cloves to boiling water.
2. Inhale the aromatic steam for 5–10 minutes.

Uses: Provides antibacterial benefits and relieves congestion.

Storage Tips: Use immediately.

197. Licorice Root Steam

Ingredients:

- 1 tsp dried licorice root
- 1 liter boiling water

Instructions:

1. Add licorice root to boiling water.
2. Inhale the steam for 10 minutes.

Uses: Soothes the throat and reduces respiratory inflammation.

Storage Tips: Consume fresh.

198. Lemongrass and Mint Steam

Ingredients:

- 1 tbsp dried lemongrass
- 1 tsp dried mint leaves
- 1 liter boiling water

Instructions:

1. Add herbs to boiling water.
2. Inhale the steam deeply for 10 minutes.

Uses: Refreshes the respiratory system and clears nasal passages.

Storage Tips: Prepare fresh for each use.

199. Holy Basil (Tulsi) and Ginger Steam

Ingredients:

- 1 tbsp dried holy basil leaves
- 1 tsp fresh ginger slices
- 1 liter boiling water

Instructions:

1. Add tulsi and ginger to boiling water.
2. Cover your head with a towel and inhale deeply.

Uses: Supports respiratory wellness and relieves congestion.

Storage Tips: Discard after use.

200. Eucalyptus and Cinnamon Steam

Ingredients:

- 2 drops eucalyptus essential oil
- 1 cinnamon stick
- 1 liter boiling water

Instructions:

1. Add eucalyptus oil and cinnamon to boiling water.
2. Inhale the steam for 10 minutes.

Uses: Improves lung function and fights respiratory infections.

Storage Tips: Use immediately.

201. Mullein and Rosemary Steam

Ingredients:

- 1 tbsp dried mullein leaves
- 1 tbsp dried rosemary leaves
- 1 liter boiling water

Instructions:

1. Combine herbs with boiling water in a bowl.
2. Inhale the steam deeply for 10 minutes.

Uses: Clears mucus and supports lung health.

Storage Tips: Prepare fresh for each session.

202. Calendula and Chamomile Steam

Ingredients:

- 1 tbsp dried calendula petals
- 1 tbsp dried chamomile flowers
- 1 liter boiling water

Instructions:

1. Add herbs to boiling water.
2. Inhale the steam while seated comfortably.

Uses: Soothes inflamed airways and supports healing.

Storage Tips: Use immediately.

203. Mint and Eucalyptus Steam

Ingredients:

- 2 drops eucalyptus essential oil
- 1 tsp dried mint leaves

- 1 liter boiling water

Instructions:

1. Add eucalyptus and mint to boiling water.
2. Breathe in the steam for 5–10 minutes.

Uses: Reduces nasal congestion and soothes the throat.

Storage Tips: Consume fresh.

204. Thyme and Lemon Peel Steam

Ingredients:

- 1 tbsp dried thyme
- 1 tbsp fresh lemon peel
- 1 liter boiling water

Instructions:

1. Add thyme and lemon peel to boiling water.
2. Inhale the steam deeply for 10 minutes.

Uses: Clears nasal passages and invigorates the lungs.

Storage Tips: Discard after use.

205. Fennel and Ginger Steam

Ingredients:

- 1 tbsp fennel seeds
- 1 tbsp fresh ginger slices
- 1 liter boiling water

Instructions:

1. Combine fennel and ginger with boiling water.
2. Inhale deeply for 10 minutes.

Uses: Soothes airways and reduces inflammation.

Storage Tips: Use immediately.

Recipes for Cough Syrups and Throat Soothers

Coughs and sore throats are common discomforts caused by colds, flu, allergies, or dry air. Herbal cough syrups and throat soothers provide natural relief by calming irritation, reducing inflammation, and promoting healing. Made with ingredients like honey, ginger, licorice root, and slippery elm, these remedies are gentle yet effective alternatives to over-the-counter medicines.

This chapter offers 15 easy-to-make recipes for herbal cough syrups and throat soothers. Each recipe is designed to address specific symptoms, such as dry coughs, chest congestion, or irritated throats. These remedies use simple, natural ingredients to provide comfort and support recovery.

206. Honey and Ginger Cough Syrup

Ingredients:

- 1/4 cup raw honey
- 1 tbsp fresh ginger juice
- 1 tbsp lemon juice

Instructions:

1. Mix all ingredients in a jar.
2. Take 1 teaspoon every 2–3 hours as needed.

Uses: Soothes sore throats and suppresses coughs.

Storage Tips: Store in a sealed jar in the refrigerator for up to 1 week.

207. Licorice Root Throat Soother

Ingredients:

- 1 tsp dried licorice root
- 1 cup boiling water
- 1 tsp honey

Instructions:

1. Steep licorice root in boiling water for 10 minutes.
2. Strain, add honey, and sip slowly.

Uses: Reduces throat irritation and relieves dry coughs.

Storage Tips: Prepare fresh for each use.

208. Slippery Elm and Marshmallow Root Syrup

Ingredients:

- 1 tbsp slippery elm powder
- 1 tbsp marshmallow root
- 1 cup boiling water
- 1/4 cup honey

Instructions:

1. Steep slippery elm and marshmallow root in boiling water for 10 minutes.
2. Strain and mix with honey.
3. Take 1 teaspoon as needed.

Uses: Coats the throat and relieves irritation.

Storage Tips: Store in the refrigerator for up to 5 days.

209. Lemon and Thyme Cough Syrup

Ingredients:

- 1/4 cup fresh lemon juice
- 1 tbsp dried thyme leaves
- 1/4 cup honey

Instructions:

1. Steep thyme in lemon juice for 10 minutes.
2. Strain and mix with honey.
3. Take 1 teaspoon every 3 hours.

Uses: Clears congestion and soothes coughs.

Storage Tips: Keep in the refrigerator for up to 1 week.

210. Cinnamon and Honey Throat Soother

Ingredients:

- 1/2 tsp cinnamon powder
- 1 tbsp honey

Instructions:

1. Mix cinnamon and honey into a smooth paste.
2. Take 1/2 teaspoon as needed.

Uses: Relieves throat irritation and reduces inflammation.

Storage Tips: Store in an airtight jar for up to 2 weeks.

211. Peppermint and Ginger Chest Syrup

Ingredients:

- 1 tsp dried peppermint leaves
- 1 tsp fresh ginger juice
- 1/4 cup honey

Instructions:

1. Steep peppermint in 1/4 cup boiling water for 10 minutes.
2. Strain and mix with ginger juice and honey.
3. Take 1 teaspoon as needed.

Uses: Eases chest congestion and soothes coughs.

Storage Tips: Store in the refrigerator for up to 1 week.

212. Echinacea and Lemon Balm Syrup

Ingredients:

- 1 tsp dried echinacea leaves
- 1 tsp dried lemon balm
- 1/4 cup honey

Instructions:

1. Steep echinacea and lemon balm in 1/4 cup boiling water for 10 minutes.
2. Strain and mix with honey.
3. Take 1 teaspoon every 4 hours.

Uses: Boosts immunity and calms throat irritation.

Storage Tips: Store in the refrigerator for up to 5 days.

213. Apple Cider Vinegar and Honey Cough Remedy

Ingredients:

- 1 tbsp apple cider vinegar
- 1 tbsp honey
- 1/4 cup warm water

Instructions:

1. Mix all ingredients until well combined.
2. Take 1 tablespoon every 3 hours.

Uses: Reduces mucus and soothes the throat.

Storage Tips: Prepare fresh for each use.

214. Turmeric and Ginger Cough Paste

Ingredients:

- 1 tsp turmeric powder
- 1 tsp fresh ginger juice
- 1 tbsp honey

Instructions:

1. Mix all ingredients into a smooth paste.
2. Take 1/2 teaspoon as needed.

Uses: Combats inflammation and soothes coughs.

Storage Tips: Store in a sealed jar for up to 1 week.

215. Chamomile and Honey Throat Spray

Ingredients:

- 1 tsp dried chamomile flowers
- 1/4 cup boiling water
- 1 tbsp honey

Instructions:

1. Steep chamomile in boiling water for 10 minutes.
2. Strain and mix with honey.
3. Pour into a small spray bottle and apply to the throat.

Uses: Relieves irritation and calms the throat.

Storage Tips: Store in the refrigerator for up to 3 days.

216. Basil and Ginger Syrup

Ingredients:

- 5 fresh basil leaves
- 1 tsp fresh ginger juice
- 1/4 cup honey

Instructions:

1. Crush basil leaves and steep in 1/4 cup boiling water for 10 minutes.
2. Strain and mix with ginger juice and honey.

Uses: Relieves dry coughs and soothes sore throats.

Storage Tips: Keep refrigerated for up to 5 days.

217. Garlic and Honey Immune Syrup

Ingredients:

- 3 cloves garlic (crushed)
- 1/4 cup raw honey

Instructions:

1. Mix garlic and honey in a jar.
2. Let sit for 12 hours, then strain.

Uses: Supports immunity and calms coughs.

Storage Tips: Store in the refrigerator for up to 1 week.

218. Rosemary and Lemon Throat Soother

Ingredients:

- 1 tsp dried rosemary
- 1 tsp fresh lemon juice
- 1 tbsp honey

Instructions:

1. Steep rosemary in 1/4 cup boiling water for 10 minutes.
2. Strain, add lemon juice and honey, and drink slowly.

Uses: Reduces throat irritation and clears congestion.

Storage Tips: Prepare fresh for each use.

219. Fenugreek and Licorice Root Syrup

Ingredients:

- 1 tsp fenugreek seeds
- 1 tsp dried licorice root
- 1/4 cup honey

Instructions:

1. Simmer fenugreek and licorice root in 1/4 cup water for 10 minutes.
2. Strain and mix with honey.

Uses: Loosens mucus and soothes the throat.

Storage Tips: Store in the refrigerator for up to 5 days.

220. Mint and Lavender Cough Remedy

Ingredients:

- 1 tsp dried mint leaves
- 1 tsp dried lavender flowers
- 1/4 cup honey

Instructions:

1. Steep mint and lavender in 1/4 cup boiling water for 10 minutes.
2. Strain and mix with honey.

Uses: Calms dry coughs and promotes relaxation.

Storage Tips: Keep in the refrigerator for up to 7 days.

BOOK 10

MANAGING PAIN NATURALLY

Pain is an inevitable part of life, but how we manage it can make a significant difference in our overall well-being. Whether it's sore muscles after a workout, chronic conditions that affect daily life, or the occasional headache or migraine, herbal remedies provide natural, effective solutions for relief. Unlike pharmaceutical options, these remedies work in harmony with the body, reducing inflammation, improving circulation, and soothing discomfort without unwanted side effects.

This book explores the power of herbs in pain management, offering a variety of recipes and techniques to address different types of pain. From topical salves and balms for sore muscles to teas and blends for chronic pain, you'll find practical solutions for everyday discomfort. The chapters also delve into the creation of anti-inflammatory blends and specific remedies for headaches and migraines, providing targeted support for common issues.

By incorporating these herbal practices into your routine, you can take control of your pain management naturally. Each remedy is easy to prepare and uses accessible ingredients, allowing you to build a natural first-aid kit for pain relief. Let's embark on this journey toward managing pain naturally, with the wisdom of herbal medicine as our guide.

Topical Applications for Sore Muscles

Sore muscles can result from overexertion, stress, or physical activity, leaving us feeling stiff, achy, and fatigued. While rest and hydration are essential, topical herbal applications can provide immediate relief by reducing inflammation, improving circulation, and relaxing tense muscles. These remedies, which include balms, oils, and compresses, offer natural, targeted relief without relying on synthetic chemicals.

Herbs like arnica, ginger, and peppermint are renowned for their muscle-soothing properties.

When combined with carrier oils and other complementary ingredients, they create potent remedies that penetrate the skin to address underlying tension and pain. This chapter explores 15 easy-to-make topical applications to help soothe sore muscles and restore comfort.

These recipes are simple, effective, and customizable, making them a valuable addition to any natural wellness routine. Proper preparation and storage ensure you have these remedies ready whenever you need relief.

221. Arnica and Peppermint Cooling Balm

Ingredients:

- 1/4 cup beeswax
- 1/4 cup coconut oil
- 2 tbsp arnica-infused oil
- 5 drops peppermint essential oil

Instructions:

1. Melt beeswax and coconut oil in a double boiler.
2. Stir in arnica oil and peppermint essential oil.
3. Pour into a small jar and let cool.

Uses: Relieves muscle soreness and provides a cooling effect.

Storage Tips: Store in a cool, dark place for up to 6 months.

222. Ginger and Turmeric Warming Oil

Ingredients:

- 1/4 cup sesame oil
- 1 tbsp grated fresh ginger
- 1/2 tsp turmeric powder

Instructions:

1. Heat sesame oil with ginger and turmeric over low heat for 10 minutes.
2. Strain and store in a clean bottle.
3. Massage into sore muscles.

Uses: Improves circulation and reduces inflammation.

Storage Tips: Store in a dark bottle for up to 2 weeks.

223. Rosemary and Lavender Muscle Rub

Ingredients:

- 1/4 cup olive oil
- 1 tbsp dried rosemary
- 5 drops lavender essential oil

Instructions:

1. Heat olive oil with rosemary on low heat for 10 minutes.
2. Strain and add lavender essential oil.
3. Massage onto sore areas.

Uses: Relieves muscle tension and promotes relaxation.

Storage Tips: Store in a sealed jar for up to 1 month.

224. Cayenne and Olive Oil Pain Relief Salve

Ingredients:

- 1/4 cup olive oil
- 1 tsp cayenne powder
- 2 tbsp beeswax

Instructions:

1. Heat olive oil with cayenne powder for 5 minutes.
2. Strain and mix with melted beeswax.
3. Pour into a jar and cool.

Uses: Provides a warming effect and reduces muscle pain.

Storage Tips: Keep in a cool place for up to 6 months.

225. Chamomile and Coconut Oil Massage Blend

Ingredients:

- 1/4 cup coconut oil
- 2 tbsp dried chamomile flowers

Instructions:

1. Heat coconut oil with chamomile flowers on low for 10 minutes.
2. Strain and store in a glass bottle.

Uses: Calms inflamed muscles and reduces tension.

Storage Tips: Store in a cool, dry place for up to 3 months.

226. Peppermint and Eucalyptus Cooling Compress

Ingredients:

- 5 drops peppermint essential oil
- 5 drops eucalyptus essential oil
- 1 liter cold water

Instructions:

1. Add essential oils to cold water.
2. Soak a cloth in the mixture and apply to sore muscles.

Uses: Provides instant cooling relief for muscle pain.

Storage Tips: Prepare fresh for each use.

227. Arnica and Ginger Soothing Balm

Ingredients:

- 1/4 cup arnica-infused oil
- 1 tbsp grated ginger
- 2 tbsp beeswax

Instructions:

1. Melt beeswax and mix with arnica oil and ginger.
2. Strain and pour into a jar.

Uses: Relieves muscle stiffness and soreness.

Storage Tips: Store in a dark jar for up to 3 months.

228. Mustard Seed Muscle Rub

Ingredients:

- 1 tbsp mustard seed powder
- 2 tbsp olive oil

Instructions:

1. Mix mustard seed powder with olive oil into a paste.
2. Apply to sore areas and cover with a warm cloth.

Uses: Stimulates circulation and reduces pain.

Storage Tips: Prepare fresh for each use.

229. Calendula and Mint Relief Gel

Ingredients:

- 1/4 cup aloe vera gel
- 2 tbsp calendula-infused oil
- 5 drops peppermint essential oil

Instructions:

1. Mix all ingredients thoroughly.
2. Apply to sore muscles.

Uses: Soothes inflammation and cools the skin.

Storage Tips: Store in the refrigerator for up to 1 month.

230. Lavender and Basil Warm Compress

Ingredients:

- 5 drops lavender essential oil
- 3 drops basil essential oil
- 1 liter warm water

Instructions:

1. Add essential oils to warm water.
2. Soak a cloth and apply to sore areas.

Uses: Relieves tension and reduces inflammation.

Storage Tips: Use immediately.

231. Black Pepper and Ginger Massage Oil

Ingredients:

- 1/4 cup almond oil
- 1 tsp black pepper
- 1 tsp fresh ginger juice

Instructions:

1. Heat almond oil with black pepper and ginger for 5 minutes.
2. Strain and store in a bottle.

Uses: Improves circulation and soothes sore muscles.

Storage Tips: Store in a dark, cool place for up to 1 month.

232. Turmeric and Clove Pain Relief Paste

Ingredients:

- 1 tsp turmeric powder
- 1/2 tsp clove powder
- 1 tbsp water

Instructions:

1. Mix all ingredients into a paste.
2. Apply to sore muscles and rinse off after 20 minutes.

Uses: Reduces pain and inflammation.

Storage Tips: Prepare fresh for each use.

233. Lemongrass and Arnica Massage Oil

Ingredients:

- 1/4 cup jojoba oil
- 5 drops lemongrass essential oil
- 2 tbsp arnica-infused oil

Instructions:

1. Combine all ingredients in a bottle.
2. Use for massaging sore areas.

Uses: Reduces soreness and enhances relaxation.

Storage Tips: Keep in a sealed bottle for up to 3 months.

234. Mint and Rosemary Compress

Ingredients:

- 1 tbsp dried mint leaves
- 1 tbsp dried rosemary leaves
- 1 liter hot water

Instructions:

1. Steep mint and rosemary in hot water for 10 minutes.
2. Soak a cloth and apply to muscles.

Uses: Relaxes tension and promotes circulation.

Storage Tips: Use immediately.

235. Eucalyptus and Lemon Cooling Gel

Ingredients:

- 1/4 cup aloe vera gel
- 5 drops eucalyptus essential oil
- 3 drops lemon essential oil

Instructions:

1. Mix all ingredients thoroughly.
2. Apply to muscles for a cooling effect.

Uses: Eases soreness and refreshes the skin.

Storage Tips: Store in the refrigerator for up to 2 weeks.

Herbs for Chronic Pain Management

Chronic pain can significantly affect daily life, impacting mobility, energy, and overall well-being. While pharmaceutical options are often prescribed, long-term reliance on medications can bring unwanted side effects. Herbs provide a natural and sustainable alternative for managing chronic pain. With their anti-inflammatory, analgesic, and calming properties, herbs like turmeric, willow bark, and boswellia have been used for centuries to alleviate persistent discomfort.

This chapter explores 15 herbal remedies designed to address chronic pain naturally. These remedies include teas, tinctures, and topical applications that target inflammation, improve circulation, and support the body's natural healing processes. Whether dealing with joint pain, nerve discomfort, or muscular tension, these herbal solutions offer gentle yet effective relief.

236. Turmeric and Ginger Anti-Inflammatory Tea

Ingredients:

- 1 tsp turmeric powder
- 1 tsp fresh ginger slices
- 1 cup boiling water

Instructions:

1. Steep turmeric and ginger in boiling water for 10 minutes.
2. Strain and drink warm.

Uses: Reduces inflammation and relieves joint pain.

Storage Tips: Consume fresh.

237. Willow Bark Pain Relief Tea

Ingredients:

- 1 tsp dried willow bark
- 1 cup boiling water

Instructions:

1. Steep willow bark in boiling water for 10 minutes.
2. Strain and drink warm.

Uses: Acts as a natural analgesic for chronic pain.

Storage Tips: Prepare fresh for each use.

238. Boswellia and Ashwagandha Tonic

Ingredients:

- 1 tsp boswellia powder
- 1 tsp ashwagandha powder
- 1 cup warm milk (dairy or plant-based)

Instructions:

1. Mix boswellia and ashwagandha powder into warm milk.
2. Stir well and drink before bedtime.

Uses: Reduces inflammation and supports joint health.

Storage Tips: Consume immediately.

239. Chamomile and Lavender Calming Tea

Ingredients:

- 1 tsp dried chamomile flowers
- 1 tsp dried lavender flowers
- 1 cup boiling water

Instructions:

1. Steep chamomile and lavender in boiling water for 5 minutes.
2. Strain and drink warm.

Uses: Relieves nerve pain and promotes relaxation.

Storage Tips: Drink fresh.

240. Peppermint and Rosemary Massage Oil

Ingredients:

- 1/4 cup olive oil
- 5 drops peppermint essential oil
- 3 drops rosemary essential oil

Instructions:

1. Combine all ingredients in a small bottle.
2. Massage onto painful areas.

Uses: Soothes muscular pain and improves circulation.

Storage Tips: Store in a dark glass bottle for up to 3 months.

241. Ginger and Cayenne Warming Compress

Ingredients:

- 1 tbsp grated fresh ginger
- 1/2 tsp cayenne powder
- 1 liter hot water

Instructions:

1. Mix ginger and cayenne into hot water.
2. Soak a cloth in the mixture and apply to the affected area.

Uses: Relieves deep-seated pain and stimulates circulation.

Storage Tips: Prepare fresh for each use.

242. St. John's Wort Oil

Ingredients:

- 1 cup olive oil
- 1/4 cup dried St. John's Wort flowers

Instructions:

1. Infuse St. John's Wort flowers in olive oil using the solar method for 4 weeks.
2. Strain and store in a clean bottle.

Uses: Eases nerve pain and supports healing.

Storage Tips: Keep in a cool, dark place for up to 12 months.

243. Epsom Salt and Lavender Bath Soak

Ingredients:

- 1 cup Epsom salt
- 10 drops lavender essential oil

Instructions:

1. Mix Epsom salt and lavender essential oil.
2. Add to a warm bath and soak for 20 minutes.

Uses: Relieves muscle tension and calms chronic pain.

Storage Tips: Store in an airtight jar for up to 6 months.

244. Arnica and Turmeric Pain Relief Balm

Ingredients:

- 1/4 cup beeswax
- 1/4 cup arnica-infused oil
- 1 tsp turmeric powder

Instructions:

1. Melt beeswax and mix with arnica oil and turmeric.
2. Pour into a jar and let cool.

Uses: Reduces inflammation and relieves joint pain.

Storage Tips: Store in a cool, dry place for up to 6 months.

245. Licorice Root and Ginger Tea

Ingredients:

- 1 tsp dried licorice root
- 1 tsp fresh ginger slices
- 1 cup boiling water

Instructions:

1. Steep licorice root and ginger in boiling water for 10 minutes.
2. Strain and drink warm.

Uses: Reduces inflammation and supports pain relief.

Storage Tips: Prepare fresh for each use.

246. Ashwagandha and Cinnamon Energy Tonic

Ingredients:

- 1 tsp ashwagandha powder
- 1/2 tsp cinnamon powder
- 1 cup warm milk

Instructions:

1. Mix ashwagandha and cinnamon into warm milk.
2. Stir well and drink.

Uses: Supports chronic fatigue and pain relief.

Storage Tips: Consume immediately.

247. Lemon Balm and Mint Compress

Ingredients:

- 1 tbsp dried lemon balm leaves
- 1 tbsp dried mint leaves
- 1 liter hot water

Instructions:

1. Steep lemon balm and mint in hot water for 10 minutes.
2. Soak a cloth in the mixture and apply to painful areas.

Uses: Reduces inflammation and calms nerve pain.

Storage Tips: Use immediately.

248. Clove and Cinnamon Massage Oil

Ingredients:

- 1/4 cup sweet almond oil
- 3 drops clove essential oil
- 3 drops cinnamon essential oil

Instructions:

1. Combine all ingredients in a bottle.
2. Massage onto joints and muscles.

Uses: Provides warmth and relieves deep pain.

Storage Tips: Store in a cool, dark place for up to 3 months.

249. Black Pepper and Ginger Muscle Rub

Ingredients:

- 1/4 cup coconut oil
- 1 tsp black pepper powder
- 1 tsp fresh ginger juice

Instructions:

1. Heat coconut oil with black pepper and ginger for 5 minutes.
2. Strain and store in a jar.

Uses: Improves circulation and soothes muscular pain.

Storage Tips: Store in a sealed container for up to 1 month.

250. Holy Basil and Turmeric Tea

Ingredients:

- 1 tsp dried holy basil leaves
- 1/2 tsp turmeric powder
- 1 cup boiling water

Instructions:

1. Steep holy basil and turmeric in boiling water for 10 minutes.
2. Strain and drink warm.

Uses: Reduces inflammation and chronic pain.

Storage Tips: Consume immediately.

Creating Anti-Inflammatory Blends

Inflammation is the body's natural response to injury or illness, but chronic inflammation can lead to discomfort, pain, and long-term health issues. Herbal remedies offer a natural, gentle approach to combating inflammation. By using the anti-inflammatory properties of herbs such as turmeric, ginger, chamomile, and rosemary, you can create blends that soothe discomfort and promote healing.

This chapter focuses on 15 anti-inflammatory blends, including teas, oils, and topical applications. These recipes are designed to target inflammation at its source, whether it's joint pain, skin irritation, or internal discomfort. By integrating these remedies into your routine, you can harness the power of herbs to reduce inflammation and enhance your overall well-being.

251. Turmeric and Ginger Anti-Inflammatory Tea

Ingredients:

- 1 tsp turmeric powder
- 1 tsp fresh ginger slices
- 1 cup boiling water

Instructions:

1. Steep turmeric and ginger in boiling water for 10 minutes.
2. Strain and drink warm.

Uses: Reduces joint inflammation and supports overall wellness.

Storage Tips: Prepare fresh for each use.

252. Rosemary and Chamomile Relaxation Tea

Ingredients:

- 1 tsp dried rosemary leaves
- 1 tsp dried chamomile flowers
- 1 cup boiling water

Instructions:

1. Steep rosemary and chamomile in boiling water for 5–7 minutes.
2. Strain and drink warm.

Uses: Soothes inflammation and calms the mind.

Storage Tips: Drink fresh.

253. Peppermint and Basil Infused Oil

Ingredients:

- 1/4 cup olive oil
- 1 tsp dried peppermint leaves
- 1 tsp dried basil leaves

Instructions:

1. Heat olive oil with peppermint and basil over low heat for 10 minutes.
2. Strain and store in a clean bottle.
3. Massage onto inflamed areas.

Uses: Reduces muscle inflammation and soothes pain.

Storage Tips: Store in a dark, cool place for up to 3 months.

254. Clove and Cinnamon Warming Blend

Ingredients:

- 1/4 cup coconut oil
- 1/2 tsp clove powder
- 1/2 tsp cinnamon powder

Instructions:

1. Heat coconut oil with clove and cinnamon for 5 minutes.
2. Strain and store in a small jar.
3. Apply to sore joints and muscles.

Uses: Provides warmth and relieves deep-seated inflammation.

Storage Tips: Store in a sealed jar for up to 1 month.

255. Turmeric and Black Pepper Tonic

Ingredients:

- 1/2 tsp turmeric powder
- 1/4 tsp black pepper
- 1 cup warm almond milk

Instructions:

1. Mix turmeric and black pepper into warm almond milk.
2. Stir well and drink before bedtime.

Uses: Reduces systemic inflammation and promotes relaxation.

Storage Tips: Consume immediately.

256. Ginger and Lemongrass Compress

Ingredients:

- 1 tbsp grated fresh ginger
- 1 tbsp dried lemongrass
- 1 liter hot water

Instructions:

1. Add ginger and lemongrass to hot water.
2. Soak a cloth in the mixture and apply to inflamed areas.

Uses: Eases swelling and improves circulation.

Storage Tips: Use fresh for each application.

257. Calendula and Lavender Healing Oil

Ingredients:

- 1/4 cup calendula-infused oil
- 5 drops lavender essential oil

Instructions:

1. Mix calendula oil and lavender essential oil.
2. Apply to irritated or inflamed skin.

Uses: Reduces redness and promotes skin healing.

Storage Tips: Store in a dark glass bottle for up to 6 months.

258. Holy Basil (Tulsi) Tea

Ingredients:

- 1 tsp dried holy basil leaves
- 1 cup boiling water

Instructions:

1. Steep tulsi leaves in boiling water for 7 minutes.
2. Strain and drink warm.

Uses: Alleviates inflammation and supports respiratory health.

Storage Tips: Consume immediately.

259. Arnica and Peppermint Massage Balm

Ingredients:

- 1/4 cup arnica-infused oil
- 5 drops peppermint essential oil
- 2 tbsp beeswax

Instructions:

1. Melt beeswax and mix with arnica oil and peppermint essential oil.
2. Pour into a jar and let cool.
3. Use as needed on sore areas.

Uses: Relieves muscle inflammation and provides a cooling effect.

Storage Tips: Keep in a sealed container for up to 3 months.

260. Licorice Root and Ginger Anti-Inflammatory Tea

Ingredients:

- 1 tsp dried licorice root
- 1 tsp fresh ginger slices
- 1 cup boiling water

Instructions:

1. Steep licorice root and ginger in boiling water for 10 minutes.
2. Strain and drink warm.

Uses: Soothes internal inflammation and supports digestive health.

Storage Tips: Prepare fresh for each use.

261. Eucalyptus and Peppermint Chest Rub

Ingredients:

- 1/4 cup coconut oil
- 5 drops eucalyptus essential oil
- 3 drops peppermint essential oil

Instructions:

1. Mix all ingredients in a small jar.
2. Rub onto the chest or inflamed areas.

Uses: Reduces inflammation and soothes respiratory discomfort.

Storage Tips: Store in a cool, dry place for up to 2 months.

262. Rosemary and Lemon Peel Compress

Ingredients:

- 1 tbsp dried rosemary leaves
- 1 tbsp fresh lemon peel
- 1 liter hot water

Instructions:

1. Steep rosemary and lemon peel in hot water for 10 minutes.
2. Soak a cloth and apply to affected areas.

Uses: Reduces swelling and promotes circulation.

Storage Tips: Use immediately.

263. Ashwagandha and Turmeric Golden Milk

Ingredients:

- 1/2 tsp ashwagandha powder
- 1/2 tsp turmeric powder
- 1 cup warm coconut milk

Instructions:

1. Mix ashwagandha and turmeric into warm coconut milk.
2. Stir well and drink.

Uses: Reduces systemic inflammation and supports joint health.

Storage Tips: Consume immediately.

264. Mint and Basil Cooling Gel

Ingredients:

- 1/4 cup aloe vera gel
- 1 tsp dried mint leaves
- 1 tsp dried basil leaves

Instructions:

1. Heat aloe vera gel with mint and basil on low heat for 10 minutes.
2. Strain and store in a jar.
3. Apply to inflamed skin.

Uses: Cools irritation and reduces swelling.

Storage Tips: Store in the refrigerator for up to 1 month.

265. Clove and Ginger Soothing Oil

Ingredients:

- 1/4 cup sesame oil
- 1/2 tsp clove powder
- 1 tsp fresh ginger juice

Instructions:

1. Heat sesame oil with clove and ginger for 5 minutes.
2. Strain and store in a bottle.
3. Massage onto inflamed areas.

Uses: Reduces deep inflammation and soothes pain.

Storage Tips: Store in a dark container for up to 1 month.

Remedies for Headaches and Migraines

Headaches and migraines can disrupt daily life, causing discomfort and reducing productivity. While over-the-counter medications can provide relief, they often come with side effects. Herbal remedies offer a natural alternative, targeting the root causes of headaches, such as tension, inflammation, or hormonal imbalances. By using herbs with calming, anti-inflammatory, and circulatory properties, you can alleviate pain and prevent recurring headaches.

This chapter presents 15 effective remedies for headaches and migraines, including teas, compreses, and oils. These recipes focus on relieving pain, reducing stress, and calming the nervous system. Each remedy is easy to prepare and uses accessible, natural ingredients to provide gentle yet effective relief.

266. Peppermint and Lavender Headache Balm

Ingredients:

- 1/4 cup coconut oil
- 5 drops peppermint essential oil
- 5 drops lavender essential oil

Instructions:

1. Melt coconut oil and mix in essential oils.
2. Store in a small jar.
3. Massage onto temples and neck during headaches.

Uses: Reduces tension and provides cooling relief.

Storage Tips: Store in a cool, dry place for up to 3 months.

267. Ginger and Lemon Migraine Tea

Ingredients:

- 1 tsp fresh ginger slices
- 1 tsp fresh lemon juice
- 1 cup boiling water

Instructions:

1. Steep ginger in boiling water for 10 minutes.
2. Strain, add lemon juice, and drink warm.

Uses: Reduces inflammation and soothes migraine pain.

Storage Tips: Prepare fresh for each use.

268. Chamomile and Peppermint Compress

Ingredients:

- 1 tsp dried chamomile flowers
- 1 tsp dried peppermint leaves
- 1 liter hot water

Instructions:

1. Steep chamomile and peppermint in hot water for 10 minutes.
2. Soak a cloth in the infusion and apply to the forehead.

Uses: Relieves tension and calms the mind.

Storage Tips: Use immediately.

269. Rosemary and Clove Massage Oil

Ingredients:

- 1/4 cup almond oil
- 3 drops rosemary essential oil
- 1 drop clove essential oil

Instructions:

1. Mix all ingredients in a bottle.
2. Massage onto temples, neck, and shoulders.

Uses: Improves circulation and relieves headache pain.

Storage Tips: Store in a dark glass bottle for up to 6 months.

270. Holy Basil (Tulsi) Stress Relief Tea

Ingredients:

- 1 tsp dried holy basil leaves
- 1 cup boiling water

Instructions:

1. Steep holy basil in boiling water for 7 minutes.
2. Strain and drink warm.

Uses: Relieves stress-induced headaches and promotes relaxation.

Storage Tips: Consume fresh.

271. Eucalyptus Steam for Sinus Headaches

Ingredients:

- 5 drops eucalyptus essential oil
- 1 liter boiling water

Instructions:

1. Add eucalyptus oil to boiling water.
2. Inhale the steam for 5–10 minutes.

Uses: Clears sinus congestion and relieves headaches.

Storage Tips: Use immediately.

272. Lavender and Lemon Soothing Tea

Ingredients:

- 1 tsp dried lavender flowers
- 1 tsp fresh lemon juice
- 1 cup boiling water

Instructions:

1. Steep lavender in boiling water for 5 minutes.
2. Add lemon juice and sip slowly.

Uses: Calms the nervous system and eases headache pain.

Storage Tips: Drink fresh.

273. Ginger and Turmeric Anti-Inflammatory Paste

Ingredients:

- 1 tsp turmeric powder
- 1 tsp fresh ginger juice
- 1 tbsp honey

Instructions:

1. Mix all ingredients into a paste.
2. Take 1/2 teaspoon as needed.

Uses: Reduces inflammation and soothes migraines.

Storage Tips: Store in a sealed jar for up to 1 week.

274. Clary Sage and Lavender Oil Blend

Ingredients:

- 1/4 cup jojoba oil
- 3 drops clary sage essential oil
- 3 drops lavender essential oil

Instructions:

1. Mix all ingredients in a small bottle.
2. Apply to the wrists, temples, and back of the neck.

Uses: Relieves stress and hormonal headaches.

Storage Tips: Keep in a cool, dark place for up to 3 months.

275. Mint and Basil Cooling Compress

Ingredients:

- 1 tsp dried mint leaves
- 1 tsp dried basil leaves
- 1 liter cold water

Instructions:

1. Steep mint and basil in cold water for 10 minutes.
2. Soak a cloth in the mixture and place on the forehead.

Uses: Provides cooling relief for tension headaches.

Storage Tips: Use fresh for each application.

276. Cinnamon and Honey Migraine Remedy

Ingredients:

- 1/2 tsp cinnamon powder
- 1 tsp honey

Instructions:

1. Mix cinnamon and honey into a paste.
2. Take 1/2 teaspoon at the onset of a migraine.

Uses: Improves blood flow and reduces pain.

Storage Tips: Store in a jar for up to 2 weeks.

277. Rosemary and Lemon Bath Soak

Ingredients:

- 1/2 cup Epsom salt
- 1 tbsp dried rosemary leaves
- 1 tbsp lemon zest

Instructions:

1. Combine all ingredients and add to a warm bath.
2. Soak for 20 minutes.

Uses: Relieves tension and reduces headache pain.

Storage Tips: Store the dry mix in an airtight container for up to 3 months.

278. Licorice Root and Ginger Tea

Ingredients:

- 1 tsp dried licorice root
- 1 tsp fresh ginger slices
- 1 cup boiling water

Instructions:

1. Steep licorice root and ginger in boiling water for 10 minutes.
2. Strain and drink warm.

Uses: Reduces inflammation and soothes migraines.

Storage Tips: Prepare fresh for each use.

279. Peppermint and Chamomile Pillow Spray

Ingredients:

- 1/2 cup distilled water
- 5 drops peppermint essential oil
- 5 drops chamomile essential oil

Instructions:

1. Mix ingredients in a spray bottle.
2. Lightly spray on your pillow before bedtime.

Uses: Promotes relaxation and prevents nighttime headaches.

Storage Tips: Store in a cool, dry place for up to 1 month.

280. Black Pepper and Ginger Compress

Ingredients:

- 1 tsp black pepper powder
- 1 tsp grated fresh ginger
- 1 liter warm water

Instructions:

1. Add black pepper and ginger to warm water.
2. Soak a cloth and place it on the back of the neck.

Uses: Reduces tension and relieves migraines.

Storage Tips: Use fresh for each application.

BOOK 11

HERBAL SOLUTIONS FOR THE IMMUNE SYSTEM

A strong immune system is the cornerstone of good health, protecting the body from illnesses and infections. While modern medicine plays a vital role in addressing serious conditions, natural remedies can enhance the immune system's resilience, helping to prevent sickness and support recovery. Herbs offer a gentle yet powerful way to boost immunity, promoting overall well-being through adaptogens, nutrient-rich tonics, and daily health practices.

This book explores the wide array of herbal solutions available to strengthen the immune system naturally. From adaptogens that promote long-term resilience to tinctures and tonics for cold and flu prevention, each chapter focuses on practical, evidence-based approaches to bolstering immunity. You'll also learn how to incorporate herbal nutrition into your recovery routine and establish daily habits that nurture your body's defenses.

Whether you're looking to stay healthy during flu season or create a lifestyle that supports year-round immunity, this book provides easy-to-follow recipes and actionable advice. With accessible ingredients and time-tested techniques, these herbal solutions empower you to take charge of your health naturally, fostering a robust immune system for yourself and your loved ones.

Adaptogens for Long-Term Resilience

Adaptogens are a unique class of herbs that help the body adapt to physical, mental, and environmental stressors. Unlike conventional remedies that address specific symptoms, adaptogens work holistically to balance and support the body's systems, particularly the immune, endocrine, and nervous systems. Over time, these herbs can enhance resilience, improve energy levels, and fortify the immune system, making them a cornerstone of natural health.

Herbs such as ashwagandha, holy basil (tulsi), rhodiola, and astragalus have been used for centuries to promote vitality and long-term wellness. These herbs don't act as quick fixes; instead, they build cumulative strength, helping the body respond to stress more effectively and recover from illness more quickly. Incorporating adaptogens into your daily routine can help create a foundation for long-term health and resilience.

This chapter provides 15 recipes featuring adaptogens to support your immune system and overall well-being. From teas and tonics to powders and smoothies, these remedies are easy to prepare and integrate into your lifestyle. With consistent use, you can harness the power of adaptogens to create a balanced, resilient body that thrives in the face of life's challenges.

281. Ashwagandha and Cinnamon Immune Tonic

Ingredients:

- 1 tsp ashwagandha powder
- 1/2 tsp cinnamon powder
- 1 cup warm almond milk

Instructions:

1. Mix ashwagandha and cinnamon into warm almond milk.
2. Stir well and drink before bedtime.

Uses: Reduces stress, supports immunity, and improves sleep.

Storage Tips: Consume immediately.

282. Holy Basil (Tulsi) Stress-Relief Tea

Ingredients:

- 1 tsp dried holy basil leaves
- 1 cup boiling water

Instructions:

1. Steep tulsi leaves in boiling water for 7 minutes.
2. Strain and drink warm.

Uses: Enhances resilience and calms the nervous system.

Storage Tips: Prepare fresh for each use.

283. Astragalus and Ginger Decoction

Ingredients:

- 1 tbsp dried astragalus root
- 1 tsp fresh ginger slices
- 2 cups water

Instructions:

1. Simmer astragalus and ginger in water for 20 minutes.
2. Strain and drink warm.

Uses: Supports immune health and improves energy.

Storage Tips: Consume immediately.

284. Rhodiola and Lemon Energy Tea

Ingredients:

- 1 tsp dried rhodiola root
- 1 tsp fresh lemon juice
- 1 cup boiling water

Instructions:

1. Steep rhodiola root in boiling water for 10 minutes.
2. Strain, add lemon juice, and sip slowly.

Uses: Enhances mental focus and reduces fatigue.

Storage Tips: Drink fresh.

285. Maca and Cacao Smoothie

Ingredients:

- 1 tsp maca powder
- 1 tsp raw cacao powder
- 1 cup almond milk
- 1 tsp honey

Instructions:

1. Blend all ingredients until smooth.
2. Drink as a morning or midday energy boost.

Uses: Boosts energy and balances hormones.

Storage Tips: Consume immediately.

286. Licorice Root and Peppermint Tea

Ingredients:

- 1 tsp dried licorice root
- 1 tsp dried peppermint leaves
- 1 cup boiling water

Instructions:

1. Steep licorice root and peppermint in boiling water for 7 minutes.
2. Strain and drink warm.

Uses: Reduces inflammation and supports the adrenal system.

Storage Tips: Drink fresh.

287. Adaptogen Herbal Blend Powder

Ingredients:

- 1 tbsp ashwagandha powder
- 1 tbsp maca powder
- 1 tbsp rhodiola powder

Instructions:

1. Mix all powders in a jar.
2. Add 1 tsp to smoothies, teas, or soups daily.

Uses: Builds resilience and balances stress responses.

Storage Tips: Store in an airtight container for up to 3 months.

288. Ginseng and Lemonade Elixir

Ingredients:

- 1 tsp ginseng powder
- 1 cup fresh lemonade

Instructions:

1. Stir ginseng powder into lemonade until well combined.
2. Drink chilled.

Uses: Enhances energy and strengthens immunity.

Storage Tips: Consume immediately.

289. Eleuthero and Cinnamon Decoction

Ingredients:

- 1 tsp dried eleuthero root
- 1/2 tsp cinnamon powder
- 2 cups water

Instructions:

1. Simmer eleuthero root and cinnamon in water for 15 minutes.
2. Strain and drink warm.

Uses: Boosts stamina and reduces stress.

Storage Tips: Prepare fresh for each use.

290. Schisandra Berry Immune Tonic

Ingredients:

- 1 tsp dried schisandra berries
- 1 cup boiling water

Instructions:

1. Steep schisandra berries in boiling water for 10 minutes.
2. Strain and sip warm or cool.

Uses: Improves endurance and supports immunity.

Storage Tips: Drink fresh.

291. Turmeric and Holy Basil Golden Milk

Ingredients:

- 1 tsp turmeric powder
- 1/2 tsp holy basil powder
- 1 cup warm coconut milk

Instructions:

1. Mix turmeric and holy basil into warm coconut milk.
2. Stir well and drink before bedtime.

Uses: Reduces inflammation and calms the nervous system.

Storage Tips: Consume immediately.

292. Ashwagandha and Honey Paste

Ingredients:

- 1 tbsp ashwagandha powder
- 1 tbsp raw honey

Instructions:

1. Mix ashwagandha powder and honey into a paste.
2. Take 1/2 teaspoon daily.

Uses: Supports adrenal health and energy.

Storage Tips: Store in a sealed jar for up to 1 week.

293. Rhodiola and Mint Infusion

Ingredients:

- 1 tsp dried rhodiola root
- 1 tsp dried mint leaves
- 1 cup boiling water

Instructions:

1. Steep rhodiola and mint in boiling water for 10 minutes.
2. Strain and drink warm.

Uses: Combats fatigue and enhances focus.

Storage Tips: Drink fresh.

294. Astragalus and Lemon Tonic

Ingredients:

- 1 tsp astragalus powder
- 1 cup fresh lemon water

Instructions:

1. Mix astragalus powder into lemon water.
2. Drink as a morning immune booster.

Uses: Strengthens immunity and promotes energy.

Storage Tips: Consume immediately.

295. Schisandra Berry and Ginger Decoction

Ingredients:

- 1 tsp dried schisandra berries
- 1 tsp fresh ginger slices
- 2 cups water

Instructions:

1. Simmer schisandra berries and ginger in water for 15 minutes.
2. Strain and drink warm.

Uses: Improves circulation and reduces stress.

Storage Tips: Prepare fresh for each use.

Tinctures and Tonics for Cold and Flu Prevention

Cold and flu season often brings with it the discomfort of congestion, fatigue, and a weakened immune system. Herbal tinctures and tonics offer a natural and effective way to prevent illness and bolster your body's defenses. Tinctures, which are concentrated extracts of herbs, provide quick and potent relief, while tonics work to strengthen the immune system over time. Both can be easily made at home and customized to meet individual needs.

This chapter presents 15 herbal tinctures and tonics designed to ward off colds and flu, boost immunity, and reduce the severity of symptoms. Using ingredients like elderberry, echinacea, ginger, and garlic, these remedies are easy to prepare and highly effective. Incorporating them into your wellness routine can help you navigate cold and flu season with confidence and resilience.

296. Elderberry Immune-Boosting Tonic

Ingredients:

- 1 cup fresh or dried elderberries
- 4 cups water
- 1/2 cup raw honey

Instructions:

1. Simmer elderberries in water for 30 minutes.
2. Strain and mix the liquid with honey.
3. Take 1 tablespoon daily during flu season.

Uses: Strengthens immunity and fights viral infections.

Storage Tips: Store in the refrigerator for up to 2 weeks.

297. Echinacea and Ginger Tincture

Ingredients:

- 1/4 cup dried echinacea root
- 1/4 cup fresh ginger slices
- 1 cup glycerin or apple cider vinegar

Instructions:

1. Combine echinacea and ginger in a jar.
2. Cover with glycerin or vinegar.
3. Let steep for 4 weeks, shaking daily. Strain before use.

Uses: Boosts immune function and reduces cold symptoms.

Storage Tips: Store in a dark, cool place for up to 1 year.

298. Garlic and Honey Immune Syrup

Ingredients:

- 5 cloves fresh garlic (crushed)
- 1/2 cup raw honey

Instructions:

1. Mix garlic with honey in a jar.
2. Let sit for 12 hours, then strain.
3. Take 1 teaspoon daily.

Uses: Fights infections and strengthens immunity.

Storage Tips: Refrigerate for up to 2 weeks.

299. Turmeric and Lemon Anti-Inflammatory Tonic

Ingredients:

- 1 tsp turmeric powder
- 1 tsp fresh lemon juice
- 1 cup warm water

Instructions:

1. Mix turmeric and lemon into warm water.
2. Drink in the morning as a preventive tonic.

Uses: Reduces inflammation and supports immunity.

Storage Tips: Prepare fresh for each use.

300. Elderflower and Mint Tea Tonic

Ingredients:

- 1 tsp dried elderflower
- 1 tsp dried mint leaves
- 1 cup boiling water

Instructions:

1. Steep elderflower and mint in boiling water for 10 minutes.
2. Strain and drink warm.

Uses: Soothes the throat and reduces congestion.

Storage Tips: Consume immediately.

301. Ginger and Lemon Immune Shot

Ingredients:

- 1 tsp fresh ginger juice
- 1 tsp fresh lemon juice
- 1 tbsp raw honey

Instructions:

1. Mix all ingredients into a small cup.
2. Drink in one shot for quick immune support.

Uses: Combats colds and supports recovery.

Storage Tips: Prepare fresh for each use.

302. Echinacea and Elderberry Tincture

Ingredients:

- 1/4 cup dried echinacea root
- 1/4 cup dried elderberries
- 1 cup glycerin or vinegar

Instructions:

1. Combine echinacea and elderberries in a jar.
2. Cover with glycerin or vinegar and steep for 4 weeks.
3. Strain and store.

Uses: Prevents colds and supports the immune system.

Storage Tips: Store in a dark, cool place for up to 1 year.

303. Apple Cider Vinegar and Garlic Tonic

Ingredients:

- 1/2 cup apple cider vinegar
- 5 cloves fresh garlic (crushed)
- 1/4 cup raw honey

Instructions:

1. Mix all ingredients in a jar.
2. Let steep for 3 days, then strain.
3. Take 1 tablespoon daily.

Uses: Boosts immunity and fights infections.

Storage Tips: Store in the refrigerator for up to 1 month.

304. Cinnamon and Honey Immunity Paste

Ingredients:

- 1 tsp cinnamon powder
- 1 tbsp raw honey

Instructions:

1. Mix cinnamon and honey into a paste.
2. Take 1/2 teaspoon daily.

Uses: Reduces inflammation and supports overall health.

Storage Tips: Store in an airtight jar for up to 2 weeks.

305. Licorice Root and Ginger Tonic

Ingredients:

- 1 tsp dried licorice root
- 1 tsp fresh ginger slices
- 1 cup boiling water

Instructions:

1. Steep licorice root and ginger in boiling water for 10 minutes.
2. Strain and drink warm.

Uses: Soothes the throat and supports respiratory health.

Storage Tips: Prepare fresh for each use.

306. Lemon and Cayenne Immunity Shot

Ingredients:

- 1 tsp fresh lemon juice
- 1/4 tsp cayenne powder
- 1 tsp raw honey

Instructions:

1. Mix all ingredients into a small cup.
2. Drink in one shot for quick relief.

Uses: Boosts circulation and supports the immune system.

Storage Tips: Prepare fresh for each use.

307. Holy Basil (Tulsi) Immune Tea

Ingredients:

- 1 tsp dried holy basil leaves
- 1 cup boiling water

Instructions:

1. Steep holy basil in boiling water for 7 minutes.
2. Strain and sip slowly.

Uses: Reduces stress and enhances immunity.

Storage Tips: Consume immediately.

308. Ginger and Clove Cold Tonic

Ingredients:

- 1 tsp fresh ginger slices
- 2 cloves (crushed)
- 1 cup boiling water

Instructions:

1. Steep ginger and cloves in boiling water for 10 minutes.
2. Strain and drink warm.

Uses: Reduces congestion and soothes a sore throat.

Storage Tips: Drink fresh.

309. Turmeric and Black Pepper Golden Milk

Ingredients:

- 1 tsp turmeric powder
- 1/4 tsp black pepper
- 1 cup warm coconut milk

Instructions:

1. Mix turmeric and black pepper into warm coconut milk.
2. Stir well and drink before bedtime.

Uses: Reduces inflammation and supports recovery.

Storage Tips: Consume immediately.

310. Elderberry and Honey Syrup

Ingredients:

- 1 cup fresh elderberries
- 4 cups water
- 1/2 cup raw honey

Instructions:

1. Simmer elderberries in water for 30 minutes.
2. Strain and mix the liquid with honey.
3. Take 1 teaspoon daily.

Uses: Boosts immunity and prevents colds.

Storage Tips: Refrigerate for up to 2 weeks.

Supporting Recovery with Herbal Nutrition

Recovery from illness or fatigue requires more than just rest; it calls for proper nutrition to restore energy, strengthen immunity, and rebuild the body's natural defenses. Herbs are not only medicinal but also nutritional powerhouses, packed with vitamins, minerals, and antioxidants that aid in recovery. When incorporated into meals, teas, or smoothies, these herbs can accelerate healing and rejuvenate the body.

This chapter focuses on 15 herbal recipes that combine nourishment with medicinal properties to support recovery. Using ingredients like nettle, ginger, turmeric, and garlic, these remedies are designed to replenish nutrients, reduce inflammation, and promote overall well-being. These recipes are simple to prepare and can be seamlessly integrated into your daily diet, helping you bounce back stronger and healthier.

311. Nettle and Spinach Recovery Soup

Ingredients:

- 1 cup fresh nettle leaves (or 1/2 cup dried)
- 1 cup fresh spinach
- 2 cups vegetable broth
- 1 clove garlic (minced)

Instructions:

1. Sauté garlic in a pot until fragrant.
2. Add broth, nettle, and spinach, and simmer for 10 minutes.
3. Blend until smooth and serve warm.

Uses: Provides iron, calcium, and immune-boosting nutrients.

Storage Tips: Store in the refrigerator for up to 3 days.

312. Turmeric and Ginger Healing Smoothie

Ingredients:

- 1 tsp turmeric powder
- 1 tsp fresh ginger juice
- 1 banana
- 1 cup almond milk

Instructions:

1. Blend all ingredients until smooth.
2. Drink immediately as a refreshing recovery boost.

Uses: Reduces inflammation and promotes digestion.

Storage Tips: Consume fresh.

313. Garlic and Lemon Immune-Boosting Broth

Ingredients:

- 5 cloves garlic (crushed)
- 1/2 lemon (juiced)
- 4 cups vegetable broth

Instructions:

1. Simmer garlic in broth for 20 minutes.
2. Add lemon juice before serving.

Uses: Fights infections and supports respiratory health.

Storage Tips: Refrigerate for up to 3 days.

314. Oatmeal with Chia and Cinnamon

Ingredients:

- 1/2 cup rolled oats
- 1 tbsp chia seeds

- 1/2 tsp cinnamon powder
- 1 cup almond milk

Instructions:

1. Cook oats and chia seeds in almond milk.
2. Sprinkle cinnamon on top before serving.

Uses: Provides sustained energy and reduces inflammation.

Storage Tips: Consume immediately.

315. Holy Basil (Tulsi) and Honey Tea

Ingredients:

- 1 tsp dried holy basil leaves
- 1 tsp raw honey
- 1 cup boiling water

Instructions:

1. Steep holy basil in boiling water for 7 minutes.
2. Strain and stir in honey.

Uses: Reduces stress and supports immune recovery.

Storage Tips: Drink fresh.

316. Nettle and Lemon Detox Water

Ingredients:

- 1 tbsp dried nettle leaves
- 1/2 lemon (sliced)
- 1 liter water

Instructions:

1. Steep nettle leaves in hot water for 10 minutes.
2. Add lemon slices and let cool.

Uses: Detoxifies and replenishes essential nutrients.

Storage Tips: Refrigerate and consume within 24 hours.

317. Ginger and Carrot Healing Juice

Ingredients:

- 1 cup fresh carrot juice
- 1 tsp fresh ginger juice
- 1/2 tsp turmeric powder

Instructions:

1. Combine carrot juice, ginger, and turmeric.
2. Stir well and serve chilled.

Uses: Boosts immunity and reduces inflammation.

Storage Tips: Consume immediately.

318. Fenugreek and Honey Energy Paste

Ingredients:

- 1 tsp fenugreek powder
- 1 tbsp raw honey

Instructions:

1. Mix fenugreek powder with honey into a paste.
2. Take 1 teaspoon daily.

Uses: Strengthens energy levels and promotes recovery.

Storage Tips: Store in an airtight jar for up to 1 week.

319. Beetroot and Mint Smoothie

Ingredients:

- 1/2 cup fresh beetroot juice
- 1/4 cup fresh mint leaves
- 1 cup coconut water

Instructions:

1. Blend beetroot juice, mint, and coconut water until smooth.
2. Serve chilled.

Uses: Supports blood flow and reduces fatigue.

Storage Tips: Consume fresh.

320. Turmeric and Black Pepper Tonic

Ingredients:

- 1 tsp turmeric powder
- 1/4 tsp black pepper
- 1 cup warm water

Instructions:

1. Mix turmeric and black pepper into warm water.
2. Stir well and drink.

Uses: Reduces inflammation and supports immunity.

Storage Tips: Prepare fresh for each use.

321. Cilantro and Lemon Pesto

Ingredients:

- 1 cup fresh cilantro leaves
- 1/2 lemon (juiced)
- 2 tbsp olive oil

Instructions:

1. Blend cilantro, lemon juice, and olive oil into a smooth paste.
2. Use as a topping for soups or salads.

Uses: Detoxifies and provides antioxidants.

Storage Tips: Refrigerate for up to 3 days.

322. Chamomile and Apple Cider Vinegar Tonic

Ingredients:

- 1 tsp dried chamomile flowers
- 1 tbsp apple cider vinegar
- 1 cup warm water

Instructions:

1. Steep chamomile in warm water for 5 minutes.
2. Add apple cider vinegar and drink warm.

Uses: Calms digestion and promotes relaxation.

Storage Tips: Drink fresh.

323. Ginger and Garlic Healing Rice

Ingredients:

- 1 cup cooked rice
- 1 clove garlic (minced)
- 1 tsp fresh ginger (grated)

Instructions:

1. Sauté garlic and ginger in olive oil.
2. Mix with cooked rice and serve warm.

Uses: Replenishes energy and supports digestion.

Storage Tips: Consume immediately.

324. Ashwagandha and Cinnamon Tonic

Ingredients:

- 1 tsp ashwagandha powder
- 1/2 tsp cinnamon powder
- 1 cup warm milk (dairy or plant-based)

Instructions:

1. Mix ashwagandha and cinnamon into warm milk.
2. Stir well and drink before bedtime.

Uses: Reduces fatigue and enhances recovery.

Storage Tips: Consume immediately.

325. Lemon and Ginger Detox Tea

Ingredients:

- 1 tsp fresh ginger slices
- 1/2 lemon (juiced)
- 1 cup boiling water

Instructions:

1. Steep ginger in boiling water for 5 minutes.
2. Add lemon juice and sip warm.

Uses: Cleanses the system and boosts immunity.

Storage Tips: Drink fresh.

Daily Practices for Immune Strength

A strong immune system is built on consistent, supportive habits that nurture the body and enhance resilience against illness. Incorporating herbs into daily practices not only strengthens the immune system but also promotes overall well-being. Small, mindful steps like drinking herbal teas, preparing nutrient-rich meals, and using natural remedies can create a foundation for lasting health.

This chapter offers 15 practical, easy-to-follow herbal routines to fortify immunity every day. These remedies range from immune-boosting teas and tonics to herbal oils and nutrient-packed recipes. By making these practices part of your lifestyle, you can enhance your body's natural defenses and create a robust immune system that serves you year-round.

326. Morning Nettle Tea Ritual

Ingredients:

- 1 tsp dried nettle leaves
- 1 cup boiling water

Instructions:

1. Steep nettle leaves in boiling water for 5–7 minutes.
2. Strain and drink warm every morning.

Uses: Provides vitamins and minerals to start the day.

Storage Tips: Drink fresh.

327. Turmeric and Honey Immunity Shot

Ingredients:

- 1 tsp turmeric powder
- 1 tsp raw honey
- 1 tbsp warm water

Instructions:

1. Mix turmeric and honey into warm water.
2. Drink as a quick morning boost.

Uses: Reduces inflammation and supports immunity.

Storage Tips: Prepare fresh for each use.

328. Garlic and Lemon Morning Tonic

Ingredients:

- 1 clove garlic (crushed)
- 1/2 lemon (juiced)
- 1 cup warm water

Instructions:

1. Mix garlic and lemon juice into warm water.
2. Sip slowly before breakfast.

Uses: Boosts immunity and supports digestion.

Storage Tips: Consume immediately.

329. Ginger and Cinnamon Midday Tea

Ingredients:

- 1 tsp fresh ginger slices
- 1/2 tsp cinnamon powder
- 1 cup boiling water

Instructions:

1. Steep ginger and cinnamon in boiling water for 10 minutes.
2. Strain and enjoy as a midday tea.

Uses: Improves circulation and strengthens immune defenses.

Storage Tips: Drink fresh.

330. Chamomile and Holy Basil Evening Tea

Ingredients:

- 1 tsp dried chamomile flowers
- 1 tsp dried holy basil leaves
- 1 cup boiling water

Instructions:

1. Steep chamomile and holy basil in boiling water for 7 minutes.
2. Strain and sip warm before bedtime.

Uses: Promotes relaxation and supports night-time recovery.

Storage Tips: Consume immediately.

331. Echinacea and Mint Infused Water

Ingredients:

- 1 tsp dried echinacea leaves
- 1 tsp dried mint leaves
- 1 liter water

Instructions:

1. Add echinacea and mint to water and let steep overnight.
2. Drink throughout the day.

Uses: Provides continuous immune support.

Storage Tips: Refrigerate and consume within 24 hours.

332. Ashwagandha and Cinnamon Evening Milk

Ingredients:

- 1 tsp ashwagandha powder
- 1/2 tsp cinnamon powder
- 1 cup warm almond milk

Instructions:

1. Mix ashwagandha and cinnamon into warm almond milk.
2. Drink before bedtime.

Uses: Reduces stress and enhances immune recovery.

Storage Tips: Consume fresh.

333. Daily Green Smoothie with Herbs

Ingredients:

- 1 cup spinach
- 1 tsp spirulina powder
- 1 tsp fresh ginger juice
- 1 cup coconut water

Instructions:

1. Blend all ingredients until smooth.
2. Drink as a midday snack.

Uses: Replenishes nutrients and supports energy levels.

Storage Tips: Consume immediately.

334. Lemon and Honey Morning Hydration

Ingredients:

- 1/2 lemon (juiced)
- 1 tsp raw honey
- 1 cup warm water

Instructions:

1. Mix lemon juice and honey into warm water.
2. Drink as the first thing in the morning.

Uses: Detoxifies and supports immunity.

Storage Tips: Prepare fresh for each use.

335. Garlic and Olive Oil for Cooking

Ingredients:

- 5 cloves garlic (minced)
- 1/2 cup olive oil

Instructions:

1. Mix garlic and olive oil in a jar.
2. Use as a base for cooking or drizzling over meals.

Uses: Adds flavor and boosts immune health.

Storage Tips: Store in the refrigerator for up to 1 week.

336. Calendula and Mint Foot Soak

Ingredients:

- 1 tbsp dried calendula petals
- 1 tsp dried mint leaves
- 1 liter warm water

Instructions:

1. Steep calendula and mint in warm water for 10 minutes.
2. Soak your feet for 15–20 minutes.

Uses: Reduces stress and enhances circulation.

Storage Tips: Use fresh for each session.

337. Ginger and Black Pepper Detox Tea

Ingredients:

- 1 tsp fresh ginger slices
- 1/4 tsp black pepper
- 1 cup boiling water

Instructions:

1. Steep ginger and black pepper in boiling water for 7 minutes.
2. Strain and drink warm.

Uses: Supports digestion and detoxification.

Storage Tips: Consume immediately.

338. Daily Turmeric Paste

Ingredients:

- 1/4 cup turmeric powder
- 1/2 cup water

Instructions:

1. Simmer turmeric powder in water until it forms a paste.
2. Add 1/4 teaspoon to teas, smoothies, or meals daily.

Uses: Reduces inflammation and strengthens immunity.

Storage Tips: Refrigerate paste for up to 1 month.

339. Eucalyptus and Lavender Home Steam

Ingredients:

- 5 drops eucalyptus essential oil
- 5 drops lavender essential oil
- 1 liter boiling water

Instructions:

1. Add essential oils to boiling water.
2. Inhale steam for 5–10 minutes.

Uses: Clears airways and supports respiratory health.

Storage Tips: Use immediately.

340. Black Tea with Lemon and Ginger

Ingredients:

- 1 tsp black tea leaves
- 1 tsp fresh ginger slices
- 1/2 lemon (juiced)

Instructions:

1. Steep black tea and ginger in boiling water for 5 minutes.
2. Strain, add lemon juice, and sip warm.

Uses: Provides antioxidants and strengthens immunity.

Storage Tips: Drink fresh.

BOOK 12

WOMEN'S HEALTH THROUGH HERBAL REMEDIES

Women's health is a multifaceted journey that encompasses hormonal changes, reproductive health, and overall well-being at every stage of life. From managing the natural cycles of menstruation to navigating the challenges of menopause, herbs offer gentle yet powerful support for women's unique needs. Traditional herbal remedies have long been used to alleviate discomfort, promote balance, and enhance vitality, providing natural solutions for common health concerns.

This book explores the role of herbs in supporting women's health, offering practical guidance and remedies tailored to each stage of life. From teas and tonics for menstrual relief to herbs that balance hormones, this collection of remedies is designed to empower women to take charge of their well-being. It also provides nurturing solutions for pregnancy, postpartum recovery, and the transitions of menopause, ensuring that every woman can feel supported and cared for naturally.

With safe, evidence-based practices and time-tested recipes, this book serves as a comprehensive guide to using herbal remedies for women's health. Whether you're looking to manage everyday challenges or embrace long-term wellness, these natural solutions provide the tools you need to thrive at every stage of life. Let's celebrate and nurture the unique power of women's health with the wisdom of nature.

Supporting Menstrual Health Naturally

Menstrual health is a vital aspect of overall well-being for women, yet it is often accompanied by discomforts such as cramps, bloating, mood swings, and fatigue. While these symptoms are natural, they can significantly affect daily life. Herbal remedies provide a gentle and effective way to alleviate these issues by supporting hormonal balance, reducing inflammation, and promoting relaxation.

Herbs like ginger, chamomile, red raspberry leaf, and fennel have been used for centuries to ease menstrual discomfort. These remedies work to soothe cramps, regulate cycles, and improve overall menstrual health. Incorporating them into your routine can help you manage symptoms naturally and foster a more harmonious relationship with your cycle.

This chapter introduces 15 herbal remedies designed to support menstrual health. From teas and tonics to oils and compresses, these recipes are simple to prepare and highly effective. By embracing these natural solutions, you can create a toolkit for comfort and balance throughout your cycle.

341. Ginger and Turmeric Cramp-Relief Tea

Ingredients:

- 1 tsp fresh ginger slices
- 1/2 tsp turmeric powder
- 1 cup boiling water

Instructions:

1. Steep ginger and turmeric in boiling water for 10 minutes.
2. Strain and drink warm.

Uses: Reduces inflammation and soothes cramps.

Storage Tips: Prepare fresh for each use.

342. Red Raspberry Leaf Menstrual Tea

Ingredients:

- 1 tsp dried red raspberry leaves
- 1 cup boiling water

Instructions:

1. Steep red raspberry leaves in boiling water for 5–7 minutes.
2. Strain and drink warm.

Uses: Strengthens the uterus and supports hormonal balance.

Storage Tips: Consume immediately.

343. Fennel and Chamomile Relaxation Tea

Ingredients:

- 1 tsp fennel seeds
- 1 tsp dried chamomile flowers
- 1 cup boiling water

Instructions:

1. Steep fennel seeds and chamomile in boiling water for 7 minutes.
2. Strain and sip slowly.

Uses: Relieves bloating and promotes relaxation.

Storage Tips: Drink fresh.

344. Cinnamon and Honey Menstrual Tonic

Ingredients:

- 1/2 tsp cinnamon powder
- 1 tsp raw honey
- 1 cup warm water

Instructions:

1. Mix cinnamon and honey into warm water.
2. Drink daily during your cycle.

Uses: Improves circulation and reduces cramping.

Storage Tips: Prepare fresh for each use.

345. Lavender and Peppermint Compress

Ingredients:

- 5 drops lavender essential oil
- 5 drops peppermint essential oil
- 1 liter warm water

Instructions:

1. Add essential oils to warm water.
2. Soak a cloth in the mixture and apply to the lower abdomen.

Uses: Relieves cramps and promotes relaxation.

Storage Tips: Use immediately.

346. Ginger and Lemon Detox Tea

Ingredients:

- 1 tsp fresh ginger slices
- 1 tsp fresh lemon juice
- 1 cup boiling water

Instructions:

1. Steep ginger in boiling water for 10 minutes.
2. Add lemon juice and drink warm.

Uses: Reduces bloating and supports digestion.

Storage Tips: Drink fresh.

347. Clary Sage and Almond Oil Massage Blend

Ingredients:

- 1/4 cup almond oil
- 5 drops clary sage essential oil

Instructions:

1. Mix almond oil and clary sage oil in a bottle.
2. Massage onto the lower abdomen.

Uses: Reduces cramping and relaxes muscles.

Storage Tips: Store in a dark glass bottle for up to 6 months.

348. Holy Basil (Tulsi) Stress-Relief Tea

Ingredients:

- 1 tsp dried holy basil leaves
- 1 cup boiling water

Instructions:

1. Steep holy basil in boiling water for 7 minutes.
2. Strain and sip slowly.

Uses: Reduces stress and balances hormones.

Storage Tips: Prepare fresh for each use.

349. Peppermint and Chamomile Sleep Tea

Ingredients:

- 1 tsp dried peppermint leaves
- 1 tsp dried chamomile flowers
- 1 cup boiling water

Instructions:

1. Steep peppermint and chamomile in boiling water for 5 minutes.
2. Strain and drink before bedtime.

Uses: Improves sleep and relieves tension.

Storage Tips: Consume immediately.

350. Licorice Root Hormone-Balancing Tea

Ingredients:

- 1 tsp dried licorice root

- 1 cup boiling water

Instructions:

1. Steep licorice root in boiling water for 10 minutes.
2. Strain and drink warm.

Uses: Supports hormonal balance and reduces inflammation.

Storage Tips: Drink fresh.

351. Rosemary and Lavender Bath Soak

Ingredients:

- 1/4 cup dried rosemary leaves
- 1/4 cup dried lavender flowers
- 1 cup Epsom salt

Instructions:

1. Combine all ingredients and add to a warm bath.
2. Soak for 20 minutes.

Uses: Relieves tension and reduces cramps.

Storage Tips: Store dry mix in an airtight container for up to 3 months.

352. Turmeric and Cinnamon Golden Milk

Ingredients:

- 1/2 tsp turmeric powder
- 1/2 tsp cinnamon powder
- 1 cup warm coconut milk

Instructions:

1. Mix turmeric and cinnamon into warm coconut milk.
2. Drink before bedtime.

Uses: Reduces inflammation and promotes relaxation.

Storage Tips: Consume fresh.

353. Dill Seed and Honey Tea

Ingredients:

- 1 tsp dill seeds
- 1 tsp honey
- 1 cup boiling water

Instructions:

1. Steep dill seeds in boiling water for 10 minutes.
2. Strain and stir in honey.

Uses: Relieves bloating and soothes cramps.

Storage Tips: Drink fresh.

354. Calendula and Peppermint Skin Compress

Ingredients:

- 1 tbsp dried calendula petals
- 1 tsp dried peppermint leaves
- 1 liter warm water

Instructions:

1. Steep calendula and peppermint in warm water for 10 minutes.
2. Soak a cloth in the mixture and apply to the skin.

Uses: Soothes skin irritations and relaxes muscles.

Storage Tips: Use immediately.

355. Cinnamon and Clove Herbal Tea

Ingredients:

- 1/2 tsp cinnamon powder
- 2 cloves
- 1 cup boiling water

Instructions:

1. Steep cinnamon and cloves in boiling water for 10 minutes.
2. Strain and drink warm.

Uses: Improves circulation and reduces pain.

Storage Tips: Consume immediately.

Managing Hormonal Balance with Herbs

Hormonal balance plays a critical role in women's overall health, affecting energy levels, mood, skin health, and reproductive well-being. Hormonal imbalances can arise due to stress, aging, diet, or environmental factors, leading to symptoms like fatigue, mood swings, irregular cycles, and weight fluctuations. Herbal remedies provide a gentle, natural way to support hormonal harmony by addressing the root causes and promoting balance.

Adaptogenic herbs like ashwagandha, hormone-regulating herbs such as chasteberry, and nutrient-rich options like maca root have been used for centuries to balance hormones naturally. These herbs work by supporting the endocrine system, reducing stress, and enhancing the body's ability to regulate itself. By integrating these remedies into your daily routine, you can promote equilibrium and alleviate symptoms of hormonal imbalance.

This chapter offers 15 herbal remedies, including teas, tonics, and smoothies, designed to harmonize hormones and improve overall well-being. These simple, effective recipes are a practical way to embrace a balanced, healthier lifestyle.

356. Chasteberry Hormone-Balancing Tea

Ingredients:

- 1 tsp dried chasteberry
- 1 cup boiling water

Instructions:

1. Steep chasteberry in boiling water for 10 minutes.
2. Strain and drink warm.

Uses: Regulates menstrual cycles and supports hormonal balance.

Storage Tips: Prepare fresh for each use.

357. Maca and Cinnamon Energy Smoothie

Ingredients:

- 1 tsp maca powder
- 1/2 tsp cinnamon powder
- 1 banana
- 1 cup almond milk

Instructions:

1. Blend all ingredients until smooth.
2. Drink as a morning energy boost.

Uses: Supports hormonal health and boosts energy.

Storage Tips: Consume immediately.

358. Holy Basil (Tulsi) Adaptogen Tea

Ingredients:

- 1 tsp dried holy basil leaves
- 1 cup boiling water

Instructions:

1. Steep tulsi leaves in boiling water for 7 minutes.
2. Strain and sip slowly.

Uses: Reduces stress and supports adrenal health.

Storage Tips: Drink fresh.

359. Licorice Root and Ginger Tonic

Ingredients:

- 1 tsp dried licorice root
- 1 tsp fresh ginger slices
- 1 cup boiling water

Instructions:

1. Steep licorice root and ginger in boiling water for 10 minutes.
2. Strain and drink warm.

Uses: Supports adrenal glands and improves hormonal balance.

Storage Tips: Prepare fresh for each use.

360. Ashwagandha and Turmeric Golden Milk

Ingredients:

- 1 tsp ashwagandha powder
- 1/2 tsp turmeric powder
- 1 cup warm coconut milk

Instructions:

1. Mix ashwagandha and turmeric into warm coconut milk.
2. Drink before bedtime.

Uses: Reduces cortisol levels and promotes relaxation.

Storage Tips: Consume immediately.

361. Red Clover Hormone Tea

Ingredients:

- 1 tsp dried red clover blossoms
- 1 cup boiling water

Instructions:

1. Steep red clover in boiling water for 7 minutes.
2. Strain and drink warm.

Uses: Supports hormonal balance and promotes skin health.

Storage Tips: Drink fresh.

362. Fennel and Peppermint Cooling Tea

Ingredients:

- 1 tsp fennel seeds

- 1 tsp dried peppermint leaves
- 1 cup boiling water

Instructions:

1. Steep fennel and peppermint in boiling water for 7 minutes.
2. Strain and sip slowly.

Uses: Eases bloating and promotes hormonal harmony.

Storage Tips: Consume immediately.

363. Rosemary and Lemon Infused Water

Ingredients:

- 1 tsp dried rosemary leaves
- 1/2 lemon (sliced)
- 1 liter water

Instructions:

1. Add rosemary and lemon slices to water.
2. Let steep for 2–4 hours in the refrigerator and drink throughout the day.

Uses: Detoxifies and supports hormone regulation.

Storage Tips: Consume within 24 hours.

364. Cinnamon and Ginger Hormone Tonic

Ingredients:

- 1/2 tsp cinnamon powder
- 1 tsp fresh ginger slices
- 1 cup warm water

Instructions:

1. Mix cinnamon and ginger into warm water.
2. Stir and sip slowly.

Uses: Balances blood sugar and reduces inflammation.

Storage Tips: Prepare fresh for each use.

365. Lavender and Chamomile Relaxation Tea

Ingredients:

- 1 tsp dried lavender flowers
- 1 tsp dried chamomile flowers
- 1 cup boiling water

Instructions:

1. Steep lavender and chamomile in boiling water for 5 minutes.

2. Strain and drink before bedtime.

Uses: Reduces stress and improves sleep.

Storage Tips: Drink fresh.

366. Flaxseed Hormone-Balancing Smoothie

Ingredients:

- 1 tbsp ground flaxseeds
- 1 cup spinach
- 1/2 banana
- 1 cup almond milk

Instructions:

1. Blend all ingredients until smooth.
2. Drink as a midday snack.

Uses: Supports estrogen balance and promotes skin health.

Storage Tips: Consume immediately.

367. Clary Sage Essential Oil Massage

Ingredients:

- 1/4 cup almond oil
- 5 drops clary sage essential oil

Instructions:

1. Mix almond oil and clary sage oil in a bottle.
2. Massage onto abdomen or pulse points.

Uses: Regulates hormones and eases tension.

Storage Tips: Store in a dark, cool place for up to 6 months.

368. Nettle and Lemon Tea

Ingredients:

- 1 tsp dried nettle leaves
- 1 tsp fresh lemon juice
- 1 cup boiling water

Instructions:

1. Steep nettle in boiling water for 5 minutes.
2. Add lemon juice and sip slowly.

Uses: Provides essential nutrients for hormone support.

Storage Tips: Prepare fresh for each use.

369. Dill Seed Digestive Tea

Ingredients:

- 1 tsp dill seeds
- 1 cup boiling water

Instructions:

1. Steep dill seeds in boiling water for 10 minutes.
2. Strain and drink warm.

Uses: Reduces bloating and supports hormonal balance.

Storage Tips: Consume immediately.

370. Mint and Holy Basil Morning Tonic

Ingredients:

- 1 tsp dried mint leaves
- 1 tsp dried holy basil leaves
- 1 cup boiling water

Instructions:

1. Steep mint and holy basil in boiling water for 7 minutes.
2. Strain and drink warm.

Uses: Reduces stress and supports adrenal health.

Storage Tips: Prepare fresh for each use.

Remedies for Pregnancy and Postpartum Wellness

Pregnancy and postpartum are transformative periods in a woman's life, marked by physical, emotional, and hormonal changes. While these stages bring joy and new beginnings, they can also present challenges such as fatigue, nausea, digestive discomfort, and postpartum recovery needs. Herbal remedies provide gentle and safe support during this time, offering relief and nourishment without the side effects of synthetic medications.

Herbs like ginger, red raspberry leaf, nettle, and chamomile are renowned for their ability to ease pregnancy-related symptoms and promote postpartum healing. These remedies, tailored to the unique needs of expectant and new mothers, help manage nausea, improve digestion, boost milk supply, and restore energy. However, it is essential to consult with a healthcare provider before using herbal remedies during pregnancy or while breastfeeding.

This chapter offers 15 safe and effective herbal recipes designed to support mothers through pregnancy and the postpartum period. From teas and tonics to balms and baths, these remedies nurture both body and spirit, helping women thrive during this life-changing journey.

371. Ginger and Lemon Anti-Nausea Tea

Ingredients:

- 1 tsp fresh ginger slices
- 1 tsp fresh lemon juice
- 1 cup boiling water

Instructions:

1. Steep ginger in boiling water for 10 minutes.
2. Strain, add lemon juice, and sip slowly.

Uses: Relieves morning sickness and improves digestion.

Storage Tips: Prepare fresh for each use.

372. Red Raspberry Leaf Strengthening Tea

Ingredients:

- 1 tsp dried red raspberry leaves
- 1 cup boiling water

Instructions:

1. Steep red raspberry leaves in boiling water for 7 minutes.
2. Strain and drink warm.

Uses: Strengthens the uterus and prepares the body for labor.

Storage Tips: Consume immediately.

373. Chamomile and Honey Calming Tea

Ingredients:

- 1 tsp dried chamomile flowers
- 1 tsp raw honey
- 1 cup boiling water

Instructions:

1. Steep chamomile flowers in boiling water for 5 minutes.
2. Stir in honey and drink warm.

Uses: Promotes relaxation and reduces anxiety.

Storage Tips: Drink fresh.

374. Nettle and Peppermint Digestive Tea

Ingredients:

- 1 tsp dried nettle leaves
- 1 tsp dried peppermint leaves
- 1 cup boiling water

Instructions:

1. Steep nettle and peppermint in boiling water for 10 minutes.
2. Strain and drink warm.

Uses: Provides essential nutrients and eases bloating.

Storage Tips: Consume immediately.

375. Oatmeal and Fenugreek Lactation Smoothie

Ingredients:

- 1/4 cup rolled oats
- 1 tsp fenugreek powder
- 1 banana
- 1 cup almond milk

Instructions:

1. Blend all ingredients until smooth.
2. Drink as a midday snack.

Uses: Boosts milk supply and provides energy.

Storage Tips: Prepare fresh for each use.

376. Lavender and Calendula Healing Bath

Ingredients:

- 1/4 cup dried lavender flowers
- 1/4 cup dried calendula petals
- 1 cup Epsom salt

Instructions:

1. Combine all ingredients and add to a warm bath.
2. Soak for 20 minutes.

Uses: Soothes sore muscles and promotes postpartum recovery.

Storage Tips: Store dry mix in an airtight container for up to 3 months.

377. Ginger and Turmeric Recovery Tonic

Ingredients:

- 1 tsp fresh ginger juice
- 1/2 tsp turmeric powder
- 1 cup warm water

Instructions:

1. Mix ginger and turmeric into warm water.
2. Stir well and drink in the morning.

Uses: Reduces inflammation and restores energy postpartum.

Storage Tips: Consume immediately.

378. Holy Basil (Tulsi) and Lemon Tea

Ingredients:

- 1 tsp dried holy basil leaves
- 1 tsp fresh lemon juice
- 1 cup boiling water

Instructions:

1. Steep holy basil in boiling water for 7 minutes.
2. Add lemon juice and sip slowly.

Uses: Reduces stress and boosts energy levels.

Storage Tips: Drink fresh.

379. Coconut Oil and Lavender Nipple Balm

Ingredients:

- 1/4 cup coconut oil
- 5 drops lavender essential oil

Instructions:

1. Mix coconut oil and lavender oil in a small jar.
2. Apply to sore or cracked nipples as needed.

Uses: Soothes irritation and promotes healing.

Storage Tips: Store in a cool, dry place for up to 6 months.

380. Red Raspberry and Ginger Infusion

Ingredients:

- 1 tsp dried red raspberry leaves
- 1 tsp fresh ginger slices
- 1 cup boiling water

Instructions:

1. Steep red raspberry leaves and ginger in boiling water for 10 minutes.
2. Strain and drink warm.

Uses: Supports postpartum recovery and boosts energy.

Storage Tips: Consume immediately.

381. Calendula and Olive Oil Healing Salve

Ingredients:

- 1/4 cup olive oil
- 1 tbsp dried calendula petals
- 2 tbsp beeswax

Instructions:

1. Infuse calendula in olive oil over low heat for 20 minutes.
2. Strain and mix with melted beeswax.
3. Pour into a small jar and let cool.

Uses: Promotes healing of minor tears or stitches postpartum.

Storage Tips: Store in a sealed jar for up to 3 months.

382. Fennel and Lemon Digestive Tea

Ingredients:

- 1 tsp fennel seeds
- 1 tsp fresh lemon juice
- 1 cup boiling water

Instructions:

1. Steep fennel seeds in boiling water for 10 minutes.
2. Add lemon juice and drink warm.

Uses: Reduces bloating and supports digestion.

Storage Tips: Drink fresh.

383. Ginger and Honey Energy Shot

Ingredients:

- 1 tsp fresh ginger juice
- 1 tsp raw honey
- 1/4 cup warm water

Instructions:

1. Mix all ingredients in a small cup.
2. Drink as a quick pick-me-up.

Uses: Restores energy and supports recovery.

Storage Tips: Prepare fresh for each use.

384. Chamomile and Oatmeal Skin Soother

Ingredients:

- 1/4 cup dried chamomile flowers
- 1/4 cup oatmeal (ground)

Instructions:

1. Blend chamomile and oatmeal into a fine powder.
2. Mix into a warm bath and soak for 15 minutes.

Uses: Soothes itchy or irritated skin postpartum.

Storage Tips: Store dry mix in an airtight container for up to 3 months.

385. Nettle and Peppermint Recovery Tea

Ingredients:

- 1 tsp dried nettle leaves
- 1 tsp dried peppermint leaves
- 1 cup boiling water

Instructions:

1. Steep nettle and peppermint in boiling water for 10 minutes.
2. Strain and sip slowly.

Uses: Provides nutrients and relieves fatigue.

Storage Tips: Consume immediately.

Natural Solutions for Menopause

Menopause marks a significant transition in a woman's life, often accompanied by symptoms such as hot flashes, night sweats, mood swings, and fatigue. While these changes are natural, they can be challenging to manage. Herbal remedies offer gentle and effective support, helping to balance hormones, reduce discomfort, and enhance overall well-being during this phase.

Herbs like black cohosh, red clover, sage, and chamomile have been traditionally used to address menopausal symptoms. These herbs help to regulate hormonal fluctuations, cool the body, and promote relaxation. With consistent use, they can make the menopausal journey more comfortable and empowering.

This chapter provides 15 herbal remedies specifically designed to support women through menopause. From teas and tonics to compresses and baths, these recipes are simple, natural, and tailored to meet the unique needs of this transformative stage of life.

386. Sage and Lemon Hot Flash Tea

Ingredients:

- 1 tsp dried sage leaves
- 1 tsp fresh lemon juice
- 1 cup boiling water

Instructions:

1. Steep sage leaves in boiling water for 7 minutes.
2. Strain, add lemon juice, and sip slowly.

Uses: Reduces hot flashes and cools the body.

Storage Tips: Prepare fresh for each use.

387. Black Cohosh Hormone-Balancing Tea
Ingredients:

- 1 tsp dried black cohosh root
- 1 cup boiling water

Instructions:

1. Steep black cohosh root in boiling water for 10 minutes.
2. Strain and drink warm.

Uses: Balances hormones and eases menopausal symptoms.

Storage Tips: Drink fresh.

388. Chamomile and Lavender Sleep Tea
Ingredients:

- 1 tsp dried chamomile flowers
- 1 tsp dried lavender flowers
- 1 cup boiling water

Instructions:

1. Steep chamomile and lavender in boiling water for 5 minutes.
2. Strain and drink before bedtime.

Uses: Promotes relaxation and improves sleep.

Storage Tips: Consume immediately.

389. Red Clover and Mint Hormone Tea
Ingredients:

- 1 tsp dried red clover blossoms
- 1 tsp dried mint leaves
- 1 cup boiling water

Instructions:

1. Steep red clover and mint in boiling water for 7 minutes.
2. Strain and sip slowly.

Uses: Supports hormonal balance and soothes the nervous system.

Storage Tips: Drink fresh.

390. Peppermint and Lemon Cooling Compress
Ingredients:

- 5 drops peppermint essential oil
- 1 liter cool water
- 1/2 lemon (sliced)

Instructions:

1. Add peppermint oil and lemon slices to cool water.
2. Soak a cloth in the mixture and apply to the forehead or neck.

Uses: Reduces hot flashes and provides instant cooling relief.

Storage Tips: Use immediately.

391. Ashwagandha and Cinnamon Stress-Relief Tonic
Ingredients:

- 1 tsp ashwagandha powder
- 1/2 tsp cinnamon powder
- 1 cup warm almond milk

Instructions:

1. Mix ashwagandha and cinnamon into warm almond milk.
2. Stir well and drink in the evening.

Uses: Reduces stress and supports hormonal balance.

Storage Tips: Consume fresh.

392. Nettle and Lemon Detox Tea
Ingredients:

- 1 tsp dried nettle leaves
- 1 tsp fresh lemon juice
- 1 cup boiling water

Instructions:

1. Steep nettle leaves in boiling water for 5 minutes.
2. Add lemon juice and sip warm.

Uses: Provides essential nutrients and supports detoxification.

Storage Tips: Prepare fresh for each use.

393. Black Cohosh and Sage Hormone Tonic
Ingredients:

- 1 tsp dried black cohosh root
- 1 tsp dried sage leaves
- 1 cup boiling water

Instructions:

1. Simmer black cohosh and sage in boiling water for 10 minutes.
2. Strain and drink warm.

Uses: Balances hormones and reduces hot flashes.

Storage Tips: Consume immediately.

394. Rosemary and Lavender Bath Soak

Ingredients:

- 1/4 cup dried rosemary leaves
- 1/4 cup dried lavender flowers
- 1 cup Epsom salt

Instructions:

1. Combine all ingredients and add to a warm bath.
2. Soak for 20 minutes to relax and soothe.

Uses: Relieves tension and promotes relaxation.

Storage Tips: Store dry mix in an airtight container for up to 3 months.

395. Flaxseed and Honey Smoothie

Ingredients:

- 1 tbsp ground flaxseeds
- 1 tsp raw honey
- 1 banana
- 1 cup almond milk

Instructions:

1. Blend all ingredients until smooth.
2. Drink as a breakfast smoothie.

Uses: Supports hormonal balance and provides energy.

Storage Tips: Consume fresh.

396. Holy Basil (Tulsi) Adaptogen Tea

Ingredients:

- 1 tsp dried holy basil leaves
- 1 cup boiling water

Instructions:

1. Steep holy basil in boiling water for 7 minutes.
2. Strain and drink warm.

Uses: Reduces stress and balances hormones.

Storage Tips: Prepare fresh for each use.

397. Ginger and Turmeric Anti-Inflammatory Tea

Ingredients:

- 1 tsp fresh ginger slices
- 1/2 tsp turmeric powder
- 1 cup boiling water

Instructions:

1. Steep ginger and turmeric in boiling water for 10 minutes.
2. Strain and drink warm.

Uses: Reduces inflammation and relieves joint pain.

Storage Tips: Drink fresh.

398. Calendula and Olive Oil Skin Salve

Ingredients:

- 1/4 cup olive oil
- 1 tbsp dried calendula petals
- 2 tbsp beeswax

Instructions:

1. Infuse calendula in olive oil over low heat for 20 minutes.
2. Strain and mix with melted beeswax.
3. Pour into a small jar and let cool.

Uses: Soothes dry or irritated skin during menopause.

Storage Tips: Store in a cool, dry place for up to 3 months.

399. Lemon Balm and Peppermint Tea

Ingredients:

- 1 tsp dried lemon balm leaves
- 1 tsp dried peppermint leaves
- 1 cup boiling water

Instructions:

1. Steep lemon balm and peppermint in boiling water for 7 minutes.
2. Strain and drink warm.

Uses: Promotes relaxation and soothes digestive discomfort.

Storage Tips: Prepare fresh for each use.

400. Cinnamon and Clove Warming Tonic

Ingredients:

- 1/2 tsp cinnamon powder
- 2 cloves
- 1 cup warm almond milk

Instructions:

1. Steep cloves in warm almond milk for 5 minutes.
2. Stir in cinnamon powder and drink warm.

Uses: Supports circulation and balances hormones.

Storage Tips: Consume immediately.

BOOK 13

HERBS FOR MENTAL CLARITY AND FOCUS

In today's fast-paced world, staying focused and maintaining mental clarity can be challenging. Whether it's the demands of work, studies, or everyday life, our minds often feel overstimulated and fatigued. Herbs offer a natural way to enhance cognitive function, sharpen focus, and boost creative thinking. By supporting brain health, improving circulation, and reducing mental fatigue, these natural remedies can help you unlock your full potential.

This book explores a variety of herbs known for their ability to support mental clarity and focus. From adaptogens like rhodiola and ashwagandha that reduce stress to cognitive-boosting herbs like ginkgo biloba and gotu kola, you'll discover how these time-tested plants can improve memory, enhance problem-solving, and energize the mind. Each chapter is filled with practical recipes and techniques designed to fit seamlessly into your routine.

Whether you're looking to overcome mental fatigue, improve concentration, or spark creativity, this book provides the tools you need to achieve mental sharpness naturally. With easy-to-follow recipes for teas, tonics, and other herbal preparations, you can harness the power of nature to keep your mind clear, focused, and ready for whatever challenges come your way. Let's delve into the world of herbs for mental clarity and focus!

Cognitive-Boosting Blends for Concentration

Maintaining concentration is essential for productivity and focus, especially in a world filled with distractions. Herbs offer a natural and effective way to enhance cognitive function, improve memory, and sharpen concentration. Herbal remedies can support the brain by improving blood flow, reducing stress, and enhancing energy levels. Incorporating these blends into your routine can help create a state of mental clarity and focus, making everyday tasks easier and more efficient.

Herbs like ginkgo biloba, rosemary, and gotu kola are renowned for their ability to support brain health. Adaptogens like ashwagandha and rhodiola combat stress, which often hinders concentration, while energizing herbs like peppermint and green tea provide a gentle mental boost. The recipes in this chapter are designed to enhance cognitive function naturally, offering a variety of teas, tonics, and infusions to suit your preferences and needs.

These herbal blends are not only practical but also customizable, allowing you to experiment with combinations that work best for you. With consistent use, these remedies can help you achieve better focus, improved memory, and enhanced productivity.

401. Ginkgo Biloba and Green Tea Memory Tonic

Ingredients:

- 1 tsp dried ginkgo biloba leaves
- 1 tsp green tea leaves
- 1 cup boiling water Instructions:

1. Steep both herbs in boiling water for 5–7 minutes.
2. Strain and drink warm. Uses: Enhances memory and boosts mental alertness.

402. Rosemary and Peppermint Focus Tea

Ingredients:

- 1 tsp dried rosemary leaves
- 1 tsp dried peppermint leaves
- 1 cup boiling water Instructions:

1. Steep the herbs in boiling water for 7 minutes.
2. Strain and sip slowly. Uses: Improves focus and promotes mental clarity.

403. Ashwagandha and Cinnamon Morning Latte

Ingredients:

- 1 tsp ashwagandha powder
- 1/2 tsp cinnamon powder
- 1 cup warm almond milk Instructions:

1. Mix all ingredients in warm almond milk.
2. Stir well and drink in the morning. Uses: Reduces stress and enhances mental energy.

404. Gotu Kola and Lemon Tonic

Ingredients:

- 1 tsp dried gotu kola leaves
- 1 tsp fresh lemon juice
- 1 cup boiling water Instructions:

1. Steep gotu kola leaves in boiling water for 10 minutes.
2. Add lemon juice and sip warm. Uses: Supports brain health and concentration.

405. Rhodiola and Ginger Energy Tonic

Ingredients:

- 1 tsp dried rhodiola root
- 1 tsp fresh ginger slices
- 1 cup boiling water Instructions:

1. Simmer rhodiola and ginger in boiling water for 10 minutes.
2. Strain and drink warm. Uses: Reduces mental fatigue and boosts energy.

406. Peppermint and Green Tea Infusion

Ingredients:

- 1 tsp dried peppermint leaves
- 1 tsp green tea leaves
- 1 cup boiling water Instructions:

1. Steep both herbs in boiling water for 5 minutes.
2. Strain and drink warm or iced. Uses: Enhances focus and provides gentle energy.

407. Ginseng and Lemonade Elixir

Ingredients:

- 1 tsp dried ginseng root
- 1 cup fresh lemonade Instructions:

1. Steep ginseng in boiling water for 10 minutes.
2. Mix with lemonade and drink chilled. Uses: Boosts stamina and sharpens concentration.

408. Basil and Mint Brain Tonic

Ingredients:

- 1 tsp fresh basil leaves

- 1 tsp fresh mint leaves
- 1 cup boiling water Instructions:

1. Steep basil and mint in boiling water for 7 minutes.
2. Strain and drink warm. Uses: Reduces mental fatigue and supports clarity.

409. Matcha and Ginger Energizing Drink

Ingredients:

- 1 tsp matcha powder
- 1/2 tsp fresh ginger juice
- 1 cup warm water Instructions:

1. Mix matcha and ginger in warm water.
2. Stir well and drink. Uses: Provides sustained energy and improves focus.

410. Lemon Balm and Rosemary Concentration Tea

Ingredients:

- 1 tsp dried lemon balm leaves
- 1 tsp dried rosemary leaves
- 1 cup boiling water Instructions:

1. Steep both herbs in boiling water for 10 minutes.
2. Strain and sip slowly. Uses: Calms the mind and enhances concentration.

411. Holy Basil (Tulsi) and Lemon Tea

Ingredients:

- 1 tsp dried holy basil leaves
- 1 tsp fresh lemon juice
- 1 cup boiling water Instructions:

1. Steep holy basil leaves in boiling water for 7 minutes.
2. Add lemon juice and sip slowly. Uses: Reduces stress and enhances mental clarity.

412. Ginger and Turmeric Brain Health Tea

Ingredients:

- 1 tsp fresh ginger slices
- 1/2 tsp turmeric powder
- 1 cup boiling water Instructions:

1. Steep ginger and turmeric in boiling water for 10 minutes.
2. Strain and drink warm. Uses: Improves circulation to the brain and reduces inflammation.

413. Lavender and Chamomile Relaxation Blend

Ingredients:

- 1 tsp dried lavender flowers
- 1 tsp dried chamomile flowers
- 1 cup boiling water Instructions:

1. Steep lavender and chamomile in boiling water for 5 minutes.
2. Strain and drink before a focus-intensive task. Uses: Calms the mind and sharpens concentration.

414. Mint and Cacao Smoothie

Ingredients:

- 1 tsp raw cacao powder
- 1 tsp fresh mint leaves
- 1 cup almond milk Instructions:

1. Blend all ingredients until smooth.
2. Drink chilled for a refreshing mental boost. Uses: Provides energy and improves focus with antioxidants.

415. Cinnamon and Black Pepper Tonic

Ingredients:

- 1/2 tsp cinnamon powder
- 1/4 tsp freshly ground black pepper
- 1 cup warm water Instructions:

1. Mix cinnamon and black pepper into warm water.
2. Stir well and sip slowly. Uses: Enhances memory and boosts brain function.

Reducing Mental Fatigue Naturally

Mental fatigue is a common challenge in today's fast-paced world, resulting from overwork, stress, or lack of restful sleep. Persistent mental exhaustion can impair focus, memory, and productivity, leaving you feeling drained and disconnected. Herbal remedies provide a natural solution, helping to calm the nervous system, improve mental clarity, and boost energy levels.

This chapter introduces 15 effective herbal remedies designed to combat mental fatigue. From revitalizing teas and tonics to soothing oils and smoothies, these remedies incorporate herbs such as ashwagandha, rhodiola, peppermint, and ginseng to help restore energy and resilience.

With consistent use, these blends can help reduce mental fatigue and support sustained mental clarity and focus.

416. Ashwagandha and Cinnamon Morning Latte

Ingredients:

- 1 tsp ashwagandha powder
- 1/2 tsp cinnamon powder
- 1 cup warm almond milk

Instructions:

1. Mix ashwagandha and cinnamon into warm almond milk.
2. Stir well and drink in the morning.

Uses: Combats stress and restores mental energy.

Storage Tips: Prepare fresh for each use.

417. Rhodiola and Lemon Tea

Ingredients:

- 1 tsp dried rhodiola root
- 1 tsp fresh lemon juice
- 1 cup boiling water

Instructions:

1. Steep rhodiola in boiling water for 10 minutes.
2. Strain, add lemon juice, and sip slowly.

Uses: Reduces fatigue and enhances focus.

Storage Tips: Consume immediately.

418. Peppermint and Rosemary Refreshing Tea

Ingredients:

- 1 tsp dried peppermint leaves
- 1 tsp dried rosemary leaves
- 1 cup boiling water

Instructions:

1. Steep both herbs in boiling water for 7 minutes.
2. Strain and drink warm.

Uses: Revitalizes the mind and promotes mental clarity.

Storage Tips: Drink fresh.

419. Lemon Balm and Honey Relaxation Tea

Ingredients:

- 1 tsp dried lemon balm leaves
- 1 tsp raw honey
- 1 cup boiling water

Instructions:

1. Steep lemon balm in boiling water for 7 minutes.
2. Stir in honey and sip slowly.

Uses: Calms the mind and restores focus.

Storage Tips: Consume immediately.

420. Matcha and Ginger Energy Boost

Ingredients:

- 1 tsp matcha powder
- 1/2 tsp fresh ginger juice
- 1 cup warm water

Instructions:

1. Mix matcha and ginger in warm water.
2. Stir well and drink.

Uses: Provides gentle energy and reduces fatigue.

Storage Tips: Prepare fresh for each use.

421. Ginseng and Lemonade Energizer

Ingredients:

- 1 tsp dried ginseng root
- 1 cup fresh lemonade

Instructions:

1. Steep ginseng in boiling water for 10 minutes.
2. Mix with lemonade and drink chilled.

Uses: Boosts stamina and reduces mental fog.

Storage Tips: Drink fresh.

422. Basil and Mint Brain Tonic

Ingredients:

- 1 tsp fresh basil leaves
- 1 tsp fresh mint leaves
- 1 cup boiling water

Instructions:

1. Steep basil and mint in boiling water for 7 minutes.
2. Strain and drink warm.

Uses: Enhances mental alertness and calms stress.

Storage Tips: Prepare fresh.

423. Chamomile and Lavender Evening Tea

Ingredients:

- 1 tsp dried chamomile flowers
- 1 tsp dried lavender flowers
- 1 cup boiling water

Instructions:

1. Steep chamomile and lavender in boiling water for 5 minutes.
2. Strain and sip slowly before bedtime.

Uses: Promotes restful sleep and reduces fatigue.

Storage Tips: Drink fresh.

424. Holy Basil (Tulsi) and Lemon Detox Tea

Ingredients:

- 1 tsp dried holy basil leaves
- 1 tsp fresh lemon juice
- 1 cup boiling water

Instructions:

1. Steep holy basil leaves in boiling water for 7 minutes.
2. Add lemon juice and sip slowly.

Uses: Supports energy levels and mental clarity.

Storage Tips: Prepare fresh for each use.

425. Nettle and Mint Cooling Tea

Ingredients:

- 1 tsp dried nettle leaves
- 1 tsp dried peppermint leaves
- 1 cup boiling water

Instructions:

1. Steep nettle and peppermint in boiling water for 10 minutes.
2. Strain and drink warm.

Uses: Provides essential nutrients and refreshes the mind.

Storage Tips: Consume immediately.

426. Turmeric and Cinnamon Warm Tonic

Ingredients:

- 1/2 tsp turmeric powder
- 1/2 tsp cinnamon powder
- 1 cup warm almond milk

Instructions:

1. Mix turmeric and cinnamon into warm almond milk.
2. Stir well and drink in the evening.

Uses: Reduces inflammation and supports mental recovery.

Storage Tips: Drink fresh.

427. Lemon and Peppermint Iced Tea

Ingredients:

- 1 tsp dried peppermint leaves
- 1/2 lemon (sliced)
- 1 cup boiling water

Instructions:

1. Steep peppermint in boiling water for 7 minutes.
2. Add lemon slices, chill, and enjoy iced.

Uses: Provides a refreshing boost and combats fatigue.

Storage Tips: Drink within 12 hours if chilled.

428. Rosemary and Sage Memory Blend

Ingredients:

- 1 tsp dried rosemary leaves
- 1 tsp dried sage leaves
- 1 cup boiling water

Instructions:

1. Steep both herbs in boiling water for 10 minutes.
2. Strain and sip slowly.

Uses: Improves memory and enhances focus.

Storage Tips: Consume immediately.

429. Flaxseed and Cacao Smoothie

Ingredients:

- 1 tbsp ground flaxseeds
- 1 tsp raw cacao powder
- 1 banana
- 1 cup almond milk

Instructions:

1. Blend all ingredients until smooth.
2. Drink as a breakfast smoothie.

Uses: Provides sustained energy and brain-boosting nutrients.

Storage Tips: Drink fresh.

430. Ginger and Honey Energizing Shot

Ingredients:

- 1 tsp fresh ginger juice
- 1 tsp raw honey
- 1/4 cup warm water

Instructions:

1. Mix all ingredients in a small cup.

2. Drink as a quick energy boost.

Uses: Reduces fatigue and enhances alertness.

Storage Tips: Prepare fresh for each use.

Herbs for Creative Thinking and Problem Solving

Creativity and problem-solving are essential for navigating challenges, pursuing innovation, and expressing individuality. However, mental blocks, stress, and fatigue can often hinder creative thinking. Herbs can help by enhancing focus, improving brain function, and calming the mind, creating the ideal conditions for creativity to flourish. With their unique ability to balance energy and mental clarity, herbs like gotu kola rosemary, ginkgo biloba, and holy basil are excellent allies for unlocking your creative potential.

This chapter introduces 15 herbal remedies designed to stimulate creative thinking and enhance problem-solving skills. These blends include teas, tonics, and aromatherapy applications that support cognitive flexibility, reduce mental fatigue, and inspire imaginative thought. Whether you're brainstorming ideas, working on a complex project, or seeking inspiration, these remedies will help you think outside the box.

431. Rosemary and Lemon Memory Boost Tea

Ingredients:

- 1 tsp dried rosemary leaves
- 1 tsp fresh lemon juice
- 1 cup boiling water

Instructions:

1. Steep rosemary in boiling water for 10 minutes.
2. Add lemon juice and sip slowly.

Uses: Improves memory retention and enhances focus.

Storage Tips: Consume immediately.

432. Gotu Kola and Mint Brain Tonic

Ingredients:

- 1 tsp dried gotu kola leaves
- 1 tsp dried peppermint leaves
- 1 cup boiling water

Instructions:

1. Steep both herbs in boiling water for 7 minutes.
2. Strain and drink warm.

Uses: Boosts mental clarity and stimulates creative thought.

Storage Tips: Drink fresh.

433. Holy Basil (Tulsi) and Ginger Relaxation Tea

Ingredients:

- 1 tsp dried holy basil leaves
- 1 tsp fresh ginger slices
- 1 cup boiling water

Instructions:

1. Steep holy basil and ginger in boiling water for 10 minutes.
2. Strain and sip slowly.

Uses: Reduces stress and fosters innovative thinking.

Storage Tips: Prepare fresh for each use.

434. Ginkgo Biloba and Honey Energy Tea

Ingredients:

- 1 tsp dried ginkgo biloba leaves
- 1 tsp raw honey
- 1 cup boiling water

Instructions:

1. Steep ginkgo biloba in boiling water for 10 minutes.
2. Add honey and stir before drinking.

Uses: Enhances brain function and supports problem-solving.

Storage Tips: Consume immediately.

435. Lavender and Lemon Balm Calming Tea

Ingredients:

- 1 tsp dried lavender flowers
- 1 tsp dried lemon balm leaves
- 1 cup boiling water

Instructions:

1. Steep lavender and lemon balm in boiling water for 7 minutes.
2. Strain and sip before brainstorming sessions.

Uses: Calms the mind and encourages creative flow.

Storage Tips: Drink fresh.

436. Ashwagandha and Cinnamon Focus Tonic

Ingredients:

- 1 tsp ashwagandha powder
- 1/2 tsp cinnamon powder
- 1 cup warm almond milk

Instructions:

1. Mix ashwagandha and cinnamon into warm almond milk.
2. Stir well and drink in the morning.

Uses: Improves focus and reduces mental fatigue.

Storage Tips: Consume immediately.

437. Peppermint and Rosemary Essential Oil Blend

Ingredients:

- 5 drops peppermint essential oil
- 5 drops rosemary essential oil
- 1 diffuser

Instructions:

1. Add essential oils to your diffuser.
2. Use while working on creative tasks.

Uses: Enhances mental clarity and inspires problem-solving.

Storage Tips: Store oils in a dark, cool place.

438. Matcha and Turmeric Creativity Latte

Ingredients:

- 1 tsp matcha powder
- 1/2 tsp turmeric powder
- 1 cup warm coconut milk

Instructions:

1. Mix matcha and turmeric into warm coconut milk.
2. Stir well and enjoy.

Uses: Provides a sustained energy boost and supports brain health.

Storage Tips: Prepare fresh for each use.

439. Sage and Lemon Infusion

Ingredients:

- 1 tsp dried sage leaves
- 1/2 lemon (sliced)
- 1 cup boiling water

Instructions:

1. Steep sage leaves in boiling water for 7 minutes.
2. Add lemon slices and drink warm.

Uses: Improves cognitive flexibility and memory.

Storage Tips: Drink fresh.

440. Flaxseed and Cacao Brain-Boosting Smoothie

Ingredients:

- 1 tbsp ground flaxseeds
- 1 tsp raw cacao powder
- 1 banana
- 1 cup almond milk

Instructions:

1. Blend all ingredients until smooth.
2. Drink as a morning snack.

Uses: Provides brain-nourishing nutrients and improves focus.

Storage Tips: Consume immediately.

441. Lemon Balm and Peppermint Cooling Tea

Ingredients:

- 1 tsp dried lemon balm leaves
- 1 tsp dried peppermint leaves
- 1 cup boiling water

Instructions:

1. Steep both herbs in boiling water for 10 minutes.
2. Strain and sip slowly.

Uses: Refreshes the mind and promotes mental clarity.

Storage Tips: Prepare fresh for each use.

442. Turmeric and Ginger Brain Tonic

Ingredients:

- 1 tsp turmeric powder
- 1 tsp fresh ginger juice
- 1 cup warm water

Instructions:

1. Mix turmeric and ginger in warm water.
2. Stir well and drink.

Uses: Reduces inflammation and enhances brain function.

Storage Tips: Consume immediately.

443. Ginseng and Lemon Energizing Tea

Ingredients:

- 1 tsp dried ginseng root
- 1 tsp fresh lemon juice
- 1 cup boiling water

Instructions:

1. Simmer ginseng in boiling water for 10 minutes.
2. Add lemon juice and drink warm.

Uses: Boosts stamina and sharpens focus.

Storage Tips: Drink fresh.

444. Cinnamon and Black Pepper Creativity Booster

Ingredients:

- 1/2 tsp cinnamon powder
- 1/4 tsp black pepper powder
- 1 cup warm almond milk

Instructions:

1. Mix cinnamon and black pepper into warm almond milk.
2. Stir well and drink.

Uses: Enhances memory and stimulates innovative thinking.

Storage Tips: Consume immediately.

445. Mint and Basil Infused Water

Ingredients:

- 1 tsp fresh mint leaves
- 1 tsp fresh basil leaves
- 1 liter water

Instructions:

1. Add mint and basil to water and let steep for 2 hours.
2. Drink throughout the day.

Uses: Refreshes the mind and promotes cognitive clarity.

Storage Tips: Refrigerate and consume within 24 hours.

Recipes for Brain Health Tonics

Brain health is essential for maintaining focus, memory, and cognitive function throughout life. With the right nutrition and natural remedies, you can enhance mental clarity, reduce cognitive decline, and support overall brain wellness. Herbal tonics offer a powerful way to nourish the brain, combining the benefits of herbs, adaptogens, and superfoods into easy-to-consume remedies.

This chapter provides 15 recipes for brain health tonics, incorporating herbs like ginkgo biloba, ashwagandha, and turmeric, alongside nutrient-rich ingredients such as flaxseeds and cacao. These tonics are designed to improve circulation to the brain, reduce inflammation, and provide the nutrients needed for optimal mental performance. Whether you're preparing for a big task, looking to improve memory, or aiming to sustain long-term cognitive health, these recipes are perfect additions to your wellness routine.

446. Ginkgo Biloba and Lemon Brain Boost Tonic

Ingredients:

- 1 tsp dried ginkgo biloba leaves
- 1 tsp fresh lemon juice
- 1 cup boiling water

Instructions:

1. Steep ginkgo biloba leaves in boiling water for 10 minutes.
2. Add lemon juice and sip slowly.

Uses: Enhances memory and improves blood flow to the brain.

Storage Tips: Consume immediately.

447. Turmeric and Ginger Golden Milk

Ingredients:

- 1 tsp turmeric powder
- 1 tsp fresh ginger juice
- 1 cup warm coconut milk

Instructions:

1. Mix turmeric and ginger into warm coconut milk.
2. Stir well and drink before bedtime.

Uses: Reduces inflammation and supports long-term brain health.

Storage Tips: Prepare fresh for each use.

448. Ashwagandha and Honey Stress-Relief Tonic

Ingredients:

- 1 tsp ashwagandha powder
- 1 tsp raw honey
- 1 cup warm almond milk

Instructions:

1. Mix ashwagandha and honey into warm almond milk.
2. Stir and enjoy as a calming evening drink.

Uses: Lowers cortisol levels and promotes relaxation.

Storage Tips: Consume immediately.

449. Gotu Kola and Peppermint Tonic

Ingredients:

- 1 tsp dried gotu kola leaves
- 1 tsp dried peppermint leaves
- 1 cup boiling water

Instructions:

1. Steep gotu kola and peppermint in boiling water for 10 minutes.
2. Strain and drink warm.

Uses: Boosts cognitive function and mental clarity.

Storage Tips: Drink fresh.

450. Matcha and Lemon Energizing Drink

Ingredients:

- 1 tsp matcha powder
- 1/2 tsp fresh lemon juice
- 1 cup warm water

Instructions:

1. Mix matcha and lemon juice into warm water.
2. Stir well and drink in the morning.

Uses: Provides sustained energy and sharpens focus.

Storage Tips: Consume immediately.

451. Rhodiola and Honey Brain Tonic

Ingredients:

- 1 tsp dried rhodiola root
- 1 tsp raw honey
- 1 cup boiling water

Instructions:

1. Steep rhodiola in boiling water for 10 minutes.
2. Add honey and stir before sipping.

Uses: Reduces mental fatigue and enhances focus.

Storage Tips: Drink fresh.

452. Basil and Lemon Infused Water

Ingredients:

- 1 tsp fresh basil leaves
- 1/2 lemon (sliced)
- 1 liter water

Instructions:

1. Add basil leaves and lemon slices to water.
2. Let steep for 2 hours and drink throughout the day.

Uses: Refreshes the mind and supports cognitive health.

Storage Tips: Refrigerate and consume within 24 hours.

453. Flaxseed and Cacao Smoothie

Ingredients:

- 1 tbsp ground flaxseeds
- 1 tsp raw cacao powder
- 1 banana
- 1 cup almond milk

Instructions:

1. Blend all ingredients until smooth.
2. Drink as a morning snack.

Uses: Provides brain-nourishing nutrients and improves memory.

Storage Tips: Consume immediately.

454. Lemon Balm and Lavender Relaxation Tonic

Ingredients:

- 1 tsp dried lemon balm leaves
- 1 tsp dried lavender flowers
- 1 cup boiling water

Instructions:

1. Steep lemon balm and lavender in boiling water for 7 minutes.
2. Strain and sip slowly.

Uses: Calms the mind and enhances creative thinking.

Storage Tips: Drink fresh.

455. Rosemary and Cinnamon Brain Boost Tea

Ingredients:

- 1 tsp dried rosemary leaves
- 1/2 tsp cinnamon powder
- 1 cup boiling water

Instructions:

1. Steep rosemary in boiling water for 10 minutes.
2. Add cinnamon and stir before drinking.

Uses: Improves memory and promotes focus.

Storage Tips: Prepare fresh for each use.

456. Ginger and Lemon Energy Shot

Ingredients:

- 1 tsp fresh ginger juice
- 1 tsp fresh lemon juice
- 1/4 cup warm water

Instructions:

1. Mix all ingredients in a small cup.
2. Drink as a quick energy boost.

Uses: Enhances alertness and reduces fatigue.

Storage Tips: Consume immediately.

457. Nettle and Mint Revitalizing Tea

Ingredients:

- 1 tsp dried nettle leaves
- 1 tsp dried peppermint leaves
- 1 cup boiling water

Instructions:

1. Steep nettle and peppermint in boiling water for 10 minutes.
2. Strain and drink warm.

Uses: Provides essential nutrients for brain health.

Storage Tips: Drink fresh.

458. Sage and Honey Memory Tonic

Ingredients:

- 1 tsp dried sage leaves
- 1 tsp raw honey
- 1 cup boiling water

Instructions:

1. Steep sage leaves in boiling water for 7 minutes.
2. Stir in honey and sip slowly.

Uses: Enhances memory retention and mental clarity.

Storage Tips: Prepare fresh for each use.

459. Holy Basil (Tulsi) and Cinnamon Stress Tonic

Ingredients:

- 1 tsp dried holy basil leaves
- 1/2 tsp cinnamon powder
- 1 cup boiling water

Instructions:

1. Steep holy basil in boiling water for 7 minutes.
2. Add cinnamon and stir before sipping.

Uses: Reduces stress and promotes mental sharpness.

Storage Tips: Drink fresh.

460. Lemon and Peppermint Cooling Tonic

Ingredients:

- 1 tsp dried peppermint leaves
- 1/2 lemon (sliced)
- 1 cup boiling water

Instructions:

1. Steep peppermint in boiling water for 7 minutes.
2. Add lemon slices and let cool before drinking.

Uses: Refreshes the mind and enhances focus.

Storage Tips: Consume within 12 hours if chilled.

BOOK 14

SKINCARE SOLUTIONS FROM NATURE

Skincare doesn't have to rely on expensive products laden with synthetic chemicals. Nature provides a treasure trove of ingredients that can cleanse, nourish, and rejuvenate your skin. Herbs, oils, and natural extracts have been used for centuries to treat common skin issues, from acne and dryness to aging and irritation. By tapping into the power of natural remedies, you can create effective, eco-friendly skincare solutions tailored to your needs.

This book is your guide to crafting herbal and botanical remedies for glowing, healthy skin. Each chapter is dedicated to addressing specific skin concerns, from clearing blemishes with gentle herbal cleansers to soothing sunburns and irritation. You'll learn how to create anti-aging masks, luxurious body scrubs, and moisturizing lotions using easy-to-find ingredients like aloe vera, chamomile, lavender, and shea butter. These remedies not only nourish the skin but also help reduce environmental waste and harmful chemical exposure.

Whether you're dealing with acne, seeking a youthful glow, or simply wanting to pamper yourself with natural skincare, this book provides practical, step-by-step recipes for every need. Embrace the wisdom of nature and transform your skincare routine into a holistic, nurturing experience. Your skin—and the planet—will thank you!

Treating Acne with Herbal Cleansers

Acne is one of the most common skin concerns, affecting people of all ages. It is often caused by clogged pores, excess oil production, hormonal imbalances, or bacterial growth. While conventional treatments can be effective, they may also strip the skin of natural oils or cause irritation. Herbal cleansers offer a gentle, natural alternative, using the power of plants to cleanse, soothe, and restore balance to the skin.

Herbs like neem, tea tree, chamomile, and lavender are known for their antibacterial, anti-inflammatory, and healing properties. They can help reduce redness, calm irritation, and prevent future breakouts without over-drying the skin. These herbal cleansers are easy to make at home and can be tailored to suit your skin type.

This chapter introduces 10 herbal remedies for treating acne, focusing on cleansers that remove impurities while nurturing the skin. With consistent use, these remedies can help you achieve a clearer, healthier complexion naturally.

10 Remedies for Treating Acne with Herbal Cleansers

461. Neem and Aloe Vera Face Wash

Ingredients:

- 1 tsp neem powder
- 2 tbsp aloe vera gel
- 1 tbsp rose water

Instructions:

1. Mix neem powder, aloe vera gel, and rose water into a paste.
2. Massage onto your face in circular motions and rinse with warm water.

Uses: Reduces inflammation and kills acne-causing bacteria.

Storage Tips: Store in the refrigerator for up to 5 days.

462. Chamomile and Honey Cleanser

Ingredients:

- 1 tsp dried chamomile flowers
- 2 tbsp raw honey

Instructions:

1. Infuse chamomile in a small amount of hot water for 5 minutes.
2. Mix the strained infusion with honey and apply to the face.

Uses: Soothes irritated skin and reduces redness.

Storage Tips: Use immediately.

463. Tea Tree and Oatmeal Exfoliating Cleanser

Ingredients:

- 1 tsp tea tree oil
- 2 tbsp ground oatmeal
- 1 tbsp yogurt

Instructions:

1. Mix all ingredients into a thick paste.
2. Apply to your face, gently exfoliate, and rinse with cool water.

Uses: Clears pores and reduces excess oil.

Storage Tips: Use immediately.

464. Lavender and Apple Cider Vinegar Toner

Ingredients:

- 1/4 cup apple cider vinegar
- 1/4 cup distilled water
- 5 drops lavender essential oil

Instructions:

1. Mix all ingredients in a small spray bottle.
2. Apply to a cotton pad and gently wipe your face.

Uses: Balances skin pH and reduces acne-causing bacteria.

Storage Tips: Store in a cool, dark place for up to 1 month.

465. Calendula and Rose Cleansing Milk

Ingredients:

- 1 tsp dried calendula petals
- 1 cup raw milk
- 1 tsp rose water

Instructions:

1. Infuse calendula petals in warm milk for 10 minutes.
2. Strain, add rose water, and use to cleanse the face.

Uses: Hydrates while calming inflamed skin.

Storage Tips: Refrigerate and use within 3 days.

466. Turmeric and Yogurt Spot Treatment

Ingredients:

- 1/4 tsp turmeric powder
- 1 tbsp plain yogurt

Instructions:

1. Mix turmeric powder and yogurt into a paste.
2. Apply to blemishes and leave on for 10 minutes before rinsing.

Uses: Reduces inflammation and lightens scars.

Storage Tips: Use fresh.

467. Peppermint and Green Tea Cleanser

Ingredients:

- 1 tsp dried peppermint leaves
- 1 cup brewed green tea

Instructions:

1. Steep peppermint in hot green tea for 5 minutes.
2. Use the cooled mixture to wash your face.

Uses: Refreshes and reduces oiliness.

Storage Tips: Use immediately.

468. Basil and Lemon Acne Wash

Ingredients:

- 1 tsp dried basil leaves
- 1 tsp fresh lemon juice
- 1/4 cup distilled water

Instructions:

1. Steep basil leaves in hot water for 10 minutes.
2. Add lemon juice to the cooled infusion and apply to the face.

Uses: Fights bacteria and clears blemishes.

Storage Tips: Refrigerate for up to 3 days.

469. Witch Hazel and Aloe Toner

Ingredients:

- 2 tbsp witch hazel
- 2 tbsp aloe vera gel

Instructions:

1. Mix witch hazel and aloe vera gel in a small bottle.
2. Apply to a cotton pad and cleanse your face.

Uses: Soothes and hydrates acne-prone skin.

Storage Tips: Store in the refrigerator for up to 1 month.

470. Cinnamon and Honey Anti-Acne Mask

Ingredients:

- 1/4 tsp cinnamon powder

- 1 tbsp raw honey

Instructions:

1. Mix cinnamon and honey into a smooth paste.
2. Apply to the face and leave on for 15 minutes before rinsing.

Uses: Kills bacteria and reduces inflammation.

Storage Tips: Use immediately.

Creating Anti-Aging Masks and Serums

Aging is a natural part of life, but maintaining youthful, glowing skin doesn't require harsh chemicals or expensive treatments. Anti-aging herbal masks and serums nourish the skin with natural ingredients, reduce the appearance of fine lines, improve elasticity, and promote hydration. By incorporating herbs rich in antioxidants, vitamins, and minerals, you can protect your skin from free radical damage and support its renewal process.

Herbs like rose, chamomile, aloe vera, and lavender, combined with nourishing oils like jojoba and argan, offer powerful anti-aging benefits. These natural ingredients hydrate the skin, stimulate collagen production, and enhance overall skin texture. In this chapter, you'll discover 10 easy-to-make recipes for masks and serums that rejuvenate your skin and restore its youthful vitality.

10 Remedies for Anti-Aging Masks and Serums

471. Rose and Honey Hydrating Mask

Ingredients:

- 1 tbsp dried rose petals (ground into powder)
- 1 tbsp raw honey
- 1 tbsp yogurt

Instructions:

1. Mix rose petal powder, honey, and yogurt into a smooth paste.
2. Apply to your face and leave on for 15 minutes.
3. Rinse with lukewarm water.

Uses: Hydrates the skin and enhances elasticity.

Storage Tips: Use fresh.

472. Aloe Vera and Vitamin E Serum

Ingredients:

- 2 tbsp aloe vera gel
- 1 tsp vitamin E oil
- 5 drops lavender essential oil

Instructions:

1. Mix all ingredients in a small dropper bottle.
2. Apply a few drops to your face before bedtime.

Uses: Repairs skin and promotes collagen production.

Storage Tips: Store in the refrigerator for up to 2 weeks.

473. Green Tea and Chamomile Anti-Aging Mask

Ingredients:

- 1 tsp matcha green tea powder
- 1 tsp dried chamomile flowers
- 1 tbsp plain yogurt

Instructions:

1. Grind chamomile flowers into a fine powder.
2. Mix with matcha and yogurt to form a paste.
3. Apply to your face and leave on for 15 minutes.

Uses: Fights free radicals and reduces wrinkles.

Storage Tips: Use immediately.

474. Turmeric and Milk Brightening Mask

Ingredients:

- 1/2 tsp turmeric powder
- 2 tbsp milk (or almond milk)

Instructions:

1. Mix turmeric and milk into a smooth consistency.
2. Apply to your face and leave on for 10 minutes.

Uses: Brightens the skin and reduces age spots.

Storage Tips: Prepare fresh for each use.

475. Argan Oil and Rosehip Serum

Ingredients:

- 2 tbsp argan oil
- 2 tbsp rosehip oil
- 5 drops frankincense essential oil

Instructions:

1. Combine all ingredients in a dark glass bottle with a dropper.

2. Massage 2–3 drops into your skin daily.

Uses: Reduces fine lines and promotes skin regeneration.

Storage Tips: Store in a cool, dark place for up to 6 months.

476. Lavender and Honey Soothing Mask

Ingredients:

- 1 tbsp raw honey
- 5 drops lavender essential oil

Instructions:

1. Mix honey and lavender oil.
2. Apply to your face and leave on for 20 minutes.

Uses: Soothes irritation and hydrates dry skin.

Storage Tips: Use immediately.

477. Cucumber and Aloe Hydration Mask

Ingredients:

- 1/4 cucumber (blended into juice)
- 2 tbsp aloe vera gel

Instructions:

1. Mix cucumber juice and aloe vera gel.
2. Apply to your face with a cotton pad and leave for 15 minutes.

Uses: Refreshes and hydrates tired skin.

Storage Tips: Use fresh.

478. Frankincense and Jojoba Oil Serum

Ingredients:

- 2 tbsp jojoba oil
- 5 drops frankincense essential oil

Instructions:

1. Combine jojoba oil and frankincense in a small bottle.
2. Apply a few drops nightly to reduce wrinkles.

Uses: Improves skin elasticity and reduces fine lines.

Storage Tips: Store in a cool, dark place for up to 6 months.

479. Banana and Olive Oil Nourishing Mask

Ingredients:

- 1/2 ripe banana (mashed)
- 1 tsp olive oil

Instructions:

1. Mix banana and olive oil into a smooth paste.
2. Apply to your face and leave on for 15 minutes.

Uses: Softens skin and restores moisture.

Storage Tips: Use immediately.

480. Calendula and Coconut Oil Healing Serum

Ingredients:

- 1 tbsp dried calendula petals
- 2 tbsp coconut oil

Instructions:

1. Infuse calendula petals in warm coconut oil for 20 minutes.
2. Strain and store in a small jar.
3. Apply a small amount to your face nightly.

Uses: Promotes healing and reduces skin damage.

Storage Tips: Store in a cool, dry place for up to 3 months.

DIY Body Scrubs and Lotions

Achieving smooth, hydrated skin doesn't require chemical-laden products when nature offers powerful ingredients that can exfoliate and moisturize effectively. DIY body scrubs and lotions allow you to nourish your skin with natural, toxin-free alternatives that are tailored to your preferences and needs. These simple, homemade remedies combine exfoliating agents like sugar or salt with moisturizing oils and herbs to gently remove dead skin cells, improve circulation, and deeply hydrate.

Herbs like lavender, chamomile, and calendula infuse these scrubs and lotions with healing and soothing properties, while oils like coconut, shea butter, and almond restore the skin's natural glow. By incorporating these treatments into your skincare routine, you can achieve softer, healthier skin while enjoying the therapeutic benefits of creating your own products.

This chapter features 10 easy-to-make recipes for scrubs and lotions, each designed to exfoliate, hydrate, and revitalize your skin. These natural, sustainable remedies will leave your skin feeling pampered and rejuvenated.

10 Remedies for DIY Body Scrubs and Lotions

481. Lavender and Sugar Exfoliating Scrub

Ingredients:

- 1/2 cup granulated sugar
- 1/4 cup coconut oil
- 5 drops lavender essential oil

Instructions:

1. Mix all ingredients in a bowl until well combined.
2. Massage onto damp skin in circular motions, then rinse off with warm water.

Uses: Gently exfoliates and calms irritated skin.

Storage Tips: Store in an airtight container for up to 1 month.

482. Coffee and Vanilla Energizing Scrub

Ingredients:

- 1/2 cup used coffee grounds
- 1/4 cup almond oil
- 1 tsp vanilla extract

Instructions:

1. Mix coffee grounds, almond oil, and vanilla extract.
2. Apply to the skin, scrub gently, and rinse thoroughly.

Uses: Improves circulation and reduces the appearance of cellulite.

Storage Tips: Store in a cool, dry place for up to 2 weeks.

483. Chamomile and Shea Butter Lotion

Ingredients:

- 1/4 cup shea butter
- 2 tbsp almond oil
- 1 tsp dried chamomile flowers (finely ground)

Instructions:

1. Melt shea butter and almond oil together over low heat.
2. Stir in ground chamomile flowers and let cool.
3. Whip the mixture until creamy and apply to the skin.

Uses: Soothes and deeply hydrates dry skin.

Storage Tips: Store in an airtight jar for up to 3 months.

484. Sea Salt and Rosemary Detox Scrub

Ingredients:

- 1/2 cup sea salt
- 1/4 cup olive oil
- 1 tsp dried rosemary (crushed)

Instructions:

1. Mix all ingredients thoroughly in a bowl.
2. Massage onto the body, focusing on rough areas, and rinse off.

Uses: Detoxifies and refreshes the skin.

Storage Tips: Store in a sealed container for up to 1 month.

485. Calendula and Honey Healing Lotion

Ingredients:

- 1/4 cup calendula-infused oil
- 1 tbsp raw honey
- 2 tbsp aloe vera gel

Instructions:

1. Combine all ingredients in a small bowl.
2. Apply generously to the skin and let it absorb.

Uses: Hydrates and heals dry or damaged skin.

Storage Tips: Refrigerate for up to 2 weeks.

486. Brown Sugar and Peppermint Cooling Scrub

Ingredients:

- 1/2 cup brown sugar
- 1/4 cup coconut oil
- 5 drops peppermint essential oil

Instructions:

1. Mix sugar, coconut oil, and peppermint oil in a bowl.
2. Massage onto skin for a refreshing exfoliation.

Uses: Exfoliates and cools the skin, leaving it soft and refreshed.

Storage Tips: Store in a cool, dry place for up to 1 month.

487. Almond and Oatmeal Gentle Scrub

Ingredients:

- 1/4 cup ground oatmeal
- 2 tbsp almond oil
- 1 tbsp honey

Instructions:

1. Mix all ingredients into a paste.
2. Gently scrub onto the skin and rinse with warm water.

Uses: Ideal for sensitive skin, providing gentle exfoliation and hydration.

Storage Tips: Use immediately.

488. Cocoa Butter and Vanilla Body Lotion

Ingredients:

- 1/4 cup cocoa butter
- 2 tbsp coconut oil
- 1 tsp vanilla extract

Instructions:

1. Melt cocoa butter and coconut oil together over low heat.
2. Stir in vanilla extract, let cool, and whip until creamy.

Uses: Deeply moisturizes and leaves a subtle vanilla scent.

Storage Tips: Store in a cool, dry place for up to 3 months.

489. Green Tea and Lemon Detox Scrub

Ingredients:

- 1/4 cup brewed green tea (cooled)
- 1/2 cup sugar
- 1 tsp fresh lemon juice

Instructions:

1. Mix green tea, sugar, and lemon juice into a scrub.
2. Apply to damp skin and rinse thoroughly.

Uses: Brightens the skin and removes impurities.

Storage Tips: Use within 1 week if refrigerated.

490. Aloe Vera and Lavender Body Lotion

Ingredients:

- 1/4 cup aloe vera gel
- 2 tbsp jojoba oil
- 5 drops lavender essential oil

Instructions:

1. Combine all ingredients in a small jar and mix well.
2. Apply generously to the skin after bathing.

Uses: Hydrates and soothes the skin, leaving it soft and refreshed.

Storage Tips: Refrigerate for up to 2 weeks.

Remedies for Sunburn and Skin Irritations

Sunburn and skin irritations can leave your skin feeling tender, inflamed, and in need of soothing care. While over-the-counter treatments can provide relief, natural remedies offer gentle, effective solutions to heal the skin and reduce discomfort. Herbs like aloe vera, calendula, chamomile, and lavender are known for their anti-inflammatory and cooling properties, making them ideal for calming irritated skin and accelerating recovery.

This chapter provides 10 herbal remedies designed to alleviate sunburn and skin irritations. From soothing gels and sprays to healing balms and compresses, these recipes are simple to prepare and use. Whether you're treating a sunburn, a rash, or a minor irritation, these remedies can restore comfort and promote skin healing naturally.

10 Remedies for Sunburn and Skin Irritations

491. Aloe Vera and Lavender Soothing Gel

Ingredients:

- 2 tbsp fresh aloe vera gel
- 5 drops lavender essential oil

Instructions:

1. Mix aloe vera gel and lavender oil in a small bowl.
2. Apply gently to sunburned or irritated skin.

Uses: Soothes inflammation and promotes skin healing.

Storage Tips: Refrigerate for up to 1 week.

492. Calendula and Chamomile Healing Spray

Ingredients:

- 1 tsp dried calendula petals
- 1 tsp dried chamomile flowers
- 1 cup distilled water

Instructions:

1. Steep calendula and chamomile in boiling water for 10 minutes.
2. Strain, let cool, and pour into a spray bottle.

3. Mist onto affected areas as needed.

Uses: Calms redness and reduces irritation.

Storage Tips: Refrigerate and use within 1 week.

493. Peppermint and Green Tea Cooling Compress

Ingredients:

- 1 tsp dried peppermint leaves
- 1 cup brewed green tea (cooled)

Instructions:

1. Steep peppermint leaves in green tea for 10 minutes.
2. Soak a clean cloth in the mixture and apply to irritated skin.

Uses: Provides a cooling effect and reduces inflammation.

Storage Tips: Use fresh.

494. Oatmeal and Honey Skin Soother

Ingredients:

- 1/4 cup ground oatmeal
- 2 tbsp raw honey

Instructions:

1. Mix oatmeal and honey into a paste.
2. Apply to the affected area and leave on for 15 minutes.

Uses: Relieves itching and hydrates dry, irritated skin.

Storage Tips: Use immediately.

495. Cucumber and Aloe Cooling Mask

Ingredients:

- 1/4 cucumber (blended into juice)
- 2 tbsp fresh aloe vera gel

Instructions:

1. Mix cucumber juice and aloe vera gel.
2. Apply to the skin and leave on for 15 minutes.

Uses: Hydrates and cools sunburned skin.

Storage Tips: Use fresh.

496. Witch Hazel and Rose Water Toner

Ingredients:

- 2 tbsp witch hazel
- 2 tbsp rose water

Instructions:

1. Mix witch hazel and rose water in a small bottle.
2. Apply to the skin with a cotton pad.

Uses: Reduces inflammation and soothes irritated skin.

Storage Tips: Store in a cool, dark place for up to 1 month.

497. Coconut Oil and Lavender Balm

Ingredients:

- 1/4 cup coconut oil
- 5 drops lavender essential oil

Instructions:

1. Melt coconut oil and mix with lavender essential oil.
2. Let cool and apply to affected skin.

Uses: Moisturizes and promotes healing.

Storage Tips: Store in an airtight jar for up to 3 months.

498. Baking Soda and Chamomile Soothing Bath

Ingredients:

- 1/4 cup baking soda
- 1/4 cup dried chamomile flowers

Instructions:

1. Add baking soda and chamomile to a warm bath.
2. Soak for 20 minutes.

Uses: Relieves itching and reduces redness.

Storage Tips: Use immediately.

499. Aloe Vera and Tea Tree Gel

Ingredients:

- 2 tbsp fresh aloe vera gel
- 3 drops tea tree essential oil

Instructions:

1. Mix aloe vera gel and tea tree oil in a small container.
2. Apply to irritated skin for relief.

Uses: Soothes and disinfects minor skin irritations.

Storage Tips: Store in the refrigerator for up to 1 week.

500. Lavender and Epsom Salt Bath Soak

Ingredients:

- 1/4 cup Epsom salt
- 5 drops lavender essential oil

Instructions:

1. Add Epsom salt and lavender oil to a warm bath.
2. Soak for 15–20 minutes.

Uses: Relaxes the body and soothes inflamed skin.

Storage Tips: Store dry ingredients in an airtight container for up to 3 months.

BOOK 15
SUPPORTING DIGESTIVE HEALTH

Digestive health is fundamental to overall well-being, influencing everything from energy levels to immune function. Yet, modern lifestyles and diets can often lead to common digestive issues such as bloating, gas, nausea, or heartburn. Fortunately, herbs offer natural, effective solutions to support the digestive system, relieve discomfort, and promote long-term gut health.

This book explores the powerful role of herbs in maintaining and improving digestive health. With their ability to soothe the stomach, reduce inflammation, and balance gut flora, herbs like peppermint, ginger, fennel, and chamomile have been trusted for centuries as natural remedies for digestive concerns. In addition to providing immediate relief, herbs can help cleanse the digestive system and support detoxification for lasting wellness.

Each chapter focuses on a specific aspect of digestive health, from alleviating everyday discomforts like gas and bloating to strengthening the gut with probiotic-rich herbs and detoxifying blends. You'll find easy-to-follow recipes for teas, tonics, and infusions that are simple to incorporate into your daily routine.

Whether you're seeking quick relief or looking to nurture your digestive system for long-term vitality, this book offers practical, natural solutions to help you achieve and maintain optimal gut health.

Herbs to Relieve Bloating and Gas

Bloating and gas are common digestive complaints that can cause discomfort, abdominal distension, and even pain. These symptoms often result from overeating, poor digestion, or certain food sensitivities. While over-the-counter medications are readily available, herbs provide a natural, gentle way to alleviate bloating and gas without unwanted side effects.

Herbs like peppermint, fennel, ginger, and cham-omile are renowned for their carminative properties, which help to reduce gas buildup and promote healthy digestion. These herbs work by relaxing intestinal muscles, easing digestion, and reducing inflammation in the gut. By incorporating these remedies into your routine, you can find relief from bloating and gas while supporting overall digestive health.

This chapter presents 10 effective herbal remedies, including teas, tinctures, and compresses, to help you combat bloating and gas naturally. These recipes are easy to prepare and use, making them a practical addition to your wellness toolkit.

10 Remedies for Bloating and Gas

501. Peppermint and Ginger Tea

Ingredients:

- 1 tsp dried peppermint leaves
- 1 tsp fresh ginger slices
- 1 cup boiling water

Instructions:

1. Steep peppermint and ginger in boiling water for 10 minutes.
2. Strain and drink warm after meals.

Uses: Relaxes intestinal muscles and improves digestion.

Storage Tips: Consume fresh.

502. Fennel and Chamomile Digestive Tea

Ingredients:

- 1 tsp fennel seeds
- 1 tsp dried chamomile flowers
- 1 cup boiling water

Instructions:

1. Steep fennel and chamomile in boiling water for 7 minutes.
2. Strain and sip slowly.

Uses: Reduces gas and soothes an upset stomach.

Storage Tips: Drink immediately.

503. Lemon and Cumin Warm Water

Ingredients:

- 1 tsp cumin seeds
- 1 tbsp fresh lemon juice
- 1 cup warm water

Instructions:

1. Simmer cumin seeds in water for 5 minutes.
2. Strain, add lemon juice, and drink warm.

Uses: Eases bloating and supports digestion.

Storage Tips: Prepare fresh.

504. Dill Seed and Mint Tea

Ingredients:

- 1 tsp dill seeds
- 1 tsp dried mint leaves
- 1 cup boiling water

Instructions:

1. Steep dill seeds and mint in boiling water for 10 minutes.
2. Strain and enjoy warm.

Uses: Relieves gas and improves digestion.

Storage Tips: Consume immediately.

505. Cardamom and Ginger Tonic

Ingredients:

- 1/2 tsp cardamom powder
- 1 tsp fresh ginger juice
- 1 cup warm water

Instructions:

1. Mix cardamom and ginger juice in warm water.
2. Stir and drink after meals.

Uses: Reduces gas buildup and aids digestion.

Storage Tips: Prepare fresh for each use.

506. Warm Caraway Seed Compress

Ingredients:

- 1 tbsp caraway seeds
- 1 cup warm water
- A clean cloth

Instructions:

1. Steep caraway seeds in warm water for 5 minutes.
2. Soak the cloth in the mixture and apply to the abdomen.

Uses: Relaxes the stomach muscles and relieves gas.

Storage Tips: Use immediately.

507. Apple Cider Vinegar and Honey Tonic

Ingredients:

- 1 tbsp apple cider vinegar
- 1 tsp raw honey
- 1 cup warm water

Instructions:

1. Mix apple cider vinegar and honey into warm water.
2. Drink before meals to prevent bloating.

Uses: Improves digestion and reduces bloating.

Storage Tips: Prepare fresh for each use.

508. Parsley and Lemon Infusion

Ingredients:

- 1 tsp fresh parsley (chopped)
- 1 tsp fresh lemon juice
- 1 cup boiling water

Instructions:

1. Steep parsley in boiling water for 10 minutes.
2. Strain, add lemon juice, and drink warm.

Uses: Reduces bloating and detoxifies the digestive system.

Storage Tips: Consume immediately.

509. Coriander and Ginger Digestive Tea

Ingredients:

- 1 tsp coriander seeds
- 1 tsp fresh ginger slices
- 1 cup boiling water

Instructions:

1. Simmer coriander and ginger in boiling water for 10 minutes.
2. Strain and drink warm.

Uses: Eases digestion and reduces gas.

Storage Tips: Drink fresh.

510. Warm Clove and Cinnamon Water

Ingredients:

- 2 cloves
- 1/2 tsp cinnamon powder
- 1 cup warm water

Instructions:

1. Steep cloves and cinnamon in warm water for 7 minutes.
2. Strain and sip slowly.

Uses: Relieves bloating and promotes healthy digestion.

Storage Tips: Consume immediately.

Remedies for Nausea and Heartburn

Nausea and heartburn are common digestive discomforts that can be caused by stress, overeating, pregnancy, or certain foods. While these conditions are often temporary, they can significantly impact daily life if not managed effectively. Herbal remedies offer a natural, gentle way to soothe nausea and alleviate heartburn without the potential side effects of medications.

Herbs like ginger, peppermint, chamomile, and licorice root are known for their calming and anti-inflammatory properties. These herbs help to relax the stomach muscles, reduce acid reflux, and improve digestion. By incorporating these remedies into your routine, you can find relief from nausea and heartburn in a natural and effective way.

This chapter introduces 10 herbal recipes, including teas, tonics, and lozenges, to help you manage nausea and heartburn. These simple remedies are easy to prepare and can provide quick relief when you need it most.

10 Remedies for Nausea and Heartburn

511. Ginger and Lemon Anti-Nausea Tea

Ingredients:

- 1 tsp fresh ginger slices
- 1 tsp fresh lemon juice
- 1 cup boiling water

Instructions:

1. Steep ginger in boiling water for 10 minutes.
2. Strain, add lemon juice, and sip slowly.

Uses: Soothes nausea and improves digestion.

Storage Tips: Consume immediately.

512. Peppermint and Honey Soothing Tea

Ingredients:

- 1 tsp dried peppermint leaves
- 1 tsp raw honey
- 1 cup boiling water

Instructions:

1. Steep peppermint in boiling water for 5 minutes.
2. Strain, stir in honey, and drink warm.

Uses: Calms the stomach and reduces heartburn.

Storage Tips: Drink fresh.

513. Chamomile and Fennel Digestive Tea

Ingredients:

- 1 tsp dried chamomile flowers
- 1 tsp fennel seeds
- 1 cup boiling water

Instructions:

1. Steep chamomile and fennel in boiling water for 7 minutes.
2. Strain and drink slowly.

Uses: Eases nausea and relieves acid reflux.

Storage Tips: Consume immediately.

514. Licorice Root and Mint Cooling Tea

Ingredients:

- 1 tsp dried licorice root
- 1 tsp dried mint leaves
- 1 cup boiling water

Instructions:

1. Steep licorice root and mint in boiling water for 10 minutes.
2. Strain and sip warm.

Uses: Soothes the esophagus and reduces heartburn.

Storage Tips: Drink fresh.

515. Apple Cider Vinegar and Honey Tonic

Ingredients:

- 1 tbsp apple cider vinegar
- 1 tsp raw honey
- 1 cup warm water

Instructions:

1. Mix apple cider vinegar and honey into warm water.

2. Drink before meals to prevent heartburn.

Uses: Balances stomach acid and prevents reflux.

Storage Tips: Prepare fresh for each use.

516. Lemon Balm and Ginger Nausea Relief Tea

Ingredients:

- 1 tsp dried lemon balm leaves
- 1 tsp fresh ginger slices
- 1 cup boiling water

Instructions:

1. Steep lemon balm and ginger in boiling water for 10 minutes.
2. Strain and sip slowly.

Uses: Relieves nausea and promotes relaxation.

Storage Tips: Consume immediately.

517. Clove and Cinnamon Heartburn Tonic

Ingredients:

- 2 cloves
- 1/2 tsp cinnamon powder
- 1 cup warm water

Instructions:

1. Steep cloves and cinnamon in warm water for 7 minutes.
2. Strain and drink slowly.

Uses: Reduces acid reflux and soothes the stomach.

Storage Tips: Prepare fresh.

518. Cucumber and Aloe Cooling Drink

Ingredients:

- 1/4 cucumber (blended into juice)
- 2 tbsp fresh aloe vera gel

Instructions:

1. Mix cucumber juice and aloe vera gel in a glass.
2. Drink chilled for immediate relief.

Uses: Cools the stomach and alleviates heartburn.

Storage Tips: Drink fresh.

519. Cardamom and Ginger Tonic

Ingredients:

- 1/2 tsp cardamom powder
- 1 tsp fresh ginger juice
- 1 cup warm water

Instructions:

1. Mix cardamom and ginger juice into warm water.
2. Stir and sip slowly.

Uses: Eases nausea and prevents bloating.

Storage Tips: Consume immediately.

520. Warm Milk and Turmeric Anti-Reflux Drink

Ingredients:

- 1/2 tsp turmeric powder
- 1 cup warm milk (dairy or plant-based)

Instructions:

1. Mix turmeric powder into warm milk.
2. Stir well and drink before bedtime.

Uses: Reduces inflammation and soothes acid reflux.

Storage Tips: Prepare fresh.

Supporting Gut Health with Probiotic Herbs

Gut health is the cornerstone of overall well-being, influencing digestion, immunity, mental health, and even skin health. A balanced gut microbiome is essential for efficient digestion, nutrient absorption, and protection against harmful bacteria. Probiotic herbs, along with fermented foods, play a vital role in maintaining and restoring this balance by introducing beneficial bacteria to the digestive system.

Herbs like dandelion, chicory root, and burdock are rich in prebiotics, which feed healthy gut bacteria. Others, like ginger and fennel, soothe the digestive tract, while certain fermented herbal preparations enhance the gut's probiotic population. This chapter explores how to incorporate probiotic herbs into your diet with teas, tonics, and simple recipes that nurture a thriving gut microbiome.

The following 10 herbal remedies are designed to promote a balanced gut, prevent digestive discomfort, and support long-term digestive health. By incorporating these remedies into your routine, you can foster a healthy, resilient gut and enjoy the benefits of enhanced well-being.

10 Remedies for Supporting Gut Health with Probiotic Herbs

521. Dandelion Root and Ginger Gut Tonic

Ingredients:

- 1 tsp dried dandelion root
- 1 tsp fresh ginger slices
- 1 cup boiling water

Instructions:

1. Steep dandelion root and ginger in boiling water for 10 minutes.
2. Strain and sip slowly.

Uses: Encourages healthy gut bacteria and soothes the stomach.

Storage Tips: Drink fresh.

522. Burdock Root and Fennel Tea

Ingredients:

- 1 tsp dried burdock root
- 1 tsp fennel seeds
- 1 cup boiling water

Instructions:

1. Simmer burdock root and fennel in boiling water for 10 minutes.
2. Strain and drink warm.

Uses: Supports digestion and feeds beneficial gut bacteria.

Storage Tips: Consume immediately.

523. Fermented Ginger and Lemon Tonic

Ingredients:

- 1 tbsp grated fresh ginger
- 1 tbsp fresh lemon juice
- 1 cup warm water

Instructions:

1. Combine ginger, lemon juice, and warm water in a jar.
2. Leave uncovered for 12 hours, then refrigerate and drink.

Uses: Introduces natural probiotics and calms the digestive system.

Storage Tips: Refrigerate and consume within 3 days.

524. Chamomile and Chicory Prebiotic Tea

Ingredients:

- 1 tsp dried chamomile flowers
- 1 tsp dried chicory root
- 1 cup boiling water

Instructions:

1. Steep chamomile and chicory root in boiling water for 7 minutes.
2. Strain and sip warm.

Uses: Nourishes gut bacteria and reduces digestive discomfort.

Storage Tips: Drink immediately.

525. Aloe Vera and Mint Digestive Smoothie

Ingredients:

- 2 tbsp fresh aloe vera gel
- 1 tsp dried mint leaves
- 1 cup coconut water

Instructions:

1. Blend all ingredients until smooth.
2. Drink chilled for a refreshing gut-boosting treat.

Uses: Soothes the stomach and supports gut hydration.

Storage Tips: Consume immediately.

526. Probiotic Dill and Garlic Fermented Water

Ingredients:

- 1 tsp dried dill
- 1 clove garlic (smashed)
- 1 cup filtered water

Instructions:

1. Combine all ingredients in a jar.
2. Cover with a breathable cloth and ferment for 24 hours.
3. Strain and drink in small amounts.

Uses: Promotes a healthy gut microbiome and aids digestion.

Storage Tips: Refrigerate and use within 1 week.

527. Licorice Root and Cinnamon Digestive Tea

Ingredients:

- 1 tsp dried licorice root
- 1/2 tsp cinnamon powder
- 1 cup boiling water

Instructions:

1. Steep licorice root and cinnamon in boiling water for 10 minutes.
2. Strain and drink warm.

Uses: Reduces inflammation and supports gut health.

Storage Tips: Drink fresh.

528. Fenugreek and Lemon Hydration Drink

Ingredients:

- 1 tsp fenugreek seeds
- 1 tsp fresh lemon juice
- 1 cup warm water

Instructions:

1. Soak fenugreek seeds in warm water for 12 hours.
2. Strain, add lemon juice, and drink.

Uses: Improves digestion and boosts gut hydration.

Storage Tips: Prepare fresh.

529. Kombucha with Herbal Infusion

Ingredients:

- 1 cup plain kombucha
- 1 tsp dried peppermint leaves

Instructions:

1. Add dried peppermint leaves to kombucha.
2. Let steep for 1 hour, strain, and drink.

Uses: Combines probiotics with digestive-supporting herbs.

Storage Tips: Consume immediately.

530. Yogurt and Chamomile Digestive Bowl

Ingredients:

- 1 cup plain yogurt
- 1 tsp dried chamomile flowers
- 1 tsp honey

Instructions:

1. Grind chamomile flowers into a fine powder.
2. Mix yogurt, chamomile powder, and honey.
3. Enjoy as a probiotic-rich snack.

Uses: Boosts gut health and soothes the stomach.

Storage Tips: Refrigerate and consume within 2 days.

Cleansing and Detoxifying the Digestive System

A healthy digestive system is essential for detoxifying the body and maintaining overall wellness. Toxins from processed foods, environmental pollutants, and stress can accumulate in the digestive tract, leading to sluggishness, bloating, and other health issues. Cleansing and detoxifying the digestive system with herbs can help remove waste, improve gut function, and boost energy levels.

Herbs like dandelion, fennel, ginger, and licorice root are renowned for their detoxifying properties. These herbs stimulate digestion, cleanse the liver, and promote regular bowel movements, ensuring the efficient elimination of toxins. By incorporating these natural remedies into your routine, you can support your body's natural detox processes and enhance overall digestive health.

This chapter introduces 10 herbal remedies, including teas, tonics, and infusions, to help cleanse and detoxify your digestive system. These easy-to-prepare recipes are a practical way to restore balance and vitality to your digestive health.

10 Remedies for Cleansing and Detoxifying the Digestive System

531. Dandelion and Lemon Detox Tea

Ingredients:

- 1 tsp dried dandelion root
- 1 tsp fresh lemon juice
- 1 cup boiling water

Instructions:

1. Steep dandelion root in boiling water for 10 minutes.
2. Strain, add lemon juice, and sip slowly.

Uses: Stimulates liver detoxification and improves digestion.

Storage Tips: Consume immediately.

532. Ginger and Turmeric Cleansing Tonic

Ingredients:

- 1 tsp fresh ginger slices
- 1/2 tsp turmeric powder
- 1 cup warm water

Instructions:

1. Mix ginger and turmeric into warm water.
2. Stir well and drink in the morning.

Uses: Reduces inflammation and aids in digestive cleansing.

Storage Tips: Prepare fresh.

533. Peppermint and Fennel Detox Tea

Ingredients:

- 1 tsp dried peppermint leaves
- 1 tsp fennel seeds
- 1 cup boiling water

Instructions:

1. Steep peppermint and fennel in boiling water for 7 minutes.
2. Strain and drink warm.

Uses: Relieves bloating and promotes gut detoxification.

Storage Tips: Drink fresh.

534. Aloe Vera and Cucumber Detox Drink

Ingredients:

- 2 tbsp fresh aloe vera gel
- 1/4 cucumber (blended into juice)
- 1 cup water

Instructions:

1. Blend aloe vera, cucumber juice, and water.
2. Drink chilled for a refreshing detox.

Uses: Hydrates and soothes the digestive system.

Storage Tips: Use immediately.

535. Parsley and Green Tea Detox Infusion

Ingredients:

- 1 tsp fresh parsley leaves (chopped)
- 1 cup brewed green tea

Instructions:

1. Add parsley to brewed green tea and steep for 5 minutes.
2. Strain and drink warm or chilled.

Uses: Flushes out toxins and supports digestion.

Storage Tips: Consume immediately.

536. Cinnamon and Licorice Root Cleansing Tea

Ingredients:

- 1 tsp dried licorice root
- 1/2 tsp cinnamon powder
- 1 cup boiling water

Instructions:

1. Steep licorice root and cinnamon in boiling water for 10 minutes.
2. Strain and sip slowly.

Uses: Soothes the gut and aids in detoxification.

Storage Tips: Drink fresh.

537. Lemon and Apple Cider Vinegar Morning Tonic

Ingredients:

- 1 tbsp apple cider vinegar
- 1 tsp fresh lemon juice
- 1 cup warm water

Instructions:

1. Mix all ingredients in a glass.
2. Drink on an empty stomach in the morning.

Uses: Stimulates digestion and detoxifies the gut.

Storage Tips: Prepare fresh for each use.

538. Burdock Root and Chamomile Digestive Tea

Ingredients:

- 1 tsp dried burdock root
- 1 tsp dried chamomile flowers
- 1 cup boiling water

Instructions:

1. Steep burdock root and chamomile in boiling water for 10 minutes.
2. Strain and enjoy warm.

Uses: Promotes liver detox and soothes the stomach.

Storage Tips: Drink fresh.

539. Cilantro and Mint Cleansing Infusion

Ingredients:

- 1 tsp fresh cilantro leaves (chopped)
- 1 tsp fresh mint leaves (chopped)
- 1 cup boiling water

Instructions:

1. Steep cilantro and mint in boiling water for 5 minutes.
2. Strain and drink warm.

Uses: Helps eliminate heavy metals and supports digestion.

Storage Tips: Consume immediately.

540. Warm Water and Sea Salt Cleanse

Ingredients:

- 1/4 tsp sea salt
- 1 cup warm water

Instructions:

1. Dissolve sea salt in warm water.
2. Drink on an empty stomach in the morning.

Uses: Stimulates bowel movements and flushes out toxins.

Storage Tips: Use immediately.

BOOK 16

HERBAL SOLUTIONS FOR STRESS RELIEF

Stress is a natural part of life, but when it becomes chronic, it can take a toll on both the mind and body. While modern life often demands quick fixes, herbs offer a gentle, sustainable way to manage stress, promote relaxation, and restore emotional balance. By incorporating natural remedies into your daily routine, you can create a sense of calm and resilience that supports your overall well-being.

This book explores the powerful role of herbs in stress management, highlighting their ability to soothe anxiety, ease tension, and enhance emotional resilience. Nervines like chamomile, valerian, and passionflower calm the nervous system, while adaptogens like ashwagandha and holy basil help the body adapt to stress over time. Through aromatherapy, teas, tinctures, and long-term herbal practices, you can cultivate a sense of inner peace and emotional stability.

Each chapter offers practical, easy-to-follow recipes for managing stress naturally. Whether you're looking for immediate relief or long-term solutions, this book provides the tools you need to navigate life's challenges with greater ease. Embrace the healing power of herbs and discover a more balanced, harmonious approach to stress relief. Your journey to tranquility starts here.

Calming Nervines for Anxiety and Tension

Anxiety and tension are common responses to the challenges of modern life. When left unmanaged, they can lead to physical and emotional strain, impacting overall health. Calming nervines are a category of herbs that directly support the nervous system, helping to ease stress, promote relaxation, and restore balance. These herbs work gently, making them ideal for daily use without the risk of dependency.

Herbs like chamomile, passionflower, valerian, and lemon balm are known for their ability to calm the mind, reduce physical tension, and encourage restful sleep. By incorporating these nervines into your routine, you can address both the mental and physical symptoms of anxiety, creating a greater sense of peace and resilience.

This chapter introduces 10 herbal remedies designed to relieve anxiety and tension naturally. From soothing teas to relaxing baths and inhalation blends, these remedies provide simple, effective ways to bring calm into your daily life.

10 Remedies for Calming Nervines

541. Chamomile and Honey Relaxation Tea

Ingredients:

- 1 tsp dried chamomile flowers
- 1 tsp raw honey
- 1 cup boiling water

Instructions:

1. Steep chamomile in boiling water for 5 minutes.
2. Stir in honey and drink warm.

Uses: Calms the mind and reduces physical tension.

Storage Tips: Consume immediately.

542. Lemon Balm and Lavender Calming Infusion

Ingredients:

- 1 tsp dried lemon balm leaves
- 1 tsp dried lavender flowers
- 1 cup boiling water

Instructions:

1. Steep lemon balm and lavender in boiling water for 7 minutes.
2. Strain and sip slowly.

Uses: Eases anxiety and promotes relaxation.

Storage Tips: Drink fresh.

543. Passionflower and Peppermint Tea

Ingredients:

- 1 tsp dried passionflower
- 1 tsp dried peppermint leaves
- 1 cup boiling water

Instructions:

1. Steep passionflower and peppermint in boiling water for 10 minutes.
2. Strain and drink warm before bedtime.

Uses: Relieves mental stress and supports restful sleep.

Storage Tips: Use immediately.

544. Valerian Root and Ginger Tonic

Ingredients:

- 1 tsp dried valerian root
- 1 tsp fresh ginger slices
- 1 cup boiling water

Instructions:

1. Steep valerian root and ginger in boiling water for 10 minutes.
2. Strain and sip slowly.

Uses: Reduces tension and eases restlessness.

Storage Tips: Consume immediately.

545. Holy Basil (Tulsi) and Lemon Relaxation Drink

Ingredients:

- 1 tsp dried holy basil leaves
- 1 tsp fresh lemon juice
- 1 cup boiling water

Instructions:

1. Steep holy basil in boiling water for 7 minutes.
2. Add lemon juice and sip slowly.

Uses: Balances stress hormones and promotes calmness.

Storage Tips: Prepare fresh for each use.

546. Lavender and Epsom Salt Bath Soak

Ingredients:

- 1/4 cup Epsom salt
- 5 drops lavender essential oil

Instructions:

1. Add Epsom salt and lavender oil to a warm bath.
2. Soak for 20 minutes to relax muscles and reduce stress.

Uses: Relieves physical tension and calms the mind.

Storage Tips: Store dry ingredients in an airtight container for up to 6 months.

547. Peppermint and Rosemary Steam Inhalation

Ingredients:

- 1 tsp dried peppermint leaves
- 1 tsp dried rosemary leaves
- 1 bowl boiling water

Instructions:

1. Add peppermint and rosemary to boiling water.
2. Cover your head with a towel and inhale the steam for 5 minutes.

Uses: Clears the mind and reduces stress.

Storage Tips: Use immediately.

548. Chamomile and Lavender Sleep Sachet

Ingredients:

- 1 tbsp dried chamomile flowers
- 1 tbsp dried lavender flowers
- A small cloth bag

Instructions:

1. Mix chamomile and lavender and place them in the cloth bag.
2. Keep the sachet near your pillow at night.

Uses: Promotes restful sleep and reduces nighttime anxiety.

Storage Tips: Replace herbs every 2–3 months.

549. Lemon Balm and Orange Essential Oil Diffuser Blend

Ingredients:

- 5 drops lemon balm essential oil
- 3 drops orange essential oil

Instructions:

1. Add oils to a diffuser and run for 30 minutes.

Uses: Creates a calming atmosphere and reduces anxiety.

Storage Tips: Store oils in a cool, dark place.

550. Valerian Root and Cinnamon Warming Drink

Ingredients:

- 1 tsp dried valerian root
- 1/2 tsp cinnamon powder
- 1 cup warm almond milk

Instructions:

1. Steep valerian root in warm almond milk for 10 minutes.
2. Strain, add cinnamon, and sip slowly.

Uses: Relieves tension and promotes relaxation.

Storage Tips: Consume fresh.

Aromatherapy Blends for Relaxation

Aromatherapy is a powerful tool for relaxation, offering immediate and soothing relief from stress and anxiety. The therapeutic properties of essential oils work through the sense of smell, directly influencing the nervous system to promote calmness, reduce tension, and enhance emotional well-being. Blending essential oils is an art that allows you to create personalized scents tailored to your needs and preferences.

Oils like lavender, chamomile, ylang-ylang, and bergamot are renowned for their calming effects, while citrus oils like orange and lemon add a refreshing touch. When combined thoughtfully, these oils create blends that transform your environment into a peaceful retreat. Aromatherapy can be used in diffusers, bath soaks, massage oils, and sprays, making it a versatile addition to your relaxation routine.

This chapter introduces 10 aromatherapy blends specifically designed to ease stress and promote relaxation. With simple recipes and easy application methods, these blends are perfect for helping you unwind and find tranquility in your day.

551. Lavender and Chamomile Diffuser Blend

Ingredients:

- 5 drops lavender essential oil
- 3 drops chamomile essential oil

Instructions:

1. Add oils to your diffuser with water as directed.
2. Run for 30 minutes to fill your space with a calming aroma.

Uses: Promotes relaxation and restful sleep.

Storage Tips: Store essential oils in a cool, dark place.

552. Ylang-Ylang and Orange Room Spray

Ingredients:

- 5 drops ylang-ylang essential oil
- 5 drops orange essential oil
- 1 cup distilled water
- 1 tsp witch hazel

Instructions:

1. Mix all ingredients in a spray bottle.
2. Shake well and spray around your room.

Uses: Uplifts mood and reduces tension.

Storage Tips: Store in a cool, dry place for up to 3 months.

553. Bergamot and Cedarwood Relaxation Massage Oil

Ingredients:

- 5 drops bergamot essential oil
- 3 drops cedarwood essential oil
- 2 tbsp carrier oil (such as almond or jojoba oil)

Instructions:

1. Mix essential oils with the carrier oil in a small bottle.
2. Use for a soothing massage.

Uses: Relaxes muscles and calms the mind.

Storage Tips: Store in an airtight container for up to 6 months.

554. Frankincense and Rose Bath Soak

Ingredients:

- 5 drops frankincense essential oil
- 5 drops rose essential oil
- 1 cup Epsom salt

Instructions:

1. Mix oils with Epsom salt and add to a warm bath.
2. Soak for 20 minutes to relax your body and mind.

Uses: Reduces stress and enhances skin health.

Storage Tips: Store dry ingredients in a sealed container for up to 3 months.

555. Lemon and Peppermint Cooling Blend

Ingredients:

- 5 drops lemon essential oil
- 3 drops peppermint essential oil

Instructions:

1. Add oils to a diffuser or inhale directly from a tissue.

Uses: Refreshes the mind and reduces tension headaches.

Storage Tips: Keep essential oils tightly sealed in a dark, cool place.

556. Clary Sage and Geranium Calming Lotion

Ingredients:

- 5 drops clary sage essential oil
- 5 drops geranium essential oil
- 1/4 cup unscented lotion

Instructions:

1. Mix essential oils with the lotion in a small jar.
2. Apply to your hands and neck for relaxation.

Uses: Balances emotions and hydrates skin.

Storage Tips: Store in an airtight container for up to 3 months.

557. Sandalwood and Lavender Relaxing Inhaler

Ingredients:

- 5 drops sandalwood essential oil
- 5 drops lavender essential oil
- 1 aromatherapy inhaler stick

Instructions:

1. Add essential oils to the inhaler stick's cotton wick.
2. Seal and inhale deeply as needed.

Uses: Reduces anxiety and promotes focus.

Storage Tips: Keep the inhaler sealed for up to 6 months.

558. Vetiver and Lemon Grounding Spray

Ingredients:

- 5 drops vetiver essential oil
- 3 drops lemon essential oil
- 1 cup distilled water

Instructions:

1. Combine all ingredients in a spray bottle.
2. Shake well and spray around your space.

Uses: Provides grounding and reduces overwhelm.

Storage Tips: Store in a cool, dry place for up to 3 months.

559. Eucalyptus and Lavender Steam Therapy

Ingredients:

- 5 drops eucalyptus essential oil
- 5 drops lavender essential oil
- 1 bowl boiling water

Instructions:

1. Add essential oils to boiling water.
2. Cover your head with a towel and inhale the steam for 5 minutes.

Uses: Relieves tension and opens airways.

Storage Tips: Use immediately.

560. Jasmine and Chamomile Pillow Spray

Ingredients:

- 5 drops jasmine essential oil
- 5 drops chamomile essential oil
- 1/2 cup distilled water
- 1 tsp witch hazel

Instructions:

1. Mix all ingredients in a spray bottle.
2. Lightly mist your pillow before bedtime.

Uses: Enhances relaxation and promotes deep sleep.

Storage Tips: Store in a cool, dark place for up to 2 months.

Crafting Stress-Relief Tinctures and Teas

Stress can affect both the body and mind, but crafting your own stress-relief tinctures and teas can be a powerful way to find calm and balance. These herbal remedies are easy to prepare, highly effective, and can be tailored to suit individual needs. Tinctures are concentrated herbal extracts made using alcohol or non-alcoholic alternatives like glycerin, while teas provide a gentle, soothing way to incorporate stress-relieving herbs into your daily routine.

Herbs like ashwagandha, passionflower, chamomile, and lemon balm are known for their calming effects, while adaptogens like holy basil and rhodiola support the body's ability to cope with stress. These herbal remedies not only calm the nervous system but also help reduce cortisol levels, promote relaxation, and restore emotional equilibrium.

This chapter provides 10 easy-to-follow recipes for tinctures and teas designed to alleviate stress and promote tranquility. With a combination of quick tinctures and comforting teas, you'll have an arsenal of natural remedies to help manage stress whenever it arises.

561. Lemon Balm and Chamomile Stress-Relief Tea

Ingredients:

- 1 tsp dried lemon balm leaves
- 1 tsp dried chamomile flowers
- 1 cup boiling water

Instructions:

1. Steep lemon balm and chamomile in boiling water for 7 minutes.
2. Strain and sip slowly.

Uses: Calms the mind and promotes relaxation.

Storage Tips: Drink fresh.

562. Holy Basil (Tulsi) and Ginger Tonic Tea

Ingredients:

- 1 tsp dried holy basil leaves
- 1 tsp fresh ginger slices
- 1 cup boiling water

Instructions:

1. Steep holy basil and ginger in boiling water for 10 minutes.
2. Strain and enjoy warm.

Uses: Supports stress resilience and soothes tension.

Storage Tips: Use immediately.

563. Passionflower and Lavender Calming Tea

Ingredients:

- 1 tsp dried passionflower
- 1 tsp dried lavender flowers
- 1 cup boiling water

Instructions:

1. Steep passionflower and lavender in boiling water for 8 minutes.
2. Strain and drink before bedtime.

Uses: Promotes relaxation and restful sleep.

Storage Tips: Consume immediately.

564. Ashwagandha and Cinnamon Adaptogen Tincture

Ingredients:

- 1/4 cup dried ashwagandha root
- 1 cup vegetable glycerin (non-alcoholic base)
- 1/2 cup water

Instructions:

1. Combine ashwagandha root, glycerin, and water in a glass jar.
2. Let steep for 4 weeks, shaking daily.
3. Strain and store in a dark glass bottle.

Uses: Reduces cortisol levels and enhances emotional resilience.

Storage Tips: Store in a cool, dark place for up to 1 year.

565. Valerian Root and Peppermint Tincture

Ingredients:

- 1/4 cup dried valerian root
- 1/4 cup dried peppermint leaves
- 1 cup glycerin or vodka

Instructions:

1. Combine all ingredients in a jar and steep for 4 weeks, shaking daily.
2. Strain and store in a dropper bottle.

Uses: Eases anxiety and reduces tension.

Storage Tips: Store for up to 1 year in a dark, cool place.

566. Rhodiola and Lemon Tea

Ingredients:

- 1 tsp dried rhodiola root
- 1 tsp fresh lemon juice
- 1 cup boiling water

Instructions:

1. Simmer rhodiola root in boiling water for 10 minutes.
2. Add lemon juice and drink warm.

Uses: Improves stress resilience and enhances focus.

Storage Tips: Prepare fresh.

567. Lavender and Honey Soothing Tea

Ingredients:

- 1 tsp dried lavender flowers
- 1 tsp raw honey
- 1 cup boiling water

Instructions:

1. Steep lavender in boiling water for 5 minutes.
2. Stir in honey and sip slowly.

Uses: Calms the nerves and promotes relaxation.

Storage Tips: Drink immediately.

568. Peppermint and Rosemary Mental Clarity Tea

Ingredients:

- 1 tsp dried peppermint leaves
- 1 tsp dried rosemary leaves
- 1 cup boiling water

Instructions:

1. Steep peppermint and rosemary in boiling water for 7 minutes.
2. Strain and drink warm.

Uses: Reduces mental fatigue and promotes relaxation.

Storage Tips: Use fresh.

569. Lemon Balm and Skullcap Tincture

Ingredients:

- 1/4 cup dried lemon balm leaves
- 1/4 cup dried skullcap leaves
- 1 cup glycerin or vodka

Instructions:

1. Combine herbs and glycerin in a jar, then steep for 4 weeks, shaking daily.
2. Strain and store in a dark bottle.

Uses: Relieves stress and enhances emotional balance.

Storage Tips: Store in a cool, dark place for up to 1 year.

570. Holy Basil and Chamomile Bedtime Tea

Ingredients:

- 1 tsp dried holy basil leaves
- 1 tsp dried chamomile flowers
- 1 cup boiling water

Instructions:

1. Steep holy basil and chamomile in boiling water for 7 minutes.
2. Strain and enjoy before bed.

Uses: Supports deep relaxation and restful sleep.

Storage Tips: Consume immediately.

Herbs for Long-Term Emotional Resilience

Life's challenges can take a toll on emotional well-being, but building resilience helps us navigate stress and adversity with greater ease. Herbs play a significant role in supporting long-term emotional health by calming the nervous system, balancing stress hormones, and enhancing overall mental stability. Adaptogens like ashwagandha and rhodiola strengthen the body's ability to adapt to stress, while nervines such as chamomile and lemon balm offer consistent emotional support.

This chapter focuses on herbs that nurture emotional resilience over time, promoting a balanced and calm state of mind. These remedies are not quick fixes; instead, they work gently to build long-term stability and inner peace. Through teas, tinctures, and daily rituals, these herbs help create a solid foundation for mental and emotional health.

Here are 10 herbal remedies designed to foster emotional resilience, providing the tools needed to maintain calmness and clarity in the face of life's demands.

571. Ashwagandha and Holy Basil Adaptogen Tea

Ingredients:

- 1 tsp dried ashwagandha root
- 1 tsp dried holy basil leaves
- 1 cup boiling water

Instructions:

1. Steep ashwagandha and holy basil in boiling water for 10 minutes.

2. Strain and drink warm.

Uses: Supports stress adaptation and emotional stability.

Storage Tips: Consume fresh.

572. Rhodiola and Lemon Balm Calm Tonic

Ingredients:

- 1 tsp dried rhodiola root
- 1 tsp dried lemon balm leaves
- 1 cup boiling water

Instructions:

1. Simmer rhodiola root in boiling water for 10 minutes.
2. Add lemon balm and steep for an additional 5 minutes.
3. Strain and sip slowly.

Uses: Enhances focus and balances mood.

Storage Tips: Drink immediately.

573. Chamomile and Lavender Bedtime Tea

Ingredients:

- 1 tsp dried chamomile flowers
- 1 tsp dried lavender flowers
- 1 cup boiling water

Instructions:

1. Steep chamomile and lavender in boiling water for 7 minutes.
2. Strain and enjoy before bed.

Uses: Promotes restful sleep and reduces emotional fatigue.

Storage Tips: Use fresh.

574. Passionflower and Valerian Night Tincture

Ingredients:

- 1/4 cup dried passionflower
- 1/4 cup dried valerian root
- 1 cup glycerin or vodka

Instructions:

1. Combine all ingredients in a jar and steep for 4 weeks, shaking daily.
2. Strain and store in a dark glass bottle.

Uses: Eases tension and fosters deep relaxation.

Storage Tips: Store in a cool, dark place for up to 1 year.

575. Holy Basil and Peppermint Refreshing Tea

Ingredients:

- 1 tsp dried holy basil leaves
- 1 tsp dried peppermint leaves
- 1 cup boiling water

Instructions:

1. Steep holy basil and peppermint in boiling water for 10 minutes.
2. Strain and drink warm.

Uses: Refreshes the mind and restores balance.

Storage Tips: Consume immediately.

576. Lemon Balm and Skullcap Daily Calm Tea

Ingredients:

- 1 tsp dried lemon balm leaves
- 1 tsp dried skullcap leaves
- 1 cup boiling water

Instructions:

1. Steep lemon balm and skullcap in boiling water for 7 minutes.
2. Strain and drink as needed.

Uses: Relieves daily stress and fosters calmness.

Storage Tips: Drink fresh.

577. Ashwagandha and Cinnamon Adaptogen Tincture

Ingredients:

- 1/4 cup dried ashwagandha root
- 1 tsp cinnamon powder
- 1 cup glycerin

Instructions:

1. Combine ashwagandha, cinnamon, and glycerin in a jar.
2. Let steep for 4 weeks, shaking daily.
3. Strain and store in a dropper bottle.

Uses: Reduces cortisol levels and enhances resilience.

Storage Tips: Store in a cool, dark place for up to 1 year.

578. Rhodiola and Orange Morning Tea

Ingredients:

- 1 tsp dried rhodiola root
- 1 tsp fresh orange zest
- 1 cup boiling water

Instructions:

1. Simmer rhodiola root in boiling water for 10 minutes.
2. Add orange zest and steep for an additional 5 minutes.
3. Strain and drink.

Uses: Boosts energy and improves emotional clarity.

Storage Tips: Prepare fresh.

579. Peppermint and Rosemary Focus Tea

Ingredients:

- 1 tsp dried peppermint leaves
- 1 tsp dried rosemary leaves
- 1 cup boiling water

Instructions:

1. Steep peppermint and rosemary in boiling water for 10 minutes.
2. Strain and sip slowly.

Uses: Promotes mental clarity and reduces tension.

Storage Tips: Use immediately.

580. Lavender and Frankincense Diffuser Blend

Ingredients:

- 5 drops lavender essential oil
- 3 drops frankincense essential oil

Instructions:

1. Add essential oils to a diffuser with water as directed.
2. Run for 30 minutes to create a calming environment.

Uses: Enhances emotional grounding and relaxation.

Storage Tips: Store essential oils in a cool, dark place.

BOOK 17

SUPPORTING RESTFUL SLEEP

A good night's sleep is essential for physical and mental well-being, yet many people struggle to achieve the restful slumber their bodies need. Sleep disturbances, whether caused by stress, an overactive mind, or irregular schedules, can lead to fatigue, irritability, and reduced productivity. Herbs provide a natural and effective way to address sleep issues without the side effects of conventional medications, helping you achieve deeper, more restorative rest.

This book is dedicated to herbal remedies that support healthy sleep patterns. Nervine herbs like chamomile, valerian, and passionflower calm the nervous system, while adaptogens like ashwagandha and holy basil help regulate stress hormones that can interfere with sleep. From soothing nighttime teas to aromatic herbal pillows and remedies for jet lag, these natural solutions are designed to promote relaxation, ease anxiety, and improve the quality of your sleep.

Each chapter offers simple, practical recipes and techniques to help you create a personalized sleep routine. Whether you're seeking relief from insomnia, trying to calm an overactive mind, or recovering from fatigue, this book provides the tools to restore your sleep cycle and enhance your overall well-being. Say goodbye to sleepless nights and embrace the healing power of herbs for a peaceful slumber.

Nighttime Teas for a Peaceful Slumber

Sleep is the cornerstone of good health, yet achieving restful slumber can often feel elusive. Herbal teas are a time-tested remedy for calming the mind, soothing the body, and preparing you for a deep, restorative sleep. They work by harnessing the gentle power of nervine and sedative herbs, which help to relax the nervous system, ease anxiety, and reduce physical tension.

Chamomile, valerian, passionflower, and lavender are some of the most effective herbs for promoting relaxation and sleep. Combined with complementary ingredients like honey, lemon balm, or mint, these teas not only taste delightful but also create a comforting ritual that signals your body it's time to wind down.

This chapter introduces 10 nighttime tea recipes specifically designed to promote a peaceful slumber. These blends are easy to prepare and can be customized to suit your preferences. Sip these teas in the evening as part of your bedtime routine to enjoy their soothing effects and wake up feeling refreshed.

581. Chamomile and Honey Sleep Tea

Ingredients:

- 1 tsp dried chamomile flowers
- 1 tsp raw honey
- 1 cup boiling water

Instructions:

1. Steep chamomile in boiling water for 5 minutes.
2. Strain and stir in honey before drinking.

Uses: Calms the mind and promotes restful sleep.

Storage Tips: Drink fresh.

582. Lavender and Lemon Balm Relaxation Tea

Ingredients:

- 1 tsp dried lavender flowers
- 1 tsp dried lemon balm leaves
- 1 cup boiling water

Instructions:

1. Steep lavender and lemon balm in boiling water for 7 minutes.
2. Strain and sip slowly.

Uses: Relaxes the nervous system and eases tension.

Storage Tips: Consume immediately.

583. Valerian Root and Mint Sleep Aid Tea

Ingredients:

- 1 tsp dried valerian root
- 1 tsp dried peppermint leaves
- 1 cup boiling water

Instructions:

1. Steep valerian root in boiling water for 10 minutes.
2. Add peppermint leaves and steep for another 5 minutes.
3. Strain and drink warm.

Uses: Relieves anxiety and supports deep sleep.

Storage Tips: Use fresh.

584. Passionflower and Orange Zest Bedtime Tea

Ingredients:

- 1 tsp dried passionflower
- 1 tsp fresh orange zest
- 1 cup boiling water

Instructions:

1. Steep passionflower and orange zest in boiling water for 10 minutes.
2. Strain and drink 30 minutes before bedtime.

Uses: Reduces overactive thoughts and promotes calmness.

Storage Tips: Drink immediately.

585. Holy Basil (Tulsi) and Ginger Sleep Tonic

Ingredients:

- 1 tsp dried holy basil leaves
- 1 tsp fresh ginger slices
- 1 cup boiling water

Instructions:

1. Steep holy basil and ginger in boiling water for 7 minutes.
2. Strain and sip slowly.

Uses: Balances stress hormones and aids relaxation.

Storage Tips: Consume fresh.

586. Cinnamon and Nutmeg Warming Sleep Tea

Ingredients:

- 1/2 tsp cinnamon powder
- 1/4 tsp nutmeg powder
- 1 cup warm almond milk

Instructions:

1. Mix cinnamon and nutmeg into warm almond milk.
2. Stir well and enjoy before bed.

Uses: Soothes the body and encourages drowsiness.

Storage Tips: Prepare fresh.

587. Lemon and Peppermint Calming Tea

Ingredients:

- 1 tsp dried peppermint leaves
- 1 tsp fresh lemon juice
- 1 cup boiling water

Instructions:

1. Steep peppermint in boiling water for 5 minutes.
2. Add lemon juice and drink warm.

Uses: Refreshes the mind and promotes relaxation.

Storage Tips: Use immediately.

588. Skullcap and Chamomile Serenity Tea

Ingredients:

- 1 tsp dried skullcap leaves
- 1 tsp dried chamomile flowers
- 1 cup boiling water

Instructions:

1. Steep skullcap and chamomile in boiling water for 8 minutes.
2. Strain and sip slowly before bed.

Uses: Calms the nervous system and reduces nighttime restlessness.

Storage Tips: Drink fresh.

589. Rose and Vanilla Comfort Tea

Ingredients:

- 1 tsp dried rose petals
- 1/4 tsp vanilla extract
- 1 cup boiling water

Instructions:

1. Steep rose petals in boiling water for 5 minutes.
2. Add vanilla extract and stir before drinking.

Uses: Promotes emotional calmness and relaxation.

Storage Tips: Consume immediately.

590. Ginger and Lemon Balm Digestive Sleep Tea

Ingredients:

- 1 tsp fresh ginger slices
- 1 tsp dried lemon balm leaves
- 1 cup boiling water

Instructions:

1. Steep ginger and lemon balm in boiling water for 10 minutes.
2. Strain and sip slowly.

Uses: Eases digestion and prepares the body for sleep.

Storage Tips: Drink fresh.

Remedies for Insomnia and Overactive Minds

Insomnia and an overactive mind can disrupt your sleep cycle, leaving you feeling drained and irritable. Persistent thoughts, anxiety, or even physical restlessness can make it difficult to relax and fall asleep. Herbal remedies offer a natural and gentle solution to calm the mind, soothe the body, and promote a deeper, more restful sleep.

Herbs like valerian root, passionflower, and chamomile are known for their sedative and calming effects, while others like ashwagandha and skullcap support stress relief and emotional balance. When combined in tinctures, teas, or even topical applications, these remedies help quiet the mind and ease the transition to sleep.

This chapter introduces 10 herbal remedies specifically designed to combat insomnia and overactive thoughts. These simple recipes provide effective ways to unwind, relax, and restore your natural sleep patterns.

591. Valerian Root and Lemon Balm Tonic

Ingredients:

- 1 tsp dried valerian root
- 1 tsp dried lemon balm leaves
- 1 cup boiling water

Instructions:

1. Steep valerian root and lemon balm in boiling water for 10 minutes.
2. Strain and drink 30 minutes before bedtime.

Uses: Reduces anxiety and induces drowsiness.

Storage Tips: Use immediately.

592. Passionflower and Chamomile Relaxation Tea

Ingredients:

- 1 tsp dried passionflower
- 1 tsp dried chamomile flowers
- 1 cup boiling water

Instructions:

1. Steep passionflower and chamomile in boiling water for 8 minutes.
2. Strain and sip slowly.

Uses: Calms the nervous system and promotes restful sleep.

Storage Tips: Drink fresh.

593. Ashwagandha and Nutmeg Sleep Elixir

Ingredients:

- 1 tsp ashwagandha powder
- 1/4 tsp nutmeg powder
- 1 cup warm almond milk

Instructions:

1. Mix ashwagandha and nutmeg into warm almond milk.
2. Stir well and drink before bed.

Uses: Reduces cortisol levels and encourages relaxation.

Storage Tips: Prepare fresh.

594. Skullcap and Lavender Bedtime Tincture

Ingredients:

- 1/4 cup dried skullcap leaves
- 1/4 cup dried lavender flowers
- 1 cup glycerin (or vodka for alcohol-based tincture)

Instructions:

1. Combine all ingredients in a jar and steep for 4 weeks, shaking daily.
2. Strain and store in a dark dropper bottle.
3. Take 1–2 droppers of tincture before bed.

Uses: Relieves tension and soothes an overactive mind.

Storage Tips: Store in a cool, dark place for up to 1 year.

595. Chamomile and Rose Sleep Spray

Ingredients:

- 5 drops chamomile essential oil
- 3 drops rose essential oil
- 1/2 cup distilled water
- 1 tsp witch hazel

Instructions:

1. Mix all ingredients in a spray bottle.
2. Shake well and mist onto pillows or bedding.

Uses: Creates a calming atmosphere and supports restful sleep.

Storage Tips: Store in a cool, dry place for up to 3 months.

596. Holy Basil and Ginger Relaxation Tea

Ingredients:

- 1 tsp dried holy basil leaves
- 1 tsp fresh ginger slices
- 1 cup boiling water

Instructions:

1. Steep holy basil and ginger in boiling water for 10 minutes.
2. Strain and drink warm.

Uses: Balances stress hormones and promotes calmness.

Storage Tips: Consume immediately.

597. Lavender and Frankincense Aromatherapy Blend

Ingredients:

- 5 drops lavender essential oil
- 3 drops frankincense essential oil

Instructions:

1. Add essential oils to a diffuser with water as directed.
2. Run for 30 minutes before bedtime.

Uses: Calms the mind and prepares the body for sleep.

Storage Tips: Store essential oils in a cool, dark place.

598. Peppermint and Lemon Balm Steam Inhalation

Ingredients:

- 1 tsp dried peppermint leaves
- 1 tsp dried lemon balm leaves
- 1 bowl boiling water

Instructions:

1. Add herbs to a bowl of boiling water.
2. Cover your head with a towel and inhale deeply for 5 minutes.

Uses: Clears the mind and promotes relaxation.

Storage Tips: Use fresh.

599. Valerian and Cinnamon Sleepy Time Tea

Ingredients:

- 1 tsp dried valerian root
- 1/2 tsp cinnamon powder
- 1 cup boiling water

Instructions:

1. Steep valerian root in boiling water for 10 minutes.
2. Add cinnamon, stir well, and drink warm.

Uses: Eases restlessness and supports deep sleep.

Storage Tips: Prepare fresh for each use.

600. Chamomile and Lemon Balm Dream Tea

Ingredients:

- 1 tsp dried chamomile flowers
- 1 tsp dried lemon balm leaves
- 1 cup boiling water

Instructions:

1. Steep chamomile and lemon balm in boiling water for 7 minutes.
2. Strain and sip before bed.

Uses: Promotes peaceful sleep and reduces night-time anxiety.

Storage Tips: Drink fresh.

Crafting Herbal Pillows for Sleep Aid

Herbal pillows, also known as dream pillows or aromatherapy pillows, have been used for centuries as a natural way to promote restful sleep. Filled with a blend of calming and soothing herbs, these small pillows release gentle aromas that help relax the mind and body, making them an ideal companion for bedtime. The fragrant oils from the herbs work as a form of aromatherapy, gently easing stress and promoting relaxation.

Creating herbal pillows is simple and allows for personalization based on individual preferences. Common herbs like lavender, chamomile, lemon balm, and hops are popular choices for their calming properties, while other herbs like rose petals or mint can add a touch of refreshing or uplifting scent. These pillows can be used under or next to your regular pillow, or even placed on your nightstand to diffuse their soothing fragrance.

This chapter provides 10 easy-to-make recipes for herbal pillows that cater to different sleep needs, from relieving insomnia to calming anxiety. These handmade creations not only improve your sleep quality but also add a personal touch to your bedtime routine.

10 Recipes for Crafting Herbal Pillows

601. Lavender and Chamomile Sleep Pillow

Ingredients:

- 1/4 cup dried lavender flowers
- 1/4 cup dried chamomile flowers
- 1 small cloth pouch

Instructions:

1. Mix lavender and chamomile flowers in a bowl.
2. Fill the cloth pouch with the mixture and seal tightly.

Uses: Promotes relaxation and reduces nighttime restlessness.

Storage Tips: Replace herbs every 3–4 months.

602. Lemon Balm and Mint Refreshing Pillow

Ingredients:

- 1/4 cup dried lemon balm leaves
- 1/4 cup dried peppermint leaves
- 1 small cotton bag

Instructions:

1. Combine lemon balm and mint leaves in a bowl.
2. Stuff the mixture into the cotton bag and secure it.

Uses: Calms the mind and provides a refreshing scent.

Storage Tips: Store in a dry place and replace herbs after 3 months.

603. Hops and Rose Relaxation Pillow

Ingredients:

- 1/4 cup dried hops
- 1/4 cup dried rose petals
- 1 small fabric sachet

Instructions:

1. Mix hops and rose petals together in a bowl.
2. Fill the sachet with the blend and sew or tie it closed.

Uses: Promotes relaxation and reduces mild anxiety.

Storage Tips: Refresh the herbs every 2–3 months.

604. Lavender and Clove Dream Pillow

Ingredients:

- 1/4 cup dried lavender flowers
- 1 tbsp dried cloves
- 1 small muslin bag

Instructions:

1. Combine lavender and cloves in a bowl.
2. Add the mixture to a muslin bag and secure tightly.

Uses: Encourages restful sleep and adds a comforting aroma.

Storage Tips: Replace herbs every 4 months.

605. Chamomile and Cinnamon Calming Pillow

Ingredients:

- 1/4 cup dried chamomile flowers
- 1 tsp cinnamon powder
- 1 small cloth pouch

Instructions:

1. Mix chamomile flowers and cinnamon powder.
2. Fill the cloth pouch with the blend and tie it closed.

Uses: Soothes the mind and provides a warm, relaxing scent.

Storage Tips: Refresh herbs every 3 months.

606. Rose and Lemon Verbena Aromatherapy Pillow

Ingredients:

- 1/4 cup dried rose petals
- 1/4 cup dried lemon verbena leaves

- 1 fabric sachet

Instructions:

1. Mix rose petals and lemon verbena leaves in a bowl.
2. Add the mixture to the sachet and secure tightly.

Uses: Reduces stress and adds a floral, uplifting aroma.

Storage Tips: Replace herbs every 3–4 months.

607. Valerian Root and Lavender Deep Sleep Pillow

Ingredients:

- 1/4 cup dried valerian root
- 1/4 cup dried lavender flowers
- 1 small cotton bag

Instructions:

1. Combine valerian root and lavender in a bowl.
2. Fill the cotton bag with the mixture and tie it closed.

Uses: Supports deep, uninterrupted sleep and calms anxiety.

Storage Tips: Replace herbs every 2–3 months.

608. Peppermint and Rosemary Focus Pillow

Ingredients:

- 1/4 cup dried peppermint leaves
- 1/4 cup dried rosemary leaves
- 1 small fabric pouch

Instructions:

1. Mix peppermint and rosemary leaves in a bowl.
2. Stuff the mixture into the fabric pouch and secure it.

Uses: Eases mild headaches and clears the mind before sleep.

Storage Tips: Store in a dry place and replace herbs after 3 months.

609. Lavender and Orange Zest Pillow

Ingredients:

- 1/4 cup dried lavender flowers
- 1 tbsp dried orange zest
- 1 small muslin bag

Instructions:

1. Combine lavender and orange zest in a bowl.
2. Add the mixture to a muslin bag and secure tightly.

Uses: Brightens mood and promotes restful sleep.

Storage Tips: Refresh herbs every 3 months.

610. Skullcap and Lemon Balm Serenity Pillow

Ingredients:

- 1/4 cup dried skullcap leaves
- 1/4 cup dried lemon balm leaves
- 1 fabric pouch

Instructions:

1. Mix skullcap and lemon balm leaves together.
2. Stuff the mixture into the fabric pouch and seal it.

Uses: Calms an overactive mind and reduces mild insomnia.

Storage Tips: Replace herbs every 3–4 months.

Natural Solutions for Jet Lag and Fatigue

Traveling across time zones or dealing with demanding schedules can disrupt the body's natural rhythm, leading to jet lag and persistent fatigue. Symptoms like insomnia, irritability, and sluggishness can take a toll on both your physical and mental well-being. Natural remedies provide a gentle and effective way to reset your internal clock, boost energy, and help your body recover from travel or exhaustion.

Herbs like valerian root, lemon balm, and chamomile can promote sleep when adjusting to a new time zone, while adaptogens such as ashwagandha and ginseng enhance energy and resilience during the day. Paired with hydration, light exposure, and movement, these herbal solutions can ease the transition and combat fatigue naturally.

This chapter introduces 10 remedies tailored for jet lag and fatigue, from teas and tinctures to aromatherapy blends. These recipes offer practical ways to restore balance, re-energize your body, and help you adjust more smoothly to changes in your routine.

611. Valerian Root and Chamomile Sleep Tea

Ingredients:

- 1 tsp dried valerian root
- 1 tsp dried chamomile flowers
- 1 cup boiling water

Instructions:

1. Steep valerian root and chamomile in boiling water for 10 minutes.
2. Strain and sip slowly before bedtime.

Uses: Promotes restful sleep and helps adjust to a new time zone.

Storage Tips: Consume immediately.

612. Lemon Balm and Peppermint Rebalancing Tea

Ingredients:

- 1 tsp dried lemon balm leaves
- 1 tsp dried peppermint leaves
- 1 cup boiling water

Instructions:

1. Steep lemon balm and peppermint in boiling water for 7 minutes.
2. Strain and drink during the day to refresh and uplift.

Uses: Eases mental fatigue and clears the mind.

Storage Tips: Drink fresh.

613. Ashwagandha and Cinnamon Adaptogen Latte

Ingredients:

- 1 tsp ashwagandha powder
- 1/4 tsp cinnamon powder
- 1 cup warm almond milk

Instructions:

1. Mix ashwagandha and cinnamon into warm almond milk.
2. Stir well and drink in the morning for a gentle energy boost.

Uses: Supports resilience and combats daytime fatigue.

Storage Tips: Prepare fresh.

614. Lavender and Orange Pillow Spray

Ingredients:

- 5 drops lavender essential oil
- 3 drops orange essential oil
- 1/2 cup distilled water
- 1 tsp witch hazel

Instructions:

1. Combine all ingredients in a spray bottle.
2. Shake well and mist onto pillows or bedding.

Uses: Creates a calming atmosphere and aids relaxation.

Storage Tips: Store in a cool, dry place for up to 3 months.

615. Ginseng and Lemon Energy Tea

Ingredients:

- 1 tsp dried ginseng root (sliced or powdered)
- 1 tsp fresh lemon juice
- 1 cup boiling water

Instructions:

1. Simmer ginseng root in boiling water for 10 minutes.
2. Add lemon juice and sip slowly in the morning.

Uses: Boosts energy and improves mental clarity.

Storage Tips: Consume immediately.

616. Rosemary and Peppermint Energy Mist

Ingredients:

- 5 drops rosemary essential oil
- 3 drops peppermint essential oil
- 1/2 cup distilled water

Instructions:

1. Mix all ingredients in a spray bottle.
2. Shake well and spray on your face or wrists for an instant refresh.

Uses: Reduces fatigue and enhances alertness.

Storage Tips: Store for up to 3 months.

617. Ginger and Honey Travel Tonic

Ingredients:

- 1 tsp fresh ginger slices
- 1 tsp raw honey
- 1 cup warm water

Instructions:

1. Steep ginger in warm water for 10 minutes.
2. Stir in honey and drink during travel to ease fatigue.

Uses: Refreshes and supports digestion during long trips.

Storage Tips: Consume immediately.

618. Holy Basil (Tulsi) and Lemon Balm Restorative Tea

Ingredients:

- 1 tsp dried holy basil leaves
- 1 tsp dried lemon balm leaves
- 1 cup boiling water

Instructions:

1. Steep holy basil and lemon balm in boiling water for 10 minutes.
2. Strain and drink in the evening to support restful sleep.

Uses: Balances stress and promotes relaxation.

Storage Tips: Drink fresh.

619. Eucalyptus and Lavender Steam Inhalation

Ingredients:

- 3 drops eucalyptus essential oil
- 3 drops lavender essential oil
- 1 bowl boiling water

Instructions:

1. Add essential oils to a bowl of boiling water.
2. Cover your head with a towel and inhale deeply for 5 minutes.

Uses: Clears the mind and reduces travel-induced tension.

Storage Tips: Use immediately.

620. Rhodiola and Lemon Morning Tonic

Ingredients:

- 1 tsp dried rhodiola root
- 1 tsp fresh lemon juice
- 1 cup warm water

Instructions:

1. Simmer rhodiola root in water for 10 minutes.
2. Add lemon juice and drink in the morning for an energy boost.

Uses: Supports stress resilience and combats fatigue.

Storage Tips: Prepare fresh for each use.

BOOK 18

HERBS FOR CHILDREN

Caring for children often involves navigating a range of minor ailments, from colds and tummy troubles to scraped knees and restless nights. While conventional remedies are widely available, many parents seek natural alternatives to support their child's health gently and effectively. Herbs, with their long history of safe use, offer a versatile and nurturing way to care for little ones.

This book is a guide to using herbs safely and effectively for children. It covers kid-friendly remedies for common ailments, such as herbal syrups for coughs, soothing teas for upset stomachs, and balms for cuts and bruises. You'll also learn how to incorporate nutrient-dense herbs into your child's diet to support their growth and development. These remedies are crafted with children's unique needs in mind, prioritizing gentle, safe, and easy-to-use preparations.

Designed for parents, caregivers, and anyone interested in holistic health, this book provides practical tips for introducing herbal remedies to children and making them a natural part of family wellness. With simple recipes and clear guidance, you'll gain the confidence to care for your children using the wisdom of nature. Let herbs become your partner in raising happy, healthy, and resilient kids.

Kid-Friendly Remedies for Common Ailments

Children are naturally resilient, but they often experience minor ailments like colds, fevers, stomachaches, and scrapes. While these conditions are usually mild, they can cause discomfort and disrupt a child's routine. Herbal remedies provide gentle, effective solutions that can soothe symptoms, promote healing, and boost overall well-being without harsh chemicals or synthetic ingredients.

When treating children, it's important to use remedies tailored to their unique needs. Herbs like chamomile, ginger, calendula, and elderberry are safe and effective options for kids. These herbs can be incorporated into teas, syrups, salves, and other preparations that are both palatable and easy to administer. Additionally, incorporating remedies into playful rituals can make the experience more enjoyable for children.

Below are 10 simple herbal remedies designed to address common childhood ailments. These recipes are quick to prepare and offer natural support for your little one's health.

621. Elderberry and Honey Immune Syrup

Ingredients:

- 1/4 cup dried elderberries
- 2 cups water
- 1/4 cup raw honey

Instructions:

1. Simmer elderberries in water for 30 minutes.
2. Strain the liquid and let cool.
3. Stir in honey and store in a glass jar.

Uses: Boosts immunity and soothes colds.

Storage Tips: Refrigerate for up to 2 weeks.

622. Chamomile Tea for Restful Sleep

Ingredients:

- 1 tsp dried chamomile flowers
- 1 cup boiling water

Instructions:

1. Steep chamomile flowers in boiling water for 5 minutes.
2. Strain and cool slightly before serving.

Uses: Calms the mind and promotes restful sleep.

Storage Tips: Use fresh.

623. Ginger and Lemon Tummy Soother

Ingredients:

- 1 tsp fresh ginger slices
- 1 tsp fresh lemon juice
- 1 cup warm water

Instructions:

1. Steep ginger in warm water for 10 minutes.
2. Add lemon juice and serve warm.

Uses: Eases nausea and stomach discomfort.

Storage Tips: Consume immediately.

624. Calendula Salve for Cuts and Scrapes

Ingredients:

- 1/4 cup dried calendula flowers
- 1/2 cup olive oil
- 1 tbsp beeswax

Instructions:

1. Infuse calendula flowers in olive oil over low heat for 30 minutes.
2. Strain, mix with melted beeswax, and pour into a small tin.

Uses: Promotes healing and soothes irritated skin.

Storage Tips: Store in a cool place for up to 6 months.

625. Peppermint Steam for Congestion

Ingredients:

- 1 tsp dried peppermint leaves
- 1 bowl boiling water

Instructions:

1. Add peppermint to boiling water.
2. Let your child inhale the steam for 5 minutes under supervision.

Uses: Clears nasal passages and eases breathing.

Storage Tips: Use immediately.

626. Honey and Ginger Cough Syrup

Ingredients:

- 1 tsp grated ginger
- 1/4 cup raw honey

Instructions:

1. Mix grated ginger with honey in a small jar.
2. Give 1/2 tsp to your child as needed for a cough.

Uses: Soothes throat irritation and reduces coughing.

Storage Tips: Refrigerate for up to 1 week.

627. Lemon Balm and Honey Calming Tea

Ingredients:

- 1 tsp dried lemon balm leaves
- 1 tsp raw honey
- 1 cup boiling water

Instructions:

1. Steep lemon balm in boiling water for 7 minutes.
2. Strain and stir in honey before serving.

Uses: Reduces stress and calms anxiety.

Storage Tips: Use fresh.

628. Lavender Compress for Fevers

Ingredients:

- 1 cup warm water
- 5 drops lavender essential oil
- A clean cloth

Instructions:

1. Mix lavender oil into warm water.
2. Soak the cloth in the mixture and place it on your child's forehead.

Uses: Lowers mild fevers and promotes relaxation.

Storage Tips: Use immediately.

629. Marshmallow Root Sore Throat Tea

Ingredients:

- 1 tsp dried marshmallow root
- 1 cup boiling water

Instructions:

1. Steep marshmallow root in boiling water for 10 minutes.
2. Strain and let cool slightly before serving.

Uses: Coats the throat and relieves irritation.

Storage Tips: Drink fresh.

630. Aloe Vera and Calendula Skin Soother

Ingredients:

- 2 tbsp fresh aloe vera gel
- 1 tsp calendula-infused oil

Instructions:

1. Mix aloe vera gel and calendula oil in a small container.
2. Apply to sunburns or skin irritations.

Uses: Soothes irritated or sunburned skin.

Storage Tips: Refrigerate for up to 1 week.

Syrups, Teas, and Balms Safe for Little Ones

Children's bodies are delicate and constantly growing, which makes finding gentle and effective remedies essential for their health and comfort. Herbal syrups, teas, and balms are ideal for little ones because they are easy to administer, soothing, and specifically designed to address common ailments like colds, coughs, and minor skin irritations. These remedies are simple to prepare at home, allowing parents to control the ingredients and ensure their child receives safe, natural care.

Herbal syrups, made with herbs and honey, are sweet and appealing, making them particularly well-suited for children. Teas are another excellent option, offering hydration and gentle relief for issues like an upset stomach or restlessness. Balms, created with soothing herbs and oils, provide external care for cuts, scrapes, or dry skin. Each of these preparations can be tailored to suit your child's specific needs and preferences.

This chapter introduces 10 easy recipes for syrups, teas, and balms that are safe for children. These remedies use mild, effective herbs like chamomile, calendula, and elderberry to promote healing and well-being. With these simple herbal solutions, parents can confidently care for their little ones while fostering a holistic approach to family health.

631. Elderberry Immune Syrup

Ingredients:

- 1/4 cup dried elderberries
- 2 cups water
- 1/4 cup raw honey

Instructions:

1. Simmer elderberries in water for 30 minutes.
2. Strain the liquid and let cool.
3. Stir in honey and store in a jar.

Uses: Boosts immunity and helps with colds.

Storage Tips: Refrigerate for up to 2 weeks.

632. Chamomile and Honey Tea

Ingredients:

- 1 tsp dried chamomile flowers
- 1 tsp raw honey
- 1 cup boiling water

Instructions:

1. Steep chamomile flowers in boiling water for 5 minutes.
2. Strain and stir in honey before serving.

Uses: Soothes upset stomachs and promotes relaxation.

Storage Tips: Use fresh.

633. Calendula Healing Balm

Ingredients:

- 1/4 cup dried calendula flowers
- 1/2 cup olive oil
- 1 tbsp beeswax

Instructions:

1. Infuse calendula in olive oil over low heat for 30 minutes.
2. Strain, add melted beeswax, and pour into tins.

Uses: Promotes healing of cuts and scrapes.

Storage Tips: Store in a cool, dry place for up to 6 months.

634. Ginger Tummy-Soothing Tea

Ingredients:

- 1 tsp fresh ginger slices
- 1 tsp raw honey
- 1 cup warm water

Instructions:

1. Steep ginger in warm water for 10 minutes.
2. Strain, add honey, and serve warm.

Uses: Eases nausea and stomach discomfort.

Storage Tips: Prepare fresh.

635. Lavender and Coconut Oil Balm

Ingredients:

- 1/4 cup coconut oil
- 5 drops lavender essential oil

Instructions:

1. Melt coconut oil and mix with lavender oil.
2. Pour into a small jar and let cool.

Uses: Calms irritated skin and promotes relaxation.

Storage Tips: Store for up to 3 months in a cool place.

636. Lemon Balm Relaxation Tea

Ingredients:

- 1 tsp dried lemon balm leaves
- 1 cup boiling water

Instructions:

1. Steep lemon balm in boiling water for 7 minutes.
2. Strain and serve slightly cooled.

Uses: Calms anxiety and promotes restful sleep.

Storage Tips: Drink immediately.

637. Peppermint and Chamomile Cooling Tea

Ingredients:

- 1 tsp dried peppermint leaves
- 1 tsp dried chamomile flowers
- 1 cup boiling water

Instructions:

1. Steep peppermint and chamomile in boiling water for 5 minutes.
2. Strain and serve warm or slightly cooled.

Uses: Relieves mild fevers and digestive upset.

Storage Tips: Use fresh.

638. Marshmallow Root Sore Throat Syrup

Ingredients:

- 1/4 cup dried marshmallow root
- 2 cups water
- 1/4 cup raw honey

Instructions:

1. Simmer marshmallow root in water for 30 minutes.
2. Strain, cool, and mix with honey.

Uses: Coats the throat and soothes irritation.

Storage Tips: Refrigerate for up to 1 week.

639. Calendula and Aloe Skin Balm

Ingredients:

- 1 tbsp calendula-infused oil
- 2 tbsp fresh aloe vera gel

Instructions:

1. Mix calendula oil and aloe vera gel in a small jar.
2. Apply to dry or irritated skin.

Uses: Heals and hydrates delicate skin.

Storage Tips: Refrigerate for up to 1 week.

640. Cinnamon and Ginger Warming Syrup

Ingredients:

- 1 tsp ground cinnamon
- 1 tsp fresh ginger slices
- 1 cup water
- 1/4 cup honey

Instructions:

1. Simmer cinnamon and ginger in water for 20 minutes.
2. Strain, cool, and stir in honey.

Uses: Relieves cold symptoms and boosts circulation.

Storage Tips: Store in the refrigerator for up to 2 weeks.

Tips for Encouraging Herbal Use in Children

Introducing herbal remedies to children can be both a rewarding and challenging experience. While many herbs offer gentle, safe, and effective ways to address minor ailments, children may initially resist trying unfamiliar tastes or incorporating new routines. However, with creativity, patience, and knowledge, you can make herbal remedies an enjoyable and integral part of your child's life. This chapter provides practical tips for encouraging herbal use in children, ensuring that they not only accept but also appreciate the natural healing benefits of herbs.

1. Start with Familiar and Pleasant Flavors

Children are often sensitive to new or strong flavors. Herbs like chamomile, lemon balm, and peppermint are mild and naturally appealing to most kids. Start with teas or syrups made from these herbs, and sweeten them with a touch of honey (for children over one year old) or a splash of fruit juice. Gradually introduce more complex or bitter herbs by blending them with sweeter flavors.

For example, if you're introducing elderberry syrup, which has a slightly tart taste, consider mixing it with a bit of apple juice or diluting it with water. Making the experience pleasant from the start will encourage your child to trust and accept herbal remedies.

2. Involve Children in the Process

Engage your child in preparing herbal remedies. Let them pick herbs from the garden, measure ingredients, or stir a pot of tea. When children are involved, they feel a sense of ownership and are more likely to try the finished product. You can also teach them simple facts about herbs, such as how chamomile helps with sleep or how mint can soothe an upset tummy.

For older children, explain how herbal remedies align with their interests. For example, teach a budding scientist about the medicinal properties of plants, or show an artistic child how to craft herbal sachets or decorate jars for storing remedies.

3. Use Playful Presentation

Children are drawn to things that are fun and imaginative. Turn herbal remedies into a game or part of a story. For example:

- Create a "magic potion" using a brightly colored herbal tea.
- Call elderberry syrup "dragon juice" to spark curiosity.
- Incorporate herbal remedies into pretend play, such as "serving tea" to stuffed animals or dolls.

Herbs can also be incorporated into activities like making herbal crafts or creating DIY bath bombs with lavender or chamomile. These playful approaches make herbs seem less like medicine and more like a special treat.

4. Make Remedies Convenient and Accessible

Children are more likely to use herbal remedies if they are easy to consume. Syrups, gummies, and lozenges are excellent forms for delivering herbal benefits in a way that feels like a snack rather than a treatment. For instance, elderberry gummies are not only tasty but also fun to eat.

Store teas, syrups, or tinctures in brightly labeled bottles with cheerful designs. Encourage your child to personalize their remedy containers with stickers or drawings, turning the storage into an exciting element of the process.

5. Create Herbal Rituals

Consistency and routine help children adapt to new practices. Create rituals around using herbal remedies, such as having "tea time" before bed or taking a spoonful of elderberry syrup every morning. Explain how these habits are part of keeping their body strong and healthy.

Incorporate herbs into daily life in non-medical ways. For example, use herbal bath soaks with calming lavender or chamomile for evening relaxation. These routines help normalize the use of herbs and make them feel less like a chore.

6. Address Resistance with Patience

It's natural for children to be wary of new things, especially if they associate them with being unwell. If your child refuses an herbal remedy, don't force it. Instead, look for alternative ways to introduce the herb. For example:

- Blend the herb into smoothies or juice.
- Infuse the herb into honey and use it as a topping for toast or yogurt.
- Offer herbal popsicles made with tea or syrup.

Praise your child when they try a remedy and focus on positive reinforcement. Over time, their comfort and familiarity with herbs will grow.

7. Share the Benefits

Explain to your child how herbs work and how they will make them feel better. Use simple, relatable terms such as "This tea will help your tummy feel happy again," or "This syrup is like a superhero for your body, helping to fight off colds." Connecting the remedy to a positive outcome can make children more willing to try it.

For older kids, you can provide more detail, teaching them about the history or science behind the herbs. This not only fosters curiosity but also helps them develop a deeper respect for natural healing methods.

8. Use Stories and Books

Children love stories, and weaving herbal remedies into a tale can make them more appealing. Tell a bedtime story about how chamomile flowers help fairies fall asleep or how elderberries give dragons their strength. You can also explore books on herbs designed for children, which feature colorful illustrations and simple explanations.

Books and stories about nature and plants can also help children feel more connected to herbs and the environment. A trip to the library to explore these topics can spark their interest and excitement.

9. Keep Safety in Mind

Always ensure that the herbs you use are age-appropriate and safe for children. Some herbs, such as peppermint and chamomile, are gentle enough for most children, while others, like valerian root or licorice, should be used with caution. Start with small doses and monitor for any reactions.

Consult a healthcare provider or herbalist if you're unsure about the safety of a particular herb for your child. Education and awareness are key to ensuring that your child benefits from herbal remedies safely and effectively.

10. Set an Example

Children often emulate what they see adults doing. If they see you drinking herbal teas or applying a calendula salve, they are more likely to be curious and willing to try it themselves. Make herbs a natural part of your family's lifestyle, and your child will likely follow suit.

Encouraging children to use herbal remedies requires creativity, patience, and a thoughtful approach. By introducing pleasant flavors, involving them in the process, and making herbal remedies fun and accessible, you can foster a positive association with natural healing. Over time, your child will grow comfortable with herbs and may even develop their own curiosity about their benefits. Incorporating herbs into their daily lives not only supports their health but also teaches them to value the gifts of nature—a lesson they can carry into adulthood.

Supporting Growth with Nutrient-Dense Herbs

Children grow rapidly, and their bodies require a consistent supply of essential nutrients to support physical, cognitive, and emotional development. While a balanced diet is the cornerstone of healthy growth, nutrient-dense herbs can play a complementary role in filling nutritional gaps and boosting overall health. These herbs are rich in vitamins, minerals, and beneficial compounds that not only support growth but also strengthen immunity, enhance digestion, and improve energy levels.

Herbs like nettle, alfalfa, dandelion, and moringa are nutritional powerhouses. They provide vital nutrients such as calcium, magnesium, iron, and vitamins A, C, and K, which are critical for building strong bones, maintaining healthy blood, and supporting the nervous system. By incorporating these herbs into your child's daily routine, you can help them thrive during their formative years.

This chapter explores the most effective nutrient-dense herbs for children and provides practical ways to include them in meals and remedies. With recipes and tips, you can confidently support your child's growth and ensure they receive the nourishment they need.

1. The Role of Nutrient-Dense Herbs in Growth

Nutrient-dense herbs are plants that offer a high concentration of vitamins, minerals, and phytonutrients relative to their weight. Unlike synthetic supplements, these herbs provide nutrition in a bioavailable form, meaning the body can absorb and utilize the nutrients more effectively.

For example:

- Calcium and magnesium in herbs like nettle and alfalfa are crucial for bone development and muscle function.
- Iron found in dandelion and moringa supports healthy blood and energy levels.
- Antioxidants in herbs like parsley and hibiscus protect growing cells from oxidative stress.

Incorporating these herbs into your child's diet can prevent deficiencies, improve energy, and support overall health.

2. Nutrient-Dense Herbs for Growth

Here are some of the most effective nutrient-dense herbs for children:

1. Nettle (Urtica dioica)

Nettle is a rich source of calcium, magnesium, iron, and vitamin C, making it excellent for bone health, blood production, and immune support.

2. Alfalfa (Medicago sativa)

Alfalfa is packed with vitamins A, C, and K, as well as trace minerals like zinc and manganese. It supports healthy skin, bones, and digestion.

3. Dandelion (Taraxacum officinale)

Dandelion leaves are high in potassium and iron, promoting healthy blood and detoxification.

4. Moringa (Moringa oleifera)

Known as a "superfood," moringa provides protein, calcium, iron, and vitamin A, making it a powerful herb for overall growth and development.

5. Parsley (Petroselinum crispum)

Parsley is an excellent source of vitamin K and folate, which are essential for bone health and cellular growth.

6. Hibiscus (Hibiscus sabdariffa)

Rich in vitamin C, hibiscus helps boost immunity and supports skin and connective tissue development.

3. Easy Ways to Incorporate Nutrient-Dense Herbs

Children may not always be eager to try new herbs, so it's important to introduce them in creative and palatable ways:

- Smoothies: Blend herbs like moringa powder or nettle infusion into fruit smoothies for a nutrient boost.
- Soups: Add dandelion leaves or parsley to soups and stews.
- Herbal Teas: Make mild teas with herbs like nettle, alfalfa, or hibiscus, and sweeten them with honey.
- Herbal Powders: Sprinkle powdered moringa or parsley into rice, pasta, or scrambled eggs.
- Herbal Gummies: Create kid-friendly gummies using herbal infusions and gelatin.

By integrating these herbs into familiar foods and drinks, you can ensure your child enjoys the benefits without resistance.

641. Nettle and Honey Tea

Ingredients:

- 1 tsp dried nettle leaves
- 1 cup boiling water
- 1 tsp raw honey

Instructions:

1. Steep nettle leaves in boiling water for 10 minutes.
2. Strain, let cool, and stir in honey before serving.

Uses: Provides calcium and iron to support bone and blood health.

Storage Tips: Use fresh.

642. Moringa Smoothie

Ingredients:

- 1 tsp moringa powder
- 1 banana
- 1/2 cup milk (dairy or plant-based)
- 1/4 cup spinach

Instructions:

1. Blend all ingredients until smooth.
2. Serve as a nutritious snack or breakfast.

Uses: Boosts energy and provides essential nutrients.

Storage Tips: Consume immediately.

643. Dandelion and Parsley Soup

Ingredients:

- 1/2 cup fresh dandelion leaves (chopped)
- 1/4 cup fresh parsley (chopped)
- 2 cups vegetable broth

Instructions:

1. Simmer dandelion and parsley in broth for 15 minutes.
2. Blend until smooth and serve warm.

Uses: Detoxifies the body and supports digestion.

Storage Tips: Refrigerate for up to 2 days.

644. Alfalfa and Lemon Herbal Tea

Ingredients:

- 1 tsp dried alfalfa leaves
- 1 cup boiling water
- 1 tsp fresh lemon juice

Instructions:

1. Steep alfalfa leaves in boiling water for 7 minutes.
2. Strain, add lemon juice, and serve warm.

Uses: Provides vitamins and supports overall growth.

Storage Tips: Use fresh.

645. Hibiscus Vitamin-C Drink

Ingredients:

- 1 tsp dried hibiscus flowers
- 1 cup boiling water
- 1 tsp raw honey

Instructions:

1. Steep hibiscus flowers in boiling water for 5 minutes.
2. Strain, cool, and sweeten with honey.

Uses: Boosts immunity and promotes healthy skin.

Storage Tips: Refrigerate for up to 2 days.

646. Moringa Energy Bites

Ingredients:

- 1 tbsp moringa powder
- 1 cup oats
- 1/4 cup peanut butter
- 2 tbsp honey

Instructions:

1. Mix all ingredients in a bowl.
2. Form into small balls and refrigerate for 1 hour.

Uses: Provides a nutrient-rich energy boost.

Storage Tips: Store in the refrigerator for up to 1 week.

647. Parsley and Lemon Juice

Ingredients:

- 1/4 cup fresh parsley (chopped)
- 1/2 cup water
- 1 tsp fresh lemon juice

Instructions:

1. Blend parsley with water.
2. Strain, add lemon juice, and serve chilled.

Uses: Detoxifies and provides essential vitamins.

Storage Tips: Consume immediately.

Nutrient-dense herbs are a powerful way to support children's growth and development naturally. By incorporating these herbs into daily meals and remedies, you can ensure your child receives essential vitamins and minerals in a bioavailable form. With creative recipes and thoughtful preparation, these herbs can become a delicious and enjoyable part of your child's diet, fostering a lifetime of health and wellness.

BOOK 19

HERBAL REMEDIES FOR MEN'S HEALTH

Men's health often takes a backseat in discussions about wellness, yet men face unique challenges that can impact their vitality, hormonal balance, stress levels, and physical appearance. Incorporating herbal remedies into daily routines provides a natural and effective way to address these concerns, promoting overall health and resilience.

This book explores the powerful role of herbs in supporting men's well-being. From herbal tonics that boost energy and stamina to remedies that promote prostate health and balance hormones, these natural solutions are designed to address the specific needs of men. Adaptogenic herbs like ashwagandha and ginseng enhance vitality and stress resistance, while saw palmetto and nettle root support prostate health and hormonal balance. For busy lifestyles, stress-relief remedies provide a much-needed sense of calm and focus. Additionally, this book covers herbal tips for maintaining healthy skin and hair, addressing common issues like dryness, irritation, and hair loss.

With practical recipes and actionable advice, this book empowers men to take charge of their health through nature's wisdom. Whether you're seeking to boost vitality, manage stress, or enhance your daily grooming routine, these herbal remedies offer simple and effective solutions for living your healthiest life.

Supporting Vitality with Herbal Tonics

Vitality is the foundation of a healthy and active life. For men, maintaining energy, stamina, and overall wellness is crucial to meet the demands of work, family, and personal goals. While modern life often leads to fatigue and stress, herbal tonics offer a natural way to enhance vitality, strengthen the body, and improve resilience against daily challenges.

Herbal tonics are crafted to nourish and support the body over time, helping to boost energy, stamina, and overall health. Adaptogenic herbs like ashwagandha, ginseng, and rhodiola improve endurance and promote stress resistance, while nutrient-rich herbs such as nettle and moringa provide essential vitamins and minerals to fuel the body. These tonics are ideal for daily use, working gently yet effectively to restore balance and vitality.

This chapter introduces 10 easy-to-prepare herbal tonics designed specifically for men. These recipes combine herbs known for their energizing, restorative, and strengthening properties, offering a natural boost to physical and mental well-being. Whether you're looking to enhance your workout, recover from fatigue, or simply maintain optimal health, these tonics are an excellent addition to your wellness routine.

648. Ashwagandha and Cinnamon Energy Tonic

Ingredients:

- 1 tsp ashwagandha powder
- 1/2 tsp cinnamon powder
- 1 cup warm almond milk

Instructions:

1. Mix ashwagandha and cinnamon into warm almond milk.
2. Stir well and drink in the morning or evening.

Uses: Boosts energy and promotes resilience to stress.

Storage Tips: Consume immediately.

649. Ginseng and Lemon Refreshing Tonic

Ingredients:

- 1 tsp dried ginseng root
- 1 tsp fresh lemon juice
- 1 cup boiling water

Instructions:

1. Simmer ginseng root in boiling water for 10 minutes.
2. Strain, add lemon juice, and sip warm.

Uses: Enhances endurance and mental clarity.

Storage Tips: Drink fresh.

650. Nettle and Honey Nutritive Tonic

Ingredients:

- 1 tsp dried nettle leaves
- 1 tsp raw honey
- 1 cup boiling water

Instructions:

1. Steep nettle leaves in boiling water for 10 minutes.
2. Strain, stir in honey, and drink warm.

Uses: Provides essential nutrients and supports overall health.

Storage Tips: Use immediately.

651. Rhodiola and Mint Cooling Tonic

Ingredients:

- 1 tsp dried rhodiola root
- 1 tsp dried mint leaves
- 1 cup boiling water

Instructions:

1. Simmer rhodiola root in boiling water for 10 minutes.
2. Add mint leaves and steep for another 5 minutes.
3. Strain and drink warm or chilled.

Uses: Reduces fatigue and improves focus.

Storage Tips: Consume fresh.

652. Holy Basil (Tulsi) and Ginger Immune Tonic

Ingredients:

- 1 tsp dried holy basil leaves
- 1 tsp fresh ginger slices
- 1 cup boiling water

Instructions:

1. Steep holy basil and ginger in boiling water for 7 minutes.
2. Strain and drink warm.

Uses: Enhances immunity and reduces stress.

Storage Tips: Use immediately.

653. Moringa and Lemon Uplifting Tonic

Ingredients:

- 1 tsp moringa powder
- 1 tsp fresh lemon juice
- 1 cup warm water

Instructions:

1. Mix moringa powder into warm water.
2. Add lemon juice and stir well before drinking.

Uses: Boosts energy and provides essential nutrients.

Storage Tips: Prepare fresh.

654. Licorice Root and Cardamom Tonic

Ingredients:

- 1 tsp dried licorice root
- 1/2 tsp cardamom powder
- 1 cup boiling water

Instructions:

1. Steep licorice root and cardamom in boiling water for 10 minutes.
2. Strain and enjoy warm.

Uses: Supports adrenal health and improves vitality.

Storage Tips: Drink immediately.

655. Fenugreek and Honey Strength Tonic

Ingredients:

- 1 tsp fenugreek seeds
- 1 tsp raw honey
- 1 cup warm milk (dairy or plant-based)

Instructions:

1. Soak fenugreek seeds in warm milk for 10 minutes.
2. Strain, stir in honey, and drink.

Uses: Improves stamina and muscle recovery.

Storage Tips: Use fresh.

656. Hibiscus and Orange Vitamin Tonic

Ingredients:

- 1 tsp dried hibiscus flowers
- 1/2 tsp fresh orange zest
- 1 cup boiling water

Instructions:

1. Steep hibiscus flowers and orange zest in boiling water for 7 minutes.
2. Strain and drink warm or chilled.

Uses: Boosts immunity and reduces oxidative stress.

Storage Tips: Consume fresh.

657. Parsley and Apple Green Tonic

Ingredients:

- 1/4 cup fresh parsley leaves (chopped)
- 1 cup fresh apple juice

Instructions:

1. Blend parsley leaves with apple juice until smooth.
2. Strain and serve chilled.

Uses: Detoxifies and energizes the body.

Storage Tips: Drink immediately.

Remedies for Prostate and Hormonal Health

Maintaining prostate and hormonal health is essential for men's overall well-being. As men age, they may face challenges such as hormonal imbalances, prostate enlargement (benign prostatic hyperplasia, or BPH), and other related concerns that can impact their energy levels, urinary health, and quality of life. Herbal remedies provide a natural and effective way to support these areas, promoting balance and long-term health.

Herbs like saw palmetto, nettle root, and pygeum are well-known for supporting prostate health by reducing inflammation and improving urinary function. Meanwhile, adaptogens like ashwagandha and ginseng help regulate hormones and enhance energy levels. By incorporating these herbs into daily routines through teas, tinctures, and tonics, men can address hormonal and prostate health in a safe, sustainable manner.

This chapter provides 10 simple remedies tailored for prostate and hormonal health. These recipes harness the power of nature to promote balance, reduce discomfort, and support overall vitality.

658. Saw Palmetto and Nettle Root Prostate Tonic

Ingredients:

- 1 tsp dried saw palmetto berries
- 1 tsp dried nettle root
- 1 cup boiling water

Instructions:

1. Steep saw palmetto and nettle root in boiling water for 10 minutes.
2. Strain and drink warm.

Uses: Supports prostate health and reduces urinary discomfort.

Storage Tips: Drink immediately.

659. Pumpkin Seed and Lemon Vitality Snack

Ingredients:

- 1/4 cup raw pumpkin seeds
- 1 tsp fresh lemon juice

Instructions:

1. Toss pumpkin seeds with lemon juice.
2. Eat as a healthy snack.

Uses: Provides zinc and antioxidants to support prostate health.

Storage Tips: Store seeds in an airtight container for up to 1 week.

660. Pygeum and Ginger Tea

Ingredients:

- 1 tsp dried pygeum bark
- 1 tsp fresh ginger slices
- 1 cup boiling water

Instructions:

1. Simmer pygeum bark and ginger in boiling water for 10 minutes.
2. Strain and sip slowly.

Uses: Reduces inflammation and supports urinary function.

Storage Tips: Use fresh.

661. Ashwagandha and Cinnamon Hormone Balancer

Ingredients:

- 1 tsp ashwagandha powder
- 1/2 tsp cinnamon powder
- 1 cup warm almond milk

Instructions:

1. Mix ashwagandha and cinnamon into warm almond milk.
2. Stir well and drink before bed.

Uses: Regulates stress hormones and enhances energy.

Storage Tips: Consume immediately.

662. Green Tea and Lycopene Booster

Ingredients:

- 1 tsp green tea leaves
- 1/4 cup tomato juice

Instructions:

1. Steep green tea leaves in boiling water for 5 minutes.
2. Cool and mix with tomato juice.

Uses: Provides antioxidants that support prostate health.

Storage Tips: Drink fresh.

663. Nettle Root and Peppermint Infusion

Ingredients:

- 1 tsp dried nettle root
- 1 tsp dried peppermint leaves
- 1 cup boiling water

Instructions:

1. Steep nettle root and peppermint leaves in boiling water for 10 minutes.
2. Strain and drink warm.

Uses: Improves urinary flow and reduces inflammation.

Storage Tips: Use immediately.

664. Flaxseed and Honey Hormonal Balance Drink

Ingredients:

- 1 tbsp ground flaxseed
- 1 tsp raw honey
- 1 cup warm water

Instructions:

1. Mix flaxseed and honey into warm water.
2. Stir well and drink in the morning.

Uses: Balances hormones and promotes overall health.

Storage Tips: Prepare fresh daily.

665. Turmeric and Black Pepper Anti-Inflammatory Tonic

Ingredients:

- 1/2 tsp turmeric powder
- 1/4 tsp black pepper
- 1 cup warm coconut milk

Instructions:

1. Mix turmeric and black pepper into warm coconut milk.

2. Stir well and sip slowly.

Uses: Reduces prostate inflammation and boosts immunity.

Storage Tips: Consume fresh.

666. Fenugreek and Lemon Hormonal Tea

Ingredients:

- 1 tsp fenugreek seeds
- 1 tsp fresh lemon juice
- 1 cup boiling water

Instructions:

1. Steep fenugreek seeds in boiling water for 10 minutes.
2. Strain, add lemon juice, and drink warm.

Uses: Supports testosterone balance and energy levels.

Storage Tips: Drink immediately.

667. Rosemary and Olive Oil Prostate Massage Oil

Ingredients:

- 1/4 cup olive oil
- 5 drops rosemary essential oil

Instructions:

1. Mix olive oil with rosemary essential oil.
2. Use as a massage oil for lower back and abdomen.

Uses: Improves circulation and supports prostate health.

Storage Tips: Store in an airtight container for up to 3 months.

Natural Stress Management for Busy Lifestyles

Modern life often brings a whirlwind of responsibilities, leaving little time for rest and self-care. For men balancing work, family, and personal commitments, stress can take a significant toll on both physical and mental health. Over time, chronic stress can lead to fatigue, irritability, poor sleep, and even long-term health conditions. Fortunately, nature offers a variety of herbs and remedies that can help manage stress and restore balance.

Adaptogenic herbs like ashwagandha, rhodiola, and holy basil are renowned for their ability to regulate the body's stress response and improve resilience. Nervines like chamomile and passion-flower calm the nervous system and promote relaxation, making them effective for immediate relief. These remedies can be incorporated into daily routines as teas, tinctures, or aromatherapy blends to help manage stress naturally and sustainably.

This chapter introduces 10 herbal remedies specifically designed to alleviate stress for busy men. These practical recipes are easy to prepare and use, offering a calming, grounding effect that supports mental clarity and emotional well-being even during the most demanding days.

668. Ashwagandha and Cinnamon Anti-Stress Tea

Ingredients:

- 1 tsp ashwagandha powder
- 1/2 tsp cinnamon powder
- 1 cup boiling water

Instructions:

1. Steep ashwagandha and cinnamon in boiling water for 10 minutes.
2. Strain and drink warm.

Uses: Enhances resilience to stress and balances cortisol levels.

Storage Tips: Consume immediately.

669. Rhodiola and Mint Energy Tonic

Ingredients:

- 1 tsp dried rhodiola root
- 1 tsp dried mint leaves
- 1 cup boiling water

Instructions:

1. Simmer rhodiola root in boiling water for 10 minutes.
2. Add mint leaves, steep for 5 minutes, and strain.

Uses: Reduces fatigue and improves mental focus.

Storage Tips: Drink fresh.

670. Holy Basil (Tulsi) and Lemon Calming Tea

Ingredients:

- 1 tsp dried holy basil leaves
- 1 tsp fresh lemon juice
- 1 cup boiling water

Instructions:

1. Steep holy basil in boiling water for 7 minutes.
2. Add lemon juice and drink warm.

Uses: Eases anxiety and promotes relaxation.

Storage Tips: Prepare fresh daily.

671. Passionflower and Chamomile Relaxation Tea

Ingredients:

- 1 tsp dried passionflower
- 1 tsp dried chamomile flowers
- 1 cup boiling water

Instructions:

1. Steep passionflower and chamomile in boiling water for 10 minutes.
2. Strain and sip before bedtime.

Uses: Calms the mind and promotes restful sleep.

Storage Tips: Use fresh.

672. Lemon Balm and Peppermint Stress-Relief Infusion

Ingredients:

- 1 tsp dried lemon balm leaves
- 1 tsp dried peppermint leaves
- 1 cup boiling water

Instructions:

1. Steep lemon balm and peppermint in boiling water for 7 minutes.
2. Strain and drink warm.

Uses: Soothes digestive discomfort caused by stress.

Storage Tips: Consume immediately.

673. Lavender and Rosemary Aromatherapy Spray

Ingredients:

- 5 drops lavender essential oil
- 3 drops rosemary essential oil
- 1/2 cup distilled water
- 1 tsp witch hazel

Instructions:

1. Mix all ingredients in a spray bottle.
2. Shake well and mist onto your workspace or pillow.

Uses: Creates a calming and focused environment.

Storage Tips: Store for up to 3 months in a cool, dry place.

674. Ginseng and Ginger Morning Energy Drink

Ingredients:

- 1 tsp dried ginseng root
- 1 tsp fresh ginger slices
- 1 cup boiling water

Instructions:

1. Simmer ginseng and ginger in boiling water for 10 minutes.
2. Strain and drink to start your day.

Uses: Boosts energy and reduces mental fatigue.

Storage Tips: Use immediately.

675. Valerian and Lavender Sleep Tonic

Ingredients:

- 1 tsp dried valerian root
- 1 tsp dried lavender flowers
- 1 cup boiling water

Instructions:

1. Steep valerian root and lavender in boiling water for 10 minutes.
2. Strain and drink an hour before bed.

Uses: Promotes restful sleep and reduces night-time anxiety.

Storage Tips: Drink fresh.

676. Chamomile and Orange Essential Oil Diffuser Blend

Ingredients:

- 5 drops chamomile essential oil
- 3 drops orange essential oil

Instructions:

1. Add essential oils to a diffuser with water as directed.
2. Run for 30 minutes to relax and uplift your mood.

Uses: Reduces stress and promotes a sense of calm.

Storage Tips: Keep oils in a cool, dark place.

677. Adaptogen Smoothie for Stress Relief

Ingredients:

- 1 tsp ashwagandha powder
- 1/4 cup spinach
- 1/2 banana
- 1 cup almond milk

Instructions:

1. Blend all ingredients until smooth.
2. Serve as a quick, nourishing snack.

Uses: Provides energy and balances stress hormones.

Storage Tips: Consume immediately.

BOOK 20

AGING GRACEFULLY WITH HERBAL MEDICINE

Aging is a natural part of life, but it doesn't have to mean a decline in health and vitality. With the right care and attention, aging can be a graceful and empowering journey. Herbal medicine offers a time-tested approach to supporting the body and mind as they adapt to the changes that come with age. From easing joint pain to improving cognitive function, sleep quality, and overall longevity, herbs can enhance the aging process by promoting wellness, resilience, and balance.

This book is designed to provide practical guidance and remedies tailored to the needs of seniors. It explores herbal solutions for maintaining mobility, enhancing mental clarity, addressing sleep challenges, and supporting overall health. Adaptogenic herbs like ashwagandha and rhodiola build resilience to stress and promote cognitive function, while anti-inflammatory herbs like turmeric and ginger help alleviate joint pain and improve mobility. Longevity tonics incorporating nutrient-rich herbs offer holistic support for a vibrant life.

Whether you're looking to maintain your energy, improve your sleep, or support your mental and physical health, this book provides simple and effective herbal remedies to help you age with confidence and grace. Embrace the wisdom of nature and thrive in every stage of life.

Remedies for Joint Pain and Mobility

Joint pain and reduced mobility are common concerns as we age, often caused by conditions like arthritis, inflammation, or general wear and tear on the body. These issues can affect daily activities and overall quality of life. While conventional treatments may provide temporary relief, herbal remedies offer a natural, long-term approach to reducing pain, improving flexibility, and supporting joint health.

Herbs with anti-inflammatory and pain-relieving properties, such as turmeric, ginger, and boswellia, are particularly effective for joint health. Nutrient-rich herbs like nettle and horsetail support the body by providing essential minerals for bone and cartilage strength. Incorporating these remedies into your daily routine can help restore mobility, reduce discomfort, and enhance overall well-being.

This chapter introduces 10 herbal remedies for joint pain and mobility, ranging from teas and tinctures to topical applications. These simple and effective recipes provide natural relief, helping you stay active and enjoy life to the fullest.

688. Turmeric and Black Pepper Anti-Inflammatory Tonic

Ingredients:

1/2 tsp turmeric powder

1/4 tsp black pepper

1 cup warm coconut milk

Instructions:

Mix turmeric and black pepper into warm coconut milk.

Stir well and drink once daily.

Uses: Reduces inflammation and supports joint health.

Storage Tips: Consume immediately.

689. Ginger and Lemon Pain-Relief Tea

Ingredients:

1 tsp fresh ginger slices

1 tsp fresh lemon juice

1 cup boiling water

Instructions:

Steep ginger slices in boiling water for 10 minutes.

Add lemon juice, strain, and drink warm.

Uses: Relieves joint pain and improves circulation.

Storage Tips: Use fresh.

690. Boswellia and Honey Tincture

Ingredients:

1/4 cup dried boswellia resin

1 cup vegetable glycerin or vodka

Instructions:

Combine boswellia resin and glycerin in a jar.

Steep for 4 weeks, shaking daily.

Strain and store in a dark bottle.

Uses: Reduces arthritis-related inflammation and pain.

Storage Tips: Store in a cool, dark place for up to 1 year.

691. Nettle Infusion for Joint Health

Ingredients:

1 tsp dried nettle leaves

1 cup boiling water

Instructions:

Steep nettle leaves in boiling water for 10 minutes.

Strain and drink daily.

Uses: Provides essential minerals to strengthen bones and joints.

Storage Tips: Drink fresh.

692. Eucalyptus and Lavender Massage Oil

Ingredients:

5 drops eucalyptus essential oil

5 drops lavender essential oil

2 tbsp carrier oil (such as almond or olive oil)

Instructions:

Mix all ingredients in a small bottle.

Massage onto affected joints as needed.

Uses: Reduces pain and improves flexibility.

Storage Tips: Store for up to 6 months in a cool, dry place.

693. Horsetail and Mint Tea

Ingredients:

1 tsp dried horsetail

1 tsp dried mint leaves

1 cup boiling water

Instructions:

Steep horsetail and mint in boiling water for 10 minutes.

Strain and drink warm.

Uses: Strengthens cartilage and supports joint mobility.

Storage Tips: Use immediately.

694. Arnica and Olive Oil Topical Balm

Ingredients:

1/4 cup dried arnica flowers

1/2 cup olive oil

1 tbsp beeswax

Instructions:

Infuse arnica flowers in olive oil over low heat for 30 minutes.

Strain, mix with melted beeswax, and pour into a container.

Uses: Relieves pain and reduces swelling in joints.

Storage Tips: Store in a cool, dry place for up to 6 months.

695. Cayenne and Coconut Oil Warm Rub

Ingredients:

1/4 tsp cayenne pepper powder

2 tbsp coconut oil

Instructions:

Mix cayenne pepper into coconut oil.

Apply to affected joints and leave for 10–15 minutes.

Rinse thoroughly.

Uses: Stimulates blood flow and reduces stiffness.

Storage Tips: Store in a sealed container for up to 3 months.

696. Willow Bark and Chamomile Pain-Relief Tea

Ingredients:

1 tsp dried willow bark

1 tsp dried chamomile flowers

1 cup boiling water

Instructions:

Simmer willow bark in boiling water for 10 minutes.

Add chamomile flowers, steep for 5 minutes, and strain.

Uses: Relieves joint pain and inflammation.

Storage Tips: Drink fresh.

697. Rosemary and Olive Oil Joint Compress

Ingredients:

1/4 cup fresh rosemary leaves

1/2 cup olive oil

A clean cloth

Instructions:

Warm olive oil and rosemary leaves over low heat for 10 minutes.

Soak the cloth in the mixture and apply to the affected joint for 20 minutes.

Uses: Reduces inflammation and improves circulation.

Storage Tips: Use immediately.

Cognitive Support with Adaptogens

As we age, maintaining cognitive function becomes increasingly important for overall quality of life. Challenges like memory lapses, reduced focus, and mental fatigue can impact daily activities and emotional well-being. While a healthy diet, regular exercise, and mental stimulation are key components of brain health, adaptogenic herbs provide an additional layer of support by enhancing the body's resilience to stress and improving cognitive function.

Adaptogens are a unique class of herbs that help the body adapt to physical, mental, and emotional stress. They regulate cortisol levels, protect brain cells from oxidative damage, and improve blood flow to the brain, all of which are critical for preserving mental clarity and focus. Herbs like ashwagandha, rhodiola, ginseng, and holy basil have been widely studied for their cognitive-enhancing properties and are known to support memory, concentration, and mental energy.

This chapter delves into the benefits of adaptogens for cognitive health, explaining how they work and providing practical ways to incorporate them into your routine. Additionally, you'll find 10 recipes that make it easy to enjoy the cognitive benefits of these powerful herbs.

How Adaptogens Support Cognitive Health

Adaptogens work on multiple levels to support brain health:

Regulating Cortisol Levels: Chronic stress elevates cortisol, a hormone that can impair memory and reduce focus. Adaptogens like ashwagandha and rhodiola balance cortisol levels, helping you stay calm and focused.

Enhancing Neuroprotection: Adaptogens protect brain cells from oxidative stress, which can lead to cognitive decline. Antioxidant-rich adaptogens such as ginseng and holy basil reduce the damage caused by free radicals.

Improving Circulation: Herbs like ginkgo biloba and rhodiola enhance blood flow to the brain, ensuring it receives the oxygen and nutrients needed for optimal function.

Boosting Neurotransmitter Activity: Adaptogens promote the production of neurotransmitters like dopamine and serotonin, which improve mood, memory, and cognitive sharpness.

Best Adaptogens for Cognitive Support

1. Ashwagandha (Withania somnifera)

Benefits: Reduces stress, improves memory, and enhances focus.

Best Uses: Teas, powders, and capsules.

2. Rhodiola (Rhodiola rosea)

Benefits: Increases mental energy, reduces fatigue, and enhances memory.

Best Uses: Teas and tinctures.

3. Ginseng (Panax ginseng)

Benefits: Boosts concentration, reduces mental fatigue, and supports long-term brain health.

Best Uses: Teas and tonics.

4. Holy Basil (Ocimum sanctum, or Tulsi)

Benefits: Improves mood, reduces anxiety, and enhances mental clarity.

Best Uses: Teas and infusions.

5. Bacopa (Bacopa monnieri)

Benefits: Supports memory retention and cognitive processing speed.

Best Uses: Teas and tinctures.

698. Ashwagandha and Cinnamon Memory Tea

Ingredients:

1 tsp ashwagandha powder

1/2 tsp cinnamon powder

1 cup boiling water

Instructions:

Steep ashwagandha and cinnamon in boiling water for 10 minutes.

Strain and drink warm.

Uses: Reduces stress and enhances memory.

Storage Tips: Use fresh.

699. Rhodiola and Lemon Energy Tonic

Ingredients:

1 tsp dried rhodiola root

1 tsp fresh lemon juice

1 cup boiling water

Instructions:

Simmer rhodiola root in boiling water for 10 minutes.

Add lemon juice, strain, and drink warm.

Uses: Improves focus and mental energy.

Storage Tips: Consume immediately.

700. Ginseng and Honey Focus Tea

Ingredients:

1 tsp dried ginseng root

1 tsp raw honey

1 cup boiling water

Instructions:

Steep ginseng root in boiling water for 10 minutes.

Strain, add honey, and sip slowly.

Uses: Boosts mental clarity and reduces fatigue.

Storage Tips: Drink fresh.

701. Holy Basil and Mint Clarity Infusion

Ingredients:

1 tsp dried holy basil leaves

1 tsp dried mint leaves

1 cup boiling water

Instructions:

Steep holy basil and mint in boiling water for 7 minutes.

Strain and drink warm.

Uses: Reduces anxiety and improves focus.

Storage Tips: Prepare fresh daily.

702. Bacopa and Hibiscus Brain Tonic

Ingredients:

1 tsp dried bacopa leaves

1 tsp dried hibiscus flowers

1 cup boiling water

Instructions:

Steep bacopa and hibiscus in boiling water for 10 minutes.

Strain and drink warm.

Uses: Enhances memory and reduces oxidative stress.

Storage Tips: Drink immediately.

703. Adaptogen Smoothie Bowl

Ingredients:

1 tsp ashwagandha powder

1/2 banana

1/2 cup spinach

1/2 cup almond milk

Instructions:

Blend all ingredients until smooth.

Serve in a bowl and top with nuts or seeds.

Uses: Provides a nutrient-rich start to the day and boosts cognitive function.

Storage Tips: Consume immediately.

704. Rhodiola and Ginger Brain Booster Tea

Ingredients:

1 tsp dried rhodiola root

1 tsp fresh ginger slices

1 cup boiling water

Instructions:

Simmer rhodiola and ginger in boiling water for 10 minutes.

Strain and drink warm.

Uses: Reduces mental fatigue and enhances focus.

Storage Tips: Use fresh.

705. Holy Basil and Lavender Relaxation Tonic

Ingredients:

1 tsp dried holy basil leaves

1/2 tsp dried lavender flowers

1 cup boiling water

Instructions:

Steep holy basil and lavender in boiling water for 7 minutes.

Strain and sip slowly.

Uses: Relieves stress and promotes mental clarity.

Storage Tips: Consume immediately.

706. Ginseng and Turmeric Golden Latte

Ingredients:

1 tsp ginseng powder

1/2 tsp turmeric powder

1 cup warm coconut milk

Instructions:

Mix ginseng and turmeric into warm coconut milk.

Stir well and drink in the evening.

Uses: Reduces inflammation and supports brain health.

Storage Tips: Drink fresh.

707. Bacopa and Lemon Balm Cognitive Tonic

Ingredients:

1 tsp dried bacopa leaves

1 tsp dried lemon balm leaves

1 cup boiling water

Instructions:

Steep bacopa and lemon balm in boiling water for 10 minutes.

Strain and drink warm.

Uses: Enhances memory and calms the mind.

Storage Tips: Use immediately.

Herbal Solutions for Sleep Challenges in Seniors

Sleep plays a crucial role in maintaining physical and mental well-being, yet many seniors struggle with issues like insomnia, fragmented sleep, or waking up too early. These challenges can result from hormonal changes, increased stress, or age-related health conditions. While prescription medications are often used to treat sleep disorders, they may come with side effects such as grogginess or dependency. Herbal remedies offer a gentle, natural alternative to improve sleep quality and address the underlying causes of sleep disturbances.

Certain herbs like valerian root, chamomile, and passionflower have been used for centuries to calm the mind, relax the body, and promote restful sleep. Additionally, adaptogens like ashwagandha and holy basil help reduce stress and balance hormones, making it easier to achieve deep, restorative sleep. These remedies can be consumed as teas, tinctures, or topical applications, offering versatile and effective solutions for various sleep challenges.

This chapter provides 10 simple and effective herbal remedies to help seniors achieve better sleep. By incorporating these natural solutions into your nightly routine, you can create a peaceful environment that supports relaxation and rejuvenation.

708. Valerian and Chamomile Bedtime Tea

Ingredients:

1 tsp dried valerian root

1 tsp dried chamomile flowers

1 cup boiling water

Instructions:

Steep valerian root and chamomile in boiling water for 10 minutes.

Strain and drink 30 minutes before bed.

Uses: Promotes relaxation and eases anxiety for a peaceful night's sleep.

Storage Tips: Use fresh.

709. Lavender and Lemon Balm Calming Infusion

Ingredients:

1 tsp dried lavender flowers

1 tsp dried lemon balm leaves

1 cup boiling water

Instructions:

Steep lavender and lemon balm in boiling water for 7 minutes.

Strain and sip slowly.

Uses: Reduces stress and prepares the body for restful sleep.

Storage Tips: Consume immediately.

710. Ashwagandha Sleep Tonic

Ingredients:

1 tsp ashwagandha powder

1/2 tsp cinnamon powder

1 cup warm almond milk

Instructions:

Mix ashwagandha and cinnamon into warm almond milk.

Stir well and drink before bedtime.

Uses: Balances stress hormones and promotes restorative sleep.

Storage Tips: Prepare fresh.

711. Passionflower and Peppermint Relaxation Tea

Ingredients:

1 tsp dried passionflower

1 tsp dried peppermint leaves

1 cup boiling water

Instructions:

Steep passionflower and peppermint in boiling water for 10 minutes.

Strain and drink warm.

Uses: Calms an overactive mind and helps induce sleep.

Storage Tips: Use fresh.

712. Hops and Honey Nighttime Tea

Ingredients:

1 tsp dried hops

1 tsp raw honey

1 cup boiling water

Instructions:

Steep hops in boiling water for 7 minutes.

Strain, stir in honey, and drink before bed.

Uses: Reduces restlessness and promotes deep sleep.

Storage Tips: Consume immediately.

713. Holy Basil and Ginger Relaxation Drink

Ingredients:

1 tsp dried holy basil leaves

1 tsp fresh ginger slices

1 cup boiling water

Instructions:

Steep holy basil and ginger in boiling water for 10 minutes.

Strain and sip slowly.

Uses: Lowers stress and encourages relaxation.

Storage Tips: Use fresh.

714. Lavender and Eucalyptus Pillow Spray

Ingredients:

5 drops lavender essential oil

3 drops eucalyptus essential oil

1/4 cup distilled water

Instructions:

Mix all ingredients in a spray bottle.

Shake well and spritz onto pillows or bedding before bedtime.

Uses: Creates a calming sleep environment.

Storage Tips: Store for up to 3 months.

715. Skullcap and Lemon Balm Sleep Tea

Ingredients:

1 tsp dried skullcap leaves

1 tsp dried lemon balm leaves

1 cup boiling water

Instructions:

Steep skullcap and lemon balm in boiling water for 8 minutes.

Strain and drink warm.

Uses: Soothes the nervous system and promotes sleep.

Storage Tips: Prepare fresh daily.

716. Chamomile and Rose Herbal Bath

Ingredients:

1/2 cup dried chamomile flowers

1/4 cup dried rose petals

1 muslin bag or cheesecloth

Instructions:

Add chamomile and rose petals to the muslin bag.

Place the bag in warm bathwater and soak for 20 minutes.

Uses: Relaxes muscles and calms the mind.

Storage Tips: Use herbs immediately.

717. Nutmeg and Honey Sleep Tonic

Ingredients:

1/4 tsp ground nutmeg

1 tsp raw honey

1 cup warm milk (dairy or plant-based)

Instructions:

Mix nutmeg and honey into warm milk.

Stir well and drink 30 minutes before bed.

Uses: Induces sleep and prevents waking up during the night.

Storage Tips: Prepare fresh.

Recipes for Longevity Tonics

Longevity is about more than living longer—it's about thriving as you age, maintaining vitality, and enjoying a high quality of life. Herbal tonics, long used in traditional medicine systems around the world, can support this goal by nourishing the body, balancing energy, and protecting against the effects of aging. These remedies help strengthen the immune system, improve resilience to stress, and provide essential nutrients for optimal health.

Longevity tonics often feature adaptogenic and antioxidant-rich herbs such as ashwagandha, ginseng, and goji berries, which boost energy and protect against cellular damage. Other ingredients like turmeric, moringa, and reishi mushrooms promote inflammation control, detoxification, and overall well-being. Regularly incorporating these herbal tonics into your diet can enhance your energy, improve your immune system, and support graceful aging.

This chapter introduces 10 easy-to-make longevity tonic recipes. These blends are packed with powerful herbs to nourish your body and mind, helping you live your best life at every age.

718. Ashwagandha and Turmeric Golden Milk Tonic

Ingredients:

1 tsp ashwagandha powder

1/2 tsp turmeric powder

1/4 tsp black pepper

1 cup warm almond milk

Instructions:

Mix ashwagandha, turmeric, and black pepper into warm almond milk.

Stir well and drink in the evening.

Uses: Reduces inflammation and promotes relaxation.

Storage Tips: Prepare fresh for each use.

719. Ginseng and Goji Berry Energy Tonic

Ingredients:

1 tsp dried ginseng root

1 tbsp dried goji berries

1 cup boiling water

Instructions:

Steep ginseng root and goji berries in boiling water for 15 minutes.

Strain and sip slowly.

Uses: Boosts energy and supports immune health.

Storage Tips: Consume immediately.

720. Moringa and Lemon Refreshing Tonic

Ingredients:

1 tsp moringa powder

1 tsp fresh lemon juice

1 cup cold water

Instructions:

Mix moringa powder and lemon juice into cold water.

Stir well and serve chilled.

Uses: Provides essential vitamins and minerals for vitality.

Storage Tips: Drink fresh.

721. Reishi Mushroom and Cinnamon Immune Tonic

Ingredients:

1 tsp dried reishi mushroom slices

1/2 tsp cinnamon powder

1 cup boiling water

Instructions:

Simmer reishi slices in boiling water for 15 minutes.

Strain, add cinnamon, and drink warm.

Uses: Enhances immunity and reduces stress.

Storage Tips: Use immediately.

722. Hibiscus and Ginger Antioxidant Tonic

Ingredients:

1 tsp dried hibiscus flowers

1 tsp fresh ginger slices

1 cup boiling water

Instructions:

Steep hibiscus and ginger in boiling water for 10 minutes.

Strain and serve warm or chilled.

Uses: Protects cells from oxidative stress and supports heart health.

Storage Tips: Drink fresh.

723. Holy Basil (Tulsi) and Honey Calmness Tonic

Ingredients:

1 tsp dried holy basil leaves

1 tsp raw honey

1 cup boiling water

Instructions:

Steep holy basil leaves in boiling water for 7 minutes.

Strain, stir in honey, and drink warm.

Uses: Reduces stress and balances energy.

Storage Tips: Consume immediately.

724. Turmeric and Coconut Water Detox Tonic

Ingredients:

1/2 tsp turmeric powder

1 cup coconut water

1/2 tsp fresh lime juice

Instructions:

Mix turmeric and lime juice into coconut water.

Stir well and drink as a mid-morning refresher.

Uses: Supports detoxification and hydration.

Storage Tips: Prepare fresh daily.

725. Nettle and Lemon Vitality Tonic

Ingredients:

1 tsp dried nettle leaves

1 tsp fresh lemon juice

1 cup boiling water

Instructions:

Steep nettle leaves in boiling water for 10 minutes.

Strain, add lemon juice, and drink warm.

Uses: Provides minerals for bone and joint health.

Storage Tips: Drink fresh.

726. Rhodiola and Peppermint Cooling Tonic

Ingredients:

1 tsp dried rhodiola root

1 tsp dried peppermint leaves

1 cup boiling water

Instructions:

Simmer rhodiola root in boiling water for 10 minutes.

Add peppermint leaves, steep for another 5 minutes, and strain.

Uses: Boosts energy and mental clarity.

Storage Tips: Use immediately.

727. Aloe Vera and Lemon Hydration Tonic

Ingredients:

2 tbsp fresh aloe vera gel

1 tsp fresh lemon juice

1 cup cold water

Instructions:

Blend aloe vera gel, lemon juice, and water until smooth.

Serve chilled.

Uses: Hydrates the body and promotes digestive health.

Storage Tips: Consume immediately.

BOOK 21

SEASONAL HERBAL PRACTICES

Each season brings unique challenges and opportunities for health and wellness. Seasonal shifts affect our bodies, moods, and energy levels, often requiring adjustments in our self-care routines. Incorporating seasonal herbal practices can help align your body with the rhythms of nature, supporting overall balance and well-being throughout the year.

This book explores how to use herbs to address the specific needs of each season. In spring, herbs like dandelion and nettle aid in detoxification and renewal, helping you transition out of winter's heaviness. Summer calls for cooling and hydrating remedies, such as aloe vera and mint, to beat the heat. Fall is the perfect time to fortify the immune system with elderberry and echinacea, preparing for the challenges of winter. Finally, winter blends featuring warming spices like cinnamon and ginger provide comfort, warmth, and immune support during the colder months.

With practical recipes, seasonal insights, and herbal guidance, this book helps you embrace the healing power of nature all year long. By understanding the unique qualities of each season and the herbs best suited to support them, you can cultivate a harmonious and healthful lifestyle that thrives alongside the changing seasons.

Herbs for Spring Cleansing and Renewal

Spring is a time of renewal and growth, both in nature and within ourselves. As the earth awakens from the cold, dormant months of winter, our bodies also shift, calling for detoxification and revitalization. Spring cleansing is an ancient practice that focuses on clearing out stagnation, rejuvenating the body, and preparing for the active months ahead. Herbs play a vital role in this process, offering gentle yet powerful support to the liver, kidneys, and digestive system.

Herbs like dandelion, nettle, burdock root, and milk thistle are traditionally used during spring cleanses to aid in detoxification and promote renewal. These herbs work by supporting the body's natural elimination pathways, reducing inflammation, and replenishing essential nutrients. They are rich in vitamins, minerals, and antioxidants that help the body recover from the heavier, slower energy of winter.

In this chapter, we will explore the benefits of cleansing herbs, how they work, and practical ways to incorporate them into your routine. Whether you're sipping a dandelion detox tea, blending a nettle smoothie, or preparing a cleansing herbal broth, these remedies will help you feel refreshed, energized, and ready to embrace the vitality of spring.

Why Spring Cleansing Is Important

During winter, many people consume heavier foods and move less, which can lead to the build-up of toxins and stagnation in the body. Spring cleansing helps:

Support the Liver: The liver is the body's main detox organ. Spring herbs like dandelion and milk thistle help it process and eliminate toxins more efficiently.

Promote Kidney Health: Herbs like nettle and parsley increase urination, flushing out waste products and reducing water retention.

Improve Digestion: Burdock root and ginger stimulate digestion and support gut health, easing bloating and sluggishness.

Enhance Energy: Cleansing removes what weighs you down, leaving you feeling lighter and more vibrant.

Key Herbs for Spring Cleansing

1. Dandelion (Taraxacum officinale)

Benefits: Supports liver detoxification, promotes bile production, and acts as a gentle diuretic.

How to Use: Teas, tinctures, or added fresh to salads.

2. Nettle (Urtica dioica)

Benefits: Rich in iron, calcium, and magnesium, nettle nourishes the body while flushing out toxins.

How to Use: Teas, infusions, or blended into smoothies.

3. Burdock Root (Arctium lappa)

Benefits: Cleanses the blood, improves digestion, and reduces inflammation.

How to Use: Decoctions, soups, or roasted as a root vegetable.

4. Milk Thistle (Silybum marianum)

Benefits: Protects and regenerates liver cells, supporting long-term detoxification.

How to Use: Capsules, teas, or powdered and added to food.

5. Parsley (Petroselinum crispum)

Benefits: Acts as a diuretic, supports kidney health, and provides vitamin C and antioxidants.

How to Use: Juices, teas, or as a garnish in meals.

6. Ginger (Zingiber officinale)

Benefits: Stimulates digestion, reduces inflammation, and warms the body.

How to Use: Teas, soups, or grated fresh into dishes.

728. Dandelion and Nettle Detox Tea

Ingredients:

1 tsp dried dandelion root

1 tsp dried nettle leaves

1 cup boiling water

Instructions:

Steep dandelion root and nettle leaves in boiling water for 10 minutes.

Strain and drink warm, once daily in the morning.

Uses: Flushes out toxins and revitalizes energy.

729. Burdock Root and Parsley Cleansing Soup

Ingredients:

1/4 cup chopped burdock root

1/4 cup chopped parsley

4 cups vegetable broth

1 clove garlic (minced)

Instructions:

Simmer burdock root in vegetable broth for 20 minutes.

Add parsley and garlic, cook for another 10 minutes, and serve warm.

Uses: Nourishes while promoting detoxification.

730. Milk Thistle and Lemon Liver Tonic

Ingredients:

1 tsp milk thistle powder

1 tsp fresh lemon juice

1 cup warm water

Instructions:

Mix milk thistle powder and lemon juice into warm water.

Stir well and drink mid-morning.

Uses: Supports liver health and boosts digestion.

731. Nettle and Spinach Spring Smoothie

Ingredients:

1 cup fresh nettle leaves (steamed)

1 cup fresh spinach

1 banana

1/2 cup almond milk

Instructions:

Blend all ingredients until smooth.

Serve as a nutrient-packed breakfast.

Uses: Provides minerals and promotes detoxification.

732. Ginger and Turmeric Anti-Inflammatory Tea

Ingredients:

1 tsp grated ginger

1/2 tsp turmeric powder

1 cup boiling water

Instructions:

Steep ginger and turmeric in boiling water for 10 minutes.

Strain and drink warm.

Uses: Reduces inflammation and supports digestion.

733. Dandelion and Mint Fresh Salad

Ingredients:

1 cup fresh dandelion greens

1/4 cup fresh mint leaves

1 tbsp olive oil

1 tsp fresh lemon juice

Instructions:

Toss dandelion greens and mint with olive oil and lemon juice.

Serve as a light and refreshing side dish.

Uses: Supports digestion and detoxification.

734. Parsley and Apple Detox Juice

Ingredients:

1/4 cup fresh parsley

2 apples (juiced)

1/2 lemon (juiced)

Instructions:

Blend parsley with apple and lemon juice.

Serve chilled as a mid-day refresher.

Uses: Hydrates and provides antioxidants.

735. Burdock and Carrot Roast

Ingredients:

1/2 cup sliced burdock root

1/2 cup sliced carrots

1 tbsp olive oil

Instructions:

Toss burdock and carrots with olive oil.

Roast in the oven at 375°F (190°C) for 20 minutes.

Uses: Promotes digestive health and provides fiber.

736. Nettle Infusion Hydration Drink

Ingredients:

1 tbsp dried nettle leaves

2 cups boiling water

Instructions:

Steep nettle leaves in boiling water for 4 hours.

Strain and drink throughout the day.

Uses: Replenishes minerals and promotes hydration.

737. Milk Thistle and Ginger Tea

Ingredients:

1 tsp milk thistle seeds

1 tsp grated ginger

1 cup boiling water

Instructions:

Steep milk thistle seeds and ginger in boiling water for 10 minutes.

Strain and drink after meals.

Uses: Enhances liver function and aids digestion.

Summer Remedies for Heat and Hydration

Summer is a time of sunshine, activity, and vitality, but the rising temperatures and increased humidity can take a toll on the body. Dehydration, heat exhaustion, and skin irritation are common concerns during the hotter months. Herbal remedies offer effective and natural ways to cool the body, maintain hydration, and stay energized. By incorporating these remedies into your summer routine, you can enjoy the season while staying comfortable and refreshed.

Cooling herbs like peppermint, hibiscus, and aloe vera are ideal for combating summer heat, while hydrating herbs like cucumber, fennel, and watermelon help replenish lost fluids. These herbs can be used in teas, infusions, compresses, and even refreshing sprays to provide immediate relief from the heat. Additionally, many of these remedies are rich in vitamins and minerals, ensuring your body stays nourished and balanced.

This chapter introduces 10 simple remedies for staying cool and hydrated during summer. From cooling teas to skin-soothing spritzes, these recipes are easy to prepare and will help you embrace the warmth of summer without discomfort.

738. Hibiscus and Mint Cooling Tea

Ingredients:

1 tsp dried hibiscus flowers

1 tsp dried mint leaves

1 cup boiling water

Instructions:

Steep hibiscus and mint in boiling water for 10 minutes.

Strain, chill, and serve over ice.

Uses: Reduces body heat and hydrates.

Storage Tips: Refrigerate for up to 2 days.

739. Aloe Vera and Cucumber Hydrating Juice

Ingredients:

1/4 cup fresh aloe vera gel

1/2 cup cucumber (chopped)

1 cup cold water

Instructions:

Blend aloe vera gel and cucumber with cold water.

Strain and serve chilled.

Uses: Hydrates and soothes the body from within.

Storage Tips: Consume immediately.

740. Watermelon and Basil Refresher

Ingredients:

1 cup watermelon (cubed)

1 tbsp fresh basil leaves

1/2 cup cold water

Instructions:

Blend watermelon and basil with cold water.

Serve as a refreshing summer drink.

Uses: Hydrates and provides natural electrolytes.

Storage Tips: Prepare fresh.

741. Peppermint and Lemon Facial Mist

Ingredients:

1/2 cup distilled water

5 drops peppermint essential oil

1 tsp fresh lemon juice

Instructions:

Mix all ingredients in a spray bottle.

Mist onto the face for instant cooling.

Uses: Cools the skin and reduces redness.

Storage Tips: Store in a cool place for up to 1 week.

742. Fennel and Ginger Hydration Tea

Ingredients:

1 tsp fennel seeds

1 tsp grated ginger

1 cup boiling water

Instructions:

Steep fennel seeds and ginger in boiling water for 10 minutes.

Strain, cool, and serve over ice.

Uses: Hydrates and aids digestion.

Storage Tips: Drink fresh.

743. Chamomile and Lavender Sun Relief Compress

Ingredients:

1 tbsp dried chamomile flowers

1 tsp dried lavender flowers

1 cup boiling water

Instructions:

Steep chamomile and lavender in boiling water for 10 minutes.

Soak a clean cloth in the infusion and apply to sunburned skin.

Uses: Soothes sunburn and cools irritated skin.

Storage Tips: Use immediately.

744. Lemon Balm and Cucumber Detox Water

Ingredients:

1/2 cup cucumber slices

1 tsp dried lemon balm leaves

1 liter cold water

Instructions:

Combine cucumber slices and lemon balm leaves with cold water in a pitcher.

Let infuse in the refrigerator for 1 hour before serving.

Uses: Hydrates and supports gentle detoxification.

Storage Tips: Keep refrigerated and consume within 1 day.

745. Aloe and Mint After-Sun Gel

Ingredients:

1/4 cup fresh aloe vera gel

5 drops peppermint essential oil

Instructions:

Mix aloe vera gel with peppermint oil.

Apply to sun-exposed skin for a cooling effect.

Uses: Soothes and hydrates irritated skin.

Storage Tips: Store in the refrigerator for up to 1 week.

746. Coconut Water and Chia Seed Hydration Drink

Ingredients:

1 cup coconut water

1 tbsp chia seeds

Instructions:

Stir chia seeds into coconut water.

Let sit for 10 minutes before drinking.

Uses: Replenishes electrolytes and keeps you hydrated.

Storage Tips: Consume fresh.

747. Rose and Lemon Cooling Infusion

Ingredients:

1 tbsp dried rose petals

1 tsp fresh lemon juice

1 cup boiling water

Instructions:

Steep rose petals in boiling water for 5 minutes.

Strain, add lemon juice, and chill before serving.

Uses: Cools the body and soothes the skin.

Storage Tips: Drink fresh.

Fall Recipes for Immune Preparation

As the temperatures drop and the leaves change, fall serves as a reminder to prepare for the colder months ahead. The shift in seasons often brings an increased risk of colds, flu, and other immune challenges. Strengthening your immune system during this time is essential for staying healthy and resilient through fall and winter. Herbal remedies are a natural, effective way to boost immunity, fight infections, and support overall wellness.

Herbs like elderberry, echinacea, astragalus, and ginger are renowned for their immune-enhancing properties. These herbs work by stimulating the production of white blood cells, reducing inflammation, and providing vital antioxidants that help the body ward off illness. Incorporating them into teas, syrups, and broths allows you to enjoy their benefits while creating a seasonal self-care ritual.

This chapter introduces 10 fall recipes to prepare your immune system for the season. From soothing teas to nourishing soups, these remedies are designed to fortify your defenses and keep you thriving as the weather turns colder.

748. Elderberry Immune-Boosting Syrup

Ingredients:

1/4 cup dried elderberries

2 cups water

1/4 cup raw honey

Instructions:

Simmer elderberries in water over low heat for 30 minutes.

Strain the liquid and allow it to cool.

Stir in honey and store in a glass jar.

Uses: Boosts immunity and helps prevent colds and flu.

Storage Tips: Refrigerate for up to 2 weeks.

749. Echinacea and Lemon Immune Tea

Ingredients:

1 tsp dried echinacea leaves

1 tsp fresh lemon juice

1 cup boiling water

Instructions:

Steep echinacea leaves in boiling water for 10 minutes.

Strain, add lemon juice, and drink warm.

Uses: Strengthens the immune system and reduces cold symptoms.

Storage Tips: Use fresh.

750. Ginger and Turmeric Immunity Shot

Ingredients:

1 tsp grated ginger

1/2 tsp turmeric powder

1/4 cup fresh orange juice

Instructions:

Mix all ingredients in a small glass.

Drink in the morning as a daily immune booster.

Uses: Reduces inflammation and supports immune health.

Storage Tips: Consume immediately.

751. Astragalus and Garlic Healing Soup

Ingredients:

2 slices dried astragalus root

4 cups vegetable broth

2 cloves garlic (minced)

Instructions:

Simmer astragalus root in vegetable broth for 30 minutes.

Add minced garlic, cook for another 10 minutes, and serve.

Uses: Strengthens the immune system and wards off infections.

Storage Tips: Refrigerate for up to 3 days.

752. Lemon Balm and Honey Soothing Tea

Ingredients:

1 tsp dried lemon balm leaves

1 tsp raw honey

1 cup boiling water

Instructions:

Steep lemon balm leaves in boiling water for 7 minutes.

Strain, stir in honey, and sip slowly.

Uses: Calms the body and supports immune function.

Storage Tips: Use immediately.

753. Reishi Mushroom Immune Broth

Ingredients:

1/4 cup dried reishi mushroom slices

6 cups water

1 onion (chopped)

Instructions:

Simmer reishi mushrooms and onion in water for 1 hour.

Strain and drink the broth warm.

Uses: Enhances immunity and provides antioxidants.

Storage Tips: Refrigerate for up to 5 days.

754. Cinnamon and Clove Warming Tea

Ingredients:

1 cinnamon stick

3 cloves

1 cup boiling water

Instructions:

Steep cinnamon stick and cloves in boiling water for 10 minutes.

Strain and enjoy warm.

Uses: Warms the body and boosts circulation to fight seasonal illnesses.

Storage Tips: Drink fresh.

755. Elderberry and Hibiscus Immune Tonic

Ingredients:

1 tbsp dried elderberries

1 tsp dried hibiscus flowers

1 cup boiling water

Instructions:

Steep elderberries and hibiscus flowers in boiling water for 10 minutes.

Strain and drink warm or chilled.

Uses: Provides antioxidants and supports immune health.

Storage Tips: Refrigerate for up to 2 days.

756. Garlic and Lemon Immunity Elixir

Ingredients:

1 clove garlic (crushed)

1 tsp fresh lemon juice

1 cup warm water

Instructions:

Mix garlic and lemon juice into warm water.

Stir well and drink once daily.

Uses: Fights infections and boosts immune strength.

Storage Tips: Prepare fresh for each use.

757. Nettle and Apple Detox Juice

Ingredients:

1/4 cup fresh nettle leaves

1 apple (juiced)

1/2 lemon (juiced)

Instructions:

Blend nettle leaves with apple and lemon juice.

Strain and serve as a refreshing drink.

Uses: Provides nutrients and supports immunity.

Storage Tips: Consume immediately.

Chapter 4: Winter Blends for Warmth and Wellness

Winter brings cold weather, shorter days, and an increased risk of seasonal illnesses. It's a time when our bodies crave warmth, nourishment, and immune support to stay strong and resilient. Herbal remedies are particularly well-suited for winter, offering natural ways to warm the body, strengthen immunity, and promote overall wellness during the colder months.

Warming herbs like cinnamon, ginger, and clove increase circulation and combat the chill, while adaptogens such as ashwagandha and reishi mushroom build resilience to stress and illness. Immune-boosting herbs like elderberry, echinacea, and turmeric can help ward off colds and flu. By combining these herbs into teas, broths, and tonics, you can enjoy their comforting and healing benefits throughout winter.

This chapter introduces 10 simple and effective herbal blends designed to keep you warm, healthy, and energized all season long. These recipes provide soothing warmth, support your body's natural defenses, and offer the perfect way to embrace the coziness of winter.

758. Ginger and Cinnamon Warming Tea

Ingredients:

1 tsp fresh ginger slices

1 cinnamon stick

1 cup boiling water

Instructions:

Steep ginger and cinnamon in boiling water for 10 minutes.

Strain and drink warm.

Uses: Boosts circulation and warms the body.

Storage Tips: Prepare fresh for each use.

759. Turmeric and Black Pepper Immune Latte

Ingredients:

1/2 tsp turmeric powder

1/4 tsp black pepper

1 cup warm almond milk

Instructions:

Mix turmeric and black pepper into warm almond milk.

Stir well and enjoy in the evening.

Uses: Reduces inflammation and supports immunity.

Storage Tips: Consume immediately.

760. Elderberry and Hibiscus Immune Tea

Ingredients:

1 tbsp dried elderberries

1 tsp dried hibiscus flowers

1 cup boiling water

Instructions:

Steep elderberries and hibiscus in boiling water for 10 minutes.

Strain and drink warm.

Uses: Boosts immunity and provides antioxidants.

Storage Tips: Store in the refrigerator for up to 2 days.

761. Ashwagandha and Honey Relaxation Tonic

Ingredients:

1 tsp ashwagandha powder

1 tsp raw honey

1 cup warm water

Instructions:

Mix ashwagandha and honey into warm water.

Stir well and sip before bed.

Uses: Reduces stress and promotes restful sleep.
Storage Tips: Prepare fresh.

762. Clove and Lemon Immune Elixir

Ingredients:

3 whole cloves

1 tsp fresh lemon juice

1 cup boiling water

Instructions:

Steep cloves in boiling water for 10 minutes.

Strain, add lemon juice, and drink warm.

Uses: Combats infections and supports immunity.

Storage Tips: Use immediately.

763. Reishi Mushroom and Ginger Broth

Ingredients:

1/4 cup dried reishi mushroom slices

1 tsp grated ginger

4 cups vegetable broth

Instructions:

Simmer reishi mushrooms and ginger in vegetable broth for 30 minutes.

Strain and serve warm.

Uses: Boosts immunity and provides warmth.

Storage Tips: Refrigerate for up to 3 days.

764. Peppermint and Chamomile Comfort Tea

Ingredients:

1 tsp dried peppermint leaves

1 tsp dried chamomile flowers

1 cup boiling water

Instructions:

Steep peppermint and chamomile in boiling water for 7 minutes.

Strain and sip slowly.

Uses: Soothes digestion and promotes relaxation.

Storage Tips: Drink fresh.

765. Garlic and Onion Healing Soup

Ingredients:

2 cloves garlic (minced)

1/2 onion (chopped)

4 cups vegetable broth

Instructions:

Sauté garlic and onion until fragrant.

Add vegetable broth and simmer for 20 minutes.

Uses: Supports immunity and aids in recovery from colds.

Storage Tips: Refrigerate for up to 3 days.

766. Holy Basil (Tulsi) and Ginger Tea

Ingredients:

1 tsp dried holy basil leaves

1 tsp grated ginger

1 cup boiling water

Instructions:

Steep holy basil and ginger in boiling water for 10 minutes.

Strain and drink warm.

Uses: Reduces stress and boosts immunity.

Storage Tips: Consume immediately.

767. Cinnamon and Honey Winter Tonic

Ingredients:

1 tsp ground cinnamon

1 tsp raw honey

1 cup warm water

Instructions:

Mix cinnamon and honey into warm water.

Stir well and sip slowly.

Uses: Provides warmth and supports digestion.

Storage Tips: Use fresh for each preparation.

BOOK 22

HERBAL BEAUTY RITUALS

Embracing herbal beauty rituals allows you to nourish your body with nature's finest ingredients while creating a luxurious self-care experience. Herbs have been used for centuries in beauty routines to promote radiant skin, glossy hair, and overall wellness. By crafting your own beauty products, you can avoid harmful chemicals, tailor treatments to your needs, and infuse your self-care practices with the healing power of plants.

This book introduces you to a variety of herbal beauty recipes that are easy to make and deeply effective. From moisturizing lip balms to strengthening hair treatments, each chapter explores how natural ingredients like calendula, lavender, chamomile, and rosemary can enhance your beauty routine. Facial steams and bath soaks provide a spa-like experience at home, offering relaxation alongside visible results.

By following the recipes and tips in this book, you can create a personalized, eco-friendly beauty regimen that supports your skin, hair, and overall well-being. Whether you're looking to revitalize your glow, strengthen your hair, or simply indulge in self-care, these herbal beauty rituals are the perfect way to harness the nurturing benefits of nature while treating yourself to moments of pure bliss.

Recipes for DIY Lip Balms and Glosses

Dry, chapped lips can be uncomfortable and unsightly, but commercial lip balms often contain artificial ingredients and chemicals that may not be ideal for sensitive skin. Creating your own herbal lip balms and glosses allows you to nourish your lips naturally while enjoying the satisfaction of a handcrafted product. Using herbs like calendula, lavender, and chamomile, combined with natural moisturizers such as beeswax, shea butter, and coconut oil, you can craft luxurious lip care solutions that are as effective as they are indulgent.

Herbal lip balms and glosses are easy to customize with different scents, colors, and flavors, making them perfect for personal use or as thoughtful gifts. These recipes harness the healing properties of herbs to soothe, hydrate, and protect your lips, leaving them soft, smooth, and healthy. Additionally, making these products at home ensures they are free from synthetic additives, making them safer and more environmentally friendly.

In this chapter, you'll find 10 simple recipes for herbal lip balms and glosses, along with tips for adding natural color and scent. Whether you're looking for a nourishing balm for winter or a glossy finish for a night out, these recipes have you covered.

768. Calendula Healing Lip Balm

Ingredients:

1 tbsp dried calendula petals

2 tbsp coconut oil

1 tbsp beeswax

Instructions:

Infuse calendula petals in coconut oil over low heat for 30 minutes.

Strain, then mix with melted beeswax.

Pour into tins and let cool.

Uses: Soothes dry, cracked lips and promotes healing.

Storage Tips: Store in a cool, dry place for up to 6 months.

769. Lavender and Honey Moisturizing Balm

Ingredients:

2 tbsp shea butter

1 tbsp beeswax

3 drops lavender essential oil

1 tsp raw honey

Instructions:

Melt shea butter and beeswax together.

Stir in lavender oil and honey.

Pour into small jars and cool.

Uses: Hydrates lips and reduces inflammation.

Storage Tips: Store in a sealed container for up to 3 months.

770. Peppermint Cooling Lip Balm

Ingredients:

1 tbsp cocoa butter

2 tbsp coconut oil

5 drops peppermint essential oil

Instructions:

Melt cocoa butter and coconut oil.

Add peppermint oil, stir, and pour into containers.

Uses: Refreshes and cools lips while providing moisture.

Storage Tips: Keep in a cool place for up to 4 months.

771. Rose-Infused Gloss

Ingredients:

1 tbsp almond oil

1 tbsp castor oil

1 tsp dried rose petals

Instructions:

Infuse rose petals in almond oil for 1 hour over low heat.

Strain and mix with castor oil.

Pour into a gloss tube.

Uses: Adds shine and a subtle rose scent.

Storage Tips: Store for up to 3 months.

772. Chamomile and Vanilla Balm

Ingredients:

1 tbsp chamomile tea (brewed strong)

2 tbsp beeswax

1 tsp vanilla extract

Instructions:

Combine brewed chamomile tea with melted beeswax.

Add vanilla extract and pour into containers.

Uses: Calms irritated lips and adds a sweet scent.

Storage Tips: Use within 2 months.

773. Beetroot-Tinted Lip Gloss

Ingredients:

1 tbsp castor oil

1 tsp beetroot powder

1 tsp coconut oil

Instructions:

Mix beetroot powder with castor oil and coconut oil.

Heat gently to blend, then cool and pour into a gloss tube.

Uses: Adds a natural red tint and shine.

Storage Tips: Store for up to 2 months.

774. Lemon Balm Lip Protector

Ingredients:

1 tbsp lemon balm-infused oil

1 tbsp shea butter

1 tbsp beeswax

Instructions:

Melt shea butter and beeswax, then mix with lemon balm oil.

Pour into tins and let cool.

Uses: Protects lips from dryness and cracking.

Storage Tips: Store in a cool place for up to 4 months.

775. Orange Spice Lip Balm

Ingredients:

2 tbsp coconut oil

1 tsp beeswax

3 drops orange essential oil

1/2 tsp cinnamon powder

Instructions:

Melt coconut oil and beeswax together.

Stir in orange oil and cinnamon powder.

Pour into containers and cool.

Uses: Warms and hydrates lips with a zesty scent.

Storage Tips: Store for up to 3 months.

776. Cocoa Mint Lip Gloss

Ingredients:

1 tbsp cocoa butter

1 tbsp castor oil

5 drops peppermint essential oil

Instructions:

Melt cocoa butter and mix with castor oil and peppermint oil.

Pour into gloss tubes and cool.

Uses: Provides a glossy finish and a refreshing feel.

Storage Tips: Keep in a sealed container for up to 2 months.

777. Vanilla and Almond Shine Balm

Ingredients:

1 tbsp almond oil

1 tsp beeswax

1 tsp vanilla extract

Instructions:

Melt beeswax and mix with almond oil and vanilla extract.

Pour into tins and let cool.

Uses: Hydrates lips with a glossy shine.

Storage Tips: Store in a cool place for up to 4 months.

Natural Hair Treatments for Strength and Shine

Healthy, strong, and shiny hair is a hallmark of beauty and vitality, yet factors like environmental stress, over-styling, and harsh chemicals can leave hair looking dull and damaged. Natural hair treatments offer a gentle and effective way to restore hair health, nourish the scalp, and promote growth without exposing your hair to synthetic chemicals. By using herbal remedies, you can harness the power of nature to create treatments that strengthen strands, enhance shine, and keep your scalp healthy.

Herbs like rosemary, hibiscus, and nettle are excellent for promoting hair growth and adding luster, while aloe vera, coconut oil, and fenugreek deeply hydrate and repair damaged strands. These ingredients can be used in masks, rinses, and oils to address specific hair concerns, whether it's dryness, breakage, or thinning.

In this chapter, we provide 13 simple recipes for natural hair treatments. Each recipe is designed to strengthen and revitalize your hair, leaving it shiny, smooth, and full of life. Whether you're seeking to nourish dry hair or boost volume, these herbal treatments can help you achieve your hair goals naturally.

778. Rosemary and Olive Oil Scalp Treatment

Ingredients:

2 tbsp olive oil

5 drops rosemary essential oil

Instructions:

Warm olive oil slightly and mix with rosemary essential oil.

Massage into your scalp for 5–10 minutes.

Leave for 30 minutes before rinsing with shampoo.

Uses: Stimulates hair growth and improves scalp circulation.

Storage Tips: Store in a cool, dark place for up to 3 months.

779. Aloe Vera and Coconut Oil Hydration Mask

Ingredients:

1/4 cup fresh aloe vera gel

2 tbsp coconut oil

Instructions:

Blend aloe vera gel and coconut oil into a smooth mixture.

Apply to damp hair and leave for 20 minutes.

Rinse thoroughly with lukewarm water.

Uses: Deeply hydrates and repairs dry, damaged hair.

Storage Tips: Use immediately.

780. Hibiscus and Fenugreek Strengthening Paste

Ingredients:

1 tbsp hibiscus powder

1 tbsp fenugreek powder

1/4 cup warm water

Instructions:

Mix hibiscus and fenugreek powders with warm water to form a paste.

Apply to hair and scalp, leave for 20 minutes, then rinse.

Uses: Strengthens hair and reduces breakage.

Storage Tips: Prepare fresh for each use.

781. Nettle and Apple Cider Vinegar Rinse

Ingredients:

1 tbsp dried nettle leaves

1 cup boiling water

2 tbsp apple cider vinegar

Instructions:

Steep nettle leaves in boiling water for 15 minutes.

Strain and mix with apple cider vinegar.

Use as a final rinse after shampooing.

Uses: Adds shine and balances scalp pH.

Storage Tips: Refrigerate for up to 1 week.

782. Avocado and Honey Repair Mask

Ingredients:

1/2 ripe avocado

1 tbsp raw honey

Instructions:

Mash avocado and mix with honey until smooth.

Apply to damp hair and leave for 20 minutes.

Rinse thoroughly with warm water.

Uses: Repairs damaged hair and restores moisture.

Storage Tips: Use immediately.

783. Lavender and Chamomile Hair Mist

Ingredients:

1/2 cup distilled water

3 drops lavender essential oil

1 tsp chamomile tea (brewed strong)

Instructions:

Combine all ingredients in a spray bottle.

Mist onto hair for a refreshing boost.

Uses: Calms the scalp and hydrates hair.

Storage Tips: Store in the refrigerator for up to 2 weeks.

784. Castor Oil and Peppermint Hair Growth Serum

Ingredients:

2 tbsp castor oil

5 drops peppermint essential oil

Instructions:

Mix castor oil and peppermint oil.

Massage into your scalp and leave overnight.

Wash out with shampoo the next morning.

Uses: Encourages hair growth and thickens strands.

Storage Tips: Store for up to 3 months in a cool place.

785. Banana and Yogurt Nourishing Mask

Ingredients:

1 ripe banana

2 tbsp plain yogurt

Instructions:

Blend banana and yogurt until smooth.

Apply to damp hair, leave for 20 minutes, then rinse.

Uses: Softens hair and boosts shine.

Storage Tips: Use immediately.

786. Sage and Rosemary Volumizing Rinse

Ingredients:

1 tsp dried sage

1 tsp dried rosemary

1 cup boiling water

Instructions:

Steep sage and rosemary in boiling water for 15 minutes.

Strain and use as a final rinse after washing your hair.

Uses: Adds volume and enhances hair texture.

Storage Tips: Refrigerate for up to 3 days.

787. Cocoa Butter and Vanilla Hair Balm

Ingredients:

2 tbsp cocoa butter

1/2 tsp vanilla extract

Instructions:

Melt cocoa butter and mix with vanilla extract.

Apply to the ends of your hair and leave for 15 minutes.

Rinse with shampoo.

Uses: Prevents split ends and improves hair texture.

Storage Tips: Store for up to 3 months in a cool, dry place.

788. Coconut Milk and Aloe Deep Conditioner

Ingredients:

1/4 cup coconut milk

2 tbsp fresh aloe vera gel

1 tbsp olive oil

Instructions:

Mix coconut milk, aloe vera gel, and olive oil until well combined.

Apply to damp hair from roots to ends.

Leave on for 30 minutes and rinse with lukewarm water.

Uses: Deeply conditions, reduces frizz, and hydrates hair.

Storage Tips: Use immediately for the best results.

789. Green Tea and Honey Strength Rinse

Ingredients:

1 cup brewed green tea (cooled)

1 tbsp raw honey

Instructions:

Brew green tea and let it cool.

Mix in raw honey until dissolved.

Pour over hair after shampooing and leave for 5 minutes before rinsing.

Uses: Strengthens hair follicles and reduces breakage.

Storage Tips: Prepare fresh for each use.

790. Fenugreek and Curry Leaf Growth Tonic

Ingredients:

1 tbsp fenugreek seeds (soaked overnight)

1/4 cup fresh curry leaves

1 cup water

Instructions:

Blend soaked fenugreek seeds and curry leaves with water into a smooth mixture.

Strain and apply to the scalp.

Leave for 30 minutes, then rinse thoroughly.

Uses: Promotes hair growth and reduces hair fall.

Storage Tips: Use immediately.

Facial Steams for a Radiant Glow

Facial steams are one of the simplest yet most effective ways to rejuvenate your skin and achieve a radiant glow. This ancient beauty ritual uses the power of warm steam to open pores, promote circulation, and allow herbal infusions to deeply penetrate the skin. The result? A refreshed, hydrated, and glowing complexion.

Facial steaming is particularly beneficial for removing dirt, excess oil, and impurities, making it an excellent step in any skincare routine. Incorporating herbs such as chamomile, lavender, and calendula enhances the experience by infusing the steam with soothing, anti-inflammatory, and skin-nourishing properties. Adding essential oils, rose petals, or green tea can further amplify the benefits, creating a luxurious, spa-like experience at home.

This chapter provides 10 simple recipes for herbal facial steams designed to target different skin types and concerns, from calming irritated skin to boosting hydration and combating acne. These steams are not only effective but also offer a relaxing self-care moment, allowing you to unwind while pampering your skin.

791. Chamomile and Lavender Soothing Steam

Ingredients:

1 tbsp dried chamomile flowers

1 tbsp dried lavender flowers

4 cups boiling water

Instructions:

Add chamomile and lavender to a bowl of boiling water.

Place your face over the bowl and cover your head with a towel.

Steam for 8–10 minutes.

Uses: Soothes sensitive or irritated skin and reduces redness.

Storage Tips: Use immediately.

792. Green Tea and Mint Detox Steam

Ingredients:

2 green tea bags

1 tbsp fresh mint leaves

4 cups boiling water

Instructions:

Steep green tea and mint in boiling water for 5 minutes.

Steam your face for 10 minutes, breathing deeply.

Uses: Detoxifies the skin and tightens pores.

Storage Tips: Discard the mixture after use.

793. Rose Petal and Hibiscus Glow Steam

Ingredients:

1 tbsp dried rose petals

1 tbsp dried hibiscus flowers

4 cups boiling water

Instructions:

Add rose petals and hibiscus to boiling water.

Steam for 8–10 minutes to hydrate and brighten the skin.

Uses: Enhances natural radiance and deeply hydrates.

Storage Tips: Use fresh for each session.

794. Calendula and Aloe Soothing Steam

Ingredients:

1 tbsp dried calendula flowers

1 tsp fresh aloe vera gel

4 cups boiling water

Instructions:

Add calendula flowers and aloe to boiling water.

Steam for 10 minutes for soothing hydration.

Uses: Calms inflammation and promotes skin healing.

Storage Tips: Prepare fresh.

795. Lemon and Basil Clarifying Steam

Ingredients:

1 slice fresh lemon

1 tbsp fresh basil leaves

4 cups boiling water

Instructions:

Add lemon and basil to boiling water.

Steam for 8 minutes to clear pores and refresh skin.

Uses: Reduces oiliness and cleanses pores.

Storage Tips: Discard after use.

796. Rosemary and Eucalyptus Decongesting Steam

Ingredients:

1 tbsp dried rosemary

3 drops eucalyptus essential oil

4 cups boiling water

Instructions:

Add rosemary and eucalyptus oil to boiling water.

Steam for 10 minutes to cleanse and refresh.

Uses: Clears sinuses and rejuvenates the skin.

Storage Tips: Use immediately.

797. Turmeric and Ginger Brightening Steam

Ingredients:

1 tsp turmeric powder

1 tsp grated ginger

4 cups boiling water

Instructions:

Add turmeric and ginger to boiling water.

Steam for 8 minutes for a brighter complexion.

Uses: Reduces dullness and boosts circulation.

Storage Tips: Prepare fresh for each session.

798. Thyme and Lemon Balm Purifying Steam

Ingredients:

1 tbsp dried thyme

1 tbsp dried lemon balm

4 cups boiling water

Instructions:

Add thyme and lemon balm to boiling water.

Steam for 10 minutes to purify and balance skin.

Uses: Perfect for acne-prone or combination skin.

Storage Tips: Use fresh.

799. Sage and Lavender Anti-Aging Steam

Ingredients:

1 tbsp dried sage

1 tbsp dried lavender

4 cups boiling water

Instructions:

Add sage and lavender to boiling water.

Steam for 10 minutes to enhance elasticity and rejuvenate skin.

Uses: Fights fine lines and promotes youthful skin.

Storage Tips: Discard after use.

800. Cucumber and Peppermint Hydrating Steam

Ingredients:

1/4 cup sliced cucumber

1 tsp dried peppermint leaves

4 cups boiling water

Instructions:

Add cucumber and peppermint to boiling water.

Steam for 8 minutes to deeply hydrate and refresh.

Uses: Ideal for dry or dehydrated skin.

Storage Tips: Use immediately.

Creating Herbal Bath Soaks and Scrubs

Herbal bath soaks and scrubs offer a luxurious way to nourish your skin, relax your body, and uplift your spirit. By combining natural ingredients like dried herbs, salts, and oils, you can create spa-quality treatments that pamper your skin and leave you feeling rejuvenated. These DIY remedies are not only easy to make but also customizable to your preferences and skin type.

Bath soaks infused with herbs like lavender, chamomile, and rose petals can calm the mind, soothe tired muscles, and hydrate the skin. Meanwhile, scrubs made with sugar, salt, and moisturizing oils gently exfoliate, leaving your skin soft and radiant. Adding essential oils or dried herbs to these products enhances their benefits, whether you're seeking relaxation, detoxification, or revitalization.

This chapter introduces 10 herbal bath soak and scrub recipes that transform your bathing routine into a therapeutic and indulgent experience. These natural, chemical-free treatments are perfect for self-care days, gifts, or daily rituals to keep your skin glowing and your mind refreshed.

801. Lavender and Epsom Salt Relaxing Bath Soak

Ingredients:

1/2 cup Epsom salt

1/4 cup dried lavender flowers

5 drops lavender essential oil

Instructions:

Mix all ingredients in a bowl.

Add 1/4 cup of the mixture to warm bathwater.

Uses: Relieves stress, soothes muscles, and promotes relaxation.

Storage Tips: Store in an airtight jar for up to 3 months.

802. Chamomile and Oatmeal Skin-Soothing Soak

Ingredients:

1/4 cup dried chamomile flowers

1/4 cup oatmeal (ground)

2 tbsp baking soda

Instructions:

Combine all ingredients in a muslin bag or cheesecloth.

Place the bag in warm bathwater and soak for 20 minutes.

Uses: Soothes irritated skin and relieves dryness.

Storage Tips: Store in a cool, dry place for up to 2 months.

803. Rose and Coconut Milk Luxurious Bath Soak

Ingredients:

1/4 cup dried rose petals

1/4 cup coconut milk powder

2 tbsp pink Himalayan salt

Instructions:

Mix all ingredients thoroughly.

Add 1/4 cup of the blend to your bathwater.

Uses: Hydrates the skin and creates a spa-like experience.

Storage Tips: Keep in an airtight container for up to 3 months.

804. Peppermint and Sea Salt Energizing Bath Soak

Ingredients:

1/2 cup sea salt

1/4 cup dried peppermint leaves

5 drops peppermint essential oil

Instructions:

Combine all ingredients in a jar.

Use 1/4 cup of the mixture in your bath.

Uses: Refreshes and energizes the body.

Storage Tips: Store in a sealed jar for up to 3 months.

805. Sugar and Lemon Exfoliating Body Scrub

Ingredients:

1/2 cup granulated sugar

1/4 cup coconut oil

1 tsp fresh lemon zest

Instructions:

Mix sugar and coconut oil until well combined.

Stir in lemon zest and use to exfoliate damp skin.

Uses: Gently exfoliates and brightens skin.

Storage Tips: Store in an airtight container for up to 2 weeks.

806. Rosemary and Olive Oil Invigorating Scrub

Ingredients:

1/2 cup coarse sea salt

2 tbsp fresh rosemary leaves (chopped)

1/4 cup olive oil

Instructions:

Combine all ingredients in a bowl.

Massage onto skin in circular motions and rinse off.

Uses: Improves circulation and smooths rough skin.

Storage Tips: Keep in the refrigerator for up to 1 week.

807. Calendula and Honey Gentle Scrub

Ingredients:

1/4 cup dried calendula petals (ground)

2 tbsp honey

1/4 cup fine sugar

Instructions:

Mix all ingredients into a paste.

Use to gently exfoliate sensitive skin.

Uses: Exfoliates while nourishing and calming the skin.

Storage Tips: Use immediately.

808. Hibiscus and Coconut Oil Brightening Scrub

Ingredients:

1 tbsp hibiscus powder

1/4 cup coconut oil

1/4 cup brown sugar

Instructions:

Combine hibiscus powder, coconut oil, and brown sugar.

Gently massage onto damp skin and rinse.

Uses: Brightens skin and promotes a radiant glow.

Storage Tips: Store in a sealed container for up to 2 weeks.

809. Ginger and Eucalyptus Detox Bath Soak

Ingredients:

1/4 cup grated fresh ginger

1/2 cup Epsom salt

3 drops eucalyptus essential oil

Instructions:

Combine all ingredients in a bowl.

Add 1/4 cup of the mixture to a warm bath.

Uses: Detoxifies and revitalizes the body.

Storage Tips: Prepare fresh for each use.

810. Vanilla and Almond Oil Hydrating Scrub

Ingredients:

1/4 cup almond oil

1/2 cup sugar

1 tsp vanilla extract

Instructions:

Mix almond oil and sugar.

Stir in vanilla extract and use to exfoliate dry skin.

Uses: Moisturizes and leaves skin silky smooth.

Storage Tips: Store in an airtight container for up to 2 weeks.

BOOK 23

ADVANCED HERBAL TECHNIQUES

For those who are ready to deepen their herbal knowledge, advanced techniques offer exciting ways to enhance the potency, effectiveness, and versatility of herbal remedies. Beyond the basics, these methods focus on maximizing the benefits of individual herbs, creating synergistic blends, and exploring innovative preparations. From mastering the art of combining herbs to experimenting with fermentation and working with rare botanicals, this book provides the tools and techniques to take your herbal practice to the next level.

Combining herbs for synergistic effects allows you to create remedies that work harmoniously, amplifying their healing properties. Techniques like percolation offer a more efficient way to extract potent compounds, while making herbal wines and fermented blends opens the door to unique remedies that nourish the body and support gut health. For those drawn to rare and exotic herbs, this book provides guidance on sourcing, preparing, and safely incorporating them into your repertoire.

Whether you're an experienced herbalist or an enthusiast eager to expand your skills, this book equips you with the knowledge and confidence to explore advanced herbal techniques. Dive into these chapters to unlock the full potential of herbal medicine and create remedies that are as powerful as they are innovative.

Combining Herbs for Synergistic Effects

Imagine you're standing in a sunlit kitchen, surrounded by jars of dried herbs, their earthy aromas filling the air. On the counter are sprigs of lavender, a handful of chamomile flowers, and a small dish of dried lemon balm. You're about to embark on the artful practice of blending herbs, creating a remedy that not only soothes the body but also nurtures the soul. The concept of combining herbs isn't new—it's been practiced for centuries by herbalists who understood that, together, herbs can achieve far more than they can alone.

Combining herbs for synergistic effects is like composing a symphony. Each herb brings its unique "note" to the blend, working harmoniously to create a remedy that is balanced, effective, and often greater than the sum of its parts. It's a process that requires intuition, knowledge, and a willingness to experiment. But when done correctly, it can transform simple ingredients into a powerful tool for healing.

The Dance of Herbal Synergy

To understand synergy in herbal medicine, think of chamomile and lavender. Individually, both herbs are calming, but together, they create a soothing blend that can ease stress and promote restful sleep. This is the magic of synergy—where one herb's strengths amplify another's, creating a blend that's more than what either could achieve alone.

But synergy isn't just about adding herbs together. It's about understanding their personalities—what they offer, how they interact, and how they balance each other. For instance, a warming herb like ginger can complement a cooling herb like peppermint, creating a blend that's both invigorating and soothing. Or take echinacea and elderberry: echinacea stimulates the immune system, while elderberry provides antiviral support, making them a powerful duo for fighting colds and flu.

Herbal synergy allows you to address not just one aspect of a condition but multiple layers. For example, when crafting a remedy for stress, you might include ashwagandha for long-term resilience, lemon balm for immediate calming, and lavender to enhance the aroma and overall experience.

Crafting Your Herbal Symphony

Creating a synergistic blend begins with a clear intention. What are you hoping to achieve? Perhaps you want a tea to ease digestion after meals or a tincture to bolster your immune system during flu season. Once you've defined your goal, the process unfolds like a creative journey.

Start with a primary herb—the star of your formula. This herb addresses the main concern, such as chamomile for relaxation or peppermint for digestion. Then, add supportive herbs that enhance or complement the primary herb's action. For a digestive tea, you might choose fennel to reduce bloating or ginger to stimulate digestion. Finally, include a harmonizer—an herb that ties the blend together, improving flavor or balancing energetics. Licorice root, for instance, adds sweetness and a soothing quality.

As you blend, imagine the herbs as collaborators. Each one has its own role, but together, they create a remedy that is greater than any single ingredient.

A Real-Life Example

Let's take a practical example: crafting a blend for restful sleep. You start with valerian, a powerful sedative herb that encourages deep sleep. To support its effects, you add passionflower, which calms an overactive mind, and chamomile, known for its gentle, relaxing properties. To tie it all together, you include lemon balm, which adds a soothing citrus flavor and rounds out the energetics. The result is a tea that not only helps you drift off but also nurtures your nervous system.

Each step in this process feels intentional, almost meditative. You measure the herbs carefully, appreciating their textures and aromas. As you mix them, you imagine the final result: a warm cup of tea that soothes the mind and body.

Learning from Tradition

This practice of combining herbs isn't new—it's steeped in history. Traditional Chinese Medicine (TCM) often uses formulas with four roles: the chief herb addresses the main condition, the deputy herb supports or enhances the chief, the assistant mitigates side effects, and the envoy harmonizes the blend. Similarly, Ayurveda emphasizes the balance of energetics, ensuring that a formula isn't too heating, cooling, drying, or moistening.

Drawing from these traditions, modern herbalists can create blends that honor the wisdom of the past while addressing contemporary needs. For instance, an adaptogenic blend for modern stress might combine ashwagandha (to build resilience), holy basil (to calm the mind), and cinnamon (to enhance flavor and balance the formula energetically).

Challenges and Discoveries

Of course, the journey isn't always straightforward. Some blends might taste too bitter or feel unbalanced. Perhaps you combine peppermint and valerian, only to find that valerian's strong aroma overpowers the tea. These moments are opportunities to learn. You might adjust the proportions, add a harmonizer like lemon balm, or try a different preparation method, such as a tincture instead of a tea.

Over time, you'll develop a deeper relationship with the herbs. You'll notice how chamomile's floral scent pairs beautifully with the earthiness of ginger or how a touch of cinnamon can elevate an otherwise bland blend. This process of discovery is part of the joy of herbalism.

Advanced Techniques

Once you've mastered the basics, you can explore more advanced techniques. For example, you might experiment with:

Layering Actions: Creating blends that work on multiple systems, like combining digestive herbs (fennel, peppermint) with calming herbs (chamomile, lemon balm) for a post-meal tea.

Customizing Energetics: Balancing warming and cooling herbs to suit different constitutions.

Tincture Blends: Combining liquid extracts for fast-acting remedies that address acute conditions.

The possibilities are endless, limited only by your imagination and understanding of the herbs.

The Joy of Experimentation

What makes combining herbs so rewarding is the creative freedom it offers. Each blend is a reflection of your knowledge, intuition, and care.

Whether you're crafting a remedy for yourself, a loved one, or a client, the process is deeply personal and gratifying. You're not just mixing ingredients—you're creating something greater, something that heals and supports.

As you sip your first cup of a carefully crafted blend, you'll feel a sense of accomplishment. The flavors meld perfectly, the effects are just what you hoped for, and you realize you've tapped into a tradition that connects you to generations of herbalists before you.

This is the art of combining herbs—a practice that celebrates the power of nature, the wisdom of tradition, and the creativity of the human spirit.

Extracting Maximum Potency with Percolation

Herbal medicine thrives on the principle of effectively extracting the healing compounds of plants. Among the many methods available, percolation stands out as an advanced technique that offers maximum potency and efficiency. Known for its precision and effectiveness, percolation allows herbalists to create concentrated tinctures and extracts that are not only powerful but also consistent in quality. This chapter dives into the art and science of percolation, exploring its benefits, processes, and how to apply it in your own herbal practice.

What is Percolation?

Percolation is a method of extracting the active compounds from herbs by passing a solvent—typically alcohol or a water-alcohol mixture—through a column of powdered plant material in a controlled and steady manner. Unlike maceration, where herbs are soaked for weeks, percolation provides a faster and often more efficient means of extraction. This technique is particularly valued for its ability to yield tinctures that are both potent and uniform in their chemical composition.

In essence, percolation mimics the natural process of water passing through soil layers, carrying with it dissolved nutrients. In herbalism, this concept is applied to ensure the solvent captures the full range of beneficial compounds from the herb, leaving behind the inert materials.

Why Use Percolation?

Percolation offers several advantages over traditional extraction methods like maceration:

Efficiency: The process takes hours instead of weeks, making it ideal for preparing tinctures in a shorter timeframe.

Potency: The consistent flow of solvent ensures thorough extraction of active compounds.

Uniformity: Percolation yields extracts that are more uniform in potency, which is essential for therapeutic applications.

Resource Optimization: It often requires less plant material and solvent, reducing waste and making the process more sustainable.

Understanding the Percolation Process

The percolation method can be broken down into a series of precise steps, each critical to the success of the extraction. While the process may seem intimidating at first, mastering it will elevate your herbal practice and allow you to produce professional-grade tinctures.

Step 1: Prepare the Herb

Start by selecting the herb you wish to extract. The herb must be finely powdered to ensure maximum surface area for the solvent to interact with. This step is crucial because larger particles may hinder the solvent's ability to extract the active compounds effectively.

Step 2: Moistening the Herb

The powdered herb is moistened with a small amount of solvent (often alcohol) until it achieves a damp but not dripping consistency. This is known as the menstruum, and its role is to prime the herb for efficient extraction. The herb is allowed to sit for several hours, ensuring the solvent fully penetrates the plant material.

Step 3: Packing the Percolation Cone

The moistened herb is carefully packed into a percolation cone, which can be made from glass or stainless steel. The packing process must be done gently yet firmly to ensure there are no air pockets, as these can disrupt the flow of solvent and lead to uneven extraction.

Step 4: Adding the Solvent

The solvent is poured into the top of the cone, saturating the herb completely. The choice of solvent depends on the herb and its intended use. For example:

Alcohol is commonly used for tinctures.

Glycerin or vinegar may be used for alcohol-free extracts.

Step 5: Starting the Percolation

Once the solvent has saturated the herb, it begins to slowly drip through the bottom of the cone. The flow rate should be controlled—too fast, and the extraction may be incomplete; too slow, and the process becomes inefficient. A steady drip, often described as one drop per second, is considered ideal.

Step 6: Collecting the Extract

The solvent passing through the herb carries with it the plant's active compounds, resulting in a concentrated extract. The collected liquid is your tincture, ready to be used or further refined if necessary.

Tools and Equipment for Percolation

To perform percolation effectively, you'll need specific tools and equipment. While some items can be improvised, investing in quality materials ensures consistent results.

Percolation Cone: A cone-shaped apparatus made from glass, stainless steel, or plastic.

Filter Paper: Used to line the cone and prevent herb particles from clogging the flow.

Collection Vessel: A clean glass jar or beaker to catch the tincture as it drips from the cone.

Powder Mill or Grinder: For achieving a fine, consistent herb powder.

Graduated Cylinder: To measure the solvent accurately.

Choosing the Right Solvent

The choice of solvent, or menstruum, is critical in percolation. Each solvent has unique properties that make it suitable for extracting specific compounds:

Alcohol: Ideal for most herbs due to its ability to dissolve a wide range of compounds, including alkaloids and resins.

Glycerin: A gentle, alcohol-free alternative for ex-

tracts intended for children or those sensitive to alcohol.

Vinegar: Useful for minerals and acidic compounds, often used in tonics.

The solvent's strength (measured as a percentage) should be matched to the herb. For example, high-resin herbs may require a stronger alcohol content (70–95%), while delicate flowers might only need 40–50%.

Common Challenges and Troubleshooting

Challenge 1: Clogging

If the flow of solvent slows or stops, the herb may be packed too tightly. Try repacking the cone with less pressure.

Challenge 2: Uneven Extraction

Uneven extraction can occur if the herb isn't evenly moistened during the initial stages. Always take time to ensure the herb is uniformly damp.

Challenge 3: Weak Tincture

If the tincture is too weak, it could be due to insufficient solvent strength or too fast a percolation rate. Adjust these factors and try again.

Applications of Percolation

Percolation can be used to create a variety of herbal preparations:

Tinctures: Concentrated liquid extracts for internal use.

Liniments: External preparations for muscle pain or skin conditions.

Extracts for Recipes: Herbal extracts for use in skincare or culinary applications.

For example, a percolated tincture of echinacea provides a powerful immune boost, while a comfrey liniment can be applied topically for sore muscles.

The Benefits of Mastering Percolation

Learning the art of percolation not only enhances your herbal practice but also deepens your understanding of how plants and their active compounds interact. The ability to create potent, professional-grade extracts empowers you to tailor remedies to specific needs, ensuring efficacy and consistency.

Moreover, percolation allows you to explore herbs

in new ways, experimenting with blends, solvents, and techniques to achieve desired effects. It's a process that bridges science and tradition, combining precision with the wisdom of herbal medicine.

Percolation is a skill that requires patience, practice, and attention to detail, but the results are well worth the effort. By mastering this technique, you can create highly potent, consistent herbal extracts that elevate your remedies to a professional level. Whether you're preparing a tincture to boost immunity or an extract for skincare, percolation offers a reliable and efficient way to unlock the full potential of herbs. Embrace this advanced method and discover the transformative power of precision in herbal medicine.

Creating Herbal Wines and Fermented Blends

The tradition of creating herbal wines and fermented blends dates back centuries, intertwining the art of herbalism with the craft of fermentation. These preparations offer a unique way to extract and preserve the healing properties of herbs while creating beverages that are flavorful, aromatic, and therapeutic. Fermentation not only enhances the bioavailability of nutrients in herbs but also introduces probiotics, supporting gut health and overall well-being.

Herbal wines and fermented blends combine the nourishing qualities of herbs with the transformative process of fermentation, resulting in a product that is both medicinal and enjoyable. From elderberry wine to ginger-infused mead, the possibilities for creativity are endless. These preparations can support digestion, boost immunity, or simply provide a calming ritual for relaxation.

In this chapter, we'll explore the basics of herbal fermentation and provide 10 simple recipes to inspire your own creations. Whether you're a seasoned herbalist or a curious beginner, these recipes offer a delightful way to incorporate herbs into your daily routine.

821. Elderberry Immune-Boosting Wine

Ingredients:

2 cups fresh elderberries

1 gallon water

2 cups sugar

1 packet wine yeast

Instructions:

Mash elderberries and place them in a fermentation vessel.

Add water and sugar, stirring to dissolve.

Add wine yeast and seal with an airlock.

Ferment for 4–6 weeks, then strain and bottle.

Uses: Supports immunity and provides antioxidants.

Storage Tips: Store in a cool, dark place for up to 1 year.

822. Lavender and Lemon Fermented Tonic

Ingredients:

1/4 cup dried lavender flowers

2 lemons (sliced)

1/2 cup raw honey

1 quart water

Instructions:

Combine all ingredients in a jar.

Cover loosely and ferment at room temperature for 2–3 days.

Strain and refrigerate.

Uses: Calms the nerves and refreshes the mind.

Storage Tips: Refrigerate for up to 1 week.

823. Ginger and Turmeric Fizzy Drink

Ingredients:

1 tbsp grated ginger

1 tsp turmeric powder

1/4 cup sugar

1 quart water

1/4 tsp active dry yeast

Instructions:

Dissolve sugar in water, then add ginger, turmeric, and yeast.

Ferment for 24–48 hours, then bottle and refrigerate.

Uses: Reduces inflammation and aids digestion.

Storage Tips: Consume within 1 week.

824. Rosehip and Cinnamon Mead

Ingredients:

1 cup dried rosehips

1 cinnamon stick

1 gallon water

3 cups honey

1 packet mead yeast

Instructions:

Combine all ingredients in a fermentation vessel.

Add yeast and seal with an airlock.

Ferment for 6–8 weeks, then strain and bottle.

Uses: Supports skin health and provides immune support.

Storage Tips: Store for up to 1 year.

825. Chamomile and Vanilla Herbal Wine

Ingredients:

1/2 cup dried chamomile flowers

1 vanilla bean (split)

1 gallon water

2 cups sugar

1 packet wine yeast

Instructions:

Infuse chamomile and vanilla in water for 24 hours.

Strain, add sugar and yeast, and ferment for 4 weeks.

Uses: Promotes relaxation and aids sleep.

Storage Tips: Store in a cool place for up to 1 year.

826. Peppermint and Honey Fermented Elixir

Ingredients:

1/4 cup dried peppermint leaves

1/2 cup raw honey

1 quart water

Instructions:

Combine all ingredients in a jar.

Cover loosely and ferment for 2–3 days.

Strain and refrigerate.

Uses: Refreshes and supports digestion.

Storage Tips: Consume within 1 week.

827. Elderflower and Lemon Sparkling Wine

Ingredients:

1 cup fresh elderflowers

1 lemon (sliced)

1 gallon water

2 cups sugar

1 packet champagne yeast

Instructions:

Combine elderflowers, lemon, sugar, and water.

Add yeast and ferment for 4 weeks.

Strain and bottle.

Uses: Boosts mood and provides antioxidants.

Storage Tips: Store for up to 1 year.

828. Hibiscus and Ginger Fermented Tea

Ingredients:

2 tbsp dried hibiscus flowers

1 tbsp grated ginger

1/4 cup sugar

1 quart water

Instructions:

Dissolve sugar in water, then add hibiscus and ginger.

Ferment for 2–3 days, then strain and refrigerate.

Uses: Supports cardiovascular health and hydration.

Storage Tips: Consume within 1 week.

829. Nettle and Green Tea Kombucha

Ingredients:

1 quart brewed green tea

1/4 cup dried nettle leaves

1/4 cup sugar

1 kombucha SCOBY

Instructions:

Combine tea, nettle leaves, and sugar.

Add SCOBY and ferment for 7–10 days.

Strain and bottle.

Uses: Boosts energy and supports digestion.

Storage Tips: Store in the refrigerator for up to 1 month.

830. Basil and Orange Herbal Mead

Ingredients:

1/4 cup fresh basil leaves

1 orange (sliced)

1 gallon water

3 cups honey

1 packet mead yeast

Instructions:

Combine all ingredients in a fermentation vessel.

Add yeast and ferment for 6 weeks.

Strain and bottle.

Uses: Uplifts mood and supports overall health.

Storage Tips: Store for up to 1 year.

Working with Rare and Exotic Herbs

Herbs have been revered across cultures for their healing properties, but some of the most intriguing and powerful remedies come from rare and exotic plants that thrive in unique environments around the world. These herbs often hold the key to addressing specific health concerns, offering potent benefits not found in more common plants. However, working with these rare herbs requires a deeper level of knowledge, respect, and care.

Rare and exotic herbs, such as maca from Peru, ashwagandha from India, and rhodiola from Siberia, have traditionally been used in specific cultural and medical contexts. They often have unique properties, making them highly sought after for their adaptogenic, immune-boosting, or cognitive-enhancing effects. But with their increasing popularity, these herbs also face challenges, such as overharvesting and sustainability concerns. This chapter explores the nuances of working with rare and exotic herbs, from sourcing and preparation to ensuring ethical and sustainable use.

Understanding Rare and Exotic Herbs

Rare herbs are those that are not commonly found in local markets or gardens due to their specific growing conditions or geographical origins. They are often tied to traditional systems of medicine, such as Ayurveda, Traditional Chinese Medicine (TCM), or Indigenous practices, and carry centuries of knowledge about their cultivation and use.

Some examples of rare and exotic herbs include:

Maca (Lepidium meyenii): A Peruvian root known for its adaptogenic properties and energy-boosting effects.

Rhodiola (Rhodiola rosea): A Siberian herb prized for its ability to reduce fatigue and enhance mental clarity.

Shatavari (Asparagus racemosus): An Ayurvedic herb that supports hormonal balance and reproductive health.

Gotu Kola (Centella asiatica): A tropical herb used in Ayurveda and TCM to enhance memory and promote skin healing.

Cordyceps (Cordyceps sinensis): A fungus from the Tibetan Plateau known for its immune-boosting and energy-enhancing properties.

Sourcing Rare and Exotic Herbs

When working with rare herbs, sourcing them ethically and sustainably is critical. Overharvesting has endangered many valuable species, and unethical practices can harm the communities that cultivate these plants. Consider these tips for responsible sourcing:

Research Suppliers: Purchase from reputable suppliers who prioritize organic and sustainable practices. Look for certifications such as Fair Trade or Rainforest Alliance.

Support Local Growers: When possible, source herbs directly from communities that grow and harvest them. This not only ensures quality but also supports local economies.

Avoid Overharvested Herbs: Be aware of herbs that are endangered, such as goldenseal or wild ginseng, and seek cultivated alternatives when available.

Educate Yourself: Understand the ecological impact of using certain herbs and explore ways to reduce your footprint, such as using herbs in moderation or substituting with more sustainable options.

Preparation Techniques for Rare Herbs

Rare and exotic herbs often require specialized preparation methods to unlock their full potential.

Understanding the traditional practices associated with these herbs can guide their use.

1. Decoctions

Many roots and barks, like maca or ashwagandha, require boiling to extract their active compounds. Decoctions involve simmering the herb in water for 15–30 minutes to create a concentrated liquid.

2. Powders

Herbs like maca and shatavari are often consumed in powdered form, mixed into smoothies, teas, or food. This form allows for easy digestion and absorption.

3. Tinctures

Alcohol-based tinctures are ideal for preserving rare herbs and extracting potent compounds. Herbs like rhodiola and gotu kola are commonly prepared this way to ensure longevity and effectiveness.

4. Capsules

Encapsulating powdered herbs provides a convenient way to take precise doses of potent herbs like cordyceps or reishi mushroom.

5. Infusions

Leaves and flowers of exotic herbs, such as gotu kola, are best prepared as infusions. Steep them in hot water for 10–15 minutes to extract their delicate properties.

Incorporating Rare Herbs into Your Practice

Rare and exotic herbs can enhance your herbal practice by offering unique solutions to specific health concerns. Here are some ways to incorporate them effectively:

1. Addressing Stress and Fatigue

Adaptogens like rhodiola, ashwagandha, and maca are particularly effective in managing stress and boosting energy. Rhodiola can be taken as a tincture, while maca powder can be added to morning smoothies.

2. Supporting Hormonal Health

Shatavari is a renowned herb for balancing hormones and supporting women's reproductive health. It can be consumed as a tea or in capsule form.

3. Boosting Immunity

Cordyceps and reishi mushrooms are excellent for strengthening the immune system. They can be brewed into teas or taken as powders mixed with warm water.

4. Enhancing Cognitive Function

Gotu kola and rhodiola are popular for improving focus, memory, and mental clarity. These herbs are often used in teas or tinctures for daily brain support.

5. Promoting Skin Health

Gotu kola, known for its wound-healing and collagen-boosting properties, is used in creams and topical treatments. It can also be consumed as a tea for internal skin support.

Safety Considerations

When working with potent herbs, safety is paramount. Always consider the following:

Dosage: Exotic herbs are often more concentrated in their active compounds, so start with small doses and increase gradually.

Interactions: Some herbs may interact with medications or exacerbate certain conditions. For example, rhodiola may not be suitable for individuals with bipolar disorder.

Quality Control: Ensure the herbs are free from contaminants like heavy metals or pesticides by purchasing from trusted suppliers.

Consultation: When in doubt, consult with a qualified herbalist or healthcare professional before using rare herbs, especially if you have underlying health conditions.

Challenges in Using Rare Herbs

While rare and exotic herbs offer incredible benefits, they also come with challenges:

Cost: These herbs can be expensive due to their limited availability and high demand.

Authenticity: Adulteration is a common issue in the herbal industry. Always verify the authenticity of your herbs.

Sustainability: Overharvesting can threaten the survival of certain species. Use these herbs responsibly and explore alternatives when possible.

Exploring Cultural Significance

Rare herbs often carry deep cultural significance, being integral to the traditions and rituals of their regions of origin. For example:

Maca is a staple in Peruvian culture, where it has been used for centuries to enhance stamina and fertility.

Shatavari is revered in Ayurveda as the "queen of herbs" for women's health.

Cordyceps is considered a prized tonic in Traditional Chinese Medicine, symbolizing vitality and longevity.

Understanding and respecting these traditions adds depth to your practice and fosters a deeper connection with the plants.

Working with rare and exotic herbs is a rewarding journey that combines the richness of global herbal traditions with modern herbal practice. These plants, with their unique properties and histories, offer powerful solutions for health and wellness. However, their use demands knowledge, respect, and responsibility to ensure ethical sourcing and sustainable practices.

By mastering the preparation, application, and cultural context of rare herbs, you can unlock their full potential while honoring their origins. Whether you're blending a stress-relieving rhodiola tincture or crafting a nourishing maca smoothie, these extraordinary plants invite you to expand your herbal repertoire and deepen your connection to the natural world.

BOOK 24

NATURAL FIRST AID REMEDIES

In moments of minor injury or sudden discomfort, having access to natural first aid remedies can provide quick, effective relief while supporting your body's natural healing processes. Nature offers a powerful toolkit for addressing common first aid needs, from soothing burns and cuts to alleviating allergic reactions and easing travel-related ailments. By harnessing the healing properties of herbs, you can create a portable, eco-friendly first aid kit tailored to your family's needs.

This book empowers you to confidently handle minor emergencies using herbal remedies that are safe, effective, and easy to prepare. With a focus on practical solutions, you'll learn how to assemble a well-rounded herbal first aid kit, treat common issues like bug bites and scrapes, and manage more specific challenges such as motion sickness or mild allergic reactions. Each remedy is crafted to support healing naturally, without relying on synthetic chemicals.

Whether you're at home, traveling, or enjoying the outdoors, these natural first aid remedies will ensure you're prepared for life's little surprises. Packed with easy-to-follow recipes and tips, this book is your guide to creating a natural first response system that supports your health and well-being, wherever life takes you.

Assembling a Portable Herbal First Aid Kit

A well-prepared first aid kit is a must-have for addressing minor injuries and ailments, whether at home, on the road, or during outdoor adventures. By assembling a portable herbal first aid kit, you can harness the power of nature's remedies to handle common issues like cuts, scrapes, bug bites, and headaches in a safe, effective, and eco-friendly way. Unlike conventional kits, an herbal first aid kit focuses on natural, plant-based solutions that support the body's natural healing processes without synthetic chemicals.

In this chapter, we'll explore the essentials of cre-ating a portable herbal first aid kit, from selecting versatile herbs to organizing your supplies for maximum convenience. By the end, you'll have the knowledge and confidence to build a kit that meets your family's needs and keeps you prepared for minor emergencies.

The Essentials of a Herbal First Aid Kit

An herbal first aid kit is more than just a collection of herbs; it's a curated set of remedies tailored to your lifestyle, environment, and potential risks. The key to assembling an effective kit lies in selecting versatile herbs and natural remedies that address a wide range of situations.

Key Considerations

Portability: Choose a lightweight, compact container that is easy to carry. Options include small tackle boxes, toiletry bags, or even custom-designed herbal pouches.

Customization: Tailor your kit to your specific needs. If you hike frequently, include remedies for blisters and sunburn. For families, prioritize remedies for cuts, bruises, and children's ailments.

Durability: Use sturdy, leak-proof containers for your remedies. Ensure everything is labeled clearly for easy identification.

Core Components of Your Kit

Your herbal first aid kit should include remedies for common issues such as wounds, inflammation, digestive discomfort, and mild infections. Below are the key categories to consider:

1. Wound Care

Wounds like cuts, scrapes, and minor burns are among the most common injuries. Herbs with antimicrobial, soothing, and healing properties are essential for this category:

Calendula Salve: Known for its anti-inflammatory and antimicrobial properties, calendula is excellent for soothing cuts and promoting healing.

Comfrey Ointment: Often called "knitbone," comfrey helps accelerate the healing of minor wounds and bruises.

Lavender Essential Oil: A versatile remedy for soothing burns and reducing inflammation.

2. Pain Relief

For aches, sprains, and minor injuries, include natural pain relievers:

Arnica Gel: Reduces pain and swelling associated with bruises and sprains.

Willow Bark Tincture: A natural source of salicin, similar to aspirin, for relieving headaches and muscle pain.

3. Digestive Support

Digestive discomfort, such as nausea or indigestion, can strike unexpectedly:

Ginger Lozenges: Relieves nausea and motion sickness.

Peppermint Tea Bags: Eases bloating and digestive discomfort.

Activated Charcoal Capsules: Useful for mild food poisoning or diarrhea.

4. Skin Irritations

For rashes, bug bites, and other skin irritations:

Plantain Salve: Soothes itchy bug bites and promotes healing of minor rashes.

Bentonite Clay: A natural detoxifier for drawing out impurities from bug bites or stings.

5. Immune Support

Prepare for colds and mild infections:

Elderberry Syrup: A potent antiviral remedy for warding off colds and flu.

Echinacea Tincture: Boosts the immune system and shortens the duration of illnesses.

6. Calming Remedies

Stress, anxiety, and sleeplessness are common during emergencies:

Rescue Remedy: A Bach flower remedy for calming anxiety and shock.

Chamomile Tea Bags: Promotes relaxation and eases tension.

7. General Tools

Include tools to help administer remedies and manage first aid situations:

Tweezers (for splinters)

Small scissors (for cutting bandages or herbs)

Sterile gauze pads

Bandages of various sizes

Cotton swabs and balls

Disposable gloves

Top Herbs to Include in Your Kit

1. Calendula (Calendula officinalis)

Uses: Wound care, skin irritations, and burns.

Preparation: Infuse in oil to create a soothing salve or add to a wound spray.

2. Comfrey (Symphytum officinale)

Uses: Promotes healing of bruises, sprains, and minor fractures.

Preparation: Create an ointment or poultice for topical use.

3. Lavender (Lavandula angustifolia)

Uses: Calms the mind, soothes burns, and reduces inflammation.

Preparation: Use essential oil for direct application or add dried flowers to sachets for stress relief.

4. Plantain (Plantago major)

Uses: Draws out toxins from bug bites and soothes rashes.

Preparation: Mash fresh leaves into a poultice or create a salve.

5. Elderberry (Sambucus nigra)

Uses: Boosts immunity and fights colds.

Preparation: Make a syrup or tincture for quick administration.

6. Ginger (Zingiber officinale)

Uses: Relieves nausea, indigestion, and motion sickness.

Preparation: Use dried ginger powder for teas or include ginger candies for convenience.

7. Yarrow (Achillea millefolium)

Uses: Stops bleeding and reduces fever.

Preparation: Apply fresh yarrow leaves to wounds or brew as a tea for fevers.

Organizing Your Herbal Kit

Once you've selected your remedies, organizing them properly ensures they are easy to access in an emergency. Here are some tips:

Label Clearly: Use waterproof labels to identify each remedy, including its name, use, and dosage instructions.

Create Categories: Divide your kit into sections (e.g., Wound Care, Digestive Support) using small pouches or compartments.

Include Instructions: Add a small guide or notebook explaining how to use each remedy, especially if others may need to use the kit.

Keep It Fresh: Regularly check your kit to replace expired remedies and restock any items you've used.

Customizing Your Kit for Different Settings

Home Use

A home herbal first aid kit can be more comprehensive, including remedies like large jars of salves or tinctures. Consider adding:

Larger quantities of elderberry syrup and calendula salve.

Additional items like a thermometer and ice packs.

Travel

For a travel kit, focus on portability and versatility:

Use small containers for tinctures and salves.

Include remedies for travel-specific issues, like motion sickness (ginger) and jet lag (adaptogens like ashwagandha).

Outdoor Adventures

For hiking or camping, prioritize remedies for injuries and environmental concerns:

Add sunburn soothers like aloe vera gel.

Include natural insect repellents made from citronella or lemon eucalyptus oil.

Assembling a portable herbal first aid kit is an empowering step toward self-reliance and natural living. With thoughtfully chosen remedies and tools, you can address a wide range of minor injuries and ailments confidently and sustainably. By customizing your kit to suit your lifestyle and keeping it well-organized, you'll always be prepared for the unexpected—whether at home, on the road, or in the great outdoors. Embrace the power of herbal medicine to keep yourself and your loved ones healthy, naturally.

Remedies for Burns, Cuts, and Bug Bites

Minor burns, cuts, and bug bites are among the most common injuries in daily life. While these issues are rarely severe, they can cause discomfort, irritation, and a risk of infection if not treated properly. Herbal remedies offer gentle yet effective solutions to soothe pain, reduce inflammation, and promote healing naturally. Using the right combination of herbs, you can manage these minor emergencies without relying on synthetic chemicals.

Herbs like calendula, lavender, and plantain are excellent for wound care, thanks to their antibacterial and anti-inflammatory properties. Meanwhile, aloe vera and chamomile provide soothing relief for burns and skin irritations. These remedies not only aid the healing process but also offer an eco-friendly alternative to over-the-counter treatments.

This chapter introduces 10 herbal remedies for treating burns, cuts, and bug bites. These recipes are simple to prepare and can be stored in your first aid kit for quick access whenever needed. Whether you're soothing a child's scraped knee or calming the itch of a mosquito bite, these herbal solutions will help you handle minor injuries with confidence.

831. Aloe Vera Gel for Burns

Ingredients:

2 tbsp fresh aloe vera gel

2 drops lavender essential oil

Instructions:

Extract fresh aloe vera gel and mix with lavender oil.

Apply directly to the burn for instant cooling relief.

Uses: Soothes pain, hydrates the skin, and speeds healing.

Storage Tips: Store in the refrigerator for up to 1 week.

832. Calendula Healing Salve

Ingredients:

1/4 cup dried calendula flowers

1/2 cup olive oil

1 tbsp beeswax

Instructions:

Infuse calendula flowers in olive oil over low heat for 1 hour.

Strain and mix with melted beeswax.

Pour into tins and let cool.

Uses: Promotes healing and prevents infection in cuts and scrapes.

Storage Tips: Keep in a cool, dry place for up to 6 months.

833. Lavender Essential Oil Spray

Ingredients:

1 cup distilled water

10 drops lavender essential oil

Instructions:

Mix water and lavender oil in a spray bottle.

Shake well and spray on burns or bug bites.

Uses: Reduces pain, inflammation, and itching.

Storage Tips: Store at room temperature for up to 3 months.

834. Plantain Poultice for Bug Bites

Ingredients:

Fresh plantain leaves

Instructions:

Crush plantain leaves to release their juices.

Apply directly to bug bites and secure with a bandage.

Uses: Draws out toxins and relieves itching.

Storage Tips: Use fresh leaves as needed.

835. Chamomile Tea Compress for Cuts

Ingredients:

1 chamomile tea bag

1 cup boiling water

Instructions:

Steep the tea bag in boiling water for 10 minutes.

Allow to cool slightly, then place the tea bag on the cut.

Uses: Soothes irritation and reduces inflammation.

Storage Tips: Use immediately.

836. Honey and Turmeric Wound Paste

Ingredients:

1 tbsp raw honey

1/2 tsp turmeric powder

Instructions:

Mix honey and turmeric into a paste.

Apply to cuts and cover with a bandage.

Uses: Antibacterial properties prevent infection and promote healing.

Storage Tips: Use fresh each time.

837. Witch Hazel and Peppermint Bug Bite Relief

Ingredients:

1/4 cup witch hazel

5 drops peppermint essential oil

Instructions:

Combine witch hazel and peppermint oil.

Dab onto bug bites with a cotton ball.

Uses: Reduces itching and cools the skin.

Storage Tips: Store in a sealed container for up to 3 months.

838. Comfrey Ointment for Cuts and Scrapes

Ingredients:

1/4 cup comfrey-infused oil

1 tbsp beeswax

Instructions:

Mix comfrey oil with melted beeswax.

Pour into tins and let cool.

Uses: Promotes fast healing of minor wounds.

Storage Tips: Store in a cool place for up to 6 months.

839. Yarrow Powder for Bleeding Cuts

Ingredients:

1 tbsp dried yarrow leaves (ground into powder)

Instructions:

Sprinkle yarrow powder onto the bleeding cut.

Apply pressure to stop bleeding and promote clotting.

Uses: Stops bleeding quickly and disinfects the wound.

Storage Tips: Keep in an airtight container for up to 1 year.

840. Basil and Lemon Balm Anti-Itch Paste

Ingredients:

1 tbsp crushed fresh basil leaves

1 tbsp crushed fresh lemon balm leaves

Instructions:

Mash basil and lemon balm into a paste.

Apply to bug bites to reduce itching and swelling.

Uses: Soothes skin and reduces inflammation.

Storage Tips: Use immediately for best results.

Herbal Solutions for Travel Illnesses

Traveling can be an exciting adventure, but it often comes with unexpected challenges for the body. Whether it's motion sickness, digestive discomfort, jet lag, or exposure to unfamiliar germs, travel illnesses can quickly turn a trip into an uncomfortable experience. Fortunately, herbal remedies provide effective, natural solutions to help you feel your best while on the go.

Herbs like ginger, peppermint, and chamomile are travel-friendly and versatile, addressing issues such as nausea, fatigue, and digestive upsets. Meanwhile, immune-boosting herbs like echinacea and elderberry can protect you from seasonal illnesses or infections you might encounter in new environments. These remedies are easy to prepare and pack, making them a convenient addition to your travel kit.

This chapter presents 10 practical herbal solutions for common travel illnesses. These remedies are designed to keep you comfortable, energized, and healthy, ensuring that nothing stands in the way of your adventures.

841. Ginger Chews for Motion Sickness

Ingredients:

1/4 cup fresh ginger root (grated)

1/4 cup honey

Instructions:

Simmer grated ginger and honey over low heat for 10 minutes.

Pour onto parchment paper and let cool until solid.

Cut into bite-sized pieces.

Uses: Relieves nausea and prevents motion sickness.

Storage Tips: Store in an airtight container for up to 2 weeks.

842. Peppermint Tea for Digestive Relief

Ingredients:

1 tsp dried peppermint leaves

1 cup boiling water

Instructions:

Steep peppermint leaves in boiling water for 10 minutes.

Strain and drink warm.

Uses: Soothes bloating, gas, and indigestion.

Storage Tips: Carry tea bags for easy brewing during travel.

843. Chamomile and Lavender Sleep Aid Spray

Ingredients:

1/4 cup distilled water

5 drops chamomile essential oil

3 drops lavender essential oil

Instructions:

Combine distilled water and essential oils in a small spray bottle.

Shake well and spritz onto your pillow or bedding.

Uses: Promotes restful sleep and eases jet lag.

Storage Tips: Keep in a sealed spray bottle for up to 3 months.

844. Elderberry Syrup for Immune Support

Ingredients:

1/2 cup dried elderberries

2 cups water

1/2 cup raw honey

Instructions:

Simmer elderberries in water over low heat for 30 minutes.

Strain and mix the liquid with honey.

Uses: Boosts immunity and helps prevent colds.

Storage Tips: Refrigerate for up to 2 weeks.

845. Lemon and Ginger Hydration Tonic

Ingredients:

1/2 lemon (sliced)

1 tsp grated ginger

1 quart water

Instructions:

Combine lemon and ginger in a jar of water.

Let infuse for 1–2 hours and drink throughout the day.

Uses: Rehydrates and soothes the digestive system.

Storage Tips: Consume within 24 hours.

846. Echinacea and Honey Throat Soother

Ingredients:

1 tsp dried echinacea flowers

1 tsp raw honey

1 cup boiling water

Instructions:

Steep echinacea flowers in boiling water for 10 minutes.

Stir in honey and sip slowly.

Uses: Supports the immune system and soothes a sore throat.

Storage Tips: Prepare fresh each time.

847. Fennel and Anise Digestive Tea

Ingredients:

1 tsp fennel seeds

1 tsp anise seeds

1 cup boiling water

Instructions:

Steep seeds in boiling water for 10 minutes.

Strain and drink warm.

Uses: Relieves gas, bloating, and mild indigestion.

Storage Tips: Keep seeds in an airtight container for easy transport.

848. Holy Basil (Tulsi) Jet Lag Tea

Ingredients:

1 tsp dried holy basil leaves

1 cup boiling water

Instructions:

Steep holy basil leaves in boiling water for 10 minutes.

Strain and drink warm.

Uses: Supports energy levels and helps reset circadian rhythms.

Storage Tips: Carry pre-portioned tea bags or leaves for convenience.

849. Aloe Vera and Calendula Soothing Gel

Ingredients:

1/4 cup fresh aloe vera gel

1 tbsp calendula-infused oil

Instructions:

Mix aloe vera gel with calendula oil in a small container.

Apply to sunburns, dry skin, or minor irritations.

Uses: Hydrates and soothes skin after long flights or exposure to the elements.

Storage Tips: Keep in a cool place for up to 2 weeks.

850. Lemon Balm and Peppermint Energy Elixir

Ingredients:

1 tsp dried lemon balm leaves

1 tsp dried peppermint leaves

1 cup boiling water

Instructions:

Steep lemon balm and peppermint in boiling water for 10 minutes.

Strain and sip slowly for a refreshing energy boost.

Uses: Reduces fatigue and refreshes the mind.

Storage Tips: Prepare fresh as needed.

Emergency Care for Allergic Reactions

Allergic reactions can range from mild discomfort, such as itchy skin or sneezing, to more severe symptoms like swelling, difficulty breathing, or even anaphylaxis. While severe allergic reactions require immediate medical attention, herbal remedies can provide effective support for managing mild to moderate symptoms. Many herbs possess antihistamine, anti-inflammatory, and soothing properties that can help alleviate allergic responses naturally.

Understanding how to use these remedies in an emergency is essential, as prompt action can make a significant difference in minimizing symptoms. Herbs like nettle, chamomile, and plantain are well-known for their antihistamine effects, while soothing agents such as calendula and aloe vera can calm skin irritations caused by contact allergies. This chapter provides practical guidance on using herbal remedies to care for mild allergic reactions and offers 10 recipes for common allergy concerns.

851. Nettle Infusion for Hay Fever Relief

Ingredients:

1 tbsp dried nettle leaves

1 cup boiling water

Instructions:

Steep nettle leaves in boiling water for 10 minutes.

Strain and drink warm.

Uses: Reduces nasal congestion, sneezing, and watery eyes caused by hay fever.

Storage Tips: Use fresh each time.

852. Chamomile and Honey Allergy Tea

Ingredients:

1 tsp dried chamomile flowers

1 cup boiling water

1 tsp raw honey

Instructions:

Steep chamomile flowers in boiling water for 10 minutes.

Stir in honey and sip slowly.

Uses: Calms inflamed tissues and soothes allergic coughs.

Storage Tips: Prepare as needed.

853. Aloe Vera Gel for Skin Irritations

Ingredients:

2 tbsp fresh aloe vera gel

Instructions:

Extract fresh aloe vera gel.

Apply directly to rashes or itchy skin for cooling relief.

Uses: Reduces itching, redness, and swelling from contact allergies.

Storage Tips: Refrigerate for up to 1 week.

854. Plantain Poultice for Hives

Ingredients:

Fresh plantain leaves

Instructions:

Crush fresh plantain leaves to release their juices.

Apply directly to hives and secure with a bandage.

Uses: Soothes itching and irritation while reducing swelling.

Storage Tips: Use fresh leaves as needed.

855. Calendula and Lavender Skin Spray

Ingredients:

1/2 cup distilled water

1 tbsp calendula-infused oil

5 drops lavender essential oil

Instructions:

Combine all ingredients in a spray bottle.

Shake well and spritz onto affected areas.

Uses: Cools and calms inflamed skin caused by mild allergic reactions.

Storage Tips: Store in a cool place for up to 2 weeks.

856. Peppermint Steam for Sinus Relief

Ingredients:

1 tsp dried peppermint leaves

4 cups boiling water

Instructions:

Add peppermint leaves to a bowl of boiling water.

Lean over the bowl, cover your head with a towel, and inhale the steam for 5–10 minutes.

Uses: Clears nasal passages and eases sinus congestion.

Storage Tips: Use immediately.

857. Holy Basil Tea for Respiratory Allergies

Ingredients:

1 tsp dried holy basil leaves

1 cup boiling water

Instructions:

Steep holy basil leaves in boiling water for 10 minutes.

Strain and drink warm.

Uses: Reduces respiratory discomfort caused by allergies.

Storage Tips: Prepare fresh for each use.

858. Apple Cider Vinegar and Honey Tonic

Ingredients:

1 tbsp apple cider vinegar

1 tsp raw honey

1 cup warm water

Instructions:

Mix all ingredients in a glass.

Drink slowly to alleviate allergy symptoms.

Uses: Balances pH and supports immune response to allergens.

Storage Tips: Prepare fresh each time.

859. Licorice Root Tea for Swollen Airways

Ingredients:

1 tsp dried licorice root

1 cup boiling water

Instructions:

Steep licorice root in boiling water for 10 minutes.

Strain and drink warm.

Uses: Reduces swelling in airways and soothes irritated mucous membranes.

Storage Tips: Consume immediately.

860. Turmeric and Ginger Anti-Inflammatory Paste

Ingredients:

1 tsp turmeric powder

1/2 tsp grated ginger

1 tbsp honey

Instructions:

Mix turmeric, ginger, and honey into a paste.

Take 1/2 tsp at a time to reduce inflammation.

Uses: Calms systemic inflammation caused by allergic reactions.

Storage Tips: Refrigerate for up to 1 week.

Herbal remedies offer effective, natural support for managing mild allergic reactions. From nettle infusions for hay fever to aloe vera for itchy skin, these recipes provide safe and accessible solutions to alleviate discomfort. By incorporating these remedies into your first aid kit, you can confidently handle everyday allergies with the healing power of nature. Always monitor symptoms closely, and when in doubt, consult a healthcare professional.

BOOK 25

HERBAL NUTRITION AND SUPERFOODS

Herbs and superfoods are more than just flavorful additions to your meals—they are powerful sources of nutrition and wellness that can transform the way you eat and live. By incorporating nutrient-rich herbs into your daily diet, you can enhance energy, support immunity, and promote overall health naturally. Whether you're looking to boost vitality with adaptogens, create nourishing meals, or simply add a touch of herbal goodness to your cooking, this book provides the inspiration and tools to make it happen.

This book explores the many ways herbs can be used to enrich your diet, from simple additions like fresh parsley in salads to creative recipes featuring adaptogenic herbs like ashwagandha or maca. You'll learn how to integrate herbs into everyday dishes, craft herbal smoothies and soups, and leverage the unique nutritional profiles of culinary herbs to support specific health goals.

Packed with practical tips and delicious recipes, this book is your guide to making herbal nutrition a seamless and enjoyable part of your lifestyle. Whether you're a seasoned cook or just starting to explore the world of herbal wellness, you'll discover how simple and rewarding it is to nourish your body with the power of herbs and superfoods.

Integrating Herbs into Daily Meals

Incorporating herbs into your daily meals is one of the simplest and most effective ways to enhance both flavor and nutrition. Herbs are nutrient-dense, offering vitamins, minerals, antioxidants, and healing properties that can boost your overall well-being. By weaving them into your cooking, you not only transform everyday dishes but also create meals that support energy, immunity, and digestion.

Fresh or dried, herbs can elevate the taste of a dish while adding significant health benefits. For example, parsley is rich in vitamin C and antioxidants, making it a great addition to salads, soups,

and marinades. Similarly, basil, thyme, and rosemary bring anti-inflammatory and antimicrobial properties to your meals, while adaptogenic herbs like ashwagandha and turmeric can promote balance and reduce stress when incorporated thoughtfully.

This chapter focuses on simple ways to integrate herbs into everyday cooking, from enhancing your morning smoothie with herbal powders to infusing olive oil with your favorite fresh herbs for a nutrient-rich drizzle. Along with practical tips, you'll find 10 recipes that showcase how versatile and easy it is to incorporate these natural wonders into your meals.

861. Basil and Garlic Herb Butter

Ingredients:

1/2 cup unsalted butter (softened)

2 tbsp chopped fresh basil

1 clove garlic (minced)

Instructions:

Mix softened butter with basil and garlic.

Use as a spread for bread, or melt over roasted vegetables.

Uses: Adds flavor while providing anti-inflammatory benefits.

Storage Tips: Store in the refrigerator for up to 1 week.

862. Parsley and Lemon Detox Salad

Ingredients:

1 cup chopped fresh parsley

1/2 cup chopped cucumber

2 tbsp fresh lemon juice

1 tbsp olive oil

Instructions:

Toss all ingredients in a bowl.

Serve as a light, refreshing side dish.

Uses: Boosts digestion and provides a vitamin C-rich detox.

Storage Tips: Consume immediately for freshness.

863. Rosemary and Thyme Roasted Potatoes

Ingredients:

2 cups diced potatoes

1 tbsp olive oil

1 tsp dried rosemary

1 tsp dried thyme

Instructions:

Toss potatoes with olive oil, rosemary, and thyme.

Roast at 400°F (200°C) for 30 minutes.

Uses: A delicious side dish with antimicrobial properties.

Storage Tips: Store leftovers in the refrigerator for up to 3 days.

864. Mint and Yogurt Dip

Ingredients:

1 cup plain Greek yogurt

2 tbsp chopped fresh mint

1/2 tsp ground cumin

Instructions:

Mix all ingredients until well combined.

Serve as a dip for vegetables or bread.

Uses: Refreshes the palate and aids digestion.

Storage Tips: Refrigerate for up to 3 days.

865. Cilantro and Lime Rice

Ingredients:

2 cups cooked rice

1/4 cup chopped fresh cilantro

2 tbsp fresh lime juice

Instructions:

Toss cooked rice with cilantro and lime juice.

Serve warm as a side dish.

Uses: Supports detoxification and boosts flavor.

Storage Tips: Store in an airtight container for up to 3 days.

866. Sage and Honey Tea

Ingredients:

1 tsp dried sage leaves

1 cup boiling water

1 tsp honey

Instructions:

Steep sage leaves in boiling water for 10 minutes.

Stir in honey and drink warm.

Uses: Soothes the throat and calms the mind.

Storage Tips: Prepare fresh each time.

867. Oregano and Tomato Pasta Sauce

Ingredients:

1 can crushed tomatoes

1 tbsp olive oil

1 tsp dried oregano

1 clove garlic (minced)

Instructions:

Sauté garlic in olive oil, then add tomatoes and oregano.

Simmer for 15 minutes and serve over pasta.

Uses: Adds immune-boosting benefits to a classic dish.

Storage Tips: Refrigerate for up to 3 days.

868. Lavender-Infused Honey

Ingredients:

1 cup raw honey

2 tbsp dried lavender flowers

Instructions:

Combine honey and lavender in a jar.

Let sit for 1 week, then strain out flowers.

Uses: Drizzle over toast, yogurt, or desserts for relaxation.

Storage Tips: Store in a cool, dark place for up to 6 months.

869. Turmeric and Black Pepper Golden Milk

Ingredients:

1 cup almond milk

1/2 tsp turmeric powder

Pinch of black pepper

1 tsp honey

Instructions:

Warm almond milk and whisk in turmeric, black pepper, and honey.

Serve hot.

Uses: Reduces inflammation and promotes relaxation.

Storage Tips: Consume immediately.

870. Dill and Lemon Baked Fish

Ingredients:

2 fillets of white fish

1 tbsp chopped fresh dill

1 tbsp lemon juice

Instructions:

Place fish fillets on a baking sheet and drizzle with lemon juice.

Sprinkle with dill and bake at 375°F (190°C) for 20 minutes.

Uses: Enhances digestion and adds omega-3 benefits.

Storage Tips: Consume immediately.

Integrating herbs into daily meals is a simple and flavorful way to enhance your overall nutrition. With minimal effort, these recipes bring a variety of health benefits, from supporting digestion and boosting immunity to calming the mind and reducing inflammation. Start experimenting with these versatile recipes, and discover how the power of herbs can transform your meals into delicious, nutrient-packed creations that nourish your body and soul.

Cooking with Adaptogens for Energy and Vitality

Adaptogens are a remarkable class of herbs and mushrooms that help the body adapt to stress, increase energy levels, and restore balance. These herbs have been used for centuries in traditional systems of medicine like Ayurveda and Traditional Chinese Medicine (TCM) to support endurance, vitality, and overall well-being. Incorporating adaptogens into your meals is a simple and delicious way to enjoy their benefits daily, especially for those seeking sustained energy and resilience in a busy lifestyle.

Adaptogens like ashwagandha, maca, rhodiola, and reishi are known for their ability to reduce fatigue, enhance focus, and support the body's natural stress response. Cooking with these powerful herbs allows you to infuse their therapeutic properties into your favorite dishes, from smoothies and soups to energy bars and teas.

This chapter explores the unique properties of key adaptogens, practical tips for cooking with them, and 10 versatile recipes to help you incorporate these powerful herbs into your diet. With a little creativity, you can transform ordinary meals into nutrient-dense, energy-boosting feasts.

871. Ashwagandha Energy Balls

Ingredients:

1 cup rolled oats

2 tbsp ashwagandha powder

1/4 cup almond butter

2 tbsp honey

1/4 cup dark chocolate chips

Instructions:

Mix all ingredients in a bowl until well combined.

Roll into small balls and refrigerate for 30 minutes.

Uses: Boosts energy and reduces stress.

Storage Tips: Store in an airtight container in the refrigerator for up to 1 week.

872. Maca and Cacao Smoothie

Ingredients:

1 banana

1 cup almond milk

1 tbsp maca powder

1 tbsp cacao powder

1 tsp honey

Instructions:

Blend all ingredients until smooth.

Serve immediately.

Uses: Provides natural energy and enhances mood.

Storage Tips: Consume fresh.

873. Reishi Mushroom Soup

Ingredients:

1 cup sliced mushrooms

1 tbsp reishi mushroom powder

1 tbsp olive oil

3 cups vegetable broth

Instructions:

Sauté mushrooms in olive oil until soft.

Add reishi powder and vegetable broth. Simmer for 20 minutes.

Uses: Supports immunity and reduces fatigue.

Storage Tips: Refrigerate leftovers for up to 3 days.

874. Rhodiola Lemon Tea

Ingredients:

1 tsp rhodiola root (dried)

1 cup boiling water

1 tsp lemon juice

Instructions:

Steep rhodiola root in boiling water for 10 minutes.

Add lemon juice and stir.

Uses: Enhances focus and mental clarity.

Storage Tips: Prepare fresh each time.

875. Holy Basil (Tulsi) Stir-Fry

Ingredients:

2 cups mixed vegetables (e.g., bell peppers, carrots, broccoli)

1 tsp holy basil powder

1 tbsp soy sauce

1 tbsp olive oil

Instructions:

Heat olive oil in a pan and add vegetables.

Stir-fry until tender, then sprinkle holy basil powder and soy sauce.

Uses: Reduces stress and supports digestion.

Storage Tips: Consume immediately.

876. Shatavari Golden Milk

Ingredients:

1 cup coconut milk

1 tsp shatavari powder

1/2 tsp turmeric powder

1 tsp honey

Instructions:

Warm coconut milk and whisk in shatavari, turmeric, and honey.

Serve warm.

Uses: Balances hormones and supports vitality.

Storage Tips: Consume fresh.

877. Licorice Root Energy Bars

Ingredients:

1 cup rolled oats

1 tbsp licorice root powder

1/4 cup almond butter

1/4 cup honey

Instructions:

Mix all ingredients in a bowl until combined.

Press into a baking dish and refrigerate for 1 hour.

Uses: Provides sustained energy and supports adrenal health.

Storage Tips: Store in the refrigerator for up to 1 week.

878. Eleuthero Berry Breakfast Bowl

Ingredients:

1 cup plain yogurt

1 tbsp eleuthero berry powder

1/4 cup granola

1/4 cup mixed berries

Instructions:

Stir eleuthero powder into yogurt.

Top with granola and berries.

Uses: Improves stamina and reduces fatigue.

Storage Tips: Consume immediately.

879. Ginseng and Ginger Tea

Ingredients:

1 tsp dried ginseng root

1/2 tsp grated fresh ginger

1 cup boiling water

Instructions:

Steep ginseng root and ginger in boiling water for 10 minutes.

Strain and serve warm.

Uses: Boosts energy and enhances mental clarity.

Storage Tips: Prepare fresh each time.

880. Cordyceps Mushroom Pasta Sauce

Ingredients:

2 cups tomato sauce

1 tbsp cordyceps mushroom powder

1 tbsp olive oil

1 clove garlic (minced)

Instructions:

Sauté garlic in olive oil, then add tomato sauce and cordyceps powder.

Simmer for 10 minutes and serve over pasta.

Uses: Enhances endurance and supports immune health.

Storage Tips: Refrigerate leftovers for up to 3 days.

Tips for Cooking with Adaptogens

Start Small: Adaptogens are potent; begin with small amounts and adjust based on taste and tolerance.

Pair with Fats: Many adaptogens, such as turmeric and ashwagandha, are fat-soluble and absorb better when paired with healthy fats like coconut milk or olive oil.

Avoid Overheating: Some adaptogens lose potency when exposed to high heat for extended periods. Add powders toward the end of cooking whenever possible.

Cooking with adaptogens is a delicious and practical way to boost energy, combat stress, and support overall vitality. From smoothies and teas to soups and energy bars, these recipes make it easy to incorporate adaptogens into your diet. By experimenting with different adaptogens, you'll discover which ones best suit your needs, transforming your meals into a powerful tool for health and resilience.

Creating Herbal Smoothies and Soups

Herbs are a versatile addition to smoothies and soups, offering a delicious way to incorporate their nutritional and therapeutic benefits into your diet. Whether blended into a refreshing morning drink or simmered into a comforting bowl of soup, herbs enhance flavor while providing vitamins, minerals, and bioactive compounds that promote health and wellness.

Herbal smoothies are an easy way to kickstart your day with energy-boosting ingredients like adaptogens, greens, and fruits. Adding powdered herbs such as maca, spirulina, or moringa transforms your smoothie into a nutrient-packed powerhouse. Similarly, soups offer the perfect opportunity to include fresh or dried herbs like thyme, rosemary, or nettle for immune-boosting, anti-inflammatory, and digestive-supporting benefits.

In this chapter, you'll find tips for selecting the best herbs for your smoothies and soups, along with 10 easy recipes to inspire your culinary creativity. Whether you're seeking a quick meal replacement or a nourishing comfort dish, these herbal creations will leave you feeling revitalized and satisfied.

881. Green Energy Smoothie with Spirulina

Ingredients:

1 banana

1 cup spinach

1 tsp spirulina powder

1 cup almond milk

Instructions:

Blend all ingredients until smooth.

Serve immediately for a nutrient-packed boost.

Uses: Provides energy and detoxifies the body.

Storage Tips: Consume fresh.

882. Berry and Maca Vitality Smoothie

Ingredients:

1 cup mixed berries (blueberries, strawberries)

1 tsp maca powder

1 cup yogurt

1 tsp honey

Instructions:

Blend all ingredients until smooth.

Enjoy as a refreshing mid-day pick-me-up.

Uses: Boosts energy and supports hormonal health.

Storage Tips: Refrigerate for up to 24 hours.

883. Creamy Turmeric and Ginger Soup

Ingredients:

1 tbsp olive oil

1 tsp turmeric powder

1/2 tsp grated ginger

2 cups coconut milk

Instructions:

Heat olive oil, then add turmeric and ginger.

Stir in coconut milk and simmer for 10 minutes.

Uses: Reduces inflammation and soothes digestion.

Storage Tips: Refrigerate leftovers for up to 3 days.

884. Detoxifying Nettle and Spinach Soup

Ingredients:

1 cup fresh nettle leaves (or 1 tbsp dried nettle)

1 cup spinach

1 clove garlic (minced)

2 cups vegetable broth

Instructions:

Sauté garlic, then add nettle, spinach, and broth.

Simmer for 10 minutes, then blend until smooth.

Uses: Cleanses the body and supports energy.

Storage Tips: Refrigerate for up to 3 days.

885. Adaptogenic Ashwagandha Smoothie Bowl

Ingredients:

1 frozen banana

1/2 cup almond milk

1 tsp ashwagandha powder

1/4 cup granola

Instructions:

Blend banana, almond milk, and ashwagandha powder.

Top with granola before serving.

Uses: Reduces stress and promotes energy.

Storage Tips: Consume immediately.

886. Mushroom and Thyme Immune Soup

Ingredients:

2 cups sliced mushrooms

1 tsp dried thyme

1 tbsp olive oil

3 cups chicken or vegetable broth

Instructions:

Sauté mushrooms in olive oil.

Add thyme and broth, then simmer for 15 minutes.

Uses: Boosts immunity and supports gut health.

Storage Tips: Store in the refrigerator for up to 4 days.

887. Lemon Balm and Mint Refreshing Smoothie

Ingredients:

1 cup cucumber slices

1/2 cup fresh mint leaves

1 tsp dried lemon balm

1 cup water

Instructions:

Blend all ingredients until smooth.

Serve over ice for a refreshing drink.

Uses: Soothes stress and supports digestion.

Storage Tips: Consume immediately.

888. Herbal Tomato Basil Soup

Ingredients:

2 cups diced tomatoes

1/4 cup fresh basil leaves

1 tbsp olive oil

2 cups vegetable broth

Instructions:

Sauté tomatoes in olive oil.

Add basil and broth, then simmer for 20 minutes.

Uses: Supports immunity and provides antioxidants.

Storage Tips: Refrigerate for up to 3 days.

889. Lavender and Blueberry Smoothie

Ingredients:

1 cup blueberries

1 tsp dried lavender flowers

1 cup almond milk

1 tsp honey

Instructions:

Blend all ingredients until smooth.

Serve as a calming morning drink.

Uses: Reduces stress and provides antioxidants.

Storage Tips: Consume fresh.

890. Bone Broth with Adaptogenic Herbs

Ingredients:

4 cups bone broth

1 tsp reishi powder

1/2 tsp turmeric powder

1 clove garlic (minced)

Instructions:

Heat bone broth and stir in reishi, turmeric, and garlic.

Simmer for 15 minutes and serve warm.

Uses: Boosts immunity and promotes recovery.

Storage Tips: Store in the refrigerator for up to 5 days.

Tips for Creating Herbal Smoothies and Soups

Start Simple: When using herbs, begin with small amounts to avoid overpowering the flavor.

Balance Flavors: Pair earthy herbs like ashwagandha with sweet fruits in smoothies, or savory herbs like thyme with hearty ingredients in soups.

Use Fresh and Dried Herbs: Fresh herbs add vibrancy, while dried herbs bring concentrated flavor and benefits.

Experiment: Don't hesitate to mix herbs and ingredients to discover combinations that work best for your taste and health goals.

Herbal smoothies and soups are an easy and versatile way to incorporate the healing power of herbs into your diet. Whether you're starting your day with an adaptogen-rich smoothie or ending it with a nourishing herbal soup, these recipes provide a delicious means of supporting energy, immunity, and overall wellness. Embrace the endless possibilities of herbal cooking and create meals that heal and delight.

Nutritional Profiles of Common Culinary Herbs

Culinary herbs are more than just a way to enhance the flavor of your dishes—they are nutrient-dense powerhouses that offer a wide range of health benefits. Packed with vitamins, minerals, and antioxidants, these everyday ingredients can significantly boost your overall wellness. Understanding the nutritional profiles of common culinary herbs allows you to make informed decisions about which herbs to include in your meals to meet specific health goals.

Herbs like parsley, basil, cilantro, and oregano are often staples in kitchens worldwide. They bring much more than flavor to the table: parsley, for example, is rich in vitamin C and iron, while basil contains anti-inflammatory compounds that promote overall health. Cilantro supports detoxification, and oregano is a potent source of antioxidants. By including these herbs in your cooking, you can transform your meals into nutrient-packed creations that support digestion, immunity, and vitality.

In this chapter, we'll delve into the nutritional highlights of some of the most commonly used culinary herbs, exploring how they contribute to overall health and how best to incorporate them into your diet.

Parsley (Petroselinum crispum)

Parsley is a nutrient-dense herb commonly used in garnishes, soups, and salads. It is high in vitamin C, vitamin K, and iron, making it a great choice for boosting immunity, supporting bone health, and aiding in detoxification. The antioxidants in parsley, including flavonoids and carotenoids, help combat oxidative stress and inflammation.

Basil (Ocimum basilicum)

Known for its aromatic flavor, basil is rich in vitamin A, vitamin K, and manganese. It also contains polyphenols such as eugenol, which have anti-inflammatory properties. Basil supports cardiovascular health, aids digestion, and promotes healthy skin. It's a fantastic addition to sauces, pestos, and salads.

Cilantro (Coriandrum sativum)

Cilantro is well-known for its detoxifying properties, particularly its ability to support the removal of heavy metals from the body. Rich in vitamin A, vitamin C, and potassium, it also supports immune health and reduces bloating. Cilantro adds a fresh flavor to soups, tacos, curries, and salsas.

Oregano (Origanum vulgare)

A robust herb with a bold flavor, oregano is a source of vitamin K, calcium, and magnesium. It contains potent antioxidants like thymol and carvacrol, which have antimicrobial and immune-boosting properties. Oregano is an essential herb in Mediterranean cuisine, used in sauces, pizzas, and roasted vegetables.

Mint (Mentha spp.)

Mint is not only refreshing but also a functional herb for digestion and stress relief. High in vitamin A and iron, it contains menthol, which has a natural cooling effect. Mint is excellent for calming indigestion, freshening breath, and reducing stress. Use it in teas, smoothies, or as a garnish for desserts.

Rosemary (Rosmarinus officinalis)

Rosemary is a fragrant herb rich in vitamin B6, calcium, and manganese. It contains rosmarinic acid, a powerful antioxidant that supports memory, concentration, and circulation. Rosemary is often used in savory dishes like roasted meats, potatoes, and breads.

Thyme (Thymus vulgaris)

Thyme is packed with vitamin C, vitamin A, and copper, making it a great herb for boosting immunity and supporting respiratory health. It contains thymol, a natural antiseptic and antifungal compound. Thyme is commonly used in soups, stews, and marinades for meats.

Dill (Anethum graveolens)

Dill is a light, fragrant herb with significant health benefits. Rich in vitamin C, manganese, and folate, it supports digestion, strengthens bones, and promotes healthy skin. Dill is a popular addition to pickles, fish dishes, and creamy dips like tzatziki.

Chives (Allium schoenoprasum)

Chives are a mild member of the allium family, rich in vitamin K and vitamin A. They contain sulfur compounds that promote detoxification and cardiovascular health. Sprinkle chopped chives over baked potatoes, soups, and omelets to enhance both flavor and nutrition.

Sage (Salvia officinalis)

Sage is a versatile herb packed with vitamin K, magnesium, and zinc. Its antioxidant properties, including rosmarinic acid, support memory, reduce inflammation, and improve oral health. Sage is a favorite for stuffing, roasted meats, and herbal teas.

How to Maximize Nutrition from Culinary Herbs

Use Fresh Whenever Possible: Fresh herbs often retain more nutrients and antioxidants than dried herbs.

Add Late in Cooking: To preserve nutrients, add herbs toward the end of the cooking process.

Combine with Healthy Fats: Fat-soluble vitamins like vitamin A and K are better absorbed when paired with healthy fats, such as olive oil or avocado.

Grow Your Own: Growing herbs at home ensures freshness and gives you access to a sustainable source of nutrients.

The culinary herbs you use daily are not only flavor enhancers but also potent sources of nutrition. By understanding their health benefits, you can make intentional choices to incorporate these powerful plants into your meals. Whether you're sprinkling parsley over a salad or adding rosemary to roasted vegetables, these herbs turn your food into a vibrant, health-boosting experience. Unlock the full potential of your kitchen with these nutrient-rich additions and savor the dual benefits of taste and wellness.

BOOK 26

HERBAL REMEDIES FOR EMOTIONAL TRAUMA

Emotional trauma can leave a deep impact on the mind and body, often manifesting as stress, anxiety, fatigue, or feelings of disconnection. While time and support are vital in the healing process, nature offers a powerful ally in the form of herbs. With their soothing, grounding, and nurturing properties, herbs can help calm emotional turmoil, restore balance, and encourage resilience.

This book explores how herbal remedies can assist in processing emotional trauma and grief, providing gentle support for the heart and mind. From calming nervines like chamomile and lemon balm to grounding adaptogens like ashwagandha, these herbs work holistically to ease anxiety, uplift the spirit, and promote long-term healing. You'll also discover the transformative power of aromatherapy blends and flower essences, which can nurture emotional well-being in subtle yet profound ways.

Whether you're seeking comfort after a personal loss, support during a challenging time, or tools to help a loved one, this book offers a compassionate guide to using herbal remedies for emotional healing. By embracing the wisdom of nature, you can embark on a journey of restoration and rediscovery, finding peace and strength within yourself.

Supporting Grief with Gentle Remedies

Grief is a natural yet deeply challenging response to loss. It can leave emotional and physical impacts, including anxiety, fatigue, and a sense of disconnection. While time and support are critical, herbs offer gentle, nurturing remedies to help soothe the heart, calm the mind, and provide comfort during this difficult time. These natural allies, including chamomile, lavender, and rose, can ease emotional tension, promote relaxation, and support the healing process.

Gentle herbal teas, tinctures, and salves work holistically to address the physical and emotional symptoms of grief. Adaptogens like ashwagandha can help build resilience, while nervines like passionflower and lemon balm offer much-needed calm. This chapter provides 10 simple, effective remedies designed to support individuals during their grieving journey, offering a sense of comfort and healing through the power of nature.

891. Chamomile and Lavender Calm Tea

Ingredients:

1 tsp dried chamomile flowers

1 tsp dried lavender flowers

1 cup boiling water

Instructions:

Steep chamomile and lavender in boiling water for 10 minutes.

Strain and sip slowly.

Uses: Soothes anxiety and promotes relaxation.

Storage Tips: Use fresh each time.

892. Rose Petal Comfort Infusion

Ingredients:

1 tbsp dried rose petals

1 cup boiling water

Instructions:

Steep rose petals in boiling water for 5–7 minutes.

Strain and enjoy as a heart-soothing drink.

Uses: Provides emotional comfort and uplifts the spirit.

Storage Tips: Prepare fresh.

893. Lemon Balm Stress Relief Tea

Ingredients:

1 tsp dried lemon balm leaves

1 cup boiling water

Instructions:

Steep lemon balm leaves in boiling water for 10 minutes.

Strain and drink in moments of overwhelm.

Uses: Reduces stress and promotes calm.

Storage Tips: Best enjoyed fresh.

894. Holy Basil (Tulsi) Resilience Tincture

Ingredients:

1 tbsp dried holy basil leaves

1/2 cup glycerin

Instructions:

Combine holy basil and glycerin in a jar.

Steep for 2 weeks, shaking daily, then strain.

Uses: Builds resilience and eases tension.

Storage Tips: Store in a dark, cool place for up to 6 months.

895. Lavender and Bergamot Aromatherapy Spray

Ingredients:

1/2 cup distilled water

5 drops lavender essential oil

3 drops bergamot essential oil

Instructions:

Combine ingredients in a spray bottle.

Shake well and spritz in your space for calm.

Uses: Promotes relaxation and uplifts the mood.

Storage Tips: Store for up to 3 months.

896. Hawthorn and Cinnamon Heart Tea

Ingredients:

1 tsp dried hawthorn berries

1 small cinnamon stick

1 cup boiling water

Instructions:

Steep hawthorn berries and cinnamon in boiling water for 15 minutes.

Strain and enjoy warm.

Uses: Nurtures the heart and provides emotional strength.

Storage Tips: Consume fresh.

897. Passionflower Sleep Aid Tea

Ingredients:

1 tsp dried passionflower

1 cup boiling water

Instructions:

Steep passionflower in boiling water for 10 minutes.

Strain and drink 30 minutes before bed.

Uses: Helps with grief-related insomnia.

Storage Tips: Prepare fresh.

898. Rosemary Memory and Clarity Infusion

Ingredients:

1 tsp dried rosemary

1 cup boiling water

Instructions:

Steep rosemary in boiling water for 5 minutes.

Strain and sip to support mental clarity.

Uses: Clears the mind and strengthens memory.

Storage Tips: Best enjoyed fresh.

899. Ashwagandha Comforting Milk

Ingredients:

1 cup warm almond milk

1 tsp ashwagandha powder

1 tsp honey

Instructions:

Mix ashwagandha powder into warm almond milk.

Stir in honey and drink before bed.

Uses: Reduces stress and promotes emotional comfort.

Storage Tips: Consume immediately.

900. Calendula Healing Salve

Ingredients:

1/4 cup calendula-infused oil

1 tbsp beeswax

Instructions:

Melt beeswax and combine with calendula oil.

Pour into a small jar and let solidify.

Uses: Soothes tension-related skin irritation.

Storage Tips: Store in a cool, dry place for up to 6 months.

Herbal Allies for Emotional Stability

Emotional stability is crucial for maintaining balance in life, particularly when faced with challenges such as stress, anxiety, or emotional upheaval. Herbs offer a natural, gentle approach to fostering emotional resilience, calming the mind, and uplifting the spirit. Adaptogens, nervines, and mood-enhancing herbs work holistically to address the underlying causes of emotional instability, providing relief and supporting long-term emotional well-being.

This chapter explores key herbal allies for emotional stability and presents 10 carefully crafted recipes to incorporate these herbs into your daily routine. Each recipe is designed to be easy to prepare and effective in promoting calm, clarity, and emotional strength.

901. Chamomile and Lavender Relaxation Tea

Ingredients:

1 tsp dried chamomile flowers

1 tsp dried lavender flowers

1 cup boiling water

Instructions:

Combine chamomile and lavender in a teapot or mug.

Pour boiling water over the herbs and steep for 10 minutes.

Strain and sip slowly to enjoy its calming effects.

Uses: Reduces anxiety and promotes relaxation.

Storage Tips: Prepare fresh for maximum potency.

902. Ashwagandha Golden Milk

Ingredients:

1 cup almond milk

1 tsp ashwagandha powder

1/2 tsp turmeric powder

1 tsp honey

Instructions:

Warm almond milk in a small saucepan.

Whisk in ashwagandha powder, turmeric powder, and honey until well blended.

Serve warm as a soothing evening drink.

Uses: Reduces stress and supports restful sleep.

Storage Tips: Consume immediately.

903. Lemon Balm and Holy Basil Iced Tea

Ingredients:

1 tsp dried lemon balm leaves

1 tsp dried holy basil leaves

2 cups boiling water

1 tsp honey (optional)

Instructions:

Steep lemon balm and holy basil in boiling water for 10 minutes.

Strain, cool, and refrigerate until chilled.

Add honey if desired, and serve over ice.

Uses: Calms the mind and provides daytime stress relief.

Storage Tips: Store in the refrigerator for up to 24 hours.

904. St. John's Wort Mood-Boosting Tincture

Ingredients:

1/4 cup dried St. John's wort

1/2 cup glycerin (non-alcoholic option)

Instructions:

Combine St. John's wort and glycerin in a clean jar.

Seal tightly and let steep in a cool, dark place for 4–6 weeks, shaking daily.

Strain into a dropper bottle for easy use.

Uses: Balances mood and uplifts emotional well-being.

Storage Tips: Store in a dark, cool place for up to 6 months.

905. Lavender and Bergamot Aromatherapy Spray

Ingredients:

1/2 cup distilled water

5 drops lavender essential oil

3 drops bergamot essential oil

Instructions:

Combine distilled water and essential oils in a spray bottle.

Shake well before use.

Spritz in your space to create a calming atmosphere.

Uses: Promotes relaxation and uplifts the spirit.

Storage Tips: Store in a sealed bottle for up to 3 months.

906. Passionflower and Valerian Night Tea

Ingredients:

1 tsp dried passionflower

1/2 tsp dried valerian root

1 cup boiling water

Instructions:

Steep passionflower and valerian in boiling water for 10 minutes.

Strain and drink 30 minutes before bed.

Uses: Eases restlessness and promotes restful sleep.

Storage Tips: Prepare fresh as needed.

907. Rhodiola Energy Smoothie

Ingredients:

1 cup almond milk

1 banana

1 tsp rhodiola powder

1/2 cup frozen berries

Instructions:

Blend all ingredients until smooth.

Serve immediately as a refreshing, energy-boosting drink.

Uses: Enhances focus and reduces fatigue.

Storage Tips: Consume fresh.

908. Holy Basil Soup

Ingredients:

1 tsp dried holy basil leaves

2 cups vegetable broth

1/2 cup chopped carrots

1/2 cup chopped celery

Instructions:

Sauté carrots and celery in olive oil until tender.

Add vegetable broth and holy basil leaves.

Simmer for 15 minutes, then strain or serve as is.

Uses: Supports emotional clarity and reduces stress.

Storage Tips: Refrigerate leftovers for up to 3 days.

909. Rose Petal and Lemon Balm Infusion

Ingredients:

1 tsp dried rose petals

1 tsp dried lemon balm leaves

1 cup boiling water

Instructions:

Combine rose petals and lemon balm in a teapot or mug.

Pour boiling water over the herbs and steep for 10 minutes.

Strain and enjoy warm.

Uses: Uplifts mood and soothes anxiety.

Storage Tips: Prepare fresh each time.

910. Chamomile and Calendula Bath Soak

Ingredients:

1/2 cup dried chamomile flowers

1/2 cup dried calendula flowers

1 muslin bag

Instructions:

Fill the muslin bag with chamomile and calendula flowers.

Place the bag in warm bathwater and let steep for 10 minutes before bathing.

Uses: Relaxes the mind and nourishes the skin.

Storage Tips: Store dried herbs in an airtight container for up to 6 months.

Herbs are valuable allies in promoting emotional stability, providing support for the mind and body in times of stress or emotional imbalance. These 10 recipes offer simple yet effective ways to incorporate herbal remedies into daily life, fostering calm, resilience, and overall well-being. With these herbal allies, you can find natural and nurturing ways to navigate emotional challenges and cultivate inner peace.

Creating Comforting Aromatherapy Blends

Aromatherapy is a powerful practice that uses essential oils extracted from plants to promote emotional well-being and relaxation. The calming, uplifting, and grounding properties of these oils can create a comforting atmosphere, helping to soothe anxiety, uplift the spirit, and provide a sense of balance during emotionally challenging times. Aromatherapy blends are versatile and can be used in diffusers, sprays, massage oils, or bath soaks.

This chapter introduces 10 easy-to-make aromatherapy blends that harness the soothing qualities of essential oils like lavender, bergamot, chamomile, and frankincense. These recipes are designed to provide comfort and emotional stability, whether you're seeking relaxation, mental clarity, or a sense of grounding.

911. Lavender and Chamomile Sleep Mist

Ingredients:

1/2 cup distilled water

5 drops lavender essential oil

3 drops chamomile essential oil

Instructions:

Combine distilled water and essential oils in a spray bottle.

Shake well before use.

Spray onto your pillow or around your room before bedtime.

Uses: Promotes restful sleep and calms an overactive mind.

Storage Tips: Store in a sealed bottle for up to 3 months.

912. Bergamot and Ylang-Ylang Uplifting Diffuser Blend

Ingredients:

4 drops bergamot essential oil

3 drops ylang-ylang essential oil

Instructions:

Add the essential oils to your diffuser with the recommended amount of water.

Turn on the diffuser and enjoy the uplifting aroma.

Uses: Boosts mood and relieves stress.

Storage Tips: Use essential oils fresh each time.

913. Frankincense and Cedarwood Grounding Blend

Ingredients:

3 drops frankincense essential oil

3 drops cedarwood essential oil

1 tbsp carrier oil (e.g., sweet almond oil)

Instructions:

Mix essential oils with the carrier oil.

Apply a small amount to pulse points or use as a massage oil.

Uses: Provides grounding and emotional stability during stressful moments.

Storage Tips: Store in a dark glass bottle for up to 6 months.

914. Lemon and Rosemary Focus Spray

Ingredients:

1/2 cup distilled water

5 drops lemon essential oil

3 drops rosemary essential oil

Instructions:

Combine water and essential oils in a spray bottle.

Shake well before use.

Spritz around your workspace to promote mental clarity and focus.

Uses: Enhances concentration and reduces mental fatigue.

Storage Tips: Store for up to 3 months.

915. Peppermint and Eucalyptus Revitalizing Shower Blend

Ingredients:

3 drops peppermint essential oil

3 drops eucalyptus essential oil

Instructions:

Add the essential oils to a damp washcloth.

Place the washcloth in the corner of your shower, away from direct water flow.

Inhale the refreshing aroma as you shower.

Uses: Revitalizes energy and clears the mind.

Storage Tips: Use immediately.

916. Jasmine and Orange Joyful Diffuser Blend

Ingredients:

3 drops jasmine essential oil

4 drops orange essential oil

Instructions:

Add the essential oils to your diffuser with water.

Turn on the diffuser and enjoy the cheerful aroma.

Uses: Elevates mood and reduces feelings of sadness.

Storage Tips: Use fresh each time.

917. Chamomile and Rose Relaxation Massage Oil

Ingredients:

1 tbsp carrier oil (e.g., jojoba oil)

3 drops chamomile essential oil

2 drops rose essential oil

Instructions:

Mix the essential oils with the carrier oil.

Use as a massage oil to promote relaxation and reduce tension.

Uses: Eases stress and provides emotional comfort.

Storage Tips: Store in a glass bottle for up to 6 months.

918. Lavender and Clary Sage Stress Relief Bath Soak

Ingredients:

1 cup Epsom salts

5 drops lavender essential oil

3 drops clary sage essential oil

Instructions:

Combine Epsom salts and essential oils in a mixing bowl.

Add the mixture to warm bathwater and soak for 20 minutes.

Uses: Relieves stress and promotes relaxation.

Storage Tips: Store dry salts in a sealed jar for up to 3 months.

919. Geranium and Patchouli Mood-Balancing Blend

Ingredients:

3 drops geranium essential oil

2 drops patchouli essential oil

1 tbsp carrier oil

Instructions:

Mix the essential oils with the carrier oil.

Apply to pulse points or use in a diffuser.

Uses: Balances emotions and provides grounding.

Storage Tips: Store in a cool, dark place for up to 6 months.

920. Tea Tree and Lemongrass Refreshing Room Spray

Ingredients:

1/2 cup distilled water

5 drops tea tree essential oil

3 drops lemongrass essential oil

Instructions:

Combine water and essential oils in a spray bottle.

Shake well before use.

Spritz around your room to create a refreshing atmosphere.

Uses: Cleanses the air and uplifts the mood.

Storage Tips: Store for up to 3 months.

Aromatherapy blends are a simple yet powerful way to provide comfort, reduce stress, and uplift emotions. Whether you're diffusing oils, using them in sprays, or incorporating them into massage or bath routines, these recipes offer natural ways to create a calming and supportive environment. By tailoring these blends to your needs, you can harness the power of essential oils to nurture your emotional well-being and find peace in challenging times.

Long-Term Healing with Flower Essences

Flower essences are gentle, vibrational remedies that address the emotional and spiritual aspects of well-being. Unlike herbal infusions or tinctures, flower essences capture the energetic imprint of flowers, offering subtle but profound support for healing deep-seated emotional wounds, releasing trauma, and promoting inner peace. These remedies are particularly effective for long-term emotional healing, as they work gradually to restore balance and harmony.

Popularized by Dr. Edward Bach in the early 20th century, flower essences like Rescue Remedy, crafted from a combination of flowers, have become widely known for their calming and grounding effects. Today, many individuals turn to flower essences for support in navigating grief, fostering resilience, and building emotional stability.

This chapter introduces 10 carefully crafted flower essence combinations and provides instructions on how to use them to promote long-term healing. Each recipe is designed to target specific emotional needs, allowing you to address the root causes of emotional imbalances over time.

921. Resilience Essence

Ingredients:

2 drops oak flower essence

2 drops yarrow flower essence

2 drops sweet chestnut flower essence

Instructions:

Combine the essences in a 30 mL dropper bottle filled with spring water.

Take 4 drops under the tongue or in water, 3 times daily.

Uses: Builds emotional strength and helps cope with challenging times.

Storage Tips: Store in a cool, dark place for up to 6 months.

922. Grief Comfort Essence

Ingredients:

2 drops star of Bethlehem flower essence

2 drops willow flower essence

2 drops wild rose flower essence

Instructions:

Mix the essences in a dropper bottle with spring water.

Take 4 drops daily to ease feelings of loss and sadness.

Uses: Provides comfort and facilitates the grieving process.

Storage Tips: Keep in a sealed bottle away from direct sunlight.

923. Clarity and Focus Essence

Ingredients:

2 drops clematis flower essence

2 drops honeysuckle flower essence

2 drops white chestnut flower essence

Instructions:

Add all essences to a 30 mL bottle with spring water.

Take 4 drops in water during periods of mental fog or distraction.

Uses: Enhances focus and clears emotional confusion.

Storage Tips: Store for up to 6 months.

924. Emotional Balance Essence

Ingredients:

2 drops cherry plum flower essence

2 drops impatiens flower essence

2 drops rock rose flower essence

Instructions:

Combine essences in a dropper bottle with spring water.

Take 4 drops twice daily to maintain emotional stability.

Uses: Reduces emotional outbursts and promotes calm.

Storage Tips: Keep in a cool, dark place.

925. Confidence Booster Essence

Ingredients:

2 drops larch flower essence

2 drops mimulus flower essence

2 drops cerato flower essence

Instructions:

Mix essences in a dropper bottle filled with spring water.

Take 4 drops daily to boost self-confidence and courage.

Uses: Supports self-assurance and diminishes fear.

Storage Tips: Store for up to 6 months.

926. Inner Peace Essence

Ingredients:

2 drops white chestnut flower essence

2 drops agrimony flower essence

2 drops aspen flower essence

Instructions:

Combine essences in a dropper bottle with spring water.

Take 4 drops during stressful or unsettling times.

Uses: Promotes calm and a sense of inner peace.

Storage Tips: Keep in a sealed container away from heat.

927. Grounding and Stability Essence

Ingredients:

2 drops oak flower essence

2 drops centaury flower essence

2 drops chestnut bud flower essence

Instructions:

Mix essences in a dropper bottle with spring water.

Take 4 drops in the morning and evening to feel grounded.

Uses: Enhances emotional stability and rootedness.

Storage Tips: Store in a cool, dry place.

928. Self-Love and Compassion Essence

Ingredients:

2 drops crab apple flower essence

2 drops pink monkeyflower flower essence

2 drops holly flower essence

Instructions:

Add essences to a dropper bottle filled with spring water.

Take 4 drops daily to foster self-acceptance and love.

Uses: Cultivates self-compassion and acceptance.

Storage Tips: Keep for up to 6 months.

929. Restful Sleep Essence

Ingredients:

2 drops white chestnut flower essence

2 drops vervain flower essence

2 drops chamomile flower essence

Instructions:

Combine essences in a dropper bottle with spring water.

Take 4 drops 30 minutes before bedtime for better sleep.

Uses: Eases restlessness and promotes relaxation.

Storage Tips: Store in a dark, cool location.

930. Emotional Renewal Essence

Ingredients:

2 drops gorse flower essence

2 drops sweet chestnut flower essence

2 drops mustard flower essence

Instructions:

Mix the essences in a dropper bottle filled with spring water.

Take 4 drops daily to feel emotionally rejuvenated.

Uses: Uplifts the spirit and restores hope.

Storage Tips: Keep in a sealed bottle for up to 6 months.

Flower essences offer a gentle yet transformative approach to emotional healing, providing support for long-term balance and resilience. By selecting blends tailored to specific emotional needs, you can harness the vibrational power of flowers to nurture emotional well-being. These recipes empower you to take charge of your emotional health, creating a foundation of peace and harmony that lasts a lifetime.

BOOK 27
HERBAL SYRUPS AND HONEYS

Herbal syrups and honeys are not only delicious but also highly effective ways to deliver the healing benefits of herbs. By combining the therapeutic properties of herbs with natural sweeteners like honey or sugar, you can create remedies that are both enjoyable to consume and beneficial for addressing various health concerns. From soothing sore throats and coughs to supporting digestion and immunity, herbal syrups and honeys offer versatile solutions for everyday wellness.

This book explores the art and science of creating these natural remedies. You'll learn how to make herbal syrups for respiratory and digestive health, craft infused honeys packed with healing properties, and understand the techniques of preservation to extend the shelf life of your creations. Whether you're making a simple elderberry syrup to boost immunity or a calming chamomile-infused honey, these recipes are designed to be easy, effective, and adaptable.

Perfect for beginners and seasoned herbalists alike, this book equips you with the knowledge and skills to create a wide range of syrups and honeys for yourself and your loved ones. Embrace the tradition of herbal medicine and enjoy the sweet and soothing remedies that nature has to offer.

Making Syrups for Respiratory and Digestive Health

Herbal syrups are a time-honored way to deliver the healing benefits of herbs in a form that is both effective and enjoyable. These sweet, viscous liquids combine herbal infusions or decoctions with natural sweeteners such as honey or sugar to create remedies that are easy to take and highly palatable. Traditionally used to support respiratory and digestive health, herbal syrups can soothe sore throats, calm coughs, improve digestion, and even boost immunity.

The preparation of herbal syrups involves extracting the medicinal properties of herbs through boiling or steeping, followed by the addition of a sweetener to preserve the liquid and enhance its flavor. This simple yet versatile method makes syrups an excellent choice for children, adults, and anyone who prefers a milder, sweeter form of herbal medicine.

In this chapter, we'll guide you through the basics of making herbal syrups for respiratory and digestive health. We'll also provide 10 easy-to-follow recipes using herbs like ginger, thyme, elderberry, and fennel, known for their effectiveness in addressing common ailments. These syrups can be incorporated into your daily routine or kept on hand for seasonal wellness support.

931. Elderberry Immune-Boosting Syrup

Ingredients:

1 cup dried elderberries

4 cups water

1 cup honey

Instructions:

Simmer elderberries and water in a pot for 30–40 minutes.

Strain the liquid through a fine sieve, pressing the berries to extract all the juice.

Mix the strained liquid with honey while warm.

Store in a sterilized bottle.

Uses: Boosts immunity and supports respiratory health.

Storage Tips: Refrigerate for up to 2 months.

932. Ginger and Lemon Digestive Syrup

Ingredients:

1/4 cup fresh ginger (sliced)

2 cups water

1/2 cup honey

2 tbsp fresh lemon juice

Instructions:

Simmer ginger in water for 20 minutes.

Strain the liquid and let it cool slightly.

Stir in honey and lemon juice.

Uses: Relieves nausea and improves digestion.

Storage Tips: Keep refrigerated for up to 1 month.

933. Thyme and Honey Cough Syrup

Ingredients:

2 tbsp dried thyme

2 cups water

1 cup honey

Instructions:

Boil thyme in water for 10 minutes, then let it steep for another 10 minutes.

Strain and mix the liquid with honey.

Uses: Soothes coughs and clears respiratory pathways.

Storage Tips: Store in a glass jar in the fridge for up to 6 weeks.

934. Fennel and Peppermint Digestive Syrup

Ingredients:

1 tbsp fennel seeds

1 tbsp dried peppermint leaves

2 cups water

3/4 cup honey

Instructions:

Simmer fennel seeds and peppermint in water for 15 minutes.

Strain and combine the liquid with honey.

Uses: Reduces bloating and supports digestion.

Storage Tips: Store in a cool place for up to 1 month.

935. Marshmallow Root Sore Throat Syrup

Ingredients:

2 tbsp marshmallow root

2 cups water

1 cup honey

Instructions:

Simmer marshmallow root in water for 30 minutes.

Strain and mix the liquid with honey.

Uses: Coats the throat and alleviates irritation.

Storage Tips: Refrigerate for up to 6 weeks.

936. Chamomile and Cinnamon Tummy Syrup

Ingredients:

1 tbsp dried chamomile flowers

1 small cinnamon stick

2 cups water

3/4 cup honey

Instructions:

Steep chamomile and cinnamon in boiling water for 15 minutes.

Strain and add honey.

Uses: Calms upset stomachs and reduces inflammation.

Storage Tips: Keep refrigerated for up to 1 month.

937. Licorice Root Respiratory Syrup

Ingredients:

1 tbsp dried licorice root

2 cups water

1 cup honey

Instructions:

Simmer licorice root in water for 20 minutes.

Strain and mix the liquid with honey.

Uses: Relieves respiratory discomfort and soothes coughs.

Storage Tips: Store in the fridge for up to 6 weeks.

938. Lemon Balm and Lavender Relaxing Syrup

Ingredients:

1 tbsp dried lemon balm leaves

1 tsp dried lavender flowers

2 cups water

3/4 cup honey

Instructions:

Steep lemon balm and lavender in boiling water for 10 minutes.

Strain and stir in honey.

Uses: Reduces stress and promotes restful digestion.

Storage Tips: Refrigerate for up to 4 weeks.

939. Eucalyptus and Honey Decongestant Syrup

Ingredients:

1 tbsp dried eucalyptus leaves

2 cups water

1 cup honey

Instructions:

Boil eucalyptus leaves in water for 10 minutes, then let steep for another 10 minutes.

Strain and mix with honey.

Uses: Clears nasal passages and supports respiratory health.

Storage Tips: Store in a sealed container for up to 2 months.

940. Turmeric and Black Pepper Anti-Inflammatory Syrup

Ingredients:

1 tsp turmeric powder

1/4 tsp black pepper

2 cups water

1 cup honey

Instructions:

Simmer turmeric and black pepper in water for 10 minutes.

Strain and mix with honey.

Uses: Reduces inflammation and boosts immunity.

Storage Tips: Keep in the fridge for up to 6 weeks.

Herbal syrups are versatile remedies that combine the healing power of herbs with the natural sweetness of honey or sugar, making them easy to use and enjoyable for all ages. Whether you're soothing a cough, supporting digestion, or boosting immunity, these recipes offer effective and delicious solutions for common health concerns. By creating your own syrups, you can harness the benefits of herbs in a form that is both practical and long-lasting. With these recipes, you'll be well-equipped to support respiratory and digestive health year-round.

Crafting Herbal-Infused Honeys for Sweet Remedies

Herbal-infused honeys are a delightful and effective way to enjoy the healing properties of herbs. By infusing honey with the essence of herbs, you create a remedy that is not only medicinal but also a delicious treat. The natural sweetness of honey complements the flavors of herbs while preserving their properties, making it an ideal medium for remedies that soothe sore throats, calm the nervous system, or boost immunity.

Honey itself is a powerhouse of health benefits. It has antibacterial, antimicrobial, and antioxidant properties, which enhance the therapeutic effects of the infused herbs. The infusion process is simple: fresh or dried herbs are combined with honey and left to steep, allowing the beneficial compounds of the herbs to infuse into the honey over time.

This chapter explores the art of crafting herbal-infused honeys, offering step-by-step guidance and 10 easy-to-follow recipes. From lavender-infused honey for relaxation to ginger-honey blends for digestion, these recipes provide a versatile and delicious way to incorporate herbal remedies into your daily routine.

941. Lavender-Infused Honey

Ingredients:

1/4 cup dried lavender flowers

1 cup raw honey

Instructions:

Add dried lavender flowers to a clean jar.

Pour honey over the flowers, ensuring they are fully submerged.

Seal the jar and let it infuse for 2 weeks, shaking gently every few days.

Strain out the flowers and store the honey in a clean jar.

Uses: Promotes relaxation and improves sleep.

Storage Tips: Store in a cool, dark place for up to 1 year.

942. Ginger and Lemon Honey

Ingredients:

1/4 cup sliced fresh ginger

Zest of 1 lemon

1 cup raw honey

Instructions:

Place ginger slices and lemon zest in a jar.

Cover with honey, making sure the ingredients are submerged.

Let infuse for 1 week, then strain and store.

Uses: Aids digestion and soothes sore throats.

Storage Tips: Keep in a sealed jar for up to 6 months.

943. Thyme-Infused Honey

Ingredients:

1/4 cup dried thyme leaves

1 cup raw honey

Instructions:

Add thyme leaves to a clean jar.

Pour honey over the leaves and stir to combine.

Infuse for 2 weeks, then strain.

Uses: Supports respiratory health and relieves coughs.

Storage Tips: Store in a cool place for up to 1 year.

944. Chamomile and Vanilla Honey

Ingredients:

1/4 cup dried chamomile flowers

1 vanilla bean, split

1 cup raw honey

Instructions:

Add chamomile flowers and vanilla bean to a jar.

Cover with honey and stir well.

Infuse for 2 weeks, then strain.

Uses: Calms the mind and aids digestion.

Storage Tips: Store in an airtight jar for up to 6 months.

945. Rose and Cardamom Honey

Ingredients:

1/4 cup dried rose petals

3 crushed cardamom pods

1 cup raw honey

Instructions:

Place rose petals and cardamom pods in a jar.

Pour honey over the ingredients and mix.

Let infuse for 2 weeks, then strain.

Uses: Uplifts the mood and promotes heart health.

Storage Tips: Keep in a sealed jar for up to 1 year.

946. Cinnamon and Clove Honey

Ingredients:

2 cinnamon sticks

5 whole cloves

1 cup raw honey

Instructions:

Add cinnamon sticks and cloves to a jar.

Cover with honey and let infuse for 2 weeks.

Strain and store.

Uses: Boosts immunity and supports digestion.

Storage Tips: Store in a cool, dry place for up to 1 year.

947. Lemon Balm Honey

Ingredients:

1/4 cup dried lemon balm leaves

1 cup raw honey

Instructions:

Combine lemon balm leaves and honey in a jar.

Stir thoroughly and seal the jar.

Infuse for 1–2 weeks, then strain.

Uses: Reduces stress and promotes relaxation.

Storage Tips: Keep in a dark place for up to 6 months.

948. Orange and Rosemary Honey

Ingredients:

Zest of 1 orange

1 sprig fresh rosemary

1 cup raw honey

Instructions:

Add orange zest and rosemary to a clean jar.

Cover with honey and stir.

Infuse for 1 week, then strain.

Uses: Supports circulation and enhances mental clarity.

Storage Tips: Store in an airtight container for up to 1 year.

949. Peppermint Honey

Ingredients:

1/4 cup dried peppermint leaves

1 cup raw honey

Instructions:

Add peppermint leaves to a jar and pour honey over them.

Stir to combine and let infuse for 2 weeks.

Strain and store.

Uses: Soothes indigestion and freshens breath.

Storage Tips: Keep in a cool, dark place for up to 6 months.

950. Turmeric and Black Pepper Honey

Ingredients:

1 tsp ground turmeric

1/4 tsp ground black pepper

1 cup raw honey

Instructions:

Mix turmeric and black pepper directly into honey.

Stir until well combined.

Uses: Reduces inflammation and boosts immunity.

Storage Tips: Store in a sealed jar for up to 1 year.

Crafting herbal-infused honeys is a simple and rewarding way to combine the healing properties of herbs with the natural benefits of honey. These remedies are versatile, delicious, and easy to incorporate into daily life, whether drizzled over toast, stirred into tea, or taken by the spoonful. With these 10 recipes, you can create sweet, effective remedies for a variety of health concerns, ensuring that your herbal toolkit is as enjoyable as it is therapeutic.

The Science of Preservation in Syrups

Preservation is a critical aspect of making herbal syrups, ensuring that the final product remains effective, safe, and free from spoilage. Because syrups are typically made with water-based herbal extracts and sweeteners like honey or sugar, they are susceptible to microbial growth if not properly preserved. Understanding the science behind preservation can help you create syrups with an extended shelf life while maintaining their medicinal potency.

This chapter delves into the fundamental principles of syrup preservation, the role of sweeteners, pH levels, sterilization, and storage methods. By mastering these techniques, you can confidently craft herbal syrups that are both delicious and long-lasting.

The Role of Sweeteners in Preservation

Sweeteners like honey, sugar, and glycerin play a dual role in syrups. They not only enhance the flavor but also act as natural preservatives by creating an environment that is inhospitable to microbial growth. This is due to their hygroscopic nature, which means they draw water out of microbial cells, effectively inhibiting their ability to thrive.

Honey as a Preservative

Honey, a traditional sweetener in herbal syrups, contains natural antimicrobial compounds such as hydrogen peroxide and low moisture content. These properties make honey an excellent choice for extending the shelf life of syrups while adding its own health benefits, such as soothing sore throats and boosting immunity.

Sugar as a Preservative

Sugar, particularly in high concentrations, helps preserve syrups by increasing osmotic pressure. This prevents bacteria, yeast, and mold from growing. When making syrups with sugar, it is crucial to maintain a high enough ratio of sugar to liquid, typically 2:1, to ensure proper preservation.

Glycerin as a Preservative

Glycerin, a plant-derived compound, serves as an alternative sweetener and preservative, particularly for those avoiding sugar or honey. While less effective than sugar or honey, glycerin is ideal for making alcohol-free syrups and offers a mild sweet flavor.

pH and Preservation

The pH level of a syrup significantly affects its shelf life. Most bacteria and fungi cannot thrive in highly acidic environments, making acidity an essential factor in preservation. Adding acidic ingredients such as lemon juice, apple cider vinegar, or citric acid can lower the pH of your syrup, enhancing its resistance to microbial growth.

Testing and Adjusting pH

Ideal pH Range: Herbal syrups should ideally have a pH of 4.6 or lower to inhibit microbial growth.

Testing: Use pH test strips or a digital pH meter to measure the acidity of your syrup.

Adjusting: If the pH is too high, add small amounts of acidic ingredients until the desired level is achieved.

Sterilization Techniques

Proper sterilization is essential to prevent contamination during the syrup-making process. Contaminants such as bacteria, mold, and yeast can significantly reduce the shelf life of your syrup and compromise its safety.

Sterilizing Equipment

Cleanliness: Wash all equipment, including pots, spoons, jars, and lids, with hot, soapy water before use.

Boiling: Sterilize jars and lids by boiling them in water for 10 minutes. Allow them to air dry on a clean towel.

Alcohol Wipes: For smaller tools like spoons or droppers, use alcohol wipes to sanitize.

Handling During Preparation

Avoid touching sterilized surfaces with bare hands. Use clean utensils to handle ingredients and jars.

Ensure the workspace is clean and free from dust or contaminants.

The Role of Heat in Preservation

Heat plays a crucial role in extracting the medicinal compounds of herbs and ensuring the sterility of the syrup. However, excessive heat can degrade certain heat-sensitive compounds, reducing the syrup's therapeutic value. Striking a balance between effective heat for extraction and preserving active compounds is key.

Simmering vs. Boiling

Simmering: Use gentle simmering to extract herbs, particularly for delicate flowers and leaves. This method preserves volatile oils and minimizes nutrient loss.

Boiling: For roots, barks, and seeds, boiling is often necessary to extract the tougher constituents effectively.

Pasteurization

If you plan to store syrups for extended periods, consider pasteurizing them. Gently heating the finished syrup to 160°F–180°F (71°C–82°C) for a few minutes can kill most microorganisms without degrading the medicinal compounds.

Storage Methods for Herbal Syrups

Proper storage is essential for maintaining the freshness and potency of your syrups. Even well-preserved syrups can degrade if stored improperly.

Refrigeration

Refrigerating herbal syrups is the easiest and most effective way to extend their shelf life. Most syrups will last 4–6 weeks in the refrigerator, depending on their sugar content and acidity.

Freezing

For longer storage, freezing syrups is an excellent option. Freeze syrups in small portions, such as in ice cube trays, for easy use. Syrups stored in the freezer can last up to 6 months.

Sealed Storage

Storing syrups in sterilized, airtight glass jars or bottles helps prevent contamination. Dark-colored glass containers are preferred, as they protect the syrup from light, which can degrade its quality.

Signs of Spoilage

Despite best efforts, syrups may occasionally spoil. Recognizing the signs of spoilage is important to ensure safety.

Cloudiness: Clear syrups becoming cloudy may indicate microbial growth.

Fermentation: If the syrup has a fizzy or alcoholic smell, fermentation has likely occurred.

Mold: Visible mold growth on the surface is a clear sign of spoilage.

Unpleasant Odors: A sour or off-putting smell signals that the syrup is no longer safe to use.

Discard any syrup showing these signs to avoid health risks.

Tips for Successful Syrup Preservation

High Sweetener Ratios: Ensure a high ratio of honey or sugar to liquid to inhibit microbial growth.

Acidity: Test and adjust the pH to create an environment unsuitable for bacteria and fungi.

Clean Equipment: Use sterilized jars and tools to minimize contamination.

Small Batches: Make small batches of syrup to ensure freshness and avoid waste.

Labeling: Clearly label jars with the date of preparation and ingredients for easy tracking.

Understanding the science of preservation is essential for creating safe, effective, and long-lasting herbal syrups. By mastering the roles of sweeteners, pH, heat, and storage methods, you can confidently craft syrups that retain their potency and flavor for weeks or even months. With these preservation techniques, you'll not only extend the life of your remedies but also ensure their safety and effectiveness, empowering you to embrace the art of herbal medicine with confidence.

Recipes for All-Natural Cough Syrups

Coughing is a natural reflex that helps clear the airways, but persistent coughing can be uncomfortable and disruptive. Herbal cough syrups are a gentle, natural way to soothe irritation, reduce inflammation, and promote respiratory health. By combining therapeutic herbs with the preservative power of honey or glycerin, these syrups provide effective relief while avoiding the harsh ingredients found in many over-the-counter remedies.

The recipes in this chapter harness the healing properties of herbs like thyme, ginger, marshmallow root, and mullein. These ingredients work synergistically to coat the throat, ease discomfort, and calm the cough reflex. Whether addressing a dry, tickly cough or a productive, phlegm-filled one, these syrups are designed to support the body's natural healing process.

951. Ginger and Honey Throat Soother

Ingredients:

1/4 cup sliced fresh ginger

2 cups water

1 cup honey

Instructions:

Simmer ginger in water for 20 minutes.

Strain and let the liquid cool slightly.

Mix with honey and store in a sterilized jar.

Uses: Soothes irritation and reduces coughing.

Storage Tips: Refrigerate for up to 6 weeks.

952. Thyme and Lemon Cough Syrup

Ingredients:

2 tbsp dried thyme

2 cups water

1/2 cup lemon juice

1 cup honey

Instructions:

Simmer thyme in water for 15 minutes, then strain.

Mix the strained liquid with lemon juice and honey.

Uses: Clears congestion and calms the cough reflex.

Storage Tips: Keep refrigerated for up to 1 month.

953. Marshmallow Root and Cinnamon Syrup

Ingredients:

2 tbsp marshmallow root

1 small cinnamon stick

2 cups water

1 cup honey

Instructions:

Simmer marshmallow root and cinnamon in water for 30 minutes.

Strain and mix the liquid with honey.

Uses: Coats the throat and reduces dryness.

Storage Tips: Store in a cool, dark place for up to 6 weeks.

954. Eucalyptus and Peppermint Syrup

Ingredients:

1 tbsp dried eucalyptus leaves

1 tsp dried peppermint leaves

2 cups water

1 cup honey

Instructions:

Simmer eucalyptus and peppermint in water for 10 minutes.

Strain and mix the liquid with honey.

Uses: Opens airways and soothes coughs.

Storage Tips: Refrigerate for up to 1 month.

955. Licorice Root and Ginger Syrup

Ingredients:

1 tbsp dried licorice root

1/4 cup sliced fresh ginger

2 cups water

1 cup honey

Instructions:

Simmer licorice root and ginger in water for 20 minutes.

Strain and mix with honey.

Uses: Reduces inflammation and soothes the throat.

Storage Tips: Keep refrigerated for up to 6 weeks.

956. Elderberry Immune Cough Syrup

Ingredients:

1/2 cup dried elderberries

3 cups water

1 cup honey

Instructions:

Simmer elderberries in water for 30 minutes.

Strain and mix the liquid with honey.

Uses: Boosts immunity and relieves coughs.

Storage Tips: Store in the refrigerator for up to 2 months.

957. Mullein and Honey Respiratory Syrup

Ingredients:

2 tbsp dried mullein leaves

2 cups water

1 cup honey

Instructions:

Steep mullein leaves in boiling water for 20 minutes.

Strain and combine with honey.

Uses: Clears mucus and supports lung health.

Storage Tips: Refrigerate for up to 1 month.

958. Chamomile and Lemon Balm Syrup

Ingredients:

1 tbsp dried chamomile flowers

1 tbsp dried lemon balm leaves

2 cups water

1 cup honey

Instructions:

Steep chamomile and lemon balm in boiling water for 15 minutes.

Strain and mix the liquid with honey.

Uses: Calms coughs and promotes relaxation.

Storage Tips: Store in a sealed jar for up to 6 weeks.

959. Garlic and Honey Antimicrobial Syrup

Ingredients:

2 cloves garlic (crushed)

1 cup honey

Instructions:

Add crushed garlic to honey in a jar.

Let infuse for 1 week, then strain.

Uses: Fights infections and soothes coughs.

Storage Tips: Keep in a sealed container for up to 6 weeks.

960. Turmeric and Black Pepper Anti-Inflammatory Syrup

Ingredients:

1 tsp turmeric powder

1/4 tsp black pepper

2 cups water

1 cup honey

Instructions:

Simmer turmeric and black pepper in water for 10 minutes.

Strain and mix with honey.

Uses: Reduces inflammation and soothes irritation.

Storage Tips: Refrigerate for up to 1 month.

All-natural cough syrups provide a gentle, effective way to relieve coughs and soothe respiratory discomfort. By combining the healing power of herbs with the sweetness of honey, these recipes deliver relief while nourishing the body. With the versatility and ease of these syrups, you can tailor remedies to suit your needs and support your respiratory health naturally.

BOOK 28

DETOXIFYING WITH HERBS

In today's world, exposure to environmental toxins, processed foods, and daily stress can burden the body's natural detoxification systems. Detoxifying with herbs offers a gentle yet powerful way to support the body's ability to cleanse, rejuvenate, and restore balance. Herbal remedies can assist the liver, kidneys, lymphatic system, and other organs in their crucial roles of eliminating toxins and maintaining optimal health.

This book explores the art of detoxification through the use of herbs, guiding you in creating safe, effective remedies to cleanse the body naturally. You'll learn about herbs like milk thistle, dandelion root, and burdock that strengthen and protect the liver, as well as natural solutions to support kidney function and lymphatic drainage. Recipes for detox teas, juices, and adaptogenic blends will provide practical ways to incorporate these cleansing herbs into your routine.

Whether you're seeking relief from fatigue, digestive issues, or simply aiming to reset your body, this book equips you with the knowledge to embark on a gentle and sustainable detox journey. By harnessing the power of herbs, you can rejuvenate your body and embrace a healthier, more balanced lifestyle.

Supporting the Liver with Detox Herbs

The liver is one of the most vital organs for detoxification, working tirelessly to filter toxins, metabolize nutrients, and regulate hormones. Supporting liver health with herbs can optimize its function, improve digestion, and enhance overall well-being. Herbal remedies, known for their gentle yet effective detoxifying properties, can assist in cleansing and protecting the liver from oxidative stress and damage caused by toxins.

Detox herbs like milk thistle, dandelion root, burdock, and artichoke have been used for centuries in traditional medicine to promote liver health. These herbs stimulate bile production, aid in the breakdown of fats, and help flush toxins from the liver. They also offer anti-inflammatory and antioxidant benefits, which protect liver cells and support regeneration.

This chapter explores 10 powerful herbal remedies designed to support the liver. Whether taken as teas, tinctures, or capsules, these remedies provide a natural way to detoxify and fortify your liver for better health and vitality.

961. Milk Thistle Liver Tonic

Ingredients:

1 tsp milk thistle seeds (ground)

1 cup boiling water

Instructions:

Steep milk thistle seeds in boiling water for 10 minutes.

Strain and drink once daily.

Uses: Protects liver cells and aids regeneration.

Storage Tips: Use freshly ground seeds for maximum potency.

962. Dandelion Root Detox Tea

Ingredients:

1 tsp dried dandelion root

1 cup boiling water

Instructions:

Simmer dandelion root in boiling water for 15 minutes.

Strain and enjoy as a morning tea.

Uses: Stimulates bile production and supports digestion.

Storage Tips: Store dried dandelion root in an airtight container for up to 6 months.

963. Burdock Root and Ginger Infusion

Ingredients:

1 tsp dried burdock root

1/2 tsp grated fresh ginger

1 cup boiling water

Instructions:

Combine burdock root and ginger in a teapot.

Steep in boiling water for 15 minutes, then strain.

Uses: Aids liver detoxification and reduces inflammation.

Storage Tips: Consume fresh for best results.

964. Artichoke Leaf Liver Booster

Ingredients:

1 tsp dried artichoke leaves

1 cup boiling water

Instructions:

Steep artichoke leaves in boiling water for 10 minutes.

Strain and drink before meals.

Uses: Enhances bile flow and improves fat digestion.

Storage Tips: Store dried leaves in a sealed container for up to 1 year.

965. Turmeric Golden Detox Milk

Ingredients:

1 cup warm almond milk

1/2 tsp turmeric powder

Pinch of black pepper

Instructions:

Mix turmeric powder and black pepper into warm almond milk.

Stir well and drink before bedtime.

Uses: Reduces inflammation and protects liver cells.

Storage Tips: Prepare fresh each time.

966. Schisandra Berry Tincture

Ingredients:

1/4 cup dried schisandra berries

1/2 cup glycerin

Instructions:

Combine schisandra berries and glycerin in a jar.

Let steep for 2 weeks, shaking daily, then strain into a dropper bottle.

Uses: Enhances liver detoxification and resilience.

Storage Tips: Store in a cool, dark place for up to 6 months.

967. Lemon and Beet Detox Juice

Ingredients:

1/2 fresh beetroot (grated)

Juice of 1/2 lemon

1 cup water

Instructions:

Blend beetroot and water, then strain the juice.

Add lemon juice and stir well.

Uses: Supports liver detox and improves energy.

Storage Tips: Consume immediately.

968. Rosemary Liver Support Tea

Ingredients:

1 tsp dried rosemary leaves

1 cup boiling water

Instructions:

Steep rosemary leaves in boiling water for 10 minutes.

Strain and drink in the afternoon.

Uses: Stimulates circulation and aids liver function.

Storage Tips: Store dried rosemary in a cool, dry place for up to 1 year.

969. Chicory Root Liver Cleanse

Ingredients:

1 tsp dried chicory root

1 cup boiling water

Instructions:

Simmer chicory root in water for 15 minutes.

Strain and drink before meals.

Uses: Encourages bile production and liver detoxification.

Storage Tips: Keep in an airtight jar for up to 6 months.

970. Cilantro and Parsley Detox Shot

Ingredients:

1/4 cup fresh cilantro leaves

1/4 cup fresh parsley leaves

1/2 cup water

Instructions:

Blend cilantro, parsley, and water until smooth.

Strain and drink as a quick detox shot.

Uses: Supports heavy metal detox and liver health.

Storage Tips: Consume fresh within 24 hours.

Herbs offer a natural and effective way to support the liver's vital detoxification processes. From teas and tinctures to nourishing juices, these remedies help cleanse and protect the liver while improving digestion and overall well-being. Incorporating these simple recipes into your routine can enhance your body's ability to eliminate toxins and maintain optimal health. By giving your liver the care it deserves, you empower your body to thrive naturally.

Kidney and Lymphatic Cleansing with Natural Solutions

The kidneys and lymphatic system play a vital role in the body's detoxification process. The kidneys filter blood, removing toxins and waste products, while the lymphatic system works to drain excess fluid and transport immune cells throughout the body. Supporting these systems with natural solutions helps to maintain balance, reduce inflammation, and enhance overall health.

Herbal remedies are an effective way to promote kidney and lymphatic cleansing. Diuretic herbs like nettle and parsley increase urine output, helping to flush out toxins from the kidneys. Meanwhile, lymphatic herbs like cleavers and red clover stimulate lymph flow, reducing fluid retention and promoting detoxification. Combining these herbs into teas, tinctures, or juices creates a gentle yet powerful approach to maintaining these systems' health.

This chapter provides insight into the importance of kidney and lymphatic cleansing, along with practical advice and 10 herbal remedies to support these critical detox pathways. By integrating these natural solutions into your routine, you can promote better circulation, reduce bloating, and strengthen your body's natural defenses.

971. Nettle Leaf Diuretic Tea

Ingredients:

1 tsp dried nettle leaves

1 cup boiling water

Instructions:

Steep nettle leaves in boiling water for 10 minutes.

Strain and drink 1–2 cups daily.

Uses: Supports kidney function and flushes toxins.

Storage Tips: Store dried nettle leaves in an airtight container for up to 1 year.

972. Parsley and Lemon Kidney Flush

Ingredients:

1/4 cup fresh parsley (chopped)

Juice of 1/2 lemon

1 cup warm water

Instructions:

Blend parsley and water, then strain.

Add lemon juice and drink fresh.

Uses: Encourages diuresis and supports kidney health.

Storage Tips: Consume immediately.

973. Cleavers Lymphatic Tea

Ingredients:

1 tsp dried cleavers

1 cup boiling water

Instructions:

Steep cleavers in boiling water for 10 minutes.

Strain and drink once daily.

Uses: Stimulates lymphatic drainage and reduces fluid retention.

Storage Tips: Keep dried cleavers in a sealed jar for up to 6 months.

974. Red Clover Detox Infusion

Ingredients:

1 tsp dried red clover blossoms

1 cup boiling water

Instructions:

Steep red clover in boiling water for 15 minutes. Strain and enjoy as a gentle detox tea.

Uses: Supports lymphatic flow and detoxifies the blood.

Storage Tips: Store in a cool, dry place for up to 1 year.

975. Dandelion and Ginger Cleansing Tonic

Ingredients:

1 tsp dried dandelion root

1/2 tsp grated fresh ginger

1 cup boiling water

Instructions:

Simmer dandelion root and ginger in water for 10 minutes.

Strain and drink warm.

Uses: Stimulates kidney function and reduces inflammation.

Storage Tips: Consume fresh for best results.

976. Burdock Root and Lemon Detox Water

Ingredients:

1 tbsp dried burdock root

2 cups water

Juice of 1/2 lemon

Instructions:

Simmer burdock root in water for 20 minutes.

Strain and mix with lemon juice.

Uses: Cleanses the blood and supports kidney health.

Storage Tips: Refrigerate for up to 24 hours.

977. Peppermint and Horsetail Herbal Blend

Ingredients:

1 tsp dried horsetail

1 tsp dried peppermint

1 cup boiling water

Instructions:

Combine horsetail and peppermint in boiling water.

Steep for 10 minutes, then strain.

Uses: Promotes kidney function and reduces fluid retention.

Storage Tips: Store dried herbs in a cool, dark place.

978. Yellow Dock Root Detox Tea

Ingredients:

1 tsp dried yellow dock root

1 cup boiling water

Instructions:

Steep yellow dock root in boiling water for 15 minutes.

Strain and drink once daily.

Uses: Enhances lymphatic detoxification and liver support.

Storage Tips: Keep dried yellow dock root in an airtight container for up to 6 months.

979. Cilantro and Cucumber Hydration Juice

Ingredients:

1/4 cup fresh cilantro leaves

1/2 cucumber (sliced)

1 cup water

Instructions:

Blend cilantro, cucumber, and water until smooth.

Strain and drink immediately.

Uses: Hydrates and supports kidney detox.

Storage Tips: Consume fresh within 24 hours.

980. Licorice Root and Fennel Digestive Tea

Ingredients:

1 tsp dried licorice root

1/2 tsp fennel seeds

1 cup boiling water

Instructions:

Simmer licorice root and fennel seeds in boiling water for 15 minutes.

Strain and enjoy warm.

Uses: Promotes detoxification and reduces bloating.

Storage Tips: Store in a sealed jar for up to 6 months.

Supporting the kidneys and lymphatic system

with natural solutions is an essential step in detoxifying the body and promoting overall wellness. These herbal remedies work to flush toxins, reduce fluid retention, and enhance circulation, making them a valuable addition to your self-care routine. By integrating these simple recipes into your lifestyle, you can maintain a healthy balance and give your body the tools it needs to thrive.

Recipes for Gentle Detox Teas and Juices

Detox teas and juices are a refreshing and effective way to cleanse the body, boost energy, and support overall health. These beverages are crafted with nutrient-rich herbs, fruits, and vegetables that promote natural detoxification. Unlike harsh cleanses, gentle detox teas and juices work with the body's systems, supporting the liver, kidneys, and digestive tract to eliminate toxins without causing stress or discomfort.

Herbs like dandelion, nettle, and ginger pair beautifully with hydrating fruits and vegetables like cucumber, lemon, and apple, offering a harmonious blend of flavors and benefits. These recipes are easy to prepare and versatile, making them suitable for daily detox support or as part of a periodic cleanse.

In this chapter, you'll find 10 carefully curated recipes for gentle detox teas and juices. Each one is designed to be flavorful, nourishing, and effective in promoting a sense of vitality and balance.

981. Dandelion and Lemon Detox Tea

Ingredients:

1 tsp dried dandelion root

1 slice fresh lemon

1 cup boiling water

Instructions:

Steep dandelion root in boiling water for 10 minutes.

Add the lemon slice and sip warm.

Uses: Supports liver detoxification and improves digestion.

Storage Tips: Prepare fresh each time.

982. Nettle and Mint Cleansing Tea

Ingredients:

1 tsp dried nettle leaves

1 tsp dried peppermint leaves

1 cup boiling water

Instructions:

Combine nettle and peppermint in a teapot.

Pour boiling water over the herbs and steep for 10 minutes.

Strain and enjoy warm or chilled.

Uses: Flushes out toxins and promotes hydration.

Storage Tips: Consume immediately or refrigerate for up to 12 hours.

983. Ginger and Turmeric Tonic Tea

Ingredients:

1/2 tsp grated fresh ginger

1/2 tsp turmeric powder

1 cup boiling water

Instructions:

Add ginger and turmeric to boiling water.

Steep for 5–7 minutes, then strain.

Uses: Reduces inflammation and supports digestion.

Storage Tips: Prepare fresh for maximum benefits.

984. Lemon and Cucumber Detox Water

Ingredients:

3 slices fresh cucumber

2 slices fresh lemon

1 cup water

Instructions:

Combine cucumber and lemon slices in a glass of water.

Let infuse for 30 minutes before drinking.

Uses: Hydrates and supports gentle detoxification.

Storage Tips: Refrigerate for up to 12 hours.

985. Green Apple and Parsley Juice

Ingredients:

1 green apple (cored)

1/4 cup fresh parsley

1 cup water

Instructions:

Blend apple, parsley, and water until smooth.

Strain or drink as is.

Uses: Boosts kidney health and provides antioxidants.

Storage Tips: Consume immediately.

986. Hibiscus and Rosehip Antioxidant Tea

Ingredients:

1 tsp dried hibiscus flowers

1 tsp dried rosehips

1 cup boiling water

Instructions:

Steep hibiscus and rosehips in boiling water for 10 minutes.

Strain and serve warm or over ice.

Uses: Flushes out toxins and provides vitamin C.

Storage Tips: Store in the fridge for up to 24 hours.

987. Beetroot and Carrot Cleansing Juice

Ingredients:

1/2 small beetroot (peeled and diced)

1 medium carrot (peeled and diced)

1 cup water

Instructions:

Blend beetroot, carrot, and water until smooth.

Strain or enjoy as a thick juice.

Uses: Supports liver detoxification and boosts energy.

Storage Tips: Consume fresh within 24 hours.

988. Lemon Balm and Lavender Relaxing Tea

Ingredients:

1 tsp dried lemon balm leaves

1/2 tsp dried lavender flowers

1 cup boiling water

Instructions:

Steep lemon balm and lavender in boiling water for 10 minutes.

Strain and sip in the evening.

Uses: Reduces stress and promotes gentle detox.

Storage Tips: Prepare fresh each time.

989. Watermelon and Mint Hydration Juice

Ingredients:

1 cup diced watermelon

5 fresh mint leaves

1/2 cup water

Instructions:

Blend watermelon, mint, and water until smooth.

Strain and serve chilled.

Uses: Hydrates and supports kidney cleansing.

Storage Tips: Store in the fridge for up to 12 hours.

990. Celery and Lemon Green Juice

Ingredients:

2 stalks celery (chopped)

Juice of 1/2 lemon

1 cup water

Instructions:

Blend celery and water, then strain the juice.

Add lemon juice and stir well.

Uses: Cleanses the digestive system and reduces bloating.

Storage Tips: Consume immediately.

Gentle detox teas and juices are a simple and enjoyable way to support the body's natural cleansing processes. Whether hydrating with infused water, sipping antioxidant-rich teas, or enjoying fresh juices, these recipes provide effective, natural detoxification. Incorporating these into your daily routine not only boosts your energy and vitality but also enhances overall health.

Addressing Fatigue with Cleansing Adaptogens

Fatigue, whether physical, mental, or emotional, is a common sign of a body under strain. Chronic stress, toxin buildup, and overexertion can drain the body's energy reserves, leaving you feeling sluggish and depleted. Cleansing adaptogens provide a natural solution by supporting detoxification while enhancing the body's ability to adapt to stress and restore balance.

Adaptogens are a unique class of herbs that help

the body manage stress and improve resilience. When combined with detoxifying properties, adaptogens like ashwagandha, schisandra, rhodiola, and holy basil can address the root causes of fatigue by improving liver function, balancing hormones, and enhancing cellular energy production. These herbs not only cleanse but also replenish, making them ideal for addressing fatigue during or after a detox program.

In this chapter, we explore how cleansing adaptogens can combat fatigue and boost vitality. You'll learn about the mechanisms by which these herbs support energy and detoxification, practical ways to incorporate them into your daily routine, and specific adaptogenic blends to rejuvenate your body and mind.

The Dual Role of Cleansing Adaptogens

1. Supporting Detoxification

Cleansing adaptogens aid the body's natural detoxification processes by enhancing liver and kidney function, reducing inflammation, and neutralizing free radicals. For example:

Ashwagandha reduces oxidative stress and promotes the efficient elimination of toxins.

Schisandra protects liver cells and stimulates the production of detoxifying enzymes.

2. Boosting Energy and Resilience

Adaptogens help regulate cortisol levels, improve mitochondrial function, and increase energy production, addressing the underlying causes of fatigue. Herbs like rhodiola and holy basil not only boost physical stamina but also promote mental clarity and emotional balance.

How to Use Cleansing Adaptogens

Adaptogen Teas

Herbal teas are a soothing way to incorporate adaptogens into your routine. Combine adaptogenic herbs with complementary detoxifying ingredients like ginger or lemon for enhanced effects.

Powder Blends

Adaptogens in powdered form can be added to smoothies, soups, or warm milk for a nourishing energy boost.

Capsules or Tinctures

For convenience, many adaptogens are available in capsules or tinctures, allowing you to take precise doses on the go.

Sample Daily Routine for Using Adaptogens

Morning: Start your day with a cup of schisandra berry tea to wake up your liver and energize your body.

Midday: Add rhodiola powder to a smoothie for sustained energy and focus.

Evening: Wind down with holy basil tea to reduce stress and promote restful sleep.

Adaptogenic Blends to Address Fatigue

1. Ashwagandha and Ginger Replenishing Tea

Combine 1 tsp ashwagandha powder with 1/2 tsp grated fresh ginger in 1 cup boiling water. Steep for 10 minutes, strain, and enjoy warm.

Uses: Reduces fatigue and enhances detoxification.

2. Schisandra Berry Energy Tonic

Simmer 1 tbsp dried schisandra berries in 2 cups water for 20 minutes. Strain and drink in the morning.

Uses: Boosts liver function and improves stamina.

3. Rhodiola and Lemon Revitalizing Smoothie

Blend 1 tsp rhodiola powder, 1/2 frozen banana, 1/4 cup spinach, and 1 cup almond milk until smooth.

Uses: Supports mental clarity and sustained energy.

4. Holy Basil Evening Relaxation Tea

Steep 1 tsp dried holy basil leaves in 1 cup boiling water for 10 minutes. Strain and enjoy before bed.

Uses: Reduces stress and promotes restful sleep.

5. Adaptogen Detox Elixir

Mix 1/2 tsp ashwagandha powder, 1/2 tsp turmeric powder, and a pinch of black pepper into 1 cup warm water or milk.

Uses: Combines detoxification with anti-inflammatory benefits to combat fatigue.

Practical Tips for Using Adaptogens Safely

Start Slowly: Introduce one adaptogen at a time to monitor how your body responds.

Be Consistent: Adaptogens work best when taken regularly over a period of weeks or months.

Stay Hydrated: Drink plenty of water to support the detox process.

Consult a Professional: If you have specific health concerns, consult an herbalist or healthcare provider before starting adaptogens.

Cleansing adaptogens are powerful allies in addressing fatigue and supporting detoxification. By enhancing the body's ability to adapt to stress, regulate energy production, and eliminate toxins, these herbs provide holistic support for long-term vitality. Incorporating adaptogens into your daily routine offers a natural, sustainable way to combat fatigue and restore balance to your mind and body. With their dual role in cleansing and rejuvenation, adaptogens are a cornerstone of any wellness journey.

BOOK 29

HERBAL REMEDIES FOR INFLAMMATION

Inflammation is the body's natural response to injury, infection, or irritation, but chronic or excessive inflammation can contribute to a range of health issues, including arthritis, autoimmune conditions, and cardiovascular disease. Herbal remedies offer a safe and effective way to address inflammation, supporting the body's healing process while minimizing discomfort and preventing long-term damage.

This book explores the many ways herbs can help reduce inflammation, providing practical solutions for acute and chronic conditions. From soothing teas and tinctures to cooling compresses and topical salves, these remedies harness the anti-inflammatory properties of herbs like turmeric, ginger, chamomile, and arnica. You'll also learn how to incorporate these powerful botanicals into your daily routine to support overall wellness and manage inflammation naturally.

Whether you're seeking relief from joint pain, swelling, or systemic inflammation, this book provides the knowledge and tools to create effective, personalized herbal remedies. By understanding the role of herbs in reducing inflammation, you can take control of your health and enhance your body's ability to heal naturally, without relying solely on over-the-counter medications or synthetic treatments.

Anti-Inflammatory Tinctures and Teas

Inflammation is a natural response to injury or illness, but when it becomes chronic, it can lead to discomfort and long-term health issues. Herbs with anti-inflammatory properties can offer a gentle, effective way to reduce inflammation, soothe pain, and support overall well-being. Tinctures and teas are two of the most accessible and versatile methods for incorporating these herbs into your routine, providing relief from the inside out.

Tinctures are concentrated liquid extracts of herbs, making them convenient for on-the-go use. They are particularly effective for delivering potent doses of anti-inflammatory compounds. Teas, on the other hand, are a soothing and hydrating way to enjoy the benefits of herbs, allowing their healing properties to infuse into your system gently.

In this chapter, we explore 10 simple yet effective tinctures and teas using herbs like turmeric, ginger, chamomile, and licorice root. These recipes are easy to prepare and can be tailored to your specific needs, whether you're seeking relief from joint pain, digestive discomfort, or systemic inflammation.

991. Turmeric and Ginger Anti-Inflammatory Tea

Ingredients:

1/2 tsp ground turmeric

1/2 tsp grated fresh ginger

1 cup boiling water

Instructions:

Add turmeric and ginger to boiling water.

Steep for 10 minutes, strain, and enjoy with honey.

Uses: Reduces inflammation and soothes digestive discomfort.

Storage Tips: Prepare fresh for best results.

992. Chamomile and Peppermint Digestive Tea

Ingredients:

1 tsp dried chamomile flowers

1 tsp dried peppermint leaves

1 cup boiling water

Instructions:

Steep chamomile and peppermint in boiling water for 10 minutes.

Strain and drink warm.

Uses: Calms inflammation in the digestive tract.

Storage Tips: Consume immediately.

993. Licorice Root and Cinnamon Tincture

Ingredients:

1/4 cup dried licorice root

1 small cinnamon stick

1/2 cup glycerin

Instructions:

Combine licorice root and cinnamon in a jar with glycerin.

Let steep for 2 weeks, shaking daily.

Strain into a dropper bottle.

Uses: Reduces systemic inflammation and supports adrenal health.

Storage Tips: Store in a dark, cool place for up to 6 months.

994. Rosehip and Hibiscus Tea

Ingredients:

1 tsp dried rosehips

1 tsp dried hibiscus flowers

1 cup boiling water

Instructions:

Steep rosehips and hibiscus in boiling water for 15 minutes.

Strain and serve warm or chilled.

Uses: Provides antioxidants to combat inflammation.

Storage Tips: Refrigerate for up to 24 hours.

995. Ashwagandha and Ginger Tincture

Ingredients:

1/4 cup dried ashwagandha root

1/2 cup glycerin

Instructions:

Combine ashwagandha root and glycerin in a jar.

Let steep for 2–4 weeks, shaking daily.

Strain and store in a dropper bottle.

Uses: Reduces stress-related inflammation and boosts resilience.

Storage Tips: Keep in a sealed bottle for up to 6 months.

996. Nettle and Lemon Balm Anti-Inflammatory Tea

Ingredients:

1 tsp dried nettle leaves

1 tsp dried lemon balm leaves

1 cup boiling water

Instructions:

Steep nettle and lemon balm in boiling water for 10 minutes.

Strain and enjoy warm or cool.

Uses: Eases joint pain and reduces inflammation.

Storage Tips: Drink fresh for best effects.

997. Holy Basil (Tulsi) Stress Relief Tincture

Ingredients:

1/4 cup dried holy basil leaves

1/2 cup glycerin

Instructions:

Combine holy basil leaves and glycerin in a jar.

Let steep for 2–3 weeks, shaking daily.

Strain into a dark glass bottle.

Uses: Reduces inflammation caused by stress and balances hormones.

Storage Tips: Store in a cool, dark place for up to 6 months.

998. Fennel and Ginger Digestive Tea

Ingredients:

1 tsp fennel seeds

1/2 tsp grated ginger

1 cup boiling water

Instructions:

Simmer fennel seeds and ginger in boiling water for 10 minutes.

Strain and drink after meals.

Uses: Soothes gastrointestinal inflammation.

Storage Tips: Consume immediately.

999. Lavender and Chamomile Relaxation Tea

Ingredients:

1 tsp dried lavender flowers

1 tsp dried chamomile flowers

1 cup boiling water

Instructions:

Steep lavender and chamomile in boiling water for 10 minutes.

Strain and drink in the evening.

Uses: Calms nervous system inflammation and promotes sleep.

Storage Tips: Use fresh each time.

1000. Turmeric and Black Pepper Tincture

Ingredients:

1/4 cup turmeric powder

1/8 tsp black pepper

1/2 cup glycerin

Instructions:

Mix turmeric powder and black pepper with glycerin in a jar.

Steep for 2 weeks, shaking daily, then strain.

Uses: Reduces chronic inflammation and enhances absorption of curcumin.

Storage Tips: Store in a sealed bottle for up to 6 months.

Herbal teas and tinctures provide an accessible and effective way to combat inflammation and promote overall wellness. These recipes harness the power of anti-inflammatory herbs to soothe discomfort, reduce swelling, and enhance the body's natural healing processes. Incorporate these remedies into your routine for a natural approach to managing inflammation and improving your quality of life.

Topical Salves for Joint Pain and Swelling

Joint pain and swelling can arise from a variety of conditions, such as arthritis, injuries, or chronic inflammation. Topical salves, made with anti-inflammatory and pain-relieving herbs, offer a natural and effective way to alleviate discomfort. These salves work by delivering healing compounds directly to the affected area, reducing inflammation and soothing soreness without the need for oral medications.

Salves are simple to make, requiring a base of carrier oils (like olive or coconut oil) infused with herbs, combined with beeswax or plant-based wax to create a firm texture. Essential oils can be added for additional therapeutic benefits and fragrance. Herbs like arnica, comfrey, and cayenne are particularly effective in reducing pain and swelling, while oils like peppermint and eucalyptus provide a cooling, soothing sensation.

This chapter provides 10 recipes for herbal salves designed to target joint pain and swelling. Whether you're dealing with stiff knees, sore shoulders, or aching hands, these salves can provide relief and promote healing in a natural, sustainable way.

1001. Arnica and Comfrey Healing Salve

Ingredients:

1/4 cup arnica flowers (dried)

1/4 cup comfrey leaves (dried)

1/2 cup olive oil

2 tbsp beeswax

Instructions:

Infuse olive oil with arnica and comfrey by gently heating them in a double boiler for 1–2 hours.

Strain the oil and return it to the double boiler.

Add beeswax and stir until melted.

Pour into a clean jar and let cool before sealing.

Uses: Reduces swelling and promotes tissue repair.

Storage Tips: Store in a cool, dark place for up to 6 months.

1002. Cayenne and Ginger Warming Salve

Ingredients:

1/2 tsp cayenne powder

1/2 tsp grated fresh ginger

1/2 cup coconut oil

2 tbsp beeswax

Instructions:

Heat coconut oil with cayenne and ginger in a double boiler for 1 hour.

Strain and return the oil to the double boiler.

Add beeswax and stir until melted.

Pour into a container and allow to cool.

Uses: Increases circulation and relieves joint pain.

Storage Tips: Store in a sealed container for up to 4 months.

1003. Peppermint and Eucalyptus Cooling Salve

Ingredients:

1/2 cup almond oil

2 tbsp beeswax

10 drops peppermint essential oil

10 drops eucalyptus essential oil

Instructions:

Heat almond oil and beeswax in a double boiler until melted.

Remove from heat and add essential oils.

Pour into a jar and let solidify.

Uses: Reduces inflammation and provides a cooling effect.

Storage Tips: Keep in a cool, dark place for up to 6 months.

1004. Turmeric and Black Pepper Anti-Inflammatory Salve

Ingredients:

1/2 tsp turmeric powder

1/8 tsp black pepper

1/2 cup olive oil

2 tbsp beeswax

Instructions:

Warm olive oil with turmeric and black pepper in a double boiler for 1 hour.

Strain and combine with melted beeswax.

Pour into a container and let set.

Uses: Reduces joint inflammation and stiffness.

Storage Tips: Store in a sealed jar for up to 6 months.

1005. Calendula and Lavender Soothing Salve

Ingredients:

1/4 cup calendula flowers (dried)

1/4 cup lavender flowers (dried)

1/2 cup coconut oil

2 tbsp beeswax

Instructions:

Infuse coconut oil with calendula and lavender for 1–2 hours.

Strain and mix with melted beeswax.

Pour into jars and cool.

Uses: Calms irritation and reduces mild swelling.

Storage Tips: Store in a cool, dry place for up to 6 months.

1006. Rosemary and Arnica Pain Relief Salve

Ingredients:

1/4 cup dried arnica flowers

1 tbsp dried rosemary leaves

1/2 cup olive oil

2 tbsp beeswax

Instructions:

Infuse olive oil with arnica and rosemary for 1–2 hours.

Strain and combine with melted beeswax.

Pour into a container and allow to cool.

Uses: Relieves stiffness and improves circulation.

Storage Tips: Keep in a sealed container for up to 6 months.

1007. Ginger and Lemongrass Warming Salve

Ingredients:

1/2 tsp grated fresh ginger

10 drops lemongrass essential oil

1/2 cup coconut oil

2 tbsp beeswax

Instructions:

Infuse coconut oil with ginger for 1 hour.

Strain and add lemongrass oil and beeswax.

Pour into jars and let set.

Uses: Eases joint pain and enhances mobility.

Storage Tips: Store in a cool, dry place for up to 4 months.

1008. Basil and Clove Anti-Inflammatory Salve

Ingredients:

1/4 cup dried basil leaves

5 drops clove essential oil

1/2 cup olive oil

2 tbsp beeswax

Instructions:

Heat basil and olive oil together for 1 hour.

Strain and combine with clove oil and melted beeswax.

Pour into containers and cool.

Uses: Reduces swelling and relieves deep-seated pain.

Storage Tips: Keep in a sealed jar for up to 6 months.

1009. Comfrey and Arnica Joint Relief Salve

Ingredients:

1/4 cup dried comfrey leaves

1/4 cup dried arnica flowers

1/2 cup coconut oil

2 tbsp beeswax

Instructions:

Infuse coconut oil with comfrey and arnica for 2 hours.

Strain and mix with melted beeswax.

Pour into jars and cool.

Uses: Promotes healing and reduces inflammation.

Storage Tips: Store in a cool, dark place for up to 6 months.

1010. Black Pepper and Clary Sage Warming Salve

Ingredients:

1/4 tsp black pepper

10 drops clary sage essential oil

1/2 cup almond oil

2 tbsp beeswax

Instructions:

Combine black pepper with almond oil and warm for 1 hour.

Strain and mix with clary sage oil and beeswax.

Pour into jars and let set.

Uses: Reduces stiffness and stimulates circulation.

Storage Tips: Keep in a sealed jar for up to 6 months.

Herbal salves are a powerful, natural way to target joint pain and swelling. With a few simple ingredients and techniques, you can create effective remedies that deliver anti-inflammatory and pain-relieving benefits directly where they're needed. These salves are easy to store, versatile, and safe, making them an invaluable addition to your herbal toolkit.

Herbs for Managing Chronic Conditions Naturally

Chronic conditions such as arthritis, diabetes, hypertension, and autoimmune disorders can significantly impact quality of life. While modern medicine offers solutions to manage these issues, many people seek natural alternatives or complementary therapies to reduce dependence on pharmaceuticals, alleviate side effects, and improve overall well-being. Herbs, with their diverse healing properties, provide a natural way to address chronic conditions by targeting inflammation, improving circulation, balancing hormones, and supporting organ function.

This chapter explores the role of herbs in managing chronic conditions and provides practical strategies to incorporate them into daily routines. Unlike medications that often focus on symptom management, herbs work holistically, supporting the body's natural healing processes. For instance, turmeric and ginger reduce systemic inflammation, while adaptogens like ashwagandha and rhodiola enhance resilience to stress, a common contributor to chronic illnesses.

By understanding the unique properties of specific herbs, you can create personalized remedies tailored to your needs. This chapter also emphasizes the importance of consistency, lifestyle adjustments, and consultation with healthcare professionals to ensure safe and effective integration of herbal remedies into your health plan.

Key Herbs for Managing Chronic Conditions

1. Turmeric (Curcuma longa)

Properties: Anti-inflammatory, antioxidant, liver support. Turmeric's active compound, curcumin, has been shown to reduce inflammation, making it valuable for conditions like arthritis, heart disease, and metabolic disorders.

How to Use:

Add turmeric to teas, soups, or smoothies.

Take as a tincture or capsule for concentrated benefits.

2. Ginger (Zingiber officinale)

Properties: Anti-inflammatory, digestive aid, circulatory stimulant. Ginger alleviates pain and improves circulation, making it effective for arthritis, migraines, and digestive issues.

How to Use:

Brew fresh ginger tea to reduce nausea and inflammation.

Use ginger-infused oil for joint massages.

3. Ashwagandha (Withania somnifera)

Properties: Adaptogen, stress reducer, immune modulator. Ashwagandha helps manage stress-related conditions like hypertension, diabetes, and autoimmune diseases by balancing cortisol levels and boosting resilience.

How to Use:

Take as a tincture or powder, mixed with warm milk or water.

Use daily for long-term benefits.

4. Milk Thistle (Silybum marianum)

Properties: Liver detoxifier, antioxidant, cell protector. Milk thistle supports liver function, which is critical for managing conditions like fatty liver disease and toxin buildup from chronic illnesses.

How to Use:

Brew milk thistle tea or take as a capsule.

Incorporate into detox regimens.

5. Cinnamon (Cinnamomum spp.)

Properties: Blood sugar regulator, anti-inflammatory, circulatory aid. Cinnamon helps stabilize blood sugar levels, making it a valuable herb for managing type 2 diabetes and metabolic syndrome.

How to Use:

Add cinnamon powder to meals or teas.

Use in tinctures for enhanced absorption.

6. Hawthorn (Crataegus spp.)

Properties: Heart tonic, circulatory support, antioxidant. Hawthorn strengthens the heart and improves circulation, making it ideal for managing hypertension and cardiovascular disease.

How to Use:

Brew hawthorn berry tea or use a tincture.

Take daily to improve heart health.

7. Nettle (Urtica dioica)

Properties: Anti-inflammatory, nutrient-rich, diuretic. Nettle is rich in vitamins and minerals, supports kidney function, and reduces inflammation, benefiting conditions like arthritis and gout.

How to Use:

Drink nettle tea regularly.

Use as a tincture for more potent effects.

8. Licorice Root (Glycyrrhiza glabra)

Properties: Immune modulator, anti-inflammatory, adrenal support. Licorice root supports adrenal health, making it useful for chronic fatigue syndrome, autoimmune conditions, and inflammatory disorders.

How to Use:

Brew licorice tea to soothe inflammation.

Use cautiously in cases of hypertension (consult with a healthcare provider).

9. Rhodiola (Rhodiola rosea)

Properties: Adaptogen, energy booster, mental clarity. Rhodiola helps combat chronic fatigue and stress while improving cognitive function and stamina.

How to Use:

Take as a tincture or capsule in the morning.

Combine with other adaptogens for enhanced effects.

10. Boswellia (Boswellia serrata)

Properties: Anti-inflammatory, pain reliever, joint support. Boswellia is particularly effective for arthritis and chronic inflammatory conditions, reducing swelling and pain naturally.

How to Use:

Take as a capsule or tincture.

Use in topical salves for joint pain.

Incorporating Herbs into Daily Life

1. Teas and Infusions

Sipping herbal teas throughout the day is an easy way to enjoy the benefits of anti-inflammatory and stress-relieving herbs.

2. Tinctures and Capsules

For those with busy schedules, tinctures and capsules offer a convenient way to ensure consistent dosing.

3. Culinary Integration

Adding herbs like turmeric, ginger, and cinnamon to meals enhances their flavor while providing therapeutic benefits.

Lifestyle Considerations for Managing Chronic Conditions Naturally

Balanced Diet: Focus on whole, nutrient-dense foods to support overall health.

Stress Management: Incorporate mindfulness practices like yoga or meditation alongside adaptogenic herbs.

Hydration: Stay hydrated to aid in detoxification and cellular function.

Regular Movement: Gentle exercise helps reduce inflammation and improve circulation.

Herbs offer a holistic approach to managing chronic conditions by addressing inflammation, boosting resilience, and supporting vital organ function. When integrated into a balanced lifestyle, these natural remedies provide sustainable relief and improve overall well-being. By combining knowledge, consistency, and the right herbs, you can take charge of your health and navigate chronic conditions with confidence and vitality.

Crafting Cooling Compresses for Acute Inflammation

Acute inflammation often results in swelling, redness, and heat in the affected area, whether caused by an injury, overexertion, or a medical condition like arthritis or tendinitis. While the inflammatory response is part of the body's natural healing process, excessive inflammation can cause discomfort and delay recovery. Cooling compresses, infused with anti-inflammatory and soothing herbs, provide an effective way to reduce swelling, ease pain, and promote healing.

A cooling compress is a simple yet powerful remedy that involves soaking a cloth or bandage in a cool herbal infusion, wringing it out, and applying it to the inflamed area. The herbs in the compress provide direct, localized relief, while the cooling effect helps reduce heat and swelling. Herbs like chamomile, peppermint, and calendula are excellent choices for crafting compresses because of their soothing and anti-inflammatory properties.

This chapter guides you through the process of creating herbal compresses for acute inflammation. With a few easy-to-follow recipes, you'll learn how to harness the healing power of herbs to provide immediate and effective relief.

Steps for Making Cooling Compresses

Prepare the Herbal Infusion: Choose your herbs and steep them in boiling water to extract their healing properties.

Cool the Infusion: Allow the liquid to cool to a comfortable temperature before use.

Soak the Cloth: Dip a clean, soft cloth or bandage into the infusion and wring out the excess liquid.

Apply the Compress: Place the cloth on the inflamed area and secure it if needed. Leave the compress on for 15–20 minutes, refreshing as needed.

Repeat: Use the compress 2–3 times a day for best results.

1011. Chamomile and Lavender Soothing Compress

Ingredients:

2 tbsp dried chamomile flowers

1 tbsp dried lavender flowers

2 cups water

Instructions:

Steep chamomile and lavender in boiling water for 10 minutes.

Let the infusion cool, then soak a cloth in the liquid.

Apply to the affected area for 15–20 minutes.

Uses: Reduces swelling and calms irritation.

1012. Peppermint and Witch Hazel Cooling Compress

Ingredients:

2 tbsp dried peppermint leaves

1/4 cup witch hazel

1 cup water

Instructions:

Steep peppermint in boiling water for 10 minutes.

Mix the infusion with witch hazel and let cool.

Soak a cloth and apply to the inflamed area.

Uses: Relieves heat and soothes pain.

1013. Calendula and Rose Petal Anti-Inflammatory Compress

Ingredients:

2 tbsp dried calendula flowers

1 tbsp dried rose petals

2 cups water

Instructions:

Steep calendula and rose petals in boiling water for 10 minutes.

Allow to cool, soak a cloth, and apply.

Uses: Reduces redness and supports skin healing.

1014. Green Tea and Aloe Vera Hydrating Compress

Ingredients:

1 green tea bag

2 tbsp aloe vera gel

1 cup water

Instructions:

Steep the tea bag in boiling water, then let it cool.

Mix in aloe vera gel, soak a cloth, and apply.

Uses: Cools and hydrates inflamed skin.

1015. Ginger and Turmeric Joint Relief Compress

Ingredients:

1 tsp grated fresh ginger

1 tsp turmeric powder

2 cups water

Instructions:

Simmer ginger and turmeric in water for 15 minutes.

Let the infusion cool, soak a cloth, and apply to joints.

Uses: Eases joint pain and reduces swelling.

1016. Sage and Thyme Muscle Relief Compress

Ingredients:

1 tbsp dried sage leaves

1 tbsp dried thyme leaves

2 cups water

Instructions:

Steep sage and thyme in boiling water for 10 minutes.

Cool the infusion, soak a cloth, and apply to sore muscles.

Uses: Relieves tension and reduces inflammation.

1017. Arnica and Peppermint Cooling Compress

Ingredients:

1 tbsp dried arnica flowers

1 tbsp dried peppermint leaves

2 cups water

Instructions:

Steep arnica and peppermint in boiling water for 15 minutes.

Allow to cool, then soak a cloth and apply.

Uses: Reduces bruising and soothes aches.

1018. Basil and Lemon Balm Headache Compress

Ingredients:

1 tbsp dried basil leaves

1 tbsp dried lemon balm leaves

1 cup water

Instructions:

Steep basil and lemon balm in boiling water for 10 minutes.

Cool the infusion, soak a cloth, and apply to the forehead or temples.

Uses: Relieves tension headaches and reduces inflammation.

1019. Horsetail and Comfrey Injury Compress

Ingredients:

1 tbsp dried horsetail

1 tbsp dried comfrey leaves

2 cups water

Instructions:

Steep horsetail and comfrey in boiling water for 10 minutes.

Cool the liquid, soak a cloth, and apply to sprains or bruises.

Uses: Speeds recovery and reduces swelling.

1020. Fennel and Chamomile Eye Compress

Ingredients:

1 tsp fennel seeds

1 tsp dried chamomile flowers

1 cup water

Instructions:

Steep fennel seeds and chamomile in boiling water for 10 minutes.

Cool the infusion, soak a soft cloth, and apply gently over closed eyes.

Uses: Reduces puffiness and soothes eye irritation.

Cooling compresses are an effective and natural way to address acute inflammation, delivering the healing properties of herbs directly to the affected area. These simple remedies provide immediate relief while promoting long-term healing, making them an essential part of your herbal first-aid toolkit. By incorporating these recipes into your self-care routine, you can soothe discomfort, reduce swelling, and enhance your body's natural recovery processes.

BOOK 30

HERBS FOR CARDIOVASCULAR HEALTH

The cardiovascular system is the lifeline of the body, responsible for transporting oxygen, nutrients, and essential compounds throughout. Maintaining a healthy heart and circulatory system is crucial for overall well-being, especially with the growing prevalence of heart-related issues like high blood pressure, atherosclerosis, and poor circulation. Fortunately, nature offers a variety of herbs that can strengthen the heart, regulate blood pressure, and improve circulation.

This book explores the role of herbal remedies in promoting cardiovascular health. Herbs like hawthorn, garlic, and hibiscus are renowned for their heart-protective properties, while others, such as cayenne and ginger, enhance blood flow and reduce inflammation. From tonics that nourish the heart to blends that boost circulation, these remedies are designed to support your cardiovascular system holistically and naturally.

Whether you're looking to manage an existing condition or prevent potential issues, this book provides practical insights and recipes to help you care for your heart. By incorporating these gentle yet powerful herbal remedies into your daily routine, you can strengthen your cardiovascular system, improve your energy levels, and embrace a healthier, more balanced lifestyle.

Strengthening the Heart with Natural Tonics

Herbal remedies have long been valued for their ability to support heart health, offering a natural and holistic approach to strengthening this vital organ. Tonics made from heart-healthy herbs can improve circulation, regulate blood pressure, and enhance overall cardiovascular function. Unlike synthetic medications, these remedies work gently, nourishing the body while minimizing side effects.

Heart tonics often feature herbs like hawthorn, garlic, and turmeric, which are rich in antioxidants and anti-inflammatory compounds. These herbs protect the heart by reducing oxidative stress, improving blood flow, and balancing cholesterol levels. Additionally, adaptogens like ashwagandha help manage stress, a common contributor to heart disease.

In this section, we'll explore 10 remedies that combine these powerful herbs into easy-to-prepare teas, tinctures, and tonics. Incorporating these remedies into your daily routine can promote a stronger, healthier heart and support long-term wellness.

1021. Hawthorn Berry Heart Tea

Ingredients:

1 tsp dried hawthorn berries

1 cup boiling water

Instructions:

Steep hawthorn berries in boiling water for 15 minutes.

Strain and drink once daily.

Uses: Supports heart muscle strength and improves circulation.

Storage Tips: Use dried berries and store in an airtight container for up to 1 year.

1022. Garlic and Honey Cardiovascular Booster

Ingredients:

1 clove garlic (crushed)

1 tsp honey

Instructions:

Mix garlic and honey together.

Consume daily before breakfast.

Uses: Lowers cholesterol and improves blood pressure.

Storage Tips: Use fresh garlic for best results; refrigerate honey for long-term storage.

1023. Turmeric and Ginger Heart Tonic

Ingredients:

1/2 tsp turmeric powder

1/2 tsp grated ginger

1 cup boiling water

Instructions:

Combine turmeric and ginger in boiling water.

Steep for 10 minutes, strain, and drink.

Uses: Reduces inflammation and enhances arterial health.

Storage Tips: Use freshly grated ginger and store turmeric in a sealed container.

1024. Lemon Balm Calming Tea

Ingredients:

1 tsp dried lemon balm leaves

1 cup boiling water

Instructions:

Steep lemon balm in boiling water for 10 minutes.

Strain and drink in the evening.

Uses: Reduces stress and supports heart health.

Storage Tips: Keep dried lemon balm in an airtight container.

1025. Hibiscus and Cinnamon Circulation Blend

Ingredients:

1 tbsp dried hibiscus flowers

1 cinnamon stick

2 cups boiling water

Instructions:

Steep hibiscus and cinnamon in boiling water for 15 minutes.

Strain and enjoy warm or chilled.

Uses: Lowers blood pressure and improves circulation.

Storage Tips: Refrigerate for up to 24 hours.

1026. Ashwagandha Adaptogenic Tonic

Ingredients:

1 tsp ashwagandha powder

1 cup warm almond milk

Instructions:

Mix ashwagandha powder into warm almond milk.

Stir well and drink before bed.

Uses: Reduces stress and balances cortisol levels.

Storage Tips: Use powdered ashwagandha; store in a cool, dry place.

1027. Garlic and Olive Oil Infusion

Ingredients:

2 cloves garlic (crushed)

1/2 cup olive oil

Instructions:

Combine garlic and olive oil in a jar.

Let infuse for 1 week before using.

Uses: Supports heart health and reduces inflammation.

Storage Tips: Refrigerate and use within 1 month.

1028. Hawthorn and Rosehip Immunity Tea

Ingredients:

1 tsp dried hawthorn berries

1 tsp dried rosehips

1 cup boiling water

Instructions:

Steep hawthorn and rosehips in boiling water for 10 minutes.

Strain and drink daily.

Uses: Enhances heart strength and provides antioxidants.

Storage Tips: Store dried ingredients in a sealed container.

1029. Peppermint and Ginger Digestive Tea

Ingredients:

1 tsp dried peppermint leaves

1/2 tsp grated fresh ginger

1 cup boiling water

Instructions:

Combine peppermint and ginger in boiling water.

Steep for 10 minutes, strain, and drink after meals.

Uses: Supports digestion and reduces heartburn.

Storage Tips: Use fresh ginger and store dried peppermint in a cool place.

1030. Cardamom and Black Pepper Heart Tonic

Ingredients:

1/4 tsp ground cardamom

1/8 tsp black pepper

1 cup warm milk

Instructions:

Mix cardamom and black pepper into warm milk.

Stir and drink before bed.

Uses: Improves circulation and reduces arterial stiffness.

Storage Tips: Prepare fresh for best results.

Strengthening the heart with natural tonics is a gentle, effective way to support cardiovascular health. These remedies, made from readily available herbs and spices, offer a holistic approach to enhancing circulation, reducing inflammation, and nourishing the heart. Incorporating these recipes into your daily routine can help you maintain a healthy heart and enjoy long-term vitality.

Managing Blood Pressure with Herbal Remedies

High blood pressure, or hypertension, is a common condition that increases the risk of heart disease, stroke, and other health problems. While lifestyle changes and medications are often prescribed, herbal remedies can be a powerful complementary approach to managing blood pressure naturally. Herbs with diuretic, vasodilatory, and anti-inflammatory properties help relax blood vessels, improve circulation, and reduce stress on the heart.

This chapter focuses on herbal remedies that can assist in maintaining healthy blood pressure levels. Herbs like hawthorn, hibiscus, garlic, and valerian are known for their ability to regulate blood pressure. These remedies work gently to support cardiovascular health without the side effects associated with some pharmaceutical options.

In this section, we'll explore 10 practical remedies for managing blood pressure naturally, along with tips for incorporating them into your routine.

1031. Hibiscus and Lemon Blood Pressure Tea

Ingredients:

1 tbsp dried hibiscus flowers

1 slice fresh lemon

1 cup boiling water

Instructions:

Steep hibiscus flowers in boiling water for 10 minutes.

Add the lemon slice and drink once daily.

Uses: Lowers systolic and diastolic blood pressure naturally.

Storage Tips: Store dried hibiscus flowers in an airtight container for up to 1 year.

1032. Garlic and Honey Cardiovascular Tonic

Ingredients:

2 cloves garlic (crushed)

1 tsp honey

Instructions:

Combine crushed garlic with honey.

Consume daily before breakfast.

Uses: Improves circulation and reduces blood pressure.

Storage Tips: Use fresh garlic for maximum potency.

1033. Valerian and Lavender Calming Tea

Ingredients:

1 tsp dried valerian root

1 tsp dried lavender flowers

1 cup boiling water

Instructions:

Steep valerian root and lavender in boiling water for 10 minutes.

Strain and drink in the evening.

Uses: Reduces stress-related hypertension and promotes relaxation.

Storage Tips: Store dried herbs in a cool, dark place.

1034. Hawthorn and Cinnamon Heart Tea

Ingredients:

1 tsp dried hawthorn berries

1 small cinnamon stick

1 cup boiling water

Instructions:

Steep hawthorn berries and cinnamon in boiling water for 15 minutes.

Strain and drink once daily.

Uses: Supports heart health and regulates blood pressure.

Storage Tips: Keep dried hawthorn berries in a sealed container.

1035. Nettle and Lemon Balm Relaxation Blend

Ingredients:

1 tsp dried nettle leaves

1 tsp dried lemon balm leaves

1 cup boiling water

Instructions:

Steep nettle and lemon balm in boiling water for 10 minutes.

Strain and drink in the afternoon.

Uses: Reduces stress and supports healthy circulation.

Storage Tips: Store dried nettle and lemon balm in separate airtight jars.

1036. Ginger and Turmeric Pressure Balancer

Ingredients:

1/2 tsp grated fresh ginger

1/2 tsp turmeric powder

1 cup boiling water

Instructions:

Combine ginger and turmeric in boiling water.

Steep for 5–7 minutes, strain, and drink daily.

Uses: Improves circulation and reduces arterial stiffness.

Storage Tips: Use fresh ginger and store turmeric in a sealed container.

1037. Holy Basil (Tulsi) Stress Relief Tea

Ingredients:

1 tsp dried holy basil leaves

1 cup boiling water

Instructions:

Steep holy basil in boiling water for 10 minutes.

Strain and drink in the evening.

Uses: Lowers cortisol levels and reduces stress-related hypertension.

Storage Tips: Store dried holy basil in an airtight container.

1038. Celery Seed Circulation Tea

Ingredients:

1/2 tsp celery seeds

1 cup boiling water

Instructions:

Simmer celery seeds in water for 10 minutes.

Strain and drink once daily.

Uses: Acts as a natural diuretic and supports blood pressure regulation.

Storage Tips: Store celery seeds in a cool, dry place.

1039. Olive Leaf Blood Pressure Support

Ingredients:

1 tsp dried olive leaves

1 cup boiling water

Instructions:

Steep olive leaves in boiling water for 15 minutes.

Strain and drink in the morning.

Uses: Reduces high blood pressure and improves arterial health.

Storage Tips: Keep dried olive leaves in a sealed container.

1040. Beetroot and Lemon Juice Booster

Ingredients:

1/4 fresh beetroot (grated)

Juice of 1/2 lemon

1 cup water

Instructions:

Blend beetroot and water, then strain the juice.

Add lemon juice and stir.

Uses: Boosts nitric oxide levels to improve blood flow and lower blood pressure.

Storage Tips: Consume immediately for best results.

Managing blood pressure with herbal remedies offers a safe and natural approach to cardiovascular health. By incorporating these teas, tonics, and tinctures into your daily routine, you can support healthy blood pressure levels and enhance overall well-being. These remedies, combined with a heart-healthy diet and lifestyle, provide a holistic way to care for your cardiovascular system.

Circulation-Boosting Blends for Daily Use

Good circulation is essential for overall health, ensuring that oxygen and nutrients reach every part of the body while aiding in the removal of toxins. Poor circulation can lead to cold extremities, fatigue, and even more severe conditions like varicose veins, blood clots, or cardiovascular disease. Herbal remedies can play a key role in improving blood flow, enhancing vascular health, and promoting vitality.

Circulation-boosting herbs such as cayenne, ginger, and ginkgo biloba stimulate blood flow and strengthen blood vessels. These herbs, when combined with other supportive ingredients, create powerful blends that can be consumed daily for sustained benefits. Teas, tonics, and infused oils are simple yet effective ways to incorporate these remedies into your routine.

In this chapter, we'll explore 10 circulation-boosting blends, each tailored to enhance blood flow, reduce inflammation, and promote overall vascular health.

1041. Cayenne and Ginger Circulation Tea

Ingredients:

1/4 tsp cayenne pepper

1 tsp grated fresh ginger

1 cup boiling water

Instructions:

Add cayenne and ginger to boiling water.

Steep for 10 minutes, strain, and drink.

Uses: Stimulates blood flow and warms cold extremities.

Storage Tips: Use fresh ginger; store cayenne in a sealed container.

1042. Ginkgo Biloba and Peppermint Tea

Ingredients:

1 tsp dried ginkgo biloba leaves

1 tsp dried peppermint leaves

1 cup boiling water

Instructions:

Combine ginkgo and peppermint in boiling water.

Steep for 10 minutes, strain, and enjoy.

Uses: Improves circulation to the brain and enhances focus.

Storage Tips: Store dried herbs in an airtight container.

1043. Cinnamon and Clove Warming Tonic

Ingredients:

1 cinnamon stick

2 whole cloves

1 cup boiling water

Instructions:

Steep cinnamon and cloves in boiling water for 15 minutes.

Strain and drink daily in the morning.

Uses: Promotes blood flow and reduces inflammation.

Storage Tips: Keep spices in a cool, dry place.

1044. Rosemary and Lemon Infusion

Ingredients:

1 tsp dried rosemary leaves

2 slices fresh lemon

1 cup boiling water

Instructions:

Combine rosemary and lemon in boiling water.

Steep for 10 minutes, strain, and enjoy.

Uses: Enhances circulation and reduces oxidative stress.

Storage Tips: Store rosemary in a sealed container.

1045. Garlic and Olive Oil Infusion

Ingredients:

2 cloves garlic (crushed)

1/2 cup olive oil

Instructions:

Combine garlic and olive oil in a jar.

Let infuse for 1 week.

Use as a dressing or drizzle over meals.

Uses: Supports vascular health and reduces inflammation.

Storage Tips: Refrigerate and use within 1 month.

1046. Turmeric and Black Pepper Golden Tea

Ingredients:

1/2 tsp turmeric powder

1/8 tsp black pepper

1 cup warm almond milk

Instructions:

Mix turmeric and black pepper into warm almond milk.

Stir well and drink before bed.

Uses: Improves circulation and reduces arterial stiffness.

Storage Tips: Prepare fresh for best results.

1047. Lemon and Ginger Detox Water

Ingredients:

1 slice fresh ginger

2 slices fresh lemon

1 cup warm water

Instructions:

Combine ginger and lemon in warm water.

Let steep for 5 minutes and drink.

Uses: Enhances blood flow and promotes detoxification.

Storage Tips: Prepare fresh daily.

1048. Holy Basil and Cardamom Tea

Ingredients:

1 tsp dried holy basil leaves

1/4 tsp ground cardamom

1 cup boiling water

Instructions:

Steep holy basil and cardamom in boiling water for 10 minutes.

Strain and enjoy.

Uses: Balances stress and improves circulation.

Storage Tips: Store dried holy basil in an airtight container.

1049. Beetroot and Orange Juice Booster

Ingredients:

1/2 fresh beetroot (peeled and diced)

Juice of 1 orange

1 cup water

Instructions:

Blend beetroot, orange juice, and water until smooth.

Strain if desired and drink immediately.

Uses: Boosts nitric oxide levels and enhances oxygen delivery.

Storage Tips: Consume immediately for best results.

1050. Parsley and Apple Cider Vinegar Tonic

Ingredients:

1 tbsp fresh parsley (chopped)

1 tsp apple cider vinegar

1 cup warm water

Instructions:

Combine parsley and apple cider vinegar in warm water.

Stir well and drink daily.

Uses: Improves circulation and supports detoxification.

Storage Tips: Use fresh parsley; store vinegar in a sealed bottle.

Incorporating circulation-boosting blends into your daily routine is a natural way to support cardiovascular health, enhance energy levels, and reduce the risk of complications caused by poor blood flow. These simple remedies not only improve circulation but also nourish the body with essential nutrients and antioxidants, helping you maintain vitality and wellness.

Preventing Common Cardiovascular Issues Holistically

Cardiovascular issues, including heart disease, high blood pressure, and arterial blockages, are leading causes of illness and death worldwide.

While medical treatments are often necessary for acute conditions, holistic approaches can play a critical role in prevention. By combining herbal remedies, lifestyle changes, and nutritional support, you can build a strong foundation for heart health and reduce the risk of common cardiovascular problems.

This chapter explores natural strategies to prevent cardiovascular issues. Herbs like hawthorn, garlic, and turmeric are renowned for their heart-protective properties, while lifestyle practices such as regular exercise, stress management, and balanced nutrition work synergistically to enhance cardiovascular health. By addressing the root causes of heart disease—such as chronic inflammation, poor circulation, and high cholesterol—this holistic approach offers a sustainable and proactive path to long-term wellness.

Holistic Strategies for Cardiovascular Health

1. Herbal Allies for Heart Health

Certain herbs are particularly effective in preventing cardiovascular issues by improving circulation, reducing inflammation, and balancing cholesterol levels:

Hawthorn: Strengthens the heart muscle and improves blood flow.

Garlic: Lowers cholesterol and reduces arterial plaque buildup.

Turmeric: Combats inflammation and oxidative stress.

2. A Heart-Healthy Diet

A balanced diet rich in fruits, vegetables, whole grains, and healthy fats can significantly lower the risk of heart disease. Key nutrients include:

Omega-3 fatty acids: Found in fatty fish, walnuts, and flaxseeds, these reduce inflammation and improve cholesterol levels.

Potassium: Found in bananas, sweet potatoes, and spinach, potassium helps regulate blood pressure.

Antioxidants: Found in berries, green tea, and dark chocolate, these protect against oxidative damage.

3. Regular Physical Activity

Exercise strengthens the heart, improves circulation, and helps maintain healthy blood pressure. Aim for at least 150 minutes of moderate exercise per week, such as brisk walking, cycling, or swimming.

4. Stress Management

Chronic stress contributes to hypertension and heart disease. Incorporating practices like meditation, deep breathing, and yoga can lower cortisol levels and reduce cardiovascular strain.

5. Adequate Sleep

Poor sleep is linked to an increased risk of heart disease. Aim for 7–9 hours of quality sleep per night to support overall health and recovery.

Herbal Remedies to Prevent Cardiovascular Issues

1051. Hawthorn and Lemon Balm Heart Tonic

Ingredients:

1 tsp dried hawthorn berries

1 tsp dried lemon balm leaves

1 cup boiling water

Instructions:

Steep hawthorn berries and lemon balm in boiling water for 10 minutes.

Strain and drink once daily.

Uses: Strengthens the heart and reduces stress.

1052. Garlic and Turmeric Anti-Inflammatory Blend

Ingredients:

1 clove garlic (crushed)

1/2 tsp turmeric powder

1 cup warm almond milk

Instructions:

Combine garlic and turmeric in warm almond milk.

Stir well and drink before bed.

Uses: Reduces inflammation and improves arterial health.

1053. Hibiscus and Cinnamon Blood Pressure Tea

Ingredients:

1 tbsp dried hibiscus flowers

1 small cinnamon stick

1 cup boiling water

Instructions:

Steep hibiscus and cinnamon in boiling water for 15 minutes.

Strain and enjoy warm or chilled.

Uses: Lowers blood pressure and enhances circulation.

1054. Ginger and Lemon Circulation Booster

Ingredients:

1 tsp grated fresh ginger

1 slice fresh lemon

1 cup boiling water

Instructions:

Steep ginger and lemon in boiling water for 10 minutes.

Strain and drink in the morning.

Uses: Improves circulation and reduces arterial stiffness.

1055. Nettle and Peppermint Cholesterol Tea

Ingredients:

1 tsp dried nettle leaves

1 tsp dried peppermint leaves

1 cup boiling water

Instructions:

Steep nettle and peppermint in boiling water for 10 minutes.

Strain and drink after meals.

Uses: Supports healthy cholesterol levels and digestion.

Lifestyle Tips for Preventing Cardiovascular Issues

Limit Processed Foods: Minimize consumption of sugary snacks, fried foods, and refined grains, which contribute to inflammation and heart disease.

Hydrate: Drinking plenty of water supports circulation and overall cardiovascular health.

Avoid Smoking and Excessive Alcohol: Both can damage blood vessels and increase the risk of heart disease.

Monitor Your Health: Regular check-ups and monitoring of blood pressure and cholesterol levels can help you stay proactive.

Preventing cardiovascular issues holistically involves a combination of herbal remedies, healthy lifestyle practices, and mindful nutrition. By addressing the root causes of heart disease and incorporating these strategies into your daily routine, you can support long-term cardiovascular health and reduce the risk of serious conditions. Small, consistent changes can have a profound impact on your heart's vitality, helping you enjoy a healthier, more balanced life.

BOOK 31

HERBAL CARE FOR EYES AND EARS

The eyes and ears are vital sensory organs that often go overlooked in daily wellness routines. From prolonged screen time causing eye strain and dryness to environmental factors leading to earaches and infections, modern lifestyles can take a toll on these delicate systems. Fortunately, herbal remedies offer a gentle and effective way to support and protect your vision and hearing.

This book explores the use of herbs to address common issues like eye fatigue, dryness, and irritation, as well as ear discomfort caused by infections or blockages. Herbs like chamomile, calendula, and fennel soothe and hydrate the eyes, while garlic and mullein provide relief for earaches and promote overall ear health. You'll also learn how to create herbal compresses, drops, and infusions tailored for eye and ear care.

By incorporating these natural remedies into your routine, you can nurture and protect these essential senses while reducing reliance on synthetic treatments. This book also emphasizes long-term strategies for maintaining healthy vision and hearing through herbal nutrition, lifestyle practices, and preventative care. Whether you're looking to address specific concerns or preserve your senses as you age, this guide equips you with the tools to care for your eyes and ears naturally.

Remedies for Eye Strain and Dryness

Eye strain and dryness are increasingly common issues in today's world, often resulting from prolonged screen time, environmental factors, or insufficient hydration. While these conditions are typically not severe, they can lead to discomfort, blurred vision, and difficulty concentrating. Fortunately, herbal remedies offer gentle, effective solutions to soothe and hydrate tired, dry eyes.

Herbs like chamomile, fennel, and eyebright are known for their anti-inflammatory, soothing, and hydrating properties. These herbs can be used in a variety of forms, such as teas, compresses, and rinses, to alleviate discomfort and restore moisture to the eyes. Additionally, maintaining hydration and consuming a nutrient-rich diet that includes eye-supportive vitamins like A, C, and E can enhance the effectiveness of these remedies.

This chapter provides 10 practical and easy-to-prepare remedies for relieving eye strain and dryness. These remedies are designed to be safe and gentle, offering relief while promoting long-term eye health.

1056. Chamomile Eye Compress

Ingredients:

2 chamomile tea bags

1 cup hot water

Instructions:

Steep the chamomile tea bags in hot water for 5 minutes.

Let them cool slightly, then place the tea bags over closed eyes.

Leave on for 10–15 minutes.

Uses: Reduces eye strain and soothes inflammation.

Storage Tips: Use fresh each time.

1057. Fennel Seed Eye Rinse

Ingredients:

1 tsp fennel seeds

1 cup boiling water

Instructions:

Steep fennel seeds in boiling water for 10 minutes.

Strain and allow the liquid to cool.

Use the infusion to rinse the eyes gently.

Uses: Hydrates and refreshes dry eyes.

Storage Tips: Discard any unused rinse after 24 hours.

1058. Cucumber Cooling Pads

Ingredients:

2 slices of fresh cucumber

Instructions:

Place cucumber slices in the refrigerator for 10 minutes.

Lay the slices over closed eyes for 15 minutes.

Uses: Relieves puffiness and hydrates tired eyes.

Storage Tips: Use fresh cucumber slices each time.

1059. Eyebright Tea Rinse

Ingredients:

1 tsp dried eyebright herb

1 cup boiling water

Instructions:

Steep eyebright in boiling water for 10 minutes.

Strain and let cool to room temperature.

Use a clean cotton pad to dab the rinse onto closed eyelids.

Uses: Reduces redness and soothes irritation.

Storage Tips: Prepare fresh for each use.

1060. Rose Water Eye Wash

Ingredients:

1 tsp pure rose water

1/2 cup distilled water

Instructions:

Mix rose water with distilled water.

Use as an eye wash or soak cotton pads and place them on the eyes.

Uses: Refreshes and hydrates dry eyes.

Storage Tips: Store in a sealed container for up to 1 week.

1061. Aloe Vera Eye Gel

Ingredients:

1 tsp pure aloe vera gel

Instructions:

Gently apply a small amount of aloe vera gel to the skin around the eyes.

Avoid direct contact with the eyes.

Uses: Hydrates and soothes the skin around dry, strained eyes.

Storage Tips: Store aloe vera gel in the refrigerator.

1062. Green Tea De-Puffing Pads

Ingredients:

2 green tea bags

1 cup hot water

Instructions:

Steep green tea bags in hot water for 5 minutes.

Chill the tea bags in the refrigerator, then place them over closed eyes.

Uses: Reduces puffiness and calms tired eyes.

Storage Tips: Use fresh tea bags for each application.

1063. Carrot and Spinach Eye Smoothie

Ingredients:

1 small carrot (chopped)

1/2 cup spinach

1/2 cup orange juice

Instructions:

Blend all ingredients until smooth.

Drink daily for long-term eye health.

Uses: Provides essential nutrients for eye hydration and vision health.

Storage Tips: Consume immediately for maximum benefits.

1064. Calendula Warm Compress

Ingredients:

1 tsp dried calendula flowers

1 cup boiling water

Instructions:

Steep calendula in boiling water for 10 minutes.

Soak a clean cloth in the infusion, wring out excess water, and place over closed eyes.

Uses: Reduces eye fatigue and promotes relaxation.

Storage Tips: Discard leftover infusion after use.

1065. Omega-3 Flaxseed Supplement

Ingredients:

1 tsp flaxseed oil

Instructions:

Consume flaxseed oil daily as a supplement.

Add it to smoothies or salads for easier consumption.

Uses: Supports long-term eye hydration and reduces dryness.

Storage Tips: Store flaxseed oil in the refrigerator to prevent oxidation.

Herbal remedies provide simple and effective solutions for relieving eye strain and dryness. By incorporating these recipes into your routine, you can soothe discomfort and support long-term eye health naturally. Consistent use of these remedies, paired with proper hydration and a nutrient-rich diet, can ensure your eyes remain refreshed, healthy, and resilient in the face of modern challenges.

Herbal Solutions for Earaches and Infections

Earaches and infections can be uncomfortable and disruptive, affecting people of all ages. They often result from bacterial or viral infections, fluid buildup, or irritation in the ear canal. While over-the-counter medications are commonly used, herbal remedies provide a natural and effective alternative to soothe discomfort, reduce inflammation, and support the healing process.

Herbs like garlic, mullein, and calendula have antimicrobial and anti-inflammatory properties that can help treat earaches and infections. These herbs are often used in the form of infused oils, teas, and compresses, providing relief and promoting faster recovery. It's important to use gentle, natural methods when dealing with ear issues to avoid further irritation or harm.

This chapter presents 10 herbal remedies for earaches and infections, focusing on safe, easy-to-prepare solutions that harness the healing power of nature.

1066. Garlic and Olive Oil Ear Drops

Ingredients:

2 cloves garlic (crushed)

2 tbsp olive oil

Instructions:

Warm olive oil and crushed garlic in a small pan for 10 minutes on low heat.

Strain and allow the oil to cool to a comfortable temperature.

Using a dropper, place 2–3 drops in the affected ear.

Uses: Reduces pain and fights infection with antimicrobial properties.

Storage Tips: Store in a sealed container in the refrigerator for up to 1 week.

1067. Mullein and Calendula Ear Oil

Ingredients:

1 tbsp dried mullein flowers

1 tbsp dried calendula flowers

1/4 cup olive oil

Instructions:

Infuse olive oil with mullein and calendula by heating gently in a double boiler for 1 hour.

Strain the oil and let it cool.

Use 2–3 drops in the ear as needed.

Uses: Soothes inflammation and promotes healing.

Storage Tips: Store in a sealed jar in a cool, dark place for up to 1 month.

1068. Warm Chamomile Compress

Ingredients:

1 chamomile tea bag

1 cup hot water

Instructions:

Steep the tea bag in hot water for 5 minutes.

Remove the tea bag and wring out excess water.

Place the warm tea bag over the affected ear for 10–15 minutes.

Uses: Relieves pain and reduces swelling.

Storage Tips: Use fresh each time.

1069. Onion Poultice for Ear Pain

Ingredients:

1 small onion

Instructions:

Heat the onion in the oven at 200°F (90°C) for 15 minutes.

Slice the onion and wrap it in a clean cloth.

Place the cloth over the affected ear for 10–15 minutes.

Uses: Draws out infection and reduces pain.

Storage Tips: Use fresh onion for each application.

1070. Basil and Coconut Oil Drops

Ingredients:

1 tsp fresh basil leaves (crushed)

2 tbsp coconut oil

Instructions:

Warm coconut oil and crushed basil leaves together for 10 minutes.

Strain and cool.

Use 2 drops in the affected ear.

Uses: Fights infection and soothes irritation.

Storage Tips: Store in a sealed container in the refrigerator for up to 1 week.

1071. Ginger and Olive Oil Rub

Ingredients:

1 tsp grated fresh ginger

2 tbsp olive oil

Instructions:

Heat olive oil and ginger gently for 10 minutes.

Strain and let cool.

Massage the oil around the ear (not inside).

Uses: Reduces pain and promotes circulation.

Storage Tips: Store in a sealed container for up to 1 week.

1072. Lavender and Tea Tree Oil Steam

Ingredients:

2 drops lavender essential oil

2 drops tea tree essential oil

1 bowl hot water

Instructions:

Add essential oils to the hot water.

Lean over the bowl with a towel over your head, inhaling the steam for 10 minutes.

Uses: Clears congestion and soothes ear infections.

Storage Tips: Prepare fresh for each use.

1073. Calendula Tea Rinse

Ingredients:

1 tsp dried calendula flowers

1 cup boiling water

Instructions:

Steep calendula flowers in boiling water for 10 minutes.

Strain and let cool.

Use the liquid to rinse the outer ear gently.

Uses: Cleanses the ear and reduces irritation.

Storage Tips: Use immediately after preparation.

1074. Apple Cider Vinegar and Water Solution

Ingredients:

1 tsp apple cider vinegar

1 tsp distilled water

Instructions:

Mix apple cider vinegar and water.

Soak a cotton ball in the mixture and place it gently in the ear opening (not inside).

Uses: Balances pH levels and prevents infection.

Storage Tips: Prepare fresh for each use.

1075. Turmeric and Honey Immune Booster

Ingredients:

1/2 tsp turmeric powder

1 tsp honey

1/2 cup warm water

Instructions:

Mix turmeric and honey in warm water.

Drink once daily to support the immune system.

Uses: Strengthens immunity to fight recurring ear infections.

Storage Tips: Consume immediately.

Herbal remedies offer a safe and natural approach to treating earaches and infections. By harnessing the power of antimicrobial and anti-inflammatory herbs, these remedies provide relief while supporting the healing process. Incorporate these gentle solutions into your care routine for effective, holistic ear health. Always consult a healthcare professional if symptoms persist or worsen.

Creating Compresses and Drops for Eye and Ear Care

Compresses and drops are versatile and effective tools for addressing common issues related to the eyes and ears, such as irritation, dryness, infections, and discomfort. They allow you to deliver the therapeutic properties of herbs directly to the affected area, offering localized relief. Compresses are particularly soothing for strained eyes and inflamed ears, while drops can address deeper issues like dryness or mild infections.

This chapter focuses on practical recipes for creating herbal compresses and drops tailored to eye and ear care. These remedies are simple to prepare, using natural ingredients like chamomile, calendula, garlic, and mullein to provide soothing, antimicrobial, and hydrating benefits. Proper hygiene and storage are crucial for these remedies to ensure safety and efficacy.

1076. Chamomile Eye Compress for Redness

Ingredients:

2 chamomile tea bags

1 cup hot water

Instructions:

Steep chamomile tea bags in hot water for 5 minutes.

Let them cool slightly, then place them over closed eyes.

Leave on for 10–15 minutes.

Uses: Reduces redness and soothes tired eyes.

Storage Tips: Use fresh tea bags each time.

1077. Calendula Ear Compress for Swelling

Ingredients:

1 tsp dried calendula flowers

1 cup boiling water

Instructions:

Steep calendula flowers in boiling water for 10 minutes.

Soak a clean cloth in the infusion and wring out the excess.

Apply the warm cloth to the affected ear for 10–15 minutes.

Uses: Reduces swelling and soothes ear discomfort.

Storage Tips: Discard leftover infusion after use.

1078. Fennel Eye Drops for Irritation

Ingredients:

1 tsp fennel seeds

1 cup boiling water

Instructions:

Steep fennel seeds in boiling water for 10 minutes.

Strain and cool the liquid.

Use a sterilized dropper to place 1–2 drops in each eye.

Uses: Relieves irritation and hydrates the eyes.

Storage Tips: Prepare fresh each time.

1079. Garlic Oil Ear Drops for Infections

Ingredients:

2 cloves garlic (crushed)

2 tbsp olive oil

Instructions:

Warm garlic and olive oil in a small pan for 10 minutes.

Strain the oil and let it cool.

Use a dropper to apply 2–3 drops in the affected ear.

Uses: Fights ear infections with antimicrobial properties.

Storage Tips: Store in the refrigerator for up to 1 week.

1080. Rose Water Eye Compress for Hydration

Ingredients:

1 tbsp pure rose water

1/2 cup distilled water

Instructions:

Mix rose water and distilled water.

Soak a cotton pad in the mixture and place it over closed eyes for 10 minutes.

Uses: Refreshes and hydrates dry eyes.

Storage Tips: Store the mixture in a sealed container for up to 1 week.

1081. Mullein Oil Drops for Earaches

Ingredients:

1 tbsp dried mullein flowers

1/4 cup olive oil

Instructions:

Infuse mullein flowers in olive oil by heating gently in a double boiler for 1 hour.

Strain the oil and let it cool.

Use 2–3 drops in the ear as needed.

Uses: Relieves pain and inflammation in the ear.

Storage Tips: Store in a dark, cool place for up to 1 month.

1082. Green Tea Compress for Puffy Eyes

Ingredients:

2 green tea bags

1 cup hot water

Instructions:

Steep green tea bags in hot water for 5 minutes.

Chill the tea bags in the refrigerator, then place them over closed eyes for 10–15 minutes.

Uses: Reduces puffiness and refreshes tired eyes.

Storage Tips: Use fresh tea bags each time.

1083. Lavender and Olive Oil Ear Rub

Ingredients:

2 drops lavender essential oil

2 tbsp olive oil

Instructions:

Mix lavender essential oil with olive oil.

Warm slightly and massage around the outer ear.

Uses: Soothes pain and reduces tension around the ear.

Storage Tips: Store in a sealed container for up to 1 month.

1084. Eyebright Tea Wash for Eye Irritation

Ingredients:

1 tsp dried eyebright herb

1 cup boiling water

Instructions:

Steep eyebright in boiling water for 10 minutes.

Cool and strain the liquid.

Use a cotton pad to gently wipe the eyes.

Uses: Reduces redness and irritation in the eyes.

Storage Tips: Prepare fresh each time.

1085. Basil and Coconut Oil Ear Drops

Ingredients:

1 tsp fresh basil leaves (crushed)

2 tbsp coconut oil

Instructions:

Warm coconut oil and crushed basil together for 10 minutes.

Strain and let cool.

Use 2 drops in the affected ear.

Uses: Fights infection and soothes irritation.

Storage Tips: Refrigerate and use within 1 week.

Herbal compresses and drops are simple yet effective remedies for addressing eye and ear concerns. By using these natural solutions, you can soothe irritation, reduce discomfort, and promote healing. Consistent use of these remedies, along with good hygiene and preventive care, ensures healthier eyes and ears naturally.

Long-Term Support for Vision and Hearing Health

Maintaining healthy vision and hearing over the long term requires proactive care and a combination of nutrition, lifestyle adjustments, and herbal remedies. These senses often experience gradual decline due to aging, environmental factors, and lifestyle habits, but natural solutions can help slow this process and support optimal function.

Herbs like bilberry, ginkgo biloba, and turmeric provide nutrients and antioxidants that protect against cellular damage in the eyes and ears. These remedies can help improve blood flow to the delicate structures of these organs, combat oxidative stress, and support tissue repair. In addition, incorporating healthy lifestyle practices, such as reducing screen time and protecting against loud noises, complements these herbal strategies.

This chapter provides a holistic approach to preserving your senses, featuring natural remedies, nutritional tips, and practical lifestyle changes to enhance vision and hearing health. These long-term solutions can help you maintain sharp eyesight and clear hearing as you age.

1086. Bilberry Tea for Vision Health

Ingredients:

1 tsp dried bilberry leaves or berries

1 cup boiling water

Instructions:

Steep bilberry in boiling water for 10 minutes.

Strain and drink once daily.

Uses: Improves night vision and protects against macular degeneration.

Storage Tips: Store dried bilberry in a sealed container.

1087. Ginkgo Biloba Capsules for Hearing Support

Ingredients:

1 ginkgo biloba capsule (available in health stores)

Instructions:

Take one capsule daily with water, preferably in the morning.

Uses: Enhances blood flow to the inner ear and supports hearing.

Storage Tips: Store capsules in a cool, dry place.

1088. Carrot and Spinach Smoothie for Vision

Ingredients:

1 medium carrot (chopped)

1/2 cup spinach leaves

1/2 cup orange juice

Instructions:

Blend all ingredients until smooth.

Drink daily for eye health.

Uses: Provides beta-carotene and lutein for retina health.

Storage Tips: Prepare fresh each time.

1089. Turmeric and Black Pepper Golden Milk

Ingredients:

1/2 tsp turmeric powder

1/8 tsp black pepper

1 cup warm almond milk

Instructions:

Mix turmeric and black pepper into warm almond milk.

Stir and drink before bed.

Uses: Combats oxidative stress and inflammation in sensory organs.

Storage Tips: Consume fresh.

1090. Eyebright Tea for Eye Fatigue

Ingredients:

1 tsp dried eyebright herb

1 cup boiling water

Instructions:

Steep eyebright in boiling water for 10 minutes.

Strain and drink up to twice daily.

Uses: Relieves eye strain and promotes long-term eye health.

Storage Tips: Use freshly brewed tea for best results.

1091. Omega-3 Flaxseed Supplement for Hearing

Ingredients:

1 tsp flaxseed oil

Instructions:

Take flaxseed oil daily as a supplement or add it to meals.

Uses: Reduces inflammation and supports the auditory system.

Storage Tips: Store flaxseed oil in the refrigerator.

1092. Blueberry and Kale Vision Booster Smoothie

Ingredients:

1/2 cup blueberries

1/2 cup kale leaves

1/2 cup almond milk

Instructions:

Blend all ingredients until smooth.

Drink regularly to support eye health.

Uses: Rich in antioxidants and lutein to protect vision.

Storage Tips: Prepare fresh and consume immediately.

1093. Garlic and Olive Oil Infusion for Hearing Health

Ingredients:

2 cloves garlic (crushed)

1/2 cup olive oil

Instructions:

Heat garlic and olive oil in a double boiler for 10 minutes.

Strain and use as a cooking oil or add to meals.

Uses: Improves circulation and reduces inflammation in auditory pathways.

Storage Tips: Store in the refrigerator for up to 1 month.

1094. Calendula and Rosehip Eye Compress

Ingredients:

1 tsp dried calendula flowers

1 tsp dried rosehips

1 cup boiling water

Instructions:

Steep calendula and rosehips in boiling water for 10 minutes.

Soak a clean cloth in the infusion and place over closed eyes.

Uses: Provides hydration and reduces oxidative stress in the eyes.

Storage Tips: Discard unused infusion after use.

1095. Green Tea and Lemon Hearing Support

Ingredients:

1 green tea bag

1 slice fresh lemon

1 cup boiling water

Instructions:

Steep the green tea bag in boiling water for 5 minutes.

Add lemon and drink daily.

Uses: Provides antioxidants to protect the inner ear from damage.

Storage Tips: Drink fresh each time.

Lifestyle Tips for Long-Term Vision and Hearing Health

Protect Your Eyes: Wear sunglasses to shield against UV rays and use blue light filters for screens.

Protect Your Ears: Avoid prolonged exposure to loud noises and use earplugs when needed.

Hydrate: Drink plenty of water to keep tissues in the eyes and ears hydrated.

Exercise Regularly: Improve blood circulation to sensory organs through moderate physical activity.

Limit Salt Intake: Excess salt can contribute to fluid retention, affecting hearing.

Long-term support for vision and hearing health requires a combination of herbal remedies, nutrient-rich foods, and protective habits. By incorporating these natural solutions and lifestyle adjustments into your routine, you can preserve your sensory functions and maintain quality of life as you age.

BOOK 32
AROMATHERAPY IN THE HOME APOTHECARY

Aromatherapy, the practice of using essential oils extracted from plants, is a powerful and versatile tool for enhancing physical and emotional well-being. With a wide array of applications, essential oils can be used to alleviate stress, improve focus, support relaxation, and promote emotional balance. Integrating aromatherapy into your home apothecary allows you to harness the therapeutic benefits of nature's most potent plant extracts.

This book provides a comprehensive guide to creating and using essential oil blends tailored to your specific needs. From crafting calming diffuser blends to making portable sprays and roll-ons, you'll discover how aromatherapy can enrich your daily life. Each chapter offers practical recipes and step-by-step instructions to help you confidently blend and apply essential oils.

By exploring the emotional and physical benefits of aromatherapy, you'll learn how to address common challenges like stress, fatigue, and mood imbalances. Whether you're new to essential oils or looking to expand your knowledge, this book empowers you to create a personalized, natural approach to self-care that is both effective and nurturing. Transform your home into a haven of wellness with the art and science of aromatherapy.

Blending Essential Oils for Specific Needs

Essential oils are a concentrated and versatile tool in natural healing, offering solutions for a range of physical, emotional, and mental challenges. However, their effectiveness is significantly enhanced when blended thoughtfully to target specific needs. By combining complementary oils, you can create synergies that amplify their therapeutic properties and deliver more powerful results.

Blending essential oils involves understanding the characteristics of individual oils and how they interact. Oils can be categorized into top, middle, and base notes, which not only influence the scent profile but also the therapeutic effects and longevity of the blend. For example, uplifting oils like citrus (top notes) can be paired with grounding oils like sandalwood (base notes) to create a balanced and effective blend.

This chapter explores the art of blending essential oils to address specific needs such as relaxation, focus, immunity, and mood enhancement. With these recipes, you'll gain confidence in creating personalized blends that suit your unique goals.

1096. Relaxation Blend

Ingredients:

4 drops lavender essential oil

3 drops chamomile essential oil

3 drops bergamot essential oil

Instructions:

Combine oils in a dark glass bottle.

Use in a diffuser or dilute with a carrier oil for massage.

Uses: Promotes relaxation and reduces anxiety.

1097. Focus and Concentration Blend

Ingredients:

5 drops rosemary essential oil

3 drops peppermint essential oil

2 drops lemon essential oil

Instructions:

Mix oils in a small bottle.

Add to a diffuser while working or studying.

Uses: Enhances focus and mental clarity.

1098. Immune-Boosting Blend

Ingredients:

4 drops tea tree essential oil

3 drops eucalyptus essential oil

3 drops lemon essential oil

Instructions:

Combine oils in a bottle.

Use in a diffuser or dilute with a carrier oil and apply to the chest.

Uses: Strengthens immunity and helps clear respiratory pathways.

1099. Sleep Support Blend

Ingredients:

5 drops lavender essential oil

3 drops cedarwood essential oil

2 drops vetiver essential oil

Instructions:

Mix oils in a dark bottle.

Use in a bedtime diffuser or apply to pulse points.

Uses: Encourages restful sleep and calms the mind.

1100. Energy and Uplift Blend

Ingredients:

5 drops orange essential oil

3 drops grapefruit essential oil

2 drops peppermint essential oil

Instructions:

Blend oils in a small bottle.

Use in a morning diffuser to energize your day.

Uses: Boosts energy and uplifts mood.

1101. Stress Relief Blend

Ingredients:

5 drops frankincense essential oil

3 drops lavender essential oil

2 drops ylang-ylang essential oil

Instructions:

Combine oils in a bottle.

Diffuse or dilute and apply to the temples.

Uses: Reduces stress and promotes a sense of calm.

1102. Headache Relief Blend

Ingredients:

4 drops peppermint essential oil

3 drops eucalyptus essential oil

3 drops lavender essential oil

Instructions:

Mix oils in a small container.

Apply diluted to the temples and back of the neck.

Uses: Alleviates headaches and tension.

1103. Hormonal Balance Blend

Ingredients:

5 drops clary sage essential oil

3 drops geranium essential oil

2 drops ylang-ylang essential oil

Instructions:

Combine oils in a bottle.

Diffuse or apply diluted to pulse points.

Uses: Supports hormonal balance and emotional stability.

1104. Respiratory Support Blend

Ingredients:

5 drops eucalyptus essential oil

3 drops peppermint essential oil

2 drops tea tree essential oil

Instructions:

Mix oils in a small bottle.

Use in a diffuser or dilute and apply to the chest.

Uses: Clears airways and soothes breathing.

1105. Mood Enhancer Blend

Ingredients:

5 drops bergamot essential oil

3 drops lemon essential oil

2 drops rose essential oil

Instructions:

Blend oils in a dark glass container.

Use in a diffuser or dilute for a roll-on.

Uses: Uplifts mood and creates a positive atmosphere.

Blending essential oils allows you to create customized remedies for a wide range of needs. By understanding how different oils complement one another, you can craft powerful, effective blends tailored to your lifestyle and goals. These recipes are a starting point for exploring the incredible versatility of essential oils, making them a valuable addition to your home apothecary. Always store your blends properly and follow dilution guidelines for safe use.

Creating Diffuser Blends for Relaxation and Focus

Aromatherapy through diffusers is one of the most effective and effortless ways to create a calming or invigorating environment. Essential oils, when diffused, release aromatic compounds into the air, promoting relaxation, focus, or energy depending on the blend. Whether you want to unwind after a stressful day or stay sharp during a challenging task, diffuser blends tailored to your specific needs can transform your space into a haven of tranquility or productivity.

Relaxation blends often include oils like lavender, chamomile, and ylang-ylang, known for their soothing and sedative properties. In contrast, focus blends use uplifting and stimulating oils like rosemary, lemon, and peppermint to boost alertness and mental clarity. By combining complementary oils, you can create customized diffuser recipes that address your mood and goals.

This chapter provides 10 easy-to-make diffuser blends for relaxation and focus. These recipes will help you harness the power of aromatherapy to create the perfect ambiance for unwinding or concentrating.

1106. Calm Retreat Blend

Ingredients:

4 drops lavender essential oil

3 drops cedarwood essential oil

2 drops ylang-ylang essential oil

Instructions:

Add oils to your diffuser with the recommended amount of water.

Turn on and enjoy the calming aroma.

Uses: Creates a relaxing atmosphere to unwind after a stressful day.

1107. Serenity in Bloom Blend

Ingredients:

5 drops chamomile essential oil

3 drops rose essential oil

2 drops bergamot essential oil

Instructions:

Mix oils in the diffuser.

Use during meditation or before bedtime.

Uses: Promotes emotional balance and deep relaxation.

1108. Tranquil Escape Blend

Ingredients:

4 drops sandalwood essential oil

3 drops frankincense essential oil

2 drops orange essential oil

Instructions:

Combine oils in the diffuser with water.

Turn on to create a serene ambiance.

Uses: Encourages relaxation and eases mental tension.

1109. Focused Energy Blend

Ingredients:

5 drops rosemary essential oil

3 drops peppermint essential oil

2 drops lemon essential oil

Instructions:

Add oils to the diffuser.

Diffuse while working or studying.

Uses: Enhances concentration and mental clarity.

1110. Citrus Spark Blend

Ingredients:

4 drops grapefruit essential oil

3 drops lime essential oil

3 drops basil essential oil

Instructions:

Combine oils in your diffuser with water.

Use in the morning for an energizing boost.

Uses: Uplifts mood and sharpens focus.

1111. Evening Calm Blend

Ingredients:

5 drops lavender essential oil

3 drops patchouli essential oil

2 drops clary sage essential oil

Instructions:

Add oils to the diffuser.

Turn on during your evening routine for relaxation.

Uses: Prepares the mind and body for restful sleep.

1112. Clear Mind Blend

Ingredients:

4 drops eucalyptus essential oil

3 drops peppermint essential oil

2 drops tea tree essential oil

Instructions:

Mix oils in the diffuser with water.

Use when mental clarity is needed.

Uses: Clears mental fog and invigorates the senses.

1113. Happy Heart Blend

Ingredients:

4 drops orange essential oil

3 drops lavender essential oil

2 drops geranium essential oil

Instructions:

Add oils to the diffuser.

Diffuse to create a joyful and comforting atmosphere.

Uses: Promotes positivity and emotional balance.

1114. Productive Focus Blend

Ingredients:

5 drops lemon essential oil

3 drops rosemary essential oil

2 drops thyme essential oil

Instructions:

Combine oils in the diffuser with water.

Use during work sessions for enhanced productivity.

Uses: Sharpens focus and improves mental alertness.

1115. Zen Garden Blend

Ingredients:

4 drops lavender essential oil

3 drops sandalwood essential oil

2 drops bergamot essential oil

Instructions:

Mix oils in your diffuser.

Diffuse while meditating or practicing yoga.

Uses: Creates a peaceful and grounding environment.

Tips for Using Diffuser Blends

Follow Diffuser Guidelines: Always add the recommended amount of water for your diffuser to ensure proper operation.

Clean Your Diffuser: Regularly clean your diffuser to prevent residue buildup and maintain the integrity of your blends.

Test New Blends: Start with fewer drops to test the strength of a new blend and adjust as needed.

Choose the Right Environment: Diffuse relaxation blends in the evening or during meditation and focus blends in your workspace.

Diffuser blends are a simple yet powerful way to use aromatherapy for relaxation and focus. By combining the right essential oils, you can create personalized aromas that transform your environment and enhance your mood. Experiment with these recipes and make adjustments to find the perfect blends that suit your lifestyle and needs. Whether you're seeking calm or concentration, aromatherapy can help you achieve your goals naturally.

DIY Sprays and Roll-Ons for On-the-Go Use

Aromatherapy is a versatile tool for maintaining well-being, even when you're on the move. Portable solutions like sprays and roll-ons allow you to access the benefits of essential oils anytime and anywhere. Whether you need a quick mood boost, a calming remedy, or an energizing pick-me-up, these DIY creations can be customized to suit your specific needs.

Sprays are ideal for freshening up your space, relieving stress, or promoting focus. They can be used as room sprays, pillow mists, or personal scents. Roll-ons, on the other hand, provide targeted application, allowing you to apply essential oils directly to pulse points for fast and effective results. Both options are easy to make and store, making them perfect for on-the-go use.

This chapter provides step-by-step recipes for crafting 10 sprays and roll-ons tailored for relaxation, focus, stress relief, and more. With these simple yet effective solutions, you can carry the power of aromatherapy with you wherever you go.

1116. Calming Lavender Spray

Ingredients:

10 drops lavender essential oil

2 tbsp witch hazel

1/2 cup distilled water

Instructions:

Combine all ingredients in a small spray bottle.

Shake well before each use.

Uses: Spritz on pillows or in the air for a calming effect.

Storage Tips: Store in a cool, dark place for up to 3 months.

1117. Energizing Citrus Spray

Ingredients:

8 drops orange essential oil

4 drops grapefruit essential oil

2 tbsp witch hazel

1/2 cup distilled water

Instructions:

Mix ingredients in a spray bottle.

Shake well and spray around your workspace for an energy boost.

Uses: Refreshes the air and lifts your mood.

Storage Tips: Keep in a sealed container for up to 2 months.

1118. Stress-Relief Roll-On

Ingredients:

5 drops frankincense essential oil

4 drops bergamot essential oil

2 drops lavender essential oil

10 mL carrier oil (e.g., jojoba oil)

Instructions:

Combine oils in a roll-on bottle.

Roll onto pulse points during stressful moments.

Uses: Promotes relaxation and reduces anxiety.

Storage Tips: Store in a cool, dark place for up to 6 months.

1119. Focus Booster Spray

Ingredients:

6 drops rosemary essential oil

4 drops peppermint essential oil

2 tbsp witch hazel

1/2 cup distilled water

Instructions:

Add all ingredients to a spray bottle.

Shake well and spritz in your workspace for mental clarity.

Uses: Enhances concentration and focus.

Storage Tips: Use within 3 months for best results.

1120. Sleep Support Roll-On

Ingredients:

5 drops cedarwood essential oil

5 drops lavender essential oil

10 mL carrier oil

Instructions:

Combine oils in a roll-on bottle.

Apply to wrists and temples before bedtime.

Uses: Promotes restful sleep and relaxation.

Storage Tips: Store in a cool, dark place for up to 6 months.

1121. Mood Uplift Spray

Ingredients:

5 drops lemon essential oil

5 drops geranium essential oil

2 tbsp witch hazel

1/2 cup distilled water

Instructions:

Mix ingredients in a spray bottle.

Spritz in the air for an instant mood lift.

Uses: Brightens your environment and uplifts your spirits.

Storage Tips: Keep in a sealed container for up to 3 months.

1122. Refreshing Roll-On for Headaches

Ingredients:

5 drops peppermint essential oil

3 drops eucalyptus essential oil

2 drops lavender essential oil

10 mL carrier oil

Instructions:

Add oils to a roll-on bottle.

Apply to temples and the back of your neck for headache relief.

Uses: Provides cooling relief and soothes tension headaches.

Storage Tips: Store away from direct sunlight for up to 6 months.

1123. Clean Air Spray

Ingredients:

6 drops tea tree essential oil

4 drops eucalyptus essential oil

2 tbsp witch hazel

1/2 cup distilled water

Instructions:

Combine all ingredients in a spray bottle.

Spray in rooms to purify the air.

Uses: Eliminates odors and cleanses the air.

Storage Tips: Use within 3 months for maximum effectiveness.

1124. Confidence Boost Roll-On

Ingredients:

6 drops bergamot essential oil

4 drops sandalwood essential oil

10 mL carrier oil

Instructions:

Mix oils in a roll-on bottle.

Apply to wrists and behind ears for a confidence boost.

Uses: Enhances self-assurance and emotional balance.

Storage Tips: Store in a dark place for up to 6 months.

1125. Seasonal Support Spray

Ingredients:

5 drops lavender essential oil

4 drops lemon essential oil

3 drops peppermint essential oil

2 tbsp witch hazel

1/2 cup distilled water

Instructions:

Add all ingredients to a spray bottle.

Shake and spray in your home to combat seasonal allergies.

Uses: Soothes respiratory irritation and refreshes your space.

Storage Tips: Store in a cool place for up to 3 months.

DIY sprays and roll-ons make it easy to enjoy the benefits of aromatherapy wherever you go. With these simple recipes, you can create personalized solutions for relaxation, focus, and emotional well-being. Portable, customizable, and effective, these remedies empower you to incorporate natural healing into your daily life. Always store your creations properly and enjoy the uplifting power of essential oils.

Using Aromatherapy for Emotional Balance

Emotional balance is an essential aspect of overall well-being, influencing how we respond to stress, build relationships, and manage daily challenges. Aromatherapy, the practice of using essential oils to support physical and emotional health, offers a natural and effective way to restore emotional harmony. Through their potent scents and therapeutic properties, essential oils can help reduce stress, uplift mood, and create a sense of calm or empowerment.

Essential oils work by interacting with the limbic system, the brain's emotional center. When you inhale the aroma of an essential oil, it stimulates neural pathways that influence emotions and memory. This makes aromatherapy a powerful tool for addressing anxiety, sadness, anger, and other emotional imbalances. By selecting oils with specific properties, you can tailor your aromatherapy practice to meet your unique emotional needs.

In this chapter, we will explore how to use aromatherapy for emotional balance. You'll learn about the best essential oils for managing emotions, practical ways to incorporate them into your daily routine, and tips for creating customized blends to support mental and emotional well-being.

The Best Essential Oils for Emotional Balance

Lavender: Known for its calming properties, lavender is excellent for reducing stress, promoting relaxation, and alleviating anxiety.

Bergamot: With its bright and uplifting aroma, bergamot is ideal for improving mood and easing feelings of sadness.

Ylang-Ylang: This sweet, floral oil helps soothe anger and frustration while promoting a sense of joy and peace.

Frankincense: A grounding oil that supports mindfulness and emotional clarity, often used during meditation.

Rose: A comforting and heart-opening oil that helps alleviate feelings of grief and sadness.

Peppermint: Provides mental clarity and energy, helping to combat fatigue and overwhelm.

Chamomile: Known for its soothing properties, chamomile is excellent for calming irritability and restlessness.

Incorporating Aromatherapy into Your Routine

1. Diffusion for Environmental Balance

Using a diffuser is one of the simplest ways to incorporate aromatherapy into your routine. Diffusing essential oils can create a calming or uplifting atmosphere, depending on the blend you choose. For example:

Relaxation Blend: Combine lavender, chamomile, and ylang-ylang.

Energizing Blend: Use peppermint, bergamot, and lemon.

2. Personal Inhalers for On-the-Go Support

A personal inhaler is a small, portable device that allows you to carry the benefits of aromatherapy wherever you go. Add a few drops of your chosen oils to the inhaler wick and inhale deeply whenever you need emotional support.

3. Bath Soaks for Emotional Reset

Adding essential oils to a warm bath is a luxurious way to unwind and regain balance. Use oils like lavender or rose for relaxation, or peppermint and eucalyptus for an energizing soak. Always dilute essential oils in a carrier oil before adding them to the bath to prevent skin irritation.

4. Massage for Emotional Healing

Aromatherapy massages combine the therapeutic benefits of essential oils with the calming effects of touch. Create a massage blend by adding essential oils to a carrier oil like jojoba or almond oil. Use gentle strokes to apply the blend to areas like the neck, shoulders, and temples.

Customized Blends for Emotional Balance

Calm and Relaxation Blend

5 drops lavender essential oil

3 drops ylang-ylang essential oil

2 drops frankincense essential oil

Instructions: Use in a diffuser, add to a bath, or dilute with a carrier oil for massage.

Uplifting Mood Blend

4 drops bergamot essential oil

3 drops orange essential oil

2 drops rose essential oil

Instructions: Diffuse in the morning to start your day with positivity or carry in a personal inhaler.

Stress Relief Blend

5 drops chamomile essential oil

4 drops lavender essential oil

3 drops sandalwood essential oil

Instructions: Apply diluted to pulse points or diffuse in your workspace.

Energy and Focus Blend

4 drops peppermint essential oil

3 drops rosemary essential oil

2 drops lemon essential oil

Instructions: Use in a diffuser or a roll-on for quick focus and clarity.

Emotional Grounding Blend

4 drops frankincense essential oil

3 drops cedarwood essential oil

3 drops patchouli essential oil

Instructions: Use during meditation or yoga for mindfulness and grounding.

Aromatherapy and Mindfulness

Aromatherapy pairs beautifully with mindfulness practices like meditation, yoga, or journaling. Incorporating essential oils into these activities can deepen your connection to the present moment and enhance their emotional benefits. For example:

Meditation: Diffuse frankincense or sandalwood to create a calming environment.

Yoga: Apply an uplifting blend like bergamot and peppermint to your wrists or mat.

Journaling: Use grounding oils like cedarwood and patchouli to help you process emotions and gain clarity.

Safety Tips for Emotional Aromatherapy

Dilute Properly: Always dilute essential oils with a carrier oil for topical application to prevent irritation.

Patch Test: Test new oils on a small area of skin to check for sensitivities.

Avoid Overuse: Use essential oils in moderation to avoid overstimulation.

Consult a Professional: If you're pregnant, nursing, or have medical conditions, consult an aromatherapist or healthcare provider before using essential oils.

Case Studies: Success Stories with Aromatherapy

Case 1: Overcoming Anxiety with Lavender

Sophia, a busy professional, struggled with work-related anxiety. She began diffusing lavender essential oil in her office and using a lavender roll-on during stressful meetings. Over time, she reported feeling more relaxed and better equipped to handle her workload.

Case 2: Managing Sadness with Rose Oil

After experiencing a personal loss, David found comfort in rose essential oil. He added it to his bath and used it in a diffuser during quiet moments. The nurturing aroma helped him process his grief and find emotional strength.

Aromatherapy offers a gentle and effective way to achieve emotional balance. By using essential oils thoughtfully, you can address stress, enhance your mood, and create a sense of harmony in your daily life. With the recipes, techniques, and safety tips provided in this chapter, you're equipped to make aromatherapy a powerful tool in your journey toward emotional wellness. Take time to experiment with different blends and methods, and discover how this natural practice can support your unique emotional needs.

BOOK 33

BUILDING HERBAL RITUALS FOR MINDFULNESS

Mindfulness, the practice of being present and fully engaged in the moment, can be significantly enhanced by incorporating herbs into daily rituals. Herbs have long been used to support mental clarity, emotional balance, and spiritual connection, making them a perfect complement to mindfulness practices. Whether through soothing teas, aromatic baths, or meditative ceremonies, herbs can help create meaningful rituals that ground, calm, and inspire.

This book explores the powerful synergy between herbal remedies and mindfulness. You'll learn how to integrate herbs into meditation practices, craft reflective tea ceremonies, and use herbal baths to promote mental clarity. Additionally, you'll discover herbs that can enhance spiritual practices by fostering a deeper connection to yourself and your surroundings.

Each chapter offers practical recipes, guidance, and insights to help you build personalized rituals that align with your goals. Whether you're seeking tranquility, focus, or spiritual growth, these herbal rituals provide a natural and effective way to cultivate mindfulness in your daily life. Let this book guide you in creating a nurturing and intentional practice that promotes well-being, balance, and inner peace.

Incorporating Herbs into Daily Meditation

Meditation is a powerful practice for calming the mind, cultivating awareness, and fostering inner peace. Incorporating herbs into your daily meditation routine can deepen this experience by enhancing focus, grounding energy, and encouraging relaxation. Herbs have long been revered for their ability to support mental clarity, emotional balance, and spiritual connection, making them a perfect complement to mindfulness practices.

When used intentionally, herbs can create a sensory environment that supports meditation. They can be brewed into teas, diffused as essential oils, or burned as incense to create an atmosphere conducive to stillness and contemplation. From calming chamomile to uplifting rosemary, each herb offers unique properties that can align with your meditative goals.

This chapter explores practical ways to integrate herbs into your meditation practice, offering techniques and recipes to help you establish rituals that promote mindfulness and well-being. Whether you're seeking to enhance your focus, calm anxiety, or connect with deeper spiritual energies, these herbal tools can enrich your meditation experience and bring a sense of harmony to your day.

The Role of Herbs in Meditation

Herbs have been used for centuries to support meditative and spiritual practices. Their properties can influence the body and mind in various ways:

Calming Herbs: Chamomile, lavender, and lemon balm help reduce stress and quiet the mind, making them ideal for relaxation-focused meditation.

Grounding Herbs: Frankincense, sandalwood, and vetiver provide stability and balance, aiding in deep, grounding meditative states.

Uplifting Herbs: Rosemary, peppermint, and citrus oils enhance alertness and mental clarity, helping you stay focused and present during your practice.

Techniques for Incorporating Herbs

1. Herbal Teas for Pre-Meditation

Drinking herbal tea before meditation is a simple yet effective way to prepare the mind and body. The warmth of the tea soothes the senses, while the herbal properties create the desired mental state.

Relaxation Tea: Brew chamomile, lemon balm, and lavender for a calming effect.

Focus Tea: Combine rosemary, peppermint, and green tea to enhance clarity.

Grounding Tea: Use ginger, cinnamon, and ashwagandha to promote stability.

Recipe Example:

1 tsp dried chamomile

1 tsp dried lemon balm

1 cup boiling water Steep for 5–10 minutes, strain, and enjoy before your session.

2. Aromatherapy for Meditation Spaces

Diffusing essential oils in your meditation space can create an atmosphere of tranquility and focus. Aromatherapy engages the limbic system, influencing emotions and enhancing your practice.

Use calming oils like lavender or frankincense to reduce tension.

Try uplifting oils like orange or bergamot for energizing morning meditations.

Diffuse grounding oils like sandalwood or vetiver for deep introspection.

Diffuser Blend Example:

4 drops lavender essential oil

2 drops frankincense essential oil

2 drops bergamot essential oil

3. Herbal Incense and Smudging

Burning herbs or incense is a traditional practice in many cultures for cleansing energy and setting a meditative tone. Common herbs used include sage, palo santo, and cedar.

Smudging: Light a bundle of sage or palo santo, let it smolder, and waft the smoke around your meditation space.

Incense: Burn sticks of sandalwood, myrrh, or frankincense to create a calming aroma.

4. Herbal Cushions and Eye Pillows

Infused meditation cushions or eye pillows can provide a sensory experience that enhances relaxation. These can be filled with dried herbs like lavender, chamomile, or rose petals.

DIY Lavender Eye Pillow: Fill a fabric pouch with dried lavender and flaxseed. Place it over your eyes during meditation to calm the mind.

Herbs for Specific Meditative Goals

1. Enhancing Focus

Focus is essential for maintaining a meditative state, especially during challenging sessions. Herbs that stimulate the mind without overstimulating the body are ideal.

Rosemary: Improves memory and concentration.

Peppermint: Increases alertness and mental clarity.

Gotu Kola: Traditionally used in Ayurvedic practices for mental clarity.

2. Promoting Relaxation

For those seeking stress relief or deep relaxation, calming herbs help quiet the mind and ease tension.

Chamomile: Reduces stress and encourages calmness.

Lavender: Eases anxiety and promotes a sense of peace.

Valerian Root: A natural sedative for deep relaxation.

3. Grounding Energy

Grounding herbs help stabilize emotions and anchor your focus, making them perfect for centering meditations.

Vetiver: Known as the "oil of tranquility."

Sandalwood: Creates a deep sense of connection and peace.

Ashwagandha: A grounding adaptogen that reduces stress.

4. Spiritual Connection

Herbs that enhance spiritual awareness can deepen meditative practices focused on intuition and mindfulness.

Frankincense: Supports spiritual insight and connection.

Mugwort: Traditionally used for dream work and intuition.

Tulsi (Holy Basil): Revered in Ayurvedic traditions for its ability to harmonize the mind and spirit.

Creating a Daily Herbal Meditation Ritual

Consistency is key to building a meditation practice. Adding herbal rituals can make your routine more intentional and enjoyable:

Prepare Your Space: Cleanse your space with smudging or incense.

Set Your Intention: Choose an herb or blend based on your meditative goal (e.g., relaxation, focus).

Engage the Senses: Brew a tea, diffuse an oil, or light an herbal incense to create a sensory experience.

Begin Your Practice: Sit comfortably, breathe deeply, and focus on the herb's aroma or taste as a grounding anchor.

Tips for Safely Using Herbs in Meditation

Choose High-Quality Herbs: Use organic, pesticide-free herbs and essential oils to ensure purity.

Test for Sensitivities: Patch-test essential oils and avoid ingesting herbs you're unfamiliar with.

Start Small: Introduce one herb at a time to understand its effects.

Avoid Overuse: Rotate herbs to prevent over-stimulation or desensitization.

Case Study: How Herbs Enhanced a Meditation Journey

Sara, a graphic designer, struggled with staying focused during her meditation sessions. After learning about rosemary's focus-enhancing properties, she began diffusing rosemary essential oil in her meditation space. She also incorporated a tea blend of rosemary and peppermint before her practice. Over time, Sara noticed improved concentration and a deeper sense of presence in her meditations.

Incorporating herbs into daily meditation is a simple yet transformative practice. Herbs can deepen your connection to the present moment, enhance your focus, and create a sensory-rich environment that supports mindfulness. Whether you sip on calming teas, diffuse uplifting oils, or use grounding incense, these natural tools bring balance and intention to your meditation journey. Explore these practices and create your own herbal rituals to nourish your mind, body, and spirit.

Crafting Tea Ceremonies for Reflection

Tea ceremonies are an ancient practice rooted in mindfulness, reflection, and the art of being present. By intentionally preparing and enjoying tea, you can create a ritual that fosters inner peace and clarity. When paired with herbs that support relaxation, focus, and spiritual connection, tea ceremonies become a powerful tool for self-care and reflection.

Crafting a tea ceremony is more than simply brewing tea; it's about embracing the process, from selecting herbs to savoring each sip. This ritual encourages you to slow down, center yourself, and engage your senses. Whether you're seeking calmness, mental clarity, or an opportunity to connect with your thoughts, the right herbal blends can elevate your tea ceremony experience.

This chapter provides practical guidance and 10 herbal tea recipes to inspire your reflective tea rituals. These blends are designed to support various goals, such as relaxation, grounding, and emotional balance.

1126. Serenity Blend

Ingredients:

1 tsp dried chamomile

1 tsp dried lavender

1 cup boiling water

Instructions:

Combine chamomile and lavender in a teapot.

Pour boiling water over the herbs and steep for 10 minutes.

Strain and enjoy slowly.

Uses: Promotes relaxation and calms the mind.

Storage Tips: Store dried herbs in an airtight container for up to 1 year.

1127. Clarity Tea

Ingredients:

1 tsp dried rosemary

1 tsp dried peppermint

1 cup boiling water

Instructions:

Steep rosemary and peppermint in boiling water for 7 minutes.

Strain and sip while journaling or reflecting.

Uses: Enhances focus and clears mental fog.

Storage Tips: Keep herbs in a cool, dry place.

1128. Emotional Balance Tea

Ingredients:

1 tsp dried rose petals

1 tsp dried lemon balm

1 cup boiling water

Instructions:

Combine rose petals and lemon balm in a mug.

Add boiling water and steep for 8–10 minutes.

Strain and savor each sip.

Uses: Uplifts the spirit and balances emotions.

Storage Tips: Store dried rose petals in a sealed container away from sunlight.

1129. Grounding Herbal Tea

Ingredients:

1 tsp dried ginger slices

1 tsp dried turmeric

1 cup boiling water

Instructions:

Add ginger and turmeric to boiling water.

Simmer for 5 minutes, then strain.

Sip slowly, focusing on your breath.

Uses: Grounds energy and supports mindfulness.

Storage Tips: Keep dried ginger and turmeric in an airtight jar.

1130. Dreamer's Blend

Ingredients:

1 tsp dried mugwort

1 tsp dried chamomile

1 cup boiling water

Instructions:

Steep mugwort and chamomile in boiling water for 8 minutes.

Strain and enjoy in the evening.

Uses: Encourages vivid dreams and introspection.

Storage Tips: Store mugwort in a sealed container.

1131. Spiritual Connection Tea

Ingredients:

1 tsp dried holy basil (tulsi)

1 tsp dried spearmint

1 cup boiling water

Instructions:

Combine holy basil and spearmint in a teapot.

Steep in boiling water for 10 minutes.

Strain and drink during meditation.

Uses: Enhances spiritual awareness and focus.

Storage Tips: Keep tulsi leaves in a dark, cool place.

1132. Calming Citrus Tea

Ingredients:

1 tsp dried orange peel

1 tsp dried lemon balm

1 cup boiling water

Instructions:

Add orange peel and lemon balm to a teapot.

Steep in boiling water for 8 minutes.

Strain and enjoy warm.

Uses: Relieves stress and boosts mood.

Storage Tips: Store orange peel in an airtight container.

1133. Heart-Opening Blend

Ingredients:

1 tsp dried hibiscus flowers

1 tsp dried rose petals

1 cup boiling water

Instructions:

Steep hibiscus and rose petals in boiling water for 10 minutes.

Strain and sip while practicing gratitude.

Uses: Encourages emotional openness and self-love.

Storage Tips: Keep hibiscus in a cool, dry place.

1134. Energy and Focus Tea

Ingredients:

1 tsp dried green tea leaves

1 tsp dried lemon verbena

1 cup boiling water

Instructions:

Combine green tea and lemon verbena in a mug.

Add boiling water and steep for 5 minutes.

Strain and enjoy during morning reflection.

Uses: Boosts energy and enhances mental clarity.

Storage Tips: Store green tea in a sealed pouch.

1135. Introspective Tea

Ingredients:

1 tsp dried valerian root

1 tsp dried lavender

1 cup boiling water

Instructions:

Add valerian root and lavender to a teapot.

Steep in boiling water for 10 minutes.

Strain and drink before journaling or meditating.

Uses: Calms the mind and promotes deep reflection.

Storage Tips: Keep valerian root in an airtight container.

How to Conduct a Tea Ceremony for Reflection

Prepare Your Space: Choose a quiet, comfortable area. Light a candle or incense to set the mood.

Select Your Herbs: Choose a tea blend that aligns with your intention for reflection.

Brew with Intention: As you prepare the tea, focus on your intention. Infuse the process with mindfulness.

Savor Each Sip: Drink slowly, engaging your senses. Focus on the aroma, taste, and warmth of the tea.

Reflect: Use this time to journal, meditate, or simply sit in stillness and connect with your thoughts.

Tea ceremonies offer a beautiful way to incorporate mindfulness and reflection into your daily routine. By crafting herbal blends and engaging in intentional rituals, you can create a sacred space for self-discovery, emotional balance, and spiritual growth. These recipes and practices are tools to help you slow down, focus inward, and embrace the present moment.

Using Herbal Baths for Mental Clarity

Herbal baths are an age-old practice that combines the therapeutic properties of herbs with the soothing effects of warm water. These baths go beyond physical relaxation, offering a space for mental clarity, stress relief, and emotional renewal. By immersing yourself in a thoughtfully prepared herbal bath, you can calm a cluttered mind, enhance focus, and reconnect with your inner self.

The warmth of the bath opens your pores, allowing the beneficial compounds in herbs to penetrate the skin and deliver their therapeutic properties. Aromatic herbs, such as rosemary, peppermint, and lavender, release calming scents that engage the limbic system, promoting mental clarity and emotional balance. Meanwhile, adaptogenic and grounding herbs like ashwagandha or chamomile work to reduce stress and improve cognitive focus.

In this chapter, we'll explore the art of crafting herbal baths to boost mental clarity. You'll find 10 easy-to-make recipes that cater to different needs, along with tips on how to enhance your bathing experience for maximum benefit.

1136. Rosemary and Peppermint Energizing Bath

Ingredients:

1/4 cup dried rosemary

1/4 cup dried peppermint

2 tbsp Epsom salt

Instructions:

Add rosemary and peppermint to a muslin bag or cheesecloth.

Tie the bag securely and place it in your bathtub.

Fill the tub with warm water and dissolve the Epsom salt.

Uses: Revitalizes the mind and enhances focus.

Storage Tips: Store dried herbs in an airtight container.

1137. Lavender and Chamomile Relaxation Bath

Ingredients:

1/4 cup dried lavender flowers

1/4 cup dried chamomile flowers

1 tbsp coconut oil

Instructions:

Combine lavender and chamomile in a muslin bag.

Add the bag and coconut oil to a warm bath.

Soak for 20–30 minutes.

Uses: Reduces mental fatigue and promotes calmness.

Storage Tips: Keep herbs in a cool, dry place.

1138. Basil and Lemon Refreshing Bath

Ingredients:

1/4 cup dried basil leaves

1 sliced lemon

2 tbsp sea salt

Instructions:

Add basil leaves and lemon slices to a muslin bag.

Place the bag in warm bathwater and add sea salt.

Uses: Clears mental fog and uplifts mood.

Storage Tips: Use fresh lemon slices for each bath.

1139. Eucalyptus and Sage Clearing Bath

Ingredients:

1/4 cup dried eucalyptus leaves

1/4 cup dried sage leaves

2 tbsp baking soda

Instructions:

Combine eucalyptus and sage in a muslin bag.

Add the bag and baking soda to warm bathwater.

Uses: Clears the mind and relieves tension.

Storage Tips: Store herbs in a sealed container.

1140. Mint and Ginger Invigorating Bath

Ingredients:

1/4 cup dried mint leaves

2 tbsp grated fresh ginger

Instructions:

Place mint leaves and ginger in a muslin bag.

Add the bag to warm bathwater and stir.

Uses: Boosts circulation and sharpens mental clarity.

Storage Tips: Use fresh ginger for maximum potency.

1141. Rose and Holy Basil Serenity Bath

Ingredients:

1/4 cup dried rose petals

1/4 cup dried holy basil leaves

2 tbsp Himalayan pink salt

Instructions:

Add rose petals and holy basil to a muslin bag.

Place the bag in your bath and dissolve the pink salt.

Uses: Balances emotions and fosters peace of mind.

Storage Tips: Store dried rose petals in a cool, dark place.

1142. Lemongrass and Green Tea Detox Bath

Ingredients:

1/4 cup dried lemongrass

2 green tea bags

2 tbsp apple cider vinegar

Instructions:

Add lemongrass and green tea bags to a muslin bag.

Place the bag in warm bathwater and stir in apple cider vinegar.

Uses: Detoxifies the body and refreshes the mind.

Storage Tips: Replace green tea bags with fresh ones each time.

1143. Calendula and Oatmeal Soothing Bath

Ingredients:

1/4 cup dried calendula flowers

1/4 cup oatmeal

1 tbsp jojoba oil

Instructions:

Combine calendula and oatmeal in a muslin bag.

Add the bag and jojoba oil to warm bathwater.

Uses: Relieves stress and nourishes the skin.

Storage Tips: Store oatmeal in a sealed container to avoid moisture.

1144. Pine and Cedarwood Grounding Bath

Ingredients:

1/4 cup dried pine needles

1/4 cup cedarwood chips

2 tbsp Epsom salt

Instructions:

Add pine needles and cedarwood to a muslin bag.

Place the bag in warm bathwater and dissolve Epsom salt.

Uses: Grounds energy and promotes mental focus.

Storage Tips: Keep dried pine needles in an airtight jar.

1145. Orange Peel and Cinnamon Comfort Bath

Ingredients:

1/4 cup dried orange peel

1 cinnamon stick

2 tbsp honey

Instructions:

Add orange peel and cinnamon to a muslin bag.

Place the bag in warm bathwater and stir in honey.

Uses: Uplifts mood and soothes the senses.

Storage Tips: Store orange peel in a dry, sealed container.

Enhancing the Bathing Experience

Set the Mood: Dim the lights, light candles, or play calming music to create a tranquil environment.

Mindful Soaking: Focus on your breathing and the scents around you to deepen relaxation.

Post-Bath Ritual: Journal or meditate after your bath to capture insights and mental clarity.

Herbal baths are more than a way to relax; they are a pathway to mental clarity and emotional balance. By thoughtfully selecting herbs and creating an intentional environment, you can transform a simple bath into a rejuvenating ritual. Explore these recipes and adapt them to your needs, making herbal baths a regular practice in your self-care routine.

Herbs to Enhance Spiritual Practices

Herbs have been intertwined with spiritual practices across cultures for centuries. From burning sacred herbs during rituals to using herbal teas for meditation, these plants serve as powerful tools to enhance spiritual experiences. Whether you seek clarity, grounding, or connection to higher energies, herbs can elevate your spiritual journey by creating an atmosphere of mindfulness, healing, and transcendence.

The natural properties of herbs like sage, frankincense, and mugwort can help open the mind, calm the spirit, and establish a deeper connection to your inner self and the world around you. Herbs may be incorporated into your practices through smudging, teas, baths, anointing oils, or simply as companions in sacred spaces. They act as bridges between the physical and spiritual realms, offering guidance, protection, and inspiration.

This chapter delves into how herbs can support spiritual practices, with practical ways to incorporate them into rituals and ceremonies. You'll also find a selection of herbal recipes and rituals to deepen your spiritual connection and bring balance to your mind, body, and soul.

How Herbs Support Spiritual Practices

Herbs can enhance spiritual practices by influencing the body, mind, and environment. Here's how they play a role in spiritual enhancement:

Cleansing and Protection: Sage, palo santo, and cedar are commonly used for smudging, helping to cleanse negative energies and create a sacred space.

Grounding and Centering: Herbs like vetiver, sandalwood, and patchouli bring grounding energy, anchoring you to the present moment.

Enhancing Intuition: Mugwort and bay leaf are known for stimulating intuition, dreams, and inner wisdom.

Promoting Tranquility: Chamomile, lavender, and holy basil calm the mind, preparing it for meditation or prayer.

Herbal Methods for Spiritual Enhancement

1. Smudging and Incense

Burning herbs is a traditional way to purify spaces, enhance focus, and set a sacred tone for rituals.

How to Smudge: Light the end of a sage bundle or palo santo stick. Allow it to smolder, and waft the smoke around yourself or your space with intention.

Incense for Focus: Burn frankincense, sandalwood, or myrrh during meditation to deepen concentration.

2. Herbal Teas for Inner Connection

Sipping herbal tea before or during spiritual practices can help center your mind and prepare your body for stillness or reflection.

Example Tea: Brew a blend of chamomile, rose petals, and lavender to calm the mind and open the heart.

3. Sacred Baths

Herbal baths cleanse the body and spirit, removing negativity and creating a state of balance. Add herbs like calendula, rosemary, or mugwort to your bathwater to amplify spiritual energy.

4. Herbal Anointing Oils

Create anointing oils by infusing herbs in a carrier oil, such as jojoba or olive oil. Use these oils to bless yourself, candles, or objects in your rituals.

Example Blend: Infuse frankincense, myrrh, and cinnamon in olive oil for a grounding and protective anointing oil.

5. Sacred Spaces with Herbs

Place dried herbs like lavender, rosemary, or sage in your meditation or prayer area. Their presence can create a calming, spiritually charged environment.

1146. Sage and Lavender Smudge Stick

Ingredients:

5 sprigs dried sage

3 sprigs dried lavender

Instructions:

Bundle the sage and lavender together tightly with twine.

Allow to dry completely for 1–2 weeks.

Light the bundle and let it smolder, wafting the smoke in your space.

Uses: Cleanses negativity and promotes peace.

1147. Mugwort Dream Tea

Ingredients:

1 tsp dried mugwort

1 tsp dried chamomile

1 cup boiling water

Instructions:

Combine mugwort and chamomile in a teapot.

Steep in boiling water for 10 minutes.

Strain and drink before bedtime.

Uses: Enhances dreams and intuition.

1148. Holy Basil Meditation Oil

Ingredients:

2 tbsp dried holy basil

1/4 cup olive oil

Instructions:

Gently heat the olive oil and holy basil in a double boiler for 1 hour.

Strain and store in a dark glass bottle.

Apply to pulse points before meditation.

Uses: Promotes focus and spiritual connection.

1149. Frankincense and Myrrh Incense

Ingredients:

1 tsp frankincense resin

1 tsp myrrh resin

Instructions:

Place the resins on a charcoal disk in an incense burner.

Light the charcoal and allow the resins to smolder.

Uses: Creates a sacred atmosphere and enhances prayer.

1150. Lavender and Rose Heart-Opening Tea

Ingredients:

1 tsp dried lavender

1 tsp dried rose petals

1 cup boiling water

Instructions:

Steep lavender and rose petals in boiling water for 8–10 minutes.

Strain and sip slowly.

Uses: Opens the heart and fosters emotional connection.

1151. Rosemary and Bay Leaf Protection Spray

Ingredients:

1 tsp dried rosemary

1 bay leaf

1 cup distilled water

Instructions:

Boil rosemary and bay leaf in water for 10 minutes.

Strain and pour into a spray bottle.

Use to cleanse and protect your space.

Uses: Clears negative energy and protects sacred spaces.

1152. Sandalwood and Vetiver Grounding Oil

Ingredients:

5 drops sandalwood essential oil

3 drops vetiver essential oil

2 tbsp jojoba oil

Instructions:

Combine all ingredients in a small bottle.

Apply to the soles of your feet before grounding rituals.

Uses: Anchors energy and enhances presence.

1153. Calendula and Chamomile Sacred Bath

Ingredients:

1/4 cup dried calendula flowers

1/4 cup dried chamomile

Instructions:

Place herbs in a muslin bag and add to bathwater. Soak for 20–30 minutes.

Uses: Cleanses the spirit and promotes emotional healing.

1154. Citrus and Peppermint Energy Mist

Ingredients:

5 drops orange essential oil

5 drops peppermint essential oil

1 cup distilled water

Instructions:

Combine oils and water in a spray bottle.

Shake well and mist around your space.

Uses: Energizes and uplifts the mind.

1155. Vetiver and Mugwort Dream Sachet

Ingredients:

1 tbsp dried mugwort

1 tsp dried vetiver

Instructions:

Place mugwort and vetiver in a small fabric pouch.

Keep the sachet under your pillow for vivid dreams.

Uses: Enhances dream work and spiritual insight.

Herbs are powerful allies for enhancing spiritual practices, offering support for grounding, cleansing, and connecting to higher energies. By incorporating these herbal rituals into your routine, you can create meaningful experiences that nourish the soul and deepen your spiritual journey. Explore the recipes and techniques in this chapter, and let the natural power of herbs guide your path to mindfulness and connection.

BOOK 34

PETS AND HERBAL REMEDIES

Our pets are beloved members of our families, and their health and well-being are just as important as our own. Just as humans benefit from the healing power of herbs, so too can animals. Herbal remedies offer a natural and gentle way to address common pet issues, from anxiety to skin irritations, while supporting their overall wellness. When used responsibly, herbs can complement veterinary care, providing safe and effective solutions for many of your pet's needs.

This book explores the role of herbs in pet care, offering guidance on safe dosages, practical remedies, and preventive care. You'll learn how to craft herbal remedies tailored to your pet's unique needs, including calming blends for anxiety, soothing treatments for skin and coat health, and natural repellents for fleas and ticks. Each chapter provides step-by-step instructions and tips to ensure that these remedies are both safe and effective.

Whether you're looking to support your pet's health naturally or reduce reliance on synthetic products, this book empowers you with the knowledge and tools to make informed decisions. With the right herbs and care, you can enhance your pet's quality of life and nurture their health, naturally and holistically.

Safe Dosages and Herbs for Common Pet Issues

Herbal remedies can be a wonderful way to support your pet's health, but ensuring safety is paramount. Animals have different physiological responses to herbs than humans, and their smaller sizes require careful attention to dosages. This chapter provides essential guidance on choosing safe herbs and administering them in appropriate amounts to address common pet issues, such as digestive problems, anxiety, and minor wounds.

Understanding Dosages for Pets

Determining the correct dosage for your pet depends on their size, species, and specific needs. A general rule of thumb is to adjust herbal dosages proportionally based on the animal's weight compared to an average human adult (approximately 150 pounds). Here's a simple formula:

Small dogs or cats (10–20 lbs): Use 1/8 of the human dose.

Medium dogs (20–50 lbs): Use 1/4 of the human dose.

Large dogs (50–100 lbs): Use 1/2 of the human dose.

Always start with the lowest possible dose, especially if you're introducing a new herb, and observe your pet for any adverse reactions. It's crucial to consult a veterinarian before using herbs, particularly if your pet has underlying health conditions or is on medication.

Safe Herbs for Pets

Several herbs are safe and beneficial for pets when used properly. Here are some commonly used herbs for addressing everyday issues:

1. Chamomile

Benefits: Calms anxiety, soothes digestive upset, and reduces inflammation.

Uses: Brew as a weak tea and add a small amount to your pet's water or food.

2. Ginger

Benefits: Relieves nausea and supports digestion.

Uses: Grate fresh ginger and mix a tiny pinch into your pet's food for motion sickness.

3. Calendula

Benefits: Heals minor wounds and reduces skin irritation.

Uses: Create a diluted tincture or infusion and apply topically to cuts and scrapes.

4. Dandelion

Benefits: Supports liver function and acts as a mild diuretic.

Uses: Add small amounts of fresh or dried leaves to your pet's food.

5. Milk Thistle

Benefits: Protects and detoxifies the liver.

Uses: Provide a powdered supplement mixed with food for pets with liver conditions.

6. Oat Straw

Benefits: Calms nervous pets and soothes itchy skin.

Uses: Brew a tea for topical use or as a water additive.

Common Pet Issues and Herbal Solutions

1. Digestive Upset

Symptoms like diarrhea, constipation, or bloating can often be eased with herbs.

Remedy:

1/8 tsp slippery elm powder (for small pets, adjust for larger pets) mixed with a small amount of water to form a paste.

Administer orally to soothe the stomach lining.

2. Anxiety and Stress

Separation anxiety, loud noises, and changes in routine can stress pets.

Remedy:

Brew a weak tea with 1 tsp chamomile flowers in 1 cup boiling water.

Cool and add 1–2 tsp to your pet's water bowl.

3. Skin Irritations

Hot spots, minor cuts, and insect bites can cause discomfort.

Remedy:

Infuse calendula and chamomile in warm water.

Apply the cooled infusion to affected areas with a clean cloth.

4. Fleas and Ticks

Herbs can help repel pests naturally.

Remedy:

Create a powder with equal parts diatomaceous earth and powdered neem leaf.

Sprinkle lightly onto your pet's coat, avoiding the face.

5. Joint Pain and Arthritis

Older pets often suffer from stiffness and joint discomfort.

Remedy:

Mix 1/8 tsp turmeric powder (for small pets, adjust for size) with coconut oil.

Administer with food to reduce inflammation.

How to Administer Herbal Remedies

In Food: Mix powdered or fresh herbs directly into your pet's food. Ensure the herbs are finely ground to prevent rejection.

In Water: Brew herbal teas and add them to your pet's water bowl in small amounts. Make sure the tea is weak and cooled.

Topical Application: Use herbal infusions, salves, or sprays for skin issues or wounds. Always dilute appropriately.

Capsules: For pets resistant to the taste of herbs, capsules can be a convenient option. Choose pet-safe dosages.

Precautions and Warnings

While many herbs are safe for pets, some can be toxic or harmful if misused. Avoid these herbs unless advised by a veterinarian:

Garlic (in large amounts): Can cause anemia in cats and dogs.

Onion: Toxic to pets in any form.

Essential Oils: Undiluted oils can be harmful, especially to cats.

Nutmeg: Can cause tremors and seizures.

Always research thoroughly before using any herb and consult a veterinarian if unsure.

Case Studies

Case 1: Bella's Calming Chamomile Remedy

Bella, a 7-year-old terrier, suffered from separation anxiety. Her owner started adding 1 tsp of chamomile tea to her water bowl during stressful times. Within a week, Bella appeared calmer, and her excessive barking reduced.

Case 2: Max's Skin Soothing Solution

Max, a Labrador with itchy hot spots, found relief with a calendula and chamomile infusion. His owner applied the solution to affected areas twice daily, and Max's skin showed noticeable improvement within a few days.

Building a Pet-Friendly Herbal Toolkit

To keep your pet's herbal needs covered, consider stocking the following in your pet-friendly apothecary:

Chamomile: For anxiety and digestive upset.

Calendula: For wounds and skin irritation.

Slippery Elm Powder: For digestive issues.

Milk Thistle: For liver support.

Neem Powder: For pest control.

Herbs can provide gentle, natural solutions for common pet health concerns when used responsibly. By understanding safe dosages and selecting appropriate herbs, you can support your pet's well-being while minimizing reliance on synthetic products. With proper care and guidance, herbal remedies can enhance your pet's quality of life and strengthen the bond you share. Always monitor your pet closely when introducing new remedies and consult with a veterinarian for specific needs or conditions.

Creating Herbal Remedies for Anxiety in Animals

Anxiety in pets is a common concern, manifesting as restlessness, excessive barking, hiding, or destructive behavior. Triggers may include separation, loud noises, travel, or changes in routine. While medications are often used, herbal remedies offer a gentle, natural alternative to calm anxious animals without side effects.

Herbs like chamomile, valerian root, and passionflower are known for their calming properties. These herbs work by soothing the nervous system and reducing stress responses. Incorporating these herbs into your pet's routine can help alleviate anxiety and improve their overall emotional well-being.

This chapter provides practical guidance on creating herbal remedies for anxiety in animals, including teas, infusions, and sprays. With these 10 simple recipes, you can help your pet feel more secure and at ease during stressful situations.

1156. Chamomile Tea for General Calmness

Ingredients:

1 tsp dried chamomile flowers

1 cup boiling water

Instructions:

Steep chamomile in boiling water for 5–7 minutes.

Cool and add 1–2 tsp to your pet's water bowl.

Uses: Promotes relaxation and reduces mild anxiety.

Storage Tips: Use fresh tea each time; do not store.

1157. Lavender and Valerian Infusion Spray

Ingredients:

5 drops lavender essential oil (diluted)

1 tsp valerian root infusion

1 cup distilled water

Instructions:

Brew valerian root in 1/4 cup hot water and cool.

Mix the infusion and lavender oil with distilled water in a spray bottle.

Lightly mist your pet's bedding or favorite resting area.

Uses: Calms anxiety during travel or loud noises.

Storage Tips: Store in the refrigerator for up to 1 week.

1158. Passionflower Treats

Ingredients:

1 tsp dried passionflower

1/4 cup natural peanut butter

1/2 cup rolled oats

Instructions:

Grind passionflower into a fine powder.

Mix with peanut butter and oats to form small treats.

Serve one treat during stressful moments.

Uses: Helps soothe stress and nervousness.

Storage Tips: Store in an airtight container for up to 1 week.

1159. Lemon Balm Tea Additive

Ingredients:

1 tsp dried lemon balm

1 cup boiling water

Instructions:

Brew lemon balm in boiling water for 10 minutes.

Cool and add 1–2 tsp to your pet's drinking water.

Uses: Reduces tension and calms hyperactivity.

Storage Tips: Use immediately after brewing.

1160. Oatmeal and Lavender Bath Soak

Ingredients:

1/2 cup colloidal oatmeal

1/4 cup dried lavender flowers

Instructions:

Add oatmeal and lavender to a muslin bag.

Place the bag in warm bathwater and soak your pet for 10–15 minutes.

Uses: Soothes the body and mind, reducing physical and emotional tension.

Storage Tips: Use fresh ingredients for each bath.

1161. Calming Herbal Pillow

Ingredients:

1/4 cup dried chamomile flowers

1/4 cup dried lavender flowers

1 small fabric pouch

Instructions:

Combine dried chamomile and lavender in the fabric pouch.

Place the pouch in your pet's bed or favorite resting spot.

Uses: Provides a calming aroma to reduce anxiety.

Storage Tips: Replace herbs every 1–2 weeks.

1162. Skullcap Relaxation Drops

Ingredients:

1 tsp dried skullcap

1/4 cup boiling water

Instructions:

Brew skullcap in boiling water for 10 minutes.

Cool and give 1–2 drops orally for small pets, adjusting for size.

Uses: Helps manage acute anxiety.

Storage Tips: Use fresh and discard leftovers.

1163. Rose Petal Comfort Infusion

Ingredients:

1 tsp dried rose petals

1 cup boiling water

Instructions:

Steep rose petals in boiling water for 5–7 minutes.

Cool and add a small amount to your pet's water.

Uses: Provides emotional comfort and reduces stress.

Storage Tips: Discard unused portions after 24 hours.

1164. Holy Basil (Tulsi) Relaxing Chew

Ingredients:

1 tsp dried holy basil

1/4 cup mashed sweet potato

Instructions:

Mix holy basil with mashed sweet potato.

Form small, chewable bites.

Offer one during high-stress situations.

Uses: Supports emotional balance and calms nerves.

Storage Tips: Store in the refrigerator for up to 3 days.

1165. Peppermint and Chamomile Spray

Ingredients:

1/2 cup chamomile tea (cooled)

2 drops peppermint essential oil (diluted)

Instructions:

Brew chamomile tea and allow it to cool.

Mix with diluted peppermint oil in a spray bottle. Lightly spray around your pet's environment.

Uses: Refreshes the space and reduces anxiety.

Storage Tips: Store in the refrigerator for up to 1 week.

Tips for Using Herbal Remedies for Anxiety

Start Small: Introduce one remedy at a time and observe your pet's reaction.

Consistency Matters: Use remedies regularly, especially for pets with chronic anxiety.

Create a Calming Routine: Combine remedies with a predictable routine to help your pet feel secure.

Herbal remedies offer a gentle, effective way to support your pet's emotional well-being. By using calming herbs like chamomile, lavender, and valerian, you can help reduce anxiety in stressful situations. These natural solutions are simple to prepare and provide an excellent alternative to synthetic medications. With thoughtful care and observation, you can create a peaceful environment where your pet feels safe and secure.

Natural Solutions for Skin and Coat Health

A pet's skin and coat are indicators of their overall health. Shiny, soft fur and clear, healthy skin reflect a well-balanced diet, proper care, and a stress-free lifestyle. However, pets often experience issues such as dry skin, itchiness, dandruff, or even infections, which can affect their comfort and appearance. While veterinary care is crucial for severe conditions, herbal remedies can be a safe, effective, and natural solution for maintaining your pet's skin and coat health.

Herbs like calendula, aloe vera, and neem are celebrated for their soothing, moisturizing, and antimicrobial properties. These natural ingredients can be used in shampoos, rinses, sprays, and balms to relieve irritation, promote healing, and prevent common skin problems. Additionally, dietary support with omega-rich herbs and seeds can enhance your pet's coat health from the inside out.

This chapter provides practical recipes and remedies to address various skin and coat issues, ensuring your pet looks and feels their best.

1166. Calendula Skin Soothing Spray

Ingredients:

1/4 cup dried calendula flowers

1 cup boiling water

Instructions:

Steep calendula flowers in boiling water for 10 minutes.

Cool and strain into a spray bottle.

Spray directly on irritated or itchy skin.

Uses: Reduces inflammation and soothes minor skin irritations.

Storage Tips: Store in the refrigerator for up to 1 week.

1167. Oatmeal and Lavender Shampoo

Ingredients:

1/2 cup ground oatmeal

1/4 cup castile soap

5 drops lavender essential oil

Instructions:

Mix ground oatmeal, castile soap, and lavender oil in a bottle.

Use as a gentle shampoo during baths.

Uses: Moisturizes dry skin and reduces itchiness.

Storage Tips: Store in a cool, dry place for up to 1 month.

1168. Coconut Oil and Neem Balm

Ingredients:

2 tbsp coconut oil

1 tsp neem oil

Instructions:

Melt coconut oil and mix with neem oil.

Apply a small amount to dry or flaky areas of your pet's skin.

Uses: Hydrates skin and combats bacterial or fungal infections.

Storage Tips: Store in a sealed container at room temperature.

1169. Herbal Coat Rinse

Ingredients:

1/4 cup dried rosemary

1/4 cup dried chamomile

1 liter boiling water

Instructions:

Steep rosemary and chamomile in boiling water for 15 minutes.

Cool and pour over your pet's coat after shampooing.

Uses: Enhances coat shine and soothes the skin.

Storage Tips: Prepare fresh before each use.

1170. Aloe Vera Healing Gel

Ingredients:

2 tbsp fresh aloe vera gel

Instructions:

Extract gel from a fresh aloe vera leaf.

Apply a thin layer to areas of irritation or minor wounds.

Uses: Heals small cuts, reduces redness, and soothes skin.

Storage Tips: Store in the refrigerator for up to 3 days.

1171. Flaxseed Supplement for Coat Health

Ingredients:

1 tsp ground flaxseed

Instructions:

Add ground flaxseed to your pet's food daily.

Mix well to ensure even distribution.

Uses: Promotes a shiny coat and hydrates the skin from within.

Storage Tips: Store flaxseed in an airtight container.

1172. Apple Cider Vinegar Rinse

Ingredients:

1/4 cup apple cider vinegar

1 cup distilled water

Instructions:

Dilute apple cider vinegar with water.

Apply as a final rinse after shampooing.

Uses: Balances pH and reduces dandruff.

Storage Tips: Use fresh for each application.

1173. Chamomile and Green Tea Compress

Ingredients:

1 chamomile tea bag

1 green tea bag

1 cup boiling water

Instructions:

Steep both tea bags in boiling water for 10 minutes.

Let the solution cool, then soak a clean cloth in the tea.

Apply the compress to irritated or inflamed areas.

Uses: Soothes redness and reduces swelling.

Storage Tips: Discard unused tea after 24 hours.

1174. Burdock Root Skin Tonic

Ingredients:

1 tsp dried burdock root

1 cup boiling water

Instructions:

Steep burdock root in boiling water for 10 minutes.

Cool and give 1–2 tsp orally (adjust for pet size).

Uses: Supports skin health by detoxifying the body.

Storage Tips: Store dried burdock root in a sealed container.

1175. Vitamin E Spot Treatment

Ingredients:

1 vitamin E capsule

Instructions:

Puncture the capsule and apply the oil directly to dry patches.

Uses: Promotes healing and hydrates dry skin.

Storage Tips: Store capsules in a cool, dry place.

Tips for Maintaining Skin and Coat Health

Balanced Diet: Ensure your pet's diet includes omega fatty acids, found in fish oil, flaxseed, and chia seeds, to support healthy skin and fur.

Regular Grooming: Brush your pet frequently to distribute natural oils and prevent tangling.

Bathing Routine: Bathe your pet only when necessary to avoid stripping natural oils from their coat. Use mild, pet-safe shampoos.

Hydration: Encourage your pet to drink plenty of water to keep their skin hydrated.

Natural solutions can significantly improve your pet's skin and coat health, addressing common issues like dryness, itchiness, and minor irritations. By incorporating herbal remedies into their care routine, you can provide soothing relief while enhancing their overall well-being. With these simple recipes and tips, your pet's skin and coat will remain healthy, shiny, and radiant. Always monitor for allergic reactions and consult your veterinarian for persistent or severe skin conditions.

DIY Flea and Tick Repellents

Fleas and ticks are among the most common nuisances for pets, causing discomfort, irritation, and potential health risks. These pests can lead to serious conditions like Lyme disease, anemia, and dermatitis if not addressed promptly. While conventional chemical treatments are effective, they often come with risks of side effects, such as skin irritation or toxicity. DIY natural flea and tick repellents offer a safer alternative, harnessing the power of herbs and essential oils to protect your pets effectively.

Herbs like neem, rosemary, and lavender, along with natural ingredients like apple cider vinegar and diatomaceous earth, are excellent for repelling fleas and ticks. These ingredients are not only safe for pets when used correctly but also gentle on their skin and the environment. This chapter explores a range of DIY repellents, from sprays to powders, that you can easily make at home to keep pests at bay.

Understanding the Role of Natural Ingredients

Natural flea and tick repellents rely on the properties of specific herbs and ingredients to deter pests:

Neem Oil: Contains azadirachtin, a compound that disrupts the lifecycle of fleas and ticks.

Apple Cider Vinegar: Alters the pH of your pet's skin, making it less appealing to pests.

Essential Oils: Oils like lavender, cedarwood, and citronella are potent repellents but must be diluted to avoid skin irritation.

Diatomaceous Earth: A natural powder that dehydrates and kills fleas and ticks on contact.

How to Use DIY Flea and Tick Repellents Safely

Dilution is Key: Always dilute essential oils before applying them to your pet. A 1% dilution is generally safe for pets (1 drop of essential oil per teaspoon of carrier oil).

Spot Test: Before widespread use, apply a small amount of the remedy to a test area on your pet to check for reactions.

Avoid Certain Oils: Essential oils like tea tree, clove, and eucalyptus can be toxic to pets if misused, especially for cats.

Monitor Closely: Observe your pet for any signs of discomfort, redness, or irritation.

DIY Flea and Tick Repellent Recipes

1176. Neem Oil Spray

Ingredients:

1 tsp neem oil

1 cup distilled water

1 tsp mild dish soap (optional, as an emulsifier)

Instructions:

Combine neem oil, water, and dish soap in a spray bottle.

Shake well before each use.

Lightly mist your pet's coat, avoiding the face.

Uses: Effective for repelling fleas and ticks while soothing the skin.

Storage Tips: Store in a cool, dark place for up to 2 weeks.

1177. Apple Cider Vinegar Rinse

Ingredients:

1/2 cup apple cider vinegar

1/2 cup water

Instructions:

Mix equal parts apple cider vinegar and water in a bottle.

Use as a final rinse after bathing your pet.

Uses: Deters fleas and ticks while balancing skin pH.

Storage Tips: Prepare fresh for each use.

1178. Herbal Flea Collar

Ingredients:

2 drops lavender essential oil (diluted)

2 drops cedarwood essential oil (diluted)

A plain cotton pet collar

Instructions:

Dilute essential oils with 1 tbsp carrier oil (e.g., olive oil).

Apply the mixture to the cotton collar.

Allow to dry before placing it on your pet.

Uses: Repels fleas and ticks naturally while leaving a pleasant scent.

Storage Tips: Reapply essential oils weekly for effectiveness.

1179. Rosemary Infusion Spray

Ingredients:

1/4 cup dried rosemary

1 cup boiling water

Instructions:

Steep rosemary in boiling water for 15 minutes.

Strain and pour into a spray bottle.

Lightly spritz your pet's coat.

Uses: Repels fleas and ticks and leaves a fresh scent.

Storage Tips: Store in the refrigerator for up to 1 week.

1180. Diatomaceous Earth Dusting Powder

Ingredients:

1 cup food-grade diatomaceous earth

Instructions:

Sprinkle a small amount of diatomaceous earth on your pet's coat.

Work it into the fur, avoiding the face.

Uses: Kills fleas and ticks by dehydrating them.

Storage Tips: Store in a sealed container in a dry place.

1181. Lemongrass and Citronella Spray

Ingredients:

3 drops lemongrass essential oil

3 drops citronella essential oil

1 cup distilled water

Instructions:

Dilute essential oils in water and pour into a spray bottle.

Shake well before each use.

Spray on your pet's coat and bedding.

Uses: Repels fleas and ticks with its citrusy scent.

Storage Tips: Store in a cool place for up to 2 weeks.

1182. Mint and Vinegar Repellent

Ingredients:

1/4 cup fresh mint leaves

1/2 cup apple cider vinegar

1 cup water

Instructions:

Simmer mint leaves in water for 10 minutes.

Strain and mix with apple cider vinegar.

Spray on your pet's coat.

Uses: Refreshes the coat and keeps pests away.

Storage Tips: Store in the refrigerator for up to 1 week.

1183. Coconut Oil Balm

Ingredients:

2 tbsp coconut oil

1 drop lavender essential oil

Instructions:

Mix coconut oil and lavender essential oil.

Rub a small amount onto your pet's fur, focusing on areas prone to ticks.

Uses: Repels pests while moisturizing the coat.

Storage Tips: Store in a cool, dry place.

1184. Citrus Repellent Spray

Ingredients:

1 lemon (sliced)

1 cup boiling water

Instructions:

Add lemon slices to boiling water and steep overnight.

Strain and pour into a spray bottle.

Lightly mist your pet's coat.

Uses: Naturally repels fleas with a citrus aroma.

Storage Tips: Use within 3 days and keep refrigerated.

1185. Cedar and Eucalyptus Pet Bedding Spray

Ingredients:

3 drops cedarwood essential oil

2 drops eucalyptus essential oil (diluted)

1 cup distilled water

Instructions:

Combine oils and water in a spray bottle.

Shake well and spray on pet bedding.

Uses: Keeps pests away from your pet's resting area.

Storage Tips: Store for up to 2 weeks in a cool place.

Natural flea and tick repellents provide a safe and eco-friendly way to protect your pets from pests. With ingredients like neem oil, lavender, and apple cider vinegar, these DIY solutions are easy to prepare and highly effective. Regular application, combined with good grooming and hygiene, will keep your pets comfortable and pest-free. Always test remedies for sensitivity and consult your veterinarian for persistent infestations or concerns.

BOOK 35

HERBAL REMEDIES FOR HORMONAL HEALTH

Hormonal health is a cornerstone of overall well-being, influencing energy levels, mood, metabolism, and more. When hormonal imbalances occur, they can lead to a range of challenges, including fatigue, weight fluctuations, and mood swings. While conventional treatments can be effective, herbal remedies offer a natural and supportive approach to restoring balance and promoting long-term endocrine health.

This book explores how herbs and adaptogens can be used to address common hormonal concerns, such as thyroid function, blood sugar regulation, adrenal fatigue, and overall endocrine support. With centuries of traditional use and increasing scientific backing, herbs like ashwagandha, licorice root, and holy basil provide gentle yet powerful solutions for managing hormonal health.

Each chapter delves into specific aspects of the endocrine system, offering insights, practical advice, and recipes for teas, tinctures, and tonics. Whether you're looking to support your thyroid, stabilize blood sugar, or find natural ways to manage stress, this book equips you with tools and knowledge to take control of your hormonal health. By embracing the wisdom of herbal medicine, you can create a personalized path toward balance, vitality, and long-lasting wellness.

Supporting Thyroid Function with Adaptogens

The thyroid gland plays a vital role in regulating metabolism, energy levels, and overall hormonal balance. When the thyroid is underactive (hypothyroidism) or overactive (hyperthyroidism), it can lead to a host of health challenges, including fatigue, weight changes, and mood disturbances. While medical treatment is often necessary for severe thyroid disorders, adaptogenic herbs can provide supportive care by modulating the body's stress response and promoting overall endocrine harmony.

Adaptogens are a class of herbs that help the body adapt to stress, balance hormones, and maintain homeostasis. By reducing the impact of chronic stress—a key contributor to thyroid dysfunction—adaptogens like ashwagandha, rhodiola, and holy basil can support thyroid health and improve symptoms associated with imbalance.

In this chapter, we explore the thyroid's role in hormonal health, the benefits of adaptogens for thyroid support, and practical ways to incorporate these powerful herbs into your daily routine. Whether you're managing a diagnosed thyroid condition or looking to enhance overall wellness, adaptogens offer a natural and effective solution.

The Thyroid Gland and Its Functions

The thyroid, a butterfly-shaped gland located at the base of the neck, produces hormones that regulate:

Metabolism: Controls how the body uses energy.

Body Temperature: Maintains thermoregulation.

Heart Rate: Influences cardiovascular health.

Mood and Cognition: Affects mental clarity and emotional stability.

Thyroid dysfunction is often categorized into:

Hypothyroidism: Characterized by fatigue, weight gain, and sluggishness.

Hyperthyroidism: Marked by anxiety, weight loss, and an overactive metabolism.

How Adaptogens Support Thyroid Health

1. Stress Reduction

Chronic stress triggers the release of cortisol, which can suppress thyroid function over time.

Adaptogens help lower cortisol levels, creating a healthier environment for the thyroid.

2. Hormonal Balance

Adaptogens work holistically to balance the endocrine system, supporting the thyroid in conjunction with the adrenal glands and hypothalamus.

3. Immune Modulation

Many thyroid disorders, such as Hashimoto's and Graves' disease, are autoimmune in nature. Adaptogens like holy basil and ashwagandha have immune-modulating properties, helping to regulate an overactive immune response.

Key Adaptogens for Thyroid Support

1. Ashwagandha

Benefits: Enhances thyroid hormone production, reduces stress, and combats fatigue.

How to Use: Brew ashwagandha root tea or take it as a powdered supplement.

Example Recipe:

1 tsp ashwagandha root powder

1 cup warm milk (dairy or plant-based)

1/2 tsp honey Mix and drink before bed to promote relaxation and support thyroid function.

2. Rhodiola Rosea

Benefits: Improves energy, reduces stress, and enhances cognitive function.

How to Use: Take as a tincture or capsule.

Example Recipe:

Add 5–10 drops of rhodiola tincture to herbal tea for a mid-afternoon energy boost.

3. Holy Basil (Tulsi)

Benefits: Balances hormones, reduces inflammation, and supports the immune system.

How to Use: Brew as a tea or use fresh leaves in cooking.

Example Recipe:

1 tsp dried holy basil leaves

1 cup boiling water Steep for 10 minutes and enjoy as a calming tea.

4. Schisandra

Benefits: Protects against oxidative stress, enhances energy, and supports liver detoxification (important for thyroid health).

How to Use: Add schisandra powder to smoothies or teas.

Example Recipe:

1 tsp schisandra powder

1 cup green tea Blend and sip for enhanced vitality.

5. Licorice Root

Benefits: Supports adrenal health and combats fatigue, indirectly aiding the thyroid.

How to Use: Prepare as a tea or include in herbal blends.

Example Recipe:

1 tsp dried licorice root

1 cup boiling water Steep for 5–7 minutes, strain, and drink.

Dietary Support for the Thyroid

While adaptogens are invaluable, a thyroid-supportive diet can further enhance their benefits. Incorporate these foods into your meals:

Iodine-Rich Foods: Seaweed, fish, and eggs support thyroid hormone production.

Selenium Sources: Brazil nuts and sunflower seeds aid in converting thyroid hormones to their active form.

Anti-Inflammatory Foods: Turmeric, ginger, and berries reduce inflammation associated with thyroid disorders.

Practical Tips for Using Adaptogens

Consistency Matters: Adaptogens work best when taken regularly over time.

Start Slowly: Introduce one adaptogen at a time to monitor your body's response.

Pair with Lifestyle Changes: Incorporate stress-reducing practices like meditation or yoga to complement herbal support.

Sample Daily Routine for Thyroid Support

Morning: Start the day with a holy basil and ashwagandha tea to reduce morning fatigue and balance cortisol. **Afternoon**: Add rhodiola tincture to a light herbal tea for an energy boost. **Evening**: Drink warm milk with ashwagandha powder before bed to promote relaxation and thyroid recovery.

Precautions and Contraindications

Consult a Healthcare Provider: Especially if you have a diagnosed thyroid condition or are on medication.

Avoid Overuse: High doses of adaptogens may overstimulate certain individuals.

Monitor Symptoms: Regularly assess your energy levels, mood, and other thyroid-related symptoms.

Case Study: Emily's Thyroid Wellness Journey

Emily, a 35-year-old freelance writer, experienced fatigue and weight gain due to hypothyroidism. After consulting her doctor, she incorporated ashwagandha and holy basil into her routine. She drank a nightly ashwagandha latte and sipped holy basil tea during stressful moments. Within three months, Emily noticed improved energy levels, better sleep, and more stable mood patterns.

Adaptogens offer a holistic and effective approach to supporting thyroid function, helping to balance hormones, reduce stress, and improve overall well-being. By integrating these herbs into your daily routine and combining them with a nutrient-rich diet and lifestyle practices, you can create a strong foundation for thyroid health. With time, consistency, and the right adaptogens, you can empower yourself to manage thyroid challenges naturally and effectively.

Herbs for Managing Blood Sugar Levels

Maintaining healthy blood sugar levels is crucial for overall well-being and preventing conditions like diabetes, metabolic syndrome, and chronic inflammation. While a balanced diet and regular exercise are foundational, certain herbs can offer additional support by improving insulin sensitivity, regulating glucose metabolism, and reducing sugar absorption. These natural solutions have been used for centuries in traditional medicine and are now backed by modern research.

This chapter explores the most effective herbs for managing blood sugar, their mechanisms of action, and how to incorporate them into your daily life. By following practical instructions, you can harness the benefits of these natural remedies to support metabolic health and maintain glucose balance.

How to Use Herbs for Blood Sugar Management

1. Cinnamon

Purpose: Enhances insulin sensitivity and reduces fasting blood sugar levels.

How to Use: Add 1 teaspoon of cinnamon powder to oatmeal, smoothies, or baked goods. Alternatively, steep it in hot water for tea. Consume once or twice daily.

2. Fenugreek

Purpose: Slows sugar absorption and improves glucose tolerance.

How to Use: Soak 1 tablespoon of fenugreek seeds overnight in water. In the morning, strain the seeds and drink the water on an empty stomach. You can also grind the seeds into powder and add to meals.

3. Bitter Melon

Purpose: Mimics insulin activity and lowers blood glucose levels.

How to Use: Juice fresh bitter melon and consume 1/4 to 1/2 cup daily. If fresh bitter melon is unavailable, boil sliced pieces in water to make tea and drink once a day.

4. Gymnema Sylvestre

Purpose: Reduces sugar cravings and improves insulin function.

How to Use: Brew 1 teaspoon of dried gymnema leaves in hot water to make tea. Drink daily after meals. Alternatively, take it as a tincture or supplement under the guidance of a professional.

5. Turmeric

Purpose: Reduces inflammation and supports insulin activity.

How to Use: Add 1/2 teaspoon of turmeric powder to soups, curries, or smoothies. For better absorption, mix with black pepper and a healthy fat like olive oil.

6. Ginger

Purpose: Improves glucose metabolism and reduces insulin resistance.

How to Use: Grate fresh ginger and steep 1 teaspoon in boiling water to make tea. Drink 1–2 cups daily, or add fresh ginger to stir-fries, soups, and juices.

7. Holy Basil (Tulsi)

Purpose: Lowers blood sugar and reduces stress-induced glucose spikes.

How to Use: Brew 1 teaspoon of dried tulsi leaves in hot water to make tea. Drink once or twice daily, preferably in the morning or before bedtime.

8. Aloe Vera

Purpose: Enhances glucose metabolism and supports liver health.

How to Use: Extract 2 tablespoons of fresh aloe vera gel and blend it with a cup of water. Drink once daily.

9. Berberine (from Goldenseal)

Purpose: Activates enzymes involved in glucose metabolism.

How to Use: Take berberine as a capsule or tincture, typically in doses of 500 mg, two to three times a day. Consult a healthcare provider for personalized advice.

10. Dandelion Root

Purpose: Supports liver detoxification and promotes blood sugar stability.

How to Use: Brew 1 teaspoon of dried dandelion root in hot water to make tea. Drink 1–2 cups daily, ideally before meals.

Tips for Success

Start Small: Begin with one herb at a time to monitor its effects and avoid interactions.

Consistency Matters: Herbs work best when taken regularly. Incorporate them into your daily routine for sustained benefits.

Combine with Healthy Habits: Pair herbal remedies with a balanced diet, regular exercise, and stress management for optimal results.

Hydration: Drinking plenty of water enhances the body's ability to flush excess glucose.

Precautions

Monitor Glucose Levels: Herbal remedies can lower blood sugar significantly. Regular monitoring is essential to avoid hypoglycemia, especially if you're on medication.

Consult a Professional: Always consult your healthcare provider before starting herbal remedies, particularly if you have a pre-existing condition or are taking medications like insulin.

Avoid Overuse: Some herbs, such as berberine, may cause gastrointestinal discomfort if taken in excessive amounts. Stick to recommended doses.

Herbs provide a natural, effective way to manage blood sugar levels and support metabolic health. By incorporating cinnamon, fenugreek, bitter melon, and other glucose-regulating herbs into your routine, you can take proactive steps toward maintaining balanced glucose levels. Remember to combine these remedies with a healthy lifestyle and consult your healthcare provider for personalized guidance.

Remedies for Adrenal Fatigue and Cortisol Balance

Adrenal fatigue, often caused by chronic stress, occurs when the adrenal glands become overworked and struggle to produce adequate amounts of cortisol and other essential hormones. Symptoms may include fatigue, difficulty concentrating, irritability, cravings for salty or sugary foods, and disrupted sleep patterns. While lifestyle changes like stress management, a balanced diet, and proper sleep are key to recovery, herbal remedies can play a vital role in restoring adrenal health and balancing cortisol levels.

Adaptogens like ashwagandha, rhodiola, and holy basil help the body adapt to stress and regulate cortisol production, while nourishing herbs like licorice root and schisandra berries support adrenal gland function. These herbs work synergistically to reduce stress, enhance energy, and promote overall hormonal balance.

This chapter provides 10 natural remedies designed to combat adrenal fatigue and promote cortisol balance. From teas and tinctures to tonics and capsules, these recipes are easy to incorporate into your daily routine to support adrenal recovery and improve vitality.

1186. Ashwagandha and Holy Basil Tea

Ingredients:

1 tsp dried ashwagandha root

1 tsp dried holy basil leaves

1 cup boiling water

Instructions:

Combine ashwagandha root and holy basil leaves in a teapot.

Pour boiling water over the herbs and steep for 10 minutes.

Strain and enjoy warm, preferably in the evening.

Uses: Reduces stress and promotes relaxation.

Storage Tips: Use fresh tea each time; do not store.

1187. Rhodiola Energy Tincture

Ingredients:

1 tsp rhodiola root (dried)

1/2 cup vodka (or glycerin for non-alcoholic version)

Instructions:

Place rhodiola root in a glass jar and cover with vodka or glycerin.

Seal and let steep in a dark place for 4–6 weeks, shaking occasionally.

Strain and take 10–15 drops daily in water or tea.

Uses: Boosts energy and regulates cortisol levels.

Storage Tips: Store in a dark glass bottle for up to 1 year.

1188. Licorice Root and Ginger Decoction

Ingredients:

1 tsp dried licorice root

1 tsp fresh ginger (sliced)

2 cups water

Instructions:

Simmer licorice root and ginger in water for 15 minutes.

Strain and drink in the morning.

Uses: Supports adrenal health and improves energy levels.

Storage Tips: Prepare fresh for each use.

1189. Schisandra Berry Tonic

Ingredients:

1 tsp dried schisandra berries

1 cup boiling water

Instructions:

Steep schisandra berries in boiling water for 10 minutes.

Strain and drink once daily.

Uses: Enhances energy and reduces stress-induced fatigue.

Storage Tips: Store dried berries in an airtight container.

1190. Adaptogen Smoothie

Ingredients:

1/2 tsp ashwagandha powder

1/2 tsp maca powder

1 cup almond milk

1/2 banana

Instructions:

Blend all ingredients until smooth.

Consume as a morning or mid-afternoon boost.

Uses: Provides sustained energy and supports adrenal recovery.

Storage Tips: Drink immediately after preparation.

1191. Holy Basil Infused Honey

Ingredients:

1/4 cup dried holy basil leaves

1/2 cup raw honey

Instructions:

Combine holy basil leaves and honey in a glass jar.

Let infuse for 2 weeks, stirring occasionally.

Strain and use the honey in teas or on toast.

Uses: Promotes relaxation and reduces cortisol spikes.

Storage Tips: Store in a cool, dark place for up to 6 months.

1192. Lavender and Chamomile Bath Soak

Ingredients:

1/4 cup dried lavender flowers

1/4 cup dried chamomile flowers

1/2 cup Epsom salt

Instructions:

Combine lavender, chamomile, and Epsom salt in a muslin bag.

Place the bag in warm bathwater and soak for 20 minutes.

Uses: Reduces stress and promotes restful sleep.

Storage Tips: Store dried herbs in a sealed container.

1193. Turmeric Golden Milk

Ingredients:

1/2 tsp turmeric powder

1/4 tsp cinnamon

1 cup warm milk (dairy or plant-based)

Instructions:

Mix turmeric and cinnamon into warm milk.

Sweeten with honey if desired.

Uses: Reduces inflammation and supports hormonal balance.

Storage Tips: Prepare fresh for each use.

1194. Ginseng and Lemon Energy Tea

Ingredients:

1 tsp ginseng root (dried or powdered)

1 tsp fresh lemon juice

1 cup boiling water

Instructions:

Steep ginseng root in boiling water for 10 minutes.

Add lemon juice and drink in the morning.

Uses: Boosts energy and mental clarity.

Storage Tips: Store dried ginseng root in a cool, dry place.

1195. Oat Straw Relaxation Infusion

Ingredients:

1 tbsp dried oat straw

1 cup boiling water

Instructions:

Steep oat straw in boiling water for 15 minutes.

Strain and drink before bedtime.

Uses: Soothes the nervous system and promotes deep relaxation.

Storage Tips: Use immediately after brewing.

Tips for Supporting Adrenal Recovery

Balanced Diet: Include foods rich in magnesium, vitamin C, and B vitamins to nourish the adrenals.

Stress Management: Practice mindfulness, yoga, or meditation to lower cortisol levels.

Regular Sleep: Aim for 7–9 hours of quality sleep to restore adrenal function.

Limit Stimulants: Reduce caffeine and sugar, which can strain the adrenal glands.

Adrenal fatigue and cortisol imbalances can significantly impact your energy, mood, and overall well-being. By incorporating adaptogenic and nourishing herbs into your routine, you can naturally support adrenal recovery and promote hormonal balance. With these remedies and a commitment to self-care, you'll be on your way to restoring vitality and resilience. Always consult a healthcare provider before starting new remedies, especially if you have an existing condition.

Long-Term Strategies for Endocrine Support

The endocrine system is a network of glands that regulates hormones, controlling everything from metabolism and growth to mood and reproductive health. While short-term interventions can address specific imbalances, long-term strategies are essential for maintaining overall endocrine health. Consistent care and prevention can help the body adapt to life's stressors, recover from hormonal disruptions, and promote long-term vitality.

Incorporating holistic practices, such as dietary changes, stress management, and herbal remedies, can significantly enhance endocrine function. These strategies not only address current imbalances but also create a foundation for resilience against future disruptions. By supporting the adrenal glands, thyroid, pancreas, and reproductive organs, you can achieve a more balanced and harmonious endocrine system.

This chapter outlines practical, long-term strategies to promote hormonal health and introduces the best herbs, lifestyle adjustments, and practices for sustaining endocrine balance.

Key Principles for Endocrine Health

1. Prioritize Stress Management

Chronic stress is one of the leading causes of endocrine dysfunction. Prolonged stress elevates cortisol levels, which can suppress thyroid function, disrupt reproductive hormones, and increase blood sugar. Long-term stress management techniques are vital for endocrine support:

Mindfulness Practices: Meditation, yoga, and deep-breathing exercises help regulate stress hormones.

Consistent Sleep: Aim for 7–9 hours of restful sleep to support hormone production and adrenal recovery.

Adaptogens: Herbs like ashwagandha, rhodiola, and holy basil help the body adapt to stress and maintain cortisol balance over time.

2. Support Nutritional Needs

The endocrine system requires specific nutrients to function optimally. Nutritional deficiencies can impair hormone production and regulation, so a nutrient-rich diet is essential:

Magnesium: Supports adrenal and thyroid health. Found in leafy greens, nuts, and seeds.

Zinc: Essential for reproductive hormones and immune function. Found in pumpkin seeds, shellfish, and legumes.

Iodine: Necessary for thyroid hormone production. Found in seaweed, fish, and iodized salt.

Vitamin D: Regulates calcium and supports hormone balance. Sun exposure and fortified foods are good sources.

Long-Term Herbal Strategies

Herbs offer gentle, sustainable support for endocrine health, working synergistically with the body to restore balance over time. Here are some key herbs for specific glands and hormones:

Adrenal Support

Ashwagandha: Balances cortisol and reduces adrenal fatigue.

Licorice Root: Supports adrenal function by prolonging the effects of cortisol. Use cautiously under supervision.

Schisandra Berries: Improve resilience against stress and protect the adrenal glands.

Usage: Incorporate these herbs into teas, tinctures, or capsules, and take consistently for several weeks.

Thyroid Support

Holy Basil: Modulates thyroid function and reduces stress-induced imbalances.

Bladderwrack: Rich in iodine, supports thyroid hormone production in cases of hypothyroidism.

Guggul: Traditionally used in Ayurveda to balance thyroid hormones.

Usage: Include thyroid-supportive herbs in your diet or supplement regimen, following professional guidance.

Pancreatic Support for Blood Sugar Regulation

Cinnamon: Enhances insulin sensitivity and regulates blood sugar.

Fenugreek: Slows sugar absorption and supports glucose metabolism.

Bitter Melon: Mimics insulin activity and supports healthy glucose levels.

Usage: Add these herbs to meals or teas to promote long-term blood sugar stability.

Reproductive Hormones

Vitex (Chaste Tree Berry): Regulates menstrual cycles and supports progesterone production.

Maca Root: Enhances libido and balances reproductive hormones.

Black Cohosh: Eases menopausal symptoms and supports hormonal transitions.

Usage: Take as capsules or tinctures over several months to support reproductive health.

Lifestyle Practices for Hormonal Balance

1. Consistent Physical Activity

Regular exercise helps regulate blood sugar, reduce stress, and promote healthy hormone production. Incorporate a mix of strength training, cardiovascular exercise, and low-impact activities like yoga for optimal results.

2. Reduce Environmental Toxins

Endocrine-disrupting chemicals (EDCs) found in plastics, pesticides, and household products can interfere with hormone production.

Use Glass or Stainless Steel: Avoid plastic containers and bottles.

Choose Organic Produce: Reduce exposure to pesticide residues.

Switch to Natural Cleaning Products: Minimize contact with harmful chemicals.

3. Establish Healthy Sleep Patterns

The endocrine system relies on a consistent sleep-wake cycle to regulate hormone production. Create a bedtime routine that includes:

Avoiding screens an hour before bed.

Using calming herbal teas like chamomile or lavender.

Ensuring a cool, dark, and quiet sleep environment.

10 Herbal Remedies for Long-Term Endocrine Support

1196. Adaptogenic Tea for Daily Stress Relief

Ingredients:

1 tsp ashwagandha root

1 tsp holy basil leaves

1 tsp dried chamomile flowers

Instructions:

Combine all ingredients and steep in 1 cup boiling water for 10 minutes.

Strain and drink once daily in the evening.

Uses: Supports adrenal recovery and reduces cortisol levels.

1197. Thyroid-Boosting Seaweed Salad

Ingredients:

1 cup mixed seaweed (e.g., wakame, nori)

1 tbsp sesame seeds

1 tsp soy sauce

Instructions:

Soak seaweed in water for 10 minutes to rehydrate.

Toss with sesame seeds and soy sauce.

Uses: Provides iodine for thyroid hormone production.

1198. Schisandra and Lemon Tonic

Ingredients:

1 tsp dried schisandra berries

1 slice fresh lemon

1 cup boiling water

Instructions:

Steep schisandra berries in boiling water for 10 minutes.

Add lemon slice and drink daily.

Uses: Enhances energy and stress resilience.

1199. Cinnamon and Fenugreek Blood Sugar Tea

Ingredients:

1 tsp cinnamon powder

1 tsp fenugreek seeds

Instructions:

Steep ingredients in 1 cup boiling water for 10 minutes.

Strain and drink before meals.

Uses: Promotes blood sugar stability and insulin sensitivity.

1200. Maca Energy Smoothie

Ingredients:

1 tsp maca powder

1 banana

1 cup almond milk

Instructions:

Blend all ingredients until smooth.

Drink as a morning boost.

Uses: Balances reproductive hormones and improves energy.

1201. Golden Turmeric Latte

Ingredients:

1/2 tsp turmeric powder

1/4 tsp cinnamon

1 cup warm milk

Instructions:

Mix ingredients into warm milk and sweeten with honey if desired.

Uses: Reduces inflammation and supports hormonal balance.

1202. Licorice Root Tea

Ingredients:

1 tsp dried licorice root

1 cup boiling water

Instructions:

Steep licorice root in boiling water for 10 minutes.

Strain and enjoy once daily.

Uses: Supports adrenal health and combats fatigue.

1203. Lavender and Oat Bath Soak

Ingredients:

1/4 cup dried lavender flowers

1/4 cup oatmeal

Instructions:

Combine lavender and oatmeal in a muslin bag.

Add to warm bathwater and soak for 20 minutes.

Uses: Reduces stress and promotes relaxation.

1204. Bladderwrack Thyroid Support Tincture

Ingredients:

1 tsp dried bladderwrack

1/2 cup vodka or glycerin

Instructions:

Combine bladderwrack and liquid in a jar.

Let steep for 4 weeks, strain, and take 5 drops daily.

Uses: Supports thyroid health with natural iodine.

1205. Chamomile Sleep Tea

Ingredients:

1 tsp dried chamomile flowers

1 cup boiling water

Instructions:

Steep chamomile in boiling water for 10 minutes.

Strain and drink before bedtime.

Uses: Promotes restful sleep and endocrine recovery.

Long-term endocrine health requires a multifaceted approach that integrates herbal remedies, proper nutrition, and lifestyle practices. By incorporating these strategies into your daily routine, you can support hormonal balance, enhance resilience, and promote overall well-being. With consistency and care, you'll create a foundation for enduring endocrine health and vitality.

BOOK 36

CRAFTING HERBAL DRINKS BEYOND TEA

Herbal beverages offer endless possibilities beyond traditional teas, inviting creativity and innovation into your daily routine. Whether you're seeking a refreshing soda, a health-boosting kombucha, a celebratory mocktail, or a soothing coffee alternative, herbal drinks can cater to every occasion and preference. These versatile creations allow you to enjoy the benefits of herbs in unique, flavorful ways that go beyond the typical tea cup.

This book explores how to craft a variety of herbal beverages to suit your lifestyle and taste. From sparkling herbal tonics and fermented drinks like kombucha and kefir to cocktails and mocktails infused with nature's finest flavors, these recipes are designed to elevate your beverage repertoire. Additionally, we'll dive into herbal coffee alternatives, offering a caffeine-free solution for those seeking a healthier start to their day.

Each chapter provides step-by-step guidance, practical tips, and customizable recipes, making it easy to create drinks that align with your needs. Whether you're looking to impress guests, support your health, or simply try something new, this book equips you with the knowledge to craft delicious herbal beverages that are as functional as they are flavorful. Let's embark on this journey to discover the endless possibilities of herbal drinks!

Recipes for Herbal Sodas and Tonics

Herbal sodas and tonics are refreshing, health-boosting beverages that combine the benefits of herbs with effervescent fizz or flavorful blends. These drinks not only quench your thirst but also provide a creative way to incorporate the therapeutic properties of herbs into your daily life. Whether you're looking to energize, relax, or support digestion, herbal sodas and tonics can be tailored to your specific needs.

Herbal sodas use sparkling water or natural carbonation from fermentation, while tonics often feature bold herbal infusions mixed with sweeteners, citrus, or other flavor enhancers. With a little preparation, you can create your own delicious herbal beverages at home, free from artificial additives and tailored to your tastes.

This chapter provides 10 simple, customizable recipes for herbal sodas and tonics, offering a range of benefits from immune support to mood enhancement. You'll also find tips on crafting the perfect balance of flavors and carbonation to suit any occasion.

1206. Lemon Balm Sparkling Cooler

Ingredients:

1/4 cup fresh lemon balm leaves

2 tbsp lemon juice

1 tsp honey

1 cup sparkling water

Instructions:

Muddle lemon balm leaves with lemon juice and honey in a glass.

Add ice and top with sparkling water.

Stir gently and garnish with a lemon slice.

Uses: Promotes relaxation and uplifts mood.

1207. Ginger Turmeric Digestive Tonic

Ingredients:

1 tsp fresh grated ginger

1/2 tsp turmeric powder

1 tbsp honey

1 cup warm water

Instructions:

Mix ginger, turmeric, and honey in warm water until dissolved.

Let cool, then pour over ice.

Uses: Supports digestion and reduces inflammation.

1208. Lavender Blueberry Fizz
Ingredients:

1/4 cup fresh blueberries

1/2 tsp dried lavender flowers

1 tsp agave syrup

1 cup sparkling water

Instructions:

Muddle blueberries and lavender with agave syrup.

Add sparkling water and stir gently.

Strain if desired or leave blueberries for added texture.

Uses: Calms nerves and provides antioxidants.

1209. Rosemary Citrus Soda
Ingredients:

1 sprig fresh rosemary

1/4 cup orange juice

1 tsp simple syrup

1 cup sparkling water

Instructions:

Muddle rosemary with orange juice and simple syrup.

Strain and pour into a glass with ice.

Top with sparkling water and garnish with a rosemary sprig.

Uses: Energizes and boosts circulation.

1210. Mint Lime Cooler
Ingredients:

1/4 cup fresh mint leaves

2 tbsp lime juice

1 tsp sugar

1 cup sparkling water

Instructions:

Muddle mint leaves with lime juice and sugar.

Fill a glass with ice and pour sparkling water over the mixture.

Stir gently and garnish with a lime wedge.

Uses: Refreshes and aids digestion.

1211. Elderflower Tonic
Ingredients:

1 tbsp dried elderflowers

1 cup boiling water

1 tsp honey

1/2 cup sparkling water

Instructions:

Steep elderflowers in boiling water for 10 minutes.

Strain, cool, and mix with honey.

Add sparkling water before serving.

Uses: Supports immune health and soothes the throat.

1212. Hibiscus Citrus Spritz
Ingredients:

1 tbsp dried hibiscus flowers

1 cup boiling water

1 tbsp orange juice

1 tsp sugar

1/2 cup sparkling water

Instructions:

Steep hibiscus flowers in boiling water for 10 minutes.

Strain, cool, and mix with orange juice and sugar.

Add sparkling water and serve over ice.

Uses: Refreshes and provides antioxidants.

1213. Basil Cucumber Soda
Ingredients:

1/4 cup fresh basil leaves

2 slices cucumber

1 tsp simple syrup

1 cup sparkling water

Instructions:

Muddle basil leaves and cucumber slices with simple syrup.

Add ice and top with sparkling water.

Uses: Hydrates and promotes calmness.

1214. Cardamom Honey Tonic

Ingredients:

1/4 tsp ground cardamom

1 tbsp honey

1 cup warm water

Instructions:

Mix cardamom and honey in warm water until dissolved.

Cool and serve over ice.

Uses: Supports digestion and balances blood sugar.

1215. Chamomile Vanilla Soda

Ingredients:

1 tsp dried chamomile flowers

1 cup boiling water

1/2 tsp vanilla extract

1 tsp honey

1/2 cup sparkling water

Instructions:

Steep chamomile in boiling water for 10 minutes.

Strain, cool, and mix with vanilla extract and honey.

Add sparkling water before serving.

Uses: Promotes relaxation and soothes the mind.

Tips for Crafting Herbal Sodas and Tonics

Balance Flavors: Combine herbal, sweet, and tart flavors for a well-rounded drink.

Experiment: Mix and match herbs to create unique blends.

Use Fresh Ingredients: Fresh herbs and citrus enhance flavor and aroma.

Presentation: Garnish with fresh herbs, fruit slices, or edible flowers to elevate the experience.

Herbal sodas and tonics are a delightful way to enjoy the health benefits of herbs while exploring creative flavor combinations. These recipes offer something for everyone, from refreshing coolers to nourishing tonics. Experiment with these ideas and adjust them to suit your taste, making herbal sodas and tonics a regular part of your wellness routine.

Crafting Fermented Herbal Kombucha and Kefir

Fermented herbal beverages like kombucha and kefir are not only delicious but also packed with probiotics and beneficial compounds that support gut health, immunity, and overall well-being. When combined with herbs, these drinks gain additional therapeutic properties, making them a perfect addition to a holistic lifestyle.

Kombucha, a fermented tea made with a symbiotic culture of bacteria and yeast (SCOBY), is a tangy, effervescent drink that can be infused with a variety of herbal flavors. **Kefir**, a fermented milk or water-based beverage, is slightly creamy and offers a probiotic boost with a different spectrum of beneficial microbes. Both are versatile, customizable, and easy to make at home.

This chapter provides an overview of how to craft herbal kombucha and kefir, from selecting the right herbs to mastering the fermentation process. Whether you're a beginner or an experienced fermenter, these recipes and techniques will guide you toward creating nutrient-rich, flavorful beverages that support your health and delight your taste buds.

Step-by-Step Guide to Herbal Kombucha

Ingredients:

1 SCOBY (symbiotic culture of bacteria and yeast)

1 gallon water

1 cup sugar

8–10 black or green tea bags (or 2 tbsp loose leaf tea)

1 cup starter kombucha (from a previous batch or store-bought)

1/2 cup dried or fresh herbs for flavoring (e.g., hibiscus, chamomile, ginger)

Instructions:

Prepare Sweet Tea: Boil 1 gallon of water and dissolve 1 cup sugar. Add tea bags and steep until cooled to room temperature.

Add SCOBY: Transfer the tea to a large glass jar. Add the starter kombucha and place the SCOBY on top.

Ferment: Cover the jar with a cloth and secure

with a rubber band. Allow to ferment at room temperature (68–78°F) for 7–10 days.

Infuse with Herbs (Optional Second Fermentation): Remove the SCOBY and pour the kombucha into bottles. Add 1–2 tbsp of herbs per bottle for flavor. Seal tightly and ferment for an additional 2–3 days.

Strain and Serve: Strain out the herbs, refrigerate, and enjoy your flavored kombucha.

5 Herbal Kombucha Recipes

1216. Hibiscus Ginger Kombucha

Ingredients:

2 tbsp dried hibiscus flowers

1 tbsp grated fresh ginger

Instructions:

Add hibiscus and ginger during the second fermentation.

Ferment for 2–3 days, strain, and refrigerate.

Uses: Supports digestion and provides antioxidants.

1217. Chamomile Lavender Kombucha

Ingredients:

1 tbsp dried chamomile flowers

1 tbsp dried lavender flowers

Instructions:

Add chamomile and lavender during the second fermentation.

Strain after 2–3 days for a calming, floral drink.

Uses: Promotes relaxation and better sleep.

1218. Mint Lime Kombucha

Ingredients:

1/4 cup fresh mint leaves

2 tbsp fresh lime juice

Instructions:

Muddle mint and lime juice before adding to the kombucha.

Ferment for 2 days and strain.

Uses: Refreshing and digestive aid.

1219. Rosemary Citrus Kombucha

Ingredients:

1 sprig fresh rosemary

1/4 cup fresh orange juice

Instructions:

Add rosemary and orange juice during the second fermentation.

Strain and refrigerate after 2–3 days.

Uses: Energizes and boosts immunity.

1220. Basil Strawberry Kombucha

Ingredients:

1/4 cup fresh basil leaves

1/2 cup chopped strawberries

Instructions:

Add basil and strawberries to the kombucha and ferment for 2 days.

Strain and enjoy.

Uses: Sweet and refreshing with antioxidant benefits.

Step-by-Step Guide to Herbal Kefir

Ingredients:

1/4 cup kefir grains (milk or water-based)

4 cups milk (for milk kefir) or sugar water (for water kefir)

1/4 cup fresh or dried herbs for flavoring (e.g., mint, lemon balm)

Instructions:

Prepare the Base: If using milk, ensure it's at room temperature. For water kefir, dissolve 1/4 cup sugar in 4 cups water.

Add Kefir Grains: Place kefir grains into the liquid.

Ferment: Cover with a cloth and let ferment at room temperature for 24–48 hours.

Strain and Flavor: Strain the kefir grains and transfer the liquid to a bottle. Add herbs for flavor and let sit for 1–2 additional days for a secondary fermentation.

Strain and Serve: Remove herbs, refrigerate, and enjoy.

5 Herbal Kefir Recipes

1221. Lemon Balm Water Kefir

Ingredients:

1/4 cup fresh lemon balm leaves

Instructions:

Add lemon balm during the second fermentation.

Strain after 1–2 days for a refreshing, citrusy kefir.

Uses: Uplifts mood and supports digestion.

1222. Ginger Turmeric Milk Kefir

Ingredients:

1 tsp grated fresh ginger

1/2 tsp turmeric powder

Instructions:

Mix ginger and turmeric into milk kefir.

Let sit for 1 day before serving.

Uses: Anti-inflammatory and digestive support.

1223. Lavender Honey Kefir

Ingredients:

1 tsp dried lavender flowers

1 tsp honey

Instructions:

Stir honey and lavender into kefir during the second fermentation.

Strain and enjoy after 1–2 days.

Uses: Calms and soothes the body.

1224. Mint Cucumber Water Kefir

Ingredients:

1/4 cup fresh mint leaves

2 slices cucumber

Instructions:

Add mint and cucumber to water kefir for the second fermentation.

Strain and serve chilled.

Uses: Hydrating and refreshing.

1225. Orange Spice Milk Kefir

Ingredients:

1/4 tsp cinnamon

1/4 tsp ground cloves

1/4 cup orange juice

Instructions:

Add spices and orange juice to milk kefir during the second fermentation.

Let sit for 1 day before serving.

Uses: Warming and immune-boosting.

Tips for Success with Fermented Herbal Drinks

Use Quality Ingredients: Fresh herbs and organic tea or milk yield the best results.

Monitor Fermentation: Over-fermentation can lead to overly sour flavors. Taste regularly to find your preference.

Experiment with Flavors: Combine different herbs and fruits to create unique blends.

Fermented herbal drinks like kombucha and kefir offer an exciting, healthful way to incorporate herbs into your diet. With endless flavor possibilities and numerous health benefits, these beverages are a perfect addition to your wellness journey. By mastering the fermentation process, you'll create vibrant, probiotic-rich drinks that nourish your body and delight your senses.

Herbal Cocktails and Mocktails for Special Occasions

Herbal cocktails and mocktails offer a sophisticated, alcohol-free way to celebrate special occasions while promoting wellness. By combining the flavors of fresh herbs, fruits, and natural sweeteners, you can craft delicious drinks that are as healthful as they are festive. These beverages bring out the therapeutic qualities of herbs, offering calming, energizing, or refreshing benefits tailored to your needs.

This chapter provides 10 unique herbal mocktail recipes that focus on fresh, natural ingredients without using alcohol. Whether it's a refreshing lavender lemon fizz or a warming ginger spice mule, these recipes showcase how herbs can elevate your beverage experience. They're perfect for parties, quiet evenings, or as a creative alternative to traditional drinks.

1226. Lavender Lemon Fizz

Ingredients:

1 cup sparkling water

1 tbsp lavender syrup

1 tbsp lemon juice

Ice cubes

Instructions:

Combine lavender syrup and lemon juice in a glass.

Add ice and top with sparkling water.

Garnish with a sprig of fresh lavender.

Uses: Promotes relaxation and uplifts mood.

1227. Rosemary Citrus Spritzer

Ingredients:

1/4 cup fresh grapefruit juice

1 sprig fresh rosemary

1/2 tsp honey

1 cup sparkling water

Instructions:

Muddle rosemary with grapefruit juice and honey in a glass.

Add ice and top with sparkling water.

Garnish with a rosemary sprig.

Uses: Boosts energy and circulation.

1228. Basil Cucumber Cooler

Ingredients:

1/4 cup fresh basil leaves

3 slices cucumber

1 tbsp lime juice

1 tsp simple syrup

1 cup sparkling water

Instructions:

Muddle basil leaves, cucumber slices, lime juice, and simple syrup in a glass.

Add ice and top with sparkling water.

Stir gently and garnish with a cucumber slice.

Uses: Refreshes and aids digestion.

1229. Mint Mojito Mocktail

Ingredients:

1/4 cup fresh mint leaves

2 tbsp lime juice

1 tsp sugar

1 cup soda water

Instructions:

Muddle mint leaves, lime juice, and sugar in a glass.

Add ice and top with soda water.

Garnish with a lime wedge and mint sprig.

Uses: Energizing and cooling for hot days.

1230. Chamomile Honey Cooler

Ingredients:

1 cup chamomile tea (cooled)

1 tbsp honey

1 tbsp lemon juice

Ice cubes

Instructions:

Brew chamomile tea and allow it to cool.

Mix honey and lemon juice into the tea.

Serve over ice with a lemon slice garnish.

Uses: Calms the mind and soothes the stomach.

1231. Spiced Ginger Mule Mocktail

Ingredients:

1 oz ginger syrup

1 tbsp lime juice

3 oz ginger beer (non-alcoholic)

Ice cubes

Instructions:

Combine ginger syrup and lime juice in a glass with ice.

Top with non-alcoholic ginger beer and stir gently.

Garnish with a lime wheel and a slice of fresh ginger.

Uses: Aids digestion and provides a warming sensation.

1232. Hibiscus Berry Mocktail

Ingredients:

1 cup hibiscus tea (cooled)

1/4 cup mixed berries (muddled)

1 tbsp simple syrup

1 cup sparkling water

Instructions:

Muddle mixed berries and simple syrup in a glass.

Add hibiscus tea and ice, then top with sparkling water.

Garnish with fresh berries.

Uses: Antioxidant-rich and refreshing.

1233. Thyme Lemon Refresher

Ingredients:

1 tbsp lemon juice

1 tsp thyme-infused honey

1 cup sparkling water

Instructions:

Mix lemon juice and thyme-infused honey in a glass.

Add ice and top with sparkling water.

Garnish with a fresh thyme sprig.

Uses: Uplifting and aromatic.

1234. Sage Pear Sparkler

Ingredients:

1/2 cup pear juice

1 tsp sage-infused honey

1/2 cup sparkling water

Ice cubes

Instructions:

Mix pear juice and sage-infused honey in a glass.

Add ice and top with sparkling water.

Garnish with a fresh sage leaf.

Uses: Supports digestion and immunity.

1235. Cardamom Rose Lassi

Ingredients:

1 cup plain yogurt (or dairy-free alternative)

1/2 tsp ground cardamom

1 tbsp rosewater

1 tbsp honey

Ice cubes

Instructions:

Blend yogurt, cardamom, rosewater, honey, and a few ice cubes until smooth.

Serve in a chilled glass with a sprinkle of cardamom on top.

Uses: Cooling and aids digestion.

Tips for Crafting Herbal Mocktails

Balance Flavors: Experiment with herbal, sweet, sour, and bitter notes for complex, satisfying drinks.

Use Fresh Ingredients: Fresh herbs and juices enhance flavor and aroma.

Garnish Thoughtfully: A sprig of herb, a slice of fruit, or an edible flower adds elegance.

Herbal mocktails bring flavor, health benefits, and a touch of sophistication to any gathering or quiet moment of self-care. With their vibrant colors and fresh flavors, they're perfect for impressing guests or elevating your own beverage experience. These recipes provide inspiration for creating alcohol-free drinks that are both delicious and nourishing. Experiment with different herbs and fruits to craft your own signature blends!

Blending Herbal Coffee Alternatives

For those looking to reduce caffeine intake or simply explore new flavors, herbal coffee alternatives provide a satisfying and healthful substitute for traditional coffee. Made from roasted roots, grains, seeds, and herbs, these alternatives mimic the rich, robust flavors of coffee while offering additional health benefits. Herbal coffee alternatives can support digestion, reduce inflammation, and provide a calming or energizing effect without the jitters associated with caffeine.

This chapter introduces you to the art of blending herbal coffee substitutes, highlighting key ingredients like dandelion root, chicory, carob, and roasted barley. Each recipe is carefully crafted to deliver a delicious, coffee-like experience with unique herbal twists. Whether you prefer a simple cup of roasted dandelion coffee or a spiced latte-style drink, these blends will satisfy your taste buds and nourish your body.

Key Ingredients for Herbal Coffee Alternatives

Dandelion Root: A roasted root with a slightly bitter flavor, supporting liver health and digestion.

Chicory Root: Adds a rich, nutty taste and promotes gut health with its prebiotic content.

Carob Powder: A sweet, chocolaty flavor that adds depth and natural sweetness.

Barley or Rye: Roasted grains mimic the robust flavor of coffee and enhance digestion.

Cinnamon, Cardamom, and Nutmeg: Spices that add warmth and complexity to herbal blends.

Blending Techniques

Base Ingredient: Start with a primary base like roasted dandelion root or chicory for a coffee-like flavor.

Flavor Enhancers: Add carob, cacao, or spices to tailor the blend to your taste preferences.

Preparation Methods: Brew herbal coffee alternatives like traditional coffee—using a French press, drip coffee maker, or boiling on the stove.

10 Herbal Coffee Alternative Recipes

1236. Classic Dandelion Coffee

Ingredients:

2 tbsp roasted dandelion root

1 cup water

Instructions:

Simmer roasted dandelion root in water for 5–7 minutes.

Strain and enjoy as a simple coffee alternative.

Uses: Supports liver detoxification and digestion.

1237. Chicory and Carob Blend

Ingredients:

1 tbsp roasted chicory root

1 tbsp carob powder

1 cup water

Instructions:

Combine chicory root and carob powder in a pot with water.

Simmer for 5 minutes, strain, and serve.

Uses: A rich, chocolaty flavor to curb coffee cravings.

1238. Spiced Herbal Latte

Ingredients:

1 tbsp roasted dandelion root

1/2 tsp cinnamon

1/4 tsp cardamom

1 cup almond milk

Instructions:

Simmer dandelion root and spices in almond milk for 5 minutes.

Strain and froth for a latte-like experience.

Uses: A warm, comforting drink to replace coffee.

1239. Barley and Chicory Mocha

Ingredients:

1 tbsp roasted barley

1 tbsp roasted chicory root

1 tsp cacao powder

1 cup water

Instructions:

Simmer barley, chicory, and cacao in water for 7 minutes.

Strain and enjoy.

Uses: A robust, mocha-flavored alternative for coffee lovers.

1240. Vanilla Almond Dandelion Brew

Ingredients:

2 tbsp roasted dandelion root

1 tsp vanilla extract

1 cup almond milk

Instructions:

Simmer dandelion root in almond milk for 5–7 minutes.

Add vanilla extract and stir.

Uses: A soothing drink with a hint of sweetness.

1241. Chai-Spiced Herbal Coffee

Ingredients:

1 tbsp roasted chicory root

1/4 tsp ground ginger

1/4 tsp cinnamon

2 cardamom pods

1 cup water

Instructions:

Simmer all ingredients in water for 7 minutes.

Strain and enjoy as a chai-inspired coffee alternative.

Uses: Energizes without caffeine while supporting digestion.

1242. Cocoa Mint Herbal Brew

Ingredients:

1 tbsp roasted barley

1 tsp cacao powder

1 tsp dried mint leaves

1 cup water

Instructions:

Simmer all ingredients in water for 5 minutes.

Strain and serve warm or chilled.

Uses: Refreshing and soothing for the digestive system.

1243. Hazelnut Chicory Coffee

Ingredients:

1 tbsp roasted chicory root

1 tsp hazelnut extract

1 cup water

Instructions:

Brew chicory root in water for 5 minutes.

Add hazelnut extract and stir.

Uses: A nutty, aromatic alternative for coffee lovers.

1244. Carob Coconut Latte

Ingredients:

1 tbsp carob powder

1 cup coconut milk

1 tsp honey

Instructions:

Heat coconut milk and whisk in carob powder and honey.

Serve warm for a creamy, caffeine-free treat.

Uses: Provides natural sweetness and energy without caffeine.

1245. Cinnamon Turmeric Dandelion Blend

Ingredients:

2 tbsp roasted dandelion root

1/2 tsp turmeric powder

1/4 tsp cinnamon

1 cup water

Instructions:

Simmer all ingredients in water for 5–7 minutes.

Strain and enjoy.

Uses: Anti-inflammatory and detoxifying.

Tips for Perfect Herbal Coffee Blends

Adjust Ratios: Customize the blend's strength by increasing or decreasing the amount of roasted herbs.

Experiment with Spices: Try nutmeg, cloves, or anise for additional depth.

Froth Milk Alternatives: Frothing almond, oat, or coconut milk adds a café-like experience.

Sweeten Naturally: Use honey, maple syrup, or stevia for added sweetness without refined sugar.

Herbal coffee alternatives are a delicious, healthful way to enjoy a coffee-like experience without caffeine. These blends offer a variety of flavors and therapeutic benefits, making them a versatile addition to your daily routine. Experiment with these recipes to discover your favorite combination, and enjoy the rich, aromatic world of herbal coffee substitutes.

BOOK 37

ZERO-WASTE HERBALISM

In a world where sustainability is more critical than ever, zero-waste herbalism offers a mindful approach to making the most of nature's gifts while minimizing environmental impact. By embracing this philosophy, you can reduce waste, maximize the use of your herbal materials, and contribute to a healthier planet. Whether it's turning herb scraps into compost, finding creative uses for infused oils, or crafting eco-friendly packaging, zero-waste herbalism ensures that nothing goes to waste.

This book is your guide to incorporating sustainable practices into your herbal journey. It explores practical techniques like upcycling herb waste, repurposing spent herbs, and implementing eco-conscious foraging and gardening methods. You'll also discover how to make beautiful, DIY packaging for herbal gifts that reflect your commitment to the environment.

Each chapter provides actionable steps and creative ideas to help you reduce waste while enhancing your connection to nature. By adopting zero-waste herbalism, you not only honor the earth but also create a more mindful and resourceful approach to herbal crafting. Whether you're an experienced herbalist or just starting, this book will inspire you to embrace sustainability and make every herb count.

Upcycling Herb Waste into Compost and Mulch

As an herbal enthusiast, you may find yourself with leftover stems, leaves, or herb scraps after creating tinctures, infusions, or salves. While these remnants may seem like waste, they are actually a valuable resource for your garden and overall sustainability efforts. Upcycling herb waste into compost and mulch not only reduces your environmental footprint but also enriches the soil, supporting healthy plant growth for future herbal endeavors.

This chapter explores practical methods for transforming herb waste into compost and mulch. By embracing these practices, you can close the loop in your herbal journey, ensuring that no part of the plant goes unused.

Why Upcycling Herb Waste Matters

Herbs are rich in nutrients, including essential minerals and organic matter, that can benefit your soil. Upcycling herb waste into compost or mulch helps to:

Reduce Landfill Waste: Organic matter decomposing in landfills generates methane, a potent greenhouse gas. Composting diverts waste and minimizes environmental harm.

Improve Soil Health: Herb scraps decompose into nutrient-rich humus, enhancing soil structure, water retention, and fertility.

Support Circular Herbalism: By returning herb waste to the soil, you create a sustainable cycle that nourishes the plants you grow.

Step 1: Composting Herb Waste

Composting is one of the most effective ways to recycle herb scraps. Here's how to get started:

1. Choose Your Composting Method

Traditional Composting: A backyard compost pile or bin is perfect for processing larger volumes of herb waste.

Vermicomposting: Worm bins work well for smaller amounts of waste, and the worms produce nutrient-rich castings.

Bokashi Composting: This anaerobic method is ideal for breaking down herb scraps quickly, even in small spaces.

2. Balance Carbon and Nitrogen

Herb scraps are considered "greens" (nitrogen-rich materials). To create a healthy compost pile, balance them with "browns" (carbon-rich materials), such as:

Dry leaves

Straw

Shredded paper

A good ratio is approximately 2–3 parts browns to 1 part greens.

3. Prepare Your Herb Scraps

Chop larger stems and branches into smaller pieces to speed up decomposition.

Avoid adding diseased plants, invasive weeds, or herb scraps treated with pesticides.

4. Monitor the Pile

Turn your compost pile regularly to aerate it and ensure even decomposition. Keep the pile moist but not waterlogged. Within a few months, you'll have dark, crumbly compost ready to use in your garden.

Step 2: Creating Mulch from Herb Waste

Mulch is another excellent way to upcycle herb scraps, providing a protective layer for your garden soil. It helps retain moisture, suppress weeds, and regulate soil temperature. Herb-based mulch adds organic matter as it decomposes, enriching the soil over time.

How to Make Herbal Mulch

Dry Your Herb Waste: Spread herb scraps, stems, and leaves in a sunny, well-ventilated area to dry. This prevents mold and speeds up decomposition once applied to the soil.

Chop or Shred: Use garden shears or a shredder to break down larger pieces for easier application.

Layer the Mulch: Apply a 2–3 inch layer of dried herb scraps around your plants, avoiding direct contact with stems to prevent rot.

Specific Herb Waste Uses

Certain herbs offer unique benefits when composted or mulched, thanks to their properties:

Lavender and Rosemary: Their antimicrobial compounds can help deter pests and fungi.

Mint and Lemon Balm: Deter ants and other insects when used as mulch.

Chamomile: Adds calcium and potassium to the soil.

Tips for Successful Upcycling

Avoid Harmful Additions: Do not compost or mulch herb waste that contains essential oils in high concentrations (e.g., large amounts of eucalyptus or tea tree), as these can inhibit microbial activity.

Separate Seed Heads: Herb waste with seeds, like dill or fennel, can sprout in your compost or mulch. Remove seeds if you don't want them to grow.

Use in Moderation: When mulching, mix herb scraps with other materials like straw or wood chips to ensure a balanced breakdown.

Additional Uses for Herb Waste

If composting or mulching isn't feasible, consider these alternative ways to upcycle herb scraps:

Herbal Cleaning Solutions: Soak citrus peels and herb stems in vinegar to create a natural household cleaner.

Potpourri or Sachets: Dry herb scraps like lavender, mint, or lemon balm for aromatic sachets or potpourri.

Herbal Dyes: Use certain herbs, like chamomile or turmeric, to create natural dyes for fabric or paper.

Case Study: Emily's Garden Transformation

Emily, an herbal enthusiast, faced an issue with leftover herb stems and trimmings cluttering her workspace. By starting a backyard compost bin, she transformed her waste into rich compost that revitalized her herb garden. She also began using dried lavender and rosemary scraps as mulch, which not only nourished her plants but also deterred pests. Emily now enjoys a thriving garden while reducing her environmental impact—a testament to the power of upcycling herb waste.

Upcycling herb waste into compost and mulch is a simple yet impactful way to embrace sustainability in herbalism. These practices allow you to honor the full life cycle of your plants while enriching your soil and supporting future growth. With just a few adjustments, your herb scraps can become a valuable resource, contributing to a more eco-friendly and rewarding herbal journey. Start today, and watch your garden—and the planet—thrive!

Reusing Infused Oils and Spent Herbs Creatively

Herbal infusions, whether in oils, water, or alcohol, are a cornerstone of herbalism. However, after creating your salves, tinctures, or teas, you might find yourself left with spent herbs and infused oils that seem to have served their purpose. Instead of discarding them, these materials can be reused in creative ways, extending their life cycle and reducing waste. By thinking outside the box, you can maximize the value of your ingredients and discover new uses for these herbal byproducts.

This chapter explores innovative methods for re-purposing infused oils and spent herbs, turning them into practical, beautiful, and sustainable creations. With a bit of creativity, what was once seen as waste can become a treasure for your home, skincare routine, or garden.

Why Reuse Infused Oils and Spent Herbs?

Reusing infused oils and spent herbs aligns with the principles of zero-waste herbalism by:

Reducing Waste: Prevents valuable materials from ending up in the trash.

Saving Resources: Maximizes the benefits of your herbs and oils, making them more cost-effective.

Encouraging Creativity: Opens opportunities for crafting unique products and solutions.

Reusing Infused Oils

Infused oils are versatile and retain much of their herbal properties even after their initial use. Here are creative ways to reuse them:

1. Make a Multi-Purpose Cleaning Oil

Leftover infused oils, especially those with antimicrobial herbs like lavender, rosemary, or tea tree, can be turned into natural cleaning oils.

How to Use: Mix the infused oil with equal parts vinegar and a few drops of citrus essential oil. Use it to polish wood or clean stainless steel surfaces.

2. Create Aromatherapy Candles

Infused oils can be used to make candles that emit a gentle herbal aroma.

How to Use: Combine the oil with melted soy or beeswax, add a wick to a glass jar, and pour in the mixture. Allow it to harden before use.

3. Formulate a Protective Lip Balm

Even lightly used infused oils can be the base for nourishing lip balms.

How to Use: Melt 1 part infused oil with 1 part beeswax and a few drops of honey. Pour into small tins and allow to set.

4. Make a Herbal Bath Oil

Transform infused oils into a luxurious bath additive to nourish your skin.

How to Use: Add a few tablespoons of the oil to a warm bath. Use soothing oils like chamomile, calendula, or lavender for best results.

5. Create a Massage Blend

Infused oils still hold therapeutic properties that can benefit the body when used in massage.

How to Use: Mix the oil with a carrier oil, such as almond or coconut, for a relaxing massage experience.

Reusing Spent Herbs

The herbs left behind after infusions or teas often retain significant nutritional and therapeutic value. Here's how to give them a second life:

1. Herbal Compost Booster

Spent herbs are an excellent addition to your compost pile. They decompose quickly and add nutrients to the soil.

How to Use: Spread the herbs in your compost bin, balancing with carbon-rich materials like leaves or straw.

2. Herbal Sachets and Potpourri

Spent herbs with a pleasant aroma can be dried and repurposed into sachets or potpourri.

How to Use: Mix dried herbs with dried flowers and essential oils. Place them in small fabric bags for use in drawers or closets.

3. Make a Second Infusion

Some herbs, such as chamomile, rose, and mint, can be infused a second time for a milder tea or bath soak.

How to Use: Re-steep the herbs in hot water for a lighter flavor or therapeutic bath.

4. Herb-Infused Vinegar

Spent herbs can be infused in vinegar to create a cleaning solution or a hair rinse.

How to Use: Place the herbs in a jar, cover with vinegar, and let sit for 2–4 weeks. Strain and use as desired.

5. DIY Face and Body Scrub

Exfoliating scrubs made with spent herbs are gentle on the skin and environmentally friendly.

How to Use: Combine dried, ground herbs with sugar, salt, and coconut oil. Use in the shower to exfoliate and moisturize.

Combining Infused Oils and Spent Herbs

For a truly zero-waste approach, you can use both infused oils and spent herbs together to create new products:

1. Herbal Soap Bars

Combine infused oils and finely ground spent herbs to craft nourishing soap bars.

How to Use: Mix the oil and herbs with a soap base (like glycerin or goat's milk), pour into molds, and let harden.

2. Garden Care Spray

Create a natural garden spray using antimicrobial herb-infused oils and a tea made from spent herbs.

How to Use: Dilute the oil and tea in water and use as a natural pesticide or plant spray.

3. Scented Drawer Liners

Combine the dried herbs and a small amount of infused oil to create herbal-scented paper for drawer liners.

How to Use: Infuse plain paper or fabric with the herbs and oil, then place in drawers to freshen clothes.

Tips for Reusing Oils and Herbs

Store Properly: Keep infused oils in dark, airtight containers to prevent rancidity.

Dry Thoroughly: Dry spent herbs completely before repurposing them to avoid mold.

Experiment Freely: Be creative in finding new uses for these materials—it's part of the zero-waste journey.

Case Study: Sarah's Creative Reuse Journey

Sarah, a home herbalist, noticed that her spent chamomile and lavender flowers were piling up after making teas and infused oils. Instead of discarding them, she began drying the herbs for sachets and potpourri, turning her waste into aromatic gifts for friends. She also repurposed her leftover infused lavender oil into massage blends and bath oils, finding joy in her resourceful approach. Sarah's efforts reduced her herbal waste to almost zero while giving her more products to share and enjoy.

Reusing infused oils and spent herbs is not only environmentally friendly but also a creative and rewarding aspect of herbalism. These materials still hold therapeutic and practical value, allowing you to craft new products for your home, self-care routine, or garden. By thinking resourcefully and embracing a zero-waste mindset, you can extend the life of your herbal ingredients and contribute to a more sustainable lifestyle. Every leftover drop and scrap has potential—use them wisely and reap the benefits!

Making DIY Packaging for Herbal Gifts

Creating herbal gifts is a thoughtful and personal way to share the benefits of herbs with loved ones. To make these gifts even more special, designing your own sustainable and creative packaging can elevate the experience while reinforcing your commitment to zero-waste practices. Whether it's handmade herbal teas, bath salts, or infused oils, beautiful DIY packaging adds a touch of artistry and care to your gifts.

This chapter focuses on practical, eco-friendly ideas for crafting personalized packaging using recycled and natural materials. From fabric wraps to upcycled jars, these options are both visually appealing and environmentally conscious. By using what you already have or sourcing sustainable materials, you can craft packaging that reflects your love for herbalism and the planet.

Benefits of DIY Packaging

Reduces Waste: Avoids single-use plastics and unnecessary packaging materials.

Personalized Touch: Adds a unique, creative element to your herbal gifts.

Cost-Effective: Repurposes materials you already have, saving money.

Eco-Friendly: Reinforces sustainability by using natural, recyclable, or biodegradable materials.

Eco-Friendly Materials for DIY Packaging

1. Glass Jars and Bottles

Ideal for: Herbal teas, bath salts, infused oils, and creams.

How to Source: Reuse jars from your pantry or purchase in bulk from thrift stores or online shops.

Customization: Add hand-drawn labels, paint, or decorative ribbons.

2. Kraft Paper and Cardboard

Ideal for: Wrapping soaps, sachets, or bundles of dried herbs.

How to Use: Wrap items in kraft paper and secure with twine or washi tape. Stamp or write on the paper for a personal touch.

3. Fabric Scraps or Furoshiki Wraps

Ideal for: Loose-leaf teas, dried herbs, or small gift bundles.

How to Use: Wrap items in fabric, tie with a ribbon, or knot in the Japanese furoshiki style. Use scraps from old clothes or linens.

4. Recycled Cardboard Boxes

Ideal for: Gift sets or larger items like soap bars or tinctures.

How to Use: Decorate plain boxes with hand-drawn designs, stamps, or recycled paper cutouts.

5. Mason Jars with DIY Lids

Ideal for: Multipurpose packaging that can be reused by the recipient.

How to Customize: Add a fabric circle under the lid ring, tie a handwritten tag, or paint the jar for a rustic look.

DIY Packaging Ideas for Herbal Gifts

1. Herbal Tea Sampler in Glass Tubes

Materials Needed: Glass test tubes, cork stoppers, twine, and small labels.

How to Assemble:

Fill each tube with a different herbal tea blend.

Seal with a cork stopper and tie a label around the neck with twine.

Place the tubes in a small recycled box lined with kraft paper.

2. Hand-Stitched Sachet Bags

Materials Needed: Fabric scraps, needle, thread, and dried herbs.

How to Assemble:

Sew small rectangular pouches from fabric scraps.

Fill with dried herbs like lavender, chamomile, or mint.

Stitch the opening closed or tie with a ribbon.

3. Kraft Paper Herb Bundles

Materials Needed: Kraft paper, twine, and fresh or dried herb sprigs.

How to Assemble:

Lay herb sprigs on a sheet of kraft paper.

Roll the paper around the herbs and secure with twine.

Add a small handwritten note or label to identify the herbs.

4. Infused Oil in Upcycled Bottles

Materials Needed: Glass bottles, corks, and ribbon or raffia.

How to Assemble:

Fill the bottle with infused oil and seal with a cork or screw cap.

Tie a ribbon or raffia around the neck and attach a label with instructions for use.

5. Bath Salt Jars with Natural Accents

Materials Needed: Mason jars, dried flowers, and kraft paper tags.

How to Assemble:

Fill the jar with herbal bath salts.

Add a decorative band of dried flowers around the lid.

Attach a kraft paper tag with the ingredients and instructions.

Tips for Personalizing Your Packaging

Add Handwritten Notes: Include a card with the benefits of the herbs and how to use the gift.

Incorporate Dried Herbs: Use sprigs of rosemary, lavender, or thyme as decoration.

Use Natural Colors: Stick to earth tones, greens, and other natural hues for an eco-friendly aesthetic.

Repurpose Materials: Turn old jars, fabric scraps, and paper into beautiful packaging with a little creativity.

Practical Examples

Case Study: A Zero-Waste Gift Set

Maria, an herbalist, wanted to create a zero-waste holiday gift set. She packaged her lavender bath salts in mason jars with handmade fabric lids, tied bundles of dried herbs with twine, and made herbal sachets from leftover cotton fabric. By adding handwritten tags and small dried flower accents, her gifts looked polished and personal, all while minimizing waste.

DIY packaging for herbal gifts is a wonderful way to combine creativity, sustainability, and thoughtfulness. By using eco-friendly materials and incorporating personal touches, you can create gifts that are as beautiful as they are meaningful. These ideas not only elevate your herbal creations but also align with the principles of zero-waste living, making them a win for both your recipient and the environment. Explore these methods, and let your packaging reflect the care and love you've put into your herbal gifts.

Sustainable Foraging and Gardening Practices

As herbalists and nature enthusiasts, our relationship with the earth is central to our craft. Sustainable foraging and gardening practices ensure that we can harvest the bounty of nature without depleting resources or damaging ecosystems. By practicing mindfulness and stewardship, we contribute to the health of the environment while enjoying the benefits of its gifts.

This chapter delves into sustainable approaches to foraging and gardening, highlighting techniques that preserve biodiversity, promote soil health, and support thriving plant communities. By following these guidelines, you can cultivate a respectful and symbiotic connection with the natural world, ensuring that it continues to provide for generations to come.

Understanding Sustainable Foraging

Foraging is the practice of gathering wild plants for food, medicine, or other uses. While foraging connects us to ancient traditions and provides access to potent, natural ingredients, it must be approached responsibly to prevent overharvesting and harm to ecosystems.

1. Research Local Laws and Regulations

Before heading out, familiarize yourself with the rules governing foraging in your area. Some regions protect specific plants or prohibit foraging in certain locations, such as national parks. Adhering to these laws helps conserve sensitive ecosystems and rare species.

2. Identify Plants with Confidence

Responsible foraging begins with proper plant identification. Misidentifying plants can lead to harvesting non-native invasives or, worse, toxic species. Invest in a good field guide, take classes, or forage with an experienced mentor to ensure safe and accurate identification.

3. Harvest Mindfully

When harvesting, always ask yourself:

Is this plant abundant? Avoid taking plants that are rare or endangered in your region.

Am I leaving enough? Never take more than 10% of a plant population to allow it to regenerate.

Am I causing harm? Harvest in a way that doesn't damage the plant or its environment. For example, use sharp tools to minimize stress on roots and avoid trampling nearby vegetation.

4. Choose Abundant or Invasive Species

Focus on plants that are prolific or considered invasive, such as dandelion, garlic mustard, or nettle.

Harvesting these species can support ecosystem health by preventing overgrowth.

5. Leave No Trace

Practice "leave no trace" principles while foraging. This includes packing out all trash, not disturbing wildlife, and avoiding areas where your presence might cause harm, such as wetlands or fragile habitats.

Sustainable Gardening Practices

For those who prefer cultivating herbs at home, sustainable gardening practices can help you grow a thriving, eco-friendly garden that supports biodiversity and reduces waste.

1. Plan Your Garden Wisely

Select Native Plants: Native plants are well-adapted to your region, requiring less water, fertilizer, and maintenance. They also support local pollinators and wildlife.

Choose Perennials: Perennial herbs like thyme, mint, and sage reduce the need for frequent replanting, saving resources.

2. Build Healthy Soil

Soil health is the foundation of sustainable gardening. Practices like composting, mulching, and crop rotation replenish nutrients and prevent erosion.

Composting: Use kitchen scraps, herb waste, and yard trimmings to create nutrient-rich compost.

Mulching: Apply a layer of organic mulch, such as straw or dried leaves, to retain soil moisture, suppress weeds, and improve soil quality over time.

3. Practice Water Conservation

Water is a precious resource, and conserving it is essential for sustainable gardening.

Install a Rain Barrel: Collect rainwater to reduce dependency on municipal supplies.

Use Drip Irrigation: Drip systems deliver water directly to plant roots, minimizing evaporation.

Plant in Zones: Group plants with similar water needs to optimize irrigation.

4. Attract Beneficial Insects

Incorporate plants that attract pollinators and predatory insects to maintain a healthy garden ecosystem.

Pollinator-Friendly Plants: Include flowers like calendula, echinacea, and lavender to attract bees and butterflies.

Encourage Predators: Provide habitat for ladybugs and lacewings, which help control pests naturally.

5. Minimize Chemical Use

Avoid synthetic pesticides, herbicides, and fertilizers, which can harm beneficial insects, contaminate water supplies, and disrupt soil health. Instead, opt for natural solutions like:

Neem Oil: A biodegradable, plant-based insecticide.

Companion Planting: Pairing certain plants together to repel pests (e.g., marigolds to deter aphids).

Homemade Remedies: Use soap sprays or garlic infusions to control pests.

Ethical Harvesting in Your Garden

Even in your own garden, harvesting with care ensures the longevity of your plants and the continued health of your soil.

Prune Selectively: Harvest herbs in a way that encourages regrowth, such as trimming leaves instead of pulling entire plants.

Rotate Crops: Change the location of annual herbs each year to prevent soil depletion.

Allow Seed Production: Let some plants go to seed to promote natural regeneration.

Blending Foraging and Gardening

Combining sustainable foraging and gardening practices creates a harmonious approach to herbalism. By supplementing your garden with foraged plants, you can enjoy a broader range of herbs while reducing pressure on wild populations. Similarly, cultivating native plants in your garden supports local ecosystems and offers a convenient alternative to foraging.

Additional Practices for Sustainability

1. Seed Saving

Saving seeds from your garden reduces reliance on store-bought seeds and preserves heirloom varieties.

How to Save Seeds: Allow flowers to dry and collect seeds from mature pods or heads. Store them in a cool, dry place for future planting.

2. Compost Tea

Enhance your garden's fertility by making compost tea, a nutrient-rich liquid made from steeping compost in water. Use it to feed your plants naturally.

3. Encourage Biodiversity

Diverse plantings create a resilient garden that can withstand pests, diseases, and climate changes. Incorporate a mix of herbs, vegetables, flowers, and shrubs to mimic natural ecosystems.

Case Study: Anna's Holistic Herb Garden

Anna, an herbalist in Oregon, combined foraging and gardening to create a sustainable herbal practice. She foraged abundant plants like nettle and dandelion while cultivating native herbs like yarrow and bee balm in her backyard. By composting her herb waste and practicing crop rotation, Anna enriched her soil naturally. Her rain barrel provided water for her garden, and she used companion planting to minimize pests. With these practices, Anna not only reduced her environmental impact but also enjoyed a flourishing garden and access to wild herbs year-round.

Challenges and Solutions

Overharvesting Risks: Stick to the 10% rule and focus on abundant species to avoid depleting wild populations.

Limited Space for Gardening: Use vertical gardening techniques or container gardening to maximize small spaces.

Learning Curve: Sustainable practices take time to master. Start small and expand your efforts as you gain experience.

Sustainable foraging and gardening practices are essential for ensuring the longevity and health of our natural resources. By respecting the environment and cultivating with care, you create a positive impact that goes beyond your own herbal practice. Whether you're harvesting from the wild or tending to your garden, these mindful practices empower you to work in harmony with nature while enjoying its abundant gifts. Together, sustainable foraging and gardening pave the way for a greener, more balanced future.

BOOK 38

HERBAL SUPPORT FOR CHRONIC CONDITIONS

Living with chronic conditions often requires a multifaceted approach to manage symptoms, improve quality of life, and support overall well-being. While modern medicine provides essential tools, herbal remedies offer complementary support that addresses the root causes of many chronic issues, such as inflammation, fatigue, and immune system imbalances. These natural solutions have been used for centuries to help people manage persistent health challenges in a holistic, sustainable way.

This book explores the role of herbs in supporting chronic conditions, offering practical, evidence-based strategies to integrate them into your care routine. From anti-inflammatory herbs for arthritis to adaptogens for chronic fatigue and autoimmune support, each chapter provides targeted remedies tailored to specific conditions. You'll also learn how to develop long-term holistic care plans that align with your body's natural rhythms and promote overall health.

Whether you're looking to alleviate discomfort, boost energy, or enhance your resilience, this book provides the knowledge and tools to harness the power of herbs effectively and safely. With a focus on sustainability and self-care, Herbal Support for Chronic Conditions empowers you to take an active role in managing your health while honoring the wisdom of nature.

Managing Arthritis with Anti-Inflammatory Herbs

Arthritis, characterized by joint inflammation and pain, is one of the most common chronic conditions, affecting millions worldwide. While medical treatments can provide relief, integrating anti-inflammatory herbs into your routine offers a natural and holistic approach to managing symptoms. Herbs can help reduce inflammation, alleviate pain, and promote joint health, complementing conventional therapies and enhancing overall well-being.

This chapter explores the best anti-inflammatory herbs for arthritis and how to use them effectively. Whether consumed as teas, tinctures, or topical applications, these herbs provide versatile solutions tailored to individual needs.

Understanding Arthritis and Inflammation

Arthritis encompasses a range of conditions, with osteoarthritis and rheumatoid arthritis being the most prevalent.

Osteoarthritis (OA): Caused by wear and tear on joints, leading to cartilage breakdown.

Rheumatoid Arthritis (RA): An autoimmune condition where the immune system attacks joint tissues.

Both forms involve chronic inflammation, which contributes to pain, stiffness, and reduced mobility. Addressing inflammation is key to managing symptoms, and herbs are a powerful ally in this process.

Key Anti-Inflammatory Herbs for Arthritis

1. Turmeric (Curcuma longa)

Turmeric is renowned for its active compound, curcumin, which has potent anti-inflammatory and antioxidant properties.

How It Helps: Curcumin inhibits inflammatory pathways, reducing swelling and joint pain.

How to Use:

Tea: Steep 1 tsp turmeric powder with a pinch of black pepper in hot water.

Golden Milk: Mix turmeric with warm milk and honey for a soothing drink.

Capsules: Take standardized curcumin supplements for concentrated doses.

2. Ginger (Zingiber officinale)

Ginger is another powerful anti-inflammatory herb that works similarly to non-steroidal anti-inflammatory drugs (NSAIDs).

How It Helps: Blocks enzymes that cause inflammation and reduces pain in joints.

How to Use:

Tea: Simmer fresh ginger slices in water for 10 minutes.

Compress: Use warm ginger-infused water as a compress on affected joints.

3. Boswellia (Boswellia serrata)

Also known as Indian frankincense, boswellia is prized for its anti-inflammatory effects, particularly for rheumatoid arthritis.

How It Helps: Blocks the production of inflammatory molecules, reducing stiffness and improving mobility.

How to Use:

Capsules: Take a standardized boswellia extract as directed.

Topical Cream: Apply boswellia-based creams to affected areas for localized relief.

4. Devil's Claw (Harpagophytum procumbens)

Native to Africa, devil's claw is widely used for its anti-inflammatory and pain-relieving properties.

How It Helps: Reduces swelling and improves joint function.

How to Use:

Tea: Steep dried devil's claw root in hot water.

Capsules: Available as a supplement for convenient daily use.

5. Willow Bark (Salix alba)

Often called "nature's aspirin," willow bark contains salicin, a compound that reduces pain and inflammation.

How It Helps: Eases arthritis pain and stiffness.

How to Use:

Tea: Brew willow bark in water for a mild, effective remedy.

Incorporating Herbs into Your Daily Routine

Herbal Teas and Decoctions

Herbal teas are a simple and effective way to integrate anti-inflammatory herbs into your daily life. Prepare a blend of turmeric, ginger, and cinnamon for a warming, joint-soothing drink.

Topical Applications

Many herbs can be applied directly to painful joints. Create a soothing poultice with fresh ginger or turmeric, or use boswellia-based creams for targeted relief.

Dietary Integration

Incorporate anti-inflammatory herbs into meals. Add turmeric and ginger to soups, stews, or smoothies for a flavorful and medicinal boost.

Supplements

Standardized supplements offer a concentrated dose of active compounds. Consult a healthcare provider for guidance on proper dosage and safety.

Lifestyle Practices to Enhance Herbal Benefits

While herbs are a powerful tool, combining them with lifestyle changes can amplify their effects:

Anti-Inflammatory Diet: Emphasize whole foods like leafy greens, fatty fish, nuts, and seeds while minimizing processed foods and sugar.

Regular Exercise: Low-impact activities like swimming, yoga, and walking improve joint mobility and reduce stiffness.

Stress Management: Chronic stress exacerbates inflammation. Practice mindfulness, meditation, or deep breathing to support overall well-being.

Precautions and Considerations

While herbs are generally safe, it's important to use them mindfully:

Allergies: Test for any sensitivities, especially when using topical applications.

Interactions: Some herbs, like willow bark, may interact with blood thinners or other medications. Consult a healthcare professional before use.

Dosage: Stick to recommended dosages to avoid side effects like stomach upset.

Case Study: Sarah's Arthritis Relief Journey

Sarah, a 55-year-old yoga instructor, struggled with osteoarthritis in her knees, making her daily practice challenging. After incorporating turmeric and ginger into her routine, she noticed significant improvements in her joint pain and flexibility. By drinking turmeric tea twice daily and using a boswellia cream, she reduced inflammation and regained mobility, allowing her to continue her yoga practice with ease.

Managing arthritis with anti-inflammatory herbs offers a natural, effective way to alleviate pain and improve joint health. Herbs like turmeric, ginger, and boswellia not only reduce inflammation but also support overall well-being. By integrating these remedies into your daily routine and adopting complementary lifestyle practices, you can take control of arthritis symptoms and enhance your quality of life. Always consult with a healthcare provider to ensure safe and effective use, and let the wisdom of herbs guide you on your path to relief.

Natural Remedies for Chronic Fatigue Syndrome

Chronic Fatigue Syndrome (CFS), also known as Myalgic Encephalomyelitis (ME), is a complex condition characterized by extreme fatigue that doesn't improve with rest and often worsens with physical or mental exertion. Accompanied by symptoms like brain fog, muscle pain, sleep disturbances, and immune dysfunction, CFS significantly impacts quality of life. While its exact cause remains unclear, a holistic approach that includes natural remedies can provide symptom relief and enhance energy levels.

This chapter explores herbs, lifestyle adjustments, and nutritional strategies to manage CFS naturally. By supporting the body's energy systems, addressing underlying inflammation, and nurturing the nervous system, these remedies help restore balance and vitality.

Key Herbal Remedies for CFS

Herbs can support energy production, reduce inflammation, and strengthen the body's resilience against stress. Here are some of the most effective options:

1. Adaptogens: Enhancing Resilience

Adaptogenic herbs help the body adapt to stress and improve energy levels by supporting adrenal and immune function.

Ashwagandha (Withania somnifera)

How It Helps: Reduces cortisol levels, supports energy balance, and combats fatigue.

How to Use: Take as a capsule or powder mixed into smoothies or teas.

Rhodiola (Rhodiola rosea)

How It Helps: Boosts mental clarity and physical stamina by improving oxygen utilization in cells.

How to Use: Brew as a tea or take as a standardized extract.

Holy Basil (Ocimum sanctum)

How It Helps: Reduces stress and promotes calmness, supporting restful sleep and sustained energy.

How to Use: Drink as an herbal infusion or use in cooking.

2. Anti-Inflammatory Herbs

Chronic inflammation is often a factor in CFS, contributing to fatigue and pain.

Turmeric (Curcuma longa)

How It Helps: Contains curcumin, a potent anti-inflammatory compound that reduces oxidative stress.

How to Use: Incorporate turmeric into meals, teas, or golden milk.

Ginger (Zingiber officinale)

How It Helps: Soothes inflammation and supports digestion, which is often compromised in CFS.

How to Use: Brew ginger tea or add freshly grated ginger to dishes.

3. Nervines: Supporting the Nervous System

CFS often involves nervous system dysregulation, leading to heightened stress responses and poor sleep.

Chamomile (Matricaria chamomilla)

How It Helps: Promotes relaxation and improves sleep quality.

How to Use: Drink as a soothing tea before bedtime.

Skullcap (Scutellaria lateriflora)

How It Helps: Calms an overactive nervous system and reduces anxiety.

How to Use: Take as a tincture or tea in the evening.

Nutritional Support for Energy and Recovery

CFS can often be exacerbated by nutritional deficiencies. Supporting the body with key nutrients enhances energy production and overall health.

1. Magnesium

Magnesium is essential for energy metabolism and muscle relaxation. Deficiency is common in people with CFS.

Sources: Leafy greens, nuts, seeds, and Epsom salt baths.

2. Vitamin B Complex

B vitamins play a crucial role in cellular energy production and neurological health.

Sources: Whole grains, eggs, fish, and fortified cereals.

3. Omega-3 Fatty Acids

Omega-3s reduce inflammation and support brain health, which can improve symptoms like brain fog.

Sources: Fatty fish, flaxseeds, walnuts, and fish oil supplements.

4. Coenzyme Q10 (CoQ10)

CoQ10 is involved in cellular energy production and has been shown to improve fatigue in some people with CFS.

Sources: Found in organ meats, fatty fish, and supplements.

Lifestyle Adjustments for Managing CFS

Herbal remedies work best when paired with lifestyle changes that promote rest, recovery, and balance.

1. Prioritize Restorative Sleep

Poor sleep exacerbates fatigue and impairs the body's ability to heal.

Herbal Aids: Use chamomile or valerian tea to support sleep.

Sleep Hygiene: Establish a consistent bedtime routine and create a calming environment.

2. Practice Gentle Movement

While intense exercise can worsen symptoms, gentle activities can improve circulation and energy levels.

Options: Try restorative yoga, tai chi, or short walks.

3. Manage Stress

Stress management is critical for reducing fatigue and preventing flare-ups.

Herbal Support: Adaptogens like ashwagandha and holy basil help reduce stress.

Techniques: Practice mindfulness, meditation, or deep breathing exercises.

4. Implement Pacing Strategies

Overexertion can lead to post-exertional malaise (PEM), a hallmark of CFS.

How to Pace: Divide activities into smaller, manageable tasks with frequent breaks to conserve energy.

Topical and Aromatherapy Remedies

1. Essential Oils for Energy and Relaxation

Essential oils can provide a quick boost or promote relaxation depending on your needs.

Peppermint Oil: Inhalation can invigorate and reduce brain fog.

Lavender Oil: Diffuse or apply topically for relaxation and better sleep.

2. Herbal Compresses for Muscle Pain

Chronic fatigue often comes with muscle aches and tension. Herbal compresses offer localized relief.

How to Use: Soak a cloth in a warm infusion of chamomile or ginger and apply to sore areas.

Case Study: Emily's Journey to Balance

Emily, a 42-year-old teacher, was diagnosed with CFS after years of debilitating fatigue and brain fog. With the help of a holistic practitioner, she incorporated herbal teas like ashwagandha and chamomile into her daily routine, added magnesium-rich foods to her diet, and practiced pacing to avoid overexertion. Within a few months, Emily noticed improvements in her energy levels and mental clarity. By continuing these practices, she found a sustainable way to manage her symptoms and regain control of her life.

Precautions and Considerations

While natural remedies can be effective, they should be used thoughtfully:

Consult a Professional: Work with a healthcare provider to ensure safety, especially if taking medications or managing other conditions.

Start Slowly: Introduce herbs and supplements gradually to monitor how your body responds.

Listen to Your Body: Adjust your approach based on your energy levels and symptoms.

Chronic Fatigue Syndrome is a challenging condition, but natural remedies offer a supportive and holistic approach to managing symptoms. Herbs like ashwagandha and ginger, combined with targeted nutrition and lifestyle changes, can restore balance and promote resilience. By addressing underlying inflammation, nourishing the nervous system, and practicing mindfulness, you can create a path toward renewed energy and vitality. Remember, small, consistent changes can make a profound difference in your journey to wellness.

Herbs for Supporting Autoimmune Wellness

Autoimmune diseases occur when the immune system mistakenly attacks the body's tissues, causing chronic inflammation, pain, and dysfunction. Conditions like lupus, rheumatoid arthritis, Hashimoto's thyroiditis, and multiple sclerosis are examples of autoimmune disorders that affect millions worldwide. While managing these conditions often requires medical intervention, herbs can play a supportive role in regulating immune responses, reducing inflammation, and promoting overall wellness.

This chapter explores herbs that support autoimmune health by balancing the immune system, soothing inflammation, and aiding in stress reduction. Used thoughtfully, these herbs can complement conventional treatments, helping to improve quality of life for those with autoimmune conditions.

Understanding Immune Modulation

In autoimmune diseases, the immune system becomes overactive, targeting the body's own tissues. The goal of herbal support is not to suppress the immune system entirely but to modulate it—helping to calm overactivity while maintaining its ability to protect against infections. Herbs that achieve this balance are known as **immunomodulators**.

Key Herbs for Autoimmune Support

1. Ashwagandha (Withania somnifera)

Ashwagandha is an adaptogenic herb that reduces stress, a common trigger for autoimmune flare-ups.

How It Helps: Calms an overactive immune response, reduces inflammation, and supports adrenal function.

How to Use: Take as a capsule, powder, or tea. Mix the powder into warm milk for a soothing bedtime drink.

2. Turmeric (Curcuma longa)

Turmeric is rich in curcumin, a powerful anti-inflammatory compound.

How It Helps: Inhibits inflammatory pathways and reduces oxidative stress.

How to Use: Add turmeric to meals, teas, or prepare golden milk with black pepper to enhance absorption.

3. Licorice Root (Glycyrrhiza glabra)

Licorice root is both an anti-inflammatory and an adaptogen, supporting the immune system and adrenal health.

How It Helps: Protects tissues from inflammation and supports energy levels.

How to Use: Brew as a tea or take as a tincture. Avoid prolonged use if you have high blood pressure.

4. Reishi Mushroom (Ganoderma lucidum)

Known as the "mushroom of immortality," reishi is an adaptogen with immunomodulatory properties.

How It Helps: Balances immune activity, reduces fatigue, and supports overall vitality.

How to Use: Take as a powder, capsule, or tea.

5. Nettle (Urtica dioica)

Nettle is a nourishing herb packed with vitamins and minerals, making it ideal for overall immune and inflammatory support.

How It Helps: Reduces inflammation and provides nutrients that support tissue repair.

How to Use: Drink as a tea or use fresh nettles in soups and salads.

6. Cat's Claw (Uncaria tomentosa)

Cat's claw is a potent anti-inflammatory herb often used for autoimmune conditions like rheumatoid arthritis.

How It Helps: Reduces inflammatory markers and supports immune balance.

How to Use: Take as a tincture or capsule.

Herbal Teas for Autoimmune Wellness

Combining herbs into teas is a simple way to incorporate them into your routine. Try this **Autoimmune Support Blend**:

Ingredients: 1 tsp each of nettle, licorice root, and turmeric powder; 1 cup hot water.

Instructions: Steep herbs in hot water for 10 minutes, strain, and enjoy.

Lifestyle Tips to Enhance Herbal Benefits

1. Manage Stress

Stress is a common trigger for autoimmune flares.

Herbal Support: Use adaptogens like ashwagandha and holy basil to regulate stress responses.

Practice Mindfulness: Meditation, yoga, and deep breathing can calm the nervous system.

2. Prioritize Nutrition

Nourishing your body with anti-inflammatory foods supports healing.

Focus on Whole Foods: Incorporate leafy greens, fatty fish, nuts, and seeds.

Avoid Triggers: Reduce processed foods, refined sugars, and potential allergens.

3. Gentle Movement

Exercise can improve circulation and reduce inflammation.

Options: Choose low-impact activities like walking, swimming, or tai chi to avoid overexertion.

4. Get Adequate Rest

Poor sleep can worsen autoimmune symptoms.

Herbal Aid: Drink chamomile or valerian tea to support restful sleep.

Precautions When Using Herbs for Autoimmune Wellness

While herbs can provide significant support, it's important to use them thoughtfully:

Consult Your Doctor: Some herbs may interact with medications, such as immunosuppressants or blood thinners.

Start Slowly: Introduce one herb at a time to monitor your body's response.

Be Patient: Herbal remedies often take time to show their full effects.

Case Study: Amanda's Path to Balance

Amanda, a 37-year-old graphic designer, struggled with lupus, experiencing chronic fatigue and joint pain. She began incorporating licorice root tea and turmeric into her daily routine while practicing mindfulness to reduce stress. Over time, Amanda noticed a reduction in flare-ups and an increase in energy. By pairing these herbs with a nutrient-dense diet and light yoga, she regained a sense of control over her condition and felt empowered by her progress.

Managing autoimmune conditions requires a holistic approach, and herbs offer valuable tools for promoting wellness. From adaptogens like ashwagandha to anti-inflammatory herbs like turmeric, these natural remedies help regulate immune function and reduce inflammation. When combined with stress management, proper nutrition, and gentle movement, herbal support can improve quality of life and foster balance in the body. By using herbs thoughtfully and consistently, you can take meaningful steps toward managing autoimmune challenges and achieving a greater sense of well-being.

Long-Term Care Plans Using Holistic Remedies

Living with a chronic condition requires not just managing symptoms but also developing a sustainable, long-term care plan. Holistic remedies offer a powerful complement to conventional medicine, addressing the root causes of chronic issues while nurturing the body, mind, and spirit. A well-rounded care plan integrates herbal remedies, nutrition, lifestyle adjustments, and emotional well-being to create a balanced and supportive approach to health.

This chapter provides guidance on creating a personalized, long-term care plan using holistic remedies. By focusing on prevention, consistency, and adaptability, you can empower yourself to manage your condition effectively and improve your quality of life over time.

1. Building the Foundation: Understanding Your Needs

Before creating a care plan, it's essential to understand the specifics of your condition and your body's unique needs.

Assess Your Symptoms

Identify recurring symptoms, triggers, and patterns.

Keep a health journal to track changes over time.

Set Realistic Goals

Focus on improving daily functioning, reducing flare-ups, and enhancing overall well-being.

Goals should be specific, measurable, achievable, relevant, and time-bound (SMART).

2. Core Components of a Holistic Care Plan

A successful care plan addresses multiple aspects of health.

a. Herbal Remedies

Herbs provide long-term support for chronic conditions by reducing inflammation, regulating immune responses, and supporting energy levels.

Adaptogens: Enhance resilience to stress (e.g., ashwagandha, rhodiola).

Anti-Inflammatory Herbs: Reduce chronic inflammation (e.g., turmeric, ginger).

Nervines: Support the nervous system (e.g., chamomile, skullcap).

Example Plan:

Morning: Take a turmeric capsule or add it to a smoothie for anti-inflammatory support.

Afternoon: Sip holy basil tea to reduce stress.

Evening: Use a chamomile infusion to promote relaxation and better sleep.

b. Nutrition

A nutrient-rich diet forms the backbone of holistic care.

Anti-Inflammatory Foods: Include leafy greens, berries, fatty fish, and olive oil.

Avoid Triggers: Limit refined sugars, processed foods, and potential allergens.

Supplements: Incorporate omega-3s, magnesium, and vitamin D as needed.

Example Plan:

Breakfast: Smoothie with spinach, blueberries, flaxseeds, and almond milk.

Lunch: Salad with salmon, avocado, and olive oil dressing.

Dinner: Lentil soup with turmeric and ginger for warming nourishment.

c. Movement and Exercise

Physical activity improves circulation, reduces stiffness, and enhances mental health.

Choose low-impact exercises like yoga, tai chi, or swimming.

Focus on consistency rather than intensity to avoid overexertion.

Example Plan:

Morning yoga stretches to ease stiffness.

Evening walk to improve circulation and reduce stress.

3. Supporting Emotional Well-Being

Chronic conditions can take an emotional toll. Addressing mental health is crucial for long-term wellness.

a. Stress Management

Use mindfulness techniques, meditation, or deep breathing to reduce stress levels.

Incorporate adaptogens like ashwagandha or holy basil into your daily routine.

b. Emotional Support

Join support groups or seek therapy to connect with others who understand your experiences.

Journaling can help process emotions and identify triggers.

c. Aromatherapy

Essential oils like lavender and bergamot can reduce anxiety and promote relaxation.

Diffuse oils or apply them to pulse points for daily emotional support.

4. Long-Term Herbal Strategies

Consistency is key when using herbs for chronic conditions.

Rotating Herbs

Rotate between herbs to prevent tolerance and ensure a broad range of benefits.

For example, alternate between ashwagandha and rhodiola for stress resilience.

Seasonal Adjustments

Adjust your remedies based on seasonal needs. For instance, focus on immune-boosting herbs in winter and cooling herbs in summer.

Personalized Blends

Create herbal blends tailored to your specific symptoms and preferences.

Example: A tea blend of nettle, chamomile, and peppermint for relaxation and anti-inflammatory support.

5. Creating a Routine for Success

Developing a consistent routine ensures that holistic remedies become an integral part of your life.

Daily Practices

Start the day with a warm herbal tea to set a calming tone.

Incorporate herbs into meals, such as adding turmeric to soups or salads.

Weekly Rituals

Dedicate time to preparing remedies, like infusions or herbal oils, for the week.

Practice self-care activities such as herbal baths or meditation sessions.

Monthly Check-Ins

Review your health journal to assess progress and make necessary adjustments.

Experiment with new herbs or remedies to keep your plan dynamic and engaging.

6. Real-Life Application: Maria's Holistic Journey

Maria, a 45-year-old with rheumatoid arthritis, struggled with joint pain and fatigue. She developed a long-term care plan incorporating turmeric for inflammation, chamomile for relaxation, and a nutrient-dense diet rich in omega-3s. She practiced gentle yoga and used mindfulness techniques to manage stress. Over time, Maria noticed fewer flare-ups and improved energy, demonstrating the power of a consistent, holistic approach.

7. Challenges and Solutions

Challenge 1: Maintaining Consistency

Solution: Build habits by incorporating remedies into existing routines, like drinking herbal tea with meals.

Challenge 2: Adapting to Changes

Solution: Be flexible and adjust your plan based on your body's needs or seasonal shifts.

Challenge 3: Finding the Right Remedies

Solution: Start with one or two herbs and gradually expand as you discover what works best.

A long-term care plan using holistic remedies empowers you to take control of your health and address chronic conditions from multiple angles. By combining herbal remedies, nutrition, movement, and emotional support, you create a sustainable foundation for wellness. Remember, healing is a journey that requires patience, consistency, and adaptability. With a thoughtful approach, you can foster resilience, reduce symptoms, and enjoy a more balanced and fulfilling life.

BOOK 39

HERBAL SUPPORT FOR ATHLETES

Athletes, whether professional or recreational, push their bodies to achieve peak performance, endurance, and recovery. Herbal remedies provide a natural, effective way to enhance athletic performance, reduce fatigue, support joint health, and speed up muscle recovery. By incorporating herbs into their routines, athletes can nourish their bodies with nutrient-rich, plant-based solutions that promote stamina, flexibility, and overall resilience.

This book explores the many ways herbs can support athletic goals, from pre-workout blends that boost energy and endurance to post-workout remedies that reduce soreness and inflammation. Whether it's crafting herbal teas, muscle rubs, or energy bars, each chapter provides practical recipes and tips tailored to athletes' unique needs.

Designed to complement rigorous training schedules and active lifestyles, the remedies in this book emphasize sustainability, safety, and ease of use. With a focus on natural ingredients and time-tested herbal wisdom, athletes can take their performance to the next level while supporting long-term health. Whether you're a runner, weightlifter, yogi, or weekend warrior, Herbal Support for Athletes equips you with the tools to stay energized, recover faster, and maintain peak physical condition. Let nature's power fuel your fitness journey!

Pre-Workout Blends for Energy and Endurance

A successful workout begins with proper preparation, and pre-workout nutrition plays a vital role in fueling the body for optimal performance. While many turn to synthetic energy drinks or supplements, herbal blends offer a natural and sustainable alternative to enhance energy, endurance, and focus. Herbs like ginseng, maca, and guarana are known for their energizing properties, while adaptogens such as rhodiola and ashwagandha improve stamina and resilience.

This chapter explores herbal remedies that provide a steady energy boost without the jitters or crashes often associated with synthetic stimulants. These pre-workout blends are easy to prepare and customizable to fit your specific fitness goals and needs.

Key Herbs for Pre-Workout Blends

1. Ginseng (Panax ginseng)

How It Helps: Increases energy, reduces fatigue, and improves physical endurance.

How to Use: Brew a tea or take as a tincture 30 minutes before your workout.

2. Maca Root (Lepidium meyenii)

How It Helps: Balances hormones, enhances stamina, and boosts overall energy levels.

How to Use: Add maca powder to smoothies or mix into a pre-workout drink.

3. Rhodiola (Rhodiola rosea)

How It Helps: Improves oxygen utilization, reduces fatigue, and enhances focus.

How to Use: Take as a tea or capsule an hour before physical activity.

4. Guarana (Paullinia cupana)

How It Helps: Provides natural caffeine to boost energy and mental alertness.

How to Use: Infuse guarana powder in water or add it to a pre-workout shake.

5. Beetroot Powder (Beta vulgaris)

How It Helps: Enhances blood flow and oxygen delivery to muscles, improving endurance.

How to Use: Mix beetroot powder into water or juice for a nitrate-rich boost.

1236. Energizing Herbal Tea

Ingredients:

1 tsp dried ginseng root

1 tsp dried rhodiola root

1/2 tsp guarana powder

1 cup boiling water

Instructions:

Steep ginseng and rhodiola in boiling water for 10 minutes.

Add guarana powder, stir well, and strain.

Drink 30 minutes before exercise.

Benefits: Enhances energy and focus for intense workouts.

1237. Maca Smoothie

Ingredients:

1 tbsp maca powder

1 banana

1 cup almond milk

1 tsp honey

Instructions:

Blend all ingredients until smooth.

Serve chilled before your workout.

Benefits: Provides sustained energy and supports endurance.

1238. Beetroot and Ginger Shot

Ingredients:

2 tbsp beetroot powder

1 tsp grated ginger

1/2 cup orange juice

Instructions:

Mix beetroot powder and ginger with orange juice.

Drink 20 minutes before exercise.

Benefits: Enhances circulation and reduces fatigue.

1239. Adaptogenic Pre-Workout Tea

Ingredients:

1 tsp ashwagandha powder

1 tsp cinnamon

1 tsp honey

1 cup hot water

Instructions:

Dissolve ashwagandha and cinnamon in hot water.

Stir in honey and enjoy.

Benefits: Reduces stress and boosts physical endurance.

1240. Guarana Citrus Water

Ingredients:

1 tsp guarana powder

1 cup cold water

1 tbsp lemon juice

Instructions:

Mix guarana powder with cold water.

Add lemon juice and stir well.

Benefits: Provides a natural caffeine boost for alertness.

1241. Cacao Energy Boost

Ingredients:

1 tsp cacao powder

1 tsp maca powder

1 cup oat milk

1 tsp maple syrup

Instructions:

Heat oat milk and whisk in cacao and maca powders.

Sweeten with maple syrup and serve warm.

Benefits: Increases energy and supports recovery.

1242. Mint Beet Smoothie

Ingredients:

1 cup beet juice

1/4 cup fresh mint leaves

1 tbsp chia seeds

Instructions:

Blend all ingredients until smooth.

Serve immediately.

Benefits: Improves oxygen delivery and provides hydration.

1243. Herbal Pre-Workout Shot

Ingredients:

1 tsp ginseng tincture

1 tsp rhodiola tincture

1 tbsp apple cider vinegar

1/2 cup water

Instructions:

Mix all ingredients in a small glass.

Drink 20 minutes before physical activity.

Benefits: Boosts energy and sharpens focus.

1244. Lemon Ginger Energizer

Ingredients:

1 tsp grated ginger

1 tsp honey

1 cup warm water

1 tbsp lemon juice

Instructions:

Mix ginger and honey into warm water.

Add lemon juice and stir well.

Benefits: Wakes up your system and supports digestion.

1245. Green Tea Energy Boost

Ingredients:

1 tsp matcha green tea powder

1 cup almond milk

1 tsp honey

Instructions:

Heat almond milk and whisk in matcha powder.

Sweeten with honey and enjoy.

Benefits: Provides clean energy and antioxidants.

Tips for Effective Pre-Workout Herbal Use

Time It Right: Consume herbal pre-workout blends 30–60 minutes before exercise for optimal absorption.

Start Slow: If new to herbs like ginseng or guarana, start with small amounts to gauge your body's response.

Stay Hydrated: Combine herbal blends with adequate water intake to prevent dehydration.

Herbal pre-workout blends provide a natural, effective way to fuel your body and mind for exercise. By incorporating herbs like ginseng, rhodiola, and maca into your routine, you can boost energy and endurance while avoiding artificial stimulants. These easy-to-make recipes ensure you're ready to perform at your best while prioritizing your health and well-being. With consistency and experimentation, you'll find the perfect blend to power your fitness journey!

Remedies for Muscle Recovery and Soreness

After intense physical activity, muscle soreness and fatigue are common. While it's a natural part of building strength and endurance, prolonged soreness can hinder performance and recovery. Herbal remedies offer an effective, natural way to support muscle recovery, reduce inflammation, and ease discomfort. From herbal teas to soothing salves, these remedies can help athletes and active individuals recover faster and get back to their routines.

This chapter focuses on key herbs, practical recipes, and tips for relieving muscle soreness and promoting recovery. By integrating these remedies into your post-workout routine, you can enhance muscle repair, reduce inflammation, and support long-term physical health.

Key Herbs for Muscle Recovery

1. Arnica (Arnica montana)

How It Helps: Reduces inflammation, relieves pain, and improves circulation.

How to Use: Apply arnica gel or cream directly to sore muscles for localized relief.

2. Turmeric (Curcuma longa)

How It Helps: Contains curcumin, a powerful anti-inflammatory compound that speeds up recovery.

How to Use: Add turmeric to meals, teas, or golden milk.

3. Ginger (Zingiber officinale)

How It Helps: Reduces muscle pain and inflammation while improving circulation.

How to Use: Brew ginger tea or incorporate fresh ginger into your diet.

4. Peppermint (Mentha piperita)

How It Helps: Soothes muscle tension and provides a cooling sensation.

How to Use: Apply peppermint oil diluted in a carrier oil to affected areas or enjoy as a tea.

5. Chamomile (Matricaria chamomilla)

How It Helps: Relaxes muscles and reduces spasms.

How to Use: Drink chamomile tea or add dried flowers to a warm bath.

6. Devil's Claw (Harpagophytum procumbens)

How It Helps: Reduces pain and inflammation, particularly in joints and muscles.

How to Use: Take as a tincture or capsule post-workout.

10 Herbal Remedies for Muscle Recovery

1246. Arnica Massage Oil

Ingredients:

1/4 cup arnica-infused oil

5 drops lavender essential oil

5 drops eucalyptus essential oil

Instructions:

Mix arnica oil with essential oils in a small bottle.

Massage into sore muscles for relief.

Benefits: Reduces pain, inflammation, and tension in muscles.

1247. Turmeric Recovery Tea

Ingredients:

1 tsp turmeric powder

1/2 tsp ginger powder

1 cup hot water

1 tsp honey

Instructions:

Mix turmeric and ginger into hot water.

Add honey and stir well.

Drink warm after a workout.

Benefits: Reduces inflammation and supports muscle repair.

1248. Ginger Compress

Ingredients:

1/4 cup grated ginger

1 quart hot water

Instructions:

Steep grated ginger in hot water for 10 minutes.

Soak a cloth in the infusion, wring out excess water, and apply to sore muscles.

Benefits: Improves circulation and reduces stiffness.

1249. Peppermint Cooling Spray

Ingredients:

1/2 cup distilled water

10 drops peppermint essential oil

5 drops eucalyptus essential oil

Instructions:

Combine ingredients in a spray bottle.

Shake well and spritz onto sore areas for a cooling effect.

Benefits: Provides instant relief from muscle tension and inflammation.

1250. Chamomile Bath Soak

Ingredients:

1 cup dried chamomile flowers

1 cup Epsom salt

Instructions:

Mix chamomile flowers and Epsom salt in a bowl.

Add the mixture to a warm bath and soak for 20 minutes.

Benefits: Relaxes muscles and reduces stress.

1251. Devil's Claw Infusion

Ingredients:

1 tsp dried devil's claw root

1 cup boiling water

Instructions:

Steep the devil's claw root in boiling water for 10 minutes.

Strain and drink warm.

Benefits: Reduces pain and inflammation in muscles and joints.

1252. Lavender and Arnica Balm

Ingredients:

1/4 cup beeswax

1/2 cup arnica-infused oil

10 drops lavender essential oil

Instructions:

Melt beeswax in a double boiler and mix with arnica oil.

Add lavender oil, stir, and pour into a small jar.

Apply to sore muscles as needed.

Benefits: Soothes pain and promotes relaxation.

1253. Anti-Inflammatory Smoothie

Ingredients:

1 banana

1/2 cup spinach

1/2 tsp turmeric powder

1/2 tsp ginger powder

1 cup almond milk

Instructions:

Blend all ingredients until smooth.

Drink post-workout.

Benefits: Reduces inflammation and supports recovery.

1254. Peppermint and Ginger Rub

Ingredients:

2 tbsp coconut oil

5 drops peppermint essential oil

1 tsp grated ginger

Instructions:

Warm coconut oil and mix with peppermint oil and grated ginger.

Massage into sore muscles for relief.

Benefits: Relieves pain and stimulates circulation.

1255. Herbal Ice Pack

Ingredients:

1/2 cup witch hazel

10 drops peppermint essential oil

1 clean cloth

Instructions:

Soak the cloth in witch hazel mixed with peppermint oil.

Place the cloth in the freezer for 10 minutes.

Apply to inflamed muscles.

Benefits: Reduces swelling and provides cooling relief.

Tips for Muscle Recovery

Hydration: Drink plenty of water or herbal teas to flush out toxins and keep muscles hydrated.

Stretching: Gentle post-workout stretching prevents stiffness and improves flexibility.

Rest: Allow adequate time for recovery to avoid overtraining and further soreness.

Muscle recovery is an essential part of any fitness routine, and herbal remedies offer a natural, effective way to speed up the process. By incorporating herbs like arnica, turmeric, and chamomile into your recovery plan, you can reduce soreness, inflammation, and tension while promoting relaxation. These remedies, combined with proper hydration, stretching, and rest, will help you maintain peak performance and support long-term physical health.

Herbal Solutions for Joint Health and Flexibility

Joint health and flexibility are critical for maintaining mobility, reducing discomfort, and supporting an active lifestyle. Whether you're dealing with stiffness, inflammation, or age-related wear and tear, herbal remedies can play a significant role in improving joint function and alleviating discomfort. Herbs with anti-inflammatory, analgesic, and regenerative properties can help protect joints, soothe pain, and enhance flexibility.

This chapter explores effective herbal solutions for joint health, including teas, salves, and tinctures. With these natural remedies, you can nurture your joints, prevent further damage, and promote long-term mobility.

Key Herbs for Joint Health

1. Turmeric (Curcuma longa)

How It Helps: Curcumin, the active compound, reduces inflammation and protects cartilage.

How to Use: Add turmeric to meals, make golden milk, or take as a supplement.

2. Boswellia (Boswellia serrata)

How It Helps: Known as Indian frankincense, boswellia inhibits inflammatory pathways and reduces joint stiffness.

How to Use: Take as a capsule, tincture, or topical cream.

3. Ginger (Zingiber officinale)

How It Helps: Eases joint pain by reducing inflammation and improving circulation.

How to Use: Drink ginger tea, use in cooking, or apply as a warm compress.

4. Devil's Claw (Harpagophytum procumbens)

How It Helps: Effective for reducing pain and inflammation in osteoarthritis and rheumatoid arthritis.

How to Use: Take as a tea, capsule, or tincture.

5. Nettle (Urtica dioica)

How It Helps: Rich in minerals like calcium and magnesium, nettle strengthens bones and supports joint repair.

How to Use: Drink as a tea or use fresh leaves in cooking.

6. Willow Bark (Salix alba)

How It Helps: Contains salicin, a natural pain reliever that reduces inflammation.

How to Use: Brew as a tea or take as a tincture.

1256. Turmeric and Ginger Tea

Ingredients:

1 tsp turmeric powder

1 tsp grated ginger

1 cup hot water

1 tsp honey

Instructions:

Steep turmeric and ginger in hot water for 10 minutes.

Strain, add honey, and drink.

Benefits: Reduces inflammation and improves joint flexibility.

1257. Boswellia Capsules

Ingredients:

500 mg boswellia extract capsules

Instructions:

Take one capsule with water twice daily.

Benefits: Alleviates joint pain and stiffness in conditions like arthritis.

1258. Ginger Compress

Ingredients:

1/4 cup grated ginger

1 quart hot water

Instructions:

Steep grated ginger in hot water for 10 minutes.

Soak a cloth in the infusion and apply to sore joints for 15 minutes.

Benefits: Eases stiffness and improves circulation.

1259. Nettle Tea

Ingredients:

1 tsp dried nettle leaves

1 cup hot water

Instructions:

Steep nettle leaves in hot water for 10 minutes.

Strain and enjoy.

Benefits: Strengthens bones and supports joint repair.

1260. Herbal Joint Salve

Ingredients:

1/4 cup arnica-infused oil

1/4 cup beeswax

10 drops ginger essential oil

10 drops lavender essential oil

Instructions:

Melt beeswax and arnica oil in a double boiler.

Add essential oils, stir, and pour into a jar.

Apply to joints as needed.

Benefits: Relieves joint pain and promotes flexibility.

1261. Devil's Claw Infusion

Ingredients:

1 tsp dried devil's claw root

1 cup boiling water

Instructions:

Steep devil's claw root in boiling water for 10 minutes.

Strain and drink warm.

Benefits: Reduces joint inflammation and pain.

1262. Willow Bark Tea

Ingredients:

1 tsp dried willow bark

1 cup boiling water

Instructions:

Steep willow bark in boiling water for 10 minutes.

Strain and drink.

Benefits: Provides natural pain relief for joint discomfort.

1263. Anti-Inflammatory Smoothie

Ingredients:

1/2 cup spinach

1/2 tsp turmeric powder

1/4 tsp black pepper

1 cup almond milk

Instructions:

Blend all ingredients until smooth.

Drink as a post-workout recovery aid.

Benefits: Supports joint health and reduces inflammation.

1264. Chamomile Bath Soak

Ingredients:

1 cup dried chamomile flowers

1 cup Epsom salt

Instructions:

Mix chamomile flowers and Epsom salt in a bowl.

Add the mixture to a warm bath and soak for 20 minutes.

Benefits: Relaxes joints and eases stiffness.

1265. Ginger and Boswellia Paste

Ingredients:

1 tsp ginger powder

1 tsp boswellia powder

2 tbsp water

Instructions:

Mix ginger and boswellia powder with water to form a paste.

Apply to sore joints and leave for 20 minutes before rinsing.

Benefits: Reduces pain and improves flexibility.

Tips for Supporting Joint Health

Stay Active: Regular low-impact exercise like yoga or swimming helps maintain flexibility and strengthen muscles around joints.

Maintain a Healthy Weight: Reducing excess weight alleviates stress on weight-bearing joints.

Eat Joint-Friendly Foods: Incorporate omega-3 fatty acids, leafy greens, and bone-supporting minerals like calcium and magnesium.

Herbal remedies offer a natural, effective way to support joint health and flexibility, reducing pain and inflammation while promoting mobility. By incorporating these herbs into your routine through teas, salves, and compresses, you can nurture your joints and maintain an active lifestyle. Paired with a healthy diet and regular movement, these remedies can help you stay strong, flexible, and pain-free for years to come.

Creating Energy Bars and Drinks with Herbs

Energy bars and drinks are essential tools for athletes and active individuals seeking a convenient source of fuel before, during, or after workouts. While store-bought options are often packed with refined sugars and synthetic ingredients, homemade herbal energy bars and drinks offer a natural, nutrient-dense alternative. Infused with herbs that promote energy, endurance, and recovery, these recipes are as functional as they are flavorful.

This chapter focuses on creating easy-to-make herbal energy bars and drinks that cater to your specific fitness needs. By combining whole foods and herbs, you can craft customized solutions that enhance your performance and support your active lifestyle.

Key Herbs for Energy Bars and Drinks

1. Maca Root (Lepidium meyenii)

How It Helps: Boosts energy and endurance while balancing hormones.

How to Use: Add maca powder to energy bar mixtures or smoothies.

2. Ashwagandha (Withania somnifera)

How It Helps: Reduces stress and supports sustained energy.

How to Use: Incorporate ashwagandha powder into energy bars or teas.

3. Cacao (Theobroma cacao)

How It Helps: Provides natural caffeine and antioxidants for an energy boost.

How to Use: Use cacao powder or nibs in bars and drinks.

4. Ginseng (Panax ginseng)

How It Helps: Enhances stamina and reduces fatigue.

How to Use: Include ginseng tea or powder in pre-workout drinks.

5. Matcha (Camellia sinensis)

How It Helps: Supplies clean, long-lasting energy with antioxidants.

How to Use: Add matcha powder to drinks or energy bar glazes.

6. Adaptogenic Herbs

Examples: Rhodiola rosea, holy basil

How They Help: Improve endurance and recovery by balancing the body's stress response.

1266. Maca and Cacao Energy Bars

Ingredients:

1 cup rolled oats

1/2 cup almond butter

1/4 cup honey

2 tbsp cacao powder

1 tbsp maca powder

1/4 cup chia seeds

Instructions:

Mix all ingredients in a bowl until evenly combined.

Press the mixture into a square pan and refrigerate for 1 hour.

Cut into bars and store in an airtight container.

Benefits: Provides a quick energy boost and sustained endurance.

1267. Matcha Coconut Bliss Balls

Ingredients:

1 cup shredded coconut

1/2 cup dates (pitted)

1 tbsp matcha powder

1 tbsp almond butter

Instructions:

Blend all ingredients in a food processor until sticky.

Roll into small balls and refrigerate for 30 minutes.

Benefits: Offers a clean energy boost with antioxidants.

1268. Ashwagandha Honey Granola Bars

Ingredients:

1 cup rolled oats

1/4 cup honey

2 tbsp ashwagandha powder

1/4 cup sunflower seeds

1/4 cup dried cranberries

Instructions:

Mix oats, seeds, and cranberries in a bowl.

Heat honey and stir in ashwagandha powder.

Combine wet and dry ingredients, press into a pan, and refrigerate.

Benefits: Supports recovery and reduces post-workout stress.

1269. Ginseng Energy Tea

Ingredients:

1 tsp dried ginseng root

1 cup boiling water

1 tsp honey

Instructions:

Steep ginseng root in boiling water for 10 minutes.

Add honey and enjoy warm or chilled.

Benefits: Enhances stamina and mental clarity.

1270. Cacao Matcha Latte

Ingredients:

1 tsp matcha powder

1 tsp cacao powder

1 cup almond milk

1 tsp honey

Instructions:

Heat almond milk and whisk in matcha and cacao powders.

Sweeten with honey and serve warm.

Benefits: Provides a balanced energy boost with antioxidants.

1271. Adaptogen Energy Smoothie

Ingredients:

1 banana

1 tbsp almond butter

1 tsp ashwagandha powder

1 cup almond milk

Instructions:

Blend all ingredients until smooth.

Serve immediately.

Benefits: Enhances energy and recovery while reducing stress.

1272. Spiced Beet Energy Drink

Ingredients:

1/2 cup beet juice

1 tsp grated ginger

1 tsp honey

1 cup water

Instructions:

Mix all ingredients in a blender or shaker.

Chill and serve.

Benefits: Improves circulation and endurance.

1273. Chia Energy Water

Ingredients:

1 tbsp chia seeds

1 cup water

1 tbsp lemon juice

Instructions:

Soak chia seeds in water for 10 minutes.

Stir in lemon juice and enjoy.

Benefits: Hydrates and provides a natural energy boost.

1274. Holy Basil Lemonade

Ingredients:

1 tsp dried holy basil leaves

1 cup boiling water

1 tbsp lemon juice

1 tsp honey

Instructions:

Steep holy basil leaves in boiling water for 10 minutes.

Strain, add lemon juice and honey, and serve chilled.

Benefits: Reduces stress and boosts focus.

1275. Rhodiola Recovery Drink

Ingredients:

1 tsp rhodiola powder

1 cup coconut water

1 tsp honey

Instructions:

Mix rhodiola powder into coconut water.

Sweeten with honey and serve over ice.

Benefits: Improves endurance and speeds recovery.

Tips for Creating Herbal Energy Bars and Drinks

Adjust Sweetness: Use natural sweeteners like honey, dates, or maple syrup for energy without refined sugar.

Balance Flavors: Combine earthy herbs like ashwagandha with sweet or citrus ingredients for a more palatable taste.

Prep Ahead: Make bars and drinks in batches to save time and have them ready when needed.

Store Properly: Keep bars in airtight containers and refrigerate drinks for freshness.

Herbal energy bars and drinks are a versatile and natural way to fuel your body for peak performance and recovery. By using nutrient-dense ingredients and energizing herbs like maca, ginseng, and matcha, you can create delicious, functional snacks and beverages tailored to your needs. Whether you're prepping for a workout or recovering after one, these recipes provide the nourishment and energy you need to stay active and strong. Let nature power your performance!

BOOK 40

PRESERVING AND SHARING HERBAL KNOWLEDGE

Herbalism is an ancient practice rooted in tradition, wisdom, and a deep connection to nature. Preserving and sharing this knowledge is essential for ensuring that future generations can benefit from the healing power of plants. By documenting your experiences, passing down family remedies, teaching others, and creating a lasting legacy, you contribute to the timeless art of herbal healing.

This book guides you through practical ways to preserve and share herbal knowledge, from keeping a detailed herbal journal to teaching friends and your community. You'll discover how to document your journey, refine your skills, and share your insights in meaningful ways. Whether you're organizing family remedies into a cherished heirloom or building a home apothecary for generations to use, every step you take helps ensure the continuity of herbal traditions.

Designed for both beginner and experienced herbalists, this book emphasizes sustainability, collaboration, and creativity. It empowers you to celebrate your journey while inspiring others to explore the world of herbs. Together, we can honor the wisdom of the past, adapt it for the present, and preserve it for the future. Let's keep the spirit of herbalism alive and thriving.

Keeping a Herbal Journal for Long-Term Learning

A herbal journal is an invaluable tool for anyone embarking on or deepening their journey into herbalism. Whether you are a beginner experimenting with simple remedies or an experienced herbalist refining your craft, documenting your observations, recipes, and reflections can significantly enhance your learning and understanding. A well-maintained herbal journal serves as a repository of knowledge, a source of inspiration, and a personalized reference guide.

Why Keep a Herbal Journal?

1. Documentation and Learning

Herbalism is a hands-on practice that thrives on experimentation and observation. Keeping a journal allows you to document your discoveries, such as the effects of specific herbs, the outcomes of new recipes, and the subtleties of growing and harvesting plants. By recording your experiences, you create a resource you can revisit and build upon.

2. Reflection and Growth

A journal is a space to reflect on your journey. It reveals patterns, highlights successes, and illuminates areas where improvement is needed. Over time, these reflections help refine your skills and deepen your understanding of herbalism.

3. Building a Legacy

A herbal journal is more than just a learning tool—it can become a family heirloom or a resource for your community. Sharing your documented experiences ensures that your knowledge and wisdom endure.

What to Include in a Herbal Journal

A well-rounded herbal journal is more than a collection of recipes. It can encompass various aspects of your herbal practice, from plant identification to reflections on your journey.

1. Plant Profiles

Create detailed profiles for each herb you encounter. Include the following information:

Scientific and Common Names: To accurately identify the plant.

Properties and Benefits: Note medicinal uses, energetic properties, and other applications.

Growing Conditions: Record where and how the

plant thrives, including soil type, sunlight, and watering needs.

Harvesting Tips: Detail the best time and method for harvesting to ensure potency.

Preparations: Document how the herb is best used, such as in teas, tinctures, or salves.

2. Recipes and Remedies

Write down recipes for teas, tinctures, salves, syrups, and more. Be specific about measurements, preparation methods, and storage instructions. Include notes on how well the recipe worked and any modifications you made.

3. Observations and Experiments

Record your personal experiences with herbs. For example:

How did a chamomile tea affect your sleep?

Did a salve help alleviate muscle pain? Document side effects, unexpected benefits, or noticeable patterns.

4. Seasonal Notes

Track the seasonal availability of herbs in your area. Note when certain plants flower, go to seed, or are ready for harvest. Seasonal records help you plan your foraging or gardening efforts.

5. Sketches and Photos

Visual aids like sketches, pressed flowers, or photographs can enrich your journal. They help with plant identification and add a creative, personal touch.

How to Start Your Herbal Journal

1. Choose Your Format

Select a format that works for your lifestyle and preferences. Options include:

Traditional Notebook: A physical journal offers tactile appeal and creative freedom.

Digital Journal: Apps and document editors provide searchable entries and easy organization.

Combination: Use a notebook for creative entries and a digital tool for detailed records.

2. Organize Your Journal

Structure your journal in a way that makes it easy to navigate. Suggested sections include:

Plant Profiles

Recipes and Remedies

Observations and Notes

Seasonal Charts

Reflection and Growth

3. Set a Routine

Consistency is key to maintaining a useful journal. Dedicate time weekly or monthly to update it with your observations, new recipes, or seasonal insights.

Tips for Effective Journaling

1. Be Detailed

Include as much detail as possible, especially in recipes and plant profiles. Specifics like dosages, preparation times, and personal reactions are invaluable for future reference.

2. Stay Consistent

Even if you can't journal daily, regular entries ensure you capture your learning journey. Short, consistent notes are better than infrequent, lengthy ones.

3. Reflect Often

Revisit older entries to track your growth and rediscover forgotten insights. Reflection deepens your understanding and helps refine your practices.

4. Add Personal Touches

Make your journal uniquely yours by incorporating creative elements like doodles, pressed flowers, or inspirational quotes.

Examples of Herbal Journal Entries

Plant Profile: Lavender (Lavandula angustifolia)

Common Uses: Calming tea, sleep aid, wound healing.

Harvesting Tips: Best harvested in mid-morning when flowers are fully bloomed.

Personal Notes: Lavender-infused oil worked well

for soothing dry skin but needed longer steeping for full fragrance.

Recipe Entry: Elderberry Syrup

Ingredients: 1 cup dried elderberries, 4 cups water, 1 cinnamon stick, 1 cup honey.

Method: Simmer elderberries, water, and cinnamon for 45 minutes. Strain, add honey, and store in a sterilized jar.

Effectiveness: Effective for preventing colds during flu season.

The Long-Term Benefits of a Herbal Journal

Personal Growth: A journal reveals how your understanding of herbs evolves over time.

Knowledge Sharing: Your journal can inspire and guide others, from family members to fellow herbalists.

A Lifelong Resource: As your collection of entries grows, it becomes a treasure trove of herbal wisdom.

A herbal journal is an essential companion on your journey into herbalism. It captures your unique experiences, documents your learning, and preserves valuable insights for the future. By dedicating time and care to your journal, you create a resource that not only supports your growth but also contributes to the enduring legacy of herbal knowledge. Start today, and let your journal become a living record of your connection to nature and the healing power of plants.

Passing Down Family Remedies and Traditions

The tradition of passing down family remedies is a time-honored way to preserve cultural heritage, connect generations, and ensure that the wisdom of natural healing remains accessible. These remedies, often crafted with care and love, are more than practical solutions for everyday ailments— they are symbols of resilience, knowledge, and connection to nature. By sharing these traditions, you preserve the legacy of your ancestors while adapting the wisdom to meet modern needs.

The Value of Family Remedies

1. A Connection to Heritage

Family remedies often carry stories and traditions unique to your ancestry. They reflect the environment, resources, and cultural practices of past generations. Each recipe is a window into the lives of those who came before you, offering insights into their values, struggles, and triumphs.

2. Proven Reliability

Passed down through generations, family remedies have stood the test of time. They are trusted solutions, often accompanied by anecdotal evidence of their effectiveness, providing a sense of comfort and familiarity.

3. Building Relationships

Sharing family remedies strengthens bonds among relatives. It fosters communication, collaboration, and a shared commitment to health and well-being, particularly when teaching younger generations.

Steps to Preserve Family Remedies

1. Collecting Recipes

Gathering recipes from elders or family members is the first step in preserving this knowledge. Approach them with curiosity and respect to uncover the stories and experiences tied to these remedies.

Interview Relatives: Ask about remedies they used, why they were effective, and how they were prepared.

Document Everything: Write down exact instructions, ingredient lists, and preparation methods. Include anecdotes or memories associated with the remedies to preserve their personal touch.

2. Modernizing Recipes

While staying true to tradition is important, some remedies may need adjustments for modern lifestyles or ingredient availability.

Substitute Ingredients: Replace hard-to-find herbs with accessible alternatives while maintaining the remedy's intent.

Ensure Safety: Verify dosages and preparation

methods with current herbal knowledge to ensure safe use.

Adjust for Preferences: Adapt recipes to suit dietary restrictions or individual preferences, such as creating non-alcoholic tinctures.

3. Creating a Family Herbal Guide

Compile your collected remedies into a family herbal guide, which can serve as a treasured heirloom.

Include Key Details: Add plant profiles, stories, and images alongside each recipe.

Organize by Purpose: Divide remedies into sections like digestive health, immune support, or skincare.

Incorporate Modern Additions: Include new remedies inspired by traditional ones to keep the guide evolving.

Sharing Family Remedies

1. Teaching Through Practice

The best way to ensure family remedies are passed down is by teaching others how to prepare and use them. Practical, hands-on experiences leave a lasting impression.

Host Workshops: Invite family members to gatherings where they can learn to make remedies together.

Create Starter Kits: Assemble basic ingredients and instructions for new herbal enthusiasts.

Demonstrate Techniques: Show how to harvest, prepare, and use remedies, emphasizing safety and effectiveness.

2. Digital Preservation

Technology offers new ways to safeguard and share family remedies.

Record Videos: Create tutorials that demonstrate the preparation process step-by-step.

Build a Digital Archive: Use cloud storage or a family website to store and share recipes, photos, and notes.

Social Media: Share simplified versions of family remedies to inspire others while preserving your unique traditions.

Incorporating Family Traditions Into Modern Life

1. Seasonal Practices

Integrate remedies into seasonal traditions to keep them relevant. For example:

Use elderberry syrup during winter for immune support.

Prepare cooling herbal teas like mint and lemon balm in summer.

2. Create Rituals

Infuse remedies into everyday routines or special occasions:

Brew herbal teas as part of a daily mindfulness practice.

Prepare salves together during family gatherings or holidays.

3. Pass Down Stories

Share the origins and stories behind remedies as part of the tradition. This creates emotional connections that enhance the value of the remedies.

Case Study: Restoring a Family Tradition

Maria, a third-generation herbalist, rediscovered her grandmother's recipe for calendula salve, a remedy used to treat minor cuts and burns. After modernizing the recipe by adding beeswax for easier application, Maria began teaching her children how to make it during weekend kitchen sessions. The salve is now a staple in their household, symbolizing both practical healing and a cherished family bond.

Challenges in Preserving Family Remedies

1. Lost Knowledge

Over time, some remedies may be incomplete or forgotten.

Solution: Collaborate with multiple family members to fill in gaps and combine memories.

2. Generational Gaps

Younger generations may lack interest in traditional practices.

Solution: Present remedies in engaging, modern ways, like hosting DIY workshops or creating digital content.

3. Accessibility of Ingredients

Certain ingredients used in traditional remedies may no longer be readily available.

Solution: Research substitutions or explore online resources for sourcing hard-to-find herbs.

The Importance of Adaptability

While preserving traditions is essential, flexibility ensures these remedies remain practical and relevant. Adapting recipes to modern contexts doesn't dilute their significance—it enhances their longevity. By honoring the intent behind family remedies while embracing new knowledge, you create a tradition that bridges the past and future.

Passing down family remedies and traditions is a powerful way to preserve heritage, foster connections, and share the healing power of herbalism. By collecting, modernizing, and teaching these remedies, you create a legacy that celebrates your family's unique wisdom while inspiring future generations to embrace natural healing. Start today by documenting your own favorite remedies, sharing them with loved ones, and keeping the rich tradition of herbalism alive.

Teaching Herbal Skills to Friends and Community

Teaching herbal skills is a meaningful way to share knowledge, inspire others, and build a community connected to natural healing. Herbalism, rooted in centuries of tradition, thrives when passed on through demonstration and practice. Sharing your expertise helps others develop a deeper connection with nature while empowering them to take control of their health and well-being. This chapter explores practical ways to teach herbal skills effectively, whether to friends, small groups, or larger communities.

The Importance of Sharing Herbal Knowledge

Herbalism is a tradition that has long been passed down through generations. Sharing this knowledge creates a ripple effect, allowing more people to benefit from nature's healing power. Teaching also helps deepen your understanding of herbalism, as explaining concepts and demonstrating techniques reinforces your own learning. Beyond the personal benefits, it strengthens community bonds, fosters collaboration, and ensures that herbal wisdom continues to thrive.

Preparing to Teach

Effective teaching begins with preparation. Ensuring clarity, simplicity, and engagement in your teaching methods makes the experience rewarding for both you and your audience.

1. Define Your Focus

Choose specific skills or topics that suit your audience's level of knowledge and interest. Examples include:

Making herbal teas or infusions.

Preparing salves and balms.

Identifying common local herbs.

Understanding herbal safety basics.

2. Gather Materials

Provide the tools and supplies needed for hands-on activities. For example:

Dried herbs, carrier oils, beeswax, or tincture bases.

Measuring spoons, jars, and labels for participants.

Visual aids such as charts, plant samples, or photos.

3. Create a Teaching Plan

Outline your session with clear steps. A well-structured plan keeps the class flowing smoothly. Divide your session into:

Introduction: Briefly explain the topic and its benefits.

Demonstration: Show the process step-by-step while explaining each action.

Practice: Allow participants to try the technique themselves.

Questions and Discussion: Create space for engagement and feedback.

Methods of Teaching Herbal Skills

1. Hosting Workshops

Workshops are an interactive and engaging way to teach herbal skills. They can range from small, informal gatherings to more structured community events.

Example Workshop: Teaching participants how to make a calendula salve.

Demonstrate the process: infusing oil with calendula flowers, melting beeswax, and combining the ingredients.

Provide participants with small kits to make their own salve during the session.

2. Leading Herbal Walks

Herbal walks allow participants to learn about plants in their natural habitat.

Teach plant identification, including key features like leaves, flowers, and growth patterns.

Explain ethical harvesting practices and seasonal availability.

Share anecdotes about the historical uses of each herb.

3. Offering One-on-One Mentoring

Personalized instruction is ideal for friends or family members who want to dive deeper into herbalism.

Tailor the lessons to their interests, such as growing herbs, creating remedies, or crafting herbal skincare products.

4. Leveraging Digital Platforms

Online teaching expands your reach to a broader audience.

Create video tutorials demonstrating techniques like tincture-making or herbal oil infusions.

Host virtual workshops using platforms like Zoom to engage participants in real-time.

Share recipes and tips through blogs or social media to inspire others.

Encouraging Engagement

To ensure your audience remains engaged and motivated, incorporate interactive elements into your teaching.

1. Hands-On Activities

Participants retain more information when they actively engage in the process.

Provide materials for everyone to follow along, such as jars, herbs, and tools.

Encourage creativity by letting participants customize their remedies with different herbs or scents.

2. Use Storytelling

Share personal experiences or historical anecdotes about the herbs you're teaching. Stories make the learning experience memorable and relatable.

3. Provide Takeaways

Offer written instructions, recipe cards, or small samples for participants to take home. This reinforces what they've learned and gives them the tools to practice on their own.

Teaching Herbal Safety

Herbal education must include a focus on safety to build trust and ensure responsible use.

Dosage Guidelines: Explain appropriate dosages and the importance of moderation.

Contraindications: Highlight potential interactions with medications or conditions.

Sustainable Practices: Emphasize ethical harvesting and avoiding overuse of wild plants.

Case Study: A Community Herbal Class

In a small town, an herbalist organized a workshop on herbal teas for immune support. Participants learned to mix herbs like elderberry, echinacea, and ginger to create personalized blends. Each attendee received a kit containing dried herbs, a tea strainer, and a recipe booklet. The event fostered enthusiasm for herbalism, and several participants later started their own tea-making practices, sharing their knowledge with others.

Overcoming Challenges

Teaching herbal skills comes with unique challenges, but they can be addressed with thoughtful planning.

1. Addressing Skepticism

Some participants may doubt the efficacy of herbal remedies.

Share evidence-based information and your own positive experiences.

2. Managing Group Dynamics

Larger groups may present logistical challenges.

Use smaller breakout groups for hands-on activities to ensure everyone receives guidance.

3. Staying Inclusive

Ensure the session is welcoming to all skill levels.

Begin with simple concepts before introducing more advanced techniques.

Creating a Legacy Through Teaching

Teaching herbal skills extends your impact far beyond your own practice. Each participant who learns from you becomes part of a growing network of people who value natural healing. By fostering curiosity, providing tools for learning, and creating meaningful connections, you ensure that herbal knowledge continues to flourish.

Teaching herbal skills to friends and your community is a fulfilling way to share your passion while empowering others to embrace natural wellness. Through workshops, herbal walks, or digital platforms, you can inspire curiosity, build connections, and pass on the timeless art of herbalism. As you teach, you not only deepen your own understanding but also contribute to a growing tradition that values the healing power of nature. By sharing your knowledge, you plant seeds of inspiration that will continue to grow in the lives of others.

Creating a Legacy with Your Home Apothecary

A home apothecary is more than a collection of jars and bottles filled with herbs and remedies; it's a tangible expression of your herbal journey and a legacy that can be passed down for generations. By curating and organizing your apothecary with care, you not only ensure access to natural solutions for everyday ailments but also preserve a wealth of knowledge and traditions for the future. Your apothecary becomes a living testament to the healing power of nature and the wisdom you've cultivated along the way.

Building the Foundation of Your Home Apothecary

Creating a meaningful and functional apothecary requires thoughtful planning and dedication. The goal is to design a space that reflects your unique needs and preferences while being accessible and easy to maintain.

1. Choosing a Location

Your apothecary should be a dedicated space in your home where herbs and remedies can be stored safely and organized efficiently.

Consider Accessibility: Choose a location that is easy to reach, such as a pantry, kitchen shelf, or dedicated cabinet.

Avoid Heat and Humidity: Keep herbs away from direct sunlight, heat, and moisture to preserve their potency.

2. Organizing Your Apothecary

An organized apothecary ensures that you can quickly locate the herbs and remedies you need.

Use Clear Labels: Clearly mark jars with the herb name, date of preparation, and storage instructions.

Group by Category: Arrange items by type, such as teas, tinctures, salves, and dried herbs.

Use Airtight Containers: Store herbs in glass jars with tight lids to maintain freshness.

3. Stocking Essentials

Start with a selection of versatile, commonly used herbs and remedies tailored to your household's needs.

Teas and Infusions: Chamomile, peppermint, nettle, and elderflower.

Tinctures and Extracts: Echinacea, valerian, and turmeric.

Topicals: Calendula salve, arnica oil, and aloe vera gel.

Specialized Remedies: Include items for specific concerns, such as cold and flu relief or stress management.

Personalizing Your Apothecary

A home apothecary is deeply personal, reflecting your unique approach to herbalism. By adding personalized touches, you create a space that feels meaningful and inspires continued practice.

1. Incorporating Family Remedies

Include recipes and remedies passed down through your family. These heirloom practices honor your heritage and give your apothecary a sense of history and tradition.

2. Documenting Your Recipes

Create a companion herbal guide or journal where you document the recipes stored in your apothecary. Include:

Ingredients and preparation methods.

Usage instructions and dosages.

Notes on effectiveness or adaptations.

3. Adding Creative Elements

Visual Appeal: Use decorative jars, wooden shelves, or chalkboard labels to make your apothecary inviting.

Inspiration: Display books, quotes, or art that reflect your connection to herbalism.

Maintaining Your Apothecary

A well-maintained apothecary is essential for ensuring that your remedies remain effective and safe to use.

1. Regular Inventory Checks

Check expiration dates on tinctures and dried herbs.

Rotate older stock to the front to ensure it's used before newer batches.

2. Restocking Supplies

Keep track of frequently used items and replenish them as needed. Stock up on seasonal essentials before demand peaks (e.g., elderberry for winter months).

3. Cleaning and Organizing

Dust shelves and jars regularly to maintain a clean and appealing space.

Dispose of expired or degraded items responsibly, such as composting expired dried herbs.

Sharing Your Apothecary

Your home apothecary can extend its benefits to others through thoughtful sharing and teaching.

1. Hosting Family and Friends

Invite loved ones to explore your apothecary and learn about its contents. Demonstrate how to prepare simple remedies like teas or salves.

2. Creating Starter Kits

Assemble small herbal kits with remedies for common concerns, such as stress relief or immune support, to gift to friends or family members.

3. Teaching Through Your Apothecary

Use your apothecary as a hands-on teaching tool during workshops or herbal classes. Show how to create remedies from start to finish using the resources you've gathered.

Preserving Your Legacy

A home apothecary is more than a personal resource; it's a legacy that can inspire future generations. By taking steps to document and preserve your work, you ensure that your knowledge lives on.

1. Creating a Family Herbal Guide

Compile your remedies, recipes, and notes into a comprehensive guide. This heirloom document can include:

Stories or histories behind specific remedies.

Photos of plants you've foraged or grown.

Instructions for maintaining the apothecary.

2. Teaching Younger Generations

Pass down the skills and knowledge required to sustain the apothecary. Involve children or family members in the preparation of remedies, teaching them the value of herbalism through hands-on experience.

3. Expanding Your Reach

Consider donating resources or sharing your guide with local libraries, community centers, or herbal organizations to inspire others beyond your immediate circle.

A Case Study: Sarah's Home Apothecary Legacy

Sarah, a dedicated herbalist, spent years building her apothecary and documenting her work. She created a detailed herbal guide that included her favorite remedies, notes on her gardening practices, and family recipes passed down from her grandmother. Before her retirement, she began teaching her grandchildren how to use the apothecary, sharing stories about the herbs and their uses. Today, her apothecary continues to serve her family, ensuring that her legacy remains alive and thriving.

Creating a home apothecary is an act of empowerment, creativity, and care. It serves as a personal resource for wellness, a tool for teaching, and a symbol of your connection to the natural world. By curating, organizing, and sharing your apothecary with intention, you create a lasting legacy that honors the wisdom of the past while inspiring future generations to embrace the healing power of herbs. Whether you're just beginning or refining an established collection, your apothecary is a testament to the enduring art of herbalism and the positive impact it can have on the world.

CONCLUSION

Herbalism is more than a practice—it's a connection to nature, a bridge between past and present, and a gift to future generations. As we journey through the art and science of working with plants, we uncover not just remedies, but stories, traditions, and a profound understanding of how deeply intertwined our lives are with the natural world. The work of preserving and sharing herbal knowledge is not just about ensuring that remedies endure; it is about safeguarding a way of life that values balance, respect, and harmony.

Imagine standing in your garden or at your apothecary shelves, each jar and bottle holding more than dried leaves or infused oils. They hold your time, your effort, and your love for this craft. Each preparation carries the weight of tradition and the promise of healing. And in those moments, you realize that herbalism is more than recipes and techniques—it is a legacy you are crafting with every decision to blend, infuse, or brew. It's a legacy built on the care you put into understanding each herb, the respect you show for its power, and the creativity you use to adapt it to meet the needs of today.

There is something magical in this continuity. When you prepare a chamomile tea to soothe someone's restless night, you are not simply making a drink; you are participating in a tradition that stretches back thousands of years. When you teach someone to make a calendula salve for their dry skin, you are planting seeds of knowledge that may flourish in ways you'll never fully see. This is the enduring beauty of herbalism—it connects us to our ancestors while allowing us to shape its future.

As you grow in your herbal journey, you come to see the small yet profound ways this practice changes you. It slows you down, asking you to notice the delicate veins on a plant's leaf or the way its fragrance shifts as it dries. It teaches patience, whether waiting for tinctures to steep or for a garden to bloom. And it instills humility as you learn to listen—truly listen—to the wisdom of the natural world and the lessons it offers. In the process, you become not just a practitioner of herbalism but a steward of its wisdom.

The act of sharing this knowledge is equally transformative. When you teach a friend how to prepare an infusion or guide a child in identifying their first wild plant, you see how herbalism sparks curiosity and empowerment. These moments remind us that herbalism is not about one person holding all the knowledge; it's about a shared journey where we each contribute to something greater than ourselves. Every time you pass on a recipe, explain the use of a plant, or invite someone to join you on an herb walk, you add to this growing tapestry of wisdom.

Yet, herbalism is not without its challenges. There will be moments of doubt—when a remedy doesn't work as expected or when someone questions the validity of what you do. There will be times when the scope of what you don't yet know feels overwhelming. But these moments are opportunities for growth. They remind you that herbalism, like nature, is dynamic, evolving, and always offering more to learn. They teach resilience, creativity, and the importance of approaching your practice with humility and an open heart.

There will also be moments of profound joy. The first time someone tells you a remedy you shared truly helped them. The day you see a plant you've tended bloom with vibrant life. The quiet satisfaction of watching your apothecary shelves fill with jars that hold not just herbs, but years of dedication and care. These moments make all the effort worthwhile, grounding you in the purpose of your work and inspiring you to continue.

As you move forward, remember that the legacy of herbalism is not measured solely in the remedies you create or the knowledge you share. It is reflected in how you live—your choices to nurture the earth, to embrace curiosity, to foster community, and to honor the balance between humans and nature. Your herbal journey is as much about who you become as it is about what you do.

The world today needs herbalists. It needs people who look to nature not as a resource to exploit, but as a partner to cherish. It needs the wisdom of plants to remind us of our interconnectedness and our capacity to heal, not just ourselves, but the earth that sustains us. By continuing this journey, you take part in a tradition that is as ancient as it is vital, contributing to a future where nature's wisdom is valued and preserved.

Let this be your encouragement: keep going. Keep exploring, experimenting, and sharing. Keep tending your garden, your apothecary, and your community. Keep learning, not just about plants, but about yourself and the world around you. Your efforts matter. Every herb you grow, every remedy you make, and every person you teach adds to a legacy of healing and hope.

Herbalism is a gift—one you've chosen to embrace and one you have the power to pass on. It's a quiet revolution, a gentle but profound act of care for yourself, others, and the earth. And in that act, you leave behind more than remedies; you leave a legacy of wisdom, connection, and love. That, in the end, is the true essence of herbalism—a practice that heals and inspires, not just for today, but for generations to come.

APPENDICES

Appendix A: Herb Safety Guidelines

Understanding and respecting the safety aspects of herbal remedies is essential for their effective use. Here are some key safety principles to guide your herbal practice:

Start Small: Always begin with a small dose to observe how your body reacts to a new herb.

Know Your Source: Use high-quality, organic herbs from reputable suppliers to avoid contamination.

Allergies and Sensitivities: Be mindful of potential allergic reactions, especially with herbs in the daisy family (e.g., chamomile, echinacea).

Pregnancy and Breastfeeding: Consult a healthcare professional before using herbs during pregnancy or lactation.

Medication Interactions: Some herbs, like St. John's Wort, can interact with prescription medications. Research and consult with a professional if unsure.

Age and Health Considerations: Adjust dosages based on age, weight, and overall health.

Proper Storage: Keep herbs in airtight containers, away from heat, light, and moisture to preserve their potency.

Appendix B: Dosage Recommendations for Different Age Groups

Dosage varies depending on age, weight, and health condition. Below are general guidelines:

Infants (0–12 months)

Use mild teas like chamomile or fennel (1–2 teaspoons per day, diluted).

Avoid strong herbs and alcohol-based tinctures.

Children (1–12 years)

Use teas, syrups, or glycerite-based tinctures.

Dosage: 1/4 to 1/2 of the adult dose depending on weight and age.

Teens (13–18 years)

Can tolerate adult dosages for most remedies.

Adjust based on body weight and sensitivity.

Adults

Standard dosages apply unless underlying health conditions warrant adjustments.

Examples: 1 cup of herbal tea (3 times daily), 30–60 drops of tincture.

Seniors (65+ years)

Start with lower doses, as metabolism and tolerance may vary.

Monitor for interactions with medications or health conditions.

Appendix C: Conversion Charts for Herbal Preparations

Tinctures and Extracts

1 ml = 20 drops (approx.)

1 teaspoon = 5 ml

1 tablespoon = 15 ml

Dry Herbs to Fresh Herbs

1 part dried herb = 3 parts fresh herb (by weight).

Infusion and Decoction Ratios

Standard Tea: 1–2 teaspoons dried herb per 1 cup boiling water.

Strong Infusion: 1–2 tablespoons dried herb per 1 cup boiling water.

Weight to Volume

1 ounce = 28 grams.

1 cup dried herb (light herbs like chamomile) = 1 ounce.

Oils and Salves

1 part beeswax to 4 parts infused oil for firm salves.

1 part beeswax to 6 parts infused oil for softer balms.

Appendix D: Glossary of Herbal Terms

Adaptogen: Herbs that help the body adapt to stress and promote overall balance (e.g., ashwagandha, rhodiola).

Decoction: A method of extraction by simmering tougher plant materials, like roots or bark, in water.

Glycerite: A herbal extract made with glycerin instead of alcohol.

Infusion: A method of steeping herbs, typically leaves or flowers, in hot water to extract their properties.

Poultice: A moist preparation of crushed herbs applied directly to the skin to soothe or heal.

Tincture: A concentrated herbal extract made by soaking herbs in alcohol or a non-alcoholic solvent like vinegar.

Volatile Oils: Essential oils found in plants that evaporate easily and are used for their therapeutic properties.

Appendix E: Resources for Further Learning

Books

The Herbal Medicine-Maker's Handbook by James Green.

Medicinal Plants of the Pacific West by Michael Moore.

Herbal Healing for Women by Rosemary Gladstar.

Websites and Online Courses

Herbal Academy: Comprehensive online courses for beginners and advanced learners.

American Botanical Council: Research-based herbal information.

Mountain Rose Herbs Blog: Tutorials, recipes, and sustainable sourcing tips.

Herbal Organizations

American Herbalists Guild (AHG): Professional organization for herbalists.

United Plant Savers: Focuses on the conservation of at-risk medicinal plants.

Communities and Forums

Local herb walks and workshops (check libraries or community centers).

Social media groups dedicated to herbalism and natural health.

These appendices serve as practical tools to deepen your understanding of herbalism and enhance your practice. With safety guidelines, dosage recommendations, preparation tips, and additional resources, you'll have everything you need to continue your herbal journey with confidence.

GET YOUR EXCLUSIVE BONUS

Scan the QR-CODE below and get your exclusive bonus

Made in the USA
Las Vegas, NV
01 March 2025

18854978R00208